P9-DKD-439

COMMUNISM AND REVOLUTION

The Strategic Uses of Political Violence

Other books published for
The Center of International Studies
Woodrow Wilson School of Public and International Affairs

Gabriel A. Almond, *The Appeals of Communism*

Gabriel A. Almond and James S. Coleman, editors, *The Politics of the Developing Areas*

Cyril E. Black and Thomas P. Thornton, editors, *Communism and Revolution: The Strategic Uses of Political Violence*

Robert J. C. Butow, *Tojo and the Coming of the War*

Bernard C. Cohen, *The Political Process and Foreign Policy: The Making of the Japanese Peace Settlement*

Bernard C. Cohen, *The Press and Foreign Policy*

Charles De Visscher, *Theory and Reality in Public International Law*, Second Edition, translated by P. E. Corbett

Frederick S. Dunn, *Peace-making and the Settlement with Japan*

Richard A. Falk and Richard J. Barnet, editors, *Security in Disarmament*

Herman Kahn, *On Thermonuclear War*

W. W. Kaufmann, editor, *Military Policy and National Security*

Klaus Knorr, *The War Potential of Nations*

Klaus Knorr, editor, *NATO and American Security*

Klaus Knorr and Sidney Verba, editors, *The International System: Theoretical Essays*

Sidney J. Ploss, *Conflict and Decision-Making in Soviet Russia*

Lucian W. Pye, *Guerrilla Communism in Malaya*

James N. Rosenau, *International Aspects of Civil Strife*

James N. Rosenau, *National Leadership and Foreign Policy: A Case Study in the Mobilization of Public Support*

Rolf Sannwald and Jacques Stohler, *Economic Integration: Theoretical Assumptions and Consequences of European Unification*, translated by Herman F. Karreman

Richard L. Sklar, *Nigerian Political Parties: Power in an Emergent African Nation*

Glenn H. Snyder, *Deterrence and Defense*

Thomas P. Thornton, editor, *The Third World in Soviet Perspective: Studies by Soviet Writers on the Developing Areas*

Sidney Verba, *Small Groups and Political Behavior: A Study of Leadership*

Myron Weiner, *Party Politics in India*

COMMUNISM AND REVOLUTION

The Strategic Uses of Political Violence

EDITED BY CYRIL E. BLACK
AND THOMAS P. THORNTON

PRINCETON UNIVERSITY PRESS
PRINCETON · NEW JERSEY
1964

L.C. Card No. 63-18640

Second Printing, 1967

Printed in the United States of America

Preface

For the past three years, the Center of International Studies at Princeton University has been engaged in studies of internal war. This project has followed a multi-faceted approach, considering the tactical problems of guerrilla warfare, armed uprisings, *coups d'état* and other forms of revolutionary activity. It has also been concerned with the historical settings in which such revolutions have occurred, and in the general environment which seems to breed or inhibit them and influence their outcome. A research activity of such intent and dimension must necessarily concern itself with the role which communism and Communists play in these events. The actuality of the problem today derives especially from the challenge of Communist-directed revolutions. In addition, it is precisely the Communists who have had some of the most extensive experience with internal war over the past decades and who have provided considerable theoretical and practical material for the student of revolution.

The purpose of the present symposium is to describe the nature of the Communist experience in influencing political change by violent methods, and to investigate to what extent this experience is pertinent in the present and foreseeable future. The setting of the symposium, within the Center's internal war studies, necessarily influenced the general approach taken by the various contributors. It was not our objective to study the tactics of Communist revolutions in detail. This is indeed an interesting field, but it has been covered at least adequately by others and we feel that an excessive preoccupation with tactics would tend to overlook the more significant factors which determine the strategy of revolutions. Similarly, we have not been particularly concerned with presenting a historical survey of communism. This can be read for background in various sources, and although the ups and downs and ins and outs of the movement's history have great significance for the role which communism has played in revolutions, we have tended to assign these to a peripheral position.

Though we are primarily interested in violence, most political and social change does not, of course, result from violent revolution. Indeed, patterns of non-violent change have assumed ever greater importance in Communist theory and practice and, particularly when we deal with the fairly contemporary scene, they are given commensurate attention. Even in the optimal situation of coexistence as defined by the Communists, however, violence plays a crucial, if de-emphasized, role. We feel that the option of violence continues to be of major importance to Communist strategy—not only because of the Chinese position on the subject—and have oriented our presentations to the role played by revolution rather than evolution. Our preoccupation with revolution is not meant to denigrate the importance or possibility either of peaceful change or of the role played by international war in helping the Communists to power. These factors are necessarily present, implicitly or explicitly, in any survey of Communist revolution, mostly implicitly in ours, which is specifically concerned with this subject.

In a field thus narrowed, we have felt that there are two aspects of Communist revolutionary activity which merit special attention. The first is quite obviously the Communists' own appraisal of their role. The Communists are required by their precepts of action and cognition to ascribe a high role to experience in the formulation of policy, and do in fact devote great effort to policy-oriented historical research. To the extent possible we have viewed the Communists' historical experience as they themselves view it. Similarly, there is a wealth of Communist material available on many of the areas of the world in which they may see possibility for revolutionary action in the fairly near future. This material has been used, and in evaluating likely Communist courses of action we would hope insofar as possible to be making an estimate of their estimate, rather than attempting to anticipate their actions in an ideological framework of our own.

On the other hand, our view of revolutions is strongly influenced by our view of the one great revolution characteristic of our time: the pervasive tide of modernization which has involved the entire world, Communist and non-Communist, backward and advanced, in one general historical process. Communism and democracy themselves are manifestations of this process. Communism, and perhaps democracy as well, are in a sense incidental to the course of modernization. While tactics and strategy will do much to determine the success or failure of Communist ventures, it is in the last analysis the degree to which the leaders of the major competing systems are able to understand and identify themselves with the process of modernization that will determine the outcome of the competition.

The contributors have been left a maximum of freedom to approach their particular topics within the general outlines set forth above. For both subjective and objective reasons, these approaches should and do vary considerably. The authors have sought to emphasize those points which can contribute most to our understanding of communism and revolution as viewed in the context of their individual problem areas. The structure of the volume also necessarily affected the points of emphasis proper to each chapter. The first section provides historical and doctrinal background for what is to come later. Black has described the basic premises of the volume, Janos has provided a brief summary of the ideological background to the Communists' use of violence, and Thornton has surveyed the experience which Communists had with violence up until about the time of the Second World War. The second part, a series of case studies of Communist revolutionary activity, brings the range of Communist experiences up approximately to the death of Stalin. Taken together with the first part, it provides the experiential background of the present-day Communist leadership. Proceeding from this, the third section concerns itself with interpreting the Communist estimate of the prospects for revolution in the present-day world. The concluding chapter is in the nature both of a summary and an outlook, tying together the material which has been presented in the rest of the book and giving consideration to the challenge of Communist revolutions in a modernizing world.

We are of course well aware that in each case a distinction must be drawn between that which is reasonably understandable and that which is not. History is to a considerable extent understandable, as is the Communists' appraisal of history. To a rather lesser extent, the current state of the world is ascertainable and we also know much about how the Communists view this. Indeed, the Communists have consistently been quite obliging in stating their views and objectives in such a direct and open manner that hardly anyone has been willing to believe them. The body of facts which can be brought together from these various sources can show the general direction which we feel Communist activities—violent or non-violent—are likely to take.

At the same time, it would be naive to expect to make specific predictions or, in the historical sense, to state unequivocally why this or that happened in the way it did. Since we are not determinist in our outlook, we readily acknowledge that the best laid of plans, and even the best analyses of these plans, are subject to the whim of chance. Shifts in Communist ideology, technological advances, economic and political developments outside the Communist orbit: all of these and many other factors could change radically and rapidly the range of options open to Communist policy. Although on occasion we have indicated some of the changes which are more likely than others, a prognosis which incorporates such variables must be left to the computers of some future date.

If the imponderables are kept in mind, however, this study of Communist policy should serve to elucidate a number of important features of communism both as a discrete phenomenon and as a factor in contemporary politics, while at the same time clarifying the nature of political revolution as a feature of modernization in the years ahead.

This volume is the result of the individual efforts of authors representing a wide range of experience and talents, and of three conferences at which opinions were exchanged at several stages in the preparation of these chapters. Comments and advice were also sought of a number of specialists who were not able to attend the conferences. In making available its facilities for the production of this volume, the Center of International Studies is grateful for the assistance of the Carnegie Corporation, which has supported this program of research.

CYRIL E. BLACK
Princeton, New Jersey
THOMAS P. THORNTON
McLean, Virginia

May 15, 1963

Contents

PART I

The Perspective of History

Abbreviations

The following abbreviations are used in the footnotes:

CDSP—*Current Digest of the Soviet Press*—New York

GWY—*Guoji Wenti Yanjiu* (*Kuo-chi Wen-t'i Yen-chiu*) [Study of International Affairs]—Peking

IntAff—*International Affairs*—Moscow

JPRS—Joint Publications Research Service—Washington

MEIMO—*Mirovaya Ekonomika i Mezhdunarodnye Otnosheniya* [World Economics and International Relations]—Moscow

NAIA—*Narody Azii i Afriki* [Peoples of Asia and Africa]—Moscow

PR—*Peking Review*—Peking

PV—*Problemy Vostokovedeniya* [Problems of Oriental Studies]—Moscow

SGIP—*Sovetskoye Gosudarstvo i Pravo* [Soviet State and Law]—Moscow

SV—*Sovetskoye Vostokovedeniye* [Soviet Oriental Studies]—Moscow

WMR—*World Marxist Review*—Toronto

Note: *Sovetskoye Vostokovedeniye, Problemy Vostokovedeniya,* and *Narody Azii i Afriki,* are successive names for essentially the same periodical.

1

Revolution, Modernization, and Communism

CYRIL E. BLACK

Introduction

"Our epoch, the main content of which is the transition from capitalism to socialism begun by the Great October Socialist Revolution, is an epoch of struggle between the two opposing social systems, an epoch of socialist revolutions and national-liberation movements, an epoch of the downfall of imperialism and abolition of the colonial system, an epoch of transition of more and more peoples to the path of socialism, of the triumph of socialism and communism on a world scale."[1]

This definition of the modern epoch was adopted at a conference of eighty-one Communist parties (exclusive of the Yugoslav party) held in Moscow in November 1960, and was cited by the Communist Party of the Soviet Union in its open letter of July 14, 1963 on the Sino-Soviet dispute as "the basis for a correct approach in drawing up the strategy and tactics of the world Communist movement."[2]

This statement has the familiar ring of the many proclamations of the inevitability of revolution that have been issued by advocates of communism since Marx first suggested this theme in 1848, and it raises a number of questions that are relevant to the contemporary international scene. To what extent is there a common body of revolutionary strategy and tactics to which all Communist parties are committed? Are the various Communist parties in agreement in identifying which revolutions deserve support and in allocating the resources necessary to provide it? Do the Communists mean what they say when they declare their support for revolution, or are they simply enunciating a ritual doctrine that has become an inseparable part of their system of beliefs?

There is no easy answer to these questions, and many specific problems must be clarified before even a qualified answer can be formulated. Under what circumstances are revolutions in fact likely to occur, regardless of Communist policies? How does the Com-

[1] *CDSP,* XII (December 28, 1960), 3.
[2] *New York Times* (July 15, 1963), 14.

munist understanding of the problem of change in the modern world differ from other interpretations? What has in fact been the policy of the various Communists parties over the years in regard to revolutions in other countries? What strategic and tactical doctrines have the Communists evolved that are likely to be applicable in the foreseeable future?

Revolution

Revolution is used here as a general term to denote the wide range of circumstances—from mere threats of force to major civil wars—in which illegitimate violence is employed within a country to effect political change. It is not necessary to emphasize that violence in the realm of politics has been in some degree characteristic of all societies, and that in many it is still the most common means of effecting change. Revolutions have varied widely in purpose, scope, and intensity, but they have in common several characteristics which may serve as a basis for an introductory analysis: they result from a breakdown in the legitimate means of effecting political change; they involve the use of illegitimate violence, from within or from without; they so disrupt the consensus necessary for the orderly conduct of society that a major effort is required to legitimatize the policies of the victor; and they tend to become an issue in international relations.[3]

The legitimate means of effecting change breaks down when the incumbent political leaders are trying to effect a change that significant elements of the population are not willing to accept, or when insurgents have goals that cannot be achieved by the legally available means. Underlying every revolution there is therefore an issue of policy or ideology, which forms the rallying point for the forces that become engaged in the conflict. Not infrequently the conflict itself generates new issues, especially resentment against

[3] The following papers, prepared in connection with the Internal War Project of the Center of International Studies at Princeton University, have been particularly useful: Harry Eckstein, ed., *Internal War: Problems and Approaches* (New York 1964); and James Rosenau, ed., *International Aspects of Civil Strife* (forthcoming); Andrew Janos, "Unconventional Warfare: Framework and Analysis," *World Politics*, XV (July 1963), 636-646; and Richard Falk, "Indirect Aggression and Disarmament" (mimeographed 1963). See also Franklin A. Lindsay, "Unconventional Warfare," *Foreign Affairs*, XL (January 1962), 264-274; Chalmers A. Johnson, "Civilian Loyalties and Guerrilla Conflict," *World Politics*, XIV (July 1962), 646-661; and H. L. Nieburg, "The Threat of Violence and Social Change," *American Political Science Review*, LVI (December 1962), 865-873.

the ramifications of violence, and a myriad of motives of revenge may arise to becloud the original causes of the conflict. Granting the role that chance events, external influences, and miscellaneous personal motives and conspiracies frequently play in the initiation and conduct of revolutions, one may properly ask what types of issue provoke the initial breakdown of authority. This question, in turn, leads one directly to theories of social change—an area where many points of view have been advanced and few have met with general acceptance. Yet the question cannot be avoided, and reference will be made later in this essay to the general character of the modern era and to Communist interpretations of it. Suffice it for the moment to say that the causes of revolutions vary greatly from country to country and from period to period, and that individual cases must be examined very carefully before they can serve as a basis for generalization and comparison. A glance at the many explanations that have been advanced for such explosions of political violence as the French revolution and the American civil war, will serve as a warning to those who seek easy answers to these complex issues.

Another characteristic common to revolutions is the threat or employment of illegitimate violence. This may take a wide variety of forms, and one of the virtues of the comparative study of revolutions is that it brings under systematic consideration many different types of domestic conflict. In cases where insurgents have successfully prepared their positions, the mere massing of forces may constitute such an obvious threat of violence that the incumbents in effect surrender without an overt struggle. In some degree, the threat of violence is an initial element in all revolutionary situations, but if the threat is not effective violence breaks out.

If the violence is well organized, it will frequently result in a *coup d'état* in which the insurgents—by means of sudden and rapid political measures—are able to defeat the incumbents and take their place. The Bolshevik revolution on October 25/November 7, 1917 was of this type, and it effected a transfer of power in the main centers of authority within a very short time and with relatively little loss of life. In such cases, and there are many other examples, the violence is usually organized by an insurgent group that is already well established and equipped with instruments of power. Most typically, insurgent military leaders backed by sizable elements of the armed forces are often able to topple incumbent regimes without a great deal of bloodshed. In cases where *coups d'état* are not successful, or where the insurgents do not have the capacity to attempt them, the revolutionary struggle is likely to become prolonged. It may then take the form of loosely organized agrarian *jacqueries* or industrial strikes; or systematic guerrilla operations, in which the insurgents are able to operate from sizable areas which they control; or full-fledged civil wars where each side has a government, armed forces, and a well defined territory. Not many civil wars have had the dimensions of the American (1861-1865), the Spanish (1936-1939), or the Chinese (1945-1949), which in many respects reached the proportion of international wars in duration, casualties, and consequences. Nor need one think of the different types of revolution as existing in distinct categories. Many, particularly the major ones, have involved all of these forms of violence in a variety of combinations.

Since only illegitimate violence is in question, one usually thinks of insurgents rather than incumbents as initiating the employment of violence. Incumbent governments have at their disposal legitimate forms of violence, particularly armies and the police, which they can use to give effect to their policies. In this sense, incumbents always have the threat of violence at their disposal to preserve the status quo or to enforce change, depending on their policy. Use of legitimate forms of violence may reach the point of terrorism, however, and incumbents may also resort to illegitimate violence. They may carry out assassinations and other atrocities, or institute widespread purges, and if these fail they may conduct themselves like an army in occupation of enemy territory. As the revolutionary struggle develops, incumbents may lose all of the advantages accorded to those wielding legitimate authority, and find themselves fighting it out with the insurgents on a more or less equal basis and with similar methods and resources.

Violence in support of a revolutionary program may also originate in part or even entirely outside of a country. In an extreme case a foreign army of occupation may bring with it a provisional government led by exiled revolutionaries, or after the occupation it may form one composed of local opponents of the defeated government. Through such a provisional government, and using the army of occupation as a domestic instrument of coercion, a revolutionary program may thus be implemented by a foreign state. There is usually some basis in domestic politics for the personnel and program of such a revolution, but the role of the foreign army of occupation may be so disproportionate to that of the local insurgents that the revolution is in effect imported rather than domestic.

A third characteristic of revolutions is the legitimation of the results after a settlement has been achieved. A well-ordered society is founded on a general agreement as to objectives, laws, and norms of behavior, and it is this fundamental consensus that is most frequently disrupted, especially by protracted revolutions. No doubt violence would not have broken out if there had not already been serious divisions, but the introduction of the element of violence tends to widen the rift and to make more difficult the establishment of a new consensus at the end of the war. Revolutions may thus be ultimately effective in reallocating political power in a society, but they frequently result in extensive social disorganization. If the incumbents are in the end victorious, it may take a long time before the wounds of civil strife are sufficiently healed to permit the reestablishment of orderly government. When the insurgents are victorious, especially if they represent a minority point of view, the problems are frequently much more serious. They may find themselves in control of formal political power, but lacking in any of the informal attributes of tradition and loyalty that hold together the fabric of society. This they can achieve only after they have educated a generation or two of citizens to an acceptance of their policies. In some cases this is never achieved, violence begets more violence, and a society may squander its resources for many years on unproductive strife.

Revolutions are limited by definition to violence within the boundaries of a single country, but this does not mean that they are necessarily conducted in isolation from international relations. More often than not, the outcome of a revolution after the onset of violence is affected by the action of outside states. International law has supported incumbent governments by maintaining that other states may have only such relations with insurgents as are required by practical necessity. Other states may deal with insurgents on a *de facto* basis in such matters as the protection of the property of their nationals, although international law does not define insurgency with much precision. If other states wish to support the cause of the insurgents, however, they cannot do so directly without in effect interfering in the internal affairs of the state concerned. States desiring to help insurgents have therefore often resorted to a series of ostensibly legitimate measures that have come in recent years to be known as indirect aggression. These measures include supporting insurgents with money and arms, sending in agents for purposes of subversion, and attempting to undermine the incumbent government by means of propaganda and political and economic pressure. Such interference may, of course, take place in the absence of actual internal war, but it is particularly significant after the outbreak of violence. Indirect aggression has not as yet been defined by international agreement, and states giving such assistance to insurgents must calculate the risks involved.

If the insurgents gain control over a considerable amount of national territory, are able to administer it in an orderly manner, and can conduct their armed forces in a responsible fashion, then other states whose interests are affected by the revolutionary struggle may grant the insurgents the status of belligerency. The incumbent government itself may wish to invoke belligerency in order to impose a blockade or take other measures against the insurgents that affect the interests of other states. In this event the belligerents are for many purposes treated as sovereign states and other states must conduct themselves as neutrals if they do not wish to risk an international war. Other states may, finally, recognize the insurgents as the legitimate government and withdraw recognition from the incumbent government, although premature recognition is regarded as interference in the domestic affairs of the country and entitles the incumbent government to take retaliatory measures. This decision, like the recognition of insurgency and of belligerency, is one that other states must take in the light of the facts and of their own interests.

The extent to which a revolution may become an issue of international relations varies greatly, and only on a few occasions involving major civil wars has the question of the recognition of a status of belligerency arisen. In circumstances such as those existing today, however, even minor domestic conflicts are likely to become a subject of international concern. When two extensive coalitions of states confront each other in a struggle to control the balance of power, a revolution even in a very small state may become a significant factor of power or prestige affecting the balance. It is under these circumstances that revolutions become a substitute for international war, and other states go to great lengths to influence their outcome.

Modernization

It is important to consider analytically the common features of revolutions as a historical phenomenon, but those concerned with the contemporary scene must also view them within the context of the worldwide process that is variously known as Europeanization, Westernization, social change, the revolution of rising expectations, and modernization. Modernization is the most comprehensive of these terms, and will be employed here to refer to this process in all of its complexity. There is no generally accepted doctrine as to the nature and course of this process, and students of this subject must arrive at their own interpretation with such assistance as they can obtain from the wide variety of available views and theories.[4]

Modernization is a recent form of the age-old process of innovation; and it gains its special character in modern times from the unprecedented growth in man's knowledge and in the resulting technology, with their pervasive effects on all human affairs. Underlying this process is a profound change in man's outlook toward the nature of the world and his destiny in it. The modern outlook assumes that man can understand his environment by means of scientific investigation, can control and alter it for purposes of human betterment, and can adapt his institutions to the new circumstances. This enthusiastic acceptance of the view that change is feasible and desirable has affected all aspects of human activity. The desire for greater control in human affairs has led to a marked centralization and bureaucratization of policy-making, in both the governmental and the private spheres. Governments have taken on a wide range of responsibilities, and have come to administer directly or indirectly a large share of the national wealth. Business enterprises and other private organizations have also tended to become national and even international in the scope of their activities. The tendency to centralize policy-making has led to a much sharper definition of the organizational basis of political integration, which has generally been found in nationality or in some equally effective common experience. Thus traditional multi-national empires have tended to be dissolved when they cannot be held together by force, and scattered peoples of the same nationality, religion, or other common experience have been drawn together.

In some respects the most dramatic aspect of modernization has been the economic. The development of science and technology have made possible the mechanization of agriculture, industry, commerce, and communications, with the result that per capita production has increased very rapidly. It has in fact been estimated that the world's industrial output in the past century has been several times greater than that of the entire preceding history of mankind. This rapid growth

[4] Much has been written on this subject. This section is based on Cyril E. Black, *Modernization: Essays in Comparative History* (forthcoming), which includes a bibliographical essay.

has given rise to the prospect that man may eventually be able to satisfy all of his material needs, and that an era of universal abundance is within reach.

The social aspect of this process has been no less significant, and many hitherto isolated or dormant forces have been mobilized. In modern countries millions of people have learned to read and write, and have gone on to secondary and higher education; a large proportion of the population has moved from relatively isolated areas to large cities; health has been greatly improved, and population has grown rapidly. A more cosmopolitan approach to human relations has evolved that tends to judge individuals on the basis of personal achievement rather than of religion, race, nationality, family, or status. Consequently the relatively rigid social and economic strata of traditional societies are being dissolved into new groupings based on criteria of ability, training, and efficiency. There has evolved in the advanced countries what is sometimes called a "mass society," in which the common problems and needs of the entire population play a much greater role in the calculations of their leaders than ever before. In the course of this process the personality of the individual also undergoes a transformation as a result of changes in the social environment in which the personality is formed. It becomes necessary for the individual to become adjusted to a much wider range of norms of behavior than in the past, and to be able to play a much larger variety of roles. This requires greater individualism and adaptability, and offers new opportunities for self-fullfilment.

Modernization thus opens up unprecedented opportunities for the betterment of human life, but it also affords new possibilities of large-scale destruction. The new science and technology can make nuclear weapons as well as machines and medicines. The centralization of policy-making can be put to evil ends as well as to good. The possibilities for economic growth are not equally distributed, and the struggle for raw materials and markets can lead to great disorder. Social integration through new institutions takes place at the cost of the disintegration of many old and valued ways of doing things. The freedom of the individual from traditional constraints may lead to a purposeless atomization or to a search for new and self-defeating forms of group identification.

Modernization, with its great potential for both construction and destruction, affects all aspects of a society; and a common pattern, that may be referred to as "modernity," tends to be established in advanced countries. Nevertheless, much variety remains. No two countries undergo transformation at the same time, and at any given moment many levels of development exist side by side. In the countries of Western Europe and the English-speaking world, the origins of the break with the traditional way of life may be traced to the Middle Ages, and political leaders committed to modernization gained power between the seventeenth and the early nineteenth centuries. In other countries, including such important ones as Russia, Japan, Turkey, India, and China, traditionally-minded political leaders remained in power until the late nineteenth and early twentieth centuries. The other peoples of the world are still predominantly under the influence of traditional ideas and institutions.

More significant than the stages of development of the various countries, in explaining the differences among them, is the heritage of traditional institutions that continues to have a profound influence on the ways in which they go about tackling the problems characteristic of the modern age. Even countries closely related in stage of development and institutional heritage, such as France and England, or the Netherlands and Denmark, differ significantly in the institutional methods by which they seek to accomplish similar tasks. It must be anticipated that the Chinese and the Indians, or the Japanese and the Turks, will also differ significantly from each other and from other countries even when they are far advanced on the road to modernization. One cannot foresee when or even whether the universal attributes of modernity will ever completely absorb the many particularisms of the diverse countries that make up the world. It would nevertheless seem that for the foreseeable future, diversity among societies, and within them as well, will be a predominant characteristic of human affairs in the modern world.

On the one hand, there are certain functions in regard to intellectual outlook, policy implementation, economic growth, social mobilization, and personality adjustment that may be thought of as universal characteristics of modernity. On the other hand, the methods by which societies perform these functions are evolved through the adaptation to the requirements of modernity of their very diverse traditional institutions, generally under the influence of the experience and example of other societies. It is this process of adaptation in its political aspect that is the most characteristic cause of revolutions in modern times. Rarely have the readjustment of sovereignties, the formation and dissolution of complex societies, the displacement of entrenched political leaders, the integration of local and regional authorities into national bureaucratic systems, and the conduct of relations among states which remain jealous of their sovereignty even though they are becoming increasingly interdependent—rarely have these complex and interrelated changes taken place without violence. No age has seen more international, local, and civil wars, revolutions, *coups d'état,* assassinations, purges, and other forms of violence than the modern. Violence in its various manifestations has been characteristic of political modernization in most countries.

The principal reason for this strife has been the fact that political modernization is by its very nature a profoundly unsettling process. It is usually not a question of replacing one political party with another by means of an election, but of displacing traditional political leaders representing interests that for many generations have directed and controlled a society. The entire economic and social position of these leaders, and frequently their lives as well, depend on their political control. The traditional political leaders are therefore inclined to resist the modernizers to the bitter end, and violence ensues more often than not. Once a country has set its course on the road to modernization, the most disputed issues of domestic politics are such questions as how the leaders should be selected, how the powers of government should be allocated, how the burdens of taxation should be distributed, how government revenue should be spent, and what should be the proper relationship between the state, the individual, and the many non-governmental organizations that make up a society. It is not surprising that in regard to these issues also, violence is frequently resorted to.

Each country must ultimately solve these problems in its own way, but only the countries that were first to modernize had to find truly original solutions. Other countries were able initially to borrow and adapt from those that modernized first, although in the long run it has been found that borrowing and adaptation are not enough and no society can avoid confrontation with the original problems posed by modernization for its particular institutional heritage. We think of ourselves as living in a modern world, and there are doubtless by now few countries where the political leaders have not in some sense decided to modernize, but the question as to how to modernize is in most of the newer states still largely unresolved. Whether they be countries under colonial rule trying to gain independence; or new African countries seeking to establish orderly government on the basis of a tribal system and with an inexperienced and largely illiterate population; or a country like India, constructing a modern state from several hundred political entities and numerous languages and religions; or countries like those of the Near East and Latin America, where the oligarchies that have traditionally held power are reluctant to give up their privileges; or countries like Poland and Hungary, where resentment against the oppressiveness of Soviet rule has led to violent efforts to seek redress—in all these countries, and also in the more stable ones where violence seems less likely to occur, the question of how to modernize is one that provokes endless controversy.

These controversies are ultimately solved by political leaders who hold or gain political power, and they in turn are influenced less by personal solutions than by adaptations of ideas and institutions borrowed from other countries. A compelling program of modernization that can demonstrate successful domestic solutions to the characteristic problems of the modern era and can propagate its view by an effective organization abroad, may exert a decisive influence on the programs of modernization in many countries. Indeed, many of the newer countries have no alternative but to borrow not only personnel and techniques, but also ideologies and institutions from the more modern countries. When political violence develops in one of these countries, the ensuing revolutionary situation immediately becomes involved in the web of international affairs. This involvement frequently becomes a decisive factor in determining the outcome.

It is one of the inherent contradictions of the process of modernization that it has had the effect of concentrating unprecedented authority in the governments of individual countries, at the same time that it has led to an increasing interdependence of peoples. It has been possible to transfer sovereignty to international bodies for certain limited purposes, but the great differences among countries in levels of development and in policy have made this difficult as a general resolution of this contradiction. In the short run, political integration can be attempted only by states sharing common norms and interests, or dominated by the overwhelming military power of a larger state. In the much longer run, the peoples of the world will be confronted by the problem of finding the means of preserving their diversity of cultures in a community of societies which in most respects will function on a world-wide basis. The seriousness with which individual leaders and societies devote their attention to this problem is one of the principal tests for judging their capacity for world leadership.

Communism

In this competition among programs of modernization, with all its attendant controversies, communism has played an important role. Russian leaders originally looked primarily to Western or Central Europe for models, and indeed Marxism itself reached Russia as a result of this search for guidance. At the time of the Bolshevik seizure of power Lenin and his colleagues assumed that a Marxist revolution could succeed only within the context of an anticipated European-wide revolution. Only later did it come to be recognized that a more or less original program would have to be developed. In the course of time a characteristically Bolshevik set of policies was devised, in the aims and methods of which one can find much that is familiar to students both of the Tsarist government and of the radical ideologies of the last decades of the empire. These policies also included significant elements of European socialism, as interpreted by Russian leaders who were guided by a system of values quite different from those of the earlier socialist theorists. The resulting program of modernization, which for want of a better term may be called Marxism-Leninism, has had a significant influence on other countries. The radical and dramatic character of some of Soviet policies, the boldness of official propaganda in exaggerating achievements and underplaying human costs, and the crisis which a European-dominated world has been undergoing since the First World War, are all factors that have served to place Marxism-Leninism in a strategic position in relation to rival programs.

The Communists do not accept the view of modernization that has been advanced here, nor do they use the term in this sense. Instead they believe that societies pass through slavery, feudalism, and capitalism, occasionally skipping stages, before making the transition to socialism. Although these stages bear familiar labels, they are defined by the Communists in a manner that frequently bears only an incidental resemblance to the way that these terms are used in the West where they originated. It is therefore often necessary to put these terms in quotation marks, so as to remind the reader of the very special connotation that "capitalism" and "socialism" have in Marxist-Leninist terminology. In the Communist view, Russia was the first country in the world to make the transition to "socialism" as a result of the Bolshevik seizure of power in Petrograd on October 25/November 7, 1917. According to this interpretation, the Soviet Union is the most progressive country in the world and is destined to lead the other countries toward their predetermined destiny. Within the framework of this general agreement as to objectives, there is nevertheless plenty of room for disagreement among Communist leaders in regard to a wide range of policies. Khrushchev, Mao, Gomulka, and Tito, for example, do not agree on how socialist societies should be organized or how they should conduct their relations with each other. This lack of agreement has led to some very vigorous controversies, and these have important consequences for the study of the Communist attitude toward revolutions.

In discussing the nature of communism, it is important to make a distinction between the means by which the Communist leaders expect to achieve political power, the policies which they favor once they achieve power, and the theoretical approach to change in the modern world which goes by the name of Marxism-Leninism. Our primary concern here is with the means employed by the Communists to achieve power, but these can best be understood in the light of the system which they expect to establish and of the theoretical bases of that system.

The Communist system envisages the complete centralization of all political power, and the administration of this power by the state under policies determined by the leaders of the Communist party. The pattern of policies now generally accepted as Communist was not evolved in the Soviet Union until a decade after the Revolution of 1917, and it is significant that Marxism did not provide any more than very general indications as to the policies of the new state. These had to be worked out by trial and error, and did not take their present form until the inauguration of the First Five-Year Plan in 1928. Communist policy as it has evolved in the Soviet Union thus represents a form of modernization in which the party and state bureaucracies attempt to assert complete control over all political and economic activities, as well as over all cultural and social institutions. In very considerable measure this attempt to establish totalitarian control has been successful, even though there are important areas of personal belief and aspiration that have resisted control.

The central purpose of the Communist domestic program is rapid industrialization, with particular emphasis on heavy industry and supporting programs of technical education and public health. The most characteristic feature of the Communist domestic program is that it contemplates the rapid development of producer goods over several generations without a commensurate emphasis on consumer goods. It has been estimated, for example, that in the 1950's in the Soviet Union about 40 percent of the national product was allocated for uses other than consumption—that is to say, for investment, defense, and government administration—as compared with some 33 percent in the United States. Since the Soviet national product was probably less than one-half that of the United States, while its population was somewhat larger, the amount remaining for consumption per capita in the Soviet Union was less than one-third that available in the United States. This comparison, which refers to a relatively prosperous phase of Soviet growth, illustrates the limitations imposed on the individual by the Communist method of industrialization. Although the population is poorer to start with, it is forced to set aside for reinvestment and other purposes a substantially larger share of its earnings than in the more affluent countries. The Communist program thus imposes an unprecedented burden on the individual, and it is only through strict regimentation and harsh police methods that the population can be mobilized to work so hard for so little direct compensation. The Communists have elaborated a policy of modernization which places a very high priority on industrialization, scientific and technical education, and public health, and a very low priority on legality, the standard of living, and consumer goods. Communist policies are in principle more oppressive of the individual in the political and economic sense than those of any other fully formulated program of modernization.

Communist policies have been successful in the Soviet Union in building an industrial economy which characteristically is better equipped to make intercontinental missiles and space vehicles than to manufacture shoes or to grow food. Because of its success in the realm of heavy industry the Soviet Union is sometimes thought of as a model that other countries could follow, but such proposals overlook the fact that the Bolsheviks inherited in 1917 a country which was comparatively far more advanced than the underdeveloped countries are today. By the First World War Russia had a large and rapidly growing industrial plant and it was virtually self-sufficient in regard to mining, and the manufacture of railroad equipment, shipping, and armaments. It also produced in normal years an export surplus of grain. Most of the countries now regarded as underdeveloped are much worse off in terms of industry and food than Russia was in 1917, or for that matter in the 1860's and 1870's when the modern phase of industrialization was initiated in Russia. Only in the Soviet Union has the Communist system been in operation long enough to permit one to draw substantial conclusions from it. In other countries, its results have depended very largely on the extent of industrialization at the time that the Communists seized power. In such countries as Czechoslovakia and Hungary in Europe, and North Korea in Asia, a very substantial industrial plant had been built up before the arrival of the Communists. Here they have been in considerable measure successful in pressing further the development of industry, characteristically at the expense of consumer goods. In the other countries of Eastern Europe and Asia, the particular emphasis on industry has tended to disrupt the earlier pattern of economic growth. In China, which again is a somewhat exceptional case, the attempt at rapid industrialization has brought the economy to a point of collapse. The relative success of the Communist program of modernization thus varies greatly from country to country, and its record in the Soviet Union must be interpreted in terms of Russian conditions rather than as a typical example of Communist policy.

The theoretical bases of the Communist system stem primarily from the conception of modernization set forth by Marx and Engels, although there have been further elaborations of the theory by Communist leaders in Russia and elsewhere. Marx and Engels conceived of the process of change after the victory of the proletariat in terms of a transition from socialism to communism as a result of several concurrent and interacting developments: the disappearance of class differences, the transformation of the individual, the withering away of the state, and the merging of all countries into a single world republic.[5]

The disappearance of class differences is perhaps the most fundamental feature of the transition to communism, since in the Marxist view class conflict has been the motivating force of history. The peculiarly Marxist view of "class" is one that is related solely to the possession of the means of production. By definition, therefore, the disappearance of class differences means the transfer of the means of production from private hands to the common control of "society." What this involves in practice is the collectivization or nationalization of the means of production, and the administration of the national economy on a centralized basis. Inequalities other than those arising

[5] For useful introductions to this subject, see Elliot R. Goodman, *The Soviet Design for a World State* (New York 1960), 1-24; and Iring Fetescher, "Marx, Engels, and the Future Society," *The Future Communist Society*, ed. by Walter Laqueur and Leopold Labedz (New York 1962), 100-110.

from "class"—those due to the division of labor, differences in physical and intellectual ability, and so on—are expected to continue to be reflected in inequalities of income in the early phase known technically as "socialism." Later, when a high rate of per capita production is achieved, society will be able to distribute commodities to all individuals on the basis of need regardless of their unequal ability to contribute to society. This is the higher, and ultimate, phase known technically as "communism."

Marx and Engels anticipated that, as the individual became emancipated from what they regarded as "exploitation"—that is to say, working in a "capitalist" society—the new social environment would transform his way of life. He would be working for "society" rather than for "exploiters," and his activity would be inspired by a hitherto unknown spontaneity. The burdens of marriage, child-rearing, and family would be removed, and individuals would be free to undertake human relationships on the basis of their changing predilections. The preparation of food and the rearing of children would be handled by "society." Working hours would be gradually reduced, and the individual in his new freedom would be able to devote himself to art, education, recreation, and leisure.

The withering away of the state has been the subject of a good deal of irony and wit on the part of critics of communism, especially in the light of developments in the U.S.S.R., but much of this criticism has been misplaced. The Marxists, at least in this context, use the term "state" in a very special sense. By "state" they mean not the entire administrative apparatus, but the state as an instrument of the oppression of one class by another. It is simply a matter of definition that the state as an instrument of class oppression will disappear as soon as all classes depart from the stage of history. To say this is not to say anything very interesting, although "the withering away of the state" seems startling at first glance. The entire apparatus of administration will remain in any event, and indeed Marx and his successors recognized that a very complex administrative system would be necessary to supervise a planned economy and society on a world-wide basis. To this extent, at least, there is nothing particularly utopian about communism. So long as one is willing to use some other term than "state" to describe the complex bureaucracy of the future, the conception of "the withering away of the state" does not conflict with reality—even though it introduces an element of logical gymnastics that most students of modernization have found superfluous, if not actually confusing.

Communism was generally discussed by Marx and Engels in an abstract fashion, but they expected that the socialist revolution would start in the more industrialized societies and gradually be extended to embrace the entire world. They came eventually to recognize the revolutionary potential of Tsarist Russia, but assumed that a revolution in Russia would only be successful as part of a more general European revolutionary movement. In any event, they expected that the evolution of communism would ultimately lead to the establishment of a centralized world republic in which all of mankind would live in peace and prosperity, classless and stateless, but highly organized.

The leaders of the Bolshevik movement in Russia, no less than the Mensheviks and the European Social Democrats, were thoroughly imbued with the approach of Marx and Engels to the problems of modernization. They differed from their socialist colleagues, however, in two important respects. One was that from the start they were dominated by the personality of Lenin, who brought to Marxism much of the extremism and violence of the peculiarly Russian radicalism that flourished in the last decades of the nineteenth century. Lenin's conceptions and formulations were Marxist, but the spirit in which he interpreted them was in a significant measure alien to that of European socialism. Words like democracy, dictatorship, and even socialism, took on a different meaning when used by Lenin. In the second place the Bolsheviks, alone among Marxist socialists, faced after 1917 the practical problems of administering a government over a long period of time. Under the circumstances they could no longer deal merely in abstractions, but had to translate these abstractions into practical policies in the particular conditions in which Russia found itself. A considerable amount of attention was given by the Bolsheviks both before and after the revolution to problems of theory —particularly by Lenin, Trotsky, Bukharin, and Stalin—but in general they were too much concerned with practical affairs to produce more than glosses on the writings of Marx and Engels.[6] On two issues

[6] Valuable material on this aspect of Soviet social thought is available in the following typescript essays on deposit in the Columbia University Library: William Frederick Beachner, "Lenin's View of the Future Communist Society" (Certificate essay, Russian Institute, Columbia University, 1955); Thomas P. Farrelly, "Trotsky's Conception of the Future Communist Society" (Certificate essay, Russian Institute, Columbia University, 1955); Sidney Heitman, "Bukharin's Conception of the Transition to Communism in Soviet Russia: An Analysis of His Basic Views, 1923-

of particular concern to this essay—the withering away of the state, and the future world socialist republic—they nevertheless had some interesting ideas.

The problem of interpreting the doctrine of "the withering away of the state" has placed a considerable burden on Marxism-Leninism. Stalin in particular felt it necessary to justify the great concentration of power in the state during his long tenure as secretary-general of the Communist party. His justification was based on two arguments. The first was that the Soviet state must be strengthened to defend the homeland of socialism against the encircling capitalists. The second was that the state in the hands of the proletariat was a necessary instrument for effecting domestic change during the long period before any considerable part of the world would be ready for communism. This latter argument has been regarded by some critics as a deviation from Marxist doctrine, in so far as it appears to give the initiative in social change to the political super-structure of society rather than to the economic base. Marxist doctrine maintains that economic forces will be only "ultimately" determining, however, and it is not difficult to justify Stalin's views on this basis. The successors of Stalin have confronted this problem in a much more straightforward fashion, and the new program of the Communist Party of the Soviet Union adopted on October 31, 1961, refers to the ultimate administrative system as "public communist self-government." It goes on to say that "The agencies for planning, accounting, economic management, and cultural development, now government bodies, will lose their political character and will become agencies of public self-government."[7] This formulation remains somewhat abstract, but at least it contains the seeds of a reasonably understandable point of view.

The question of the withering away of the state is still a matter of the distant future, but that of the formation of a world socialist republic has been of some practical concern. From the statement of Stalin in 1922 that the establishment of the Union of Soviet Socialist Republics in that year was "the prototype of the future World Soviet

---

1928" (Certificate essay, Russian Institute, Columbia University, 1952); David J. Nelson, "The Views of N. Bukharin on the Future Communist Society" (Certificate essay, Russian Institute Columbia University, 1952); Hester C. Cole, "Stalin's View of the Future 'Good Society' 1901–January 1924" (Certificate essay, Russian Institute, Columbia University, 1950); and Thomas H. Rothchild, "The Highest Phase of Communism According to the Works of Joseph Stalin, 1924-1936" (M.A. essay, Faculty of Political Science, Columbia University, 1950).

[7] *CDSP*, XIII (December 13, 1961), 14.

Socialist Republic,"[8] to the declaration in the Party program of 1961 that "The majestic edifice of the new world being built by the heroic labors of the free peoples of vast areas of Europe and Asia [i.e., the Communist countries] is the prototype of the new society, of the future of all mankind,"[9] the objective of a world-wide Communist system has been consistently maintained in official documents. Until 1943 Mongolia was the only country under Communist rule other than the U.S.S.R., and it was still nominally under the suzerainty of China. During and after the Second World War, however, Communists came to power in twelve other countries. The fourteen Communist countries now have a population of well over one billion.

This Communist system of states—divided though it is in many important respects—may be thought of as a nucleus for a future world-wide system, and it has already evolved some of the attributes of such a system. Twelve Communist states—apart from Yugoslavia and Cuba—had by 1960 worked out arrangements which gave their system a significant cohesion and made it to a considerable degree independent of the outside world. Over two-thirds of their foreign trade was within the system, and in many social and cultural matters they had succeeded in creating a separate world. They organized several system-wide intergovernmental organizations, and also a number of regional organizations within the system. At the same time they supported a variety of world-wide nongovernmental organizations, which serve as transmission belts to convey their ideas to other countries. They are members of the United Nations—with the exception of the People's Republics of China, Korea, and Viet Nam—but they do not permit it to interfere in their affairs. There have been numerous conflicts among the Communist countries, but except for the Soviet-Hungarian war of 1956 they have been handled by consultation among Communist party leaders. This Communist system of states is of course far from being the world-wide system predicted by Marx and Lenin, and serious doubts have been cast on its viability by the Sino-Soviet controversy that has arisen since 1960, but it deserves careful study as a preliminary form of the international institutions that the Communists envisage for the future.[10]

[8] Cited in Goodman, 37.

[9] *CDSP*, XIII (December 6, 1961), 7.

[10] George Modelski, "The Communist International System," Research Monograph No. 9, Center of International Studies, Princeton University (December 1, 1960); Zbigniew Brzezinski, "The Organization of the Communist Camp," *World Politics*, XIII (January 1961), 175-209; and Paul Shoup, "Communism, Nationalism and the Growth of the Communist Community of Nations after World War II," *American Political Science Review*, LVI (December 1962), 886-898.

Conclusion

The Communist interpretation of change in the modern world resembles in significant respects the views of modernization held in the West, and this is natural since both approaches are concerned with the same general subject and are derived from a common intellectual background. Both recognize the unprecedented prospects for human betterment, and the possibility of an abundant life for all mankind at some future time. Both are aware that countries still in the early stages of modernization will be looking to the more advanced countries for assistance. Both see the need for an international system of states that will seek to resolve the contradictions between national diversity and international interdependence.

The differences are nevertheless profound. The Western approach to modernization—if one may presume to postulate such an approach in the absence of a consensus—is fundamentally pragmatic in addressing itself to new problems, and maintains that human costs should be the principal consideration in the elaboration of long-term plans. The West is profoundly influenced by its own experience over the centuries with the political complexities of economic and social change and is impressed by the wide diversity of ideas and institutions on the basis of which the various peoples of the world have regulated their affairs. It believes that the evolution of the world toward a modern way of life is a long process the course of which can be foreseen only in its most general outlines. It sees the solution to the many problems raised by modernization not in inexorable laws of history that can be known in advance, but in the interpretation and application of the accumulated experience of mankind by fallible human beings. The West offers the European Economic Community as a solution to the problems of international cooperation for states that are prepared for closer integration, and supports the United Nations as the evolving framework within which the larger world must seek to resolve its differences.

The Communist approach, by contrast, rejects the emphasis on the diversity of traditional ideas and institutions and hence the diversity of forms that a modern society may take. It also rejects any scheme of periodization that would regard certain countries of Europe and the English-speaking world as more advanced on the road to modernization than Russia. Most emphatically of all it rejects the view that any program or leadership other than that provided by the Communists is capable of understanding the modern world. The Communists assert in a most doctrinaire fashion that Marxism-Leninism, with its emphasis on class struggle and all that this implies, is scientifically true and that the course of events that it predicts is inevitable.

One can only speculate why the Communists take such an extremely doctrinaire view of these matters. It is probably due in part to the fact that, since Russia was a relative latecomer to modernity, its leaders spent a century or more speculating about the problems of modernization on the basis of the West European experience before they tackled these problems themselves in the practical realm. Moreover, in the early nineteenth century they came under the intellectual influence of the Germans, whose philosophical approach was particularly significant for the Marxist movement. Not all nineteenth century Russian intellectuals were theorists, of course, but the long-term influence of theoretical abstractions was much greater than in Western or Central Europe.

The Communist emphasis on doctrine may also derive from the fact that, as an ideology of relatively later-modernizing countries, it provides a justification for vigorous policies that violate accepted norms. The earlier revolutions in Britain, the American colonies, and France were also justified by a body of social theory, but the countries that modernized first were not under the pressure of more advanced models and had many generations in which to make their experiments. The pressure for rapid change is much greater in the countries that modernize later, and where the traditional government is rigid and slow-moving a revolutionary movement may be attracted by extreme radicalism. At the same time, it must be recognized that the popular appeal of communism is more as a practical program for economic and social development than as a social theory. The leaders of the movement may well be concerned with the theoretical problems of the organization of society under "socialism" and "communism," but its appeal to the intermediate leaders and to the rank and file is based on its claims of performance in the realm of industrialization, agricultural improvement, education, and more generally in the provision of a better way of life.

It is important to understand the theoretical outlook of the Communist leaders toward change in the modern world, because it reflects their view of reality and informs all of their thinking. In a simplified form their theories are taught at all levels in educational institutions, and only exceptional Communists are familiar in any detail with alternative interpretations of the modern world. At the same time, the formulation of foreign policy is a much more complex matter than simply implementing a social theory, however important the latter may be in conditioning the minds of the policy-makers. It must take into account the resources and needs of the country concerned, and the intentions and capabilities of other countries. It will also reflect in considerable measure the personalities and predilections of the policy-makers. Moreover, Marxism-Leninism provides only a general guide to action, and the policy-makers themselves must use their imagination in applying it to specific situations.

It is therefore not surprising that Communist leaders should differ in their interpretations of Marxism-Leninism. The Soviet Union and the other Communist countries have been rent by numerous and bloody controversies on this subject. The differences among the various national Communist parties have been equally pronounced. In the early postwar years the power and authority of Stalin was so great that Communist countries gave the impression of monolithic unity and were often referred to as a "bloc." This appearance of unity covered a multitude of differences, however, which came to the surface before Stalin's death. Stalin's successors have adopted a somewhat less rigid approach to the problem of uniformity, and in 1956 Khrushchev recognized that there were "many roads to socialism," and that the conditions in individual countries had to be taken into consideration. Particular concessions in this regard were made to Poland, but the extent of diversity permitted has strict limits. With Mao and his colleagues, Khrushchev has been engaged in a very bitter controversy that involves vital issues of both domestic and foreign policy. Tito has gone his own way to the point that Yugoslavia did not sign the statement of eighty-one Communist parties in 1960 and is not considered by the Chinese to be a Communist state at all. The Soviet Union does not approve of Tito's domestic policies, but the two countries cooperate to a limited extent in matters of foreign policy.

No doubt most of the controversies among Communist leaders are over matters of policy, like those that frequently occur among leaders elsewhere, and are expressed in doctrinal terms to maintain the consensus necessary for social stability. It is nevertheless important to recognize, in considering the attitude of Communists toward revolution, that Marxism-Leninism does not offer solutions to many vital issues raised by modernization, and that each Communist party must work out its own solutions to problems of practical policy. In this sense the term "Communist" is itself an abstraction that must be interpreted anew in the light of each particular situation. Except at a very general level, it does not help much to know only one's Marxism-Leninism if one wishes to interpret Communist policies. There is thus no shortcut to understanding the attitude of Communists toward revolution, and one cannot make a judgment in a specific instance without full knowledge of the interests and personalities immediately involved.

2

The Communist Theory of the State and Revolution

ANDREW C. JANOS

Communist ideology, as the term is generally understood, includes three distinct but closely interrelated elements: a dialectical philosophy, an economic theory of history, and a theory of the state and revolution.[1] This last aspect of ideology refers to two types of analytic constructs: theories of what are the dynamics of revolutionary movements, and operational theories prescribing what should be done to bring about a Communist revolution. In Marxist-Leninist doctrine, the distinction between the two becomes especially vague. Although it has been emphasized that the prescriptive rules of operational theory do not represent "scientific truth," they are frequently vested in the same garb of historical inevitability as the propositions of the social theory.

Strategy (as well as tactics) is an art of applying means to the achievement of particular objectives. As an art, strategy does not preclude the subjective element of skill. On the other hand, the relation of ends and means as well as certain conditions attending the application of means form a certain logical relationship, and as such they form the core of a theory of strategy.

The theory of knowledge accepted by Communists views the development of man's cognition as a "gradual movement from ignorance to knowledge."[2] There is a great stress on practice as the "basis and purpose" of the cognitive process. "Theory arises in response to the requirements of social life and of the class struggle, and

[1] In discussing theory and ideology I will distinguish among (1) Marxism, (2) Orthodox Marxism, (3) Revisionist Marxism, and (4) Marxism-Leninism. The first is meant to refer to the doctrine that emerged from the collaboration of Marx and Engels; the second to the interpretation of the doctrine by some of Marx's younger contemporaries like Kautsky and Plekhanov; the third to the revision of Marxism by Bernstein and the European socialists; the last to the revision of Marxism by Lenin and his followers. The ideology of Communism is thus Marxism-Leninism, a particular form of Marxism.

[2] *Fundamentals of Marxism-Leninism* (Moscow 1961), 111.

in its turn, [theory] influences the social process."[3] Such a view is obviously apt to create a great awareness of the importance of adjusting strategies and tactics to a changing environment, and indeed, in terms of this general framework, Communists make constant and systematic efforts to improve the methods by which they can manipulate the environment to their ends. Tactics are defined as the "political behavior of the Party, or the character, tendency, methods of its political activity."[4] In order to improve them, experiences are painstakingly evaluated and fed back into the theory for future guidance. "Tactical resolutions are adopted by party congresses for the purpose of determining what the political behavior of the party as a whole should be in regard to new tasks."[5]

The particular methods of the struggle, the question of how single Communist parties or the Communist leadership respond to particular situations, will be the principal concern of this volume of essays. It is therefore opportune to discuss why, with some observable regularity, certain strategic choices were made. Instead of reviewing particular strategies and tactics, the current chapter will undertake the task of summarizing the general principles that guide the selection of methods of adjustment to a changing environment. While the former is subject to change in the course of the revolutionary struggle, the latter is, presumably, immutable and universally relevant, a view that might lead to important clues concerning past and future Communist behavior.

Philosophy, Social Theory, and Strategy

The philosophical foundations of Communist social theory postulate the existence of a general trend of qualitative change in the world, and this change always represents "development" or "progress" from "lower" to "higher" stages. The process of development, in both nature and society, takes place through the struggle of opposites. The development of societies follows a definite pattern and proceeds through five typical stages: primitive communism, slavery, feudalism, capitalism, and socialism.

The character of society and the stage of social development are, above all, determined by the economic "base" comprising the "productive forces" (manpower, resources, technology) and the "produc-

[3] *Ibid.*, 114.

[4] Vladimir I. Lenin, "Two Tactics of Social Democracy in the Democratic Revolution," *Selected Works*, III (Moscow-New York n.d.), 45.

[5] *Ibid.*, 45.

tive relations" by which is meant the organization and control of production. Politics, art, morality, and legal standards, on the other hand, belong to the "superstructure," the character of which reflects the structure of the economic base and follows developments within the former. Politics is dictated by economic interest, and the ultimate source of political power is economic power.

Following traditional Marxist analysis, the Communist concepts of the state and political power are closely related. The liberal notion of the state as the guardian of common interests is rejected. The function of the state is to act as the agent of special class interests inherent in the productive relations between "exploiters" and "exploited." Authority accrues from effective power, and from effective power alone. "The state arises when and where and to the extent that class antagonisms are irreconcilable."[6] Marx, Engels, and later Lenin regarded the state as an instrument of class rule, a "special organization of force . . . the organizational [sic] violence for some class," whose main agents are "special bodies of armed men, bureaucracies, armies, police forces."[7]

On the whole, this theory views the economic and political structures of society as a system that would tend toward an equilibrium were it not for the inexorable operation of economic laws that produce "contradictions" between the two. "Contradictions" within the economic base create new forms of production and ownership that are no longer appropriate to the system of political control. While the base reaches a higher stage of economic development, the political super-structure lags behind, and at a certain point becomes incompatible with the base. At this point the downfall of the old state and the substitution of new legal norms and instruments of coercion becomes inevitable. Thus, although revolution follows causally from a process of economic and social disorganization, the process itself is essentially political. A revolutionary change takes place, and a new type of society emerges, when and where effective political power is transferred from one class to another. The Communist theory of revolution is the theory of the collapse of the system of political controls, and, on the operational level, a theory of seizing the instruments of coercion.

Of course, as has frequently been pointed out by critics, the de-

[6] Vladimir I. Lenin, "The State and the Revolution," *The Essentials of Lenin* (London 1947), 144.

[7] *Ibid.*, 144.

terministic universe of Marxism-Leninism should obviate the need for an operational doctrine. This contradiction between theory and practice has never been, and never can be, satisfactorily resolved. The need for strategic doctrine and the elaborate political preparations for the revolution cannot be reconciled with the social theory without giving considerable concessions to the role of the actors' will, reflecting their perceptions rather than the "objective reality" of their material environment. According to the explanation given by standard Communist texts, the social laws laid down by Marx do not operate "mechanically" ignoring the "human element" of the situation. Contradictions are reflected by growing class antagonisms between the exploiters and the exploited and "sooner or later social forces interested in the realization of these [social] laws will arise and these forces will by their struggle put these laws in effect."[8]

The Concept of the Revolutionary Situation

The definition of the role of strategy arises out of this curious combination of determinism and voluntarism. In terms of time-honored phraseology the Communist is the "midwife of the revolution," insofar that the conditions of a revolution are produced by history and by "material social forces," but once a revolutionary situation presents an opportunity, it is the highest moral duty of the forces of progress to "push the situation further forward" toward its logical conclusion.[9]

The concept of the revolutionary situation—defined by conditions warranting active interference with historical processes—is therefore most crucial in revolutionary theory. If it is true that a revolution cannot be created at will, but can be "pushed forward" at certain times then, as Trotsky observes, the revolutionary leaders are presented with the task of correct diagnosis.[10] Misjudgment of the right moment may spell disaster if set too early and cause the missing of a historical opportunity if set too late.

For Marx and the Orthodox protagonists of his doctrine—such as Kautsky and Plekhanov—the definition of the revolutionary situation tended to be in social and economic terms. While conditions for a revolution might exist in a variety of situations, conditions for a social-

[8] *Fundamentals,* 166.

[9] Lenin, "The Two Tactics of Social Democracy in the Democratic Revolution," *Selected Works,* III, 69.

[10] Leon Trotsky, *The Russian Revolution,* selected and edited by F. W. Dupee (New York 1959), 309. Although Trotsky was later disavowed by the Soviet leadership he was, next to Lenin, the foremost strategist of the movement at the time of the October revolution and many years after, and his influence as a theorist loomed large even after his expulsion from the Soviet Union.

ist revolution could not exist unless capitalism had run its full course, leaving no room for further development within its own social framework. The bourgeois revolutions of the eighteenth and nineteenth centuries came at a time when feudalism as an economic system had already been dissolved, and the viability of the feudal mode of production had been challenged by capitalist economies that, after the political act of the revolution, could serve as the base for bourgeois society.

Nineteenth century Marxism regarded socialism as a "higher" stage of social development characterized by economic egalitarianism and political democracy, which they knew could not be realized in the absence of the physical preconditions of high productivity and general abundance. They hypothesized correctly that the strains of enforcing economic and social development would raise the danger of dictatorship. Moreover, the idea of creating an economic base through the power instruments of the state would have been an anomaly to all who firmly believed in the primacy of the base and the secondary nature of the superstructure. A situation conducive to a socialist revolution, it was believed, could arise only in the most highly developed capitalist societies.

Whatever Marx's own views were on the subject of the revolutionary situation—and his pronouncements were ambiguous to say the least—they were reformulated by western socialist theoreticians shortly after his death with much emphasis on specific social and economic requirements and relatively peaceful political change. When Bernstein laid down his so called "revisionist" principles, these reflected a general tendency in European socialist movements and were inspired by the belief that instead of political revolution, socialist parties should attempt to promote programs that would accelerate the development of the social and economic "base," thereby creating the conditions for the downfall of capitalism and for the rise of socialist society.

Whereas Orthodox Marxism was revised in Europe by the less radical wing of the socialist movement, Russia produced her own brand of revisionism, a theory that became unconditionally accepted by Communist movements after 1918. At a time when the popularity of revolutionary radicalism seemed to have waned in the West, Lenin and the Bolsheviks applied the precepts of Marxism to conditions prevailing in Russia, inevitably blending the theory with certain elements of the rich non-Marxist Russian revolutionary tradition.

The most striking "objective condition" of Russian society, from the point of view of a socialist thinker, was the country's backwardness in comparison to Western Europe. Russia had a relatively weak bourgeoisie and a small, although concentrated, industrial proletariat. The development of capitalism did not follow the Western pattern of private initiative and free market. Instead it was encouraged, protected, and occasionally directed by a bureaucratic state apparatus. At the prevailing rate of development it could have taken many decades before capitalism would have run its full course.

To wait patiently for many decades contenting oneself with the acceleration of the development of capitalism—as indeed some of the more academically inclined Russian Marxists advocated—did not fit in with the Russian revolutionary tradition. Nechayev's apotheosis of violence and the terrorism of the Populists loomed large in Russian life at the turn of the century, and the obvious weaknesses of autocracy invited more immediate solutions. Was it not Marx, after all, who once openly advocated the solution of a Blanquist *coup d'état* to bring about a revolution—to be sure a "bourgeois" revolution—in Russia?[11]

Then, there was an additional factor without which the Bolshevik revision of Marxism cannot be properly evaluated. The political environment of Russian society was that of a tyranny. The strong and oppressive state was an unpleasant but inevitable fact of life for Russians. And while in the West the autonomous development of society seemed to have shaped the political system—which led Marx to hypothesize about the primacy of the base—the Russian experience suggested that the causal relationship might be reversed. Was it not the Tsarist state and its instruments of coercion that set the pace for economic change and paved the way for capitalist society, rather than the other way round?

The conclusion that Lenin and his followers, a handful at that time, drew from these observations was that socialist society, too, could be built up from above. The state should therefore be seized for this end whenever the opportunity presented itself. Whereas it was not openly admitted that, by inference, this refuted the theory of the primacy of the base "in effect, Lenin substituted the conquest of political power, the destruction of the existing state and all its works, for socialism as the goal or end-in-view of the socialist movement. Socialism as a form of social organization and as an ideal of fraternity

[11] See, for instance, "Marx to F. A. Sorge" (September 27, 1877), and "Marx to the Editorial Board of the 'Otechestvenniye Zapiski'" (November 1877) in Karl Marx and Frederick Engels, *Selected Correspondence* (Moscow-London 1956), 374-375 and 376-380.

can only become an end-in-view after political power has been won."[12]

As a corollary, Lenin radically transformed the concept of the revolutionary situation from a tool of social analysis into a clear-cut military analogy. He now came to refer to a favorable balance of forces that enables the insurgents to seize power and retain it. The arguments for the Bolshevik revolution run entirely in terms of opportunity and a favorable political transition. "The Bolsheviks can, and must, take over the power of the government," he contended in September 1917, ". . . because the active majority of the revolutionary elements of the people of both capitals is large enough to carry the masses, to overcome the resistance of the adversary, to smash him and to conquer power and retain it."[13] In another of his essays he further argued that in July 1917 no revolutionary situation existed because the Bosheviks "could not have retained power either physically or politically."[14]

A revolutionary situation may thus be brought about by the force of a popular movement, but in its absence, also by skillful maneuvers and the exploitation of a power vacuum by a small but well-organized minority. A revolutionary situation arises when the Communist insurgents are relatively strong, and their opponents relatively weak. Active support for the insurgent Communists is less important than the lack of support for their opponent. With this idea of the revolution, the isolation of the incumbent and the neutralization of any potential source of power became the most crucial intermediary strategies.

The Categories of Strategic Theory

What are the implications of this military analogy for the theory of strategy that Communists subscribe to? First, that there is no analytic difference between political and military forms of the class struggle—a principle that Engels had already discovered in Clausewitz with great satisfaction[15]—and second, that the methods of military analysis, the study of objectives, capabilities and conditions, are relevant in the context of any political conflict situation.

The objective, and principal determinant, of revolutionary strategy is the conquest of the state, or the "seizure" of the opponent's instrument of coercion. The first task of the strategist is, therefore, to

[12] Sidney Hook, *Marx and the Marxists* (Princeton 1955), 77.

[13] Lenin, "The Bolsheviks Must Assume Power," *Selected Works,* vi, 215.

[14] Lenin, "Marxism and Insurrection," *Selected Works,* vi, 220.

[15] Letter of Engels to Marx (September 25, 1857); quoted in Sigmund Neumann, "Engels and Marx: Military Concepts of Social Revolutionaries," in E. M. Earle, ed. *Makers of Modern Strategy* (Princeton 1943), 156.

assess the structure of the instruments of coercion and select his operational targets accordingly. In this context, Marx, Engels, and Lenin attached prime importance to the armed forces. Lenin, applying the Clausewitzian metaphor, designated them as the "key to the country." Trotsky reaffirmed Engels' and Lenin's thesis and stated that the first task of every revolution was to bring the army over to its side.[16] In modern industrial societies, the structure and distribution of political power is more complex. Trade unions, political, professional organizations, may be effective instruments of power due to their ability to mobilize their membership, order strikes, or act as paramilitary organizations. The army is thus not the only institutional target. The experience of East European countries after the Second World War also demonstrates that the struggle for power may also bypass the armed forces. In some of these countries the strategy of takeovers was based on the infiltration of bureaucracies and the preestablished control over special security police forces.

What then are the available means to attain the objective of the "seizure of power," and what importance is assigned to them in determining the prevailing balance of forces in society? Whereas power (German *Macht*, Russian *vlast'*) refers to what we might regard the authoritative power of the state as embodied in an institutional framework, "forces" (German *Kräfte*, Russian *sily*) refer to a combination of political and military capabilities to capture the state or to resist it. The "balance of social forces" refers to a ratio of armies, paramilitary and political organizations, and popular support. In the heyday of nineteenth century revolutionary idealism, the forces of revolution usually referred to the actively participating masses. At that time there was also a strong belief among revolutionaries that in order to be successful, their movement must be supported by the majority of the population. In contrast, experience convinced the Bolsheviks and their disciples that a revolution could be successful without the support of majorities or even against them. This trend is obvious in Trotsky's description of Lenin's methods of analysis at the time of the Russian revolution. "Lenin studiously followed all elections, carefully assembling those figures which would throw light on the actual correlation of forces. . . . At the same time, Lenin never identified the indexes of parliamentarism with the actual correlation of forces. He always introduced a correction in the favor of direct action."[17] The

[16] Trotsky, 318.
[17] *Ibid.*, 266.

term majority, Lenin warns, should not be understood in the "formal sense."[18] "Majorities are not counted but won over."[19] More important than general popular support may be the activities of the population in a few political centers, as were Petrograd and Moscow in the Russian case. Urban masses, intellectuals, the personnel of key industries, in general those who are easily available for mobilization, or those whose occupational or social position are strategic, are the principal popular targets of Communist movements.

Whereas in orthodox doctrine the masses figured as the backbone of revolutionary movements, Lenin replaced them in the political equation with the "organizational weapon" of the party. For Lenin, operating under extremely adverse political conditions and without the hope of ever being able to win over a great majority of the population, the party became a substitute for spontaneity and mass participation. What he needed was a disciplined core that was willing and able to perform a wide range of functions under diverse conditions, giving greater independence from wavering and unstable popular moods.[20] The party is certainly easier to mobilize and in case of need it can be used as the nucleus of an armed attack on the incumbent. "When, in pursuit of one aim, animated by one will, millions . . . change the place and the method of their activities, change their tools and weapons in accordance with the changing conditions and the requirements of the struggle—this is organization."[21] Indeed, the model for the Leninist party is the modern army, "flexible, and at the same time able to give millions a single will."[22]

Whereas it is possible to generalize about societies in terms of stages and specific levels of development, in strategy due consideration is given to certain unique elements, conditions, "characteristics or peculiarities" of a situation. In military analysis these refer to the physical conditions of the terrain attending the application of means; in political analysis, the framework has to be expanded to include social, political, and economic as well as physical-ecological factors. Writing of the October insurrection, Trotsky remarks that "its planned character grew chiefly out of objective relations, the place of Petrograd in the country, the place occupied by the government in Petrograd."[23]

[18] Lenin, "The Bolsheviks Must Assume Power," *Selected Works,* VI, 217.

[19] Trotsky, 314.

[20] The already classic analysis of the party's role in strategy is in Philip Selznick, *The Organizational Weapon* (New York 1952).

[21] Lenin, "The Collapse of the Second International," *Selected Works,* V, 215.

[22] *Ibid.,* 214.

[23] Trotsky, 431.

Lenin listed the factors of dual power and "imperialist" war as the "main peculiarities of the revolution."[24] In Mao's analysis, the "characteristics" of China's revolutionary war were, among others, "the existence of a frail capitalist economy and a preponderant semi-feudal economy," and the fact that China was a "vast semi-colonial country, unevenly developed both politically and economically."[25]

The Transfer of Power and Internal War

In essence, Communist doctrine sees revolution as a process of the transfer of power from one class to another. Although the probability of temporary setbacks is readily admitted, there is no doubt about the outcome. The ultimate change in the balance of forces is inevitable and it proceeds from "lower" to "higher" stages. Analytically one may distinguish three distinct phases: a state of disequilibrium in the favor of the incumbent, a state of equilibrium, and finally a state of disequilibrium in the favor of the insurgent. Since the pattern of strategy and tactics depends on relative power, change in the balance of forces calls for new forms of the struggle. These forms must be offensive, unless in a situation of tactical retreat, and "appropriate" to the specific stage. In the first, the main concern of the revolutionists must be the attrition of the enemy and building up their own relative strength by "political mobilization," the second and third stages, on the other hand, require a transition into full-scale attack and a strategy of annihilation.

The "inevitable" transition from attrition to annihilation can best be illustrated by Communist theories of internal war. According to these theories, violence is a particular form of the political struggle, the character of which is bound to change as the balance is turning toward the insurgents. The forms appropriate to the first stage are riots, demonstrations, and strikes. When the morale of the incumbents is sufficiently undermined and the instruments of coercion relatively disorganized, then the revolution reaches its highest stage, when the process should be consummated by calling an armed insurrection.[26]

While Lenin and European Communists thought strikes and demonstrations were the appropriate forms of the struggle for a weak

[24] Lenin, "The Tasks of the Proletariat in the Present Revolution," *Selected Works,* VI, 46-47.

[25] Mao Tse-tung, *Strategic Problems of China's Revolutionary War* (Peking 1954), 34-35.

[26] See Lenin, "Revolutionary Army and Revolutionary Government," *Selected Works,* III, 312. Also "Resolution on the Armed Uprising," *The Essentials,* 135.

insurgent, Mao, barred from the urban areas by the weakness of the Chinese working class and the effective controls of the government, but aided by special physical and demographic conditions, used guerrilla warfare as the instrument of attrition and political mobilization. He envisaged a turning point in the balance of forces and a corresponding change in the forms of the political struggle. "Guerrilla character is precisely our distinguishing feature," he wrote in 1936, "some day this character will definitely become a thing to be ashamed of and therefore to be discarded."[27] Then Mao, like Lenin, was determined to "push further forward" the revolutionary situation, although not toward an armed insurrection, but toward a full-fledged civil war of regular armies.

There may be, of course, other variations of violent tactics, such as the combination of terrorism and guerrilla warfare in the stage of attrition to be followed by armed insurrection in the second, as was contemplated and unsuccessfully applied at the time of the 1905 revolution.[28] Internal war may also start with an insurrection in the centers and be expanded by means of civil war to the periphery, as some of the Comintern strategists envisaged the course of a violent takeover.[29] But while violence may dominate the process of the transfer of power, it may—indeed it should—be substituted for by methods short of violence whenever this is possible. This, Lenin thought in 1917, was a "possibility extremely rare in history and extremely valuable,"[30] but the October revolution itself shortly thereafter provided the best example of a relatively non-violent transition. Whereas the classic strategy of the armed insurrection envisaged the seizure of the army from the barricades, the Bolsheviks accomplished this task by subverting the armed forces. Trotsky wrote that "The unique thing about the October Revolution, a thing never before observed in so complete a form, was that, thanks to a happy combination of circumstances, the proletarian vanguard had won over the garrison of the capital before the moment of insurrection."[31] As a result, the only task left for the Bolsheviks was to eliminate an already isolated political leadership very much in the manner of a police action. The

[27] Quoted in Walter D. Jacobs, "Mao Tse-tung as a Guerrilla—A Second Look," in Franklin Mark Osanka (ed.) *Modern Guerrilla Warfare* (Glencoe 1961), 172.

[28] Lenin, "Lessons of the Moscow Uprising," *Selected Works*, III, 346-356.

[29] See for instance, Alfred Lange, *The Road to Victory* (1927), reprinted in *The Communist Conspiracy*, House Report No. 2243, 84th Congress, 2nd Session (Washington, D.C. 1956), Part I, Section D, 300-335.

[30] Lenin, "Compromises," *Selected Works*, VI, 210.

[31] Trotsky, 319.

sub-violent seizure of the instruments of coercion was also supplemented by the exploitation of the legal institutional political framework for alien ends. Legally gained power positions then were used against opponents to legitimize illegal action in the "highest" stages of the political struggle.

In general, however much it may be likely in certain stages of the revolutionary struggle, violence is not the predominant aspect of the theory. Its fundamentally political (in contrast to physically violent) character is perhaps best demonstrated by the numerous arguments of Marxists against Blanqui. The latter, a pre-Marxist revolutionary, believed that a small group of men could seize the helm of the state if they were sufficiently determined and skilled. He ignored the idea of political mobilization and the necessity of a certain balance of power as a condition of revolution, and while he was concerned with the most minute details of the physical seizure of power—he worked out the tactical rules of an armed insurrection in a big city to near perfection—he overlooked the political conditions of retaining power. Thus, his Marxist critics charged, he wanted to substitute the complex process of the transfer of power with the physical act of insurrection.[32] In contrast, Marxists realized that skirmishes and battles at the barricades were only secondary aspects of the revolutionary struggle. Once, quoting Clausewitz, Engels remarked that fighting was to war what cash payment was to trade, for however important it was, it occurred only relatively rarely.[33]

For Communists and their Marxist predecessors the political process has referred to the total spectrum of the application of force, of which violence is but one variation. This specific formulation of the structure of force first appears in Clausewitz, whom Marx, Engels, and Lenin discovered separately, and whose views should be appealing to any group or individual strongly oriented toward the problem of power. But while Clausewitz maintained only that all war was politics,[34] his Communist disciples carried the formula to the logical conclusion that all politics was war.

Violence, in Communist theories, is not identical with crude physical processes of killing and pain-infliction. War, again true to the

[32] Two succinct Marxist analyses of Blanqui may be found in Frederick Engels, "Introduction to the 'Class Struggles in France, 1848-1850,'" in Karl Marx, *Selected Works*, II (New York n.d.), 169-191 and in Trotsky, 306-313.

[33] Sigmund Neumann, in Earle, 156.

[34] Carl von Clausewitz, *On War*, translated by F. J. Graham with notes of F. N. Maude (London 1918), I, 23.

Clausewitzian analysis, is an act of compulsion with the purpose of changing the opponents' state of mind. "The problem of revolution" —says Trotsky—"as of war, consists in breaking the will of the foe, forcing him to capitulate and to accept the conditions of the conqueror."[35] The destruction of an enemy involves breaking either his ability or his will to resist, thus the nature of violence is both physical and psychological.

The modern pattern of revolutionary warfare has been derived from this conceptualization of force and violence. Their use will have a psychological impact in each case it is resorted to, and the psychological impact will lesson the opponent's physical ability to resort to force. In terms of this conceptualization, the use of force by itself is meaningless, and conversely, psychological warfare is bound to fail without a show of force. But, if applied systematically, a little force can create inordinate psychological effects, an observation on which Communists build their strategies of terror and unconventional warfare.

Domestic and World Revolution

The Communist theory of revolution, one should remember, is the theory of world revolution. From its inception, the movement did not envision isolated revolutionary movements. Instead, it expected the simultaneous rising of all oppressed peoples (at least in the more advanced countries that controlled the rest of the world). At a later stage of historical development, the Bolsheviks interpreted their own role as one of initiating a world-wide insurrection by breaking "the weakest link" of the capitalist system. Since the victory of the October revolution, the leaders of the Soviet Union have regarded themselves as the principal agents of the world revolution. In terms of these images, domestic political struggle can only be viewed as an organic part of the world-wide struggle and never as an end in itself.

A country with a revolutionary situation represents only one of the many fronts on which war is conducted against the enemy. As a consequence, many revolutionary situations may be ignored, or even counteracted, should the logic of the overall strategy so desire. On the other hand, the overall strategy may be used to produce a revolutionary situation in a specific society by committing the prestige and power of Soviet Russia (or more recently of Communist China) to the revolutionary cause. Ever since 1918, the political power of

[35] Leon Trotsky, *Democracy vs. Dictatorship* (New York 1922), 54.

the Soviet state has been one of the "forces" that had to be reckoned with in domestic political equations.

The theoretical implication of this frame of reference is that the analytic categories relevant to domestic and international politics are identical. Accordingly, relations between Communist and non-Communist states are viewed as a struggle with a definitive objective, and the particular form of the overall struggle depends on the prevailing balance of forces in the world arena. The Chinese contention that "East wind has prevailed over West wind" and hence the struggle has reached its "highest" stage, is the best illustration of the point. At this, Marxist-Leninist doctrine undoubtedly supports Mao, although the Soviets may see differently and argue that nuclear weapons have changed some of the fundamental principles of strategy.

In any case, the struggle is carried on by a whole range of means, and the choice of means is limited only by the lack of power and considerations of expediency. The principal element in the struggle for power is force, although its overt, physical application may be extremely limited, and oriented more against the will of the opponent than his physical ability to fight back. The combination of massive threats and propaganda with limited violence is, indeed, the prime characteristic of prevailing international relations, that have been otherwise known as the cold war. The latter also is the best demonstration of the thesis that the internal and international strategies of the Communist movement form an integral unit, at least as long as and to the extent that, central direction can be enforced in the Communist parties inside and outside the bloc.

An Instrument of Predicting Communist Behavior

In essence, the Communist theory of revolution is a set of logical relationships combined with an empirical concept of the state. Its relevance is less likely to change than that of theoretical constructs derived inductively from a relatively limited historical experience, as, for instance, Marx's theory of capitalist society, based almost entirely on the observation of the development of *laissez faire* and the rise of the Victorian middle class in England, or Lenin's theory of imperialism, suggested by the history of the last decades of the nineteenth century. Indeed, the theory of revolution has proved perhaps the most stable aspect of the doctrine. As such, it is a useful analytic tool for outside observers. Familiarity with the theory enables the observer to assume the perspective of the Communist actors and to project their responses to diverse political situations.

Nevertheless, it has frequently been argued that the precepts of the theory have existed only for the purposes of progaganda. Another view is that, like many other aspects of the doctrine, it is merely suitable as a tool of *ex post facto* analysis, lacking any consistently applicable predictive value.

There is, of course, an element of truth in each of these statements. The precepts of strategy have been used to justify policies, and even to liquidate unwanted rivals within the movement. But, on the other hand, the writings of Lenin, Trotsky, Mao, and of many of the principal actors in the Cominform era, show that the theory of revolution has consistently influenced tactics. One must also realize that whole generations of Communist *cadres* have been brought up on its fundamental precepts at various levels of their formal education. Such intensive exposure, especially in the absence of access to alternatives, is bound to leave an imprint on the categories in which an individual habitually evaluates his environment.

Above all, however, one should not lose sight of the fact that the theory is not a blueprint that individuals are supposed to follow blindly. The Communist theory of revolution, as indeed all strategic theory, is relevant only as an ideal type that an individual might (or might not) want to approximate. The knowledge of the theory on the part of observers is a key to understanding, but only one of many factors that ultimately enables them to predict behavior with some degree of reliability. The projection of the actions of an opponent also requires knowledge of a great number of social and cultural factors, tradition, personal experience, and irrational influences that might bear on the behavior of leaders and masses.

3

The Emergence of Communist Revolutionary Doctrine*

THOMAS P. THORNTON

The Foundations: Success in Russia and Failure in Germany

Looking back at their own experience in seizing power, Soviet Russian historians have singled out six elements which were responsible for their success: the "leading role played by the working class," the alliance of the workers and the peasantry, the dual power structure of the soviets, the weakness of the Russian bourgeoisie, the disunity of foreign opposition, and the correct policies of Lenin's "party of a new type."[1] Granted the special meaning attached to the terms "working class" and "bourgeoisie," these points provide a valid summary of the factors which brought success to the Bolsheviks, even though they tend to underemphasize the exceptionally favorable conditions enjoyed by them as a result of the wartime chaos which gripped Russia in 1917.[2] At the beginning of the Russian Revolution

* In addition to sources indicated in the footnotes throughout this chapter, and materials listed in the bibliography, there are several works which deal specifically with the history of the Comintern period and provide historical background which readers may find helpful. Hugh Seton-Watson's *From Lenin to Khrushchev* (New York 1960) is the best overall history of Communism. It is readable, accurate and objective. This book has appeared in England under the title *The Pattern of Communist Revolution,* and an earlier American edition was entitled *From Lenin to Malenkov*. Stefan T. Possony's *Century of Conflict* suffers from the author's tendency to editorialize, but is an exceptionally well-documented survey, with emphasis on military and political theory. Theodor Arnold's *Der revolutionäre Krieg* (Pfaffenhofen/Ilm 1961) is not available in English. It provides a very selective but useful survey of the Communist experience with revolutions.

[1] This list is derived from both Stalin's and Khrushchev's party histories: *The History of the Communist Party of the Soviet Union (Bolsheviks): Short Course* (1st ed., Moscow 1938), 262-263 in the 1950 edition; and the *History of the Communist Party of the Soviet Union* (Moscow 1960), 258-259. Each of the lists consists of five points, four of which are identical. The soviets are not given credit in the Stalin version, however, nor is a significant role ascribed to the international situation in the 1960 book.

[2] There are many good accounts of the Bolshevik revolution, ranging from Alan Moorehead's popular *The Russian Revolution* (New York 1958) to E. H. Carr's three-volume *The Bolshevik Revolution* (New York 1951-1953). Robert H. McNeal's "Soviet Historiography on the October Revolution: A Review of Forty Years," *American Slavic and East European Review,* XVII (October 1958), 269-281, is a useful bibliography. The reverse view is provided in I. I. Mints, *Zarubezhnaya Literatura ob Oktyabr'skoy Revolyutsii* [Foreign Literature on the October Revolution] (Moscow 1961).

—the collapse of the empire in February 1917—the Bolsheviks were not even significant actors in the process. Lenin and Trotsky were abroad, many others were in exile, and only a few third-echelon leaders were available to exploit the suddenly changed situation in Petrograd. The membership of the Bolshevik faction of the Social Democratic Party was about 23,000, and in the first Petrograd Soviet the Bolsheviks controlled only 40 of the 400 members.[3] In these terms, little could haeve been expected from the group, but the strength of the party lay more in its nature than in its numbers.

Since shortly after the turn of the century, Lenin had placed his faith in the organization of a relatively small party which was characterized by strict organization and discipline—the "general staff of the proletariat." He disdained the idea of political success through reliance upon the spontaneity of the masses or upon the terrorism of the *Narodniks*. In the highly restrictive conditions of Tsarist Russia, he also saw little prospect for the success of an open mass party. The conspiratorial nature of his "new type of party" was a necessity if the Bolsheviks were to be a group which could survive Tsarist persecution and act forcefully in a situation of opportunity.[4]

The opportunity for action was to come about in a "two stage revolution,"[5] the first stage marked by the assumption to power of a moderate and progressive "bourgeois" government which would guarantee freedom of political activity. Against such an opponent, the new type of party should be able to move toward the second stage—the seizure of power—in a way which would be impossible against the Tsarist autocracy. As events developed in 1917, the February revolution was the first stage; the second was the *coup d'état* of the October revolution which carried Lenin and his party to power. The concept of the "new type of party" appeared fully vindicated by events, and even today remains the most sacred tenet of Communism.

Lenin's success would have been impossible against a determined and competent adversary. The moderates who held power between February and October lacked the determination of Lenin and showed little competence in combatting the threat of the Bolsheviks. The

[3] Former datum from *Bol'shaya Sovetskaya Entsiklopediya* (1st ed., Moscow 1930), XI, 531; the latter from Leon Trotsky, *The Russian Revolution* (New York 1959), 213.

[4] The early years of the CPSU are well described by Leonard Schapiro in Part One of *The Communist Party of the Soviet Union* (New York 1960).

[5] Elaborated in Lenin's *Two Tactics of Social Democracy in the Democratic Revolution* (1905).

Provisional Government was faced with the incompatible tasks of establishing a new order within Russia, and at the same time of continuing the war against Germany in the west. Either one of the tasks would have taxed the powers of a genius—to do both simultaneously was impossible. Lenin attacked the government on both fronts. Upon returning to Russia in April 1917, he announced that not only were the Bolsheviks for immediate peace on almost any terms, but that they intended to move rapidly toward the second stage of the revolution. The peace slogan was a powerful propaganda weapon, for the war was discredited as a patriotic undertaking and showed no hope of success. The Government, loath to reintroduce restrictions smacking of Tsardom, hesitated to take action against the Bolsheviks, and it was not until July that Bolshevik activity began to be circumscribed. Even measures instituted then were half-hearted, and when a military take-over was attempted by General Kornilov in September, the Government tacitly accepted the Bolsheviks as a lesser danger than a possible right-wing coup.

Lenin's small party clearly needed support for its seizure of power. Through painstaking work the Bolsheviks had been successful in mobilizing strength in the Petrograd and Moscow proletariat and had formed an armed "Red Guard," which ostensibly was to defend factories, but in fact was intended as the Bolshevik military arm. The proletariat of Russia was too insignificant a force to seize power by itself, however, a fact which Lenin had come to realize following the failure of the 1905 Revolution. Allies had to be found, and the most obvious reservoir was the Russian peasantry.

In contrast to the peasantry of Europe proper, which Marx and Engels had counted as "reserves of the reactionary force," the Russian peasantry was a revolutionary force in its own right. Western Europe had substantially solved its agrarian problem in the course of the industrial revolution, but agrarian conditions in Russia were still in the early stage of the emergence from serfdom. The land was overpopulated and poorly utilized, and the peasantry stood in open opposition to the landholders. The urgent need of land reform after the overthrow of the Tsar was admitted by all parties. The Provisional Government decided to postpone redistribution until a constitutional government had been formed, but the Bolsheviks urged immediate and egalitarian distribution of land to the peasants. Although the Bolsheviks did not succeed in gaining extensive positive support among the peasantry in the countryside, and indeed did not require it until the Civil War period, this policy ensured that the peasantry neither opposed them nor presented any problem to their seizure of power.

A substantial and important portion of the Russian peasantry was not in the countryside in 1917, but was serving with the army, which had suffered badly at the hands of the Germans and was thoroughly demoralized. The February Revolution fractured the army's command structure and the peasant soldiers feared that they would come off poorly in land distribution in their home villages if they were absent at the front. The desertion rate was high and disobedience posed a severe obstacle to military operations. There were still loyal and efficient units, but these were few in number.

While in hiding after July 1917, Lenin had set forth in *State and Revolution* his view of the importance of the army, the "key to the country." In his plan for the Russian army he realized that the barricade tactics of nineteenth century Europe were not necessary; political measures would suffice. The direct approach of the Bolsheviks toward the army was an intensive and extensive propaganda campaign directed at the troops, designed to erode still further the disciplinary structure of the army and prevent the command from bringing the army into action against a Bolshevik move for power. Actual political support within the army was a secondary objective; it would be quite enough if the soldiers would remain neutral at the crucial moment and refuse to obey the orders of the Government and the officers.

In addition, the Bolsheviks utilized the institution of the soviets (councils) in their campaign to neutralize the army. On the very first day of the February revolution in 1917, soviets were spontaneously created under the leadership of the non-Bolshevik left. They were initially political organs of the more radical parties, and existed parallel to the power structures of the Provisional Government. As long as the soviets and the Provisional Government were controlled by politically like-minded forces, the danger to orderly government which the dual power structure posed was minimal. Throughout the summer of 1917, the authority of the soviets increased steadily at the expense of that of the Provisional Government, and in the course of the period between July and October, the Bolsheviks were successful in gaining decisive influence in the most important ones—especially in Petrograd and Moscow, and in a number of army units. The Bolsheviks were thus able to assert their influence over the most important elements of the army even before the October revolution, despite the nominal control of the Provisional Government. When October came, the army for the most part remained neutral, and those elements which joined the fighting did so almost entirely on the side of the Bolsheviks.

The citizenry also was given the moral option of deciding which power structure to obey—the Provisional Government or the soviets. Given their organizational diligence, it was relatively easy for the Bolsheviks to rally the bulk of the politically active public behind the soviets. Even to the extent that the citizens—or the army—did not back the Bolshevik-dominated soviets, the conflict of orders from two duly constituted centers of authority could not help but impede implementation of the polices of the Provisional Government. As a result of circumstances and the skill of Lenin and his "new type of party," the final blow of the October revolution was nothing more than a *coup d'état*. The moderates and non-Bolshevik left could scarcely produce a few hundred supporters in Petrograd when the assault came. It was over in a matter of a few hours.

The real fighting was still to come, in three years of struggle between the Bolsheviks and rival political groups in a conventional civil war. The Bolsheviks could now, however, assume the role of the legitimate government of Russia and claim to represent all of the left-wing and liberal forces against the restoration of the Tsarist system. These were hard years and often the outcome would appear in doubt, but by accepting temporarily the disadvantageous German peace terms of Brest-Litovsk, Lenin was able to concentrate his efforts on the consolidation of power as long as the World War continued. By the time foreign intervention did come, it was too late and too little to be effective. Even while civil war raged in Russia, the center of Communist revolutionary activity moved westward.

Aside from the short-lived Paris Commune, the October revolution was the first example of a seizure of power by Marxists or any other left-wing group. It was therefore of great importance as a model for other Communist attempts to achieve power, and still today casts its shadow as a guide for Communists. Many of the precepts which were derived from the Bolshevik experience in 1917 are of undeniable validity and must be included in the credo of any insurgent. Lenin's genius lay, however, not so much in deriving the political and military maxims which guided the actions of the Bolsheviks. Rather his achievement was in applying them to the Russian environment at the correct point in time. Much of the early history of the Communist International could be written in terms of mistaken applications of Lenin's maxims in inappropriate circumstances, for the universalistic pretensions of Communist doctrine impeded later Communists in separating out the specifically Russian components of the events of 1917.

The steady growth of working-class parties in Europe prior to the First World War, particularly in Germany and Austria, had made it evident that these parties would soon force a crisis in the existing systems, but left-wing Socialists had severe misgivings about the gradualist tactics of the majority Socialists. The latter's support of their governments in the First World War was regarded by the radicals as the ultimate betrayal and they declared themselves in opposition to both the governments and the majority Socialists. As the war drew to a disastrous close for the Central Powers, popular resentment against the government manifested itself in strikes and demonstrations, and it was obvious that major changes were inevitable. The radicals, untarnished by participation in the discredited war effort, hopefully offered themselves as the instrument of this change.

At the same time, the newly emerging Soviet state in Russia looked about desperately for signs of revolution in other countries, not only as a source of material support in the struggle against foreign and domestic enemies, but also as an ideological justification for the Bolshevik revolution as such. Many Soviet leaders, including Lenin, doubted that the Russian success could have any lasting meaning except as part of a much wider revolutionary development including at least some of the advanced Western nations. The emerging revolutionary trends, particularly the demands of the radical Socialists, seemed to provide the possibility for merging the Bolshevik revolution into such a broader movement.

The main scene of activity was inevitably in Germany, which bore particularly deep scars from the wartime experience and possessed the intellectually most advanced leadership of the workers' movement in both the radical and majority wings. The German workers' movement was the most powerful of its time, and control of it would do much to determine the course of the German state rising out of the shambles of the collapsed Empire. All through 1918, discontent had been prevalent throughout Germany, culminating by the end of the summer in demands for the abolishment of the monarchy and the end of the war. At that point, there were certain striking similarities to Russia in 1917—the nation was defeated in war, the old government discredited, the masses clamored for a decisive break with the past—and the Russian experience seemed to provide guides to action. Soviets were established in the armed forces in many factories, and the masses went into the streets seeking leadership. Communist historians and ideologists, German and Russian alike, look back to late 1918 as a period of unprecedented revolutionary potential.[6]

The absence of a "new type of party" is particularly blamed for the failure of the German revolution to pass into Communism. In November 1918, after the monarchy fell and peace was made, there was no German Communist Party (GCP), although the groups out of which it was to be formed at the end of the year were already active on the scene. Even had a "new type" of party been in existence and functioning in November 1918, however, it is hardly likely that it could have achieved power. Communist writers are quite correct in assigning the locus of their failure to the Social Democrats. Despite their identification with the war effort, the majority Socialists remained the party of the German working class and received its overwhelming support, both on traditional grounds and because the Social Democrats had been able to claim the credit for bringing peace to Germany, just as Lenin had in Russia. Even the soviets which sprang up in factories and military units were for the most part inaccessible to the pre-Communists, and in any case were quickly brought within the power structure of the government. Also, there were no real grounds for an approach to the German peasantry; the armed forces were still well organized and responsive to the orders of their officers; the bureaucracy continued to function efficiently; the victorious allies had the means and the will to frustrate any serious attempt to turn Germany into a Communist state; and the significant mass of Germans felt a sense of positive identification with the government. The right-wing groups that did not feel such identification would scarcely turn to the Communists

[6] The situation of 1918 has come in for considerable comment in the past several years, most of it revolving around theoretical questoins. Important are the articles by Walther Ulbricht: "Über den Charakter der November-revolution," *Zeitschrift für Geschichtswissenschaft,* VI (1958), 717-729; and "Die November-revolution 1918 in Deutschland (Thesen anlässlich des 40. Jahrestages)," an official statement printed in *Neues Deutschland* on October 5, 1958. Of more general interest is Otto Grotewohl's *Dreissig Jahre später* (Berlin 1953), and the symposium volume *Revolutionäre Ereignisse und Probleme in Deutschland während der Periode der grossen sozialistischen Oktoberrevolution 1917/1918* (Berlin 1957), especially the article by A. Schreiner and G. Schmidt, "Die Rätebewegung in Deutschland bis zur November-revolution," 229-308. An important Russian commentary is provided anonymously in the article "K itogam diskussii o kharaktera i osobennostyakh noyabr'skoy revolyutsii 1918 g. v Germanii [On the Results of the Discussion of the Character and Peculiarities of the November Revolution of 1918 in Germany], *Voprosy Istorii,* No. 12 (1958), 96-115.

as allies. The young GCP did ultimately join in an uprising against the government in January 1919, the so-called "Spartacus Uprising," but only unwillingly and after the uprising had already broken out in the form of riots against the removal of the last ranking radical from the state machinery. The people were tired of fighting, however, and the movement was easily quelled by the Socialist government with the support of the army; it never even spread beyond Berlin.

The Elusive Revolutionary Situation

The newly-founded GCP had one more chance to attempt a coup before post-war order could be restored in Germany, and this resulted in the short-lived "Bavarian Socialist Republic." As in Berlin, under pressure of developments beyond their control the Bavarian Communist accepted the leadership of a radical movement in Munich which for a few weeks in April 1919 attempted to push the German revolution leftwards.[7] The Communists enjoyed some initial military successes in the field and held effective control of Munich, but hoped-for assistance from the Hungarian Communists was not forthcoming and the Communist field forces were unable to offer effective resistance to the regular Germany army. By May 3, the episode was over; the Communists tacitly recognized that an unsupported uprising in such a peripheral area as Bavaria was a futile undertaking, and that the barely-formed GCP should never have allowed itself to be involved in it.

The period of rule by Béla Kun and the Hungarian Communists in 1919 lasted somewhat longer than the Bavarians', but was no more successful. Again, the Communists assumed control of a revolutionary situation which they did not create, and Communist writers lay the blame for the ultimate failure at the door of the left-wing Socialists who shared governmental responsibility with Kun. In reality, the Hungarian soviet had no chance in the face of military pressure applied by the Rumanian and Czech armies, supported by the French. Kun's doctrinaire approach to government served only to alienate the nationalist support which he originally enjoyed, and he made no attempt to enlist the support of the Hungarian peasantry. Although military pressure brought about their downfall, there is no reason to believe that under even more favorable external circumstances the Hungarian Communists would have had the ability to maintain their rule.

[7] There is no satisfactory coverage of these events. The best study appears to be that of the East German Hans Beyer, "Die bairische Räterepublik," *Zeitschrift für Geschichtswissenschaft,* II (1954), 175-215. His treatment is naturally heavily partial to the orthodox Communist actors.

The defeats in Germany and Hungary did not immediately discourage other revolutionaries, but many began to wonder whether Lenin's strategy was not in fact a magic ingredient, the secret of which reposed in Russia. Even the great German workers' movement had failed, and no other European party had been a more likely candidate to achieve success. Of course, the German workers' movement did achieve success in that its representatives—the Social Democrats—gained adequate access to power in Germany and the main points of the Socialist program were fulfilled. As a loyal opposition within the workers' movement, the Communists could have participated in this success. For the Communists, however, success was only measured in terms of their own direct ascent to power. Only they could fulfill the promise of Marx and of history.

The failures in Central Europe marked the only serious Communist attempts to capitalize on the opportunities generated directly by the First World War. Certainly by mid-1919, the "Bolshevik menace" presented no real danger to the new order in Europe, an order which differed greatly from the pre-1914 period but still was firmly embedded in the conventions of European political development. To contemporaries however, including the Russians, the issue was far from settled. The setbacks of Berlin, Budapest, and Munich were thought to be only temporary; the collapsing capitalist system would continue to provide opportunities to spread revolution in Europe, and in 1919 the Communist International (Comintern) was formed to be the general staff of this new wave of revolutions. The poor showings outside of Russia were, after all, attributable to the organizational weakness of the local radical factions. The Comintern would provide leadership for them, just as the Bolsheviks had provided it in the October revolution. The Russian experience could be brought to bear in the interests of world Communism.

The newly formed organization was not originally intended as an extension of the Russian party. Lenin's prestige guaranteed him a leading role in it, but he undoubtedly expected the heart of the future Communist system to lie in the West, no doubt in Germany.[8] Since the Comintern was to be a "Bolshevik" organization, however, it was

[8] There are numerous quotations from Lenin which illustrate this expectation. For a sample, see Hans Koch, *Theorie, Taktik, Technik des Weltkommunismus* (Pfaffenhofen/Ilm 1959), 225ff. As late as 1923, Stalin could write to the German Communist Thalheimer "The victory of the revolution in Germany will have a greater importance for the proletariat of Europe and America than the victory of the Russian revolution six years ago. The victory of the German proletariat will undoubtedly shift the center of world revolution from Moscow to Berlin." *Rote Fahne,* October 10, 1923. Not surprisingly, this letter did not appear in Stalin's collected works.

felt necessary to organize it along authoritarian lines. This type of organization was repellent to the Western radicals, and although several mass parties showed interest in the Comintern and some (such as the Italian) actually joined it, they were soon to be disillusioned. Lenin was not interested in amorphous mass parties, and by his dominating personality, as well as the absence of strong, successful leadership elsewhere, he forced the European Communists to split off from their mass support and form small conspiratorial groups.[9] Such groups might have been successful had they been in effective existence in 1918, although this is by no means certain, but in the 1920's their prospects were exceedingly poor. This situation became self-reinforcing, for the weakness of the local parties made them continually more subservient to the Russians who provided them with a source of funds and, even more important, psychological support and a sense of security.

This process of "Bolshevization" proceeded at varying speeds in the various countries. In Italy and France it was achieved by political maneuverings; in Germany it came about in connection with an attempted uprising in March 1920, which is known as the *Märzaktion*. The antecedents of this affair are not clear, and it is not firmly established to what extent the Comintern bears responsibility for it. Béla Kun did however arrive in Germany as a Comintern emissary and in this capacity stampeded the German leadership into calling for an uprising in Central Germany, utilizing provocative terrorist techniques to stimulate the non-existent revolutionary situation. The attempt was an utter fiasco, and is only noteworthy as a milestone on the road of the German party to subservience to the dictates of Moscow.[10] The more level-headed German Communists deserted the party in disgust,

[9] Good descriptions of the process in several countries can be found in the following works: Franz Borkenau, *The Communist International* (London 1938); Ruth Fischer, *Stalin and German Communism* (New York 1948); Theodore Draper, *The Roots of American Communism* (New York 1957) and *American Communism and Soviet Russia* (New York 1960); and R. Lowenthal, "The Bolshevization of the Spartacus League," *International Communism,* edited by David Footman, "St. Anthony's Papers, No. 9" (London 1960).

[10] For a devastating critique by a former GCP chairman, see Paul Levi, *Unser Weg in den Putschismus* (Berlin 1921), which led to his expulsion from the party. Levi lashed out especially at Kun, and deplored the use of second-rate Comintern functionaries to dictate to experienced leaders of foreign parties, commenting: "I have nothing against the people of Turkestan and don't wish them harm: but often I have the impression that the antics of these plenipotentiaries would cause less harm there." (46). Perhaps unwittingly (and perhaps not) Levi's statement carried a deep truth. The Soviets were beginning to look upon all foreign parties as satrapies on a level with the Central Asian regions.

leaving behind mostly those who lacked the ability or courage to pursue any sort of independent line for the development of an independent German party.

The *Märzaktion* came about too late to capitalize upon the revolutionary potentialities of the postwar period, but a delayed reaction of the war created a promising situation in Germany in 1923. This was the year of the French occupation of the Rhineland, spiralling inflation, large-scale strikes in German industry, and the National Socialist *putsch* attempt in Munich. Although discontent had abated to some extent by the time the Communists took action, there was undoubtedly a revolutionary atmosphere and an uprising was not totally inappropriate. The causes of failure lay in timing, a gross exaggeration of the intensity of the revolutionary situation, and the approach taken.[11] It was intended that the main force of the uprising be in Hamburg and in the traditionally radical central provinces of Saxony and Thuringia. Elsewhere in Germany the party would do what it could in support.

The tactics of the uprising reflected their Russian origin: reliance was to be placed primarily upon conspiratorial methods. Communist ministers were instructed to assume cabinet posts in Saxony and Thuringia so that they could gain control of arms for distribution to the workers, terroristic methods were again used to stimulate a sense of urgency, trusted cadres were given military training by Russian advisers to act as shock troops, and above all else organization was stressed as the touchstone of victory.

Conscious of the criticism that lack of organization and armed strength had been the downfall of the Spartacus uprising, strenuous attempts were made to remedy these defects in the light of the Bolshevik experience. The organizational superstructure outweighed any concrete steps taken and was more directed to intra-party organization than the establishment of ties with the mass of workers. The Communist ministers were unable to distribute arms and the military preparations were faulty. The leadership wavered, called for the up-

[11] Some will attach more importance to one aspect, some to another. Ruth Fischer —a top GCP leader in the 1920's—for instance never ceased believing that the workers were ready for revolution; only the leadership was ineffective. Hers, however, is scarcely an unbiased viewpoint. The current official interpretation is contained in Walther Ulbricht's "Die Nachkriegskrise in Deutschland und die Ereignisse des Jahres 1923," *Zur Geschichte der deutschen Arbeiterbewegung,* I (Berlin 1954), 97-153. Helmut Gast provides interesting information in "Die proletarischen Hundertschaften als Organe der Einheitsfront im Jahre 1923," *Zeitschrift für Geschichtswissenschaft,* IV (1956), 439-465. A participant in the Hamburg uprising, Walter Zeutschel, has recounted his experiences in *Im Dienste der kommunistischen Terrororganization* (Berlin 1931).

rising, postponed it, called for it again and once again postponed it, but notice of the last postponement failed to reach the Hamburg Communists. Under Ernst Thälmann they rose up and managed to get control of a few portions of the city, but without support they had to fall back into the working class quarters where they were soon liquidated by government forces. The fight of the Hamburg workers gave some luster to an otherwise inglorious performance, but this was poor consolation. It marked the end of the revolutionary tradition of German Communism, for in the following year the GCP's activities degenerated into terrorism and political infighting, with all pretension of an independent program abandoned.[12]

The uprising of the Bulgarian Communists in September 1923 was little more than a sidelight to the German experience. The Bulgarian party had been considerably restricted in its actions by the Agrarian government of Stambolisky, and when a right-wing coup was mounted the Communists stood by and let "bourgeois fight bourgeois." They soon found that the new government was even more restrictive, and under Moscow's prodding the Communists launched an uprising against it. Their revolt went wrong in almost every particular. The party was in no sense ready, and acted mainly in self-defense; Stambolisky's former supporters showed understandably little inclination to give any help to the Communists; and the whole plan was betrayed.[13] The Bulgarian Communist Party—the last "mass" party in the movement—was shattered, never again to play a major role on the Bulgarian scene until the arrival of the Russian army at the end of the Second World War. Had the Bulgarian Communists swallowed their pride and supported Stambolisky, the unified forces of Communists and Agrarians might have prevailed, but the Communists' tactical failure permitted the Bulgarian nationalists to eliminate their enemies one by one.

[12] The military failures of the Communists gave rise to much soul-searching, set forth in theoretical writings on the art of revolution. This material is discussed in detail by Stefan Possony in *A Century of Conflict* (Chicago 1953), 177-188; some of it is available in *Communist Conspiracy*. E. Thälmann, in *Zur Geschichte der KPD* (Berlin 1955), 155-157, refers to the Hamburg uprising as the "first time in Western Europe that the Marx-Engels teaching of uprising as an art was understood and realized. . . ." This theorizing was necessarily to remain sterile, however, for it presupposed in each instance that the party would have mass support in its action. The policies of the GCP were well designed to insure that such support would never be forthcoming; it was to be the Nazis who would utilize the dissatisfactions of the German people, not the Communists.

[13] Joseph Rothschild, *The Communist Party of Bulgaria* (New York 1959), esp. chapters 5-7.

To round out the picture of Communist activities in the early 1920's, it is necessary to mention their action in Estonia in December 1924—probably the grossest *putsch* they ever attempted. There is little information available on this undertaking,[14] but it is generally conceded that it was engineered completely from the Soviet Union. Russians were smuggled into Estonia to take part, and the only theoretical or historical justification claimed was the need for self-defense against rigorous anti-Communist measures being taken by the Estonian government. The insurgents were able to occupy a few buildings in Reval, but the Estonians evicted them with little difficulty and the abortive coup was crushed within a day.

No More Revolutions

An amusing sidelight to the Estonian adventure was the explanation given in Communist circles of why it failed. It seemed that the Estonian Communists misjudged history; they were unaware that the revolutionary situation in Europe had come to an end in 1923, and that the period of the "temporary stabilization of capitalism" had set in—news apparently moved slowly in the Baltic. Despite the generally high level of agitation and violence which prevailed in much of Europe in the 1920's and 1930's, the flurries of revolutionary activity in Germany and Bulgaria in 1923 can be said to mark the end of revolutionary Communism in Europe. Stalin accepted this fact,[15] and current Soviet historiography considers the years 1923-1924 to be one of the major dividing points in Soviet history.[16] The significance of this date derives from internal conditions in the Soviet Union as well as the situation abroad. Lenin—incapacitated since 1921—died in 1924. The struggle over his succession and the related questions of domestic economics and politics more than absorbed the attentions of the Russian leaders. Trostky's slogan of "permanent revolution" would have provided for a considerable degree of effort in the international scene, but it was Stalin who prevailed. His concept of "socialism in

[14] The only adequate account of the uprising in English is to be found in the *Survey of International Affairs: 1924* (Oxford 1926), 198-203. A detailed Communist version can be found in *Istoriya Estonskoy SSR* [History of the Estonian SSR] (Tallin 1958), 513-522.

[15] In 1925, Stalin outlined the forces giving strength to the Soviet position—international proletarian solidarity, the colonial question, and contradictions among the "imperialist" powers—but pointed out that for the foreseeable future, the Russian people could expect no external assistance. In effect, he wrote the international factors off, placing all reliance upon the strength of the Soviet Union; see his *Works*, VII, 26.

[16] See the historians' discussion conducted in *Int Aff.*, Nos. 3 through 8 (1958).

one country"[17] directed all Russian efforts to domestic affairs, and the Comintern was relegated to a shadowy existence. There was no question of the Russians supporting foreign parties in the spirit of "proletarian internationalism"; these parties found their justification in support of the Soviet Union, and the issues over which they fought merely reflected the factional disputes of the Soviet leadership, not questions related to the furtherance of communism in their own countries.

The complete subservience of the non-Russian Communists was justified theoretically by the argument that the preservation of the "revolutionary base" in the USSR was the prime responsibility of all Communists, and that by strengthening this base, the prospects for the spread of Communism were enhanced.[18] This argument rested on the assumption that the revolution would spread outward from the Soviet Union, sponsored by Russian military capability. The Estonian *putsch* was to some extent a sample of the type of activity which the Russians could sponsor in contiguous areas, but it was among the least successful. Already in the days of the Russian Civil War, the Soviet leaders had discovered that the Red Army was a useful instrument, not only for ensuring the victory of the revolution in the Russian areas of the former Empire, but also in spreading revolution to non-Russian areas. Although the Bolsheviks conceded the right of self-determination to the various minority races, in practice they were always able to find a small group who represented the "will of the people" and called in Soviet armed forces. Certainly no one could seriously maintain that a revolutionary situation existed in Khiva and Bokhara or in Mongolia; Soviet *raison d'état* became the substitute for it.

More portentous for the future course in the expansion of communism was the abortive attempt to communize Poland in the course of the war between the Bolsheviks and the Poles in 1920. Initiation of

[17] This doctrine was inherent in Stalin's line of thought. (See footnote 15 above.) For a valuable discussion of it, as opposed to Trotsky's "permanent revolution," see Isaac Deutscher, *Stalin: A Political Biography* (New York 1960), 282ff.

[18] "A *revolutionary* is one who is ready to protect, to defend the USSR without reservation, without qualification, openly and honestly, without secret military conferences; for the USSR is the first proletarian, revolutionary state in the world, a state which is building socialism. An *internationalist* is one who is ready to defend the USSR without reservation, without wavering, unconditionally; for the USSR is the base of the world revolutionary movement, and this revolutionary movement cannot be defended and promoted unless the USSR is defended. For whoever thinks of defending the world revolutionary movement apart from, or against, the USSR, goes against the revolution and must inevitably slide into the camp of the enemies of the revolution." Stalin (1927) *Works*, X, 53-54; italics in original.

hostilities lay with the Poles, and Poland itself had been partially incorporated in the Tsarist empire. Yet Poland in 1920 was undoubtedly a national entity, so that when the Soviets attempted a forcible establishment of communism there, they began to tread on treacherous ground. They mustered whatever Poles were available in Russia and well-disposed toward communism, to lend some color to the idea that the "revolution" was Polish in origin.[19] A shadow government was established under the Russianized Pole Feliks Dzerzhinsky,[20] but the Polish people's traditional hatred of Russia rendered the Soviet role of liberator anomalous. The Russian attempt was beaten off, partly due to faulty military planning but mostly due to the Poles' hatred of Russians, no matter what their political persuasion.[21] Stalin was deeply involved in the Polish venture and the political tactics used were to return again in 1944.

The Polish case and the Estonian misadventure demonstrated that in the face of determined opposition, Russian expansionist tactics would not be successful in countries belonging to the Western political system. If Soviet arms were to be the carriers of revolution, it could only be in a situation of international chaos or as the result of agreement on the part of the Western powers directly concerned to permit the Soviet Union to expand. In the "period of temporary stabilization of capitalism," neither of these two situations obtained. The possibilities for revolution in Europe were also negligible, as we have already seen, due to the changed situation in the area and the extreme weakness of the Communists. Despite repeated efforts to form united fronts (unions of all working class parties) during the 1920's, the Communists had only very slight success in gaining strength within the workers' movement.[22] As the Hamburg experience showed, even when the Communists were able to mobilize a considerable degree of "proletarian" support, their lack of influence in the other segments

[19] Some 5700 Poles who had joined the Bolshevik armies assigned to the Polish front according to P. A. Golub, "Pol'skiye revolyutsionnye voyska v Rossii v 1917-1920 godakh" [Polish Revolutionary Armed Forces in Russia in 1917-1920] *Voprosy Istorii,* No. 3 (1958), 44-63.

[20] A good account is available in Warren Lerner, "The Russian Plan to Sovietize Poland in 1920" (unpublished M. A. essay, Faculty of Political Science, Columbia Univ., 1954).

[21] In Stalin's time, the failure of the Polish campaign was ascribed to machinations of Trotsky. Although prime responsibility is still put on military miscalculations, the new party history admits that the traditional anti-Russianism of the Poles had been effectively exploited; *History of the CPSU,* 334.

[22] On the united front movement see Jane Degras, "United Front Tactics in the Comintern: 1921-1928" in *International Communism,* 9-22.

of the population (army, bureaucracy, and especially peasantry) rendered their position untenable.

The lack of working class support was accounted for in terms of Lenin's theory of imperialism, whereby the colonial powers used the profits derived from colonial exploitation to buy off large numbers of workers (the "labor aristocracy") and recruit them to support of the incumbent regimes.[23] Thus on all counts, the prospects for any sort of revolutionary activity based on mass urban uprisings were dim. If communism were to expand, it would be necessary to break the hold of the colonial powers over their colonies, recruit non-urban support within the metropolitan country, and probably even then bring the armed power of the USSR to bear, while neutralizing any possible intervention from a third party. Most of this could only be accomplished in the upheavals following a war.

It would be convenient to explain all further Communist behavior in terms of these requirements, leading to their limited successes at the end of the Second World War. Such an explanation would almost certainly be fallacious. Soviet actions after the rise of Stalin were directed to only one overriding objective—the security and economic development of the USSR. The Russians tried desperately to avoid becoming involved in a war with the Western powers and did very little even to stimulate dissension among the Western states. The opportunities generated in the Second World War came despite Soviet efforts, not because of them. At least until the mid-1930's, Communist policy effectively deterred the acquisition of support outside of the working class in Western Europe, and even within the working class, refusal to cooperate with the Socialists on any workable basis still further reduced the strength of the Communist parties.

It was only the actual coming to power of Hitler that galvanized the Communists into action in the search for support against a possible German attack. The German Communists had declined to cooperate with the Socialists in opposing the rise of Hitler, and he promptly crushed both parties when he had the chance. Belatedly awakened to the danger, the Comintern called for the formation of a broad anti-Fascist front wherever possible. In such countries as France, where there was a threat of domestic fascism, this "Popular Front"[24] had the responsibility of limiting the internal danger from fascism. Its main

[23] V. I. Lenin, *Imperialism, the Highest Stage of Capitalism,* Part x.

[24] While a united front comprises only working class elements, the popular front included elements from all classes. Note, however, that this distinction is no longer current in Communist usage.

task was not the promotion of communism on a local scale but the creation of a climate more conducive to the acceptance of the Soviet Union as a trustworthy ally of France and Britain in the face of the German threat.

Judged by the situation in 1939, the Popular Front was a total failure for the Communists. As the Second World War broke out, the Soviet Union's only ally was—paradoxically—Germany. The efforts expended in France to form a Popular Front government bore some fruit when Léon Blum assumed power in 1936 with Communist backing, but this was short-lived; the Communists were simply unable to cooperate with the other parties in good faith.[25] Elsewhere there had been notable signs of success as Communists became accepted as allies in the anti-fascist struggle and achieved the highest degree of political respectability they had ever enjoyed, but all of this was destroyed overnight as the Molotov-Ribbentrop pact made a mockery of the whole idea of an anti-fascist Popular Front.

The high point of the common front period had been the Spanish Civil War.[26] From the military point of view it was probably the best performance the Communists have ever given in Europe. Their recruitment, training, and general military policy were, given the circumstances, of a high order. Not only Russian advisers but Communists from many other countries in Europe and the Western Hemisphere contributed to the effort and in turn gained experience which they were to put to good use in guerrilla campaigns of the Second World War and after. From the purely political and revolutionary aspect the Communist performance was less than outstanding. They were among the least revolutionary-minded groups fighting on the Republican side, and Stalin took great pains to discourage Republican leaders from any political or economic moves which would

[25] For a fascinating, if not always reliable account of the trials of the Popular Front in France, see Franz Borkenau's *European Communism* (London 1953). For foreign policy implications, see Max Beloff, *The Foreign Policy of Soviet Russia,* I, chapters 11 and 12.

[26] The most useful coverage of the war is provided in Hugh Thomas, *The Spanish Civil War* (New York 1961). A specialized discussion of Soviet involvement is given in two books by David T. Cattell, *Communism and the Spanish Civil War* (Berkeley 1955) and *Soviet Diplomacy and the Spanish Civil War* (Berkeley 1957). Authoritative Communist treatment is scanty. Moderately interesting is the article by Dolores Ibarurri "Natsional'no-revolyutsionnaya voyna ispanskogo naroda . . ." [The National Revolutionary War of the Spanish People . . .] in *Voprosy Istorii,* No. 11 (1952), 28-47. A pro-Franco interpretation, but interesting as an application of the concepts of *guerre révolutionnaire* to the situation, is José Diaz de Villegas, *La Guerra Revolucionaria: La Técnica de la Revolución y la Acción Psicológica* (Madrid 1959).

cause consternation among the Spanish bourgeoisie, or in Britain and France. Particularly great attention was supposed to be given to organizing the peasantry, but not with the objective of stimulating its revolutionary ardor.[27]

At no time was the establishment of a Communist government in Spain a Soviet aim. Stalin's goal was the involvement of the democracies against the fascist threat and, if possible, the denial of Spain to the Axis powers. It is even questionable whether Stalin would have welcomed the establishment of a Communist state so far from his personal jurisdiction. If the Communists profited from the war, it was in terms of the experience gained and the favorable image which Soviet involvement generated in liberal circles, at least to the extent that the liberals were unaware of the bloody work of the secret police against Stalin's enemies among the Communists fighting in Spain.

In Spain and elsewhere, the Popular Front marked the indefinite postponement of any pretext of Communist hope for revolutionary activity.[28] Although the Seventh Comintern Congress resolutions on the use of the Popular Front as a prelude to the dictatorship of the proletariat have been recently resurrected as proof of a farseeing policy upon which the victories after the Second World War were based,[29] they were really nothing of the sort. By the beginning of the war, communism in Europe was no longer a force of political consequence; it operated from weakness, rather than from strength. Even the power of the Soviet Union was a great unknown in the strategic equation, and the greatest assets of the movement were only latent. Despite—or perhaps because of—the ruthless decimation of non-Russian Communists in the Stalin purges, there was available a dedicated and responsive hard core of functionaries who could be depended upon to execute Soviet policy in their home countries of Eastern and Central

[27] See Stalin's letter to Largo Caballero (a Republican leader) printed in the *New York Times*, June 4, 1939, p. 34. The peasant question is discussed by Ibarurri.

[28] Sering, *Jenseits des Kapitalismus*, 241, comments that when the Communists adopted the popular front, ". . . they gave up the tactically inhibiting model of the Soviet Revolution of 1917 . . . they ceased to be a revolutionary party in the sense of a mass uprising against the state." (Quoted by Ossip Flechtheim, "Die Internationale des Kommunismus," *Zeitschrift für Politik*, VI (N.F.), No. 3 (1959), 242.

[29] Jan Kozak, "Znacheniye natsional'noy i demokraticheskoy revolyutsii v Chekhoslovakii dlya bor'ba rabochego klassa za sotsializm (1945-1948 gg.)" [The Importance of the National and Democratic Revolution in Czechoslovakia in the Struggle of the Working Class for Socialism, 1945-1948], *Voprosy Istorii KPSS*, No. 4 (1962), 73. Kermit McKenzie accepts the Communist claims on the nature of the popular front, and presents a well-argued but unconvincing case, in "The Soviet Union, the Communist International, and World Revolution: 1937," *Political Science Quarterly*, LXV (1950), 214-237.

Europe, should the strength of the USSR ever be able to put them in positions of power. Also, the Popular Front had been successful in recruiting a considerable number of individuals who occupied important positions in the non-Communist countries. Although most of these became rapidly disillusioned and soon fell away, a significant number accepted Communist discipline and were able to render valuable service to the Communist cause when the Russians were ultimately forced into the Allied camp and their sins of 1939 were overlooked in the general desire to win the war. For the years of the war and its immediate aftermath, the Communists were able to capitalize on the groundwork they had laid in the 1930's, but when the Comintern ("having fulfilled its historic mission") was dissolved in 1943 as a sop to world opinion, few can have mourned its passing. The Comintern had failed and failed badly. The revolutionary international European Communist movement which grew out of the First World War had long since ceased to exist. Communism was the ideology of the Soviet State and would rise or fall in direct relationship to the military fortunes of the USSR.

Communism in Asia

The disillusionment of the Comintern with the revolutionary capabilities of the European proletariat—reflected in the move to find non-proletariat allies in the Popular Front—was matched in Asia by the spurts of activity that marked the entry of communism in that part of the world. If the European proletariat would not be the harbinger of the new age, then the alternative was to look elsewhere (socially) in Europe and elsewhere (geographically) in Asia. It is in this sense that Franz Borkenau's division of Comintern history into a "German" and "Chinese" period is to be understood. The intense concern of all levels of communism with Asian problems in the late 1920's was a reaction against the failures in Europe.[30]

Lenin's admonitions that the Communists realize the revolutionary potential in Asia were of long standing, and were emphatically restated at the Second Comintern Congress (1920). In practice, the young Soviet State directed its attention to its survival in the face of foreign and domestic attack and still nurtured hopes of revolution in

[30] Ilya Ehrenburg's pitiful anti-hero Lasik Roitschwantz believed that if he could only master the intricacies of Chinese politics he would be able to become a good Communist, despite his complete misunderstanding of the system or even of his home-town politics in the Ukraine. *The Stormy Life of Lasik Roitschwantz* (New York 1960), first published in 1928.

Europe. Communist groups in Iran and Turkey were given short shrift by Lenin, who disowned them in the hopes of gaining Riza Shah Pahlavi and Mustafa Kemal Atatürk as allies against Britain, and Comintern activities farther to the east were generally limited or ineffective.

The Asian country which in Marxist terms showed the greatest potential was Japan with its well-developed industrial base, but in the face of police repression and their own incompetence the Japanese Communists made no real headway until after the Second World War. Similarly in Korea, the party was effectively repressed and split up into feuding factions, all of which were disowned by the Comintern in disgust.[31] Although there were modest signs of communism in other Asian countries such as India, it was only in China and Indonesia (at that time the Netherlands East Indies) that the movement assumed significant proportions. Communism in Indonesia grew out of a social-democratic organization which had been founded in 1914 by Dutch residents. The revolutionaries who controlled the movement sympathized with the Bolshevik revolution, and in 1920 the party assumed the Communist name and elected its first Indonesian chairman.

The party secured an important place in the emergent Indonesian political movement, for Indonesians who were attracted to the group were encouraged by radical Dutch leaders to propagate the revolutionary socialist viewpoint within the massive but disorganized proto-nationalist grouping Sarekat Islam. This strategy resulted in a victory for the Communists, for when a break between the Sarekat Islam's radical and moderate branches took place in 1923, the Communists carried with them the greater part of the movement's active membership and became the principal vehicle of Indonesian anti-colonial sentiment. The revolutionary stance which won it followers also brought increasing government restrictions, and soon the party found itself trapped between its adherents' demands for action and the authorities' threats of repression. Both the Comintern and the top local leadership seem to have argued for caution; but by this time arrests, banishments, and difficulty in communication had placed effective control in the

[31] For the early stages of Communism in Japan see R. Swearingen and P. Langer, *Red Flag in Japan* (Cambridge, Mass. 1952). The only English language source on early Korean Communism is Glenn Paige's "Korea and the Comintern: 1919-1935," *Bulletin of the Korean Research Center* (Seoul), No. 13 (1960), 1-25. G. D. Overstreet and M. Windmiller, *Communism in India* (Berkeley and Los Angeles 1959) has several chapters on Indian Communism before the Second World War; also good on the period are the first-hand observations of M. R. Masani, *The Communist Party of India* (London 1954).

hands of impatient minor leaders who opted for revolt. In late 1926 and early in 1927 a series of badly-planned uprisings took place; in their wake came large-scale arrests and severe restrictions which resulted in the virtual extinction of the Indonesian Communist movement until after World War II.[32]

The other significant Communist movement in Asia was the Chinese Communists Party (CCP) which, like its Indonesian counterpart, rose rapidly from modest beginnings. It was founded only in 1920 by a group of intellectuals possessing little Marx and less Lenin, but it had the good fortune to find itself in the midst of a revolutionary potential of massive proportions. Ever since the fall of the Manchu dynasty in 1911, China had been in a state of constant turmoil. Although suffering to some extent from the indignities which the Western powers inflicted indiscriminately on all Asians, China lacked the firm colonial control with which the Dutch, for instance, were able to stifle overt unrest. A virtual state of anarchy prevailed throughout much of the country; the only ray of hope lay in Dr. Sun Yat-sen's Kuomintang, based uncertainly in Canton.[33]

The CCP received its inspiration from the Bolshevik revolution and was only too glad to become a thoroughly subservient member of the Communist International. The party was joined by a number of enthusiastic young men who proved themselves highly adept at contacting and organizing urban (and to some extent agrarian) masses. The Comintern soon recognized, however, that by its own efforts the CCP was unlikely to make the spectacular sort of headway which was demanded, and therefore in 1924 directed the party to make common cause with the Kuomintang, as the Indonesian Communists had with the Sarekat Islam. In a short time the CCP was integrated into the Kuomintang and Russian advisers were sent to bolster the latter group's organization and fighting qualities. The alliance was highly beneficial to both sides in its early stages. The Communists gained legitimacy and an excellent platform from which to propagandize; their organizational and material support was instrumental in making the Kuomin-

[32] See *The Communist Uprisings of 1926-1927 in Indonesia: Key Documents*, introduction by H. J. Benda and R. T. McVey (Ithaca 1960). A very brief Communist discussion can be found in D. N. Aidit, *A Short History of the Communist Party of Indonesia* (New Delhi 1955).

[33] For the early years of Chinese Communism with special attention to Soviet involvement, see A. S. Whiting, *Soviet Policies in China 1917-1924* (New York 1954); Conrad Brandt, *Stalin's Failure in China: 1924-1927* (Cambridge, Mass. 1957); and Benjamin I. Schwartz, *Chinese Communism and the Rise of Mao* (Cambridge, Mass. 1951).

tang almost overnight into the dominant force in Chinese politics.

The Communist objective was nominally to help the Kuomintang realize the "bourgeois revolution," after which the stage could be set for the next wave of activity—the proletarian revolution—but the Comintern envisioned a rather more direct course of development in which the CCP would infiltrate the Kuomintang, take over its leadership and establish Communist rule quickly without the long waiting period until a proletariat could develop. In Stalin's memorable phrase, the Communists would squeeze the Kuomintang out like a lemon and then throw them away. But when squeezing time came, Stalin was surprised. The power in the Kuomintang passed from Dr. Sun (who died in 1925) to his young disciple Chiang Kai-shek. Chiang had been to Moscow, had a clear picture of the CCP's objectives, and moved to eliminate its growing power. The CCP was aware of Chiang's objectives, but the Comintern—which by now was becoming synonymous with Stalin—continued to place trust in the ability of Communists to outwit their enemies. The CCP was also directed to concentrate its efforts in urban areas, so that when Chiang struck in 1927 he was able to liquidate the CCP in its urban strongholds of Canton and Shanghai with little difficulty.

The eulogy which at that point seemed appropriate for the CCP would have been premature, or at least should have taken into account the possibility of miraculous resurrection. The CCP as the party of the Chinese proletariat, the sometime ally of the Kuomintang, and the blind instrument of the Comintern had truly died. The role as catalyst of the Chinese revolution was taken up by a movement which was none of these three things, but still proclaimed itself to be Communist—the new Communist party of Mao Tse-tung. In his early career, Mao was already identified with the exploitation of peasant unrest. Following Lenin, the CCP hierarchy accepted the idea of the peasantry as a potentially useful reserve for the revolution, but showed little inclination to allot it a leading role. Mao, however, sought to extract the maximum from the potential of the Chinese peasantry, and although clothing himself fairly adequately in the garb of Marxist orthodoxy, he held views on the role of the peasantry which were probably heretical.[34] His views, however, are of less interest than his actions. His first venture into the literature of revolutionary

[34] For a discussion of Mao's "originality" in this regard see the debate between Karl A. Wittfogel and Benjamin I. Schwartz in the first two issues of *China Quarterly* (1960). See also Arthur A. Cohen, "How Original is Maoism," *Problems of Communism*, x (November/December 1961), 34-42.

strategy, the essay "The Peasant Movement in Hunan,"[35] was theoretically unobjectionable enough to be reprinted in *Pravda,* and sufficiently undistinguished that Borodin, the Soviet adviser in China, apparently had never heard of it.[36] Mao's preoccupation with peasant violence did, however, bring him into disfavor in the late 1920's and he was demoted in the party hierarchy. Only after Chiang Kai-shek's liquidation of the CCP in its urban bases did Mao and the band of guerrillas which he had been gathering, assume prime importance. They were simply all that remained of the CCP and, after a period of internal maneuverings, Mao was by 1935 able to establish himself as the unquestioned leader of the party. It is a token of the complete collapse of the CCP as originally constituted that the Comintern and Stalin found themselves compelled to accept Mao's dominance, even though he could not have been ideologically palatable to the International and was certainly not sufficiently subservient to be fully acceptable to Stalin.

The course of Mao's victory in China showed certain tactical variations, many occasioned by the Sino-Japanese hostilities which lasted for nearly ten years. In its triumphal final stages, from 1947 to 1949, it increasingly assumed the form of conventional warfare, but the significant characteristics of the political and military aspects of "Maoism" are best seen in the context of the guerrilla warfare which laid the base for later large-scale Communist success. In reviewing the failures of the CCP's activities in the 1920's, Mao emphasized three main errors. First, by subjecting itself to the Kuomintang the CCP had forfeited the leadership of the revolution and left itself vulnerable. Second, insufficient emphasis had been placed on the role of the peasantry. Finally, there had been insufficient emphasis on armed struggle, especially as waged by the peasantry.[37]

[35] The original text can be found in Brandt, Fairbank and Schwartz, *A Documentary History of Chinese Communism* (Cambridge, Mass. 1952).

[36] Louis Fischer, *The Soviets in World Affairs* (Princeton 1951), 647.

[37] Wang Shih and others, *A Brief History of the Chinese Communist Party* [Chung-kuo Kung-ch'an-tang Li-shih Chien-pien] (Shanghai 1958), translated in JPRS, 8756, 91-94. It must be noted that in all of his formulations, Mao always insists on the proletarian leadership of the revolution. In practice, this meant only that the CCP—the surrogate of the proletariat—must lead the revolution. We will do little violence to Mao's intent if we disregard this particular sophistry. A fascinating portrayal of the strategy and tactics of the Communists in the 1930's—written by Li Wei-han, a leading figure in the Peking government—appeared in *Hongqi,* No. 3-4 (1962) and was serialized in issues 8-12 of the *Peking Review* (February and March 1962), under the title "The Struggle for Proletarian Leadership in the New-Democratic Revolution in China," and subsequently published as a pamphlet (Peking 1962).

With these points in mind, Mao went on to formulate his own analysis of the Chinese situation and the potentialities for a CCP victory. In view of the superior strength of the Kuomintang armed forces, he decided that the proper course for the CCP was protracted guerrilla warfare, during which the imbalance could be redressed. The guerrilla campaign would be made possible by the vast size of China, its lack of development, and the absence of a centralized authority which could take effective measures against the guerrillas. Finally, he noted that China was in the midst of a great revolutionary movement, essentially agrarian in nature, which would provide invaluable political and military support to the party which most effectively espoused its cause. Under Mao, the CCP was to be that party.[38]

Like so many of Mao's utterances, these insights are not very profound. Yet they present very well the basic problems of the successful conduct of internal war—the physical setting, the revolutionary situation, the tactics which these call forth—and in his practical application of the principles Mao showed a degree of real genius.[39] Above all they represent a common sense approach and are, as Mao's hagiographers never tire of repeating, a creative application of the tenets of Marxism-Leninism to the specific conditions of China.

At the beginning of his ascendancy, Mao found himself in charge of a small group of followers in East Central China, on the border between Kiangsi and Hunan provinces. He rejected the idea of taking the battle to the Kuomintang urban strongholds and concentrated his little "soviet's" efforts on building up local support among the peasantry as a base for future expansion.[40] His tactical position was good because he occupied a relatively isolated area that was difficult of access. Nevertheless, the so-called "Kwangsi Soviet" was too near the centers of Kuomintang power and yet was isolated from any possibility of external support or area of retreat. Thus when Chiang Kai-shek and his German advisers brought full force to bear on the CCP, its position became strategically untenable.

[38] *Selected Works* (New York 1954) I, 193ff. It is interesting to compare this list of factors–dating from 1936–with a similar list drawn up by Mao in 1928 (*ibid.*, 63ff.) The earlier one, although similar, is much more conventional in its Marxist outlook.

[39] Mao has written a number of works (mostly included in Vol I of the *Selected Works*) dealing with internal war. The most concise presentation can be found in *Yu Chi Chan*, not in the *Selected Works*, but translated by S. B. Griffith as *Mao Tse-tung on Guerrilla Warfare* (New York 1961).

[40] Wang Shih, *Brief History*, 104, discusses the futility of military action which is not supported from a base area.

In 1934, the famous "long march" was undertaken which moved the entire CCP force to the Yenan area of Kansu province, far from the sources of Kuomintang power and comfortably close to the Russian satellite state of Outer Mongolia.[41] Here the CCP again settled down to the business of indoctrinating the local population, establishing effective government, and above all, building an army. Mao's political approach was highly pragmatic and attempted to garner the support of the largest number of people—virtually regardless of class—as a means of supporting his military machine.[42]

The CCP was, in a very real sense, tied to the peasantry. Even more, it was identical with the Red Army, and the party and army leaderships interlocked closely. Basic political indoctrination of troops and party members was emphasized and there can be no doubt that the CCP managed to capture the imagination and support of much of the peasantry in the areas which it occupied. Material incentives were few, but by example and teaching the CCP was able to establish close identification between itself and the people, the main prerequisite of guerrilla warfare.

Given normal circumstances it is perhaps questionable that the CCP could have ultimately defeated the Kuomintang and the forces that that party represented. Circumstances in China were decidedly not normal, however. The Japanese war (1937-1945) wiped out the tenuous position which Chiang Kai-shek had laboriously established in the vital areas of north and east China, and diverted the main Kuomintang effort away from the CCP. Ultimately the CCP and Kuomintang established a sort of common front against the Japanese, within which the CCP adroitly presented itself as the most patriotic and anti-Japanese organization in China, without seriously exposing its military strength. In fact, the CCP utilized this "popular front" and the unsettled conditions of the wartime period to harass the civilians and military loyal to the Nationalists, and to establish its authority over a much broader area than had been previously possible.

The CCP utilized its potential well, and by the end of the war

[41] The best description of Chinese Communism before the Second World War is still Edgar Snow's *Red Star Over China* (New York 1938). The author's view of the Chinese Communists was extremely sympathetic and must be suitably discounted, but he attempted to render an honest report.

[42] Anna Louise Strong, "The Thought of Mao Tse-tung," *Amerasia*, XI (1947), 161-174, is the classic portrayal of the "agrarian reformist" Chinese Communist party with only nominal ties to international Communism. As such it is interesting, and is a valuable source for this period of Chinese Communist development. It is obviously Communist propaganda and should be read as such.

it represented a much more serious challenge to the Nationalist government than it had in 1937. On the face of it, however, the issue of the struggle for control of China was not immediately obvious in the 1945-1947 period, during which the CCP and Kuomintang maneuvered for political and strategic superiority. Stalin apparently discouraged the CCP from attempting to seize power in China and considered that they had "no prospect."[43] The CCP leadership itself did not expect to achieve the easy victory which was to deliver China into its hand by 1949.[44] They were determined to exploit the chaotic postwar conditions, however, and moved quickly to secure the most advantageous position possible. By centering their base of operations in Manchuria—occupied by the Soviet Union after the Japanese withdrawal—they were able to take advantage of the natural strength of that area as well as to acquire considerable supplies of Japanese war material handed over to them by the departing Soviets.

Undoubtedly the greatest advantage that accrued to the CCP was the corruption and inefficiency of the Nationalists. It is difficult to avoid the conclusion that it was more a matter of the Nationalists losing the Civil War than of the Communists winning it. To the CCP, however, must go full credit for exploiting the Nationalist weaknesses in its drive for power. The plan of strategy drawn up by Mao in late 1947 for the pursuit of his goals was well calculated to maximize the strengths of the Communist position and the weaknesses of the Natonalists'.[45] Even at this late stage, the guerrilla experiences of the CCP determined the tactics and strategy to be used in large-scale warfare. The large cities were to be left in the hands of the Kuomintang until they were completely isolated; positional warfare was to be avoided; and the main source of supplies and recruits was to be the front line—i.e. the capture of Nationalist matériel and the conversion of prisoners to the Communist cause.

The success of the Communist tactics is a matter of record.[46] In less than two years, the Communist regime was installed in Peking, the ruler of all of mainland China. But the military success was only a formality. The real victory had been achieved by the policies implemented over the previous twenty years which gave Mao the tools

[43] V. Dedijer, *Tito* (New York 1953), 322.

[44] See Chow Ching-wen, *Ten Years of Storm* (New York 1960), 12-13, on the pessimism evinced by Chou En-lai, and Mao's estimate that the war would last at least until 1952.

[45] Mao Tse-tung, "The Present Situation and Our Tasks," *Selected Works* (Peking 1961), 161ff.

[46] Documented in F. F. Liu, *A Military History of Modern China: 1924-1949* (Princeton 1956), especially chapter 19.

—the army and the party—to exploit the critical weakness inflicted on the Kuomintang by the Second World War.

The Chinese revolution was of a completely different order than the one which brought the Bolsheviks to power. Both revolutions had the advantage of operating in wartime chaos, and both took place in countries which were ripe for change. However, the Chinese success resulted from a protracted civil war rather than a *coup d'état*. The difference between their revolutionary experiences was to be of major importance in differentiating the attitudes of the two major Communists states towards revolution. The Russian model established a form of seizing power in which a small party works within an amorphous mass and picks off the fruits of a concurrent revolution. The Chinese, having failed with this method in the 1920's, developed a revolutionary model in which the Communists assert hegemony over a faction of the mass movement at an early stage and then fight their way to power by military means. Such a divergence of experience provided international communism with a considerable degree of flexibility in exploiting revolutionary situations which emerged after World War II.

The Retrospect

Between the October revolution and the Second World War the Communists had a quarter of a century to absorb and re-evaluate the lessons of the Bolshevik seizure of power and to find new approaches to revolution. Let us review the points with which this chapter began —the six reasons for the success of the October revolution—to see what new meaning these had acquired in the intervening years, and what we may reasonably assume the Communists' state of knowledge to have been as they faced the possibilities and responsibilities thrust upon them in the 1940's.

Again and again, the slogan of the "party of a new type" appears as the touchstone of revolutionary success for international communism. Only the Bolsheviks had been successful, and failures in Germany, Indonesia, China, and Hungary were ascribed, not without reason, to the immaturity and organizational weakness of the local Communist parties. "New type" parties had in fact been established in almost all cases in the 1920's, and the entire Communist movement had been Bolshevized. It is easy to point out that the weakness of the Communist parties on the eve of the Second World War derived from this very process and that the brief interlude of the Popular Front had probably expanded the Communist image more than the years of conspiratorial work, but this was not the type of strength which the Communists (particularly Stalin) sought. Objectively, neither the small conspiratorial party nor the mass party had the strength to attain power. True to their tradition, the Communists opted for the smaller group, trusting to the future to provide a situation in which it could function—just as Lenin had trusted the future before 1917.

The "dual power" tactic of the soviets had not proved very useful to European or Asian communists. Indeed, the 1938 Party History (Short Course) did not include the soviets in its list of important factors contributing to the victory in 1917. It would be wrong to assume that the dual power tactic had been discarded, however, for there are many means of creating such a situation aside from soviets. A number of new types of competitive structures were to be fashioned in Eastern Europe after the war, and even in the 1930's a new type of dual power was being brought about in China. Rather than establish a second competitive structure within a geographic area controlled by the incumbents (as had been done in Petrograd), Mao was creating his dual authority in a separate geographic area. His government in the "liberated areas" presented a semi-legitimate alternate power structure which could compete effectively with the central government of the Nationalists. It did not have extensive access to individuals outside of its boundaries, but it did possess the advantage of providing a base for military operations against the Nationalists. This was the essence of Mao's doctrine of "protracted war," a new concept in Communist revolutionary thinking. Although plans for the Bulgarian uprising and the German adventures in 1920 and 1923 envisioned the establishment of rural bases of operations, these were not intended to play a political role of any consequence. In the face of adequate repressive forces and the well developed transportation networks of Europe, they could not have existed for more than a few days. Any thoughts of dual power in these instances were limited to copies of the Bolshevik model, and even these were never realized.[47]

The "leadership of the working class" was already a euphemism

[47] For example, the Comintern document *Lehren der deutschen Ereignisse* ascribes at least part of the failure in Hamburg in 1923 to the absence of workers' councils. (Quoted by Jane Degras, *The Communist International, 1919-1943: Documents* [Oxford 1960], II, 46.) The councils would have prevented the "isolation" of the uprising–i.e. they would have given the Communists a channel of access to the well-disposed but inert mass of the proletariat.

in Lenin's time, and by the mid-1920's only the barest of pretexts was maintained of working class leadership.[48] The complete alienation of the Communists from Socialists isolated the former from mass proletarian support, and the Communist objective of seizing power was of such overriding importance that it no longer mattered on whose shoulders the party rode to power. The leaders of the movement were only abstractly interested in the working class; they desired a social upheaval, but the only real goal of this transformation was to place them in positions of power. Ironically, excessive devotion to the precepts of proletarian unity had done much to undermine the position of the Chinese Communists in the 1920's, when their preoccupation with urban areas and labor problems had been a major contributing factor to the party's vulnerability. Mao, however, set matters aright by completely abandoning any thought of working with the Chinese proletariat, and moved his base to the peasantry.[49] In Asia or in Europe, if the proletariat was to have a revolution it would be imposed upon it from without.

The question of the peasant alliance was of course in Mao's case superfluous. The peasants were not the ally of the Chinese revolution—they were the revolution. In Europe, matters stood quite differently. Aside from some unimportant exceptions in France and Eastern Europe, the Communists had failed to gain support in the countryside. European communism was oriented toward urban populations despite the obvious fact that in some areas—particularly Eastern Europe—the peasantry would either have to be neutralized or won over if the revolution was to succeed. Lenin had been successful in gaining support from the Russian peasantry (granted that the support was small, it was still more than any other contestant was able to obtain) and his program of land reform gave the peasant a stake in the Bolshevik victory during the Civil War. Similarly, the Chinese peasant would stand to lose if the Nationalists returned to power and restored old land-tenure arrangements. This method of bribery, which orthodox radicals had denounced even when it was used by Lenin,

[48] The Communist view of the role of the party and the masses can be seen in the description of the October revolution as ". . . einen Anschauungsunterricht, was die Proletarier *wollen müssen* und was sie erreichen können." (Italics added), quoted by A. Schreiner und G. Schmidt, "Die Rätebewegung in Deutschland bis zur Novemberrevolution," *Revolutionäre Ereignisse und Probleme in Deutschland während der Periode der Grossen Sozialistischen Oktoberrevolution 1917/1918* (Berlin 1957). The Communists were never to admit that the proletariat might not want what theory said it had to want.

[49] For example, see Ho Kan-chih, *A History of the Modern Chinese Revolution* (Peking 1960), 189.

became the only effective means of enlisting peasant support for communism.[50]

Incumbents are at least as important to the outcome of an internal war as are the insurgents, although their role is often neglected. The assessment of the weakness of the Russian "bourgeois" incumbents by Lenin was correct. In this assessment, it was implicit that the incumbents in other European countries would be relatively stronger —and this, too, was correct. In Europe the middle classes were familiar with the techniques of ruling—they had more than a Russian spring and summer to establish themselves. They were also firmly convinced of their own legitimacy and reacted strongly to attempts to dislodge them. In this they were aided by the relatively close ties which they enjoyed with the workers and the peasantry. The armies were likewise a strong and normally loyal bulwark of the incumbent system. In the larger European countries the people had at least a minimum of access to the government, and even in the relatively new states of Eastern Europe there was too high a degree of governmental stability to be easily shaken.

The particularly weak position of the Russian Provisional Government had been due not only to its lack of authority and legitimacy among the people; it was also drastically weakened by the wartime conditions in which it had to operate. Once the chaos of the war was over, the newly-organized European Communists found themselves confronted with situations which showed a considerable degree of political stability. The Nazis were to show that the political stability of the German state could be upset, but they did this by establishing a genuine mass movement. The Communist parties in Germany and elsewhere could only hope to be successful in a situation so highly fragmentated that even a small group could wield decisive influence.

The incumbents in Asia presented a more diverse picture. On the one hand there were the colonial powers, who still had the will and the ability to repress any challenge to their authority and thus fulfilled in the colonies the same role which they played in the metropolises. Aside from Thailand (where there was no significant Communist effort) and Japan (where the incumbents were very firmly installed),

[50] Ultimately the land holdings in Russia were collectivized, but this was done only after Communist power was well established. The importance which (at least in retrospect) is assigned to the peasant question can be seen in the eagerness with which Walther Ulbricht attempts to discredit the 1923 leadership on the point while claiming a proper orientation for himself. "Die Nachkriegskrise in Deutschland", 115.

only China had a native "bourgeois" incumbent class, represented by the Kuomintang. As we have seen, Chaing Kai-shek had the will to crush the Communists, but due to the Nationalists' weakness and (especially) geographic conditions, they were unable to assert their authority completely—and this was their ultimate undoing.

In the colonial areas, the Communists were in competition with the Nationalist forces who were soon to become incumbents. Particularly after the Sixth Comintern Conference in 1929, chastened by their experience in China, the Communists condemned all nationalist movements (such as the Indian National Congress) and went their own way politically.[51] Failure to appreciate the potential of the nationalist movements was to leave the Communists isolated when, in the wake of the Second World War, one Asian country after another became independent. The experience of the Asian Communists would compel them to look upon all nationalist governments as potential Kuomintangs, and react accordingly. When independence came, and unique opportunities for political manipulation presented themselves, the Communists had no basis, ideological or political, from which to inject themselves into the situation.

The final component of Bolshevik success was the external situation prevailing in 1918—the confusion attendant upon the war and the disunity of potential foreign enemies of the Bolshevik regime. By 1939, the situation had changed only little. Despite continual Communist allegations, the Western powers (effectively Britain, France, and Germany) were at each other's throats, not attempting to form an anti-Soviet alliance. In September of 1939, Stalin was even able to play the Germans off against the British and French, and temporarily avoid involvement in an unwelcome war. Moreover, he utilized the unsettled conditions of late 1939 and 1940 to reassert the traditional Russian boundaries in the Baltic and Poland, finishing the work that the Bolsheviks had been unable to do in the early years of their tenure.

Lenin could profit from external disunity, but there was no force outside of Russia which lent him assistance. Communist parties after 1917 had such a source of assistance, at least in theory. The existence of the Soviet Union radically changed the problems facing local Communists and the choice of measures which they could take to solve their problems. Ideally, the Red Army should have been available to

[51] The early colonial policy of the Comintern is summarized in Demetrio Boersner's *The Bolsheviks and the National and Colonial Question* (Geneva 1957). The author also provides useful background on pre-1917 developments in Socialist and Bolshevik theory.

rush to the aid of embattled proletarians, but no Soviet leader—probably not even Trotsky, had he achieved power—was so quixotic as to endanger the security of Russia in dubious foreign adventures. Stalin, ever cautious, moved only when he felt completely safe. His tenure as leader of the world Communist movement was characterized by nothing so much as by restraint and an unwillingness to gamble.[52]

Foreign communists who relied upon Stalin's concept of "proletarian internationalism" were relying upon a slender hope—but a slender hope is better than none, and that is precisely what their own capabilities would have justified. The mutual aid envisioned by the traditional Marxist concept of proletarian internationalism had been replaced by Bolshevik democratic centralism, in which loyalty flowed only upward. The blind faith of foreign Communists was a glut in the market of revolutionary Communism; action from the center was in short supply, and there was little reason to hope that it would increase. Stalin would wait until the price was right before acting.

Thus the last state of Communism in 1939 was worse than its first, two decades earlier. The strength of the Soviet union was an untapped and substantially unknown potential, and even though Mao was laying the foundations of his empire in the East, few outside of Yenan appreciated the fact. In Europe, the organizational and subversive potential of the Communists had yet to be proven. The movement was shattered—its only gains in the whole period had rested upon the conquests of the Soviet army, faced with little or no opposition. The unparalleled record of Comintern failure was not without its uses, however. The Communists were conditioned by their ideology to view experience as a guide to future conduct, and their failures provided them with a wealth of negative examples.[53] It was almost inconceivable, however, that the caution of Stalin and the ineptness of the European Communists would permit them to turn this knowledge to good advantage. It would require—so it seemed—a virtual cataclysm to galvanize the Communists into action and so weaken their opponents that Communism could again become a significant force in world affairs.

[52] Stalin was of course well aware of the potentialities of war: ". . . according to the overwhelming testimony of his writings, Stalin has expected the next crop of revolutions to come during, or in the immediate aftermath of, the Second World War." Historicus, "Stalin on Revolution," *Foreign Affairs*, XXVII (1949), 191. His problem was not in recognizing the fact, but in calculating the odds.

[53] This learning process was impeded, however, by the need to find a scapegoat for every mistake and to protect the leadership from criticism. A particularly blatant example was the aftermath of the 1923 failure in Germany, described in Degras, *The Communist International*, II, 70-72. Paradoxically, Stalin's absolute power helped alleviate this situation. He was able to rewrite history on an *ad hoc* basis, thereby introducing at least some degree of flexibility into the process.

PART II

The Legacy of the Second World War

4

Eastern Europe

R. V. BURKS

Eastern Europe, with a population of some 140 million souls inhabiting an area roughly the size of the Southern Confederacy, is one of the world's most complex and differentiated areas with a long history of ethnic intermixture and conflict. While at the time of the Communist seizures the area was preponderantly agrarian, with the most rugged mountains and the greatest poverty in the south, the provinces which bordered on Germany in the north and west were industrial, some of them heavily so. The politics of the area was to a considerable extent determined by the fact that it was in effect landlocked and, moreover sandwiched in between the major Teutonic power to the northwest and the Russian colossus to the northeast.

Thus, despite the geographic compactness of the area and its historic identity, the Communists had to apply a variety of tactics in widely differing situations in seizing power. To make clear just what transpired, and what the Communists may have learned therefrom, requires an involved and multifaceted presentation. In the first section of this chapter we attempt to evaluate the role of Soviet military occupation in the Communist seizure of power. In the second we discuss some divergencies of view which appear to have arisen among the Communists as to the how and where of seizure. In section three we present a rough classification of the different types of seizure: guerrilla war, pseudo-parliamentary procedure, and the imposition of baggage-train governments. In the next two sections we deal in some detail with a guerrilla type seizure (the case of the Yugoslav Partisans) and a "peaceful transition" (the case of Czechoslovakia). In section six we describe briefly the effort of the Austrian Communists to seize power in Vienna, and how it was defeated. Finally, we try to discover what general lessons the Communists are likely to have learned from their seizure of power in Eastern Europe 1944-1948.

Soviet Military Occupation: A Necessary Precondition

Whatever may be said of the Communist seizures of power, one single feature of these seizures overshadows all the rest: they were preceded and made possible by Soviet military occupation of the area. In Eastern Europe it was not a question of whether the Communists could capture power. Rather the question was—or turned out to be—in what manner and at what time they would mount the positions of command.[1]

This was in part because the Western powers and more particularly Western public opinion did not appreciate the character of Soviet intentions toward the East Europeans. After all that had happened under Hitler the West was willing to recognize that the Soviet Union had a special security interest in the area and was therefore privileged to preponderant influence. There was also an element of horse-trading involved. Since the Western powers wished to have the final say in the Allied Control Commission for Italy and later Japan, they had to grant the Soviets final say in the Control Commissions for Hungary, Rumania, and Bulgaria. What the West did not understand was that the USSR regarded the installation of Communist dictatorships as the absolute minimum guarantee of its security interests in the East European area. This understanding came only with the Prague coup of February 1948. Before the coup the Czechs had demonstrated a capacity for democratic self-government and they had shown a willingness to follow the precepts of Moscow in foreign policy in exchange for autonomy in domestic affairs. This is why the Prague coup created

[1] Of the many general works covering this period probably the most stimulating and insightful is that by François Fejtö, *Histoire des Democraties Populaires* (Paris 1952). Hugh Seton-Watson's *East European Revolution* (London 1959), by a leading British authority, emphasizes the sovietization of the area. A useful American work is Robert L. Wolff, *The Balkans in Our Time* (Cambridge, Mass. 1956), which unfortunately excludes developments in Greece. Ernst and Rudolf Neumann, eds., *Die Sowjetisierung Ost-Mittleuropas. Untersuchungen zu Ihrem Ablauf in den Einzelnen Ländern* (Frankfurt/M 1959) is a collective work by expellees, which suffers from failure to deal with the Nazi occupation of the area as a major factor in preparing the way for sovietization. Ygael Gluckstein's *Stalin's Satellites in Europe* (London 1952) is a Marxist presentation concerned primarily with demonstrating the instability of the Communist regimes. The bibliography presented in these footnotes was compiled by Katharine M. Burks, but the comments are mine. Thanks are also due to several of my colleagues in Radio Free Europe, Munich, who have read and criticized the manuscript, in particular to Jaromir Netik, Slobodan Stanković, and Kazimierz Zamorski. None of these gentlemen, however, assumes any responsibility for the interpretation presented.

such a stir in the Western World and why it may be taken as the beginning of the cold war.[2]

It is also questionable whether the Western powers would have acted differently had there been general public understanding that Soviet security requirements entailed Communist dictatorships in Eastern Europe. During the period of military operations the British had repeatedly proposed sending Western forces into Eastern Europe. The Americans had firmly resisted all these proposals on the grounds that such diversion of forces would delay or endanger the planned landing in Normandy and might even result in a Soviet occupation of Western Europe. The Americans were in effect saying that Eastern Europe lay beyond the perimeters of Western power.[3] As it turned out, the areas of military occupation were identical with the zones of influence. The growing belief of the Russians that they were free to do in Eastern Europe largely what they pleased was in no way diminished by the speed, not to say haste, with which the bulk of the American armies were withdrawn from Western Europe after the conclusion of hostilities.

It was a cardinal principle of Soviet policy not to permit the emergence in Eastern Europe of any local centers of authority which could offset the presence of the Soviet military. This principle underlay Soviet behavior during the Warsaw rising, which took place in the late summer of 1944, after Soviet forces had pushed the Germans back to the outskirts of the former Polish capital.[4] Militarily, the rising was directed against the *Wehrmacht,* but politically it was aimed at the USSR. The Poles wished to present the oncoming Russians with a *fait accompli,* a Polish government—however rudimentary—located on Polish territory and owing nothing to Soviet assistance. It is significant that the Poles made no effort to coordinate their plans with Moscow, although such plans had been under serious consideration by the London exile government at least since Stalingrad. It is equally significant that the units of the Polish underground army which, on instructions from London, contacted the Soviet forces when they

[2] For a good discussion of the postwar settlement in Eastern Europe, see C. E. Black, "Soviet Policy in Eastern Europe," *Annals of the American Academy of Political and Social Science,* CCLXIII (1949), 152-164.

[3] A scholarly statement by a participant is Philip E. Mosely, "Hopes and Failures: American Policy toward East Central Europe, 1941-1947," in Stephen D. Kertesz, ed., *The Fate of East Central Europe: Hopes and Failures of American Foreign Policy* (Notre Dame 1956), 51-74.

[4] Probably the best brief account of the rising is that given by S. L. Sharp in his bitter but penetrating and knowledgeable *Poland: White Eagle on a Red Field* (Cambridge, Mass. 1953).

first crossed into Polish territory, were promptly disarmed and deported to the Soviet Union.

Had the Warsaw rising succeeded, the Soviets could probably not have brought in the Lublin government in their baggage-train, as they were shortly to do. This is why the Soviet Union, despite the world-wide scandal produced by its behavior, made no serious effort to come to the aid of the Polish insurgents. It is not true to say that the USSR rendered no assistance whatever; in evident embarrassment some supplies were dropped by parachute, roughly as much in quantitative terms as the Western Allies from their much more distant bases were able to bring in. At the same time the Soviets flatly refused a request that British aircraft be permitted to land on Soviet-controlled territory east of Warsaw; such landings would have sharply increased the amount of aid the British could have given. The Soviet leaders appear to have kept clearly in mind the precept that war is fought not so much to defeat the enemy as to realize certain political objectives.

Soviet policy toward the Slovak rising in the fall of 1944 was not essentially different, though owing to different circumstances it was by no means so embarrassing to the USSR. The Slovak rising represented a *mariage de convenance* between elements of the puppet army of the "independent" Slovak state and a diverse local leadership in which Communists played an important role. Had the rising shown real prospects of success, the rest of the puppet army might well have crossed over to it. In this event there would have emerged a hybrid regime with a left-oriented but independence-minded Slovak leadership resting upon a nationalist-oriented Slovak army. From the Soviet point of view such a regime would no doubt have been preferable to the nationalist-minded but anti-Communist government that a successful Warsaw rising would have produced. Nonetheless, Moscow was deeply suspicious and feared "whether even in this case it was not a mere attempt at saving Slovakia's territory for capitalism by means of a staged uprising."[5] Moscow offered the insurgents little or nothing in the way of support as the *Wehrmacht* moved in to mop up.

[5] Václav Kopecký *ČSR a KSČ* [The Czechoslovak Republic and the Communist Party of Czechoslovakia] (Prague 1960), 348. For the rising itself see Peter A. Toma "Soviet Strategy in the Slovak Uprising of 1944," *Journal of Central European Affairs*, XIX (1959), 290-298; L. Hory, "Der slowakische Partisanenkampf 1944/45," *Osteuropa*, IX (1959), 779-785; R. Urban, "Der slowakische Partisanenkampf 1944-45 (eine Ergänzung)," *Osteuropa*, X (1960), 779-785; A. L. Nedorezov, "Vostaniye Slovatskogo naroda v 1944 g." [The Uprising of the Slovak people in 1944], *Novaya i Noveyshaya Istoriya*, no. 6, (1959), 3-17. For a general consideration of the Slovak question in its relation to Communism see J. Netik and J. Franko, *Communism and Slovakia: A Documentary Analysis of Communist Policies* (Munich: Radio Free Europe 1960), in mimeograph.

The Hungarian resistance organization (*Magyar Nemzeti Függetlenségi Front*) was not sufficiently active or influential to entertain any thought of armed uprising. Its efforts to establish contact with the Soviet high command remained without result. An attempt by Horthy to go over at the last minute (October 15, 1944) failed, and although one of the Hungarian armies crossed over to the Soviet side, it was ultimately disarmed and taken prisoner.

The Rumanians had succeeded where the Hungarians failed. On August 23, 1944, some three weeks prior to Horthy's failure, they managed to take both the German and Soviet commands by surprise, change positions, and reenter the fighting on the Allied side. To judge from the attitude of the Rumanian Communist leaders then resident in Moscow, the Russians were unhappy and chagrined. The Rumanian Communist exiles argued that the "events" of August 23 made necessary an intermediate period of collaboration with the bourgeois elements, a development that these exiles frankly regarded as unfortunate. For their part, the Soviet military did not turn Northern Transylvania, which they had occupied during the course of the fighting, over to Rumanian administration until the installation (March 1945) in Bucharest of a coalition government satisfactory to Moscow. Meanwhile Moscow had apparently toyed with the idea of a separate Transylvanian state.[6]

In the case of Bulgaria, the Russians suddenly declared war (September 4, 1944) and occupied the country. Almost at once (September 9) the Communist-led Fatherland Front took over the government by *coup d'état*. The government overthrown by the Fatherland Front had been in office less than a week; it had been moderately agrarian in its political views and looked to the US and Britain for support. After the *coup* Bulgarian forces were permitted to fight alongside Partisan and Soviet troops in the liberation of Yugoslavia and Hungary.

Thus Soviet policy makers went to considerable lengths to prevent the emergence in Eastern Europe of any power centers not under Communist control. Beyond the control of the policy makers was the development of a Communist power center with political resources of its own, i.e., the Yugoslav Partisan movement with its Albanian and Slavo-Macedonian appendages. The plain and almost miraculous truth is that the Yugoslav and Albanian Partisans fought their way into power over the opposition of both the German and Italian occupying armies and also of conservative nationalist forces such as the Croa-

[6] R. V. Burks, *The Dynamics of Communism in Eastern Europe* (Princeton 1961), 155-157 and especially n. 17.

tian *Ustaša,* the Serbian *Chetniks* and the Geg *Legaliteti.* Such outside help as the Partisans received came from the Western allies. The Soviets did not even send a military mission to Tito until July 1944, when the outcome of the fighting in Yugoslavia was already clear. They had turned down repeated Partisan appeals for assistance, for shoes, medical supplies, almost anything. The Soviet reluctance was in part the result of their own pressing needs; in part it resulted from a fear that Partisan radicalism—the Partisans insisted on wearing red stars, organizing "proletarian brigades" and setting up local soviets (Committees of National Liberation)—would make Soviet cooperation with the Western allies difficult. At one point Moscow even offered to recognize the royal Yugoslav government in London. Given Stalin's suspicious nature, however, and his instinct for the political, it may also be that the Soviet dictator viewed with reserve the emergence in Eastern Europe of any power center with significant local support, whatever its ideological allegiance.[7] At any rate, Partisan-Soviet relations were not free of serious disturbance during the period of the fighting and, after the liberation of Yugoslavia, they tended to deteriorate.

Perhaps the clearest proof that Soviet occupation of Eastern Europe was the decisive element in the seizure of power is provided by the case of Greece. There was nothing to prevent the establishment of a people's democracy in Greece except the fact that in negotiations taking place in Moscow in October 1944 Greece had been allotted to the British sphere of influence, and the British insisted on bringing back to Athens the royal government in exile. When fighting broke out in Athens between the Communist-led guerrilla forces and the government troops (supported by British units), and when it became clear that the latter would soon be overwhelmed, the British rushed in the reinforcements necessary to turn the tide. Thus even where the Communists were strong enough locally to seize power under conditions of occupation and civil war, they could not accomplish the seizure in a country which lay within the sphere of influence of an unfriendly power.

We can imagine the sequence of developments had the British been

[7] We are not of course speaking of popular majorities but of irregular armies victorious in civil war which had mass following and had set up institutions of local government in the areas under their control. On the question of Soviet policy Milovan Djilas, *Conversations with Stalin* (New York 1962) varies between the view that the Soviets simply did not understand what was going on in Yugoslavia during the Partisan war (8-11) and the view that Stalin was instinctively opposed for reasons of state to the formation of revolutionary centers outside of Moscow (132, 183).

able to carry out one of their favorite wartime projects and push an Allied army through the Ljubljana gap. Allied troops would soon have been engaged with the Partisans (Tito once told Stalin that he would attack immediately any Allied troops which put foot on Yugoslav soil). Slovenia and perhaps parts of Croatia would have shortly developed pro-Western governments. Only Soviet intervention could have prevented the partition of Yugoslavia into Communist and royalist halves.[8] In short, the prerequisite of Communist rule in any country of Eastern Europe appears to have been that country's inclusion in the Soviet sphere of influence. This was true even in countries (Yugoslavia, Albania, Greece) where Communist guerrillas had defeated their opponents in civil war and commanded extensive popular support, just as it was true in countries (Poland, Rumania, East Germany) where the Communists were little more than a handful of revolutionaries without important local adherence. This is probably only another way of saying that the armies of small states, guerrilla or otherwise, cannot contend successfully with the modern armaments of great powers.[9]

Divergencies of View Among the Communists

The principal question, then, which confronted East European Communists in 1944 with regard to the seizure of power was not the whether, but the how and the when. On these issues East European Communist leaders appear to have been divided. So, apparently, was the Soviet leadership. This division did not embrace a disputed succession, though maneuvering for position in the event of Stalin's death was involved, nor was it affected by a conflict of interest between major Communist powers. It was basically an honest division of opinion on policy and was rooted in divergent estimates of the situation which confronted the Communist movement. The evidence is skimpy

[8] In this connection it is worth quoting a leading Czechoslovak Communist on the possible division of Czechoslovakia. "We left for Bratislava on May 9, 1945 . . . Beneš proceeded toward Bratislava cherishing his pet notion that U. S. troops advancing in Western Bohemia might reach Prague. We approached Bratislava in a gloomy mood; we did not want to think of the possibility of the Americans coming to Prague. For should this happen it would mean that we ourselves would have to stay away from a Prague occupied by U. S. troops. It would have meant the Kósice government stopping in either Bratislava or Brno, as well as the possibility that Czechoslovakia might be divided into two parts—just as later on happened with the territories of Germany and Austria." Kopecký, 384.

[9] Feodor T. Konstantinov, ed., *O Narodnoy Demokratii v Stranakh Evropy: Sbornik Statey* [People's Democracy in the Countries of Eastern Europe: A Collection of Essays] (Moscow 1956) emphasizes the importance of the Soviet army in the establishment of the peoples' democracies.

in its details. The broad outlines of the dispute as it developed in the early postwar years, however, seem well established and parallel closely the familiar divergencies between "revisionists" and "dogmatists."

On the one side were the radicals, who regarded their party opponents as overestimating the economic stability and military strength of the "capitalist" states, while underestimating the power and revolutionary *élan* of the "socialist" movement. The radicals advocated the early seizure of power in Eastern Europe and the open installation of proletarian dictatorships. They wished to revive the Comintern, go back on the arrangement which put Greece in the Western sphere, and thought it unnecessary to conciliate public opinion in the West.

On the other side were the moderates, who held to the view that "capitalism" had reached a new plateau of stability through reform, and would probably avoid a serious economic crisis for some time. In seizing power they wished to pick up as much local support as possible, and to conciliate Western opinion where feasible. The moderates thought in terms of coalition governments and "peoples' democracies." They opposed heavy reparations deliveries from the former enemy states of Eastern Europe. They were against stirring up guerrilla war in Greece and they first tried to put off the revival of the Comintern and then to reduce its size and importance (thus the Cominform).[10]

Obviously the argument between the two groupings varied with the circumstances of the country to be taken over. In Rumania, where popular support for the Communists was so exiguous as to exclude any thought of a free election, the argument revolved around the "events" of August 23. The Rumanian Muscovites, those who had spent at least the war years in the Soviet capital, wished to denigrate the importance of these "events", pointing out that they made necessary a period of collaboration with bourgeois elements and thus postponed the day of final reckoning. The Muscovites seemed to be sorry that Rumania had very largely escaped the devastation of actual battle, thus leaving the traditional social order and way of life intact and undisturbed. On the other hand, the "nativists," those who had spent

[10] For the divisions in the Communist camp see especially Ernst Halperin, *The Triumphant Heretic* (London 1958). Halperin fought in the International Brigade in Spain, where he learned to know many of the key Yugoslav Communists, and reported from Belgrade for the *Neue Zürcher Zeitung* in the early 1950's. *Informatsionnoye Soveshchaniye Predstaviteley Nekotorykh Kompartii v Pol'she v Kontse Sentyabrya 1947 Goda* [Conference of representatives of some Communist parties held in Poland toward the end of September 1947] (Moscow 1948) reproduces the speeches given at the founding of the Cominform and reflects the policy change involved in its establishment. See also Franz Borkenau, *Der Europäische Kommunismus. Seine Geschichte von 1917 bis zur Gegenwart* (Bern 1952).

the war years in Rumania, seemed glad that the country had come through the war with so little physical damage, praised the "events" of August 23 as decisive for the national history, and enormously exaggerated the role which the Communist party had played in them.

There was a similar divergence of views in the Czechoslovak party. One group, which seems to have been composed mainly of *apparatchiks,* wished to seize power upon the return of the government in exile to Prague (1945). Communists or fellow travellers held key positions in the administration and the army; the party was numerically much stronger than the Rumanian or Polish parties which seized power in 1944-1945; and Communism as a doctrine was identified with such popular events as the liberation of the country from the Nazis, the expulsion of the German minority, and the nationalization of industry. An opposing group, which appears to have drawn its strength from among Communists working the bureaucracy and trade unions, advocated another course. They opposed the use of force for the time being and proposed a period of collaboration with the non-Communist parties during which the Communist Party of Czechoslovakia (CPCS) would gradually build up its popular following and acquire in free elections a majority in the national parliament. After this demonstration of the popular will Communists could make the necessary arrangements for permanent tenure of office. Meantime the world would have been edified by a powerful example of peaceful transition from bourgeois to socialist democracy.

No doubt the same or a similar issue was a source of discord in other parties. There is, for example, evidence to suggest that a group in the Greek party opposed the resort to force both in December 1944, and in September 1946. But we know little that is specific about this or other comparable quarrels. Our knowledge of the Czechoslovak and Rumanian cases is largely the result of revelations made by the parties themselves for reasons of their own, in the Czech case by Gottwald shortly after the seizure of power in February 1948, and in the Rumanian case by Gheorghiu-Dej and others in the aftermath of the XXII Congress of the Soviet party (October 1961). It is worth noting, moreover, that Tito, when he was at the height of popularity and influence with the Bloc in the fall of 1947, publicly criticized those satellite Communist leaders who were unable to distinguish between a bourgeois parliamentary government and revolutionary one. But what is most important is that there were significant divergences of view within at least some of the parties concerning the timing and the method of the seizure of power in a situation in which the ultimate issue was hardly in doubt.

Typology of Take-Over

Eastern Europe is above all a variegated area, ethnically, geographically, economically. Within the framework of the generalities outlined in the preceding paragraphs the particular circumstances faced by each party during and after the Second World War often varied widely and it is instructive to categorize the parties according to the type of process by which they came to power. There is, first of all, the case in which in the circumstances of enemy occupation a party built up guerrilla forces and waged both a hit-and-run war with the occupier and a civil war with rival local guerrilla organizations. The action against the occupier did little more than discommode him and had little effect upon the outcome of the war, but it did serve to identify the Communist party with the national interest, especially since the Communists were usually more active in fighting the foreigner than were their local competitors. Having made clear their commitment to national defense the Communists were able in the long run to overcome their guerrilla enemies, who were frequently led by increasing fear of ultimate Communist seizure of power to collaborate with the foreign enemy. This in turn led the Western Allies to give more aid to the Communist resistance forces. The world was confronted with the confusing spectacle of the democratic allies giving military support to Balkan Communists (which Communist Russia failed to do) while the pro-Western anti-Communists in the Balkans collaborated with the Nazi and Fascist invaders. When the fortunes of war forced the Axis to withdraw, control of the territory thus fell almost automatically into the hands of the Communist guerrillas. In these countries there were not even important Socialist forces to deal with; the Socialists had been relatively unimportant to begin with and they were easily absorbed by the front organization which formally gave political guidance to the guerrillas. This was the situation in Yugoslavia, Albania, and Greece.[11]

[11] Yugoslavia will be dealt with at some length. For the seizure of power in Albania the most important contribution is that of Stavro Skendi. See his "Albania Within the Slav Orbit; Advent to Power of the Communist Party," *Political Science Quarterly*, LXIII (1948), 257-274; and also Skendi, ed., *Albania* (New York 1956). See also the anonymous "History of the Albanian Communist Party," *News from Behind the Iron Curtain*, IV (1955), 3-10, and V, 22-30. Julian Amery, *Sons of the Eagle: A Study in Guerrilla War* (London 1948) is an unusually penetrating eye-witness account of the Albanian civil war by a British officer who was attached

A second case is that in which local Communists enjoyed significant popular support, relatively speaking, where the party had an important history, but where it possessed nothing in the way of guerrilla troops because there had been no civil war and in fact little underground activity. The terrain was not very propitious for guerrilla activity —but in any case the local populations had tended to collaborate with the Axis, sometimes out of national self-interest, at other times in skillful accommodation to *force majeure*. Within the shadow of Soviet tanks the local Communists began to rebuild their popular following and to play the dominant role in a coalition of anti-Fascist parties which in all sincerity shared many objectives with the Communists, such as the nationalization of industry or the expulsion of German minorities. In these circumstances the party made a patient effort to attain as large a measure of popular consent as possible, even on occasion going to the extreme of holding free elections. The final take-over was thus delayed for some time. In this category we have Hungary, where the last act was the forced resignation of Prime Minister Ferenc Nagy in September 1947, and Czechoslovakia, where the final scene was the formation of a new Gottwald government in February 1948.[12]

An interesting variant of this second case is provided by Bulgaria. There the Communist party had had a long and dramatic history and had given proof of considerable popular support. There also the regime and people had collaborated with the Axis, despite strong Russophile sentiments, because the Axis permitted the Bulgarian army

---

to the Albanian royalists. The most revealing book on the Greek guerrilla struggle is undoubtedly that of C. M. Woodhouse, *Apple of Discord: A Survey of Recent Greek Politics in their International Setting* (London 1948). Woodhouse was the head of the British military mission to the Greek guerrillas. W. H. McNeill, *The Greek Dilemma: War and Aftermath* (New York 1947) is a closely reasoned presentation based on documentary sources and interviews; L. S. Stavrianos, *Greece: American Dilemma and Opportunity* (Chicago 1952) is more sympathetic to the guerrillas.

[12] The case of Czechoslovakia will be dealt with in detail. Ferenc Nagy and Stephen K. Swift, *The Struggle Behind the Iron Curtain* (New York 1948) is a biographical account of the Communist seizure of power by the Hungarian premier and leader of the Smallholders. Stephen D. Kertesz, *Diplomacy in a Whirlpool: Hungary Between Nazi Germany and Soviet Russia* (Notre Dame 1953) views the same process within the framework of international relations; Kertesz "The Methods of Communist Conquest: Hungary 1944-47," *World Politics*, III (October 1950), 20-54, is also useful. For the regime view see Deszo Nemes, *Magyarorszag Felszabadulása. Magyarorszag Fejlodése a Felszabadulás utan* [*The Liberation of Hungary. The Post Liberation Development of Hungary*], rev. ed. (Budapest 1960). A semi-official Soviet view is presented by L. N. Nezhinsky, "Iz istorii ukrepleniya Narodno-Demokraticheskogo stroya v Vengrii (1947-48 gg.)" [History of the Consolidation of People's Democracy in Hungary (1947-48)], *Novaya i Noveyshaya Istoriya*, no. 1 (1960), 92-103.

to take possession of much of Macedonia, territory that Sofia claimed for its own. The Macedonian Communists refused to take orders from Tito, who commanded them to lead a rising, and instead took their orders from the Bulgarian party, which instructed them to take service with the Bulgarian forces "in order to keep in close touch with the masses." Only toward the end of the war, when Axis defeat was a matter of time alone, did the Macedonian Communists renew their allegiance to the CPY and join in the partisan fighting.

But the Russians did not permit the Bulgarian party to negotiate its way to power through a parliamentary maze. Suspicious of the negotiations which Sofia was entertaining with the Western Allies in Cairo, though these were faithfully reported by the Westerners to Moscow, the Soviets without warning declared war on Bulgaria on September 5, 1944, occupied the country within forty-eight hours, and installed a Communist-dominated government. It is true that the BCP came to power as part of a coalition of anti-Fascist parties, and that an election was later held in which the Communists only claimed to have received 55 percent of the popular vote. But scarcely a week elapsed between the Soviet occupation of the country and the Communist take-over. Undoubtedly considerations of Soviet national security had much to do with this hastening of events.[13]

In addition to the cases of guerrilla conquest and parliamentary infiltration there is what might be called the baggage-train government. This type literally occurred in Poland and East Germany, and happened to a substantial degree in Rumania. Each of these countries had a long history of conflict with the Russians over frontier questions and two were adjacent to the Soviet Union and therefore major security concerns. Each state, furthermore, had been occupied by Russian or Soviet armies many times. Each had only a miniscule, sectarian, and slightly ridiculous Communist party, which

[13] For developments in Bulgaria see the official view as presented in *The Trial of Nikola D. Petkov. Record of the Judicial Proceedings, August 5-15, 1947* (Sofia 1947) and the opposition viewpoint as given by Michael Padev, *Dimitrov Wastes No Bullets* (London 1948). A good picture of the operations of the Bulgarian partisans is to be found in *There is a Spirit in Europe: A Memoir of Frank Thompson* (London 1948). For the strength of the Bulgarian Party see Joseph Rothschild, *The Communist Party of Bulgaria: Origins and Development 1883-1936* (New York 1959). The regime has provided us with a collection of documents, *Bulgarskata Komunisticheska Partiya v Resolyutsii i resheniya na Kongresite, Konferentsiite i plenumite na TsK* [The Bulgarian Communist Party in the Resolutions and Decisions of the Congresses, Conferences and Plenums of the CC], III (1924-1944) (Sofia 1954), IV (1944-1955) (Sofia 1955). The Soviet view is presented in F. T. Konstantinov, *Bolgariya na Put' k Sotsializmu* [Bulgaria on the Road to Socialism] (Moscow 1953).

could not overcome a taint of treason. In Poland there was—despite unsuitable terrain—a vital, hard-hitting, and daring underground army, but it was overwhelmingly anti-Communist and anti-Russian, as well as anti-German. In Rumania there was little underground activity of any sort. The Rumanian government participated in the German march to the east in the hope of territorial gain, and the strongest and most active of the extremist elements was the fascist-minded Iron Guard.

Thus in both Rumania and Poland elections were held only after the Communists were safely ensconced in power. Actually Warsaw first held a plebiscite on such questions as whether the electorate approved of the new and greatly advantageous western frontier along the Oder and Neisse rivers. Only then did Warsaw venture to rig an election. The new Polish Communist government, which came to be known as the Lublin committee, was first established on Soviet territory and subsequently advanced to Warsaw in the rear of the Soviet forces. The Warsaw rising, discussed earlier in this essay, can be viewed as a Polish attempt to forestall the arrival of the Lublin committee. The government in Bucharest was turned over to the Communists on the direct orders of Soviet Foreign Minister Vyshinsky in early March 1945. The chief of the new government was Petru Groza, a Transylvanian lawyer who had headed a Communist front as early as the 1930's. However, neither Groza nor his cabinet could have lasted throughout one day had it not been for the support of Soviet bayonets. The popular approval which either the Polish or the Rumanian party could have mustered in 1945 was minute, even in comparison with Communist popular strength in the other countries of Eastern Europe.[14]

[14] Virtually all accounts of the seizure of power in Poland are strongly partisan. Noteworthy are *The Rape of Poland* (New York 1948) by Stanislaw Mikolajczyk, the leader of the defeated Peasant party, and *I saw Poland Betrayed: An Ambassador Reports to the American People* (Indianapolis 1948) by Arthur Bliss Lane, the American ambassador in Warsaw from 1945-1947. Much more objective is the only history of the Polish Comunist party in English, M. K. Dziewanowski, *The Communist Party of Poland: An Outline of History* (Cambridge, Mass. 1959). For the regime view see W. Gora, *PPR w Walce o Utrwalenie Wlodzy Ludowej. Od PKWN do Rzadu Jednosci Narodowej* [The Polish Workers' Party in its Struggle for the Consolidation of the People's Power. From the Polish Committee of National Liberation to the Government of National Unity] (Warsaw 1958). Also W. Gora, J. Golebioroski, R. Halaba and N. Kolomejczyk, *Zarys Historii PPR: Lipiec 1944-Sierpien 1947* [Outline of the History of the Polish Workers' Party: July 1944-August 1947] (2nd. ed., Warsaw 1962). For a Soviet view see N. Fedotenkov, "K voprosu ob etapakh v. narodno-demokraticheskoy Revoliutsii v Pol'she" [The Question of Stages in the People's Democratic Revolution in Poland], *Voprosy Ekonomiki,* no. 1 (1958), 57-65. Rumanian developments are dealt with by Alex-

In many respects the East German satellite presented the clearest case of baggage-train government. The Polish and Rumanian regimes, at the least, could claim to represent historic nations each with a mythos of its own. East Germany was not a nation, but rather a rump with a population whose real interest lay in reunion with the larger West Germany. The Polish and Rumanian regimes could gain support from even anti-Communists on vital territorial issues. The government in Warsaw could and did plead that its continuing tenure was prerequisite to the retention of the Western territories, which not only constituted a fourth of the area of the reconstituted state, but also provided it with the mineral resources of the Silesian basin and, for the first time in centuries, an access to the Baltic Sea not threatened by Germans.[15] In Rumania, the imposition of the Groza government was followed at once by the return of Northern Transylvania to Rumania administration. In the winter of 1944-1945 there had emerged in this area, annexed by Hungary on August 31, 1940, a fellow-travelling local government rooted in the Hungarian minority. Until the advent of Groza, this local administration appeared to have Soviet patronage and nourished hope of some degree of continuing independence. But East Germany, in addition to being separated from its western counterpart, had to proclaim its approval of the loss of East Prussia, Pomerania, and Silesia, provinces which had been indisputably German for hundreds of years. Free elections in West Berlin indicated that the strength of the once powerful German Communists had fallen below five percent of the electorate. As long as it was physically possible for East Germans to escape westward, they would do so in great numbers. The German Democratic Republic, as the Soviets called their artificial creation, was one of the few states in the world to be characterized (until 1961 at least) by a declining population.

The East German regime had thus less in the way of popular

---

ander Cretzianu, ed., *Captive Romania—A Decade of Soviet Rule* (New York, 1956) and Ion Gheorghe, *Rumäniens Weg zum Satellitenstaat* (Heidelberg 1952). The former is a collaborative work by a group of Rumanian exiles, the latter a presentation by a Rumanian general who served during the war as military attaché in Berlin. For an official view see 30 *de Ani de Lupta a Partidului* [30 Years of Party Struggle] (Bucharest 1951) and *Lectii in Ajutorul Celor Cara Studiaza Istoria PMR* [Lessons to Aid the Study of the History of the Rumanian Workers' Party] (Bucharest 1951).

[15] For the Oder-Neisse territories see the fundamental study by Elizabeth Wiskemann, *Germany's Eastern Neighbors: Problems Relating to the Oder-Neisse Line and the Czech Frontier Regions* (New York 1956). The book has been severely criticized by German scholars.

support or national *raison d'être* than either its Rumanian or its Polish counterpart. It was in its origin almost wholly a creature of Soviet fiat, represented by some 22 Russian divisions stationed on East German territory. The Soviet blockade of West Berlin in 1948-1949 was in considerable part an effort to endow the Pankow government with greater viability by making the whole of Berlin available to the German Democratic Republic as its capital, and by simultaneously cutting off the escape hatch through which thousands of East Germans fled, thus offsetting and enfeebling the disciplinary measures taken by the regime. In one sense the periodic crises over Berlin have been the result of a Soviet effort to endow a regime installed by Moscow with some of the real attributes of sovereignty.[16]

There is a curious geographic conformity to our typology of Communist seizure of power. The guerrilla Communists, those who fought their way into power without Soviet assistance, were all located in the rugged karst highlands of the Dinaric Alpine chain, an area with a well-established tradition of insurgency, embodied in the legend of the haiduks and the klephts. This area—roughly comprising the states of Yugoslavia, Albania, and Greece—is backward, poorly endowed with natural resources, and of secondary strategic importance to the USSR. It is the most nearly comparable to the underdeveloped territories of Asia, Africa, and Latin America. The baggage-train governments, on the other hand, are located in two countries immediately adjacent to the Soviet Union, in Poland and Rumania, and in an artificial country geographically contiguous with the first of these and having unusual strategic interest from the Soviet point of view, i.e., in Eastern Germany. The parliamentary Communists—if we may thus refer to those who sought to achieve power with a maximum appearance of popular consent—are to be found in Czechoslovakia and

[16] Ernst Richert, *Macht Ohne Mandat. Der Staatsapparat in der sowjetischen Besatzungszone Deutschlands* (Cologne 1958) is a profound study of the theory and inner workings of a satellite totalitarian regime. J. P. Nettl, *The Eastern Zone and Soviet Policy in Germany 1945-50* (Oxford 1951) is a comprehensive analysis which also deals with the place of the zone in the eastern bloc. Carola Stern, *Porträt einer bolschewistischen Partei. Entwicklung, Funktion and Situation der SED* (Cologne 1957) is a useful handbook. For a Soviet view see G. N. Goroshkova, "Narodnye komitety nakanune obrazovaniya Germanskoy Demokraticheskoy Respubliki (1948-49 gg)" [The National Committees on the Eve of the Formation of the German Democratic Republic (1948-49)], *Novaya i Noveyshaya Istoriya,* No. 5 (1959), 22-40. The official interpretation is to be found in "Grundriss der Geschichte der deutschen Arbeiterbewegung," *Einheit. Zeitschrift für Theorie und Praxis des Wissenschaftlichen Sozialismus,* special issue (August 1962.)

Hungary, countries closely identified with the West that have relatively high living standards and well established parliamentary institutions. In each country there had been extensive collaboration, whether *de jure* or *de facto,* with the Axis. The territorial arrangements of 1945 gave both Hungary and Czechoslovakia a common frontier with the USSR for the first time in their history. In a way, Bulgaria fits into all three categories. It was mountainous enough, and had enough of an insurrectionary tradition to have produced a major Communist guerrilla army—had the political situation favored such a development. It had a strong enough Communist movement to have permitted the seizure of power by way of parliamentary maneuver, and it was strategically significant enough for the Soviets to have imposed a Communist government immediately upon its liberation from the Axis.

There are, however, various features of the Communist take-over in Eastern Europe which do not conform to this basic geographical pattern, but which are common to all states, or to groupings of states which are not identical with the division into baggage-train, guerrilla, and parliamentary seizures of power. One of the universal characteristics was the effort of the Communists to achieve a monopoly of popular and reformist causes, such as the breaking up of the great estates where these still existed, the nationalization of industry, and the denazification of the bureaucracy. Another was the tendency of the Communist parties to admit to their formal membership large masses of persons who were at best little more than sympathizers and at worst opportunists seeking safe haven from a Nazi past; indeed the bulk of party membership everywhere came to be made up of opportunists. A generalization which applies to the whole area except for the guerrilla states (Yugoslavia, Albania, Greece) was the development of splinter peasant parties. These were secretly controlled, or at least strongly influenced, by the Communists, and were supposed to compete with long-established peasant parties, or in any case to confuse and disorient the electorate. Two other generalizations apply to smaller areas. The forcible fusion of the Communist and Socialist parties was an important development only in those states in which Social Democracy had been a major force during the interwar period, i.e., in East Germany, Poland, Czechoslovakia, and Hungary. In the last two, which both experienced the parliamentary transition to Socialism, the possession or infiltration of key ministries by the Communists played an important role. The ministries concerned were those of interior, national defense, agriculture and education.[17]

These various eddies and patterns, however, are only overlays on the fundamental types of power seizure, guerrilla warfare, outright imposition by the occupying authority, and parliamentary manipulations. A closer examination of two of these types, guerrilla seizure and parliamentary manipulation, will reveal the infrastructure of each and will make possible a certain amount of informed speculation as to what the Communists may have learned from their experience in Eastern Europe that would affect their approach to the seizure of power in other parts of the world.

The Case of the Yugoslav Partisans

The prime case of guerrilla warfare is represented by Yugoslavia. The terrain of Yugoslavia, particularly that of the provinces of Bosnia, Herzegovina, and Montenegro, is conducive to this kind of warfare. It is rugged enough to provide good cover and safe hideouts and militates against the use of tanks and other heavy military equipment. It is also sufficiently poor and forbidding and far off the beaten track to be unattractive to an occupying authority whose major military interest in Yugoslavia was in any case the maintenance of its lines of communication, which, naturally enough, ran through the plains and the valleys. An additional element was the fact that the mountain zones are food deficit areas that normally import edibles from the plains of Serbia and the Banat. The effect of the Axis occupation was to cut off these imports and ultimately to reduce the mountaineers to the desperate expedient of raiding other villages for food.

The tradition of this mountain area in particular, and of the Yugoslav peoples in general, favored insurrection. There were not only the colorful *haiduks* of high *Turkish* times, who had nicely mixed brigandage with patriotic acts of resistance, but there was also a whole series of heroic national acts stretching far back in time. The Monte-

[17] For a sympathetic view of Communist land reform see Doreen Warriner, *Revolution in Eastern Europe* (London 1950); the nationalization of industry is dealt with by S. Doernberg in "Iz istorii bor'by dlya natsionalizatsiyu krupnoy promyshlennosti v Vostochnoy Germanni [The History of the Struggle for the Nationalization of Heavy Industry in Eastern Germany], *Novaya i Noveyshaya Istoriya,* no. 3 (1960), 104-119. An account of the destruction of the Social Democratic parties in Poland, Czechoslovakia, and Hungary is given in Denis Healey, ed., *The Curtain Falls; the Story of the Socialists in Eastern Europe. Foreword by Aneurin Bevan* (London 1951). The mass entrance of opportunists into the East European parties is described by Burks, 49-53.

negrins under their *vladika,* or prince-bishop, had by more or less constant hard fighting maintained a precarious independence throughout the five hundred years of Turkish rule in the Balkans. The Serbs of Serbia proper had undertaken the first successful rebellion against the Turks in 1804, while the Serbs of Bosnia had begun the insurrection of 1875 which led to the Russo-Turkish war and the Treaty of Berlin. The Bosnian Serbs had also assassinated the Austrian Archduke, Franz Ferdinand, in 1914 in the hope of bringing about a war of Serbian unification. The Croatians under their leader Jellačić had played a significant part in the revolutionary risings which swept through Austria in 1848, and they were recognized as providing some of the Habsburg emperors' best soldiers.

While terrain and tradition did not necessarily favor the Communists as such, taken together they did produce a state of affairs from which the Communists by training and doctrine were better able to draw profit than their opponents. When Axis reprisals for acts of resistance produced mass graves and burned-out villages, the tendency of the *Chetniks,* the nationalist-oriented Serbian resistance guerrilla force, was to draw back and limit military action. The *Chetnik* commander Mihailović was fearful that this kind of bloodletting would impair the nation's chances for political survival. The Communist reaction to Axis reprisals, however, was to undertake raids designed to provoke more of them. Most of the terrified survivors would then flee to the hills where they of necessity turned to the Communists for weapons and food.

A more important factor in the ultimate success of the Partisans, however, was the ethnic problem of Yugoslavia. The Axis occupation brought with it the disintegration of the Yugoslav state, a creation of only some twenty years standing. In the north, parts of the Voivodina were taken over by the Hungarians. Slovenia was divided between Germany and Italy. Croatia was set up as an "independent" state and given the ethnically variegated and much contested province of Bosnia-Herzegovina. To establish permanent control in this province, where the Croatians (Catholics) constituted only a minority, Zagreb coddled the Bosniaks, or Moslem population, and created a special force (*Ustaša*) which set about exterminating the Serbian (or Orthodox) element. This attempt at genocide turned out to be an important factor in the Communist seizure of power, since many of the survivors sought refuge and succor among the Partisans. Further to the south, Montenegro was restored to a shadowy existence, the Albanian-inhabited territory of Kossovo (together with a small slice of Macedonia) was given to Albania, while the bulk of Macedonia was turned over to the Bulgarians. The rump of Serbia proper resembled in size and shape the independent kingdom of 1912.

It was the dismemberment of the Yugoslav state that, as much as anything, accounts for the ultimate victory of the Communists. The *Ustaše* and the Croatian *Domobran* (or militia) represented Croatian particularism. Both the armed forces of the Nedić puppet government in Belgrade and the *Chetnik* fighters of Mihailović, centered in the hills of central Serbia, stood for the restoration of a Serb-dominated Yugoslavia as in the time of King Alexander (1921-1934). It was precisely this Serbian domination that had alienated the Croats. The Communists, on the other hand, were in their composition and outlook a truly Yugoslav movement. They had cadres and organizations in every part of the former Yugoslav state; in this respect no other force, whether resistance or collaborationist, could match them.

In the underground movement of the interwar period, the Communists had met and mastered the very problem which in the end had destroyed royal Yugoslavia, the problem of Serbian hegemony. In the early 1920's the leadership of the CPY had been predominantly Serb, though the bulk of the party following was probably non-Serb. The two elements, Serb and non-Serb, quarrelled bitterly over whether the existing Yugoslav state should be preserved in its essentials after communism came to power, or broken up into its component ethnic parts. The Comintern threw its support to the non-Serbs, since Soviet policy favored the dissolution of Royal Yugoslavia because of its membership in the Little Entente, an alliance system in part directed against the USSR, and because of King Alexander's policy of granting refuge to White Russian exiles. In the long run, the non-Serbs got the upper hand in the party leadership, thus helping to preserve for the period of Partisan fighting the truly pan-Slav character of the party. The outcome of the ethnic struggle in national politics was, of course, the reverse. The Serbs managed to maintain their dominant position in the army, the bureaucracy, and the national life. This created such dissatisfaction among the non-Serbs as to prepare the way for the military collapse of Royal Yugoslavia in 1941 and the subsequent outbreak of civil war.

Thus in the 1920's the Comintern had pressed upon the East European parties the advocacy of the principle of national self-determination, including the right of secession. In the conditions of factional conflict in the Yugoslav underground the effect of this policy was gradually to destroy the hegemony of the Serbian comrades over the Yugoslav Communist party and to replace it with a leadership of non-Serbian Communists—Croatians, Slovenians, Montenegrins, and *prechani* (members of the Serbian minorities in Croatia, Bosnia, etc.). In the midst of battle the Communists could raise the banner of national unity because their Partisan troops included Croats as well as Serbs, Slovenians as well as Montenegrins. Indeed as the fighting went on, other elements joined the Partisans in significant numbers: Bosniaks, Macedonians, ultimately even Serbs from Serbia. As the Partisans liberated this or that area they set up institutions of local government, Committees of National Liberation (similar to the Soviets of the Russian revolution) that reflected the multi-national composition of the movement. The Communists also established a central government in the mountains, the Anti-Fascist Council of National Liberation of Yugoslavia (AVNOJ).

Perhaps the success of the Communists was also in part due to what might be called the religious character of their faith and doctrine. In the Balkans there had been for many centuries a tendency to identify religion and nationality. The *Ustaše* spared the lives of those Serbs willing to accept Catholic baptism. Serbs, Croats, and Bosniaks, for example, spoke virtually identical tongues; even the dialects of the language cut across the ethnic boundaries. It could be asserted without fear of great error that a Serb was an Orthodox Croat, a Croat a Catholic Serb, and a Bosniak a Moslem Serbo-Croat. For those who joined Tito's movement, communism, replacing traditional faiths, became in a sense the hallmark of Yugoslav nationality.

Like other emergent nationalisms, that of the Yugoslavs had a dynamic and expansionist character. Already in 1941 we find Partisan emissaries organizing a Communist party in Albania. In the ensuing years this party functioned *de facto* as a section of its Yugolsav patron. Preparations were also made for the merger of the Albanian state with a federal Yugoslavia as a sixth republic alongside the republics of Slovenia, Croatia, Bosnia, Montenegro, and Serbia. In the merger, the Albanian-inhabited autonomous region of Kossovo was to be joined with the "autonomous" Albanian republic.

The Partisans also had their eyes on Slavic Bulgaria. They revived the Comintern's scheme for a Balkan federation, argued that the new Yugoslavia was a proper nucleus for it, and arrogantly invited Bulgaria to accept the status of a Croatia or a Montenegro. The Bulgarian Communists were confused and embarrassed by this proposal, since they had been the great proponents of Balkan federation in the 1920's. A more important stumbling block to the merger, however, was the disposition of Macedonia, a province divided among Yugoslavia, Bulgaria, and Greece, with a preponderantly Slavic population in the parts controlled by the Slavic powers, and an over-whelmingly Greek population in the rest. The Bulgarians claimed all the Slavs of Macedonia as their own, whereas the Partisans considered them to be a separate Slavic people. After some negotiation, the Yugoslav and Bulgarian Communists agreed that Macedonia (including its Greek inhabited seacoast) should be reunited and made a separate member of the new federation. For a time, indeed, missionaries from Yugoslav Macedonia were permitted to spread the doctrine of Slavo-Macedonian nationalism in Bulgarian Macedonia. The Greek party was brought in on the arrangement in exchange for promise of military assistance in the seizure of power and there began (1946) a Greek civil war which was largely engineered by the Yugoslav Partisans in the interests of their version of Balkan federation. Since the Yugoslavs apparently also entered into negotiations with the Hungarian and Rumanian Communist regimes, it is clear that under their aegis a new center of Communist authority was emerging in Eastern Europe. It should also be remembered that the Partisans provoked more than one crisis by their efforts to seize the city of Trieste, to serve as the Yugoslav port on the Adriatic, just as Macedonian Salonika was to have served as the outlet on the Aegean.

Two further remarks must be made about the Yugoslav case. The first of these is that the Soviet leadership did not welcome the developments that we have just described. It was not only that the Soviets were unable to aid the hard-pressed Partisans in 1941-1944; they also thought that Partisan policy ran counter to Soviet interests. By being openly revolutionary, and by settling the question of the future Yugoslav regime while the fighting was going on, the Partisans risked rousing the suspicion of Russia's Western allies and undermining their collaboration with Russia against the Germans. Instead of setting up local Soviets and organizing a government on the mountain, the Partisans should, in the Soviet view, have continued to collaborate with Mihailović and to have postponed the political issue until the fighting was over.

The Soviets, moreover, were not pleased with the Partisan scheme for organizing a Balkan confederation. They could not openly oppose the scheme, since it was a veritable part of Marxist canon, and there was factional conflict in Moscow which gave the Yugoslavs reason to hope for Kremlin support. But in actual practice the Soviets did what they could to slow down the realization of the project and in the end it was a major factor in producing an open breach between Belgrade and Moscow. Thus the revolutionary process in the Balkans was by no means under strict Soviet control, even though Moscow was the center and supreme arbiter of the doctrine in whose name the revolution proceeded. From Moscow's point of view the revolutionary movement was pretty much out of control. The schism of 1948 was only a doctrinal, and therefore public, recognition of this fact.

The second conclusion to be drawn from the Yugoslav case is that the key element in the Communist victory was the ability of the Partisans to identify themselves with a true Yugoslav nationalism, one which seemed to offer an alternative to the bloody ethnic war which had been the outcome of King Alexander's pan-Serb Yugoslavia. It is still true that the Communist party could probably not have won a majority in a free election if one had been held in 1945, and that its solution of the nationalities problem was largely (if not entirely) restricted to the Communists and their supporters. But it is also true that the Communists would probably have been the largest single party, in ballots cast, in any free election, and perhaps the only party whose electorate did not consist overwhelmingly of the members of a given ethnic *souche*. The opposition to the Communists was and remained largely particularistic, envisioning solutions which involved the disintegration of the Yugoslav state. And when after 1948 it became evident that the Communists could, and had, defended Yugoslavia's national interests with skill and devotion, a kind of popular acceptance, or at the least a confident truce, set in.[18]

[18] The most revealing single work on the Partisan War is Stephen Clissold, *Whirlwind, An Account of Marshal Tito's Rise to Power* (London, 1949). A member of the British mission to the Partisans, Clissold was evidently given access to Partisan documents. Vladimir Dedijer, *Tito Speaks: His Self-Portrait and Struggle With Stalin* (London 1953) is the official biography, and merits careful reading. For an insightful but somewhat journalistic overall interpretation, see the previously cited work by Halperin. Constantine Fotić, Yugoslav ambassador to Washington during the Second World War, strongly defends Mihailović in *The War We Lost: Yugoslavia's Tragedy and the Failure of the West* (New York 1948). Elizabeth Barker, *Macedonia, Its Place in Balkan Power Politics* (London 1950) is a nearly classic exposition. For a Soviet viewpoint, see V. K. Volkov, "Nekotorye voprosy osvoboditel'noy bor'by Yugoslavskikh narodov v gody Vtoroy Mirovoy Voiny v osveshchenii Yugoslavskoy istoricheskoy literatury" [Some Problems of the Liberation Struggle of the Yugoslav Peoples in the Second World War in the Light

Czechoslovakia and "Peaceful Transition"

Thus in Yugoslavia, guerrilla war combined with nationalism in a very complex ethnic situation to produce a Communist victory. In Czechoslovakia, by contrast, the Communist regime was not a product of guerrilla war. Compared to the Yugoslav case, resistance had been unimportant, and the Czechoslovak Communists did not dispose of anything resembling a guerrilla army. It should be recalled, however, that the postwar provisional government, in which the Communists gained a position of predominant influence, was created as a result of negotiations between Beneš, Gottwald, and Stalin in Moscow in March 1945. At that time, Subcarpathian Ruthenia had just been annexed by the Soviet Union and Soviet troops were rapidly advancing over much of the rest of the country.

It seems probable that the Czechoslovak Communists could have seized power in 1945, upon the liberation of the country from German occupation. Soviet units were stationed throughout the land. During their advance these forces had permitted the Communists to enter newly liberated areas ahead of representatives of the parties which made up the London exile government. In the liberated areas, the Communists organized local National Committees, or soviets. While all the recognized parties were represented, the Communists filled the key positions with their own followers and from the very beginning they had the upper hand in local government. Moreover, they had been given control of a number of key ministries—and important influence in others—with the formation of the first post-liberation government in negotiations conducted in the Soviet capital. The Communists had: the ministry of interior, and therefore control of the police; the ministry of information, which licensed newspapers and distributed newsprint; agriculture, which allowed them to preempt for themselves the popular cause of land reform and in particular to distribute the landed properties of the expelled Sudeten Germans to their own followers and sympathizers; social welfare, which permitted them to develop broad sympathy and support among the masses through increases in pension, medical insurance, and the like; and education. The prime minister, although a Social Democrat, was clearly

of Yugoslav Historical Writing], *Novaya i Noveyshaya Istoriya,* no. 5 (1960), 126-138. See also Burks, Chapter VI, for the available data on the ethnic composition of the Partisan army. For the Albanian party see *Cështje të ndërtimit të Partisë. Material e dokumenta.* [Questions Dealing with the Building of the Party. Materials and Documents] (Tirana 1948), Vols. I-VIII.

pro-Communist, and the chief of the Army general staff was a fellow traveller. High ranking cadres were placed in foreign affairs and other key ministries.

In these circumstances no one can doubt the ability of the Czechoslovak party to have taken power in 1945. The question is rather why the party waited for three years. This was in part because the party could afford to wait. There was throughout the country a revolutionary mood, compounded of bitterness against the treason of the minorities, who had made possible the catastrophe of 1938-1939, the disintegrative effect of seven years of Nazi despotism, and the influence and prestige of a friendly Slav power which, espousing a revolutionary doctrine, had liberated the country. The population, moreover, was socialist-minded. Virtually everyone believed in government ownership of banks and industry, in economic planning, and in a far-reaching social security program. Thus on many crucial matters of legislative policy it was very difficult for the opposition to put up much of a struggle without appearing reactionary. Furthermore, the Czechs at least did not think of the Communist party as a foreign element, alien to the national tradition. In the interwar period the party had operated legally and in the open, much as any other radical party, and had been the third or fourth largest in a field of eight major parties. And now, for a variety of reasons, the party's prestige and influence was at an all-time high. In 1945 it was evidently the single strongest party by a wide margin and it did not seem out of the question that in a free election it could carry a majority of the voters with it.

A more important factor in the evident restraint of the party in 1945 was Soviet foreign policy. In East-West relations there was an an important carry-over of wartime collaboration and the extent of Soviet-American disagreement on such important issues as the treatment of Germany and the interpretations of the Yalta accord was not yet clear. Czechoslovak democracy was held in particularly high regard by Western public opinion and Moscow very probably saw no reason to exacerbate East-West relations (already strained) by an unnecessary *coup d'état*. The Soviets permitted a free election in Hungary, a former Axis partner, in 1945. Furthermore there was a huge bonus in prestige for the international Communist movement if for once a country could be conquered by parliamentary means, especially one as highly industrialized as Czechoslovakia. Such a victory would underline the Marxist doctrine of inevitable world revolution and give new impetus to the movement. In 1945 there was much to be gained and little to be lost by refraining from taking over in Czechoslovakia. True, as has been mentioned, there were differences of view on this issue in both the Soviet and Czechoslovak party leaderships; but the radicals did not get the upper hand until the international situation had deteriorated sharply.

It is exceptionally instructive to study the tactics which the Czechoslovak Communists worked out in these circumstances. It cannot be affirmed that everything they did in the three years 1945-1948 was designed primarily to increase their popular following. Many of the measures which they took they would have taken in any case; some lines of action they continued after the opposition had been finally defeated. Much of what they did was also done by other East European parties, sometimes before, sometimes after, these parties had come to power. But it is also true that there was little the Czechoslovak Communists did from which they did not try to manufacture prestige and popularity for themselves. From the welter of these election-oriented actions, policies, and programs, two deserve particular emphasis, e.g., Communist manipulation of the party situation, and Communist exploitation of the minorities problem.

At the very beginning of the resumption of the parliamentary process, even before the liberation of the country, the Communists succeeded in outlawing certain parties as Fascist and reactionary. The most important of these were the Agrarians and the Slovak Populists. The Populists had stood for Slovak separatism and had been responsible for the government of the Nazi puppet state; they were clearly tarred with the Fascist brush. The Agrarians, on the other hand, were a peasant party with a following in both Slovakia and the Czech lands. Electorally speaking, they had been the largest party in interwar Czechoslovakia and, although relatively conservative, they could most certainly not be regarded as Fascist or even reactionary. Thus the party system presented to the voters included the parties of the center and the left, but not those of the right, and the powerful and stubborn peasant party was banned. This fact accounts in some part for the revolutionary atmosphere which prevailed.

The accepted parties, moreover, were not given freedom of operation, but were bound together in a National Front which put forward a common program. Within that Front the four parties which could claim the title "Socialist"—the Czechoslovak Communists, the Slovak Communists, the Social Democrats, and the National Socialists—formed a special inner grouping, the Catholic Populists and the Slovak

Democrats being degraded to a secondary role. The Communist cause was aided further by a split among the Social Democrats into a left wing which preferred to merge with the Communists, and a right which fought a hard battle to preserve the party's independence.

The National Front was easily dominated by the Communists. To begin with there was the size of the Communist party itself, which had more paid secretaries than all the other parties together. Furthermore the Communist leadership followed a policy of building up mass membership in order to impress the local electorate and the world with its popularity. By the time of the *coup d'état* the CPCS had some two million members, the bulk of them nominal; this membership was comparable in size to the vote cast for the Communist ticket in the free election of 1946. Approximately two of every five adults in Czechoslovakia was a member of the party.

Communist domination was also facilitated by the absence of anything like an institutional opposition. As we have seen certain parties and points of view had been eliminated from the official roster and the remaining parties were bound together in a common front with a common program. Deputies and factions which disagreed with this or that aspect of official policy could resign or retire from the field, but they could not join a public opposition or threaten the hold of the coalition in power, and thus could not affect policy. Since there was no such thing as an opposition press, the other side of any issue was rarely discussed. Voters could express, as they freely did in 1946, their preference among the official parties, but except by giving the Communists a majority they could not change the government or its policy.

As a democracy without institutionalized opposition, Czechoslovakia was a democracy without genuine debate, political alternatives, or real public life. The power struggle between the Communists and their opponents took place behind a façade of apparent agreement and cooperation. The masses of the population did not understand what was going on until after an irrevocable decision concerning their fate had already been reached. It was not until Jan Masaryk, foreign minister and son of the founder of the Czechoslovak state, committed suicide (or was murdered) that the voters understood what had actually transpired during the "parliamentary" maneuverings of February 1948.

The Communists of course did their best to persuade the voters to give them a majority. The party was instrumental in bringing about the lowering of the voting age to 18 years, on the correct assumption that this would increase the Communist share of the total vote. The Communists pushed successfully for land reform measures, although Czechoslovakia had had a thorough-going land reform in the 1920's, and although long-range party policy called for the restoration of the great estates in the form of collective farms. The Communists sponsored amplification of the existing social welfare legislation. Through their control of local government (the National Committees) they played a decisive role in the redistribution of the properties left behind by the evacuated Germans; in the 1946 election it was precisely in the border districts where the German population had been concentrated that the Communists rolled up their heaviest vote. In three such districts the Communists polled an absolute majority. It is characteristic of their tactics that in this Sudetan area they had made final title to the newly distributed properties dependent upon the outcome of the election.

Beyond the machinery and chicanery of their electioneering, however, the Communists sought to identify themselves with the interests of the Czech and Slovak nations by appealing to their primitive instincts for survival. They sponsored the expulsion of the Sudeten Germans, whose overwhelming support of the Henlein party and of Hitler had been a prerequisite of the dismemberment of 1938. It is true that the other Front parties officially took a position in favor of expulsion, but no one could mistake the fact that it was Soviet power and Soviet policy which were ultimately responsible for it, and that it was part of a broader movement of German withdrawal, expulsion, and resettlement that was occurring under Soviet aegis all over Eastern Europe. The Czechs (and those Slovaks who were also settled in the evacuated areas) were bound to an eastward orientation not only by the sharing of the booty, but by the fear that any revival of German power might bring with it the return of the three million expellees and a wreaking of vengeance. The expulsion of the Germans, moreover, greatly reduced the number of those who would vote for the non-Communist parties.

The Communists also attempted to expel the Hungarian minority in southern Slovakia. This minority, one-half million strong, had not only welcomed enthusiastically the reunion with Hungary in 1938; it also possessed some of the best farm land in Slovakia. But here the Czechoslovak party ran into the bitter opposition of the Hungarian Communists, who evidently carried the issue to Moscow on appeal. After some hesitation, Soviet military units stationed in northeastern

Hungary turned back the large numbers of the minority which the Slovak authorities had set in motion across the border. The Communists also played upon the Slovak desire for autonomy or independence, which had found expression in the clerical Fascism of Father Tiso's independent Slovakia (1939-1945). They awarded the Slovaks some separate institutions, a national council or parliament, and a board of trustees or government, which had jurisdiction in purely Slovak matters. When, however, in the general elections of 1945 some 70 percent of the Slovaks voted for other than the Communist party (as contrasted with 57 percent of the Czechs) the Communist leadership in Prague began to whittle down the concessions it had made to Bratislava. Had the effort to expel the Magyars succeeded, however, the Slovak attitude toward both Communism and the separate institutions might have undergone a different development.

The efforts of the Communists to gain a mass following in Czechoslovakia and maneuver themselves into power by parliamentary means were thus far-reaching and shrewdly calculated. Nonetheless, despite their shrewdness and planning, despite the fact that for many reasons they were working in an exceptionally favorable environment, the Communists failed to achieve their objective. They were unable to win a majority in a free election. They were forced to resort in the end to a *coup d'état*. This fact has been somewhat disguised from public view because the so-called "events of February" began with an anti-Communist parliamentary maneuver undertaken by the leaders of the other parties. This made it easier for the Communists to carry out a *coup* which, in a major reversal of policy, they had probably been intending for some time to execute in any case.

The decline in Communist electoral strength became evident in a number of ways. In student elections at the universities during 1947 the Communist percentage averaged out at no more than twelve. Union elections also revealed an unfavorable trend and the Social Democratic party, at a convention held in November, 1947, overthrew its fellow-travelling leadership. In January a confidential poll of the public, taken by the Communist-controlled ministry of information, revealed (before it was stopped) that in the country as a whole the party would attract only about 25-30 percent of the voters, as compared to the 38 percent of the general election of 1946. New elections were scheduled for May, 1948; to avoid a significant electoral defeat the Communists would have to strike in the spring.

The degeneration of East-West relations had meantime considerably reduced the Kremlin's concern for Western sensibilities and interests. Increasing international tension also strengthened the hand of the extremists in the world Communist movement; these were at last able (September 1947) to organize a truncated version of the Comintern, the Communist Information Bureau or Cominform. In December, the Greek rebels announced the establishment of a government in the mountains. In February 1948, there was the Prague *putsch*. In March, the Communists were frustrated in an attempt to seize power in Finland, as described in another chapter of this book. In April began the land blockade of Berlin. The spring of 1948 also saw the initiation or intensification of guerrilla uprisings in Burma, in Malaya, and in the Philippines. Clearly, world Communism had gone over to the offensive.

The *putsch* itself was a fairly standard operation. The stage was set by the resignation of 12 non-Communist ministers in protest against the appointment, by a Communist minister of interior, of district police chiefs in the national capital taken exclusively from the ranks of the Communist party. The opposition scheme was to force the resignation of the entire cabinet over the issue, make the Communists share the police positions with the other parties, and permit President Beneš to form a new cabinet in which the totalitarian party would have a lesser, though still prominent role.

Actually the anti-Communists had missed their great opportunity in July 1947, when Moscow had forced Prague to withdraw its acceptance of the US invitation to participate in the Marshall plan. Even the Communist ministers had favored participation. Action by the democratic leaders at this juncture and on this issue would have placed the Communists before the devastating choice of defying Moscow or standing alone against the best interests of the country. In November 1947, furthermore, the Communists were able to stage a dress rehearsal for their *coup*. By showing that some members of the Slovak Democratic party were conspiring against the republic, they provoked a crisis in the course of which the Democrats were deprived of their absolute majority in the Slovak board of trustees (cabinet), thus annulling the free election of 1946 insofar as Slovakia was concerned.

The Communists countered the resignation of the 12 non-Communist ministers by threatening the use of force. They had enough key positions in the army to make uncertain the transmittal to operational units of orders issued by the president's office. They had enough people in the state radio to make difficult and perhaps impossible a presidential appeal over the heads of the chiefs of staff. They had control of the police, who dispersed with bullets the only demonstration to be made against the *putsch*—the demonstration of the students of the University of Prague. The police also distributed arms to a Communist-organized "workers militia", which paraded ominously through the streets. Moreover, the Communists let it be understood that, in the event they were overthrown, the Soviet units stationed in eastern Germany and in Hungary would march. The threat became more palpable with the sudden and mysterious arrival in Prague of Soviet deputy foreign minister V. A. Zorin.

In addition, the Communists were able to paralyze or gain control of the other parties, their organizational headquarters, and their newspapers. Through their influence in certain ministries, notably interior, the Communists had gotten into the personal dossiers of many of the opposition political leaders. They had used this information to blackmail members of the other parties into secret collaboration. And they had sent personnel of their own to penetrate the other parties. During the crisis day of February the Communists called for the organization of action committees. Composed of Communists and fellow travellers, these committees sprang into existence and, under the shadow of the "workers militia," took over control of newspapers, banks, the headquarters of national front parties, the national committees, and other key institutions. Overnight the commanding personalities of these institutions were pushed aside and replaced by relatively unknown persons subject to Communist discipline.

Faced with this situation, President Beneš acceded to the demands of the Communists that they be permitted to form a new government without the participation of the "obstructionist" ministers. The President then *de facto* withdrew from public life. He has been severely criticized. But in all fairness certain imponderable elements in the situation which he confronted should be recalled.[19]

[19] Perhaps the most enlightening work on the seizure of power in Czechoslovakia is that of Otto Friedman, *The Breakup of Czech Democracy* (London 1950). Friedman is strongly oriented toward the psychological aspects of the Communist takeover. D. A. Schmidt, *Anatomy of a Satellite* (Boston 1952) is an analysis by a New York Times correspondent and is particularly useful for its amassing of evidence on the factional conflict within the party. I am grateful to Paul Zinner for the loan of a paper he presented at the Annual Meeting of the American Historical Association in December 1961 entitled "Communist Seizures of Power: Czechoslovakia," His "Marxism in Action: the Seizure of Power in Czechoslovakia," *Foreign Affairs,* XXVIII (July 1950), 644-658, remains essential until the appearance of his forthcoming full-length analysis. Reference should also be made to a series of articles

The alternative to surrender was probably civil war. The Communists and their supporters represented perhaps a third of the nation. They were armed, organized along totalitarian lines, and backed by Soviet Russia. In the event that Beneš successfully conspired with local Czechoslovak army commanders, he would have serious fighting on his hands; Soviet aid would almost certainly be forthcoming in whatever degree was necessary to achieve a Communist victory. Defeat was therefore inevitable unless aid could be procured from the West. After what had happened in 1938, could Western aid be counted upon?

It seems doubtful that Beneš gave serious consideration to the alternative of civil war. He had from the beginning staked the restoration of the Czechoslovak state on agreement with the Soviet Union. He did not wish his London government to be replaced with one organized in Moscow, which is what happened to the Poles. He and his advisors hoped against hope that Moscow would exchange loyal support of Soviet foreign policy, for which the predominant position of the Communists in the Czechoslovak government after 1945 served as guarantee, for a wide measure of domestic autonomy. To bolster their courage for this venture, Beneš and his associates deluded themselves with the belief that the Soviet government was somehow essentially democratic and compromise-minded. When it turned out that the Communists and Russia would accept nothing less than total power and total control, Beneš no doubt saw himself, his policy, and his country as finished.

Another ending to this chain of events is of course conceivable. But it must be kept in mind that vital Soviet interests were at stake. Successful defiance of Moscow's authority by the Czechs and Slovaks would probably have threatened Soviet control in neighboring Hungary and Poland, and perhaps in Eastern Europe generally.

In the event of civil war in Czechoslovakia and an urgent appeal

---

by Gordon Skilling, notably "Revolution and Continuity in Czechoslovakia, 1945-46," *Journal of Central European Affairs*, XX (1961), 357-377, and "The Breakup of the Czechoslovak Coalition, 1947-48," *Canadian Journal of Economics and Political Science*, XX (1960), 396-413. For the expulsion of the Sudeten Germans see the work of Wiskemann already cited. An account by one of the democratic leaders is presented in Hubert Ripka, *Czechoslovakia Enslaved: the Story of the Communist Coup d'État* (New York 1950). See also Joseph Korbel, *Communist Subversion of Czechoslovakia 1938-1948. The Failure of Coexistence* (Princeton 1959) and Edward Taborsky, *Communism in Czechoslovakia, 1948-1960* (Princeton 1961) for scholarly treatments by eyewitnesses. The official version is to be found in Chapter IX of Pavel Reiman and others, eds., *Dějiny Komunistické Strany Československa* [History of the Communist Party of Czechoslovakia] (Prague 1961).

from Beneš, Washington's reaction would have been difficult to predict. On the one hand, US policy was not yet deterred by a Soviet nuclear capability. On the other, conventional Soviet strength stationed in Europe was such as to presage early Soviet occupation of Western Europe in any general conflict. To point to American support of the royal Greek government in 1947-1949, or to American military intervention in South Korea 1950-1953, is not really germane, since both were areas that had been assigned to the Western sphere of influence. Would the United States have taken serious risk of general war in order to preserve Czechoslovak autonomy within the Communist empire? And, if it came to that, would the US have fought a general war in order to liberate Eastern Europe from Soviet control? Beneš evidently thought the answers to such questions would be in the negative. Who can with authority gainsay him?

"Peaceful Transition" in Austria

In occupied Austria the Communists faithfully applied the strategy of "peaceful transition." Here in the shadow of a Soviet occupation of eastern Austria lasting from 1945 to 1955, they sought and gained control of key ministries, such as interior and education. They launched a major effort to secure a dominant position in the trade unions and to unite their party with that of the much older and stronger Socialists. They campaigned in free elections in the expectation of demonstrating their popularity and, at a moment of climax, they did not hesitate to organize a general strike. They were aided and abetted in all this by the Soviet occupation authorities, who among other things confiscated the industrial properties formerly owned by the German government, reorganized them as joint Soviet-Austrian companies and used the resources of the new companies in part to support the Communist movement.[20]

But in Austria, despite five long years of propaganda, threat, and maneuver, the attempt of peaceful transition ended in failure. There were many reasons for this. One was the emergence of remarkable democratic leaders, such as Leopold Figl, leader of the Catholic People's party, and Adolph Schaerf and Oskar Helmer, the dominant personalities among the Socialists. Of humble origin, Helmer had risen in the Social Democratic party prior to the *Anschluss,* and for fifteen

[20] These paragraphs rest heavily on William B. Bader, "A Communist Failure: Occupied Austria 1945-50" (doctoral dissertation, Princeton University 1963). See also William Lloyd Stearman, *The Soviet Union and the Occupation of Austria: An Analysis of Soviet Policy in Austria, 1945-1955* (Bad Godesberg 1960).

years from the autumn of 1945 he served as minister of interior, succeeding a Communist. The failure of peaceful transition was in no small part due to Helmer's courage, skill, and political sagacity in the management of police affairs.

A second reason for failure was the inability of the Communists to build up a popular following. They began their campaign believing they could poll as many votes as the Socialists, but in the free election of November, 1945, they polled a mere 5.42 percent, a figure which even fell somewhat in the next election, held four years later. These percentages are to be compared with the 17 won by the Communists in neighboring Hungary in the same month of 1945 and the 38 won by the Czechoslovak Communists in June 1946. With their distinctly German heritage, the Austrian people had a strong anti-Russian bias. This was intensified by the catastrophic military defeat that they had just been dealt, together with the plunder and rape committed by the Soviet soldiery in the early days of the occupation. There was, in addition, relatively little in the way of political combustibles for the Communists to work with. There were few great estates to break up and distribute among landless but vote-possessing peasants. There was no sizable and treasonous minority to expel across the national frontier. Nor were there great territorial acquisitions made at the expense of the defeated *Reich* to defend.

A third factor in the Communist failure was military. Austria bordered on the Eastern and Western zones of influence. The occupation of her territory was shared among the four victorious belligerents. This fact alone imposed serious limitations on both the Soviet authorities and the Austrian Communists, unless the former wished to risk an armed confrontation with their allies. In 1948 the Austrian government was able, despite the vigorous protests of Soviet authorities, to participate in the Marshall Plan. And in 1950 the Soviet military failed to interfere on the side of the Communists in a general strike, although the failure of the strike meant the end of Communist hopes. Conceivably the Soviets could have overcome this division of authority as they did in Germany by organizing a separate state in the eastern part of Austria. There was fear among the Austrians that this attempt would be made. But such a state would have been even less viable than the heavily buttressed German Democratic Republic. Besides, the Soviet leaders probably did not regard themselves as having a vital interest in Austria, other than the prevention of its union with Germany.

The presence of the Allied armies also gave Austria's democrats room for maneuver and permitted them to build up positions of strength equal to or greater than those of the Communists. The best example of this is provided by the police. Before the election of 1945, the police were under Communist control and thoroughly infiltrated. After the disastrous defeat of the Communist party in this election, the party lost control of the ministry of interior to the Socialists (Helmer). In due course the new minister was able to eliminate the Communists from positions of influence in the police. The Soviets responded by insisting that the police remain virtually disarmed and by organizing in the oil fields of the Soviet zone a plant police, or *Werkschutz,* which was both heavily armed and politically reliable. Helmer and the Western Allies thereupon more or less secretly established in the Western zones a heavily armed and mobile gendarmerie which later was to serve as the core of the new Austrian army. Thus, occupied Austria ended up with three distinct police forces. Similarly, there were two competing labor movements, an official *Gewerkschaftsbund,* controlled by the Socialists, and a series of Works Councils, the most important of which in the major industrial areas were controlled by the Communists.

In the crucial general strike of September 1950, the failure of the Communists to control the press and radio turned the tide. The economic situation in Austria at the time was depressed and the Communists had, for the moment at least, acquired the sympathy and support of the broad mass of factory workers. The socialists broke the strike by using, among other facilities, the American and British radios to explain to the workers that the goal of the Communists was the overthrow of the existing government and the establishment in its place of a People's Democracy. As soon as this elemental fact was made clear to the workers they returned to the factories, despite their physical hunger and their legitimate discontent. Thus the case of Austria provides us with a veritable photographic negative of developments in Czechoslovakia and Hungary. Austria is the case of "peaceful transition" that failed to come off.

The Lessons for the Communists

Although the events in Eastern Europe described in the preceding pages represent major gains in territory and prestige for the international Communist movement, there are some general limitations on the applicability to other areas of whatever the Communists may have learned from them. The seizures of power in Eastern Europe were a direct result of the occupation of the area by Soviet armies and followed hard upon a major military upheaval which had been a traumatic experience for all the peoples involved, victors as well as vanquished. This upheaval had created a whole new political situation. Given the present nuclear stalemate between East and West it seems unlikely for the foreseeable future that there will be a general war in the course of which Soviet or Chinese forces will come in victory to occupy major new areas. Efforts to extend communism will probably be subject to a precept of limited risk, and in general the rules of the game will be different from those obtaining in Eastern Europe during 1944-1948.

It is also the case that the populations of Eastern Europe through long association with the Russians had developed deeply ingrained attitudes toward them and their political wares, whether positive, as in the case of the Bulgarians, Yugoslavs, and Czechs, or negative, as with the Rumanians, Hungarians, and Poles. Such attitudes served as major conditioning factors in the tactics and strategy of Communist take-over, as is illustrated by the imposition of a baggage-train government on the Poles and the development of "parliamentary" Communism among the Czechs. Because of the peculiarities of Soviet geography, this kind of situation could repeat itself for Moscow only in the Moslem cultural area stretching between the two cities of Istanbul and Kabul. In this general area the Turks and the Iranians would be ill-disposed towards any doctrine or movement coming from Russia, while the Kurds and the Armenians would be more favorably inclined. For the Chinese, such traditional attitudes would be found in south-east Asia and the adjacent archipelagoes. These attitudes would have been particularly affected by the local role of the overseas Chinese. Elsewhere in the vast reaches of the underdeveloped world, however, such traditional attitudes would play only a minor role.

Whatever lessons the Communists may draw from their experience in Eastern Europe will of course be filtered through the screen of their doctrine, their dogmatic convictions, and the national interests of their principal powers. The European Communists have been inclined to lay great stress on their experience in Czechoslovakia. The CPCS now presents the "February events" as its specific contribution to the common storehouse of Marxist-Leninist theory, claiming that it has shown the way to the peaceful transition to Communism that will characterize the historical epoch now beginning, that of the preponderance of the Socialist camp. The Asians in turn lay great stress on the fundamental role of wars of liberation in colonial and semi-colonial areas; these wars have their closest analogue in the Partisan experience of the Yugoslav party. The Chinese will not, however, be inclined to learn much from the Yugoslavs. Aside from having preceded the Yugoslavs in the successful conduct of guerrilla operations, they regard Tito and his party as both deviants from and traitors to the world Communist movement. The conflict between Soviet and Chinese Communists; which is reminiscent of the Bloc-wide quarrel between extremists and moderates in 1944-1948, will have a continuing influence on the tactics and strategy of Communists everywhere.

The official European Communist view of the Czechoslovak experience is that it represents a new form of the transition to the dictatorship of the proletariat. In this form, owing to the liberation of the country by outside but friendly forces, the proletariat shares control of traditional bourgeois institutions—parliament, the ministries—with the bourgeoisie. By applying pressure from above as well as from below, the proletariat secures a majority in the parliament, and legally as well as factually transforms that body into an instrument of revolution. Examples of pressure from above are the arrest of 'treacherous' opponents by a Communist-controlled police force and the propagation of revolutionary slogans through the ministry of education. Examples of pressure from below are strikes, the organization of labor brigades, or other activity of 'mass' organizations. Throughout the process the proletariat retains possession of firearms, and it is this which persuades the bourgeoisie to hold its hand until too late. Thus it becomes possible to undertake the construction of Socialism without having first to rebuild a country devastated by civil war, and this is the original and positive feature of the new transition form.[21]

Aside from the difficulty that this operational model presumes a

[21] The most authoritative Communist version is that of Jan Kozak, *How Parliament Can Play a Revolutionary Part in the Transition to Socialism and the Role of the Popular Masses. Introduction by the Right Honorable Lord Morrison of Lambeth, C. H.* (London 1961). See also his "Znacheniye natsional'noy i demokraticheskoy revolyutsii v Chekhoslovakii dlya bor'by rabochego klassa za sotsializm (1945-1948 gg.)" [The significance of the national and democratic revolution in Czechoslovakia for the struggle of the working class for socialism (1945-1948)], *Voprosy istorii KPSS*, no. 4 (1962), 72-91. I am especially indebted to H. J. Hajek of Radio Free Europe for an *ad hoc* paper entitled "Peaceful Way to Socialism: the Czechoslovak Experience" (15 June 1962).

decisive preponderance of Communist state power in the area, whether through military occupation or otherwise, the official presentation neglects mentioning other factors peculiar to the situation in Czechoslovakia. These include: the feeling of the population that it had been abandoned by the Western powers at Munich; widespread hatred of the German oppressor and fear that he would return; and a long-standing tendency passively to accept foreign rule and domination as a part of the natural order. In sharp contrast with their Polish first cousins, the Czechs have not risen in rebellion against a foreign oppressor for more than three hundred years. Insofar as parliament is the linchpin of the new transition process, there is the further difficulty that in most underdeveloped areas parliament—where it exists—is in no wise the anchor institution of the governmental system, but rather a foreign grafting without roots of its own. The Czechoslovak ideologists themselves constantly speak of their "contribution" in terms of advanced industrial countries. Only in the very broad sense that occasional situations may arise so favorable to the Communists that the threat of force will suffice to put them in power is the Czechoslovak example a useful prototype.

The Yugoslav model has a wider application. There exist many parallels between conditions in the Balkan peninsula and in the other underdeveloped areas of the world. In the karst highlands of Yugoslavia, Albania, and Greece there is poverty, economic retardation, isolation and, partly as a consequence of these, a complex and difficult ethnic situation. We are reminded of the mountainous backwardness and ethnic variegation of Indo-China, or of the harsh veldt and the mixture of races which constitute the boiling pot of South Africa. Above all there is the decisive fact that in the nuclear age guerrilla war can be carried on for months and even years without major risk of escalation into general conflict.

One of the major lessons which the Yugoslav experience suggests is the usefulness and reliability of the peasant and mountaineer as guerrilla fighters in the cause of communism. Doctrinally, the peasant guerrilla force is a far cry from the embarricaded proletarians of the Communist manifesto. But Mao and the Chinese leaders had achieved wonders with a peasant-based movement even before the outbreak of World War II, and had modified the doctrine accordingly. After the break with the Cominform the Yugoslavs allowed themselves to be openly critical of their erstwhile Greek colleagues, whom they accused of grossly underestimating the importance of the peasant in the Greek civil war. The Yugoslavs asserted that the Greek comrades persisted in believing until too late that the final and decisive assault would be carried forward by the workers in the cities.[22] In Yugoslavia as well as in Greece the overwhelming body of peasants and mountaineers came to the Communist colors without any previous indoctrination in Marxism or even without any awareness that such a creed existed. In contrast, the workers in the cities, who had been propagandized for at least a generation, worked steadily for the relatively high wages paid by the invader and sent financial contributions to the mountain fighters surreptitiously.

A second lesson suggested by the Yugoslav case is that guerrilla revolutions develop pretty much according to their own local requirements. There was in Yugoslavia serious disruption of the traditional social order. This was in the first instance the long-standing result of the impact of influences stemming from much richer and more sophisticated national cultures. The presence of communism itself as an envious reaction was one evidence of this. There was in the second place a profound ethnic and religious conflict in the country, and nowhere more profound and exacerbated than in the poverty-stricken highlands. The conflict had made impossible the governance of the state except by dictatorship. We must add to these things an ancient tradition of insurrection in the face of great odds. As the catalyst came defeat in war and occupation by foreign armies, which cut off the mountain areas from their normal sources of food imports. The multi-faceted civil war that broke out subsequent to the occupation was a phenomenon *sui generis* from which the Communists emerged victorious in considerable part because they faced up to the local requirements of battle.

Thus it is difficult to control or even to influence a guerrilla war from distant centers such as Moscow or Peiping. The guerrillas need arms and supplies from the outside, but relative to the area controlled by them and the damage done, the quantities needed are small. The Yugoslav Partisans captured most of their equipment from the enemy; the ammunition and the medical supplies dropped to them were not of Soviet or other Communist origin. The organization of local government along Soviet lines was essential to the ultimate conquest of power, and the flaunting of Communist symbols and slogans necessary to the maintenance of morale. In the view of the Partisans, such

[22] S. Vukmanović-Tempo, *Il Partito Comunista e la Lotta de Liberazione Nazionale* (n.p. 1951).

organization and such flaunting could not be foregone simply because of a temporary requirement of Soviet foreign policy for good relations with the Western allies.

The lesson for Moscow and Peiping is one of larger tolerance for the local requirements of guerrilla revolution and a willingness to accept, at least temporarily, wide variations from traditional Marxist practice. And for the local revolutionaries the lesson is the converse. They can assume from the beginning that on many issues they know better than Moscow or Peiping; that the success of the rising does not depend on getting Moscow's or Peiping's opinion on every matter of importance; and that other sources of outside arms and supplies than the capitals of world communism exist. It is not to be excluded that the Soviet experience with Yugoslavia is one of the minor factors which accounts for the increasing Soviet reliance on more traditional methods of statecraft (long-term loans, dispatch of technical personnel, gifts of military equipment) in attempting to subvert the non-Communist governments of Asia, Africa, and Central and South America. In Moscow's view the development of secondary centers of Communist power, whether based on guerrilla armies or not, is not necessarily identical at this stage of history with the best interests of the movement. Much depends on whether serious risk of military escalation is involved and on how far the subordinate center is capable of following a foreign policy of its own. At the same time Peiping has manifested an interest in promoting guerrilla wars in very nearly any and all circumstances; evidently the advantages to Peiping of a world in violent upheaval outweigh the risks of the emergence of new and independent centers of Communist power.

The final and perhaps the most important lesson of the Yugoslav guerrilla experience concerns the key role of national feeling. This is something about which Marxism-Leninism has a great deal to say, but always in a negative vein. That is, the cadres must take such feeling into account in order that it not retard the forward movement of revolutionary forces; once the exploitation of man by man has ceased, national feeling and national aspirations will expend themselves harmlessly in folk dancing and the celebration of national holidays. The lesson of Yugoslavia, however, is that nationalism is not a temporary impediment to the revolution; it is more nearly its motor force. Frontier problems, ethnic quarrels, and language issues are central to the revolutionary process and not peripheral. The Partisans won out over their better equipped and better fed local enemies in large part because they stood for Yugoslav nationalism as opposed to Croat or Serb particularism. They were able to do this probably because they represented a new (if secular) religion, which pushed aside and replaced the characteristic Catholicism, Orthodoxy, and Islam of such discrete national groups as the Croats, the Serbs, and the Bosniaks. The Bulgarian Communists, although ethnically of the same *souche* as their Yugoslav comrades, remained apart from the Partisan struggle on account of the Macedonian issue; it was this same issue that blocked the merger of the two parties and the two states after the seizures of power. Finally, much of the *élan* and vigor of the Greek guerrillas of 1946-1949 came from the small Slavo-Macedonian population of northern Greece, who thought of themselves as fighting for a united and independent Macedonia. These Slavophones, as the Greeks call them, constituted as much as two-thirds of the Greek guerrilla force.[23] This terrain of nationalism and national conflict is in the long run the most treacherous for the Communists but in the short run the most fruitful.

[23] For the role of the Slavophone see Burks, Chapter v.

5

Finland

JAMES H. BILLINGTON

The history of Finnish communism provides a rich and largely untouched field for the student of communism and internal war.[1] In less

[1] There is no reliable scholarly history of Finnish communism. The basic Communist study, *Kipinästä tuli syttyi* [From the Spark Comes the Flame] (Helsinki 1958), is a work of composite authorship. The Russian version of this work, *Iz istorii kommunisticheskoy partii Finlyandii* [From the History of Finnish Communist Party] (Moscow 1960), slightly condenses the Finnish original but adds a valuable section on the 1945-1960 period. There is little detailed writing by anti-Communist Finns on Finnish communism in the post-war period because of self-imposed censorship, though some information is contained in such works as *Punainen Valhe* [The Red Lie] (Helsinki 1962) published under the pseudonym Pohto Pohjanpoika. Important historical work on the subject is currently being undertaken by Professor Juhani Paasivirta of Turku; and there are at present at least two American Ph.D. theses in progress on Finnish communism.

A large body of sociological investigation of the continued appeal of communism to Finnish voters has recently been undertaken somewhat along the ecological lines suggested by Sven Rydenfelt's *Kommunismen i Sverige* [Communism in Sweden] (Kristenstad 1954). Particularly noteworthy are Jaakko Nousiainen, *Kommunismi Kuopion läänissä* [Communism in Kuopio Province] (Joensuu 1956) and two mimeographed studies made in 1961 at Helsinki University by Erik Allardt: "Social Factors Affecting Left Voting in Developed and Backward Areas," and (with Pertti Pesonen) "Structural and Non-structural Cleavages in Finnish Politics." For Communist criticism of such studies and a good general statement of the present Communist position see Tuure Lehén, *Kommunismin Joukkovaikutuksen Syyt* [The Reasons for Communist Popular Appeal] (Tampere 1961); for a dissident Communist viewpoint, see the review of this book by Raimo Malm in *Tilanne,* No. 1 (1961), 35-37. See also Hannu Soikkanen, *Sosialismi tulo Suomeen* [The Coming of Socialism to Finland] (Porvoo-Turku 1961).

For short English-language surveys, see three articles all entitled "Communism in Finland" by Max Mehlem in *Swiss Review of World Affairs,* 1961, May, 13-16; by Aulis Nopsanen in *The Norseman* (Jan.-Feb., 1958), 20-23; and by Onni Rantela in *Finnish Features,* No. 14, (1962) a press release of the Finnish foreign ministry. See also Marvin Rintala, "The Problems of Generations in Finnish Communism," *American Slavic and East European Review,* XVII (April 1958), 190-202; and Arvo Tuominen, "The Northern Countries and Communism," *The Norseman* (July-Aug., 1954) 217-229. The latter figure, a former Communist leader who has since joined the Social Democratic party, has written an invaluable series of memoirs—a rich source of information on Finnish Communism and a neglected major source of international Communist history. *Sirpin ja vasaran tie* [The Way of the Hammer and Sickle] (Helsinki 1956); *Kremlin kellot* [The Clocks of the Kremlin] (Helsinki 1957), dealing with the years 1933-1939, also available in Swedish (Helsinki 1958); and *Maan alla ja päällä* [Above and Under Ground] (Helsinki 1958), dealing with 1921-1933. Also valuable are the accounts of two more recent defectors from Communism: Aira Sinervo, former director of the Sirola institute, the training than a half- century of independence, the Finnish Republic has survived a civil war, two international wars, and at least one attempted *coup d'état*—all involving Communists, who even today control a larger percentage of the electorate than in any democratic country of Europe except Italy. At the same time, a large number of leaders in international Communist activity—including the late Otto Kuusinen, member of Khrushchev's Party Presidium and editor of *Fundamentals of Marxism-Leninism*—have come from the Finnish Communist movement. The richness of its practical experience, genuineness of its proletarian base, and length of its leaders' contact with the Soviet party enables it to command continuing respect in the international movement.

Finnish communism has a special interest to the non-Communist world because: (1) It represents a dramatic, almost unique illustration of Communist failure in a region where they had every right to expect success; and (2) it has been—and may well be now—an important testing ground for new Soviet tactics. We shall consider here first the long initial record of failure; and, second, the new tactics that have emerged since the death of Stalin.

Four Bids for Power, 1918-1948

Communism is probably more intimately related to internal war in Finland than in any other European country. The Communist Party of Finland was formed late in August 1918 in the aftermath of a bloody civil war that had overtaken Finland in the midst of the general revolutionary crisis of the Russian empire. About the only thing that the hundred Finnish *emigrés* who formed the party in Moscow had in common was bitter memories of the war. They had all participated in the revolutionary seizure of power in Helsinki, Tampere, and other

---

school for Finnish Communists, *Koskessa Kolisten* [Sounds in the Waterfall] (Porvoo-Helsinki, 1960); and Raoul Palmgren, 30-*luvun Kuvat* [Pictures of 30 Years] (Helsinki n.d.).

My account of the postwar period is based largely on the valuable memoirs of Yrjö Leino, former Communist minister of interior, *Kommunisti Sisä-Ministerinä* [A Communist Minister of the Interior] (Helsinki 1958), and on extensive interviews in March 1962 with a dozen leading Finnish political figures (including Tuominen, the Communist Hertta Kuusinen, the dissident Communist Jarno Pennanen, President Kekkonen, his son Matti Kekkonen, and leading representatives of all major political parties). The net conclusions winnowed from this confusing collection of evidence and testimony are, of course, my own, and should not be attributed to any of those interviewed.

major cities in January 1918, only to be driven from the country by the victorious White forces of Marshal Mannerheim.

Civil war was something unfamiliar to the orderly Finns; and it left a legacy of bitterness among the defeated not unlike that of the American civil war.[2] Although the Whites in the north and west and the Reds in the south and east each received some foreign help, it was basically an internal war fought along class lines with a sense of growing outrage and brutality on both sides. Old rural Finland with its Swedish-speaking barons, Lutheran pastors, and traditionalist military officers was pitted against the new urban Finland of industrial workers, who were joined by many tenant farmers and soldiers from the Russian service. The revolutionaries were led by red guards (originally "people's guards") that had first appeared during the revolution of 1905 in Finland, but were relatively disorganized, and called "apaches" by the Whites for their habit of summarily executing prominent landowners and officials. The Whites were led by a special security force which had been first organized by student and bourgeois elements in an attempt to defend order and property during the chaos of 1905. Spurred on in 1918 by the return from Germany of 2,000 Prussian-trained Finnish military officers, called the Jäger battalion, the Whites responded to the Red Terror with even more brutal and systematic retaliation. Although they abjured summary execution, they placed some 80,000 revolutionaries in detention camps after the war, and some 10,000 died, largely because of malnu-

[2] From the enormous literature on the civil war in Finland, see for a good general treatment, Anatole G. Mazour, *Finland Between East and West* (Princeton 1956); also P. G. La Chesnais, *La Guerre Civile en Finlande* (Paris 1919); Henning Söderhjelm, *Det röda upproret i Finland år 1918* [The Red Rebellion in Finland in 1918] (Stockholm 1918); and E. G. von Wahl, *Voina belykh i krasnykh v Finlyandii v 1918* [The War of Whites and Reds in Finland in 1918] (Tallin 1936). The White literature is discussed critically by Marvin Rintala in "The Politics of Gustaf Mannerheim," *Journal of Central European Affairs*, XXI (April 1961), esp. 69-77; and the background to the civil war is given a fresh and balanced interpretation by Paasivirta in his *Suomen itsenäisyyskysymys 1917* [The Question of Finnish Independence] (Porvoo-Helsinki 1949).

The extent to which Finland was counted upon as a base for a general White counter-attack in the Russian civil war, particularly by Kolchak, is brought out in a series of documents published in the *Krasnyi Arkhiv*, which have not been fully utilized in general histories of the civil war period. See particularly no. 31 (1928), 51-80; No. 33 (1929), 82-144; No. 98 (1940), 31-67 and 125-144; and no. 99 (1940), 15-51. See also the short study by V. S. Petrov, *Finlyandiya v planakh imperialisticheskikh derzhav v 1918-1920 godakh* [Finland in the Plans of the Imperialist States in 1918-1920] (Petrozavodsk 1961); and on the revolutionary activity of the 1905-1907 period in Finland, see M. N. Vlasova, *Proletariat Finlyandii v godakh pervoy Russkoy Revolyutsii* [The Proletariat of Finland in the Years of the First Russian Revolution] (Petrozavodsk 1961).

trition. This White reconstruction, like that of the North after the American Civil War, was even more resented than the war itself, which had taken 25,000 lives in five months.

The Finnish Communist Party emerged as the party of revenge; and the program adopted at its founding meeting in August of 1918 was more extreme and violent than most. Kuusinen, a university-trained historian, and former Social Democratic editor and parliamentarian, emerged as the theoretician and *de facto* leader of the Finnish party. As a former delegate to the Second International and one of the very few intellectuals in the Finnish party, Kuusinen probably felt under subtle pressure to demonstrate that he also was a man of action. His *The Revolt in Finland 1918: An Essay in Self-criticism* (1920) has been called the "first brochure of 'self-criticism' made under the aegis of the Comintern."[3]

In a bitter and self-flagellating manner he argued that the absence of a Leninist-type proletarian party caused the failure of Finnish revolution. It was necessary to break completely with all traditions of parliamentary action. The Social Democrats were the worst enemies of revolution, which could only be successfully completed by a tightly disciplined party closely bound with the Russian party and pledged to setting up an "iron dictatorship of the proletariat," and instituting an immediate and dramatic social transformation of the country. Zinoviev, the first head of the Communist International, praised the Finnish program as pointing the way for the conduct of the international struggle against social democracy of the old type,[4] and Kuusinen and other Finns played an important role in forming the Third International.

During the Russian Civil War the Finnish party was particularly valued by the Bolsheviks because of the knowledge that the White Armies in Russia—particularly those of Kolchak—hoped to use Finland as a base for operations. Because the status of Karelia was still in doubt the Finns also did not feel that the conflict had been fully resolved in 1918; and because of vagueness in the terms of the Treaty of Dorpat 1920, many Finns continued to believe that they had some responsibility for the region even after its absorption into the USSR.

[3] "La révolution communiste en Finlande, monopole de la famille Kuusinen," *Est et Ouest* (Dec. 16-31, 1961), 3. See also in the same issue the article by Branko Lazitch, "La crise finno-soviétique n'est pas résolue."

[4] Mazour, 57-58; Kuusinen may have felt constrained to take such an extreme position because of Trotsky's accusation that "Kuusinen was one of those who killed the Finnish revolution of 1918." See "La Révolution," 3-4.

Kuusinen was showing himself to be "more Communist than the party itself," but had avoided the "childish disease" of left-wing deviationism by his disciplined intellect—a typical Finnish quality—and his servility before the Soviet party. The hero of Finnish Communism became Yrjö Sirola, who had favored a bolder revolutionary program during the civil war and subsequently became an important figure in the Comintern effort to secure the allegiance of the Finnish Workers Party in the USA, which was the largest single component of the incipient American Communist movement of the early 1920's.

Meanwhile in December 1918, the old Social Democratic Party, which had been by far the largest in Finland prior to the civil war, reassembled under the leadership of Väinö Tanner and voted overwhelmingly to accept the independence of Finland from the USSR and the legal, democratic arena for the advancement of worker interests. Thus, the gauntlet was down. Although the Social Democrats also professed to be defenders of the defeated revolutionary cause, they no longer stood in opposition to an independent democratic Finland. Tanner became—and has remained—the absolute *bête noire* of Finnish Communism; Kuusinen referred to him as Satan in human form.[5]

Unlike the intellectual Kuusinen, Tanner is a pragmatic man of affairs whose training ground was not the university and the editorial office but the banks and consumer cooperatives of a vigorously developing economy. Tanner is in many ways a typical Finn: honest, methodical, and incredibly tough and stubborn. Like most of the older Social Democrats, he was not an anti-Russian separatist prior to the Civil War; but he was determined to keep Bolshevism out of Finland. He considered himself to be a revisionist Marxist and frankly described himself to Stalin as a "Menshevik."[6] He excluded Finnish Communists from positions of executive leadership in the Social Democratic Party and steadily increased its electoral strength throughout the 1920's. Finally, in 1926-1927, he formed a minority government—the first democratic socialist government in independent Finland.

Because of its militant posture, the Finnish Communist Party was in a poor position to make a credible show of proletarian unity with the reconstituted Social Democrats or anyone else. The Communists formed in May 1920 their own "Finnish Party of Socialist Workers,"

[5] For this and other choice epithets, see Marvin Rintala, "Väinö Tanner in Finnish Politics," *The American Slavic and East European Review*, xx (Feb. 1961), 85.

[6] *Ibid.*, 93-94.

which was soon changed into "The Finnish Labor Party" and "The Socialist Party of Workers and Small Peasants." Throughout the 1920's, these cover parties for the Moscow-based Finnish Communist movement polled between 10 and 15 percent of the votes in national elections. During the NEP period, Finland appears to have been written off as a source of much immediate hope by the international movement. The Finnish Communists concentrated on developing an effective organization, which succeeded in affiliating the major Finnish labor federation with the international Communist federation of unions in 1922.

When the international movement phased into a period of greater truculence in 1929 in concert with the beginning of the first Five Year Plan in the USSR, the Finnish party responded with an eagerness that reflected its continued doctrinal militancy and insensitivity to local conditions. The Communists seemed to be trying artificially to recreate the revolutionary situations that had arisen naturally in 1905 and 1918. The campaign of rallies and threats of violence launched by the Young Communist League of Finland and the Communist-controlled labor federation was apparently designed to culminate in a general strike like that of 1905. But the Communist campaign was soon engulfed by a counter-campaign of violence from the right—the so-called Lapua movement. Choosing to stage a large gathering of the Young Communist League in the northwestern city of Lapua, the original stronghold of the Finnish White forces, the Communists included a crude anti-religious demonstration in the program. The pietistic local agrarian populace forcibly broke up an anti-religious rally of some 400 young Communists, and were represented as national heroes by the right-wing press.

The Lapua movement which soon developed was as committed to violence as the Communist movement. Neither it nor the Finnish Fascist party which appeared later ever received a large electoral vote in Finland; but the Lapua movement did receive a large measure of tacit approval from the legal parties in 1930.[7] They were glad to have its terrorism directed against the Communists, and gratified its demands for a "purely Finnish" nation by outlawing the Communist Party in 1930. Thus began fourteen years of illegal, purge-ridden underground existence for the Finnish Communist Party. Practically all of the serious rivals to Kuusinen—including his principal opponents, Kullervo Manner and his wife—were liquidated, and the

[7] See Marvin Rintala, *Three Generations: The Extreme Right Wing in Finnish Politics* (Bloomington, Ind. 1962).

Finnish Communist Party became almost a family movement. Kuusinen's daughter Hertta assumed increasing leadership.

During the 1930's Otto Kuusinen appears to have played a role second only to that of Dimitrov in the activities of the Comintern. His absolute loyalty to the USSR and passion for organization made him an ideal party functionary of the Stalin era. He became one of the principal—and most cynical—theoreticians of united front tactics, writing bluntly in 1931 of the need to create a system of organizations and smaller committees that would revolve in controlled orbits around the sun of the Communist Party. The following year in his widely distributed pamphlet *Prepare for Power,* Kuusinen provided one of the frankest explanations ever publicly given by a leading Communist of the nature of Communist "peace" tactics. After ridiculing the "soft, pacificist backbone" of those who contend that "Communism has peace as the key point of its being," Kuusinen explained that "the revolution has, to a certain extent, veiled its offensive operations under the guise of defence in order that in this way the undecided and vacillating elements may the more easily be brought into its whirlpool. This also explains the outer semblance of defence in the character of the speeches, articles, and slogans of this period, which nonetheless, by virtue of their inner content, possess a pronounced offensive character."[8]

After long years of service to the Soviet Union, Kuusinen was made head of the puppet government of Finland set up late in 1939 by the invading Red Army in the small Baltic resort of Terijoki near the Russian border. There has probably never been a more complete failure in all the sordid history of puppet governments. Almost no one in Finland supported Kuusinen's government, as Communists in Finland generally rallied to the support of the national government. Kuusinen signed various Finno-Soviet treaties in Moscow (which he appears never to have left) promising that they would all be ratified "in the shortest possible time in the capital of Finland, the city of Helsinki."[9] In Finnish eyes the creation of such an offensive puppet regime changed the complexion of the war from a Soviet fight for limited strategic objectives to an ideological crusade for the extinction of Finnish independence. The attempt to rekindle the class passions of the civil war, the use of anachronistic terms like "the White Guard

[8] *Prepare for Power* (New York 1932), 116. This was originally a report to the 12th plenum of the executive committee of the Comintern in September 1932. For a particularly bitter later denunciation of democratic socialists, see Kuusinen's *A Warmongers' International* (Moscow 1952).

[9] *Soviet Documents on Foreign Policy* (Oxford 1953) III, 409-10.

Government"—all indicated that Kuusinen and Stalin were totally unaware of the growing sense of solidarity and national pride that had developed in twenty years of independence. As a distinguished Finnish historian has written, "a revolution did take place in Finland, but not of the kind Kuusinen had hoped for. It was a revolution of national unity. And at last the 'popular front' too came into being, though not in the Marxist sense of the term: it was the Eastern front."[10]

The resistance of Finnish troops during the bloody hundred days of the famous Winter War forced the Russians to settle for territory rather than total occupation or a puppet regime. Up until the surrender in March 1940, the Finns had managed even to hold on to the city of Viipuri (Viborg), which had been the major Soviet objective and was only a few miles from the Soviet border. During the "continuation war" of 1941-1944, in which the Finns accepted co-belligerency but not alliance with Germany in order to recapture their lost territory, the Finns also held their advanced line deep in Soviet territory until 1944. Once against they made such a protracted defence that the USSR agreed to settle for the *status quo ante bellum* rather than persist with a costly invasion and occupation. Kuusinen was left in 1944 as in 1940 to preside over the artificially enlarged Finno-Karelian "autonomous republic" inside the USSR; but almost the entire half-million population of the Karelian area that was ceded to Russia fled on both occasions to Finland with the retreating Finnish troops.

One of the terms of the 1944 settlement was the legalization of the Finnish Communist Party, which immediately attempted to break with its unproductive past advocacy of an "iron proletarian dictatorship." In October 1944, the Communists created together with a handful of dissident Social Democrats the "Finnish People's Democratic League" (SKDL), and became the first major Communist party to call for a "people's democracy" as the alternative "peaceful" road to communism to that of proletarian disctatorship.

The years 1944-1946 were probably the most dangerous of the "dangerous years" for Finland.[11] Never in all its lonely history had Finland been more completely thrown back on its own resources for

[10] Max Jakobson, *The Diplomacy of the Winter War* (Cambridge, Mass. 1961), 171.

[11] This point emerges with particular clarity from the Leino memoirs, the best single source for the complex diplomacy of the Russo-Finnish postwar settlement. The best general account of the immediate post-war years remains Lauri Hyvämäki, *Vaaran Vuodet 1944-48* [Dangerous Years, 1944-48] (Helsinki 1956); and a short general account in English is John H. Wuorinen, "Finland and the USSR—1945-1961," *Journal of International Affairs*, XVI (1962), 38-46.

survival. Thus, it is particularly interesting to examine the reasons why a Communist take-over was not effected during this period. First and perhaps most important, Russia was preoccupied with the main front south of the Baltic. Finnish resourcefulness in leaving the war early and accepting the obligation for clearing their land of German troops deprived the Russians of any pretext they might have had to occupy the country. The bitter German troops stationed in Northern Finland destroyed almost everything in sight in reprisal for the alleged Finnish treachery, and made Finnish belligerency against Hitler in the closing months of the war considerably more than a mere formality.

The second key factor was the preoccupation of the Finnish Communists with the problem of developing a mass base for their activities through front groups. Long absence from the Finnish scene had left them out of touch with Finnish reality and in need of considerable organizational work at the precinct level. Once again they ran into the indomitable Tanner, who convened the Social Democratic congress in December 1944 to expel from positions of leadership all members who were simultaneously active in the SKDL. Rather than accept this defeat as final, the Finnish Communists turned to the splinter party that developed out of the Social Democratic movement, the United Socialist Party (SYP), whose members were active within the SKDL.

Perhaps the most important deterrent force of all, however, on the Finnish Communists was the simple element of fear. When the Finnish army demobilized after the armistice with the USSR and the expulsion of the German troops in the north, two members of the general staff quietly supervised a program of securing arms caches near major centers of Communist strength and potential agitation. War-hardened anti-Russian bitterness was still strong—and the influx of virtually the entire population of Soviet-annexed Karelia during these years brought in a fresh supply of bitterly anti-Communist elements who would have been ready for violence with little left to lose. The number of arms distributed was actually very small, but when the Communists first learned of this program in the summer of 1945 they appear to have become extremely frightened. Memories of past manhandling by White forces and a realization of their own widespread unpopularity apparently led them to exaggerate the strength of their opponents. Many of them apparently feared for their own personal safety in the event of an internal Communist putsch.

In any event, the Finnish Communists decided in the summer of

1945 not to return to their previous tactics of violence. They doubtless felt encouraged by the general establishment of people's democratic fronts that was developing throughout Eastern Europe. Controlling six out of eighteen portfolios in the coalition government that emerged following the spring elections of 1945, the Communists probably believed that total victory was simply a matter of time—particularly since the Soviet-dominated Allied Control Commission in Helsinki still exercised a kind of veto power over Finnish political life, repeatedly confronting the Finns with lists of war criminals and threats about future reparation payments and peace terms.

The Soviet control commission attempted to use the war crimes trials as a vehicle for ridding Finnish political life of all strongly anti-Soviet forces, but it was frustrated by the stubborn refusal of the Finns to prosecute anyone not directly involved in engineering the alliance with Germany. Tanner and the Social Democrats were of course the prime Soviet targets. He was eventually sentenced in 1946 and acquired something of a martyr's halo by his insistence that "he had done nothing of which he was not proud", stating that he accepted imprisonment only in order to prevent greater suffering for others. The fact is that the Social Democrats and particularly Tanner had never—with a few minor exceptions—been strongly anti-Russian or sympathetic with Fascism. The Agrarian League, which was closely aligned with the more primitive peasant and chauvinist mentality, had been much more so. Ambitious Agrarian League politicians, such as the then minister of justice Urho Kekkonen, were attempting during this period to atone for an extremely anti-Russian past by over-solicitousness to Russian demands on the war trials issue.

Communist hopes focused on their ability to dominate the coalition "red earth" government of Agrarians, Communists, and Social Democrats. With the reorganization of the government in March 1946, Communist chances seemed markedly improved. The old White commander, Mannerheim, stepped down from his interim position as president in favor of J. K. Paasikivi; and the new prime minister, Mauno Pekkala, was a fellow-travelling member of the SKDL. The Soviet Union, apparently considering the new government well on the way towards becoming a people's democracy, signed in February 1947 a peace treaty which it probably considered sufficient to assure Finland's assimilation into the Bloc. In this treaty Finland was assessed a mammoth $300,000,000 reparation to be repayed by 1952, largely in manufactured materials not previously produced in Finland and marketable only in the East; the armed forces were held to a figure of about 40,000; former German assets and property in Finland were turned over to the control commission (which turned them over to the Finnish Communist Party); and two elastic clauses were included which gave the USSR a permanent pretext for reinterfering in Finnish internal affairs.

One clause provided that "Finland shall cooperate fully with the allied and associated powers with a view to ensuring that Germany may not be able to take steps outside German territory toward rearmament." The other provided that "Finland, which in accordance with the armistice agreement has taken measures for dissolving *all organizations of a Fascist type* on Finnish territory, whether political, military or para-military, *as well as other organizations conducting propaganda hostile to the Soviet Union* or to any of the other United Nations, shall not permit in the future the existence and activities of organizations of that nature which have as their aim denial to the people of their democratic rights."[12]

Late in 1947 it became apparent that the Communists were losing rather than gaining strength. Direct Soviet pressure was needed to keep even the Communist infiltrated government from accepting US aid under the Marshall plan. Preparations for the departure of the Allied Control Commission had led to a marked rise in patriotic feeling which was reflected in substantial Communist electoral losses in municipal elections of December 1947. It became apparent that a coup from above was the only realistic possibility for a Communist consolidation in Finland. In January 1948, Lieutenant General Savonenkov, Zhdanov's former deputy on the control commission and a figure well acquainted with Finland, returned to Helsinki as Soviet ambassador and Tuure Lehén returned from his long residence in the USSR.

On February 22, 1948, just a week after the Communist coup in Czechoslovakia, Stalin delivered a long note to Paasikivi virtually commanding him to negotiate a treaty of mutual assistance with the USSR against possible German aggression. He pointedly remarked that Finland was the only one "of the three who border on the USSR and waged war against it" not to sign such a pact.[13] The other two,

[12] From the official English version of the treaty text in *British and Foreign State Papers,* CXLVIII, Part II, (London 1955), 344, 342, italics added. The United States, which was never formally at war with Finland, was not a signatory; and the West was represented on the Control Commission only by British and Commonwealth spokesmen, whose role seems to have been almost completely passive.

[13] Text of the note in *New York Times,* February 22, 1948. For analysis of this crisis the major Finnish sources are Hyvämäki, and Leino, *Kommunisti,* 113ff. Hans Krosby, "The Communist Power Bid in Finland in 1948," *Political Science Quarterly,* LXXV (1960, June), 229-243, incorporates a good deal of Swedish and English-

Rumania and Hungary, had signed such pacts on the fourth and eighteenth of February respectively; but the lumping together of Finland with two nations already clearly behind the iron curtain was ominous. Stalin's curious offer to come to Helsinki personally to sign such a pact must have had ominous overtones for the Finns, since he had last been in Helsinki just prior to the *coup* attempt of January 1918. Indeed Finland had a certain sentimental interest for Stalin since he had first met Lenin at the Social Democratic conference in Tampere in 1905 and had made his first appearance as People's Commissar of Nationalities at Helsinki in December of 1917. It seemed logical to assume that he was now planning to complete the assimilation of Finland into the Communist orbit. Western newspapers took the line they have generally taken during moments of crisis for Finland: expressions of sympathy combined with "realistic" recognition that there is really no hope for Finland.

Within the government, the Communists controlled the prime ministership, and the portfolios of the interior, education, transportation, public works, social welfare, and the army. In addition, the national radio was controlled by a fellow-travelling playwright and feminist, Hella Wuolijoki. A new Communist state police force (*Valpo*) of 400 men had been formed within the ministry of the interior under the effective leadership of a completely reliable veteran Communist, Aino Aaltonen. The minister of the interior, Leino, was a Communist with an additional 1,000-man mobile police force (*Liipo*) at his disposal. The minister of transportation and public works and the minister of social welfare were Communists who had undergone long years of residence and specialized training in the USSR.[14]

By all traditional standards of revolutionary strategy, the situation seemed ripe for a Communist coup. Soviet commentators euphemisti-

language interpretive material; while Ya. S. Il'inskiy, *Finlyandiya* [Finland] (Moscow 1949) offers a detailed exposition of the standard Soviet interpretation that there was no coup attempt in 1948, and that the only change in Finnish political life was the move to the right under the new Fagerholm government of late July. See also *Iz istorii,* 174-179. The term "frosts" for these crises was actually invoked by Khrushchev himself during his trip to Helsinki in September 1960. See his speech cited in *Helsingin Sanomat,* September 4, 1960.

[14] Wuolijoki is a fascinating illustration of the complex international connections of many of those involved in the Finnish Communist movement. She was an Esthonian by birth, author of several Hollywood scripts, sister of the wife of the British Communist Palme Dutt, and a close friend of Alexandra Kollontai with whom she tried privately to negotiate a truce with the USSR during the Winter War. See Jakobson, 203-213, 272. Aaltonen later became president of the Finnish Communist Party. The richest source of detail on all these figures is the works of Tuominen.

cally noted that "wide circles of Finnish society" appreciated the need for "a significant improvement of Finno-Soviet relations" and that such an improvement depended on "a democratic direction of policies" in Finland.[15]

Yet once again a genuine revolutionary situation was absent. The Communists had failed to broaden their base of popularity, economic conditions were improving, and a sense of national identity was growing. More important, the President of Finland was capable of taking cool and clear-headed leadership of his country. He successfully stalled for time in his reply to Stalin, and excluded all of the hard-line, Soviet-trained Communists from the coalition negotiating team he sent to Moscow. There may be a grain of truth to the subsequent Communist claim that they never even intended a coup; for Communist inactivity during the first two weeks after the Stalin note reflects indecisiveness and lack of clear prior planning. It may be, however, that the decision all along had been to wait until the negotiations with Moscow had begun to open up a campaign of coordinated domestic pressure. In any case, by mid-March the Communists had decided on a campaign of increased violence; and on March 19, 1948, the day before he was scheduled to leave for the Moscow negotiating sessions, Leino, the Communist minister of the interior, took the dramatic step which may well have turned the tide of Finnish history. He paid a secret evening visit to the army chief-of-staff, Aarne Sihvo, and warned him of the forthcoming campaign of violence. Thus alerted, the strongly anti-Communist 30,000-man army cancelled all leaves, quietly increased garrison strengths near the big cities, and simply took over the arsenal of Leino's own mobile police force. The badly outnumbered state police force was afraid to act; and the possibility of a forcible coup was out of the question.

Meanwhile, a sudden *volte-face* of the Soviet leadership in the presence of the Finnish negotiating team in Moscow indicated that Stalin was either very confused, suddenly reconciled to the improbability of any coup, or else very preoccupied with other problems. With relative speed, the USSR settled for a friendship treaty based largely on the draft that Paasikivi had prepared as a working paper for the Finnish delegation. Finland was not forced to sign a military alliance, and successfully declined a Soviet offer of increased military aid. With the signing of the treaty of friendship, cooperation, and mutual assistance on April 6, the crisis ended.

[15] Il'inskiy, 19.

The defeat of Finnish communism was subsequently turned into a rout in the elections of June 1948 in which the Communists lost 11 out of 51 seats in the diet of 200 members. All Communists were—and have remained—excluded from the coalition cabinet. A new security police (*Suopo*) was created to replace both other police forces of the ministry of the interior; the national radio was placed under parliamentary control and taken away from its Communist management; and a large strike was settled and a freeze on wages introduced by the new Social Democratic premier to prevent Communist manipulation of wage demands for political purposes. Thus, not only did Finnish Communism fail in its bid for power, but it lost the substantial power position that it already had. All of this took place with no help from the West, in a nation with an 800-mile common border with the USSR and with Soviet troops stationed in a base just a short day's march from Helsinki.

As if to rub in the defeat, a number of "war criminals" who had been sentenced to prison terms at the insistence of the Soviet control commission were released from jail late in 1948, including Tanner himself, who had served less than half of his term.

Why Communism Failed in Finland

It is worth stopping at this genuine landmark in Finnish history to examine the reasons why communism failed in all four of the bids for power which it had mounted in Finland at ten-year intervals between 1918 and 1948. There are two simple explanations. One is that the Finns are a uniquely tough people, who were not as submissive as the Czechs and did not permit themselves to be intimidated. The other is that only one key element for success was present in each revolutionary situation: in 1918, a genuine mass base; in 1929, organized leadership; in 1939, the active support of a foreign army; and in 1948, positions of power inside the government. In none of these situations were the Communists able to bring their multifarious physical assets into focus on the business of obtaining power. None of these situations except the first was a naturally revolutionary situation; and in none of them were the Communists—for all their doctrinal militancy—able to terrify or intimidate their opponents.

There are also other more generic reasons why communism failed in its major bids for power during the first three decades of Finnish independence. First and perhaps most important is the willingness of its opponents to resort to the same tactics of terror and violence that the

Communists themselves employed. This is not a conclusion that is pleasing to the liberal mind; but the fact is that—apart from the period of atrocities at the end of the civil war of 1918—calculated threats of terror by otherwise humane Finns were effective, not particularly bloody, and probably indispensable for the preservation of Finnish democracy.

The weak but generally liberal and democratic coalition government in Helsinki that had proclaimed independence from Russia in 1917 was as incapable of preventing the Communist coup in Helsinki in January of 1918 as the similarly structured provisional government in Petersburg had been in November 1917. But whereas the Russian Whites were a divided and confused force of opposition, the Finnish Whites had expert and disciplined military leadership at the top and middle echelons. The Finnish Whites were outnumbered in a way that the Russian Whites never were until late in the civil war. Moreover, they had even less of a counter-program to capture the popular imagination than had the Russian Whites. But the Finns had a great military commander in Marshal Mannerheim, and a corps of well-trained officers from the 2,000-man Jäger battalion. Again in 1929, the Communists were defeated not by attempts to steal their revolutionary thunder, but by the strong-arm methods of the up-country Lapua farmers. So vivid was the Communist memory of previous anti-Communist pogroms, that they seem to have been terrified even at the height of their power in the 1944-1946 period by the fear that terroristic reprisals would greet any overly aggressive push for power. The same exaggerated fears of reprisals from hidden anti-Communist groups appears to have been a major inhibiting factor during the crisis of 1948, judging from the repeated protests of Soviet Ambassador Savonenkov about the alleged para-military function and intention of Finnish "shooting clubs" and "hunting societies."[16]

The events of 1948 also illustrate that the second key reason why the Communists consistently failed in Finland was the widespread popular identification of communism with an aggressive foreign power. Leino's decision to forewarn the army chief-of-staff is only one dramatic illustration of the choice repeatedly made by Finns at all levels to show allegiance to their country even at the expense of deep personal and ideological attachments to the Communist cause. Nationalism proved an exciting rallying cry in a newly independent nation that had long labored under the political rule of Russia and the economic and

[16] *Ibid.*, 27-28.

cultural dominance of its own Swedish-speaking minority. By subordinating itself to Moscow-trained elements and to Soviet citizens of Finnish origin like Kuusinen and Lehén, the Finnish Communist Party forfeited its chance to expand its clientele beyond the ranks of those with abiding grievances over the outcome of the civil war.

A third reason for the Communist failures in Finland was almost certainly the repeated subordination of the domestic Communist campaign to Soviet security considerations. Soviet policy towards Finland under Stalin appears to have been guided far more by *raison d'état* than by concern for the international Communist movement. Stalin's desire to annex Karelia and to establish a base first at Hanko and then at Porkkala gratified his sense of security, but deepened Finnish hatred of Russia, which was in turn directed against the domestic Finnish Communists. At the same time the Russian unwillingness to go all the way and occupy Finland—even for a short initial period—deprived the Finnish Communists of the numerous middle echelon bureaucratic positions that Czech Communists were able to assume under the initial patronage of the Red Army. At the time of both the armistice in 1944 and the 1948 crisis, the Soviet government let the Finnish goverment off with less severe terms than the Finnish Communist Party would have liked. Having burned themselves badly in 1939-1940 with their solemn attempt to deal with the Kuusinen puppet government as the legal government of Finland, the Soviets seemed unwilling to gamble on any more popular uprisings in Finland. At the same time, however, the USSR forfeited any chance of gaining popular credit for its policy of relative non-interference, by keeping alive a menacing vestige of the puppet government—the so-called Finno-Karelian autonomous republic under Kuusinen.

A final important reason for Communist failure lies in the nature of Finnish society itself. The Communist movement was unduly influenced by memories of 1918, and it developed tactics suitable for an atmosphere of confusion and chaos that was totally uncharacteristic of Finnish life. The low social mobility of an essentially orderly society, and the high degree of authority and discipline maintained by entrenched and conservative military and civil leaders, provided a strong anchor against sudden demagogic gusts from the right or left. Just as co-belligerency with Nazi Germany had not led Finland to develop a fascist movement of any size, so friendship with the USSR did not automatically lead to a great growth in Communist strength. There were plenty of Finnish sympathizers and opportunistic fellow travellers for each of these totalitarian allies; but there was a shortage of deep social tensions and economic grievances among this relatively homogeneous and adequately-fed people. In their efforts to take over organizations to enlarge their mass support, the Communists repeatedly discovered that governing boards were usually elected for some exasperatingly long period of time. It was not just the famous Finnish courage or *sisu,* but also the virtues of organization and hard work, as well as the experience of many years in dealing with Russia, that consistently frustrated this impatient and extremist movement.

The Post-Stalin Communist Campaign

The crushing defeat of communism in Finland in 1948 gave Finnish democracy a breathing space that lasted until shortly after the death of Stalin. Kuusinen went almost literally into cold storage in the bleak city of Petrozavodsk, capital of the Finno-Karelian republic. Finland had no real role to play in the Soviet strategic maneuvers of the period; and the Finnish Communist party had little potential for growth inside Finland. The Agrarians and Social Democrats, the two participants in the "red earth" cabinets of the immediate post-war period, carried on without the Communists, and President Passikivi continued to treat the USSR with tact.

Then, in the mid-1950's, changes in both Finnish and Soviet political life created new opportunities for Finnish communism and its Soviet sponsors. A new, "peaceful" Communist offensive was launched against democratic Finland—a campaign which is still underway, and the extent and seriousness of which has yet to be fully appreciated.

The change in Finnish politics resulted from the breakdown in Agrarian-Social Democratic solidarity and the sudden willingness of both parties to engage in private talks with Soviet officials. The basis for the split between the two largest democratic parties lay partly in the different economic interests of agricultural producers and industrial consumers and partly in the personal rivalry between Kekkonen and Väinö Leskinen, the most dynamic political leaders of the Agrarians and the Social Democrats respectively. With the successful paying off of Soviet reparations and the subsequent abatement of Soviet militancy after the death of Stalin, non-Communist Finnish political leaders began to indulge in the dangerous luxury of petty squabbling. Lebedev, Russian ambassador to Finland from 1954 to 1958, was one of the first "smiling ambassadors" of the post-Stalin era, and quietly began an extensive series of exploratory talks with Finnish political leaders of all persuasions. The return to Finland of the Porkkala base in 1955, a series of state visits by Voroshilov, Bulganin, and Khrushchev, and the abolition of Kuusinen's autonomous Finno-Karelian Republic inside the USSR all represented a major effort to rehabilitate the Soviet image and open up new targets of opportunity for the large but languishing Finnish Communist Party. A new era of front activities in Finland was clearly planned. The promotion of Kuusinen—for the first time—to the presidium of the Soviet Communist Party provided Khrushchev with expert coaching on Finnish affairs and indicated—if anyone needed to be shown—that the old militant objectives of communism were unchanged.

The USSR concentrated its efforts on encouraging a newly developed split in the Social Democratic Party, supporting the dissident Social Democratic League, even though it had previously been even more anti-Soviet than the regular Leskinen leadership. In 1957, the dissidents established a newspaper, *Paivan Sanomat* [Daily News], which was apparently supported financially by the USSR and printed on the press of the Finnish Communist daily, *Kansan Uutiset* [People's News]. They soon entered into a coalition government with the Agrarians in defiance of the regular Social Democratic leadership.

The Agrarian leader, Urho Kekkonen, who had been elected president of the republic in 1956 by one parliamentary vote, had been dependent upon Communist votes for his election. As the ambitious leader of a rural party in search of issues in a rapidly urbanizing society, he soon decided to play politics with the hitherto august presidential office and vie for the slippery mantel of "best able to get along with the Russians." Leading Agrarians began criticizing the idea of a united front among non-Communist parties;[17] and when Kekkonen paid a state visit to Moscow in May 1958 he was cordially received, publicly flattered by Khrushchev, and rewarded with a promise of new credits for Finland and future access to the Saimaa Canal (a waterway that runs through former Finnish territory connecting several inland lakes still in Finland with the Baltic sea).

The split in the Social Democratic movement enabled the Finnish Communists to gain seven parliamentary seats in 1958 while the Social Democrats lost six seats in the election and eleven more through post-election defections to the Social Democratic League. The Communists

[17] This line was voiced most strongly by the then party secretary Korsimo, but was also echoed even by the so-called right wing of the Agrarian Party. See, for instance, the statements by Virolainen, cited in *Hufvudstadsbladet*, November 15, 1957, 1, 17.

thus became by a very slight margin the largest single party in terms of both popular votes and parliamentary representation. Encouraged by this success, and by the general softening of the Finnish anti-Communist posture, the USSR staged the first of its "night frosts" against Finland—a series of massive pressures apparently designed to hasten the long-delayed move of Finland towards absorption into the Soviet orbit. In rapid succession late in 1958, the USSR denounced the Social Democratic premier and conservative ministers in a new coalition government; suspended the new credits it had just extended to Finland; recalled its trade mission and ambassador; and refused to accept deliveries of goods ordered in Finland or to pay for those already delivered.

Although this crisis occurred "on schedule" (i.e. after the ten-year interval that seems to separate major Finnish contests with Communist aggression), it was a new type of crisis for it involved the use of economic threats and sanctions. The immediate objective of Soviet policy was not Soviet security, but a forcible change in the complexion of the Finnish government.

In the short term this was less dangerous than earlier crises, since there was no immediate Communist bid for power. For the longer term it was more serious, since the question at issue was the Soviet right to blackmail a hitherto free people out of their right to choose their own government. From a global point of view, the crisis was also more important than past ones, because the artificially manufactured Finnish "crisis" was not—as had previous Finnish crises been for the most part—a local matter. Rather it was a subordinate part of the general probing of Western resolve that was concurrently taking place over the suddenly activated Berlin situation. The resolution of the crisis represented an unqualified success for the Communist cause in Finland, and a probable source of encouragement for those impulses within the Soviet leadership arguing for more aggressive attempts to check growing Western strength in Europe.

Finland's Western friends did not take vigorous action and waited for the dust to settle. No one apparently offered to put up even the relative pittance needed to pay for the ice-breakers and other Finnish products that the Russians had refused to buy. One prominent Western official later resigned in disgust when he discovered how passive his nation's attitude had been—concealing his anger in order not to demoralize further the embattled Finns.

Meanwhile, the previous tendency of Finns to rally together in the face of Russian threats was undermined by the Agrarians, who resigned from the coalition government early in December 1958, thus breaking the united front of non-Communist opposition to Russian pressures. The key question was what the President would do. For forty days and nights—the darkest and coldest of the long northern winter—Finland was without a government, and Kekkonen seemed willing to sit tight. Then suddenly and mysteriously, he moved in such a way as to indicate that Finnish politics were entering a new era. On January 20, 1959, just a week after an almost totally Agrarian government was formed, Kekkonen suddenly announced that he was leaving immediately for Leningrad in response to a long-standing invitation to become "acquainted with the cultural life" of the city.[18]

The principal cultural attraction turned out to be Khrushchev, who suddenly appeared in the city for another of their confidential northern summit meetings on January 22 and 23, 1959. Many Finns, including the largest Finnish newspaper, *Helsingin Sanomat,* bitterly criticized the deception and secrecy which accompanied these vital discussions of their national future. Kekkonen's Soviet hosts remarked unctuously that as a result of the meetings the snows had melted early in Leningrad,[19] while his televised report to the Finnish people was patronizing in tone and ominous in content. After expressing "complete confidence" that Khrushchev really had no other objective but "good and friendly relations," he went on to state bluntly that these relations "will never attain the degree of confidence that our interests require" without greater self-imposed censorship of the Finnish press.[20] Whatever was actually said at the Leningrad meeting, the practical consequences were that the USSR acquired a veto power against the participation in any Finnish government coalition of any regular Social Democrats or anyone else that they consider unfriendly.

Ostensibly, Finland had lost very little. Everyone was glad to see relations with the USSR normalized, and many were willing to believe that Kekkonen had adequately defended the country's interests under trying circumstances. However, the nation's ability to resist external pressure had been severely—perhaps irreparably—compromised. Paasikivi's journeys to Moscow had been carefully prepared and solemnly

[18] *New York Times,* January 14, 1959, 6; January 21, 1959, 3; January 23, 1959, 1. For a succinct account of this crisis in English, see Austin Goodrich, *Study in Sisu* (New York 1960), 134-144. See also Kent Foster, "The Finno-Soviet Crisis of 1958-1959," *International Journal* (Spring 1960); and Tuure Junnila, *Jäädytetty Demokratia* [Frozen Democracy] (Jyväskylä 1960).

[19] *Helsingin Sanomat,* January 23, 1959; *New York Times,* January 23, 1959, 6; and January 24, 1959, 1.

[20] *New York Times,* January 26, 1959, 4.

announced. He had left the Helsinki railroad station amidst thousands of hymn-singing countrymen who felt confident that he would defend all of them against the great common external threat to their independence. Now the president of Finland attended a secret, prearranged rendezvous, at which he accepted the Soviet right to exclude a significant number of his countrymen from political power, and agreed to act as an apologist for these Soviet tactics.

The Soviets were not slow in pressing their advantage. Within a few months, the Soviet press began denouncing not only Tanner and Leskinen but several other Social Democrats for violating the "spirit" of the 1948 treaty and of the Leningrad talks. Selected members of the various conservative parties were also denounced. A "house Russian" system was introduced, whereby the 250-odd members of the massive Soviet embassy and its politically-oriented trade missions apparently worked out a division of labor as to who should cultivate which Finnish political figure. Some Finnish politicians even claimed that they could tell how vacillating a member of parliament was by which Soviet official saw him most often. The new Khrushchev-Kuusinen formula was to intimidate consistently all firm anti-Communist elements, in the belief that others could be flattered into passivity. The attainment of power would thus become simply a matter of time and of finding a soothing formula for the transition.

In September 1960 Khrushchev began a concerted campaign to build up Kekkonen's prestige by inviting himself suddenly to Finland for the celebration of the Finnish president's sixtieth birthday. The two balding and earthy sexagenarians talked and joked together in a boiling Finnish *sauna* (vapor bath). Kekkonen sent him a complete *sauna* unit as a memento of their happy communal bath, and returned the visit with a trip to Moscow in November, where he was given the rare privilege of living in the Kremlin rather than a hotel. At a lavish reception Kekkonen toasted Khrushchev with words that he attributed to Schweitzer as "the only world statesman genuinely interested in peace for its own sake," and later reportedly took off his shoe and banged it on the table as a sign of accord with his Soviet host.

When a broad multi-party coalition picked an elderly non-political judge, Honka, in 1961, to oppose Kekkonen in the presidential election of 1962, Soviet officials denounced him as a front for Tanner and foe of the neutral course of Finnish foreign policy. When it began to appear that the Honka candidacy had some prospects for success, the second Soviet-manufactured "night frost" suddenly fell on Finland.

The new crisis was in many ways similar to the previous one. It followed and helped amplify the seriousness of reactivated tension over Berlin; it was accompanied by a massive and ostentateous display of Soviet strength (the lunar orbit in the first case, the resumption of nuclear tests in the second). But in certain ominous respects it was reminiscent of the crisis that brought on the Winter War, for it began by a long and menacing note demanding military consultations over an alleged "threat to peace" in Northern Europe, and it was intensified by Soviet-planted rumors that the USSR might again demand bases on Finnish soil. Apparently unable to get any clarification of Soviet intentions, the Finnish ambassador returned dejectedly from Moscow. Meanwhile the USSR broadened its campaign of intimidation by denouncing not only Honka, the Social Democrats, and other anti-Communist politicians, but also the whole system of coalition government in Finland, which allegedly made the USSR unable to be assured of the continuity of friendly policies in Finland.

Kekkonen resolved this crisis also by travelling even further into Russia to see Khrushchev in an improvised cottage near Novosibirsk in Siberia. Kekkonen had already dissolved parliament and scheduled new elections, and Honka had withdrawn from the race. Once again no one knows what transpired between Khrushchev and Kekkonen during their three-hour conversation, but Kekkonen's subsequent attitude was even more patronizing towards his subjects and ungracious towards his political opponents. He implored his people to see the situation as it looks to Russia, echoed the particularly fatuous Soviet claim that Norwegian policy had helped bring on the entire crisis, and in his televised report to the nation called for the retirement from public life of those politicians behind Honka whom Khrushchev had criticized.[21]

[21] See text of television address of November 26, 1961, also his acceptance speech on the occasion of his reelection February 15, 1962 in English translation releases by the Foreign Ministry. The Viennese Social Democratic paper *Arbeiterzeitung,* (December 1, 1961) suggested that Kekkonen had in effect staged the entire crisis with the collaboration of Khrushchev in order to insure reelection—an interpretation that is spelled out at length by Tuure Junnila, one of Kekkonen's conservative opponents in his important study *Noottikriisi—tuoreltaan tulkittuna* [The Note-Crisis—from a fresh point of view] (Helsinki 1962). Any pre-arrangement or secret collaboration seems most unlikely; but there was a good deal of congruity between Kekkonen and the Soviet press on a variety of points. Compare, for instance the list of Finnish political figures denounced by *Pravda* on January 5, 1962, and that denounced by Kekkonen in his principal election speech of January 7, 1962 (text in *Helsingin Sanomat,* January 8). The Agrarian Minister of Justice had actually denounced the Honka coalition in terms still worse than the USSR had used—comparing them with the Nazis and implying that they might even start a "revanchist" war against the USSR. See *Maakansa* (September 5, 1961), 2.

In return for his continued willingness to defend the Soviet position to his countrymen, Kekkonen was granted a release from the immediate need for military consultations with the USSR. Finland was left with explicit responsibility for keeping watch on the development of further "threats to peace" in the area and initiating talks should such a threat arise.

Contemporary Soviet Strategy

The one lesson that Soviet strategists seem to have learned in their dealings with Finland is the need to rely on the state power of the USSR rather than on the Finnish Communist Party for the advancement of Communist objectives. The biggest single weapon in the Communist armory in Finland today is the paralyzing myth of Communist inevitability which the "night frosts" have produced. Soviet theoretical writings on Finland are surprisingly scanty, but they tend to speak of Russian-Finnish relations as an "example of peaceful coexistence,"[22] and are often more lavish in praise of Kekkonen than of the Finnish Communists.

The Soviet decision to work mainly through Kekkonen has produced certain short-term discomfitures for the local Communist party. For two weeks after the Novosibirsk meeting, the Finnish Communist press insisted that both the reserve officers' association and the Conservative Party of Finland should be disbanded—a line never publicly seconded by Moscow. The increased prestige of Kekkonen probably helped the Agrarian Party wrest three parliamentary seats from the Finnish Communists in the 1962 elections.

Despite its almost unchanged Stalinist leadership and some hesitance in denouncing Stalin, the Finnish Communist Party has recently echoed Khrushchev in attacking "sterile dogmatism" and the "infantile disorder" of leftist excess. Clearly the Finnish party has no choice but to accept the line that Khrushchev has defined; and—in view of the creeping psychology of fear and apprehension among non-Communist parties—probably sees many advantages in the new approach. Both the initial confusion and the final satisfaction of the Finnish Communist Party is indicated by the movements of its leadership during and prior to the 22nd Party Congress in the USSR. Willi Pessi, the general secretary of the Finnish party, spent much of 1961 commuting

[22] N. M. Koronen, *Sovetsko-Finlyandskiye otnosheniya—primer mirnogo sosushchestvovaniya* [Soviet Finnish Relations—An Example of Peaceful Coexistence] (Leningrad 1960).

back and forth to Moscow apparently in some confusion, but ended up by denouncing Albania and playing a more prominent role in the congress than had any native Finnish Communist leader in many years. The deepening Sino-Soviet conflict may indeed be giving Finland increased importance in Soviet eyes. For it is one country in which peaceful takeover is a serious possibility, and the Chinese might be shown that peaceful coexistence is not "pacifist capitulationism," but as Pessi put it in a recent featured article in *The World Marxist Review*—"an accelerator of progress and revolution."[23]

An agreed strategy appears to have been evolved for Finland. The first preparatory tactic is the essentially negative one of eliminating the hard core of opposition to communism inside all Finnish political parties. This tactic relies on the proven efficacy of direct pressure from the USSR rather than on unrealistic efforts to renew civil strife by the local Communists. Once this process has softened up Finnish political thinking, the Communists apparently intend to proceed with a new, more sophisticated version of Kuusinen's united front tactics—"from below" if the anti-Communist leaders of the Social Democratic Party can be disposed of, "from above" if the Communists can succeed in participating in a coalition government.

In discussing the latter possibility in the spring of 1962, one Social Democrat suggested that the Communists would probably not request the ministry of interior or any of the other positions previously used for preparing a coup, but would seek only some insignificant portfolio that provides a precedent for Communist participation. Thereafter they would claim such participation as a right that could not be revoked without violating 'the spirit of the peace treaty.' Finland would thus get a coalition government in which only the Communists would have real job security.

Some hope in this otherwise depressing picture is provided by the

[23] Willi Pessi, "Creative Marxism and Revolutionary Policy," *The World Marxist Review*, Vol. VI, no. 6 (June 1963), 3-11. See also another recent article in that journal by a politburo member, Erkki Tuominen, "Parliamentary Activities of the Finnish Communists," Vol. V. no. 12 (December 1962), 32-37. Pessi is an old-line Communist who spent most of the inter-war period either in the USSR or in Finnish jails and now lives in the same Helsinki apartment building as Mrs. Kuusinen. So tightly knit is the veteran leadership of the Finnish party that there have been almost no important personnel changes since the 1930's, so secretive that lists of the politburo of the Central Committee are not published. (Note that they have not even adopted the term presidium). The only younger figure who seems to have penetrated the inner circles of the leadership is Paavo Aitio, the first vice-speaker of the parliament and Communist candidate for president of Finland in the recent elections.

postwar economic modernization of Finnish society. Although Communist voting strength has remained constant, the militancy of the party has been weakened by the growth of "strawberry communism" —the desire to cultivate one's own strawberry patch rather than work for revolution. Many Finnish Communists have become disillusioned by the revelations about Stalin and—ironically—by the increased opportunity to travel in the USSR and compare conditions there with those in Finland. The voting strength of "wasteland communism" has already begun to decline in the red bastion of Finnish Lappland where Communists long relied on ignorance and insularity as well as poverty and climate to foment discontent against the national government. Finally, in 1961, a group of disillusioned Communist intellectuals (including the recently-returned Moscow correspondent of the Finnish Communist newspaper and the chairman of the Finno-Soviet Friendship Society) formed a self-proclaimed "party of the opposition" and published a new dissident journal, *Tilanne* [Situation].[24]

On the eve of the first "night frost" in 1958, the Finnish economy was peculiarly vulnerable to Soviet trade boycotts, unemployment was relatively high, and per capita gross national product was little more than half that of neighboring Sweden. Since then, the economy has prospered and become more diversified, unemployment has declined almost to the vanishing point, and there has been a dramatic increase in popular consumer items such as television sets and automobiles. The most serious continuing economic vulnerability is the dependence of Finland on timber products for three-fourths of its exports. Finland's prosperity has been built largely on its expanding trade with the West, but it might well be driven to the East for markets if the USSR refused to permit Finland to keep its timber prices competitive with those of an expanding Common Market.

The slumless and delinquency-free cities of Finland absorbed the

[24] *Tilanne* has become a valuable medium for public communication by former communists and has introduced the works of revisionist writers like Kolakowski to Finnish left-wing thought (See *Tilanne,* No. 1, (1962), 111-116; and No. 2-3, 157-160). The first issue was timed to appear in November 1961 on the occasion of the fifth anniversary of the Hungarian revolution (See *Tilanne,* No. 1, (1961), 17). The *Tilanne* group sent a questionnaire to the entire Communist Party leadership and has succeeded in winning away a large number of its relatively few intellectual supporters. Its generally nationalistic and neutralist tone bears some points of resemblance with the Socialist Peoples Party in Denmark, a form of national communism led by Aksel Larsen (See lead editorial in *Tilanne,* No. 1 (1961), 3) which has almost totally destroyed the regular Danish Communist Party and was roundly denounced in a *Pravda* editorial reprinted in English in *New Times,* No. 22, (May 30, 1962), 33-36.

entire 10 percent population increase of the 1950's, and the manufacturing and construction industries have accounted for almost all the increase of nearly 50 percent of Finnish output. Industrialization and urbanization do not appear to have affected Communist strength one way or the other so far. Economic prosperity may decrease the appeal of domestic Communist slogans in the years ahead, but the same prosperity may render Finland increasingly vulnerable to the type of political and psychological intimidation on which the Communist campaign in Finland is currently based. Prosperity has encouraged complacency and a growing desire "not to have to think about" long-term political questions. A sceptical revision of the long sacred image of Finnish heroism has become intellectually fashionable through such recent books as *Farewell National Romanticism, National Realism,* and the third part of the epic Finnish novel *Here Under the Northern Star.*[25]

In becoming a more mobile, mechanized, and modern society, the Finns may have lost some of the qualities of dogged self-reliance and perseverance that enabled them to survive earlier challenges to their independence. Certainly there has long been a need for greater sophistication in popular thinking about foreign affairs, and there may be some justification to the contention that Kekkonen is playing a cagey game with East as well as West. But whatever the intentions of Kekkonen and his articulate young apologists, the practical effect of their policies has already been to undermine much of the national unity and determination to resist blackmail on which Finnish independence and self-respect has been built. In the world of Finnish reality (as distinct from academic realism) "farewell national romanticism" may prove the equivalent of "farewell national independence."

The speed and ruthlessness with which the USSR may push for Communist take-over in Finland will, of course, be dependent on the overall order of Soviet state priorities. The main Soviet concern in Europe is clearly Germany and the main objective in Northern Europe is encouraging the erosion of the weak northern flank of NATO. Both "night frosts" were used in part to dramatize the seriousness with

[25] Olle Tuominen, *Hyvästi Kansallisromantiikka* [Farewell National Romanticism] (Helsinki 1961); Kalervo Siikala, *Kansallinen Realismi* [National Realism] (Jyväskylä 1960); Väinö Linna, *Täällä Pohjois Tähden Alla* [Here Under the North Star] (Helsinki 1963) III. Economic statistics on Finland are taken or extrapolated from *Facts about Finland* (Helsinki 1960) and from the annual statistical reviews under Finland in the yearbook of the *Encyclopedia Americana.*

which the USSR regarded increased German strength; and the continued threat of a take-over in Finland is obviously more effective than an actual take-over would be in furthering priority objectives. These considerations—rather than the often alleged possibility of a Swedish defection to NATO—almost certainly account for the willingness of the USSR to settle for less immediate concessions from Finland than might otherwsie have been exacted from the "night frosts." The peremptory insistence of Kosygin that Finland sharply increase its trade with the USSR, during his surprise visit to Helsinki in April 1963, may be an ominous harbinger of new pressures to come.[26]

Another reason for the relative slowness of the USSR to move against Finland is the increasing prospect that Kekkonen and the Agrarian Party may half-unwittingly be converted into a semi-permanent ally of Communism. Although more conservative domestically than the Social Democratic Party, the Agrarian League is considerably less experienced in international affairs. The leadership that has emerged under Kekkonen's authoritarian guidance is noticeably more pro-Soviet than its up-country supporters. In the last few years prominent Agrarians have publicly supported the Soviet position on Berlin and even suggested that the example of Poland proves that national independence can be maintained within the Soviet orbit.[27] The left wing of the Agrarian Party under the President's son, Matti Kekkonen, favors a conscious Eastern orientation of Finnish economic policy and cultural life. Even the so-called right wing of the party leadership seems remarkably naive about the new Soviet tactics. When one leading member of this group was asked how he could be sure that the Soviet "list" of unacceptable Finnish politicians would not someday be broadened to include "unfriendly" Agrarians like himself, he replied that Ambassador Zakharov had personally assured him that the Soviet Union seeks to exclude only Tanner and Leskinen.

Many important dealings with the USSR now appear to be conducted directly between Kekkonen and Soviet officials without consulting more than a small circle of trusted appointees (such as Prime Minister Karjalainen, Kekkonen's former personal secretary). Two important Finnish-Soviet agreements since the second "night frost" were presented by Kekkonen as *faits accomplis,* and have led to plaintive if futile protests in the press and Parliament against the allegedly un-

[26] See the analysis by Werner Wiskari in *New York Times,* April 7, 1963, 33.
[27] Pentti Saarikoski, "Onko Suomesta Sillanrakintajäksi?" [Can Finland Become a Bridgebuilder?], *Maakansa* (October 21, 1961).

constitutional secret Presidential agreements with a foreign power: the marked increase in grain purchases from the USSR in the spring of 1962 and the agreement to reopen the Saimaa Canal in September of the same year. Amidst the relative calm of late 1963 and 1964 popular approval of Kekkonen grew, and Finnish Communism was increasingly plagued with internal dissension.[28] Early in 1965, however, the post-Khrushchev leadership entertained the leaders of the Finnish Communist party, and endorsed a set of proposals for increased economic interdependence between the two nations. A subsequent visit to Moscow by Kekkonen elicited some seemingly gratuitous criticism by him of Western policies and caused renewed apprehension in Finland about the fragility of its non-aligned position.[29]

Whatever the future may hold for Finland, its previous history shows (1) that an extremely exposed and isolated nation with a large Communist party can resist communism if the Communists are unable to gain a significant number of domestic collaborators, and (2) that force, intimidation, and psychological warfare are important in the achievement of political gains even where political life is ostensibly orderly and economic well-being generally assured. The Finns resisted Soviet occupation twice despite defeats in 1940 and 1944, because they proved on the battlefield that the costs in Soviet lives would be unacceptably high. The Finns held off Finnish communism successfully when it was in an aggressive mood in the high Stalin era after the war, because—for all their assets—the Finnish Communists were afraid of reprisals. If Finland capitulates to Communism in the 1960's, it will not be simply because Soviet power has increased and Soviet tactics have become more imaginative. It will take place because Finnish political leaders have become afraid or complacent, and have lost the respect that their ancestors had earned by an unwillingness to resist with comparable firmness the new and more subtle tactics of their historic adversary.

[28] Demands of younger party members for greater freedom from Soviet control and responsiveness to local conditions were voiced not only in *Tilanne*, but even in the party daily *Kansan Uutiset* and (somewhat less forcefully) in the theoretical organ *Kommunisti*. These discussions and the organizational structure of the party are treated in detail in a section of the second volume of the collection *Communism in Europe* to be published by the M.I.T. Press under the editorship of William Griffith. Useful material and analyses generally sympathetic with Kekkonen's policies are included in the invaluable collection of the Finnish Political Science Association, *Finnish Foreign Policy*, Vammala, 1963.

[29] See dispatch in *New York Times*, March 11, 1965, p. 10; and editorial March 13, 1965, p. 24.

6

The Southeast Asian Insurrectionary Movements

RUTH T. McVEY

By the summer of 1947 it was clear that the initial postwar period of Communist strategy, based on relative moderation and alliance with non-Communist groupings, was coming to an end. In Soviet comments on the colonial question, two new interpretations of the cooperation of Communists with nationalists appeared, foreshadowing a debate on Communist policy in Asia which was to contitnue for more than a year. One leaned toward the radical proletarianism of the "united front from below," which the Comintern had advocated from 1928 to 1934 and which in its colonial context rejected any compromise with non-Communist nationalism. The other, looking toward the example of the Chinese Communists' increasing success in their struggle with the Kuomintang, held that the Communists could utilize the slogans and forces of national revolution as long as final control of the revolutionary movement lay in their hands. Both views, however, agreed that there was no basis for an alliance with bourgeois nationalist groups on a basis of equality; and both agreed that there could be no compromise with those who temporized with the imperialists—i.e., the Western powers.[1]

In September 1947 the official inauguration of the new period of intransigence took place with the establishment of the Cominform and the promulgation of the so-called Zhdanov doctrine. This new dogma divided the world into two hostile camps—that of socialism, embodying those who declared openly for the Soviet side, and that of imperialism, comprising all others. Interpreting the line for Asia, the Soviet party made it clear that neutralist nationalism was to be in-

[1] For a discussion of the development of the Soviet attitude during 1947, see John H. Kautsky, *Moscow and the Communist Party of India* (New York 1956), 24-34; and Ruth T. McVey, *The Soviet View of the Indonesian Revolution* (Ithaca 1957), 24-37. For the Soviet interpretation of the two-camp doctrine for underdeveloped areas, see Ye. Zhukov, "Obostreniye krizisa kolonialnoy sistemy" [The Sharpening of the Crisis of the Colonial System], *Bol'shevik,* No. 23 (1947), 51-64.

cluded among the forces of the enemy camp, and in the ensuing months the Southeast Asian Communist movements were made aware of the hardened international view. A Communist-sponsored conference of Southeast Asian youth and students, held in Calcutta in February 1948, was one obvious point of international contact. At this meeting harsh sentiments were expressed towards all governments that compromised with the West, and Communist Chinese and Viet Minh representatives extolled the virtues of armed struggle.[2] A few days later, the Communist Party of India held its congress in the same city; its sessions, attended by several of the Southeast Asian youth conference delegates, confirmed the party's December 1947 replacement of the moderate leader Joshi with the intransigent Ranadive, and discussed the advantages of disruptive strike action in the cities, and agrarian revolt in the countryside.[3]

We do not know just what international elements made the most impression on the Southeast Asian Communists in deciding for violence: whether it was the arguments of the Soviet-sponsored two-camp doctrine; the even more intransigent stand of the Yugoslavs (then the most radical group in the Cominform and whose delegates took an active part in the Calcutta meetings); the Chinese Communist or Viet Minh revolutionary examples; or the opinions of the Indian Communist Party. What is abundantly clear, however, is that violence did occur: in March, the Burma Communist Party rose against the newly independent U Nu government; in June, the Malayan Communist Party took to the jungle in rebellion; in August, the Communist-oriented Hukbalahap renewed its insurrection against the Philippine government with the declaration that it would refuse to consider any future offers for negotiation; and a month later the Indonesian Communists engaged in a brief but bitter clash with the forces of the Republic.

[2] The major account of the conference by its sponsors is *Hands Off South East Asia: Conference of the Youth and Students of South East Asia—Fighting for Freedom and Independence, Calcutta, February 19-28, 1948* (Prague 1948). For some interpretations of the meeting and the events surrounding it, see J. H. Brimmell, *Communism in South East Asia* (London 1959), 249-263; Kautsky, 33-42; Frank N. Trager, "The Impact of Marxism," in *Marxism in Southeast Asia* (Stanford 1959), 263-273; and Ruth T. McVey, *The Calcutta Conference and the Southeast Asian Uprisings* (Ithaca 1958).

[3] For the line adopted by the congress, see Communist Party of India, *Political Thesis: Adopted at the Second Congress, Calcutta, Feb. 28—Mar. 6, 1948* (Bombay 1948); see also B.T. Ranadive, *Nehru Govt. Declares War Against Toilers* (Bombay 1948). For an analysis of the congress and the events preceding it, see Gene D. Overstreet and Marshall Windmiller, *Communism in India* (Berkeley and Los Angeles 1959), 252-275.

Though these revolts were unsuccessful, they were all of serious magnitude. While the viewpoint of Communists abroad may have persuaded hesitant leaders that they must choose for violence, it could not create rebellions out of the blue. The ingredients for insurrection were already there, in the form of frustrated party leaderships heading restive segments of the population, and it is with these local elements that we shall be concerned. The picture that we shall draw will necessarily be over-simplified—for politics, being human, is disorderly, and no set of general categories can contain all the ingredients that make a political event. Within these limits, however, we can discern certain elements that gave the revolts a common character, and others that made them very different indeed.

The Sources of Popular Support

The countries in which the revolts took place had certain common characteristics other than their geographic location. They were all predominantly agrarian societies which had been deeply affected by the development of modern cash-crop economies aimed at the world market. Control of this production lay largely in the hands of foreigners, and foreign minorities made up a good part of the commercial middle class. All of these countries were colonies prior to the Second World War and were exposed to profound social, political, and economic disorientation during the war. In the immediate postwar period they found themselves in various final stages of achieving independence and were deeply engaged by the problems of defining their future relationship with the former colonial rulers and determining a pattern of national leadership. That pattern was clearly emergent by early 1948, and it was apparent that it would lie outside Communist hands. The Communists of all these countries were therefore concerned with the problem of preventing the realization or consolidation of these patterns of control, and with preserving the wartime legacy of disorder to gain the initiative which they had lost or failed to achieve. Beyond this, however, conditions in Malaya, Burma, the Philippines, and Indonesia diverged, and the nature of the Communist movements and the character of their revolts differed accordingly.

In Burma and Indonesia, communism found its greatest response in the decade before the war among the younger nationalistically inclined members of the indigenous elite. Exposed to Western education and ideas, and oriented by tradition and opportunity toward government careers, they were well aware of the limitations which the colonial condition placed on their chances of advancement and on their country's general progress. Rejecting most of their own cultural traditions, but not prepared to accept unquestioningly the premises of the West, they found much that was attractive in the utopian promise of Marxism, in the Leninist denunciation of imperialism, and above all in the concept of a historically inevitable victory, achieved not by generations of patient development but soon and by violence.

No real Communist party existed in either country in the decade before the war, though Indonesia had had a significant Communist party based on the urban proletariat, which collapsed in the wake of an abortive uprising in 1926-1927.[4] In Burma, Marxist ideas achieved wide currency among the Thakins, a nationalist group composed mostly of students at the University of Rangoon, who were to form the core of Burma's post-colonial leadership. Some of them—Thakin Ba Hein, Thakin Soe, Thakin Thein Pe, and perhaps Thakin Than Tun—began even before the Second World War to consider themselves consciously as Communists. The nationalist association of Indonesians studying in the Netherlands, Perhimpunan Indonesia, had passed into progressively more radical hands during the 1920's, and by 1930 its control lay with leaders who were fairly thoroughly committed to communism. Former members of this association played a role in Indonesia's nationalist leadership equivalent to that of Burma's Thakins, and thus, although communism had affected only a very small group in either country prior to the Second World War, its toehold was an extremely strategic one.

The fact that Marxist-Leninist concepts were so widely shared in revolutionary nationalist circles, that the young nationalists had very few vested organizational interests, and that their minds were fixed on the overthrow of colonialism and not on the control and structure

[4] Brimmell, 120-121, states that a Communist party was founded in Burma in 1939, with Aung San as its secretary general; and Brigadier Maung Maung asserts that Aung San was one of twelve founders of a prewar Communist party, "On the March with Aung San," in Maung Maung (ed.), *Aung San of Burma* (The Hague 1962), 64. Most accounts, however, refer only to the establishment of Marxist study groups among the Thakins in this period. It is possible that if a Communist party had been organized at this time it was a pro-forma affair created by the Thakins as part of their effort to gain international revolutionary aid; they had first intended to seek such support from the Chinese Communists rather than the Japanese.

In Indonesia, an illegal Communist group was formed in 1935 by Musso, an exiled PKI leader who returned briefly from the Soviet Union for this purpose. Most of its members were soon arrested; the party seems to have continued on a semi-active basis as a sort of study group for the rest of the colonial period, but even according to Communist accounts it succeeded in accomplishing little more than its survival.

of the state after independence, all made for an extreme fluidity of the lines between Communist and non-Communist. The international character of communism was not seen by the revolutionary nationalists as antithetical to their interests, but rather as a potential source of guidance and aid for their own contemplated anti-colonial rebellions. Divisions there certainly were within the evolving political elites of Indonesia and Burma, but the meaningful ones were based on collaboration versus non-collaboration with the colonial regime, on orientation towards traditional cultural and religious values or towards secular nationalism, and not on adherence to or rejection of communism.[5]

In Malaya and the Philippines, the local elites had little reason to be attracted by Communist ideas. Malayan leadership was split into competing ethnic groups. The Malays hewed to their traditional culture and viewed the British presence as protection against the encroachment of the numerically and economically powerful Chinese. The Malayan Chinese leadership was a business elite, presiding over a highly mobile and entrepreneurially-oriented community which was concerned in its political loyalties not with Malaya but with China and the Kuomintang. The Philippine political elite was similarly conservative, consisting for the most part of great families with considerable land holdings and connections with American business interests and markets. Moreover, it was in the unique position of facing a ruling power that by the 1930's was patently eager to be rid of its dependency. The Philippine elite played a meaningful role in governing the islands, controlled the most highly developed party organizations in colonial Southeast Asia, and participated in the distribution of patronage and power. It had a definite interest in independence, but a very qualified one in social and economic change, or in the creation of any situation which might shake its pre-eminent position.

Communism in Malaya and the Philippines, therefore, possessed no apparent prospects for a road to power through the conversion of key members of the national revolutionary movements or the securing of key spots in post-colonial nationalist governments. But for all the obvious weaknesses which this gave the Communist potential for these countries, it did provide certain advantages. For one thing, it made

[5] The collection *Political Change in Underdeveloped Countries* (New York 1962), John H. Kautsky, ed., contains several illuminating discussions of the attitude of nationalist intellectuals toward revolution and communism; see especially the introductory essay by the editor, and the article by Harry J. Benda on "Non-Western Intelligentsias as Political Elites." For a general discussion of insurrection in the period after the Second World War, see Brian Crozier, *The Rebels* (Boston 1960).

the Communists aware of themselves as a distinctive force, conscious that their conflict of interest with the non-Communist national leadership was both inherent and immediate, and that their chances for power depended on forging an organizational weapon that was their own. For the fluid lines between Communist and non-Communist within the nationalist elites of Burma and Indonesia deceived not only the nationalists but also the Communists. This fluidity made the Communists less aware of the need for an organizational base on which they could firmly rely, and they derived little idea of how much popular support they could muster in a contest with the non-Communist national leadership. In general they put off the question of what would happen if a nationalist government were formed which allotted them an unsatisfactory role.

Since the Communists in the Philippines and Malaya were in general opposition to the indigenous elites, their activities took on the aspect of class struggle. Their efforts among the masses brought them very different followings, for the Philippine Communists emerged as leaders of agrarian unrest, while the Malayan party headed a proletarian movement.

Communism in Malaya arose from the left wing of the Kuomintang organization which had developed among the Singapore Chinese. Following the 1927 split between the Nationalists and Communists in China it emerged as a separate group, first called the Nan Yang (South Seas) Communist Party and then, in 1930, the Malayan Communist Party (MCP).[6] The party was illegal and therefore underground; its major source of popular strength was the Malayan Federation of Labor, which had been founded in 1926 as the Nan Yang Federation of Labor and was originally active principally among the Singapore harbor workers. Though the Communist movement was nearly extinguished in 1930 by the arrest of a Comintern emissary and the subsequent capture of many of the MCP's political and labor leaders, it had recovered sufficiently by the middle of the decade to take advantage of the general labor unrest that followed the initial recovery of industry from the effects of the Depression.

[6] For descriptions of the emergence of the MCP, see René Onraet, *Singapore—A Police Background* (London n.d.), 116-117; J. H. Brimmell, *A Short History of the Malayan Communist Party* (Singapore 1956), 11-12; and Gene Z. Hanrahan, *The Communist Struggle in Malaya* (New York 1956), 11-13, 17. The Nan Yang Communist Party was given charge over the movement in Burma, Thailand, Indonesia, and Indochina as well as Malaya itself. The MCP was designed as a purely Malayan party but was given supervision of Communist activity in the Netherlands Indies, Siam, and Burma until such time as party organizations there were able to function on their own.

For the Chinese workers in Malaya, stability and protection was customarily provided by benevolent and clan associations representing the area of their origin, and through the patronage of labor contractors. The Communist unions became competitors of these forms of association and aid, attracting those who felt the older sources of leadership to be too traditionalist or not sufficiently active in promoting the interests of the poor. Because of the existing tendency of workers to join in associations, the Malayan Communists did not face the same difficulties in organizing an amorphous proletariat as did their colleagues elsewhere in Southeast Asia, and their unions tended to be somewhat more stable and less dependent on personal leadership. Moreover, the Malayan Chinese were relatively accustomed to clandestine association, and many of the earlier traditions and techniques of the Chinese secret societies lived on in the new parties and labor organizations. The Communist labor unions had their greatest influence among the Hailamese and Hakkas, who were economically and socially on the lowest rungs of the Chinese community and whose homes in China had been centers of Left-Kuomintang and Communist sympathy in the 1920's. As immigrants of fairly recent vintage, they were also more open to the detraditionalizing effects of urbanization than were workers with settled roots in the country. This "tribal" identification helped the Communists in the difficult task of extending their labor influence beyond the major urban centers to the mines and rubber plantations in the less easily accessible parts of the country. Moreover, the Hailamese—the Sicilians of China—were noted for keeping to themselves, and the fact that they filled a considerable portion of the Communist ranks helped assure the movement of a greater capacity for sub rosa organization than the other Southeast Asian Communist movements could boast.[7]

The Philippine Communist Party also began as a labor-oriented movement, having been formed in 1930 from the Congress of Philippine Working-Men, which had split off the year before from the Philippine Labor Congress. Had this remained its field of concentration, it probably would not have developed into a serious political element, for the prospects of developing an effective revolutionary labor movement in the Philippines were dim indeed. On the other hand, the agrarian situation did provide a considerable opportunity for political action, for the indebted and landlord-ridden peasantry of

[7] See Victor Purcell, *The Chinese in Malaya* (London 1948), 215. According to Onraet, 109-111, the left wing of the Malayan Kuomintang, from which the MCP arose, was almost entirely composed of Hailamese.

Central Luzon had a long history of rebelliousness, culminating in the violent but quickly suppressed Sakdalista revolt of 1935. Various peasant movements had risen in the area; like the Sakdals, they tended to consider themselves basically outside of and opposed to the established governmental process, and they thus offered fuel for political violence. Most of them led a highly ephemeral existence; one of the more enduring ones was the KPMP (National Union of Peasants in the Philippines), which had been founded in 1924 by Jacinto Manahan, a sometime Communist leader. It was not until 1937, however, when the Philippine Communist Party emerged from five years of illegality, that it gained access to a significant peasant organization. At that time, with American Communist mediation, it began an amalgamation with the Socialist Party into a Popular Front (Frente Popular). Pedro Abad Santos, the Socialist leader, had won a large and loyal following in central Luzon through his idealistic devotion to the cause of the rural poor, and the acquisition of his agrarian adherents swung the orientation of the Communists from the cities to the countryside.[8]

The mass bases of the Philippine and Malayan Communist movements presented no restraint to political violence; indeed, the eagerness of their supporters to undertake direct action at times hampered the parties considerably in building their organizations and timing their campaigns. Thus, although the Frente Popular concentrated on electoral activities and presented itself as a reasonable reform movement in an appeal for general public support, the areas in which it was strongest were also the places where peasants burned cane fields, seized land, and attacked the local landlords. The Communists may have given informal encouragement to these outbreaks of violence, but it was not consonant with the domestic or international Popular Front philosophy. The point is that the Communists were not really in a position to stop the violence, for the peasants saw little use of organizing unless there was some prospect of action, and since they were all too conscious of their weakness in bargaining with the land-

[8] For descriptions of the origins of the Philippine Communist Party and the development of the Frente Popular, see Alvin H. Scaff, *The Philippine Answer to Communism* (Stanford 1955), 9-11, 14-16, 20-21; and Congress of the Philippines, House of Representatives, *Report on the Illegality of the Communist Party of the Philippines* (Manila 1951), 74-79, 108-109. A stimulating discussion of the causes of peasant unrest in central Luzon may be found in Frances Lucille Starner, *Magsaysay and the Philippine Peasantry* (Berkeley and Los Angeles 1961), 3-20; and see also Erich H. Jacoby, *Agrarian Unrest in Southeast Asia* (London 1961), 191-219.

lords the only activity which showed promise in their eyes was violence. This was of advantage to the Communists in promoting insurrectionary action, but hindered their efforts to appear as a moderate and reasonable element in periods when this course seemed to their greater advantage.

Both the peasant and labor associations, then and in the early postwar period, tended to be movements with a following rather than organizations with a membership; their leaders relied heavily on loyalties to their person, and this frequently necessitated emphasis on boldness and on agitational rather than organizational activity. As is common in the early stages of labor organization, the workers tended to be interested in unions only as strike weapons. It was very difficult to preserve continuing participation when no such action was in sight, and in order to preserve their momentum unions therefore undertook strikes in which the likelihood of success was extremely slim. The economic demands of the strikers were often unclear, as their action was frequently a demonstration of defiance against the existing order of things as much as an attempt to force the redress of specific grievances. The usefulness of such an attitude for revolutionary purposes is obvious. Indeed, the 1936 strike in Malay's Batu Arang coal mines took on the aspect of a miniature revolt, for the workers seized the mines and established a "soviet" government which was deposed only by force of arms.[9] The problem for the Communists therefore was not how to create a desire for direct action among their followers, but how to control and channel it without losing their loyalties.

Linked to this question was the problem of how the Communists were to expand their support beyond the deeply disaffected groups which formed their original mass base. Insofar as Communist political violence aimed at a seizure of power, the usefulness of the Malayan Chinese workers and the central Luzon peasantry had definite limitations. In a country where the proletariat was neither very large nor well organized, and where it possessed few financial resources to fall back on, violence by the workers could at best topple a government which was already in the last stages of disintegration. The agrarian base of Philippine communism had considerably more potential in this respect, for it encompassed a sizable and strategically located part of

[9] For descriptions of the Batu Arang strike and accounts of prewar labor unrest in Malaya, see Onraet, 107, 115-117; Hanrahan, 21-25; and Virginia Thompson, *Labor Problems in Southeast Asia* (New Haven 1947), 103-107. For a discussion of MCP organization of the Malayan Chinese workers in the prewar period see Lucian W. Pye, *Guerrilla Communism in Malaya* (Princeton 1956), 51-55, 58-62.

the population which could afford to resist authority for some time because it produced its own food. Nonetheless, this following represented only one sector of the population, and one contained in a fairly limited area. In order to have an effective agrarian revolution it would have been necessary to persuade other groups of the peasant population that this was also their fight, and since peasants in other areas possessed differing grievances and ambitions, and were conscious of various linguistic and cultural differences, this was not a simple matter. Both the Malayan and Philippine Communists thus confronted serious problems in maximizing the "we" of popular discontent against the "they" of constituted authority, and they were to acquire their best chance of doing so during the Second World War.

The Anti-Japanese Armies

The character of the Communist movements under discussion was already emerging before the Second World War. However, the movements' future proportions were only dimly apparent, for communism in the prewar period operated on the discontented fringes of seemingly stable and largely unpoliticized societies. It was the Japanese occupation which created the conditions for revolution by overthrowing Western colonial rule, disregarding the established channels of social and political control, and setting into violent motion the hitherto slumbering forces of change. Moreover, the rigors of the occupation were such that the Japanese provided a focus for heartfelt general resentment—a factor of considerable importance to the Communists of Malaya and the Philippines, where the colonial relationship had not resulted in sufficient antipathy to provide the impetus for general rebellion.

As entrenched elites, with no experience or interest in revolution, the Philippine and Malayan indigenous leaderships possessed little potentiality for mass agitation and organization, and they hesitated to abandon their considerable vested political and economic interest in the present for the sake of a highly uncertain future. Consequently, when the Japanese came they were ill-equipped to lead or even to play a significant part in movements of popular resistance, and the Japanese kept them well aware of the fact that they had much to lose if they did not cooperate. The leaders of the Malayan Chinese community, insofar as they were spared by the invading forces, were compelled to buy their protection in a manner that not only ruined them financially but lost them popular esteem. The Philippine political leaders remaining behind on the islands were offered the privileges and protection of participation in a formally independent government, and most of them, after initial hesitation, took advantage of the opportunity. The creation of the major organizations of popular resistance thus fell to the only political force oriented towards armed action and against the Japanese—the Communists.

During the prewar period, the Malayan Communists had acquired a certain influence beyond the proletariat through the fact that some teachers in Chinese-language schools conveyed their sympathies for the Communist movement in China to their pupils.[10] But it was with the 1937 outbreak of China's war with Japan that Malayan Communism received its greatest opportunity to secure broader support, for it set to making itself the spokesman for anti-Japanese sentiment. Being much more effective in this than the local Kuomintang, the MCP began to appear as the most active representative of Chinese nationalism in Malaya. In March 1942 the Malayan People's Anti-Japanese Army (MPAJA) was formed from Communist guerrillas who had been trained by the British but were under the command of the MCP. The MPAJA's Communist core was augmented by Chinese patriots, by suspected radicals fleeing Japanese anti-leftist roundups, and by those who preferred the hardships of a jungle existence to those of urban wartime life. The MPAJA had the general support of the rural Chinese, whose numbers were augmented greatly by those who left the cities during the war to grow their own food. It was this group—which numbered half a million by the end of the occupation—on which the MPAJA relied for supplies and intelligence. The guerrilla army established the Malayan People's Anti-Japanese Union (MPAJU) to organize this support and to provide a means of control over the village population.

The MPAJA was not, however, a peasant movement either in terms of support or orientation. The bulk of the peasantry was Malay and had little sympathy for what was so clearly a Chinese movement. Similarly, the MPAJA drew little support from the Indians, though this group comprised a considerable portion of the plantation workers, who had little reason to be satisfied with their lot. The MCP had tried to overcome the ethnic boundaries of its following quite early in its prewar career, but it had never succeeded in attracting more than a very few Malay or Indian supporters.[11] The MPAJA fared no better,

[10] See Purcell, 232; Hanrahan, 8.

[11] MCP efforts to win Indian and Malay sympathy included the establishment of a Unification Committee in 1934, which was aimed at extending activity to other ethnic groups; the party also sought to establish liaison with the Communist Party of India to further this aim. See Hanrahan, 18; Purcell, 218; Pye, 49-51, 56-57.

though it called itself the "Three-Star Army" and carried on its struggle in the name of all three ethnic groups. Thus, though the Malayan Communists succeeded to a considerable extent in overcoming their class limitations through the anti-Japanese resistance, they made their communal boundaries more distinct in the process.

The Philippine Frente Popular had, in the manner of popular fronts, declared its principal aim to be that of opposing fascism. When the American position in the islands collapsed, the leaders of the Front outlined a plan for popular resistance which was realized the following March in the form of the People's Anti-Japanese Army (Hukbong Bayan Laban Sa Hapon, or Hukbalahap) and its civilian auxiliary, the Barrio [Village] United Defence Corps. The resistance movement was based in central and parts of southern Luzon and drew its strength largely from the Popular Front's rural following. The nature of its support meant that the Hukbalahap played a dual role of anti-Japanese guerrilla army and peasant insurrectionary movement. The chaos following the ouster of the Americans had brought rural tensions to the surface; a number of landlords were killed or dispossessed by marauders and rebellious tenants, while others fled to the comparative safety of the cities. The Huks declared their amity towards "patriotic" landlords (while reducing their share in their tenants' crops) but encouraged the redistribution of lands belonging to collaborators. Since the latter group was considered to include both those who fled the countryside and those who delivered grain to the Japanese, the number of acceptable landlords was few. This class-based activity increased the Huks' support in the centers of rural unrest, but it also caused the more conservative Filipinos to look on its claims to represent anti-Japanese patriotism with considerable distrust. Their misgivings were communicated to the American forces returning to the Philippines, so that the Hukbalahap was generally not accorded recognition as a partisan group and the Huk leaders Luis Taruc and Castro Alejandrino were jailed for a time by the military as a threat to the public peace.

The Hukbalahap has often been accused of devoting more energy to its struggle with other Filipinos than to the fight against the Japanese. From the point of view of preparing for a seizure of power, however, the reverse would seem to be true. Writing with the wisdom of hindsight, Taruc declared that the two major mistakes of the wartime Hukbalahap had been that it did not emphasize its opposition to American as well as Japanese imperialism, and that it did not set up a government of its own. The first mistake, he related, meant that the Huk adherents were not prepared to continue the struggle on an anti-American basis and were not convinced that the independence received in 1946 was a sham. The Huks, he decided, should have promoted the formation of a liberation government in opposition to the puppet regime of José Laurel, and should have directed their efforts less to the harassment of the Japanese and more to the extension of their government's influence as far as possible beyond the core area of Huk support. In this way the Hukbalahap would have established its claims to legitimacy, and would not at the end of the war have placed itself in subordination to hostile political forces whose authority it was bound to contest.[12]

Whether such a course would have brought a Huk victory is open to considerable question. However, given the general social disorganization brought by the war, the popular prestige of the Hukbalahap as a resistance movement of national stature, and the fact that the Philippine political elite was deeply compromised by collaboration, a Huk-inspired anti-Japanese coalition might well have garnered considerable popular support. It is most unlikely that the returning American forces would have negotiated with a Huk-led resistance government. They had few illusions about the Huks and had a Philippine government-in-exile of their own. Nor is it likely that the Filipino population would have greeted the American invasion initially as anything but a liberation. However, Filipino nationalism was not absent, and the Japanese had already granted the country formal independence. If an anti-Japanese resistance regime had effectively established its popular claims and had demanded that the Americans negotiate with it, their refusal to do so might well have fused nationalist sentiment with the forces of social revolution into a rebellion of major proportions.

The Hukbalahap did not make a serious effort at utilizing the war for a seizure of power, however, and neither did the MPAJA. Both of them did undertake some of the functions of public administration. The Barrio United Defence Corps acted as a shadow government in the villages it controlled, while the MPAJA was the only effective governing force in Malaya during the interregnum between the Japanese surrender and the British re-occupation. The idea of establish-

[12] Luis Taruc, *Born of the People* (New York 1953), 199. For the program adopted by the Hukbalahap at the time of its formation, see Bernard Seeman and Lawrence Salisbury, *Cross Currents in the Philippines* (New York 1946), 33-34.

ing a regime under its control was also by no means foreign to either movement. The creation of an independent Malayan republic had been the first point on the MCP's 1940 and 1943 programs, and in the latter it was added that as soon as the Japanese were defeated the MPAJA should convert itself into a national army for the securing of Malaya's freedom.[13] In September 1944 the Hukbalahap declared itself for the establishment of a people's liberation government; it subsequently appointed administrations in various towns and villages under Huk control and made an effort to extend its influence beyond the area of Huk guerrilla operations. However, the Huks established no central authority and hence no claim to represent the nation as a whole, and they abandoned their efforts to extend their popular base at the time of the American landings.

With the ouster of the Japanese and the establishment of military government control, the Huks disbanded; their counter-government, once its officials were replaced by the Osmeña administration, quietly ceased even the ephemeral existence it had enjoyed. The MPAJA took a similarly diffident stand towards the seizure of power. At a conference with British military agents in January 1944, the MPAJA commanders not only promised to cooperate fully in maintaining postwar order, but also agreed to discuss no questions of postwar policy with the British military mission—thereby abstaining from demanding concessions at the point when they were most likely to obtain them.[14] The Communists quietly dropped their slogans of immediate independence, and when the British arrived the MPAJA surrendered its authority over the areas where it had established an administration and conceded, with some grumbling but no real resistance, to the disarming and disbanding of its guerrilla forces.[15]

Just why the Malayan and Philippine Communists did not use the war to bid for power remains a puzzle. Perhaps they thought that this

[13] See Purcell, 261; and Brimmell, *Communism,* 197-199, for descriptions of these programs. According to Brimmell, *A Short History,* 14-17, the MCP dropped the demand for immediate independence from its program directly following the Japanese surrender in order to allow it to assume overt activities alongside its covert ones under a postwar colonial regime.

[14] See Hanrahan, 42, for a discussion of the MPAJA's failure to make demands and the possible reasons for this.

[15] Discussions of the MPAJA's wartime career may be found in the previously-cited works on Malayan Communism; see further F. Spencer Chapman, *The Jungle is Neutral* (London 1949) and John Cross, *Red Jungle* (London 1958) for accounts by British officers who worked with the MPAJA. For a Malayan Chinese account of the occupation and resistance see Chin Kee Onn, *Malaya Upside Down* (Singapore 1946), especially 99-131, 201-205.

was not in line with the Soviet-Western alliance, though such considerations did not similarly hinder Communists in Vietnam, Albania, Greece, and Yugoslavia. Reportedly it was the Philippine Communist leader Vincente Lava who argued most strongly for the establishment of a resistance government composed of a coalition of all anti-Japanese groups. He did this against considerable opposition by those in the Hukbalahap who wished to come to an understanding with Osmeña's exile regime.[16] Since it is not at all clear that the Hukbalahap of this period was completely under Communist control, the reluctance of more moderately-inclined leaders may have played a considerable role in hindering the effective execution of such a step. The decision to cross the Rubicon of an independence declaration was in any case not an easy one to take, for the Huks would have been faced with the prospect of defying a strong American occupation force directly following the Japanese, while the MPAJA would have had to face Malay as well as British opposition. Whatever the causes of the Communists' hesitation, it meant that they passed up the opportunity to bid for power at the time of their greatest strength, only to make this bid when their popular base was much narrower and their opponents were in a considerably better position.

Resistance and Collaboration

Non-Communist political leaders in Burma and Indonesia were in a much better position than those of Malaya and the Philippines to take advantage of the Second World War, for in both these countries there was a body of revolutionary nationalists who were prepared to take advantage of the social and political changes brought by war to establish their claims to power. They considered the rapid achievement of independence to be the main thing; how this was accomplished was, in their view, a secondary issue. Consequently, the collaboration issue did not deeply divide them: the nationalists separated amicably into collaborationist and non-collaborationist groups, as in Indonesia, or switched from cooperation to resistance when Japan's fortunes declined, as in Burma. In the process they secured their claims to national leadership, and though the Communists were also to gain a popular following during this period, it was as individuals within the nationalist group and not as an organized and powerful competition.

We can speak of Communist policy in Burma and Indonesia during

[16] Brimmell, *Communism,* 213-214.

this period only with considerable trepidation, as there were no visible Communist parties,[17] and those who later emerged as Communists pursued widely varying and at times conflicting paths. Some collaborated with the Japanese and some did not. From Burma, Thein Pe, Tin Shwe, and Goshal went to India and offered their services to the British; Than Tun accepted the post of Minister of Agriculture in the Ba Maw puppet regime, while Thakin Soe established a partisan movement. In Indonesia, Amir Sjarifuddin attempted to form an anti-Japanese underground, having received money from the Dutch for that purpose; Wikana worked for the Japanese. Several of the younger generation of post-war leaders of the Indonesian Communist Party (PKI) belonged to youth groups that existed partly in collaboration with and partly in opposition to the occupying forces.

Communism in Burma and Indonesia thus emerged from the war in an amorphous state, and there was no question of an attempt by the Communists to seize power using their own organizational base at the time of the Japanese collapse. Indeed, it was extremely problematical who was a Communist at this point, for the boundaries between nationalists and Communists—and between Communists who followed their own lights versus those faithful to the international party line—were as yet largely unresolved. It was only in the postwar period, with the development of a struggle for power among Burmese and Indonesian leaders and a growing difference of opinion regarding policy towards the colonial powers, that a more ideological division became apparent. Whether final loyalties were decided by ideological affinities or whether ideological commitments arose from the development of the

[17] The Anti-Fascist Organization (AFO, later Anti-Fascist Peoples Freedom League–AFPFL), which was founded in 1944 as the Burmese nationalist resistance association, listed the Communist Party as one of its components; however, there is no indication that an organized Communist group existed at that time other than Thakin Soe's guerrilla following in the Delta. For the founding of the AFO and the activity of Burma's Communists during the occupation, see the accounts in *Aung San of Burma,* 37-39, 50-52, 69-70, 85-86; and also Thakin Nu, *Burma Under the Japanese* (London 1954), 1-3, 42-43, 62, 98-99, 102-104; Maung Maung, *Burma's Constitution* (The Hague 1961), 61-64, 128; John Seabury Thomson, "Marxism in Burma," in *Marxism in Southeast Asia,* 28-32; and John F. Cady, *A History of Modern Burma* (Ithaca 1958), 478-484.

The most complete Indonesian Communist account of activity during the Japanese occupation may be found in Sidik Kertapati, *Sekitar Proklamasi 17 Agustus 1945* [Concerning the Proclamation of August 17, 1945] (2nd. ed.; Djakarta 1961). For a general description of the period, see George McT. Kahin, *Nationalism and Revolution in Indonesia* (Ithaca 1952), 101-146: this account gives more credence to the existence of an organized Communist underground than the PKI account does.

internal struggle for power appears in many cases to be as difficult to determine as the prior existence of the chicken or the egg.

If there were no real Communist organizations in Burma and Indonesia at the war's end, there were individuals who were—or were becoming—Communists, and some of them were highly placed and possessed a considerable personal following. Their main chance for gaining domination lay in further developing their influence within the general nationalist constellation, and utilizing or pushing aside their non-Communist colleagues. Two major objects were contested in this process. One was control of the apparatus of government and the other was popular support, in particular that of the military, paramilitary, and mass organizations which—highly undisciplined and attuned to violence—formed both a threat to security and a key to power. The methods by which the proto-Communists carried out their part in this struggle largely depended on whether they commanded the nationalist apparatus governing the mass group they wished to influence or whether they competed with it, and whether in general they felt themselves to be in or out of the core group of nationalist leaders.

The Burmese and Indonesian nationalist leaderships were engaged in struggles with the returning colonial powers which involved both violence and negotiation. The Indonesian Republic was in outright rebellion against the Dutch, but its revolution consisted not of all-out war, but rather of truces riddled by minor incidents and interrupted by brief but severe armed clashes. The Republic's leaders were therefore faced with the problem of maintaining popular revolutionary élan and at the same time controlling its expression sufficiently to maintain the cease-fires and to keep order in the nationalist-controlled territory. Though the Burmese were not engaged in outright revolt, a major lever by which they sought to pry independence from the British was the demonstration of popular rebelliousness through urban strikes and rural unrest. At the same time, they could not allow these proofs of popular support for their cause to go so far as to interfere with negotiations, and as they were granted increasing powers as heirs-apparent to the colonial government they acquired added reasons to be concerned with maintaining stability.

To whip up the forces of revolution and yet keep them on the leash is no easy task; inevitably, there were groups in Burma and Indonesia who demanded more action, who did not see the need for concessions, or who felt that their interests were not being adequately served by the leaders in power. Leaders who were competing for power with those in command could make these restive elements their clientele, and, accusing their opponents of insufficient courage in the face of the colonialist enemy, could both weaken their mass support and force them to concede to their demands by the threat of violent insubordination that was implicit in the nature of their following. The revolutionary nationalist leadership in the independence struggle thus tended to divide into two main groups, with those who considered themselves adequately represented in the ruling core taking a relatively moderate stand on the question of negotiations, and those whose demands were not satisfied assuming a position of intransigence.

The Burma Communist Party (BCP), which was founded in July 1945, appeared at first to be a part of the "in" group of nationalist leaders. It was a component of the powerful AFPFL, which was headed by Aung San as the paramount nationalist leader, but whose secretary was Than Tun. The Burmese-Indian Communist H.N. Goshal headed the All-Burma Trade Union Congress, which played an important part in organizing the strike wave that the AFPFL promoted to harass the British. Both Than Tun and Thakin Soe took a major and quite successful part in bidding for the allegiance of the Burmese military and para-military units left emotionally unemployed by the ending of the war, though they could not compete in popularity among these groups with Aung San.

The Burmese peasantry also provided the Communists with a mass base of considerable importance. The All-Burma Peasant Union was led by Than Tun, who had already built up considerable rural influence in his role as the Thakins' peasant organizer before the war and as Minister of Agriculture during the Japanese occupation. The peasantry of Lower Burma provided considerable potential for a revolutionary movement. In the prewar decades there had been an extremely rapid expansion of rice production for sale abroad, which had brought with it great social changes and also considerable peasant reliance on Indian Chettyar money lenders. The latter foreclosed on the peasants' land during the Depression, and thus the greater part of Lower Burma's ricelands passed from Burmese peasant control. The Chettyar hold was broken with the Japanese invasion, but with the return of the British the peasants were left in a limbo of uncertainty as to whether the Indians' claims would be recognized, and whether the government would allow similar situations to arise again. To harass the British and improve their own positions, Than Tun and

Soe encouraged a "no rent, no taxes" campaign among the peasantry, urged the immediate expropriation of large landholdings without compensation to the landlords, and demanded that the state provide adequate and cheap rural credit.

The Burmese Communists were at first divided as to how their mass support could best be utilized. Of the three paramount BCP leaders, Thein Pe urged that the Communists continue to work within the AFPFL framework even if they did not succeed in dominating it, and he was accordingly to oppose the Party's eventual decision to revolt. Thakin Soe took the opposite tack, holding that the Communists should not be party to negotiations with the British and should take direct and uncompromising action to secure their demands. Soe very nearly succeeded in deposing Than Tun and Thein Pe in a fight over this issue, and if he had done so the BCP would very likely have revolted much earlier than it did. As it was, Soe broke with the "White Flag" Communist regulars after failing to remove his rivals and, forming the Communist Party of Burma (CPB, or "Red Flag" Communists), commenced a guerrilla struggle of his own in July 1946 from his wartime partisan base in the Delta.

Than Tun, who defeated Thakin Soe and gradually eliminated Thein Pe as a rival, was initially second only to Aung San in the ranks of the AFPFL. There had been a long-standing personal rivalry between the two leaders, and it soon became apparent that Than Tun, whose abilities were exceeded only by his ambitions, hoped to succeed Aung San as the dominant figure in the nationalist group. Aung San was well aware of this threat, and he was consequently unwilling to yield any more ground than was necessary to his rival. When called upon to form a cabinet in September 1946, he passed over Than Tun's claims to a ministerial post in favor of the more tractable but by then clearly less important Thein Pe. Seeing little advantage to the Communists and none to himself in preserving what would clearly be a subordinate relationship within the AFPFL, Than Tun denounced Aung San and his colleagues for having sold out to the British. The AFPFL leaders charged the Communists in return with trying to destroy nationalist unity and discipline. In October 1946 the BCP left both the government and the AFPFL and set itself up in opposition to them.

Now clearly an outgroup, the BCP vigorously set to exploiting the forces of unrest. Since urban and rural disorder ran high there was considerable fuel for inflammatory tactics; moreover, the Communists could hope that the AFPFL would fail to achieve prompt and complete independence, and that they could then capitalize on their more firmly anti-British stand to gain the initiative in the national struggle. Having assumed much of the responsibility of government, the AFPFL was constrained to oppose disruptive strikes and rural rejection of taxes. To combat the Communists' organizational strongholds, it gave considerable encouragement to the Socialist-sponsored All-Burma Peasants Organization and Trade Union Congress (Burma), and during 1947 a rough-and-tumble competition for popular favor ensued between the Socialist and Communist mass groups. During the course of the year it became apparent to the Communists that the AFPFL-backed mass organizations were gaining; moreover, though the BCP ran candidates only in its strongest centers during the April 1947 elections, it did not do very well even there. It could blame part of its defeat on the fact that the British used Kachin troops to "pacify" the rural areas where the Communists were most active, and that consequently the BCP's supporters were rather disorganized and cowed at the time of the vote. But the fact remained that there appeared to be little prospect of Communist electoral success and that consequently the party had no great stake in preserving the loyal aspect of its opposition.

A brief reconciliation with the AFPFL occurred in the wake of Aung San's assassination in July 1947. U Nu, the new AFPFL leader, desired to come to terms with the Communists and offered them a place in the government. He did not, however, proffer a role sufficient to satisfy Than Tun, who was now rid of his chief rival for popular affection and paramilitary support, and the Communists refused to participate. In October came the Nu-Attlee Agreement, which called for Burmese independence in January 1948, and the BCP lost its hopes of capitalizing on an AFPFL inability to produce freedom. The Communists—and other groups in Burma as well—accordingly began to consider whether it might not be better to seize power by violence before an independent government had gotten the country well under its control.

The Indonesian Communists proceeded initially in the opposite direction from their Burmese counterparts. The PKI, which was revived in November 1945, originally formed part of the radical opposition which revolved around the former Communist leader Tan Malaka and called for "100% Independence" and no concessions to the

Dutch.[18] In April 1946 the party was purged by PKI leaders returning from abroad, however; thereafter it sought influence by supporting the government. The PKI thus entered the Sajap Kiri (Left Wing) coalition that governed the Indonesian Republic until the beginning of 1948. The Communist Party itself was a minor member of the grouping, exercising little apparent leadership in government policy. Nonetheless, when the ultimate split between pro-Communists and non-Communists developed, most of the principal leaders of the component groups of the Sajap Kiri were to align themselves with the PKI, and take with them the greater part of the coalition's mass support. They announced in August 1948 that they had been secret Communist Party members all along, and there is good reason to believe that for the majority of them this claim was true.[19] Their strategy in the immediate post-war years had been, in essence, to create a front which was controlled by the Communists through the influence clandestine party members held within each component group. This front had emphasized nationalist rather than socialist revolution, and had relied on its responsible attitude towards the crucial question of negotiations with the Dutch to give it a favored position in the Republic, whose leaders were acutely aware that concessions were necessary for survival.

Undoubtedly this strategy gained the Indonesian Communists a better position than they could otherwise have hoped for, given the fact that they had been in no condition to seize control of the revolution at its outset. The coalition could appeal to a broader audience than could a Communist Party per se, and the multiplicity of the coalition's components alleviated fears of single-party domination of the govern-

[18] Tan Malaka had been a major PKI leader during the 1920's and had worked as a Comintern agent in Southeast Asia. He drifted away from the International about the end of that decade, and in the 1930's was labelled a "Trotskyite." He was not active on the Indonesian public scene until after the formation of the Republic; in his writings and activities during the revolutionary period he took a stand independent of international Communist policy, but he did not declare his opposition either to Communism or to the USSR; he and his adherents denounced the PKI not for serving the Soviet Union but for serving the Dutch. Malaka's point of view is impossible to pigeonhole with any accuracy, but it might perhaps be described as "national-Communist."

[19] These leaders included Abdulmajdid (Socialist Party), Setiadjit (Labor Party), Tan Ling Djie (Socialist Party), Wikana (Pesindo), and Amir Sjarifuddin (Socialist Party). All but the last two had been Perhimpunan Indonesia members who returned to Indonesia in 1946. They appear to have joined the Dutch Communist Party secretly while in the Netherlands. Amir Sjarifuddin and Wikana claimed to have been members of the "illegal PKI" founded in 1935 by Musso; Sjarifuddin's commitment to Communism before 1948 is, however, open to question (see Kahin, 272-275). For a description of how mass organizations were built up in a key area of the Republic, see Selosoemardjan, *Social Change in Jogjakarta* (Ithaca 1962), 166-178.

ment. Most important, the Indonesian revolutionary leaders were very much aware of the fact that the Dutch hoped to secure a free hand by persuading the United States—which played a moderating role in the conflict—that the Republic was under Communist control. Hence it was most unlikely that the PKI could have acquired a prominent position in the government under its own name, no matter how peripheral Indonesia's leaders may have felt the issue of Communism to be in the accomplishment of the revolution.

As it was, the Sajap Kiri leaders headed the four cabinets that governed the country from November 1945 to January 1948. The Left Wing dominated the provisional parliament, while its continuing presence in the government enabled its leaders to utilize official channels as well as their own organizations to increase their mass following. The Sajap Kiri's organizational strength was impressive. In addition to its political parties—the Socialist Party (Partai Sosialis) and the smaller Indonesian Labor Party (PBI) and PKI—it controlled SOBSI, the Republic's sole federation of trade unions, and Pesindo, which was by far the most powerful youth group in the Republic, and it had a controlling voice in the Republic's federation of youth groups, BKPRI. The Sajap Kiri did not possess a well-developed peasant organization—none of the Indonesian groups did at this time —but its Indonesian Peasant Front (BTI) and the smaller Indonesian Peasants' Association (RTI) were important in some areas, while Pesindo had considerable influence among the rural youth. Both SOBSI and Pesindo were important sources of paramilitary support; moreover Amir Sjarifuddin, who was Premier of the last of the Sajap Kiri cabinets and Defense Minister in all of them, had a large following among the regular and irregular troops.

The position of the Communist-oriented Left was thus impressive —so much so that in applying the two-camp doctrine to Indonesia at the end of 1947, Soviet comment labelled the Republic a people's democracy and put it forward, along with Ho Chi Minh's Vietnam, as a revolutionary example for Southeast Asia.[20] This strength was by no means as great as it seemed, however. In the first place, although the Sajap Kiri led the Republic's governments it was not their exclusive component, and as a consensus on negotiations with the Dutch became harder to secure, more and more concessions had to be made to other

[20] See Zhukov, 52, 57; and V. Vasil'eva, "Bor'ba za demokraticheskoye razvitiye Indoneziskoy respubliki" [The Struggle for the Democratic Development of the Indonesian Republic], *Voprosy ekonomiki,* No. 1 (1948), 81-82. For a discussion of these articles, see McVey, *The Soviet View,* 33-36.

parties to secure their support. The last of the Sajap Kiri governments, though it contained more pro-Communists than any others, also had more ministers who were completely outside the Sajap Kiri group. Secondly, the Sajap Kiri itself was not controlled by the Communists; although key members were Communists or became increasingly sympathetic to the movement, by no means all of its leaders were so inclined. Communist strength outside the PKI proper depended largely on the amount of influence wielded by individual pro-Communist leaders, and since parties and mass organizations in the Republic tended to be very loosely disciplined, this control was largely a matter of personal loyalties and was accordingly difficult to assess or exploit.

The reliability of the Sajap Kiri following was also rendered questionable by the fact that it stressed national rather than social revolution, and emphasized the need for loyalty and unity within the Republic and responsibility in the matter of compromise with the Dutch. Its adherents thus tended to be loyal to the government more than to the Sajap Kiri itself; they might follow the group into opposition, but whether they would follow it into revolt was another matter. The Republic by no means lacked elements willing to back a divisive and radical opposition, but these had given their loyalties elsewhere —most notably to Tan Malaka who, though he languished in jail after an attempted coup in 1946, commanded considerable prestige among the irregular armed forces. Having alienated these elements by their moderate policy, the Sajap Kiri leaders found it impossible to gain their trust later on; it was a price paid for the advantages of participation in the government, and as it turned out it was a high one.

With the question of negotiations looming so large in the Republic's politics, it was customary for cabinets to fall when new concessions were made and for their successors, even though they had opposed the agreement, to undertake its execution. In January 1948 is was Sjarifuddin's turn; signing a UN-sponsored agreement on board the *USS Renville* which involved extensive concessions to the Dutch, he also signed away his cabinet. The Sajap Kiri itself split as a result. The two Socialist leaders Sjahrir and Sjarifuddin having become increasingly estranged, Sjahrir took the occasion to resign with his following in objection to the concessions, only to back the ensuing cabinet, which undertook to execute them. This new government was not led by the Sajap Kiri. It had been difficult enough to secure adequate support even for the very broad Sjarifuddin coalition, and now, with parliament hopelessly deadlocked and the Left Wing too long identified with concessions, an extra-parliamentary cabinet was formed under Vice-President Hatta and without Sajap Kiri representation.

Licking its wounds from these severe blows, the Left Wing reorganized itself into the People's Democratic Front (FDR) and, taking up an oppositional role, accordingly reversed its position on negotiations with the Dutch. With the revolution appearing to many Indonesians to consist chiefly of retreat and bitter economic hardship, there was considerable public sympathy for an intransigent do-or-die effort against the Dutch. This was to the FDR's advantage in securing popular support, but it also meant that the new government, conscious of the explosive possibilities of another cabinet crisis and of the need to keep the armed groups in check, was more concerned than any of its predecessors with the need to preserve and strengthen its control. Stripped of their governmental positions, seeing their military and para-military support shaken by the new cabinet's efforts at rationalizing armed units, and achieving no progress in their efforts to re-enter the government or bring it to a fall, the FDR leaders' investment in legality appeared increasingly dubious. On the governmental level, tempers were frayed by the continuing quarrel over negotiations with the Dutch, and by the increasingly important question of Cold War alignment.[21] Among the general population, growing economic and social chaos combined with frustrated revolutionary energies to produce an explosive situation. By mid-1948 sporadic clashes were taking place between para-military units adhering to the various major political groupings; and in July, the government later claimed, the FDR leaders began to consider seriously the seizure of power by force.

The Rebellions

At various points between 1945 and early 1948, then, the Communists in Burma, Malaya, Indonesia, and the Philippines passed up what in retrospect appeared to be their best chances of claiming the initiative over the postwar situation. Whether any of the parties could actually have seized power and held it is another matter; the point is that it became clear to them that political control was con-

[21] The question of Cold War alignment precipitated a major crisis in the Republic's domestic politics as a result of a Soviet attempt to force through an agreement for consular relations; see Kahin, 268-269; McVey, *The Soviet View*, 47-52,

solidating in other hands. They were thus faced with the alternatives of finding a place for themselves within the emergent postwar structures or of attempting to satisfy their ambitions by force. The first alternative would have meant assuming a subordinate role, and perhaps allowing themselves to be worked out of the political picture entirely. In order to make themselves acceptable to the governments they would have had to assume a relatively moderate stand, and in doing so they might have lost their most dynamic sources of support and created serious disciplinary problems within their ranks.

The second alternative was risky: The Communists would be fighting against more powerful forces, whose claims to legitimacy were generally recognized. If power could not be seized immediately, the rebels would be fighting a war of attrition. It was not certain that they would be able to disrupt the country sufficiently to prevent the government from stabilizing the situation, nor was it at all certain that a population, weary after years of chaos, would look on a further struggle with anything but antipathy. Nonetheless, this alternative offered the clearest path to power, and it was this which the Communists chose.

The first of the movements to take the path of violence was the Hukbalahap, which had been the least successful in adjusting to the postwar situation. It had disbanded after the Japanese defeat but, since most of its units had not been recognized and rewarded as partisans, it refused to urge its members to disarm. The old problem of agrarian unrest had been compounded by years of violence and the absence of landlord control during the war; as the landowners attempted to re-assert their claims with the aid of the constabulary forces, clashes with armed villagers began to take place. The mass base of the Hukbalahap was thus engaged in conflict with government forces almost from the outset.

At first, the Communist-oriented organizations attempted to maintain a legal and moderate aspect. The Hukbalahap proclaimed itself a veterans' association, with the National Peasants' Union (PKM) as its civilian supporting arm. The Communist Party of the Philippines established itself as a separate entity, with its headquarters in Manila and its emphasis at least officially on the urban workers. In the 1946 elections these groups combined with the Democratic Alliance, an association which relied chiefly on labor union support. The Alliance based its campaign on the issue of wartime collaboration and rural reform, and backed the incumbent Naçionalista Osmeña against the Liberal ex-collaborator Roxas for the Presidency. The result of the elections was disastrous from the Communists' point of view, for it showed that the pre-war Philippine political machinery had largely succeeded in restoring itself and that the issue of collaboration, although still a subject which aroused heated emotions, had become so confused that an able campaigner like Roxas could easily defeat his colorless, if uncompromised, opponent. The elections gave the Hukbalahap little reason to be optimistic about the benefits of continued legality, and the new government did nothing to erase this impression when it refused to seat the handful of Democratic Alliance candidates (including Taruc) who had been successful in the race for Congressional office. With the limitations of moderation thus rudely revealed, Taruc returned to rural central Luzon and set about organizing the endemic agrarian conflict.

The Hukbalahap spent the next two years half in and half out of rebellion. It did not announce its intention to overthrow the government, but only to secure rural reforms, and the government itself did not outlaw the Huks until March 1948 although it openly held them to be bandits.[22] Various political figures attempted to mediate in the conflict, and when Quirino succeeded as President on Roxas' death in April 1948, he arranged a truce. Taruc returned to Manila and assumed his seat in Congress, but his discussions with the government yielded no results. The administration understandably insisted that the Huks turn over their arms. The Huks equally understandably refused to do so, since their base of support in central Luzon had if anything broadened during the conflict, while the 1946 election experience had already demonstrated the improbability of their achieving either political power or agrarian reform without the threat of violence to back them. In August, when the truce expired, Taruc returned to the field with the announcement that no further negotiations with the authorities would be of use, and the struggle was resumed with new bitterness.

The Hukbalahap was now in full revolt, but in spite of this and the tenets of the two-camp doctrine, the Philippine Communist Party did not go underground or advocate a general resort to arms. In the 1949 electoral campaign it supported the Naçionalista candidacy of José Laurel, forgiving his wartime collaboration with the Japanese in the higher interest of his current anti-American nationalism. Not

[22] For examples of the way in which the Huks and the government presented their cases to the general public in this period, see "Taruc-Roxas Correspondence," *Far Eastern Survey*, xv, (1946), 314-317.

until the beginning of 1950 did the Party declare itself openly for the armed overthrow of the government, and even then its preparations for illegality were so incomplete that when the police raided the homes and offices of party leaders later in the year they captured a good deal of important material on Communist and Huk activities. This divergence seems to have resulted not from any disagreement on strategy between the Huks and the Communists—if anything the Communist Party's hold over the peasant movement was strengthened in this period—but from the consideration that the advantages of having a window into the political world outside the rebel area outweighed those of revolutionary consistency.[23]

The Malayan Communists were initially more successful than the Hukbalahap in their adjustment to postwar legality. The MPAJA was recognized as a proper guerrilla organization; its members were rewarded with money and in return they surrendered their arms. Not all the Communists' weapons were turned in, for the MPAJA prudently hid a substantial arsenal, and though the organization disbanded, it attempted, like the Hukbalahap, to retain the ties among its participants through a veterans' association. The Communists' main effort, however, was on labor organization; returning to the cities, they took up their prewar role as spokesmen for the Chinese proletariat. In this they were initially very successful, for social dislocation and economic hardship made for a high degree of labor unrest in the first postwar years. Moreover, the colonial authorities, influenced by the presence of a Labour government at home, looked with favor on the organization of labor unions.

Increasingly, however, it became clear to the Communists that the labor movement provided at best an uncertain basis for political power. As the post-colonial form of Malaya's government took shape through successive constitutional plans, the prospect of conservative Malay domination became a growing certainty. Moreover, within the Chinese community itself the Communists began to lose the commanding stature they had enjoyed as a result of their wartime anti-Japanese leadership. With the partial restoration of the older business-leader elite and the formation of alternate Chinese organizations, popular loyalties could spread across a broader political spectrum, and even within the MPAJA veterans' organization serious splits began to occur. The MCP's posture as the representative of labor unrest speeded the alienation of the non-proletarian Chinese, while in the labor move-

[23] For descriptions of the Huk-HMB organization, see Scaff, 31-35, 141-146.

ment itself Communist accomplishments were qualified by a lack of overall success in strike activity and by difficulty in disciplining those who wanted more action than the party was producing.[24] Most serious of all, the government began to ponder the wisdom of allowing labor agitation to proceed unchecked. Increasingly it took positive action to insure economic and political order, and by early 1948 it was clear that the authorities were going to put through regulations which would greatly decrease Communist influence in the unions.

Under these circumstances it was natural that the party's moderate leadership would come under increasingly effective fire from those who had earlier wished it to pursue a revolutionary course. This opposition was strengthened by the success of the Communist revolutionary forces in China, and the intransigent two-camp line certainly did nothing to convince them that an emulation of the Chinese example would be incorrect.[25] The replacement of the more cautious MCP leadership of Lai Tek, who had headed the party since the mid-1930's, seems to have begun in late 1947, when rebellious younger leaders under Chin Peng accused the senior group of pursuing a course of right opportunism.[26] Lai Tek was formally deposed in March 1948, taking a good part of the MCP's treasury with him as a memento.

The party now undertook the promotion of a series of disruptive strikes, apparently hoping to whip up enthusiasm for a revolutionary bid for power and to create a general lack of confidence in the government's ability to preserve order. It was soon evident, however, that urban action would not provide an effective basis for revolt; the movement towards a general insurrectionary strike failed, as such efforts usually do when there is any semblance of public authority. Nonetheless, the strike wave presented a serious challenge to the government, all the more so because its spirit was communicated beyond the urban center, threatening the still shaky security of the plantation and

[24] See Pye, 80-82; Hanrahan, 59; Purcell, 267. A detailed analysis of the labor situation in postward Malaya may be found in S. S. Awbery and F. W. Dalley, *Labour and Trade Union Organization in the Federation of Malaya and Singapore,* (Kuala Lumpur 1948).

[25] For references to MCP contacts abroad which may have had bearing on the decision to revolt, see Pye, 83-84; Brimmell, *Communism,* 210; Cecil H. Sharpley, *The Great Delusion* (Melbourne 1952), 110-111; Ian Morrison, "The Communist Uprising in Malaya," *Far Eastern Survey,* XVII (1948), 282; Virginia Thompson and Richard Adloff, *The Left Wing in Southeast Asia* (New York 1950), 153-157. The most important event would seem to have been the visit of the Australian Communist leader Sharkey to Singapore following the Indian Communist Party congress of March 1948.

[26] Morrison, 283.

mining districts. Incidents of violence increased, and in June, after the murder of three British planters, the government declared a state of emergency and moved to arrest the Communist leaders.

The MCP had apparently planned its general uprising for August, but in the process of arousing enthusiasm for revolt the party had been unable to prevent its followers from engaging in premature violence. The leaders were prepared for the government's reaction, however, and eluded it by fleeing to the jungle. There they envisioned carrying out an armed struggle based partly on the MPAJA experience during the war and partly on the strategy that was bringing victory to the Communists in China. Part of the manpower necessary for this rebellion was already outside the urban centers in the form of plantation laborers, miners, and squatters, but a good deal of it was moved in from the larger towns. Though many of those who took to the woods were motivated by the desire for a fight, a prime argument used by the MCP in accomplishing the exodus appears to have been that once the Communists had launched their revolt the British would surely arrest all those who had been associated with the Party and did not elude its grasp by fleeing.[27] The Malayan insurgents were thus not primarily peasants in origin, and while they played on the Chinese squatters' desire for legal rights to the land they were occupying, they did not make a real attempt to appeal to peasant interests.[28] They operated not from the plowed areas but from the jungles, and they left the cities for strategic reasons and not because they envisioned themselves as leading an agrarian revolt.

The Indian Communists faced a problem in some ways analagous to that of the Southeast Asian parties in the immediate postwar years. Having supported the Allied cause, the CPI enjoyed legality during the Second World War while the Congress did not, and it had used this absence of competition to build up its mass organizational strength, especially among the labor unions. With the restoration of

[27] See Pye, 87-88. For accounts of the early stages of the revolt, see Morrison, 283-285; David R. Rees-Williams, "The Malayan Situation in 1948," in *Three Reports on the Malayan Problem* (New York 1949), 8-17; Victor Purcell, *Malaya: Communist or Free?* (Stanford 1955), 60-61; Lennox A. Mills, *Malaya: A Political and Economic Appraisal* (Minneapolis 1958), 50-53.

[28] See Harry Miller, *The Communist Menace in Malaya* (New York 1954), 155-158, for a description of a conflict between the Malacca MCP leader Siew Lau and the central party leadership in 1949. Siew Lau, it is stated, urged among other things that the rebels stress agrarian action, especially the distribution of plantation lands to the peasants, while the MCP executive argued that since plantations were properly industries their resources should be regarded as belonging to the state and should therefore not be declared open for private use.

the banned political groupings, this strength soon began to disperse. As moderate sources of support turned to other leadership, the Communists were increasingly tempted to abandon their stance as a loyal opposition and to concentrate instead on mobilizing the resources of radical labor unrest. This inclination received further impetus from the party's rural following, for since early 1946 the peasantry of Telengana (eastern Hyderabad) had been engaged under local CPI leadership in a struggle against the great landowners of the area which had gained steadily in vigor and scope. At first the central party leadership soft-pedaled the peasant revolt, emphasizing that it was directed at the Nizam of Hyderabad and not at the emergent Indian republic. However, as the party became increasingly dubious of the benefits of loyalty, its leaders gave serious consideration to the general promotion of agrarian revolt in the manner of the Chinese Communists. Though the party was not able to decide whether it should devote itself to rural or proletarian effort—the question was to divide it for several years—it did mean that it received the international intransigent line with favor and, deposing its moderate leadership, adopted a program of radical opposition in December 1947.[29]

The CPI Central Committee meeting which decided this was attended by the Burmese Communist leader Goshal, who on returning to Rangoon presented the BCP with theses which were based on the Indian party discussions and viewed the newly independent Burmese government in the same terms as the CPI saw Nehru's regime.[30] It is not clear whether this viewpoint envisioned non-cooperation or outright revolt, as the Indian Communists themselves did not completely abandon legality in assuming their intransigent stand. However, the Burmese Communists had little reason to boggle at full-scale war. The ability of the AFPFL to maintain unity and order after independence was becoming increasingly dubious. Outside Rangoon, dis-

[29] For a discussion of the CPI's period of radical intransigence, see Overstreet and Windmiller, 276-308. An interesting analysis of the nature of CPI support in the agrarian revolt may be found in Selig S. Harrison, "Caste and the Andhra Communists," *American Political Science Review,* L (June 1956). CPI documents reflecting the debate on rural versus urban action may be found in *Indian Communist Party Documents 1930-1956* (Bombay 1957), 49ff.

[30] See *Burma and the Insurrections* (Rangoon 1949), 5; *Is it a People's Liberation* (Rangoon 1952), 8-9; Brimmell, *Communism,* 193, 309-310; Thomson, 38-39. Thein Pe later claimed that he protested Goshal's thesis to the BCP Central Committee, but since he had virtually no influence in the party at this time his argument was ignored; see Thein Pe Myint, *Naing-gan-yay A-tway-a-Chong-myar* [My experiences in Politics] (Rangoon 1956), 332, 437-438. I am indebted to Daphne Whittam for translating relevant portions of this work for me.

order prevailed. The Red Flag Communists were already in revolt in the Delta, as were the Muslim Mujahids in northwest Burma. The Karens were threatening to take arms; the PVO, Aung San's paramilitary organization, showed increasing signs of unreliability, and regular army loyalties were questionable. As independence neared, these elements—minorities afraid of domination by the Burman majority, leaders who saw themselves destined to lesser roles, people for whom violence had become a profession and legality a myth—began to look on the nationalist leadership less as a symbol of the struggle for freedom and more as a potentially oppressive authority.

Than Tun attended the Calcutta Southeast Asian youth conference and CPI congress in February and early March 1948; what he heard there was hardly likely to have given him much pause in considering insurrection. Returning to Burma, he drew further encouragement from the great rural enthusiasm demonstrated by a giant rally held by his All-Burma Peasant Union in Pyinmana.[31] The BCP made its first moves toward revolt in Rangoon and not in the countryside, however. It had already launched a series of disruptive strikes in February; this action culminated on March 27, when Than Tun called for insurrection at a mass meeting in the capital. Weak as the government was, however, it was not to be toppled by action at the seat of its authority. Even before Than Tun's call for revolt, orders had gone out for the arrest of the BCP leaders, and it was accordingly dangerous for them to remain in the city. Outside the capital central government authority quickly dispersed, however, and accordingly the White Flag leaders decamped to Pyinmana, Than Tun's home area and a center of Communist rural support, and there rallied their adherents for a move on Rangoon.

The BCP was not alone in taking to the field; its revolt was merely one of a series of defections which by the beginning of 1949 included most of the PVO, part of the army, and the Karen and Mon ethnic minorities. The result was a melee in which the government, con-

[31] Two Yugoslav representatives to the Calcutta meetings accompanied Than Tun to Burma afterwards and attended the Pyinmana meeting; reportedly, they pressed the BCP leader to undertake an insurrection; see *Is it a People's Liberation,* 8-10; Cady, 582-583. Thein Pe Myint, 451, 474, also comments on the Yugoslav influence and notes that Than Tun attacked the Viet Minh, at Pyinmana and later, for having "gone soft." The Viet Minh representatives at Calcutta had not been advocates of non-violence, but they seem to have been attacked there by the Yugoslavs, who accused them of being more nationalist than Communist. I was told by a friend who worked for the Viet Minh in Bangkok at the time that the Vietnamese delegates, stopping off on their way home from Calcutta, related this with considerable indignation.

trolling little more than Rangoon, survived largely by grace of its opponents' disunity. Rebel units sometimes shared the occupation of various areas, and several formal alliances were concluded at the top leadership level, but such cooperation was neither enthusiastic nor enduring. For one thing, the dissident groups had very different ambitions for Burma, and this prevented them from really coordinating their military actions or presenting a united political front at a time when there was a good chance for the government's surrender. They also represented ethnic groups whose relations with each other were hardly of the best, so that marriages of convenience concluded at the leadership level had little support among the rank and file. The Karens, for example, were struggling against domination by the Burmans. Their sometime allies, the PVO and BCP, were Burman groups, the former having been responsible for anti-Karen atrocities in its previous status as the Burma Independence Army. Similarly, although the mutinous army commander Naw Seng was a part-time ally of the White Flag insurgents, he had led his Kachin troops in the repressive action against pro-Communist villages at the time of the 1947 elections, and therefore was not overly popular with this segment of White Flag support.

The Communist insurgents were active in various widely scattered areas of Burma, but since most of these districts were occupied briefly or in conjunction with other rebel groups they did not constitute more than temporary bases of military operations. An insurgent capital was established in Prome by the PVO-BCP People's Democratic Front; however, the Communists were driven out by PVO forces when that alliance collapsed in 1950, and by the following year the government was successful in reducing White Flag strength to hit-and-run guerrilla proportions. Nonetheless, the Communists did attempt to establish an agrarian base of support for their rebellion in the principal areas they occupied, carrying out the redistribution of land and farm equipment and abrogating existing debts and taxes.[32] Some of the inspiration for this action may well have come from the Chinese revolutionary example, but its main impetus was almost certainly local, deriving from Than Tun's prior campaigns for agrarian support.

The Communists were not able to secure solid peasant backing for

[32] For descriptions of the White Flags' land reform actions, see *Is It a People's Liberation,* 11-13; and Hugh Tinker, *The Union of Burma* (London 1957), 228-229, 238.

their fight against Rangoon, however. The reforms they urged were already being worked out, for the government was by no means opposed to them; as one commentator put it, Than Tun's program differed from the government's only in that it demanded the government accomplish immediately what it was trying to do as quickly as possible.[33] The passage of the Land Nationalization Act of October 1948 and of subsequent rural reform laws took away much of the Communists' argument. Moreover, the White Flag forces were dependent for survival on levies from the countryside and thus could not appear as an advocate of "no taxes" so far as they themselves were concerned. The peasants might object to the prices set by government rice purchasers and to the fact that there was little they could buy with the money they received; but the Communist forces could offer them less. In consequence, the White Flag insurrection did not develop into a real agrarian revolt; it drew strength from the social and economic disorganization of the countryside, but like the other rebel groups the Communists operated on the peasantry and not for it.

The Indonesian Communists were the last of the Southeast Asian parties to take up arms in rebellion. In August 1948, with tension within the Republic at a peak and a Dutch attack imminently expected, the long-exiled PKI leader Musso returned to Indonesia from the Soviet Union. Coming, as he declared, to set things aright, he immediately took steps for the conversion of the FDR into a massive Communist Party. The PKI, he accused, had failed to seize control of the revolution at its outset, had failed to realize that Communism could carry out a national revolution under its own name, and had acceded to compromise with the imperialists when only an all-out liberation movement under a Communist-led National Front could bring victory.

Musso made it clear that he intended to seize command of the Republic's government, though it is not certain how he hoped to accomplish this. He referred to his recipe for the assumption of power as his "Gottwald Plan"—a reference to the Czech coup which implied an interesting if very inaccurate view of the power relationships then prevailing in the Republic. Even if the nationalist leaders had been overawed by the power and aggressiveness of a massive Communist opposition, they could not have afforded to concede it a major part in the government with the Dutch needing just

[33] J. S. Furnivall, "Communism and Nationalism in Burma," *Far Eastern Survey*, XVIII (1949), 195.

such an excuse to attack. Consequently the government prepared for a showdown, one of its first moves in this direction being to release Tan Malaka from prison. Malaka's presence on the public scene was hardly likely to add to the Republic's stability, but his supporters had already demonstrated in several clashes with armed FDR units that their predeliction for violence was directed first towards the former Sajap Kiri, which they had not forgiven for its previous concessions to the Dutch.

Whatever the PKI's intentions concerning the means of achieving power, the party's hand was forced in mid-September. Local Communist leaders in the city of Madiun, east of the revolutionary capital of Jogjakarta, became unnerved by government orders for demobilization of their forces and by skirmishes with rival paramilitary groups; seizing the city, they proclaimed an insurgent soviet regime. Musso and the senior FDR leaders, then not far from the city on a tour to drum up support for the merger of the Front components into the PKI, were now faced with the problem of disowning the revolt—which might destroy the momentum for rebellion and might not preserve them from arrest—or endorsing it and risking the possibility that it might not get off the ground. They chose the latter, and it proved a fatal miscalculation.[34]

The Madiun revolt was bloody but brief; within a month it was over, and the Communist forces spent most of that time in flight. The FDR organizations did not generally join in the affair outside the immediate area of the rebellion; even the PKI itself did not fully endorse it, and the party's entire Sumatran branch refused its approval. The Communists might well have made a better showing had they had time to organize properly. On the other hand, much of the violence that did occur arose not from political allegiance to the PKI or the government but because the rebellion sparked an outburst of socio-religious conflict among the Javanese peasants of the affected area.[35]

[34] Kahin, 272-303, gives the best account of the events leading up to the Madiun Affair. The PKI has published several pamphlets giving its side of the story, one of them in English: D. N. Aidit, *Aidit Accuses Madiun Affair* (Djakarta 1955).

[35] The conflict was between *santri*—strict Muslims—and *abangan*—whose profession of Islam was strongly mixed with pre-Islamic Javanese values; see Clifford Geertz, *The Religion of Java* (Glencoe 1960) for a discussion of this division. For a study dealing with the political implications of this split, and touching on the Madiun Affair, see Robert R. Jay, "Santri and Abangan: Religious Schism in Rural Central Java" (Ph.D. Thesis, Harvard University, 1957). The Communist-oriented Left became identified with the *abangan* viewpoint, and this was to form both a basis and a boundary for the PKI's rural appeal during the 1950's.

In a sense, however, the Indonesian Communists were lucky to be defeated so swiftly and decisively, for they did not, like the other Southeast Asian insurgents, hang on to a policy of violent opposition long after it was clear that there was no hope of its success. After the end of the Indonesian revolution a year later, the younger PKI leaders were able to consider carefully the lessons of the Madiun experience. Deposing the older leaders who had survived the clash, they embarked in 1951 on a new path, which, through applying Musso's analysis by peaceful means, was in less than a decade to bring the party to a position of great if uncertain power.

Musso's criticisms of the PKI's pre-Madiun course had application to more than just the Indonesian party, for it represented a point of view concerning revolutionary strategy in Asia that was becoming increasingly popular in international Communist thinking with the successes of Mao Tse-tung's forces in China. A final choice between the "Maoist" national front strategy and the proletarianism of a "united front from below" was not made until 1949, the delay apparently being occasioned in part by the distrust of nationalist tendencies aroused by the defection of Yugoslavia from the Soviet camp. In that year, however, Soviet comment swung to a full endorsement of the proposition that the Communists should not oppose the forces of national revolution in the name of class war but should seek to gain hegemony over them.[36] Whether because of this new doctrinal emphasis, or as a result of their own consideration of the events in China and the problem of securing mass support, the Communists of Burma, Malaya, and the Philippines attempted to transform their minority rebellions into general wars by proclaiming them to be people's liberation movements, aimed against foreign imperialism and its local servants.

Initially, the Burmese Communists seemed to have the best chance of success in insurrection. U Nu's government hung by a hair, and it had no outside sources of support. However, the BCP forces were unable to maintain alliances with the other rebel groups, much less establish hegemony over them: their People's Democratic Front with the PVO and army mutineers soon broke down; the Red Flags

[36] Full public acclamation of the Chinese example came at the November 1949 conference of Asian and Australian countries sponsored by the World Federation of Trade Unions in Peking. For interpretations of the political situation in the Southeast Asian countries according to this line, see *Krizis kolonial'noy sistemy* [The Crisis of the Colonial System] (Moscow 1949). Parts of this collection have been published in English as *Crisis of the Colonial System: National Liberation Struggle of the Peoples of Eastern Asia* (Bombay 1951).

offered only fitful cooperation, and the party's advocacy of self-determination for national minorities did not succeed in cementing its tenuous alliance with the Karens. The government was able to use the respite granted by the rebel groups' internecine quarrelings to stabilize its position, and by 1950 it clearly possessed the initiative. Than Tun led his forces northward in an effort to establish a "liberated area" that could receive aid from the Chinese Communists, but the Chinese proved either uninterested or unable to abet the White Flag cause. In 1951 a new chance for creating a national front was provided by the incursion of Kuomintang troops into northeast Burma, and the BCP tried to use this both as a rallying point for the rebel groups and to persuade the government to join it in an anti-imperialist struggle against the American-backed Chinese. The Communists succeeded in neither objective, however, and gradually were driven from military to guerrilla warfare and then to impotent and nomadic terrorism. By the middle of the decade the BCP was dead as a political factor, serving only as an embarrassment to the expanding forces of Burma's legal Communist-oriented Left.[37]

In 1949 the MCP fighting units took the title of Malayan Races' Liberation Army, and in January of the following year the Hukbalahap renamed itself the People's Liberation Army (HMB). Both groups stressed that they were not concerned primarily with promoting class war but rather with ridding their countries of American imperialism and its local lackeys, the British colonial regime and the Philippine government. Having started without general support, however, the rebels were in a most disadvantageous position to transform their struggles into general civil war. Since guerrilla operations necessarily involve injury to the civilian population, general sympathy will usually accumulate on the insurgent side only if the government shows itself hopelessly corrupt or unable to maintain order. It is necessary for the guerrillas to maintain the appearance of forward

[37] According to Maung Maung, "Thakin Than Tun," *The Guardian* (Rangoon), x (1956), 36, nine leading White Flag insurgents circulated a letter in March 1955 criticising Than Tun's leadership of the rebellion on the grounds that he had undertaken it without adequate preparation and on foreign urging, that he had banked too much on the hope of aid from China, and that he had erred both in alienating other insurgent forces and in exploiting ethnic antagonisms to secure the support of the KNDO (Karen) rebels. For general accounts of the revolt, see Cady, 578-597; Tinker, 34-61; and Edward M. Law Yone and David G. Mandelbaum, "Pacification in Burma," *Far Eastern Survey*, xix (1950), 182-186. It might be noted that in spite of its rebellion the BCP was not officially outlawed by the Burmese government until 1953.

momentum if they are not to end as terrorists opposed by government and people alike, and in a protracted struggle this is most difficult to accomplish.

In Malaya and the Philippines, the rebels were better organized than their White Flag counterparts and possessed considerable prior experience in guerrilla warfare. At the same time, however, they faced governments whose positions were much less precarious than the Burmese and which had considerable outside support. This made it very difficult for the insurgents to cripple them militarily or economically, or to weaken them to the point of compromise. Of the two groups, the Philippine rebels were in a better position. Their guerrillas operated in a food-growing area and drew their manpower from the peasantry itself, so that it was relatively easy for them to secure supplies, obtain intelligence, and melt into the civilian population. Moreover, they had such solid support in the central Luzon provinces of Nueva Ecija, Bulacan, Pampanga, and Tarlac that the area was commonly referred to as "Huklandia"; they thus possessed a relatively secure base of operations in an economically and strategically important district. Initial efforts to break their rebellion were almost solely military in nature, and the actions of the constabulary and army were so callous and inept as to alienate not only the local peasantry but also general public opinion. In addition, popular disillusionment with political corruption and incompetence ran high, reaching a peak with the scandal-ridden elections of 1949. The Huks thus had some cause to hope that they could take advantage of popular alienation from the constituted authority to turn their guerrilla struggle into a general war. Proclaiming the formation of the People's Liberation Army in 1950, Taruc declared that the time for such a transformation had come, and he announced the beginning of full-scale military operations that were to bring the rebels final victory within two years.[38]

The HMB was to fail sadly in this project, for the Philippine political machinery was not so rusted in the grooves of corruption and indifference to popular discontent as to be unable to adjust to the demands of the emergency. Ramón Magsaysay, wartime guerrilla leader and a native of central Luzon, was appointed minister of defense in September 1950 and was given power to put through drastic reforms in an anti-rebel campaign which greatly in-

[38] According to one account, the Huks expected to take Manila by Christmas 1950; see Robert Aura Smith, *Philippine Freedom 1946-1958* (New York 1958), 147.

creased public confidence in the government's ability to deal with the situation. Magsaysay was noted for his honesty, and he carefully distanced himself from the political regulars who in the popular mind were stained with corruption, further restoring public faith in the government. Moreover, he appeared as an outspoken proponent of rural reform, and, having a personality well suited to appearing as a leader of the common people, soon convinced the peasantry that their salvation lay not with the insurgents but with him. In achieving this, he accomplished the most difficult task faced by governments in dealing with guerrilla movements—the separation of the insurgent core from the disaffected segment of the population on which it relies for mass support.

Between 1950 and 1953, when Magsaysay was elected President, the HMB was reduced from an established and well-coordinated force to scattered guerrilla groups which found it increasingly necessary to rely on violence to secure civilian cooperation. The rebels were divided politically as well as physically, for with Magsaysay's rise as a national leader a number of those who had joined the movement as an expression of peasant protest wished it to support him. Others, among them Taruc, considered Magsaysay such a threat to the Huk position that they urged cooperation with his political opponents. The Communist Party regulars, for their part, insisted on uncompromising opposition to all the bourgeois political elements.[39] By 1954 the rebel position was so hopeless that Taruc conceded his part in the fight; remnants of the insurgent group continued to hold out under Communist leadership, but without hope of victory and without popular support.

The problem of communal divisions complicated the Malayan rebels' attempt to convert their guerrilla struggle into a general war, and perhaps because of the difficulties posed by this factor they first aimed at demoralizing rather than persuading the populace. They sought to paralyze the country and provide an image of irresistible strength through intensive terrorist activity; concurrently, they planned to establish Yenan-style "liberated areas," from which they would extend their operations into a full-scale military campaign.[40] This program assumed a congruence between Malayan

[39] See Starner, 55. For discussions of Magsaysay's political personality and its effect on Huk fortunes see Starner, 37-40, 76-79; and Smith, 148-194.

[40] In spite of their initial emphasis on an intensive terrorist campaign, the Malayan Communists did not undertake raids on the centers of authority or the assassination of high officials (the shooting of Sir Henry Gurney was unintentional); they kept

and Chinese geography that did not exist; equally mistakenly, it assumed that time was on the rebels' side. They were in a poor position to conduct an effective protracted struggle. Malaya's agricultural area was small and the peasantry overwhelmingly Malay, unsympathetic to and distinguishable from the Communist forces. The rebels depended for food and support on the Chinese squatters whose villages lay along the jungle's edge, and the government was able to cut off this source of assistance by the drastic but feasible method of moving that portion of the population elsewhere and keeping a watchful eye on it. Although the "new villages" were provided with considerable public services in order to placate their uprooted inhabitants, the Malayan government's solution to the rebel problem was, unlike Magsaysay's, primarily military, bent on convincing the people that the government would maintain order and on isolating the rebels physically from their sources of support.

The Malayan Communists were quickly disabused of their original plan of operations, but subsequent changes of strategy brought no improvement in their fortunes. With terrorist tactics they could cow the populace, but in the process they also alienated it. Attempts at securing more positive support became increasingly impractical as the rebels were isolated politically and militarily from the outside civilian world. As the government's campaign extended into the jungle, the guerrilla forces were broken into isolated bands, and their efforts became concentrated almost exclusively on survival. Thus, although the insurgents' number remained relatively constant during the first half of the 1950's, their importance declined from that of a major threat to a stubborn but manageable nuisance.

In retrospect, it would appear that the insurrections described here failed in good part because they were undertaken at the wrong time, from weakness rather than from strength. They were attempts to take advantage of situations that had begun to change, and to seize leaderships that were already consolidating in other hands. Time was against the rebels, but—by necessity or design—they pursued victory through protracted civil wars rather than through the lightning

instead to attacks on planters, officials, and the general population in and around the areas of revolt. Purcell (*Malaya,* 232) comments on this deviation from classical terrorist strategy and suggests that the MCP might have hoped thereby to leave an opening for possible compromise with the government, or that it may have felt such an effort would spread its forces too thin. For descriptions of Malayan guerrilla organization and the successive insurgent programs, see Pye, 86-106; Hanrahan, 65-67, 73-74, 101-133; and Brimmell, *Communism,* 320-325, 327-329.

seizure of power. They assumed that their insurrections would thoroughly cripple the government and the economy, and that if outside aid came it would be for them and not their opponents, and both suppositions proved fatally wrong. If the revolts contained a common lesson for the Communists, it was that the task of transforming the insurrection of a group into a full-blown civil war was no simple one to accomplish, and certainly not when undertaken by movements whose position was on the wane. The failure of the Southeast Asian rebellions may well have contributed to the revision of the Soviet attitude toward Asian neutralist nationalism during the mid-1950's though, since this was part of a broader change in the USSR's view of international relations, it is hard to estimate its actual role. The fate of the insurrections was such, however, as to provide the Communists with food for thought on the limitations of the Chinese example which they had so enthusiastically espoused as the pattern for Asian revolution. The defeats did not disprove the basic strategy of an anti-imperialist national front, but they demonstrated that Chinese Communist success had depended not just on the policy of the CCP but also on such exterior factors as conditions of geography, the character of Kuomintang government, and the effects of the war with the Japanese. The experience of the revolts also provided ample evidence that revolutionary initiative, once lost, is not easily regained by violence, that rebellion will not necessarily create or revive a revolutionary situation, and that the setbacks suffered in adjusting to a disadvantageous peacetime situation may be less than those incurred by resorting injudiciously to violence.

The conclusion to be drawn from this evidence was not, however, necessarily one for moderation and legal actions; on the contrary, it might equally well be argued from the experience of the Southeast Asian revolts that the Communists moved too late and not too soon, and that when they built their organizations and formulated their public policies they did not do so with a mind to their direct usefulness for the seizure of power. The perennial problem of revolutionary preparedness versus the exploitation of legality thus continues; and to judge from the current Sino-Soviet debate, it is no nearer solution in Communist thought than before.

7

The Viet Minh Complex

GEORGE MODELSKI

In the past three decades the Communist Party of North Viet Nam has donned a variety of labels. After a brief period as the "Vietnamese Communist Party" it was called after 1930 the Communist Party of Indo-China (Dong-Duong Cong-San Dang), but it dissolved voluntarily in November 1945. For a number of years its members continued to meet in the so-called Indo-Chinese Association for the Study of Marxism, until setting up, in March 1951, the Viet Nam Workers' Party (Viet Nam Lao-Dong Dang), which is still in existence. The variety of labels belies the remarkable continuity of personnel and policies, shown by the group whose leader has throughout this period been Ho Chi Minh.[1]

By adopting a name widely associated with the work of the group led by Ho Chi Minh, the title of this chapter seeks to overcome the diversity of labels. But it also intends to convey the thought that we are studying the activities of this group not only in North Viet Nam proper (upon which the organizational activities of the Lao-Dong Party are focused for the present), and those of its predecessors, but also the revolutionary efforts organized and inspired by that group elsewhere in the Indo-Chinese peninsula. For instance, although a new Viet Nam People's Revolutionary Party was set up in South Viet Nam at the end of 1961, its activities no doubt are under the direction of Hanoi. In the past moreover, revolutionary developments in Laos, Cambodia, and even Thailand also have been under significant influence of the Viet Minh. Thus for a period of about thirty years Communist work in this area has formed a complex of activities whose nucleus was the group around Ho Chi Minh, and which has maintained considerable organizational, practical, and even some theoretical distinctiveness within the world-wide Communist system.

To this identifiable complex of activities it is convenient to give the name of Viet Minh even though this label is, strictly speaking,

[1] Before 1943 known as Nguyen Ai Quoc.

at least ten years out of date. The Viet Minh[2] was founded by the Indochinese Communist Party in May 1941, and it formed the Provisional Government of Viet Nam in August 1945, but it was dissolved and merged in a still wider organization, the Lien Viet, in 1951. The name, however, because it is associated with the seizure of power in 1945, stuck and is still widely used in relation to Hanoi-directed activities. Ho Chi Minh himself could have provided an alternative for the title in view of his great and continuing personal influence upon events in this area. However, the "Viet Minh Complex" was ultimately preferred principally to underscore the element of organizational continuity, especially since this complex will predictably persist even after Ho's death or retirement.

Revolutionary Situation in March 1945

World War II created revolutionary conditions in a number of countries, but in Indo-China these turned out to be particularly favorable for Communist insurgents.[3] Two circumstances conspired to make them so. The crumbling away of colonial rule, a process well advanced in all European-held colonies, had been greatly accelerated here by the stationing of Japanese troops since 1940; this semi-occupation culminated in an inglorious overthrow of the remainder of French authority by a sudden Japanese coup on the evening of March 9, 1945. Secondly, this termination of colonial control had not been joined, as it was in such areas as Burma, or Indonesia, by the emergence of strong nationalist groups. Although the Japanese had flirted with a number of Vietnamese nationalists in 1940-1945, the overthrow of French power had come too late to allow for the Cabinet formed in April 1945 by Emperor Bao Dai with Tran Trong Kim as Premier to get a hold on the country before the capitulation of Japan threw everything into a turmoil. Into this vacuum of authority, a basic condition of insurrectionary success, stepped the Viet Minh, ably led from the background by the Communist Party of Indo-China.

The Party had some sizable assets to draw upon.[4] The building up

[2] In full: *Viet* Nam Doc Lap Dong *Minh* Hoi—League for the Independence of Viet Nam.

[3] For the political situation in this period see Ellen J. Hammer, *The Struggle for Indochina* (Stanford 1954), Ch. 1, 2.

[4] The official history of the Party (so far written only up to September 1945) is *Thirty Years of Struggle of the Party*, Book One, Central Commiittee of Propaganda of Viet Nam Lao-Dong Party and Committee for the Study of the Party's History (Hanoi 1960). Ho Chi Minh's writings and speeches have been published as

of the organization began in earnest as early as December 1924 when Ho Chi Minh arrived in Canton, then the headquarters of the alliance between the Kuomintang and the Chinese Communist Party.[5] Within a few years, 250 Vietnamese members of the Young Revolutionary Comrades Association had received their political training from Ho, and began to filter back to Viet Nam. After a period of division and uncertainty, conditions were soon judged ripe for founding a permanent organization. At a Unification Meeting in Hong Kong presided over by Ho, a Communist Party—to be known after the following October as the Indochinese Communist Party—was founded on January 6, 1930. A period of revolutionary activity in 1930-1931 was followed by serious reverses and a large part of the membership found itself in prison. However, a revival occurred during the Popular Front period (1936-1939), and after some more reverses in 1939-1940 an effective organization was reestablished in 1941.

When Ho Chi Minh returned to the Sino-Vietnamese border region after a prolonged absence (1932-1941) in the USSR and in China he immediately convened a session of the Party's Central Committee on May 19, 1941, and on the following day the Viet Minh Front was officially founded. This organization gradually consolidated its position and in 1944 began seriously to consider a general uprising. The men who together with Ho Chi Minh assumed the direction of the Party in 1941 have to this day remained the leaders of the Viet Minh complex: men such as Pham Van Dong, Truong Chinh, Vo Nguyen Giap, Hoang Van Hoan, and Hoang Quoc Viet. There have been no purges and remarkably little division in the top leadership since that time. The Party membership on which these men relied was

Selected Works, Vols. I-IV, 1922-1960 (Hanoi 1960-1962). The basic source on the early years is Gouvernement d'Indochine, Direction des affairs politiques et de la sûreté générale, *Contribution à l'histoire des mouvements politiques de l'Indochine française*, Vol. 4. *Le Dong-duong Cong-san dang ou Parti communiste indochinois 1925-1933* (Hanoi 1933). See also Ph. Devillers, *Histoire du Viêt Nam de 1940 à 1952* (Paris 1952); Virginia Thompson and Thomas Adloff, *The Left-wing in Southeast Asia* (New York 1950), Ch. 2; Milton Sacks in F. N. Trager, ed., *Marxism in Southeast Asia* (Stanford 1959), 102-170.

[5] After spending more than a decade in France (where he took part in the founding of the French Communist Party in 1921), and also in the U.S.S.R. (where he studied at the University of the Toilers of the East), he attended the Fifth Congress of the Comintern (Communist International) in July 1924, and served on the executive of Krestintern, the Peasant International (1923-1924). Ho's birthdate is variously given as 1890 or 1892. For a biographical sketch see Bernard Fall, *Le Viet-Minh* (Paris 1960), 20-37. Ho Chi Minh has made it clear that "at first it was above all my patriotism, and not by any means as yet Communism which drove me toward Lenin and the Communist International": "Moy put' k Leninizmu" [My Road to Leninism], *Problemy Vostokovedeniya*, No. 2 (1960), 20.

in the meantime rising from 211 at the time of the Unification Meeting in 1930, to 1,500 at the time of the affiliation with the Comintern in 1931, and to 5,000 in 1945. By that time, organizations affiliated with the Viet Minh had an additional membership of 50,000, and in the field there were "several thousands" of guerrillas.[6]

From our point of view among the most important assets of this group was its experience in the organization and conduct of internal war. In its short career the Party had been responsible for two series of uprisings that failed and, since 1941, it had been preparing the ground for another, and this time general insurrection. The first of the earlier uprisings was a poorly organized peasant revolt in Central Viet Nam at the time of the world depression in 1930-1931. "Soviets" were organized in two provinces and proceeded to hold revolutionary tribunals and distribute the land, but within three months they were all repressed. Two conclusions were drawn from this swift defeat: the "soviet" movement was declared an instance of "adventurism" and a resort to unorganized terrorism, and it was condemned for its preoccupation with the land question and for its failure to grasp "the policy of an anti-imperalist united front."[7] In other words, the "class struggle" had been overstressed at the expense of nationalism. Secondly, the Comintern criticized Ho Chi Minh and the Indochinese Party for lax security and the failure to protect the leadership from police supervision and ultimate arrest. One more such disaster was to occur in 1939, when nearly 1,000 Party members were arrested in one police swoop. Security methods improved noticeably thereafter, reaching a high pitch of efficiency in the mid-1940's.

The second series of uprisings occurred in 1940 at a time when the arrival of Japanese troops in Indo-China and the Thai attack on Cambodia seemed to herald the end of French rule. Communist-led insurrections broke out, and failed, in Bac Son district, North Viet Nam (this was a local uprising), in Southern Viet Nam (mostly peasant *jacquerie*), and at Do Luong, Central Viet Nam (a military revolt). The southern insurrection in particular was staged on local initiative; it is claimed that orders that it should not be launched,

[6] See in particular *Thirty Years,* p. 24; Le Thanh Khoi, *Le Viet-Nam: Histoire et Civilization* (Paris 1955), 444, 465; Vo Nguyen Giap, *People's War, People's Army* (Hanoi 1961), 51.

[7] *Thirty Years,* 36; a Soviet history, "The National Liberation Movement in Viet Nam 1858-1945," A. P. Shiltova and V. F. Mordvinov [Moscow 1958] summarised in *The YUVA Newsletter,* I (January 1962), 13-15, speaks of "leftist mistakes." This issue of *The YUVA Newsletter* contains a general survey of Soviet writings on Viet Nam.

issued by the Party's Central Session which met in North Viet Nam in October, did not reach the South in time.[8] But the costly failures (100 dead and 6,000 arrests in the South alone) did not discourage the leadership. They were taken as evidence of popular desire to fight and the lessons drawn were: (1) the insurrection must be correctly timed, in order that confusion in enemy ranks and the support of the non-committed may be maximised; (2) winning over enemy soldiers is not enough, and reliance must be placed "chiefly on the great masses of the people"; (3) the importance of creating land bases.[9]

From 1941 onwards the Viet Minh once again, but this time more systematically, went about preparing for a general insurrection.[10] This took the form chiefly of political action: dissemination of propaganda, the training of cadres, and an expansion of the network of cells throughout the country. A special effort was made to build up bases for future military action in the northern border region. These were to be areas increasingly under clandestine Viet Minh political control but not as yet primarily the bases of guerrilla warfare. Nevertheless, a number of small detachments started to operate for limited periods; some suffered heavy casualties when the French launched counter-actions, others dispersed into smaller groups to carry on political work. Despite the small scale of this activity, the framework of future armed units was thus prepared, the fundamentals of guerrilla warfare (summarised in the official history as "reliance on the masses, continual growth, extreme mobility, and constant adaptation"[11]) were learned, and the foundations for seizing power were laid in the crucial years of 1941-1945.

The prerequisite of successful uprising is wide popular support, and this was clearly recognised from an early stage. In the Popular Front period independence had been abandoned as an immediate demand and this provoked criticism from the nationalists. But in October 1940 the Central Committee withdrew the slogan "To confiscate landlords' land and distribute it to the tillers," and by May 1941 the theme of "national liberation" held the center of the stage. The organizational expression of the new emphasis on the fight for independence was the Viet Minh, formed "to rally the different strata

[8] *Thirty Years*, 67-68.

[9] *Ibid.*, 65-70.

[10] Good impressions of the atmosphere of this work may be found in stories by Vo Nguyen Giap and Hoang Quoc Viet in *A Heroic People: Memoirs from the Revolution* (Hanoi 1960), 94 ff.

[11] *Thirty Years*, 73; no reference is made to Mao Tse-tung.

of the people and the national revolutionary forces in the struggle against the main enemy, that is the French and Japanese fascist imperialists."[12] That this was a major factor in the ultimate success of the "August 1945 Revolution" is clearly recognised, for instance, by Vo Nguyen Giap. He said, "It is precisely for this reason (for stressing the tasks of national liberation) that within a short period, the Viet Minh gathered together the great forces of the people and became the most powerful political organization of the broad revolutionary masses,"[13] reflecting the fact that nationalist grievances were the direct source of the revolutionary situation. By 1943, elements of the "national bourgeoisie" and the Vietnamese intelligentsia were being drawn into the Viet Minh; the party as such kept itself all this while in the background. Despite the efforts of the Kuomintang to sponsor an alternative organization[14] and later an exile government under its own control, the Viet Minh soon developed a monopoly of the national theme within the country. Nor were the groups then active in the South and collaborating with the Japanese a match for the Viet Minh.

The Party had also acquired some useful external assets. Its loyalty to the U.S.S.R. had remained unquestioned, and links with the Chinese Communist Party were strong too, dating from the Canton period.[15] But *qua* Viet Minh, and conscious of its isolation, the Party also cultivated relations with the Kuomintang and benefited in 1942-1945 from its subsidies in exchange for intelligence information about Japanese movements in Indo-China. Some five hundred Vietnamese, mostly Viet Minh members, received training in guerrilla warfare at

[12] *Ibid.*, 71.

[13] Giap, *People's War,* 75; the official history lays less stress upon nationalism as such. Giap adds however that this concern with national independence led "in the first years of the seizure of power and of the Resistance War . . . partly to the slighting of the anti-feudal task."

[14] The Viet Nam Cach Minh *Dong Minh Hoi* (The League of Revolutionary Parties of Viet Nam), comprised the Viet Minh in addition to a number of smaller groups. In February 1943 Ho was installed as Chairman of the Dong Minh Hoi; in March 1944 he joined the exile government. Viet Minh was the sole beneficiary of these efforts, and of the subsidies from the Kuomintang which they brought forth.

[15] For instance, in 1934 the Central Committee of the C.P.C. took it upon itself to address in the light of its own "ample experience of defeats and victories" an open letter to members of the Indo-Chinese Party in order to pose "certain questions relating to your 'work and your struggle'." The letter counselled the "Indo-Chinese comrades" not to succumb to panic and disarray, criticised their factionalism, and encouraged them to follow the example of Chinese soviets. *Cahiers du Bolchévisme* (Paris), XI (Aug. 14, 1934), 957-968. "Wholehearted assistance" on the part of the Eighth Route Army of the Chinese Communist forces for the Viet Minh in the China-Viet Nam border region in 1941-1945 has recently been acknowledged. (*Nhan Dan,* in *Viet Nam News Agency,* February 4, 1963, item 0603).

a Kuomintang camp at Dai Kien near Liuchow.[16] Similar relations were built up with American (including O.S.S.) missions in South China. These contacts made it possible for the Viet Minh to claim, in its propaganda within the country, to be on the "winning side of the Allies."

As pointed out, the Viet Minh was strong because its nationalist rivals in Viet Nam had been weakened by the efficiency of French repression, and because the French colonial authorities themselves were about to be liquidated by the Japanese army. The latter, in turn, had already been defeated elsewhere. But the Communist Party of Indo-China had aspirations, implicit in its name, which extended beyond Viet Nam; it had ambitions to preserve the French-created structure of the Indo-Chinese Federation under its own leadership. The name originally adopted at the Unification Meeting was that of Viet Nam Communist Party; on Comintern instructions this was changed to Indochinese Communist Party because "the Vietnamese, Cambodian, and Laotian proletariat have politically and economically to be closely related in spite of their difference in language, customs, and race."[17] The scope of political action was thus extended and delegates from Laos are reported to have attended the Party Congress in Macao in 1935. Strikes under the party's leadership in Cambodia and Laos during the Popular Front period are claimed by Hoang Quoc Viet,[18] but organizational work in the two countries remained weak and, during wartime, the Viet Minh developed strength in neither. The most important reason for this failure was that as an organization basing itself on Vietnamese nationalism it could not effectively appeal to Laotians and Cambodians. The chief element of its strength in Viet Nam thus operated as its main liability elsewhere in Indo-China and in Southeast Asia.

Two Decades of Revolutionary Activity

Space has been devoted to this account of the revolutionary situation in March 1945 because the background and experience ac-

[16] Devillers, *Histoire du Viêt-Nam,* 104.

[17] October 1930 decision quoted in *Thirty Years,* 27. The "national" question continued to be a subject for discussions through the 1930's, some party members demanding that Laos and Cambodia be granted the right of separation. The leadership interpreted the Party program calling for a "fraternal union of all the Indochinese people," in the light of Stalin's principles of national self-determination. "Vers le renforcement du Parti communiste indochinois," *Cahiers du Bolchevisme,* XI (July 1, 1934), 798-799.

[18] *A Heroic People,* 183.

cumulated by the Viet Minh prior to that date, and especially in the crucial years 1941-1945, has usually been underestimated. It is also frequently forgotten that, from the Viet Minh point of view at least, the crucial seizure of power occurred in August 1945. The fighting that followed, especially after December 1946, has the character of a resistance war.

THE "AUGUST REVOLUTION" (MARCH-SEPTEMBER 1945)

On the night of the Japanese coup, the Standing Bureau of the Central Committee met in a Hanoi suburb. On March 12 the meeting issued a directive entitled "Our Tactics in Relation to the Franco-Japanese Conflict,"[19] ordering preparations for a general uprising, to start as soon as conditions permitted. These were not judged ripe at that moment because the Japanese remained strong, the "neutral" strata of the people still needed a period of time to get used to the new situation, and the party's forces were not yet ready for action. However, conditions were changing rapidly: the Japanese were incapable of consolidating their position; the prevailing famine created dissatisfaction among the people; and the Allies' landing in Indo-China was clearly imminent. To prepare for insurrection, either at the time of Japan's capitulation or in the event of the landing of the Allies, the group issued instructions not to regard the French any longer as the chief enemy. It also called for more active forms of political action, "propaganda with arms in hand," and decided to start guerrilla warfare where the terrain permitted it.

Events moved quickly. In April, orders were issued for setting up Liberation Committees at all levels; a military conference decided to unify all armed units into the Viet Nam Liberation Army, and to proceed with the expansion of guerrilla warfare. As the Japanese hold on the country relaxed, and as the Tran Trong Kim government was failing to establish its own authority, the Viet Minh started to assume power in many localities and in June set up a Free Zone comprising six provinces of North Viet Nam. Contact was established with de Gaullists in China, and in August also with the Japanese headquarters in Hanoi. On August 13 a Party Congress convened in Thai Nguyen province in the Free Zone and decided upon launching a general insurrection. Much emphasis was laid, however, upon the

[19] see text in *Razobem Okovy: Dokumenty avgustovskoy Revolyutsii 1945 goda vo V'yetname* [Let us Break our Shackles: Documents of the August 1945 Revolution in Viet Nam] (Moscow 1960), 9-19.

principle of "timeliness." The enemy was to be demoralised and, preferably, induced to surrender before the start of fighting. A People's Congress, which followed immediately, elected the National Liberation Committee, headed by Ho Chi Minh. When the news of the Japanese surrender spread, the general insurrection was ordered and within a few days and with a minimum of fighting, power was seized by the Viet Minh throughout most of Viet Nam, including Hanoi, Hue (the Imperial capital), and Saigon. Emperor Bao Dai abdicated in favor of the Viet Minh, and Ho Chi Minh read out the Declaration of Independence of the new Democratic Republic of Viet Nam at a mass meeting in Hanoi on September 2nd.

In August 1945 and largely by its own exertions, the Viet Minh thus assumed power. It is a point of considerable significance that, thanks to Bao Dai's act, it had now become the legitimate government of the land, although it was not as yet recognised by outside powers.[20]

"CONSOLIDATION AND TRUCE" (SEPTEMBER 1945-DECEMBER 1946)

In less than a month the new regime was under heavy pressure. In the North, the Kuomintang Army moved in and, in its wake, came the exiles from South China ready to claim a share of power. In the South, British forces landed to disarm the Japanese and were soon followed by the French. Yet the Viet Minh showed great staying power despite its basic weakness. By a series of adroit maneuvers it first conciliated the Chinese and then played them off against the French; the Chinese withdrew in March 1946. Deprived of Chinese support and bitterly anti-French, the nationalists were thus isolated and by mid-1946 lost control of the five provinces of North Viet Nam that they had gained the preceding September. The British left after disarming the Japanese, and only the French remained. Although fighting broke out in Saigon on September 23, 1946 and the major centers in the South and Cambodia and Laos were soon in French hands (with the Viet Minh holding the countryside in South Viet Nam), a truce was reached on March 6, 1946 whereby France recognised Viet Nam as a "free and independent state" within the Indo-Chinese federation and the French Union in exchange for the admission of 15,000 French troops to North Viet Nam. The truce did not last long. The build up of forces continued on both sides,

[20] A Soviet collection of documents on Viet Nam features, as its first item, the act of Bao Dai's abdication, *Demokraticheskaya Respublika V'yetnam: Konstitutsiya, Zakonodatelnye Akty, Dokumenty* [Democratic Republic of Viet Nam: Constitution, Legislative Acts, Documents] (Moscow 1955), 9-10.

and when the Viet Minh concluded that the French were unprepared to concede the substance of independence and to give up control of the South, they launched the general attack of 19 December 1946. The eight year war had begun.

"RESISTANCE WAR" (1946-1954)

The Viet Minh may have hoped to throw the French troops into the sea but they misjudged the relation of forces, and launched the country into a war of extreme hardship.[21] While the French occupied all the main towns, the government withdrew into prepared resistance bases (basically, the Free Zone readied since 1941 and established in June 1945). This area remained under Viet Minh control throughout the war and was the true foundation of its ultimate success. The main army, estimated at some 30,000 in 1946, was kept intact and every effort was put into building it up into a fully trained regular force side by side with the organization of local self-defence militia and regional guerrilla units. In pursuit of a strategy of long-term resistance, as formulated by Truong Chinh in his *The Resistance Will Win* (1947),[22] guerrilla war—a disorderly war, a war without battlefronts, a war of encirclement, a war of scorched earth—was launched throughout the country. Inspired by Mao Tse-tung, Truong Chinh thus cleared the decks for a protracted conflict in three stages—defense, equilibrium, and offence—and a correspondingly gradual transition from guerrilla to mobile and positional warfare.[23]

A decisive point in the war occurred in late 1949, when Communist Chinese troops reached the borders of Viet Nam. At that moment the war passed from the stage of defence to that of equilibrium, and at the same time began to change its character from a resistance war to a civil war. The Viet Minh reacted to this decisive development by reluctantly initiating their first, and successful, offensive on French posts along the Chinese border, and by publicly revealing their Communist affiliations. The party, "dissolved" in November 1945 to

[21] See Fall, *Le Viet-Minh,* 60-61.

[22] Republished recently in an English translation, Truong Chinh's *The Resistance Will Win* (Hanoi 1960) is the best exposition of Viet Minh political strategy in the war against the French. Malcolm Salmon, in *Focus on Indo-China* (Hanoi 1961), 118, describes Truong Chinh's (and Giap's) writings as "creative application of Marxist-Leninist revolutionary military science to the conditions of Viet Nam."

[23] Truong Chinh not only based the bulk of his analysis on Chinese practice and on Mao Tse-tung's writings, but also acknowledged his debt in a number of direct references to Man's work "On the Protracted War" [in *Selected Works,* II (London 1954), 157-243]. Hanoi recently remembered Niguyen Troi, a fifteenth-century mandarin who had "formulated concrete policies for a protracted war." (*Viet Nam News Agency,* Sept. 17, 1962 (item 3239).

lull Kuomintang and French suspicions, "reappeared" in public under its new name in March 1951, and the first drastic land reform law was promulgated in 1953.[24] With Chinese and Soviet supplies coming freely across the border and large formations receiving training in China, the army (now approaching 300,000) seized the initiative and, after a premature and unsuccessful attempt in 1951, went over to the offensive in 1953 and won a crucial victory at Dien Bien Phu in 1954. In July of that year an international conference at Geneva reached agreements restoring peace to Indo-China, but despite this military success, the Viet Minh received no more than half the loaf: only North Viet Nam was given over to its complete control.

LAOS AND CAMBODIA (1950-1954)[25]

In the 1940's the Viet Minh maintained contact with Prince Souphanouvong, a leading member of the Free Lao group that seized control in September 1945, and they supported anti-French activities in Laos.[26] However, the Free Laotians were driven out the following year and had to take refuge in Thailand. In March 1949 the Prince was dismissed from the exile government in Bangkok for authorising Viet Minh bands to operate in Laotian territory. After reaching an acceptable settlement with the French, most of the exiles returned to Laos later that year and soon assumed a decisive share in the government. There were also contacts with Cambodian nationalists late in 1945, and again in 1948-1949, helped by the sizable Vietnamese minority in close touch with Saigon. Those attempts failed due to effective French counteraction and the nationalists' unwillingness to be subordinated to Viet Minh purposes. Essentially, both in Laos and in Cambodia, the nationalists refused to serve the Viet Minh. The latter, unable to press the point, and still anxious to avoid accusations of "imperialist designs" for "colonial supremacy," paid less attention to those two small countries.[27] Only in 1950 did

[24] Ho Chi Minh admitted in 1951 that the party, despite the "proclamation of voluntary dissolution, . . . in reality went underground" and "continued to lead the administration and the people." (*Selected Works,* III, 248). It was referred to as "the organization" (*Ibid.,* 98). See also Truong Chinh, *The Resistance Will Win,* 101, 137.

[25] See also Virginia Thompson and Thomas Adloff, *Minority Problems in Southeast Asia* (Stanford 1955), 170-228; Fall, *Le Viet-Minh,* 126-133; Hammer, 254-258.

[26] During the Second World War Souphanouvong, living in Vinh, Central Viet Nam, was in touch with the Viet Minh, met Ho Chi Minh, and was engaged in organizing young Laotians. W. B. Burchett, *Mekong Upstream* (Berlin 1959), 223.

[27] Speaking in September 1946 Vo Nguyen Giap sought to dismiss such accusations. Viet Nam Democratic Republic, *One Year of Revolutionary Achievement* (Bangkok 1946), 18-19.

Vo Nguyen Giap think it "a strategic mistake" not to have regarded Indo-China as a single theatre, and "a basic error in the conduct of the war" to have neglected Cambodia and Laos.[28]

The war then moved into the stage of equilibrium and, with the Viet Minh gaining new confidence, steps were taken to remedy this neglect. A Central Committee for the Liberation of the Khmer People was formed in Cambodia in April 1950, and Prince Souphanouvong founded the Neo Lao Itsala (Laotian National United Front) the following August. These groups were replicas of the Viet Minh front, and proceeded to create "Resistance Governments" in direct opposition to the French-supported, but nationalist-led legitimate authorities of those two countries. In March 1951 a conference of the United Fronts of Viet Nam, Laos, and Cambodia decided to set up an Alliance of the Peoples of Viet Nam, Khmer, and Pathet Lao with a permanent directing committee, and "called on the people of the three countries to coordinate their fight to defeat the imperialists."[29] It was after this careful political preparation that political activity preliminary to guerrilla warfare began in both areas. It was on the basis of those decisions that regular Viet Minh forces, in official communiqués always described as volunteers, entered the two countries in strength. They entered Northern Laos in a much publicised offensive early in 1953, leading to the creation of a "liberated zone" with the Prince's headquarters established at Sam Neua. They invaded Central and Southern Laos later that year and Cambodia early in 1954. Offensives in and through Laos and Cambodia played an important part in the conduct of mobile warfare in the last year of the war.[30] By 1954 substantial parts of both countries were thus under Viet Minh-Khmer-Pathet Lao control.

Despite these developments, the "Resistance Governments," obviously Viet Minh-dominated, failed to gain recognition at the Geneva Conference on Indo-China, and the agreements then reached terminated both regular and guerrilla activities. After Geneva, North Viet Nam reluctantly recognised the legitimacy of the Royal Governments of Laos and Cambodia and gave pledges of observance of the five principles of peaceful coexistence. The "Resistance Governments" were presumably dissolved and the Viet Nam-Khmer-Pathet Lao

[28] Quoted in George Tanham, *Communist Revolutionary Warfare: Viet Minh in Indochina* (New York 1961), 17.

[29] Burchett, *Mekong Upstream*, 89.

[30] See Vo Nguyen Giap, *Dien Bien Phu* (2nd ed.; Hanoi 1962).

Alliance, which in 1951 seemed the forerunner of a new Vietnamese-dominated Indo-Chinese Federation, has not been heard of since.[31]

LAOS (1955-1962)[32]

Geneva brought peace to North Viet Nam and to Cambodia, but not to Laos where the Pathet Lao were assigned by international agreement two provinces (Sam Neua and Phong Saly) as regroupment zones where they succeeded, with Viet Minh help, in consolidating their position. Intermittent but mostly small-scale warfare thus continued in Laos until 1962.

Royal Government attempts to deal with the Pathet Lao militarily having proved unavailing in 1955-1956, a political settlement was reached with the help of the International Commission in November 1957.[33] The Neo Lao Hak Xat (Lao Fatherland Front), successor to the Neo Lao Itsala, entered the government and agreed to demobilise over 5,000 men, while two battalions totaling 1,500 men were to be incorporated into the Royal Army. The peace did not last long; after an election, the government was reformed the following July without the two Neo Lao Hak Xat ministers. In May 1959 an attempt to disarm the two battalions failed partially—No. 2 battalion escaped and the civil war was on again. With logistic support from North Viet Nam an offensive was launched with the aim of regaining the base areas in Sam Neua and Phong Saly but failed possibly because of lack of the usual careful preparation.[34] A UN inquiry mission visiting Laos in September failed to find evidence of Viet Minh "aggression," and guerrilla activities remained on a small scale until Captain Kong Le's coup of August 1960 that soon brought the neutralist forces of Prince Souvanna Phouma into an alliance with the Pathet Lao fighting units. By December 1960 the civil war once again reached serious proportions, with North Vietnamese cadres and Soviet transport planes and equipment ranged on one side and Ameri-

[31] The Program of the Viet Nam Workers' Party adopted in 1951 and still in force, favors in Art. 12 a federation of the three countries "if all three so desire." (*Demokraticheskaya Respublika V'yetnam*, 45.)

[32] See also Sisouk na Champassak, *Storm over Laos* (New York 1961); A. L. Strong, *Cash and Violence in Laos* (Peking 1961); R. Fifield, *The Diplomacy of Southeast Asia 1945-58* (New York 1958), 346-357; and George Modelski, ed., *SEATO: Six Studies* (Melbourne 1962), 147-150.

[33] See esp. *Third Interim Report of the International Commission for Supervision and Control in Laos*, Cmd. 314 (London 1957), 6-20; Burchett, *Mekong Upstream*, 246-254.

[34] A good study of this episode is A. M. Halpern and H. B. Fredman, *Communist Strategy in Laos*, Rand Research Memorandum 2561 (June 14, 1960).

can military advisers and supplies on the other. Following repeated reverses sustained by the anti-Communist forces of Phoumi Nosavan, a truce was established in May 1961, and a full international settlement on the basis of neutrality and withdrawal of all foreign troops was reached in July 1962 at Geneva.[35] Once again, the Neo Lao Hak Xat entered the government, but this time in a much stronger position. This group is still very closely tied to Hanoi, but its increasing international contacts, in Peking and Moscow as well as in Geneva, may be expected to lessen its previously exclusive dependence on the Viet Minh.

SOUTH VIET NAM (1956-1962)

When the Republic of Viet Nam refused to participate in the nation-wide elections foreseen in the Final Declaration of the Geneva Conference for mid-1956, pressure from the North soon mounted again and gradually assumed the proportions of full-scale internal war.[36] At first, it took the form of intensified political work, consolidation of bases, and elimination of "traitors" (officials, village headmen, teachers).[37] The signal for the intensification of pressure was the Viet Nam Workers' Party Congress of September 1960. Conscious of the success already achieved in political preparation, assured of the support of China and the U.S.S.R.,[38] confident that the world balance of power was swinging to the side of the "camp of socialism," and flushed at the news of the August coup in Vientiane, the Congress resolved to step up action in order to "extend the people's democratic revolution to the South."[39] This would be accomplished in two stages: (1) preparatory, to upset the local balance of power; and (2) direct revolution[40]—mainly on the basis of appeals to nationalism

[35] See George Modelski, *International Conference on the Settlement of the Laotian Question 1961-2*, Working Paper No. 2, Department of International Relations, Australian National University (Canberra 1962).

[36] This is well illustrated in the rising rate of military casualties for both sides in the south; from 1,000 in 1957 to 11,000 in 1959 and to 20,000 in the first six months of 1962 (Agence France Presse dispatch from Saigon, *Agence Khmere de Presse,* July 31, 1962).

[37] For an early and perceptive account of the revival of guerrilla warfare see Bernard B. Fall, "South Viet-Nam's Internal Problems," *Pacific Affairs,* XXXI (September 1958), 255-258.

[38] N. S. Khrushchev "An example of [a war of national liberation] is the armed struggle of the Vietnamese people" "Communists support such just wars fully and without reservations" . . . "For new victories for the World Communist Movement," *Soviet News*, London (January 21, 1961), 43-44.

[39] For a selection of Hanoi statements to this effect see Department of State, *A Threat to the Peace* (Washington 1961), Part II, 1-7.

[40] *Ibid.*, 93.

(by utilising anti-American slogans) and with underemphasis of all themes likely to antagonize "bourgeois elements."[41] Within a few months a Front for the Liberation of the South, another replica of the Viet Minh Front, was formed and announced a program calling for the withdrawal of U.S. troops and aid. Operations in company and battalion strength began to be mounted and in 1961 the war reached serious dimensions. By September, the Front claimed to control over 90 percent of South Viet Nam's six thousand villages.

The prompt and determined American reaction, and the example of the settlement in Laos, soon brought a change in policy. Reunification, though not abandoned as a goal was relegated to the background. Following mid-1962, the Front aimed to secure for South Viet Nam merely the status of neutrality on the Laotian model and the participation in a "peace bloc" with neutral Cambodia and Laos.[42] Meanwhile the armed struggle remained in the stage preparatory to direct revolution.

THAILAND

The Vietnamese minority of some 70,000 in Thailand lives mostly in the northeast, and has long been a source of anxiety for the Thai government as it must be regarded as a potential auxiliary of the Viet Minh complex within its territory. In origin, this group consists mostly of political refugees from French colonial rule, many of them from the agrarian disturbances in Central Viet Nam in 1930-1931, and from the reoccupation of Laos and Cambodia in 1945-1946. Ho Chi Minh worked among them in 1928-1929, and during the Second World War they operated in accordance with the program of the Viet Minh. Guided by the General Association of Overseas Vietnamese, they gave "vigorous support" to the resistance war.[43] Completely unassimilated, they have successfully eluded the surveillance of Thai officials. In August 1959 they were reported to have been active in relation to the fighting in Laos.[44] In 1960-1961, during the troubles in Laos, "most of

[41] At the same time the Congress resolved to intensify the "struggle for socialism in the North." By the end of 1961 this had brought 88 percent of peasant households into cooperative farms. However, there has been no sign of communes.

[42] There have been reports of Sino-Soviet disagreements over this change of tactics, the Soviet Union favoring the more moderate course of negotiations (*Times of Viet Nam* (Saigon) October 3, 1962).

[43] "Situation of Overseas Vietnamese in Thailand," *Nhan Dan* (December 9, 1959), in JRPS 3147, 1-3; see also Bui Quang Tung, "Contribution à l'étude des colonies vietnamiennes en Thailand," *France-Asie* (Saigon) XV, (1958), 438-451.

[44] Halpern and Fredman, 109, 111.

the young men in the Vietnamese communities disappeared," presumably to join the fighting there, and returned when the danger was over.[45] Between 1959 and 1962, 30,000 members of the Vietnamese community of Thailand were repatriated to North Viet Nam and within a few years the exodus may be complete.

Evidence linking indigenous political activities in Thailand with the Viet Minh complex, as distinct from the Communist system in general, has so far been scant. Speculation on this subject has stressed the close links between Lao-speaking people on both sides of the Mekong River, and has pointed out that the Northeast Region of Thailand—poor, underdeveloped, and traditionally neglected—has been a prolific source of opposition politicians and is potentially a fertile ground for guerrilla warfare. Among the few hard facts on this subject have been the setting up in Laos, after the coup of August 1960, of a Thai Exiles' Association, and the arrests in the Northeast in 1961, of individuals reported to have received guerrilla training at a Pathet Lao center in southern Laos, in order that they should work for the separation of the Northeast from Thailand and union with Laos.[46] This could be a local Pathet Lao initiative, possibly uncoordinated with the activities of a Bangkok-based Communist Party of Thailand. So far, however, the activities in the Northeast are still evidently at most in the early stages of the establishment of political bases for armed action.

The Viet Minh Experience: An Evaluation

The Viet Minh activity of the past two decades is extraordinarily rich in revolutionary experience. No other Communist Party or regime, with the one and partial exception of the Chinese, has been responsible for conducting and guiding revolutionary activities for close to twenty-two years at one stretch. We should not, however, regard the entire period as of one piece; a whole variety of experiences has been associated with the Viet Minh complex during that period.

A fine example of a relatively non-violent seizure of power, a revolutionary coup executed with a minimum of violence, was the "August Revolution" of 1945. This, indeed, is the favorite revolution of the Vietnamese Party and the one both they and Moscow seem to be most proud of.[47] It would appear that this is a type of action close to what

[45] Theh Chongkhadikij, "The North-East Story," Part III, *Bangkok Post* (March 15, 1962).

[46] *Ibid.* (March 3 and 5, 1962.)

[47] Unusually full documentation of the "August Revolution" has been published both in Hanoi and in Moscow. See in particular *Thirty Years,* and *Razobem Okovy.*

recent Soviet theoretical writings refer to as "peaceful transition to socialism." Indeed, it does represent an economical method of attaining revolutionary power. Its lessons are regarded as making "a contribution to the enrichment of the treasury of revolutionary theory in a colonial and semi-feudal country, in an epoch when imperialism is in decay and socialism is victorious."[48] From the publicity it has received in Moscow we may infer that it is regarded as a correct model for seizing power in contemporary colonial and post-colonial situations.

The "lessons" of the "August Revolution," explains the official history, have been fivefold:[49] (1) careful preparation, both in the ideological and the organizational fields (including the training of cadres, building up bases of resistance, and the organization of armed forces); (2) seizing the right opportunity (i.e., timing); (3) "launching the revolutionary high tide of the whole people" (the importance of having the support of the majority of the people by including in the movement "all classes, nationalities and religions"); (4) skillful combination of forms of armed struggle with forms of political struggle (i.e., avoiding the exclusive use of either and gradually shifting from political to military methods); and (5) making full use of the contradictions in enemy ranks and spearheading forces at the main enemy. The French and Japanese imperialists having been defined as the "main enemy," most nationalist sentiment could be attracted in support of the movement.[50]

There is little in this prescription that is peculiar to Viet Minh theory or practice; basically it is a pragmatic formula of success observed by all successful insurrections. The Viet Minh had indeed distinguished themselves in the way this prescription was implemented, and in particular by the careful preparation and fine timing of their action. Their appreciation of the situation was perfect. Yet it is also beyond question that the major element in this success was the weakness of their opponents.

The "Resistance War that became a Civil War," in so far as it can be considered apart from the "August Revolution," is an instance of the "non-peaceful settlement of the question of power." While the 1945 uprising has been acclaimed as a fine success for the Indochinese Communist Party, the war that followed it, a harrowing

[48] Those are the closing words of *Thirty Years,* 102; elsewhere it is also described as a victory of Leninist theories in the "first national-liberation revolution in a colonial country." Nguyen Khanh Toan "Put' V'yetnamskoy revolyutsii" [The Course of the Vietnamese Revolution], *Problemy Vostokovedeniya,* No. 4 (1960), 19.

[49] *Thirty-Years,* 97-102.

[50] Giap, *Peoeple's War,* 71-87, makes broadly the same points, but lays greater stress on the essentially notionalist character of the revolution (see note 13 above).

experience of eight years of cruel and relentless violence, is regarded with less pride. The battle of Dien Bien Phu and the campaign of the last year of the war have been held up, and justifiably so, as examples of first class military operations;[51] but not enough is said about the preceding seven years of tremendous hardships and unlimited sacrifice.[52] These are grounds for thinking that in retrospect, the Viet Minh leaders are not at all happy about their decision to launch a general attack on the French in December 1946. One can see that they may have reached the conclusion that peace with the French was impossible because of such acts of violence as the shelling of Haiphong, with casualities running into thousands, and because of French activities indicating a design to establish a separate state in the South. In these conditions a surprise attack might have been thought to confer advantages for the subsequent conduct of a protracted war on the Chinese model. Indeed it may have been intended to forestall a French surprise attack which, if well executed, might have had disastrous consequences.[53]

Yet Viet Minh leaders must now realize that their interpretation of the Haiphong incident was probably incorrect. In the absence of the general attack, the circles favoring all-out war with the Viet Minh might not have gained such a complete victory as they did after December. The March agreement, which envisaged the withdrawal within ten years of French troops—with the exception of some naval and air bases—might have been maintained. Even though the suspicions with regard to South Viet Nam were probably correct, eight years of war also failed to bring that area under Viet Minh control. Above all, the national "Resistance War" of 1946 had by 1954 changed into a civil war; national unity, so skillfully attained in 1945, was dissipated in a paroxysm of violence.

Thus it is not at all surprising that the present-day leadership should hesitate to offer the eight years' war as an example to be widely emulated. For instance, it is not held up as a model for the present fight in South Viet Nam, for which the 1941-1945 experi-

[51] See for instance the recent publications of Vo Nguyen Giap, such as *Dien Bien Phu* and *People's War, People's Army*.

[52] Ngo Van Chieu's *Journal d'un combattant Vietminh* (Paris 1955) is the diary of a Vietminh officer and conveys a convincing picture of the hardships of jungle warfare. See also Bernard B. Fall, *Street Without Joy: Indochina at War 1946-1954* (Harrisburg, Pa. 1961).

[53] Speaking in September 1946, Vo Nguyen Giap referred to the "atmosphere of suspicion" "throughout the country" that the French Government is trying to "gain time for a 'fait accompli'." *One Year of Revolutionary Achievement*, 12, 21.

ence is regarded as the more appropriate precept (which means that more flexible strategies are now in use than during the "Resistance War"). Although marked by skillful and successful use of military force, the war was a failure politically. The partial success it achieved was no more than what the French, in the absence of a general attack, might have conceded in 1946-1947. We may only speculate about the underlying reasons for the decision to precipitate the war: overconfidence, stimulated by the easy successes of 1945 and fostering the belief that the French forces in the North might be thrown into the sea; and possibly a victory for the pro-Chinese wing led by Truong Chinh. In July 1946, after a period of negotiations with the Kuomintang, the Chinese Communist Party also decided to resume the civil war.

The Viet Minh complex also affords instructive examples of revolution from without. These are the previously mentioned cases of Cambodia and Laos (1950-1954) and Laos (1955-1962). Such insurrectionary actions that have occurred in those two countries in the past dozen years have been stimulated and encouraged, if not directed, by the Viet Minh. The 1950 decision to broaden the field of operations in Indo-China by including Laos and Cambodia, and possibly even Thailand, without and in fact against the nationalist authorities already established there, had a good deal to be said for it.[54] The first two countries were at that time still dependent upon the French, although already self-governing under traditional elites. They had been part of the Indo-Chinese Federation and their resources were used by French forces for waging war upon the Viet Minh. Finally they constituted weak and exposed positions, and an attack upon them would put pressure on the French command. For purposes of waging war in and for Viet Nam, the decision was successful; as an instance of exporting revolution it was less so.

Such success as may ultimately attend the activities of the Pathet Lao will be in large part due to Viet Minh activities in the early 1950's. Yet even this is still a matter for the future, and in the medium range view these activities cannot be regarded as having brought about their objective of installing Viet Minh-controlled or sympathizing regimes. In 1950-1954 the Pathet Lao and Khmer "Resistance Governments" were little more than a cover for Viet Minh strategic operations. In both countries, traditionally vulnerable to

[54] Tanham, 17, regards it as "mistaken" because "geographically, racially and historically" Indo-China is not homogeneous.

Vietnamese expansion, they could easily be interpreted as a threat to national survival. The ruling elites, with the help of the French, did not find it too difficult to deal with them once independence was assured and the Vietnamese troops had withdrawn in 1954. In Cambodia, where the Viet Minh had previously relied heavily upon the Vietnamese minority and had no regroupment areas, the situation was stabilized after 1954. In Laos, close to North Viet Nam's centers of power, the Pathet Lao gained two provinces as regroupment areas and during campaigns in 1955-1956, 1959, and 1960-1962 consolidated their hold on important parts of the countryside. On the first two of these occasions, which essentially were defensive phases of the "revolution from without" operation, they benefited from logistic, training, cadre, and in 1960-1962 also from direct military support of North Viet Nam. These repeated campaigns showed that "revolution from without" can have both offensive and defensive phases. They showed too that, at times other than those of general war and without military control, revolution from without is at best a slow and time-consuming process, apt to create important international complications, and to bring in compensating intervention from the other side. This kind of revolution cannot easily be accomplished by a small power. Although its position has greatly improved since its foundation, the Pathet Lao still has some way to go before it can wield control over the whole of Laos.[55]

One of the countries here discussed, Cambodia, may yet provide an example of still another type of "transition to socialism"—"from above." Since 1955 the government of that country, led by Prince Sihanouk, has pursued a policy of neutrality towards the great powers, refusal to cooperate with SEATO, and hostility towards Thailand and South Viet Nam. Cambodia has thus earned the approval of the Soviet Union and China and has secured the support of the domestic Communist group, the "Pracheachon" (People's Party).[56] The Prince has, of course, his own political organization and is anxious to keep the influence of the Pracheachon within strict limits.[57] It has been

[55] A senior Viet Minh leader, Le Van Hien (Minister of Labor in the first government of August 1945) took up his post as the first North Vietnamese ambassador to Laos in October, 1962.

[56] Burchett, 101-102, implies that the pre-1955 Communists' failure to cooperate with the Prince had been mistaken because the "Khmer Resistance groups" had "not appreciated" the efforts made by Sihanouk to secure independence.

[57] See Norodom Sihanouk, "Le Communisme au Cambodge," *France-Asie,* xv (1958), 192-206, 290-306; M. Leifer, "Cambodian Opposition," *Asian Survey,* II (April 1962), 13-15.

observed, however, that his "business-like working relations with the country's left-wing" have led to the gradual admission of many "progressive elements" into the Cambodian administration. It is also significant that a new law, which provides that "village heads shall be elected and not appointed, as in the past, by district officials,"[58] provides an opportunity for the Pracheachon to place its own appointees in village administration and thus to develop "land bases." The outcome of all this is far from certain, however, and only one thing seems clear—Sihanouk is using the weight of the USSR and China to offset Thai and Vietnamese, and this includes North Vietnamese, pressures upon the Khmers.

Reflecting the variety of revolutionary situations encountered, the models used by the Viet Minh have been various. Due to the distance from Moscow and to the circumstances of war and of clandestine existence, the local leadership could on the whole pursue policies attuned to local conditions. Yet freedom from unthinking conformity did not weaken, and indeed may have strengthened, the ties of allegiance to the international movement as led by the Soviet Party. Within the basic framework of this allegiance the methods used have largely been flexible, and did not follow any one single "model."

The Viet Minh has, of course, adhered faithfully to the central feature of the Soviet model—the dominance of the Communist Party. The party has throughout remained the brains and the organizational center of the entire Viet Minh complex. Noteworthy and unique, however, has been the length to which the Viet Minh was prepared to carry deception in order to disguise that role. During the Second World War most public activities were carried on behind the "front" provided by the Viet Minh; late in 1945 the Party voluntarily "dissolved" in order to lull foreign and domestic suspicions of its activities and affiliations. Soviet connections with Viet Nam were few and guarded. The USSR did not raise the question of Viet Nam in the United Nations, although it did at one stage raise that of Indonesia.[59] The Cominform journal *For a Lasting Peace, for a People's Democracy* in its first sixty issues (1948-1949) carried only three items from that country. It is surprising how even today North Vietnamese news sources seek to convey the impression that the South Viet Nam Liberation Front is not Communist-controlled. Yet

[58] Salmon, 249-250.

[59] The Soviet Union spoke in favor of the D.R.V.'s admission to the U.N. Economic Comission for Asia and the Far East at its meetings in late 1947 and 1948, but did not press the matter.

what is striking about the whole story is the efficiency and the purposefulness with which the Party leadership did in fact direct activities throughout this period.

The Party in Viet Nam has in fact been an orthodox Communist Party. Its early leaders were Moscow trained and its basic ideological inspiration has been Soviet. This was clearly so when the Comintern line was being followed, and continued to be so after the dissolution of that organization.[60] After 1954, North Vietnamese authors gave full credit to Soviet inspiration and rarely mentioned Chinese precepts. For instance, in a 1957 booklet especially written for publication in Moscow and entitled *October Revolution and the Liberation of the Peoples of the East,*[61] Ho Chi Minh eulogized at length upon the "significance of October"[62] and upon the role of the Soviet Union but mentioned only once the help of the French and Chinese parties (in that order). By 1960, however, the acknowledgments of help and assistance from China had become more frequent.[63] But there is so far no clear evidence to suggest that North Viet Nam has taken

[60] When Ho Chi Minh returned to Viet Nam early in 1941, his arrival was signalled through party channels as that of a representative of the Comintern, Hoang Quoc Viet, "*A Heroic People,* 199, 205-207. Ho Chi Minh had, of course, been a Comintern official for over a decade. One of the first jobs he did upon arrival was to translate Stalin's *Short History* into Vietnamese, type it himself, and distribute copies for study by cadres. (Vo Nguyen Giap, *A Heroic People,* 104, see also 111.)

[61] Ho Chi Minh, *Oktyabrskaya Revolyutsiya i osvobozhdeniye narodov Vostoka* (Moscow 1957) also reprinted in Ho Chi Minh, *Leninizm i osvobozhdeniye ugnetennykh narodov* [Leninism and the Liberation of Oppressed Peoples] (Moscow 1960), 27-41, and in *Selected Works,* IV, 260-279); this 23-page booklet has eight quotations from Lenin, two from Resolutions of the 20th C.P.S.U. Congress and one of Mao Tse-tung. This last quotation refers to China's debt to the October Revolution; it also is the only reference to Mao Tse-tung that has found its way into *Fundamentals of Marxism-Leninism* (Moscow 1961), 403.

[62] The "August Revolution" in Viet Nam was in fact an instance of a successful Communist seizure of power that did resemble to an interesting degree (and as no other did) the standard Soviet model of the "October Revolution." In both cases power was being conquered towards the end of a world war, where military defeat had decisively weakened the ruling power and where the interval between the collapse of the old order and the Communist coup was filled by a 'caretaker' national government unable to control the country. In both cases, too, the conquest of power was protected by fighting prolonged wars of intervention and a civil war.

[63] In an article entitled "Thirty years of the Viet Nam Workers Party" in *Leninizm,* 42-53; also in *Selected Works,* IV, 430-445, Ho Chi Minh gives three mentions to China and puts the Chinese Communist Party ahead of the French: "We shall always remember the generous support given to our Party and the people in their revolutionary struggle by the Communist Parties of the Soviet Union, China and France." (52). The warmest acknowledgement of Chinese influence is contained in a political report by Ho Chi Minh in 1951, at a time when China's help was of paramount importance. "Owing to geographical, historical, economic, and cultural conditions, the Chinese revolution exerted a great influence on the Vietnamese revolution which had to learn, and indeed has learned many experiences from it. Thanks to

the side of China in the Sino-Soviet controversy of recent years. Rather it has tried to steer clear of it and remain on good terms with both sides.[64]

The broad framework of ideological allegiance to the Soviet Union did not, however, prevent the Viet Minh leaders from learning from the successes of others, and in particular the Chinese. There is no need to explain this as a matter of "accepting Mao's theories," but rather as a matter of learning, where necessary, from Chinese experience. Many Viet Minh leaders have been to China and have received training there.[65] Ho Chi Minh himself lived there for periods in the 1920's, 1930's, and 1940's. Nguyen Luong Bang and Ho Tung Mau worked with the Chinese Communist Party in the late 1920's; Pham Van Dong, Truong Chinh, Vo Nguyen Giap, Hoang Van Hoan, and Vu Anh were there in the 1930's and 1940's. Little wonder then that they should notice Chinese methods and precepts and that they later should apply those thought to be suitable in Vietnamese conditions.

On the theoretical level a precept that is now mentioned as deriving from Chinese experience is the conviction, clearly articulated by Mao, that an underdeveloped country like China, or Viet Nam, did not have to "pass" through "capitalism" before reaching "socialism" —the "people's" democratic dictatorship," the dictatorship of the party in an underdeveloped country, having the capacity to move straight to socialism without submission and unnecessary concessions to the "bourgeoisie," of which the peasantry is understood to be a part.

On the practical level the most conspicuous of these lessons undoubtedly pertained to guerrilla warfare, the creation of a revolutionary army, and the setting up of "land bases" in preparation for the general insurrection. Soviet doctrine and party practice prior to 1940 did not attach much importance to these precepts. Earlier Communist doctrine had laid stress on subverting the rank and file soldiers of the enemy army, after the manner of 1917, and had devoted much thought to

---

the experiences of the Chinese revolution and to Mao Tse-tung's thoughts we have further understood the ideology of Marx, Engels, Lenin, and Stalin and consequently scored many successes. This the Vietnamese revolutionaries must engrave on their mind and be grateful for." (*Selected Works,* III, 238).

[64] If necessary, playing the one off against the other, in order to secure maximum support from both for its objectives in the South. For a historical study of Sino-Vietnamese relations see Harold C. Hinton, *China's Relations with Burma and Viet Nam* (New York 1958), 1-25.

[65] See in particular *A Heroic People,* 29-30, 95; Devillers, *Histoire du Viêt-Nam,* 72.

organizing urban rather than country areas. For a number of reasons that are now familiar, Chinese Communist practice had since the early 1930's turned in the other directions, towards the building of an army and creating "land bases" as a support for it. From 1941 onwards, following the return of a number of senior leaders from China, these also became the operational principles of the Viet Minh.[66] The build-up of the armed force and the creation of land bases, especially in Thai Nguyen and Cao Bang areas, were indeed the conditions which in 1946-1949 meant the difference between survival and annihilation.

Acknowledged though this influence is, it is not greatly over-emphasized, and Hanoi leaders have taken pains to distinguish between Chinese and Vietnamese practice in this important field. As Tran Van Lieu put it in an interesting article, "there were differences within similarities."[67] Chinese doctrine had stressed that bases could not be established without the prior existence of an armed force. "The buildup of an armed force is the most fundamental link in establishing a base area; without an armed force, or with one that is not strong enough, nothing can be done" wrote Mao Tse-tung in 1938.[68] Although the Viet Minh recognised the importance of building both bases and the army, the essential characteristic of its activities was the over-riding emphasis on political work, and the priority given to the establishment of local political networks over the premature creation of guerrilla units. It is this careful political preparation which has been so characteristic of Viet Minh activities. In contrast to the Chinese case, the "liberated areas" (the Free Zone) were organized at a late stage, shortly before the insurrection. The favorite Chinese tactics of "using the villages to encircle the towns" was then applied and when the revolt occurred it spread from the countryside and the Free Zone to the towns. After 1946, the resistance in Viet Nam once again "learned many invaluable lessons from the prolonged war against the Japanese waged by the Chinese people."[69]

[66] Late in 1941 Ho wrote a simple textbook on guerrilla warfare. (*A Heroic People*, 112). Chinese Communist inspiration is at its most obvious in Truong Chinh's *The Resistance Will Win.*

[67] "On the 40th Anniversary of the Chinese Communist Party," *Nhan Dan* (June 25 and 26, 1961), in JPRS, 10250, 88-95.

[68] "Strategic Problems in Guerrilla War," *Selected Works,* II, 140. This no more than reflected Chinese experience. Mao has had an armed force in existence ever since the late 1920's. He had yet to build his and that is why in 1941, he started by laying emphasis on political work.

[69] Tran Van Lieu in *Nhan Dan* (26 June 1961), 93. In 1951, the translation of a Soviet book on guerrilla warfare was brought out in Viet Nam, with a preface by Ho Chi Minh (*Selected Works,* III, 290-297).

Yet the broad tenor of the above-cited article and of other writings is stress upon the basic autonomy and self-choice of Viet Minh revolutionary methods and the many parallels in the development of the two parties, thus establishing more of a position of equality between them. For instance Tran Van Lieu points out that the defeat of the Japanese Army in China was as much of a prerequisite for Chinese success as the victory of the Communist Party in China was for the favorable outcome of the war in Viet Nam.[70] Here we notice one of the basic characteristics of both these internal wars. The Chinese, like the Viet Minh, benefited crucially from the contiguity of their base areas with other Communist states, as did later the Pathet Lao and the forces of South Viet Nam.

Let us glance briefly at three qualities which particularly characterize the Viet Minh complex: its skills in the use of violence; its small power situation; and its anti-colonial character.

The Viet Minh has now been engaged in war on one "front" or another for over twenty years. In that time its skill in the application of violence has grown into a fine art. In their own context the Viet Minh's military tactics of jungle warfare are nearly perfect. It is somewhat misleading to describe them as those of guerrillas, as though the forces of Viet Minh were no more than bands of irregulars. They are in fact the tactics of a fully trained and well equipped regular army, supported by regional and local units, but fighting in guerrilla style—that is exploiting the elements of surprise and flexibility of operation given by a fine intelligence system based on the political networks, and the mobility of the infantry formations based on ability to move on foot cross-country. The military skills of the Viet Minh stood up to the test of fighting, and ultimately defeating, the modern, fully trained, and excellently equipped, "industrial" French Expeditionary Corps. This must be contrasted with the Chinese who, in their own civil war, defeated, for the most part, only poorly organized local forces. The Viet Minh also won despite the air superiority of the French Command.

But the application of violence in Viet Minh tactics does not extend solely to the military targets of the enemy. It includes the deliberate elimination of all those who might in any way support, and in particular form the core of, the political opposition to its policies. Terror

[70] On the importance of Chinese aid for solving Viet Minh logistical problems see Tanham, 68-69.

had been practiced before 1945.[71] Published instructions of this period are full of orders "to destroy the traitors."[72] Early in the preparatory stage the "liquidation of traitors and the suppression of activities of evil-minded persons" were designated as essential policies to be pursued by the revolutionary regime.[73] This deliberate policy of exterminating actual and even potential opponents has been commented upon a number of times.[74] By 1957-1958 this too has been refined into a fine art, with South Vietnamese village chiefs, for instance, serving as favorite targets of wholesale campaigns of assassination. Although a certain amount of terrorism is frequent in revolutionary wars, one cannot help thinking that in Viet Minh tactics this has long passed the stage of excess and has become a vice, an intoxication with violence, one that may well be a release from the terrible and inhumanly prolonged hardships and repressions of personal interests which its adherents must undergo.

Two unique characteristics of the Viet Minh complex which Vo Nguyen Giap has rightly stressed are its small power character and its anti-colonial nature. He wrote: "The revolutionary war in Viet Nam, while advancing as in China towards the objective of a national democratic revolution, differs for the reason that it took place in a colonial country, in a much smaller country than China in both area and population."[75] Throughout their fight the Viet Minh leaders have been supremely conscious that their action was being mounted in a small country painfully dependent upon the favors of great powers, both friendly and hostile, and a good deal of their early policies of deception and dissimulation and of early concessions to France and Nationalist China were dictated by this unavoidable condition. Despite the undoubted skill with which they did, and still do carry out their policies, their experience also shows the difficulty of completing a revolution autonomously in a small country. Years of tremendous exertions had been needed to retain the gains made while

[71] Vo Nguyen Giap recounts the war-time killing of a "traitor" (for unspecified reasons) and adds "Following this, other traitors got cold feet" (*A Heroic People*, 136).

[72] "Plan of Action Prepared by the Uprising Committee" in *Razobem Okovy*, 79.

[73] "Resolution of the Tongking Military Revolutionary Conference," *Ibid.*, 39.

[74] See for instance Devillers, *Histoire du Viêt-Nam*, 181; Ph. Devillers, *Viet Nam and France* (Paris 1950) (mimeogr.), 13; Hammer, 101, 110, 158.

[75] Giap, *People's War*, see in particular 41 B-C, 68-70. Truong Chinh's analysis of 1947, by contrast, with its criticisms of "cowards" "who only see our difficulties" and with its emphasis on "self-reliance," tended to underplay Viet Nam's weakness and applied Mao Tse-tung's principles of protracted warfare in China directly to Vietnamese circumstance. *The Resistance Will Win*, esp. 80-93, 121-123.

the "big fellows weren't looking." Only the increase in Soviet and Chinese support after 1950 allowed them to go forward to a victorious solution. Yet when peace was reached in 1954, a settlement was conceded by Molotov on general Soviet policy considerations that was less favorable to the Viet Minh than was justified by their military position. Efforts to extend revolutionary action to neighboring countries have encountered great obstacles. The lessons of the Viet Minh cannot, on this account, carry much conviction with revolutionary parties in other small states, especially those situated at a distance from the centers of Communist power. China was big enough to carry off a revolution of her own. No matter what its exertions, a small country's fate depends to a great extent upon the state of the international system at large.[76]

Similar reflections apply to the other characteristic of the Viet Minh, its anti-colonial character. Unlike China, Viet Nam was a colonial country; this condition is generally recognized as the "secret" of much of the Viet Minh's early successes. By concentrating their fire on the French, the Viet Minh could rally the bulk of the population around their cause as long as France refused to concede independence. Fortunately for the Viet Minh, the French learned very slowly, even slower than the Dutch in Indonesia. Not until 1953, after a near-decade of maneuverings to preserve the substance of power behind facades of independence, was France prepared to give up control. The result was that for years the Viet Minh had no nationalist opposition to speak of, and large numbers of non-Communist nationalists rallied to the Viet Minh and the "fronts" and "associations" sponsored by it. The "national bourgeoisie," which was at one time strong in China, missed the early chance to consolidate in Viet Nam.

But the Viet Minh complex shows, too, that nationalism alone is not enough. Both sides found this out. Nationalism of the Viet Minh brand was in the end seriously checked by nationalism first aided by France and then by the United States, and outside Viet Nam itself it did not make much headway. The antidote for nationalism was nationalism. The nationalistic content has been declining in the Viet Minh since 1950, and has given way, for instance, to spectacular persecution of peasants only slightly better-off than the average,[77]

[76] But Mao Tse-tung has been, in his writings, explicitly aware of the importance of the international environment; see for instance "On the Protracted War."

[77] For a description of this "Mobilization of the Masses for Agrarian Reform" and for an account of the "trial" of a landlord, see W. B. Burchett, *North of the Seventeenth Parallel* (Delhi 1956) Ch. 7 and 8.

which gave rise to riots and disturbances in central North Viet Nam in late 1956. Thus the purely nationalist guise of the early Viet Minh stands revealed as a piece of deception that has not been entirely lost on the South Vietnamese either. In recent years, South Viet Nam could more convincingly plead the nationalist cause than North Viet Nam.

But the Viet Minh problem is not disposed of so easily. In a trial of nationalisms it is the better and the stronger that succeeds, and here the issues are still unresolved. While the Viet Minh loses for its obsession with violence, for the tremendous strain it has exerted on the body politic for the past two decades, and for its total and arbitrary control of the entire population—it scores heavily for political effectiveness and military prowess. In economics, until 1960 the record of South Viet Nam was by no means inferior, but the North has greater natural resources for industrialization, and the emergency stopped all economic development in the South. The recent nationalist gains of Saigon were being undermined again as Ngo Dinh Diem had to lean more and more upon American support. The final judgment is yet to be delivered.

To the question has the Viet Minh complex been a success, we must thus answer both yes and no. Yes, because in the nineteen years since 1945 the party has added to its strength most impressively. Its membership has risen from 5,000 in 1945 to 500,000 in 1960; it has defeated the French in pitched battle and now controls one half of Viet Nam and exerts considerable influence in Laos. Its armed forces (from a few thousand irregulars in 1945 expanded to several hundred thousand men in large formations in 1962) are probably the most effective in the whole of South-East Asia; their "extra-mural" campaigns brought the South Vietnamese regime to near collapse in 1961 and continue to exercise all-pervasive pressure on Laos, Cambodia, and even Thailand. North Viet Nam is now outside the fighting and under its complete command and can be used as the "rear" for new political operations.[78]

The answer is at the same time no, because the nineteen years since 1945 have given the Viet Minh no more than one half of what it had already achieved in August of that year. Seventeen years of struggle and sacrifice have not given it the unity of all Viet Nam, and the control of Laos is still far from certain. The consolidation of the Viet Minh complex based primarily upon North Viet Nam has gone hand in hand with the strengthening of its opponents. In 1945 opposition

[78] Except for South Vietnamese "spies and saboteurs," trials of whom were reported by the *Viet Nam News Agency* in July-August 1962.

was virtually non-existent, but it has gathered increased strength since. Whereas in 1945 the Viet Minh no more than filled the vacuum left by the departing French and Japanese, now it has to contend with established and entrenched governmental authorities in South Viet Nam, in Cambodia, and even in Laos. Under the corrosive influence of nationalism, the Viet Minh complex is loosening. Even if Communist regimes were to be established in Laos and Cambodia it is far from certain that they would wish to join an Indo-Chinese Federation dominated by the Viet Minh. The years past have given them the taste of independence and the self-confidence necessary for it. While on the tactical level of political warfare and military operations the Viet Minh has been an unqualified success, its strategies have been more questionable, especially where they have had to contend with complex international situations.

Does the Viet Minh example hold lessons for other Communist parties, especially those in small and colonial countries, as Hanoi publicists would claim?[79] This is not at all sure. The number of colonial areas remaining in the world is small, and although one must not forget southern Africa, purely colonial situations of the Vietnamese type are likely to be rare. Viet Minh experience may suggest tactical lessons for anti-government guerrillas in recently independent areas, but its overall experience is not clear cut enough to be convincing. As the experience of a small state, it is hardly attractive, except to all-out extremists. Its basic lesson is the importance of striking when legitimate authority has nearly disintegrated. Once authority has been seized, insurgents are not easily dislodged.

Viet Minh pronouncements often refer to "the struggle for peace in Southeast Asia"; this is particularly noticeable in the writings of Vo Nguyen Giap. These references usually indicate an assertion of interest in developments in Laos and Cambodia, and even in Thailand. They accord with the long standing Viet Minh involvement in these areas, and signify a determination to back up this interest with superior strength. A book published in Hanoi in 1961 refers to North Viet Nam as the "true" center of the "gravitational system" of former French Indo-China, and contrasts it with the "false" system represented by SEATO.[80] There is little doubt that the Viet Minh is in fact claiming this area as the sphere of its influence. Also worth bearing

[79] The Publisher's Note to Vo Nguyen Giap's *People's War,* hints that the book might be of special interest to Cuba which is "subject to daily provocation by the U.S.A."; presumably on account of its analysis of the Resistance War. Hanoi maintains close contact with Havana.

[80] Salmon, 277-278.

in mind is the fact that Ho Chi Minh is by far the senior Communist leader in Southeast Asia, that he himself was at one time the Comintern head for the whole of the region and that in 1930, for instance, he seems to have presided over the founding of the Thai and Malay Communist Parties.[81] As the only ruling Communist Party in this part of the world, the Lao-Dong also has a claim to superiority within the Communist international system for the whole of this area: "in Southeast Asia, we constitute the outpost of the Front of peace and democracy in the world campaigning against imperialism and war."[82]

Despite these undoubted aspirations there is doubt whether in the near future the Viet Minh would be able to project influence, even into Cambodia or Laos. Even in those two countries its influence is now overshadowed by that of Soviet and Chinese representatives. Elsewhere, its impact is even more limited for two reasons. The strength which the movement had developed in Viet Nam was based on its national appeal; to that extent its attractiveness to other Southeast Asian countries is limited. Furthermore, the absorption in the struggle in South Viet Nam leaves little energy and attention to spare for activities elsewhere. As long as South Viet Nam remains outside Hanoi's control it will remain the lightning conductor of its energies.

[81] Sacks, in Trager, *Marxism in Southeast Asia,* 318-319; in 1947, the Viet Minh took a lead in organizing the Southeast Asia League in Bangkok, J. Coast, *Some Aspects of Siamese Politics* (New York 1953), 38. Fifield, *Diplomacy,* 458.

[82] Ho Chi Minh, *Izvestiya* (January 7, 1959), in *Selected Works,* IV, p. 334.

8

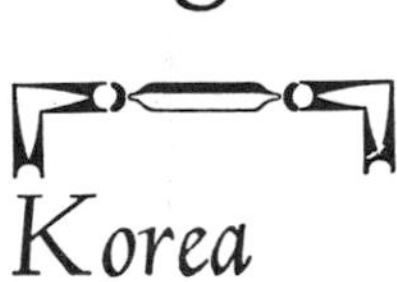

Korea

GLENN D. PAIGE

Comrade Stalin has said
that war teaches us much
KIM ILSŎNG
December 1950

Introduction

Since 1945 the Korean Communists have had considerable experience with political violence initiated either by themselves or by others. It is the purpose of this chapter to examine the interpretations which they have given to these experiences in writings used for political indoctrination, and to explore the implications of these interpretations for future Communist violence in Korea.

Events since the Second World War in Korea may well be viewed within the larger context of the social, economic, and political changes which have taken place in Korea since the end of the nineteenth century. The total population of Korea, now probably about thirty-eight million (including about twenty-seven million in South Korea) has at least tripled since 1900 and continues to grow at a rate of two to three percent each year. There has been a marked trend toward urbanization. One person in four in South Korea presently lives in communities inhabited by more than fifty thousand people, and the population of Seoul, now at least two and a half million, has increased about ten times in the past sixty years. The expansion of educational opportunity, especially after 1945, has been dramatic; whereas only a few thousand Koreans were receiving education of any kind in 1900, more than seven million (including over four a half million in South Korea) were in school in 1962. Probably more than sixty percent of the adult South Korean population can read simple texts written in the Korean alphabet. Rising education and literacy have been accompanied by increased exposure to the media of mass communication. Recent surveys in the Republic of Korea have estimated that one adult in three reads a newspaper at least occasionally, and that one household in six owns a radio. The circulation of the *Tonga Ilbo,* Seoul's largest newspaper, has at times reached three hundred thousand; that of *Sasangge,* South Korea's leading intellectual journal, has been as high as sixty thousand readers.

Half a century has also brought marked changes in the traditional social fabric of Korean Confucianism, although Japanese policy was to encourage only limited transformations. The North has suffered forced rates of change under Communist rule, while in the South the process of change has taken place in a more gradual, sometimes spasmodic, but nevertheless persistent way. Thus Koreans have experienced varying degrees of changes in attitudes toward marriage, the family, the larger kinship group, youth, the aged, and women. Economically, Koreans in both North and South have witnessed changes in traditional patterns of land ownership and the rise of modern industries which were virtually non-existent in 1910.

Politically, Koreans have witnessed the disintegration of the traditional institutions of the Yi dynasty (1392-1910). The opening of Korea by Japan in 1876 was the opening wedge for the detachment of Korea from its status as a Chinese tributary state. Struck from outside, Korea was sporadically shaken from within by outbursts of discontent such as that expressed in the great quasi-religious *Tonghak* (Eastern Learning) Rebellion of the mid-1890's which contained many features that were reminiscent of the earlier Taiping Rebellion in China. On the other hand, Korea's *Kabo* reforms of 1894-1895 seemed to anticipate Chinese attempts in 1898 to reform within the traditional order. The loss of Korean political identity which followed Japanese victory in the Russian-Japanese War brought both directed modernization, in the interests of more advanced Japan, and the intensification of Korean national sentiments expressed, for example, in the mass uprising of March 1, 1919, which sought to win self-determination through pacifist principles.

The failure of this movement led Korean leaders in the 1920's to look towards at least four sources of support and inspiration, with varying degrees of attachment and feelings of mutual exclusiveness: the Western models of Europe and America; the Bolshevik system of Soviet Russia; the potentialities of dominant Japan; and the best of Korean traditions. Hostility and hope bred reactions ranging from assassination and terror to determined efforts to save the national language. The regimentation of Korea in the 1930's as a base for military operations against China and the tightening of Japanese controls during the Pacific War served to intensify the joyous outburst of Korean aspirations which accompanied the end of Japanese rule on August 15, 1945. The shattering of Korean expectations of commanding their own national destiny in the postwar period and the Communist decision to invade the South in 1950 constituted national and international tragedies. Thus in scarcely three quarters of a century, from 1876 to 1950, four major wars, the contending forces of a dozen nations, alien rule, and internal revolt and reform had dismissed forever the political order of the Yi.

Within the broad context of historical retrospect at least four major characteristics of Korean political change since the nineteenth century can be observed. There has been a marked development of still unsatisfied Korean nationalism; a vast increase in political participation; a growth of attempts to eliminate persistent Korean factionalism; and the rough bipolarization of Korean political leadership into two groups which are divided on the issues of the rate and extent of the changes which ought to be made. One intellectual style has favored the gradual and limited; another has advocated the rapid and radical.

The character of modern Korean political history returns us to the examination of Korean Communist experience with political violence since 1945 and its implications. The Korean Communists, of course, are among those who have wished to change Korean society in immediate and far-reaching ways. Although the Soviet occupation made it possible to establish a Communist territorial base in Korea, it did not represent the beginning of Communist influence on the peninsula.[1] A Korean Communist Party was briefly active on the peninsula from 1925 until 1928 when it was decimated by Japanese police action and expelled from the Comintern largely on the grounds

[1] For the early history of the Korean Communist movement consult: Kim San and Nym Wales, *Song of Ariran* (New York 1941); Otto Kuusinen, "O koreyskom kommunisticheskom dvizhenii" [On the Korean Communist Movement], *Revolyutsionnyy vostok*, XI-XII (1931), 99-116; Chong-sik Lee, "Korean Communists and Yenan," *China Quarterly* (January-March 1962), 182-192; Glenn D. Paige, "Korea and the Comintern, 1919-1935," *Bulletin of the Korean Research Center*, No. 13 (December 1960), 1-25; and Robert A. Scalapino and Chong-sik Lee, "The Origins of the Korean Communist Movement," *Journal of Asian Studies*, XX (November 1960), 9-31, and XX (February 1961), 149-167. On postwar Korean Communism consult John Bradbury, "Sino-Soviet Competition in North Korea," *China Quarterly* (April-June 1961), 15-28; Kim Ch'angsun, *Pukhan sibonyŏn sa* [Fifteen Year History of North Korea] (Seoul 1960); Ilpyong J. Kim, "North Korea's Fourth Party Congress," *Pacific Affairs*, XXXV (Spring 1962), 37-50; Chong-sik Lee, "The 'Socialist Revolution' in the North Korean Countryside," *Asian Survey*, II (October 1962), 9-22; Lee Dong Jun, *Hwansanggwa hyŏnsil: naŭi kongsanjuŭi kwan* [Fantasy and Fact: My Observations of Communism] (Seoul 1961); Glenn D. Paige, "North Korea and the Emulation of Russian and Chinese Behavior," in A. Doak Barnett, ed., *Communist Strategies in Asia* (New York 1963); Philip Rudolph, "North Korea and the Path to Socialism," *Pacific Affairs*, XXXII (June 1959), 131-143; and Philip Rudolph, *North Korea's Political and Economic Structure* (New York 1959).

of incessant factionalism. Until 1945 there were various efforts to revive the defunct party but none of them met with appreciable success. The pre-1945 Communist movement in Korea thus seems to have been characterized by the clandestine activities of tiny Communist factions. Japanese police controls inside Korea were so effective that the Korean Communists tended to base themselves abroad in China, Manchuria, the Soviet Union, or even in Japan itself. One of these Communists was Kim Sŏngju, born on April 12, 1912, not far from P'yŏngyang. Having moved to Manchuria as an adolescent, he apparently became active as a member of an anti-Japanese guerrilla group in the 1930's. Backed by the Red Army, he was the man who was introduced in P'yŏngyang on October 14, 1945 as the nationalist hero, Kim Ilsŏng.

The Kim Ilsŏng, Guerrilla "Myth," 1931-1945

Before proceeding to examine the Korean Communist experience since 1945, it is important to consider briefly the "myth" about Kim Ilsŏng's guerrilla activities in Manchuria during the period from 1931 to 1945, which has been elaborated gradually since the installation of Communist power in North Korea by the Soviet Army. While some aspects of the myth may be verifiable, it has been treated with a measure of contempt both by Communist and non-Communist Korean critics. The former have been critical because it portrays Kim Ilsŏng as the leader of "the only true Communists," thus belittling the activities and potential claims to leadership of other Korean Communists who were active in Korea itself, Japan, China, or the Soviet Union. Non-Communist critics are skeptical mainly because the myth exaggerates the Communist role in the Korean independence movement and because virtually no veterans of Kim Ilsŏng's "army" were identifiable in post-1945 P'yŏngyang.

But whatever its historical validity, the myth about the Kim Ilsŏng partisans is an important component of the intellectual equipment of the 1.3 million members who now comprise the Korean Worker's Party (KWP). The guerrilla experience is studied solemnly in "Leader Study Rooms" throughout the northern part of the peninsula; it is glorified in the Museum of the Korean Revolution in P'yŏngyang; it is invoked in countless speeches and KWP documents; and it is a major theme of the arts. One of the most important recent articulations of the myth is contained in the *History of the Korean People's Struggle for Liberation* published by Yi Nayŏng in 1958.[2]

[2] Yi Nayŏng, *Chosŏn minjok haebang t'ujaeng sa* (Tokyo, 1960), 335 ff.

According to Yi's summation of the "historical significance" of the guerrilla experience, the following major lessons are to be derived: it is claimed that participation in partisan warfare provided valuable training and experience for the Communist leadership; it is further argued that the guerrilla war promoted organizational integration, since scattered units of the anti-Japanese resistance movement had to be brought under centralized Communist direction for effective action. The boldness of Communist action is said to have confirmed them as the "true continuators of the Korean revolutionary tradition," and to have raised the "goal consciousness" of the people. Armed violence, such as raids upon Japanese army, police, and administrative installations, and the sabotage of transportation and communications facilities, is depicted as having "weakened" an enemy of superior strength. In general, armed violence is said to have accelerated the revolutionary process by stimulating the transition from "stagnation" to "positive action." Internationally, the Korean Communists' conduct of partisan warfare is said to have brought them prestige as an "important link" in the world revolutionary movement. They fought, it is proudly claimed, both for the success of the Chinese Revolution and in defense of the Soviet Union.

Other than failure to mention Mao Tse-tung as an authority on guerrilla war, it is to be noted that the Kim Ilsŏng myth contains at least one more important omission in that nothing critical is said about the resort to violence. All of its effects are portrayed as having been completely advantageous for the Communist cause. In general, then, as an instrument of political socialization, this myth would seem conducive to a propensity to violence. As any political myth, this one can have multiple uses depending upon the purposes of its creators and purveyors. Two uses which are commonly encountered in North Korean writings are to confirm faith in the final victory of communism in Korea (even under trying circumstances the guerrillas never lost their faith in the eventual defeat of Japan) and to promote organizational loyalty (a major reason why success was possible was that the guerrillas were extremely self-sacrificing and did not engage in the factional feuding so characteristic of Korean political behavior).

There is no direct evidence that the ideas and attitudes toward violence propounded by Yi Nayŏng were actually influential after the establishment of Communist control in North Korea in 1945, but possibly the most intimate circle of Kim Ilsŏng supporters drew a rough analogy between the situation before and after the defeat of Japan. North Korea, for example, was and is described frequently as a "revolutionary democratic base," a concept reminiscent of the idea of guerrilla base areas on the Manchurian-Korean border. The target for infiltration and agitation thus changed from Japanese-dominated Korea to American-based South Korea.

The Communist experience with political violence in South Korea since 1945 was gained in four main periods: a period of demonstrations, strikes, and terrorism, 1945-1948; a period of armed guerrilla war, 1948-1950; a period of regular war, 1950-1953; and a period of "peaceful" psychological war combined with underground infiltration since 1953. Over-all Communist objectives throughout these periods may be summarized by the statement contained in the party regulations adopted by the Third Congress of the KWP in 1956: "The immediate goal of the Korean Workers Party is to carry out the tasks of the anti-imperialist, anti-feudal, democratic revolution on a national scale; the final goal is the construction of a Communist society."[3]

Demonstrations, Strikes, and Terrorism, 1945-1948

The initial Communist experience with political violence in South Korea took place during three years of United States Military Government authority. These years brought growing alienation of popular sympathy, increased antagonism of the military government, and the intensification of Communist violence. In the months immediately after liberation the Communists had considerable support, particularly among students and in rural areas where they drew strength as agrarian reformers. Often they appeared to be better organized than other political groups, but the Communist movement was not highly cohesive; the factional loyalties of the 1920's and 1930's continued to persist. The main Communist slogans of the period—similar to those being propounded in Eastern Europe—were the conduct of land reform on the basis of uncompensated confiscation, the nationalization of the property of Japanese and Japanese collaborators, and the exclusion of former collaborators from important posts such as in the police and administration. The principal Communist leader in South Korea at this time and until 1948 when he escaped to the North was Pak Hŏnyŏng who had gained fame for his underground activities against the Japanese. His main intra-party adversaries were known as the "*Taehoe* faction," a group which had organized one of two initial Communist parties during a *taehoe* (mass meeting) held

[3] *Chosŏn nodongdang kyuyak haesŏl* [Interpretation of the Korean Worker's Party Regulations], (Tokyo 1960), 1.

in Seoul on August 16, 1945 to honor Communists who had been released from Japanese prisons.

The first serious blow to Communist prestige in South Korea followed a dramatic shift in policy which apparently was undertaken in obedience to Soviet direction. In late December 1945 it was announced that the Moscow Conference of Foreign Ministers had agreed upon a plan whereby a provisional government would be established and Korea would be placed under international trusteeship for a period of five years. The news evoked a vociferous nationalist protest movement throughout South Korea, in which the Communists vigorously participated. Within days, however, the Communists abruptly threw down their protest banners and began to agitate in favor of the Moscow decisions. This apparent betrayal of Korean national interests exposed them to the scornful epithet of "puppets." Communist sympathy in rural areas was gradually dissipated by extremist acts. Early Communist tactics were to attempt to seize control of local police and administrative organizations. Attempts to eject the incumbents were often accompanied and followed by brutality and terroristic reprisals against "reactionaries." It is to be noted, however, that in the period of political instability which followed the dissolution of the Japanese control system in Korea the Communists often appeared to have been as much the victims as the initiators of violence and terror.

At first the Communists benefited from the tolerance of the American military authorities who ruled, for example, that it was not a crime to sing Communist songs in street demonstrations and that movements directed toward the amelioration of purely economic grievances were not to be treated as political in nature. But the Communist refusal to accept and to work through the military government gradually helped to place American sympathies behind a conservative Korean reaction. Whenever there was a possibility of a Soviet-American rapprochement through the work of the Joint Soviet-American Commission on Korea, Communist militancy abated, but after the breakdown of negotiations in May of 1947 and the submission of the Korean question to the United Nations by the United States in the fall of that year, the Communists increasingly resorted to strikes, demonstrations, and acts of terror.

An authoritative interpretation of Communist experience in this period is contained in the *General History of Korea,* a collective product of the Historical Research Institute of the Academy of Sciences, of the Democratic People's Republic of Korea published in 1958:

"Under the conditions of the reactionary offensive which took place in South Korea after the suspension of the Joint Soviet-American Commission, the tactical obligations of the party were to preserve carefully the party nucleus and organization from enemy attack, to combine legal and illegal forms of struggle, to set in motion mass organizations of far-reaching influence, to separate completely the American imperialists from the people, and to defeat their policy of colonial enslavement.

"However, the spy-traitor Pak Hŏnyŏng not only exposed the bare-handed masses to attack by an enemy armed to the teeth, but after the resistance had broken out, by breaking off unified and organic relationships, and scattering and isolating the forces of popular resistance, he made it easy for the enemy to crush the resistance piecemeal.

"Furthermore, after the general strike had begun, factional elements of the *Taehoe* clique obstructed the strike of the Kyŏngsŏng Electric Company workers and those of other enterprises and, even after the resistance had begun, by restraining the people, they significantly weakened the unity and solidarity of the working class and the combat power of the people.

"Nevertheless, the patriots of South Korea led by the working class launched a brave struggle under enemy fire, opposed the colonial enslavement policies of American imperialism, and fully demonstrated their unshakable determination and stubborn capabilities in the struggle for national unification and independence."[4]

The general intent of this passage, of course, seems to be to discredit the leadership of Pak Hŏnyŏng, who served as foreign minister of the northern government throughout the Korean War, but was charged with being involved in a planned coup to overthrow the Kim Ilsŏng leadership in 1953, and was finally executed in December 1955 as an "American spy." The lessons to be drawn from this experience, however, are not entirely clear. On the one hand the passage implies that Communists should not lead unarmed attacks upon heavily armed enemies; on the other it implies that once social violence occurs Communists should exert every effort to enlarge its scope, whatever the relative balance of forces. The necessity for preserving the Communist organization under all conditions seems to be understood. Thus the unqualified advantages of violence in the Kim Ilsŏng guerrilla tradition are not to be found in this interpretation, although participation in violence is depicted as being heroic.

[4] *Chosŏn t'ongsa* (Tokyo 1959), 55.

Guerrilla War, 1948-1950

The year 1948 brought an increase in the scale and intensity of Communist political violence in South Korea. By the end of the year full-fledged guerrilla bases manned partly by defectors from the South Korean army were in existence. Large scale guerrilla activity was not suppressed in South Korea until punitive expeditions by the regular army overran the guerrilla bases during the winter of 1949-1950. The principal internal war activities of the period were the general strike in opposition to the arrival of the United Nations temporary Commission on Korea in January 1948, the April 3 revolt of the people of Cheju Island, widespread Communist violence in opposition to the May 10 elections and the establishment of a separate government in South Korea, the revolt of the 14th Regiment of the ROK Army at Yŏsu and the seizure of the town of Sunch'ŏn in October, and the subsequent partisan warfare in the mountain regions.

Something of the conditions of the time can be learned from the public safety reports of the United States Military Government in Korea for the election month of May 1948.[5] These reports show that thirty-two policemen and 275 civilians had been killed during the month. Among the dead were four election candidates, fifteen election officials, and eleven other administrators. For the first time, the wives and daughters of persons connected with the election were beaten, although it had long been customary to attack the persons and property of the relatives of policemen. During the month there were fourteen labor strikes and nine strikes by students; locomotives and bridges were wrecked; power lines were sabotaged; a bomb thrown by a Communist girl disrupted communications in the port city of Inchon; and telephone exchanges were attacked and burned, in one case by youths who said they had been promised scholarships for study in the Soviet Union as a reward for the deed. The insurgents employed a wide assortment of weapons, including Japanese military equipment. According to one report, "One group of four, captured before they did any harm, was equipped with a stick of dynamite, 23 dynamite caps, one box of gunpowder, 17 homemade bombs, one bottle of gasoline, two knives, nine iron clubs, 150 pieces of metal for throwing, and one bottle of sulphuric acid."[6] The re-

[5] U. S. Military Government in Korea, *Summation of South Korean Interim Government Activities,* No. 12 (May 1948).
[6] *Ibid.,* 154.

calcitrants often posed as policemen and as members of the conservative police auxiliary. Sixty-eight election booths were attacked with homemade bombs or with bottles of burning gasoline. One bomb thrower blew off his own hand; another blew up his own house. On Cheju Island rightists and policemen were kidnapped, hanged, and beheaded, while the insurgents were gored with bamboo spears by members of a fanatic anti-Communist youth group composed of refugees from North Korea who had been brought over from the mainland.

Not all of the election month violence was the result of Communist action, but the Communists were clearly responsible for inciting it. There were a number of extreme nationalist groups which were adamantly opposed to the election on the grounds that it would impede national unification. A serious breach among the conservatives pressing for the establishment of a separate government in the south occurred when the conservative leaders Kim Koo and Kim Kyusik decided to attend the Communist-sponsored meeting of political and social leaders opposed to the separate election held in P'ŏngyang in mid-April 1948. The basic Communist strategy for the period was to be the incitement of widespread social violence, however, and not the establishment of a popular front. This is clearly shown by a statement repeatedly broadcast by P'yŏngyang radio on May 9, the day before the election: "Dear Brothers! Tomorrow is the day of the enforcement of the doomed separate election in South Korea. It is the day when the American imperialists push the people into the election booths with terrorism and suppression. Our brothers are fighting like wild beasts against this terrorism for the independence and freedom of our fatherland. Will it be all right if the 30,000,000 people kneel under the oppression of the Americans? Or should we fight against them to the end with our lives? Yes we should fight them tomorrow with all our energy.

"Dear Brothers! In front of us the American machine guns are menacing us. In the skies the American airplanes are threatening us. The reactionary police are capable of every possible terroristic action. It is time for us to rise up. . . . The world is interested to know whether we can crush down the separate election or not. Let us stand up and fight!"[7]

An important action which was undertaken by the North Korean Communists and the Soviet authorities as a protest against the May

[7] *Ibid.*, 162.

10 elections was the cessation of electric power transmission to the South which was announced on May 14. This was a serious economic blow since about 60 percent of the power consumed in the South originated in the North. Over one-third of the southern rice crop was dependent upon irrigation by electric pumps. While the Communists hoped to promote political disaffection through this move by explaining that it had been taken reluctantly because of American failure to pay proper compensation for past power deliveries, it actually had unfavorable political repercussions for them. The move seriously undermined the position of Kim Koo and Kim Kyusik who had returned from P'yŏngyang only a week earlier bearing a Communist promise that no measures would be taken to interfere with the power supply. This incident was one of the first to shake popular confidence in the protestations of reasonable readiness to negotiate which has been a continuing theme of Korean Communist propaganda.

While on the offensive in the South, the Korean Communists had to be on the defensive against subversion in the North. They were not able to prevent, for example, the effective sabotage by South Korean agents of their only oil refinery.[8]

The insurrection on Cheju Island and its violent suppression in 1948 has not been fully described from a non-Communist or non-official Korean viewpoint, but it obviously constituted a major internal war event. An American communications researcher who visited the island in January 1962 has written that the villagers told him that the repressive measures employed by the government forces were extremely cruel.[9] Inhabited areas were evidently burned out and the males of entire villages were executed for suspected sympathy with the rebels. An American military government assessment of the situation at the time suggests the complex motivations which must have led to acts of popular desperation: "The disorders broke out partly at the inspiration of the Communists opposing the South Korean election, and partly because of the islanders' long-smouldering resentment against despotic police and corrupt officials."[10] In Communist literature, Cheju-do is called "the island of heroes."

The rebellion of units of the Republic of Korea Army at the south-

[8] U. S. Department of State, *North Korea: A Case Study in the Techniques of Takeover* (Washington 1961), 90.

[9] Richard A. Garver, "Cheju-do: Communications Problems in a Korean Province," ms., 1962, 3-5.

[10] U. S. Army Military Government in Korea, 3.

ern port of Yŏsu in the fall of 1948, the capture of the town of Sunch'ŏn, and the army purge and mountainous guerrilla action which followed, was directly linked to the Cheju uprising, for officers and men refused to embark upon the ships which were to carry them to a punitive expedition against it. The rebellious men of the 14th Regiment found strong support among school students, especially those under the influence of teachers with Communist sympathies. One of the most important facts about contemporary South Korean politics which is well known to Communist Korean strategists is that the present military government of the Republic of Korea includes officers who were involved both in the Yŏsu uprising and in its suppression.

According to a Soviet specialist on Korean politics in the period after the Second World War, the guerrilla war "markedly subsided" by the end of 1949 partially due to the "demagogic" land reform enacted in 1949.[11] North Korean interpretations of the defeat of the guerrilla forces place great emphasis upon the role of American officers and American military assistance to the ROK Army. On the positive side, they assert that the guerrilla war increased anti-American sentiment among the people and contributed to dissension within the enemy ranks since there were some army units which refused to participate in the repressive campaigns. "But despite the self-sacrificing struggle of the true Workers Party members," explains the *General History of Korea,* "this kind of resistance could not achieve the desired results because of internal sabotage by the traitorous Pak Hŏnyŏng-Yi Sŭngyŏp clique, the hired spies of American imperialism. Under conditions where democratic construction was being successfully carried out in the northern part of the Republic, and in which terror and oppression by the American imperialists and their lackeys had reached an extreme, the resistance at all times should have been organized in the direction of preserving the party organization and the basic forces of the revolution and of further isolating the American imperialists from the masses by rallying the people more closely around the Workers' Party and correctly combining legal and illegal forms of struggle.

"Despite all this, the traitorous clique of Pak Hŏnyŏng and Yi Sŭngyŏp in this period, under the destructive slogan of terror against terror, drove the members of the party and the people into an ad-

[11] F. I. Shabshina, *Ocherki noveyshei istorii Korei, 1945-53* [Outlines of Recent Korean History] (Moscow 1958), 206.

venturous charge, exposed and completely destroyed the party organization, and sacrificed great numbers of party members and patriots to the bullets and bayonets of the enemy."[12]

Although this passage seems designed mainly to discredit the leadership of the former South Korean Workers' Party, and although it cannot be taken as direct evidence of the Communist estimate of the situation in 1948-1950, it appears to constitute an important injunction both against terror and against violent attacks upon an enemy of superior military strength. The necessity of preserving the party organization is stressed again as in the interpretation of the events of 1945-1947. Clearly, however, as is shown by the North Korean radio broadcast cited above, it is historically inaccurate to assign responsibility for the call to violence in South Korea solely to Pak Hŏnyŏng and his followers. Unless Pak had been given the authority to direct all operations in South Korea—which is very doubtful—both the Kim Ilsŏng leadership and the Soviet advisory group must have shared in the decision to "stand up and fight."

Regular War, 1950-1953

A fuller understanding of the choice of regular war as a means for bringing South Korea under Communist control awaits a careful reconstruction of the North Korean decisions which led up to the invasion of June 25, 1950. One of the key problems with which they as well as foreign analysts must have wrestled at the time was the question of their revolutionary capability. Apparently official American analysts had concluded that the Communist revolutionary capability in South Korean was so great that an open invasion was improbable. As Secretary of State Dean Acheson explained in 1951, "The view was generally held that since the Communists had far from exhausted the potentialities for obtaining their objectives through guerrilla and psychological warfare, political pressure and intimidation, such means would probably continue to be used rather than overt military aggression."[13] But apparently the North Koreans did not take such an optimistic view of their capabilities. While they seem to have believed that there was a large reservoir of pro-North sentiment, derived in part from South Korean revulsion against indiscriminate and harsh methods of governmental repression, they seem to have be-

[12] *Chosŏn t'ongsa,* 144.

[13] U. S. Senate, *Military Situation in the Far East,* Hearings before the Committee on Armed Services and the Committee on Foreign Relations, 82nd Congress, 1st Session (Washington 1951), 1991.

come convinced that armed guerrilla action promised no victory. The Korean experience in 1950 thus suggests that under conditions where foreign counter-intervention is considered unlikely, the suppression of internal partisan war may increase the probability of armed invasion from without.

The first radio appeal to the South Korean people by Kim Ilsŏng after the People's Army invasion had begun suggests that regular war might well have been considered as a continuation of guerrilla war by other means. Directing his exhortations to target groups within the South Korean population, Kim called for guerrillas to disrupt the enemy rear, for all to engage in civil disobedience, for workers to strike, for farmers to provide food for the guerrillas but to withhold it from the enemy, for intellectuals to agitate for a mass uprising, and for army units to defect. "The time has come to unify our country," he cried in direct evidence of the offensive nature of the military action. "Forward!"[14]

One of the first attempts to summarize the lessons of the conflict took place at a plenary meeting of the Central Committee of the KWP which was held in December, 1950. In a report to the meeting[15] Kim Ilsŏng reviewed the experience gained in the first three phases of the war: the first, in which the People's Army overran most of South Korea; the second, in which it was forced by foreign intervention to retreat; and the third, in which it was able to launch a successful counterattack with Chinese support. Strategically, Kim criticized the party's failure to prepare for fighting against a superior foreign enemy, the inadequate utilization of guerrilla forces to compensate for lack of air power and mobility, the failure to annihilate rather than rout the enemy, and the inadequate provision of rear area support. Organizationally, Kim complained that discipline in the party, army, and bureaucracy had proven weak. He argued that this resulted in defections, cowardice, and loss of popular support through wanton killings and acts of brutality committed during the period of the retreat. In this critique Kim thus revealed important awareness of the unfavorable effect of Communist violence upon popular attitudes in South Korea.

An over-all assessment of "historical significance" of the Korean

[14] *Renmin Ribao* (June 28, 1960), 1.

[15] Kim Ilsŏng, "Hyŏn chŏngsewa tangmyŏn kwaŏp," [The Present Situation and Immediate Tasks], *Kim Ilsŏng sŏnjip* [Selected works of Kim Ilsŏng] (P'yŏngyang 1954) III, 122-173. Basic source hereafter cited as *Selected Works.*

War is contained in the *General History of Korea*.[16] The conflict is depicted as the most severe in all Korean history because never before was the enemy so powerful and well equipped. Five main points of significance are asserted. First, regular war is said to have preserved the organizational identity of the Korean Democratic People's Republic and to have insured the conditions for achieving the peaceful unification of the country. Second, through the "victory" over "the United States, other foreign nations, and domestic reactionaries," the Korean people are said to have reached "unprecedented heights" of domestic and international prestige as "the shock troops of the world revolutionary and workers movements." Third, during three years of wartime experience the people, the armed forces, the party, administrative organs, social organizations, and their cadres are said to have gained invaluable experience. Fourth, the war is said to have inflicted a "great military, political, and moral defeat" upon the United States. Finally, the "victory of the Korean people" is said to have been also the "victory of the socialist camp" which is depicted as having grown in solidarity during the conflict.

It is important to note that no irredentist claims linked to the war are made: the war is described as over and as having ended in "victory" for the Korean people. This is virtually a logical necessity since the Communists depict themselves as the victims rather than the initiators of armed invasion. As explained in the *General History of Korea*, "After victory in the Fatherland Liberation War for freedom and independence, our people again turned to peaceful construction."[17] Nevertheless, from this interpretation it can be inferred that the most salient lesson derived from the war by the inner core of the North Korean leadership was that regular war as a means for the seizure of power in South Korea offers no hope of success as long as the ROK Army can count upon major foreign support. This does not mean, however, that the North Koreans have decisively rejected the idea of regular war as a method for the unification of Korea. In a 1955 speech, reproduced in his *Selected Works* in 1960, Kim Ilsŏng explicitly stated that there were two ways to unify the country; by "peaceful methods" or by "war." He further specified the conditions under which the alternative of "war" would be feasible: "If the imperialists launch a great war on a world scale we will have no choice but to fight and at that time even with our own strength we will be able to achieve

[16] *Chosŏn t'ongsa*, 165 ff.
[17] *Ibid.*, 271.

victory over the American imperialists in Korea. Whereas it would be rather difficult for us to fight all alone against American imperialism, *under conditions where they must disperse their forces on a global scale it will be comparatively easy for us to defeat them* [Emphasis added]."[18] Because of this view the North Koreans are probably highly responsive to Chinese Communist calls for widespread "wars of national liberation."

Psychological War and Underground Infiltration Since 1953

In South Korea, "March North!", the official slogan of the Liberal Party Government of President Syngman Rhee and the battle cry of many opposition politicians as well, was not abandoned until the summer of 1960. In opposition to this, the Korean Communists have since 1953, consistently emphasized the slogan of "peaceful unification." Thus North Korean strategy since the Korean Armistice may be characterized as primarily one of "peaceful" psychological warfare and underground activity. Although there was some residual guerrilla activity until the winter of 1955-1956, there has been no significant involvement of Communists in political violence in South Korea in the past decade. There are two central tactics in the Korean Communist strategy of peaceful unification. The first is to make North Korea economically and culturally attractive to the people of the South. Kim Ilsŏng has said that he wishes to evoke in the people of the South a painful yearning for participation in North Korean society such as he experienced toward the Soviet Union during his Manchurian days.[19] Therefore the North Koreans have been increasingly active in propagandizing the achievements of their three year plan for postwar reconstruction, 1954-1956; their first five year plan, 1957-1961; and their first seven year plan, 1961-1967.

Some measure of the success of this propaganda may be obtained from the reaction of the Korean population in Japan, where over 70,000 have chosen to be repatriated to the North. This response undoubtedly has reinforced the confidence of the North Korean leadership in their competitive psychological warfare positions, although other observers might wish to explain the return to North Korea more on the basis of Korean dissatisfaction with life in Japan and

[18] Kim Ilsŏng "Sasang saŏpesŏ kyojojuŭiwa hyŏngsikchuŭirŭl t'oech'ihago chuch'erŭl hwangniphal te taehayŏ," [On Exterminating Dogmatism and Formalism and Establishing Independence in Ideological Work], *Selected Works* (P'yŏngyang 1960) IV, 343.

[19] *Ibid.*, 342.

the unwillingness or inability of the Republic of Korea to absorb the island compatriots. Since North Korean publications—including pictures of the impressively reconstructed Communist capital of P'yŏngyang—are proscribed in South Korea, the full Communist propaganda capability there has not been demonstrated. Because the South Korean population has not had the opportunity to assimilate gradually and critically information about developments in the North, a form of intra-societal cultural shock is to be anticipated when materials more tangible than easily heard P'yŏngyang radio exhortations reach the hands of generations removed from the wartime experience. It is quite probable that exposure to these materials by some of the young officers studying at the National Defense College helped to propel them toward extremist measures in the seizure of power in 1961.

The second tactic of peaceful unification has been the conduct of "political work" in South Korea. Practically, this has meant the dispatching of agents, many with missions of influencing relatives in responsible positions or of assimilating themselves unobtrusively into South Korean life, the attempted underground reconstruction of the South Korean Workers' Party of which there are an estimated 30,000 former members in the South, and the dissemination of propaganda materials through such means as balloons and surreptitiously printed leaflets.

The framework of social theory which has been expounded in connection with postwar political action is that the main force of the Korean Revolution consists of the "worker-peasant alliance led by the working class." Its allies have been conceived to be all those who oppose "American imperialism" and struggle for peaceful unification. The main enemies in addition to the Americans have been "landlords, national traitors, comprador capitalists, reactionary bureaucrats," and sometimes "reactionary generals." Although sweeping changes in the North have been introduced such as the elimination of private farming, industry, and trade, immediate Communist objectives in the South are declared to be the distribution of land to individual farmers and the promotion of private economic activity. The principal themes in the Communist assault upon South Korean society are that it is caught in a linear progression of increasing poverty and unemployment, that American economic assistance is not only ineffective but actually injurious, and that the only way to recover economic viability and to regain "national honor" is to reject the American involvement on the peninsula and join with the Communist North.

It is against such a background of experience, strategy, and tactics that the two major internal war events of the post-1953 period took place: the student demonstrations of April 1960 which brought the end of the Rhee Administration; and the military coup of May 1961 which overthrew the government of Prime Minister Chang Myŏn. In neither of these events did the Communists play a direct and leading role. The basic problem for Communist strategy in recent years thus has become that of interpreting and anticipating political violence initiated by others and of developing strategies for deflecting them in favorable directions.

The Communists were apparently as much surprised by the precipitants and consequences of the police killing of students in Seoul on April 19, 1960 as was the Government of the Republic of Korea. Of those who had demonstrated against the March 15 elections, burned police boxes, attacked public buildings, and looted the homes of detested Liberal Party politicians, Nikita Khrushchev said on May 5, "They have risen so far spontaneously in an unorganized way." A Soviet analysis published in June 1960[20] attributed the failure of the April uprising to bring about a pro-Communist social revolution to lack of political leadership, organizational weakness of the working class, and failure to arouse the peasantry. The weakness of the working class was attributed to the suppression of leaders since 1945, the peasant and artisan background of new recruits to the labor force, and the small enterprise nature of South Korean industry. The lack of peasant support was attributed in part to the influence of the rich peasants who were strengthened by the land reform completed in 1951. This analysis implied some degree of "progressiveness" to the transfer of power to the Democratic Party since the "national bourgeoisie" were said to be influential in its leadership. Soviet commentaries immediately following the April demonstration stressed the theme that the United States had suffered a grave blow to its international prestige through the "smashing" of its "Asian showcase of democracy" in Korea.

Immediate Chinese Communist interpretations of the April events termed them a "preliminary victory of the Korean people against American imperialism, the root cause of all the suffering of the South

[20] V. Li, "Events in South Korea," *International Affairs* (Moscow), No. 6 (1960), 51-55.

Korean people today." Chinese commentaries significantly stressed that the events in Korea confirmed their view of the national liberation movements in Asia, Africa, and Latin America: "The South Korean people's struggle against the U. S.-Syngman Rhee clique proves that the contradictions between imperialism and the masses, and between the oppressors and the oppressed, are irreconcilable. Such contradictions can be settled only through struggle. . . . The greater the oppression and misery suffered by the people, the sharper the contradiction between them and the oppressors, the stronger their desire to change the status quo, and the more vehement their resistance will be. All oppressed nations and peoples will in the end rise up against the imperialist oppressors and strive for their freedom and independence. This is a rule of historical development independent of human will."[21]

North Korean propaganda comment on the student demonstration, the resignation of President Rhee, the activities of the interim government, and the establishment of the Democratic administration of Chang Myŏn contained a theme which was virtually absent in both the Soviet and Chinese interpretations: the gist of it was that "nothing had changed" except that Chang had replaced Rhee and the situation had become "worse." Although the Korean Communists certainly must have wished to promote widespread social disorder in South Korea during the April uprising, they seem themselves to have eschewed violence and did not commit acts of individual terror. One P'yŏngyang radio broadcast, for example, called upon the officers and men of the martial law command set up to restore social order to "throw away their bayonets" and to join the people in opposition to the government; they were not incited to turn their weapons against the government or upon their comrades in arms.[22] Communist unwillingness to become identified with acts of violence and terror might also be inferred from the fact that no personal violence was inflicted upon American citizens or upon Syngman Rhee himself, under conditions where this easily could have been accomplished. An alternative explanation to the violence-avoidance hypothesis is, of course, that the Communists simply did not have a disciplined organization with any substantial capability in South Korea. Both of these factors were probably involved. In any case, since the symbols of "Communist" and "bloodshed" are fused with horror in popular attitudes as a result of the wartime experience, it would have been suicidal to have raised

[21] Radio Peking, May 3, 1960.
[22] Radio Peking, April 20, 1960.

the blood-red banner of Communist insurrection on the streets of Seoul in the spring of 1960.

The surprise, nearly bloodless *coup d'état* of May 16, 1961 provided Communist analysts with a chain of events in which a small group of military officers successfully overthrew a freely elected constitutional government despite public opposition by the highest diplomatic and military representatives of the United States in Korea. There was a striking difference in the initial North Korean and Soviet propaganda reactions to these events.

In their first broadcast reaction to the coup on May 16, the Korean Communists reported that the "corrupt" and "puppet" government of Chang Myŏn had been overthrown, that the students of Seoul and other areas were carrying out demonstrations in support of the coup, and that General Carter B. Magruder and Minister Marshall Green had "overtly interfered in the internal affairs of South Korea." This reaction was highly favorable to the insurgents; there was no call for the militant defense of "democracy." Three factors may have led the Communists to suspect that the coup might be the signal for a pro-Communist turn of events in South Korea: First, among the announced leaders of the coup was the name of Maj. Gen. Pak Chŏnghŭi, who had been sentenced to death as a Communist sympathizer in the wake of the Yŏsu rebellion in 1948. Later his sentence was commuted to life imprisonment, apparently in part because he agreed to implicate others involved in the uprising. When the Korean War broke out, he and other officers were pardoned on the condition that they would fight loyally for the Republic of Korea. On the day of the coup the rumor swept Seoul that General Pak was the "real brains" of the junta and that he was a "Communist." Whether true or not, what was widely believed in Seoul could hardly have been disregarded in P'yŏngyang.

The second aspect of the coup which may have influenced the Communist reaction was the false report that students were acting in sympathy with the rebels. In the months preceding the coup, a small but vocal group had been agitating for a "neutral, unified Korea" and for negotiations with the students of North Korea. The Communists may well have thought that the students were now supporting army officers who held similar views. A third component of the situation which must have seemed favorable to the Communists was the opposition of the American officials. It is difficult to measure just how much the Korean Communists believe their own propaganda that South Korea is an American "colony" and that all aspects of southern society are under American domination. Certainly this view must have been reinforced by South Korean defectors who have exaggerated American influence in the South as a means of self-justification. In any case it seems likely that the North Koreans concluded that if the Americans were opposing the junta it must have contained some pro-Communist elements. The cautious and conciliatory tone which the Communists took toward the military junta is illustrated clearly by the May 17 P'yŏngyang radio commentary on the first revolutionary pledge of the rebels which was "to make anti-Communism the first national policy and to revitalize and strengthen the hitherto formlalistic and meaningless anti-Communist attitude." "Should this stand today be continued to be pursued," the Communists admonished, "there is the hidden danger that the people's struggle for the peaceful unification of the fatherland will be suppressed and that South Korea will become more fascist." Not until May 19 did the Communists hold a mass meeting in P'yŏngyang in opposition to the coup.

The immediate Soviet propaganda response was strikingly different; there was no suggestion that the junta might be amenable to negotiation. On May 16 Moscow Radio broadcast in the Korean language to South Korea: "The reactionary clique intends to fasten its tyrant rule over the people through the coup by the armed forces." A May 17 Soviet commentary referred to the coup as "clearly ultra-reactionary in character" and as designed to establish a "military fascist dictatorship." Early Soviet commentaries differed from those of the North Koreans in at least two other respects: they credited the Chang Myŏn administration with having made some democratic progress when they explained that it had been overthrown in part because it had gone "too far in playing democracy;" and they revealed some appreciation of American embarrassment with the military government. The Chinese Communists seemed generally to follow the North Korean lead, but within a week all three sets of Communist propagandists were synchronized in attacking the "fascist, murderous, military clique" in South Korea.

Korean Communist experiences with the April student demonstrations and the May military coup were authoritatively summarized in the report of the work of the Ceneral Committee of the Korean Worker's Party given by Kim Ilsŏng at the Fourth Congress of the KWP in P'yŏngyang in September 1961. The theme of his report was that the success of the socialist transformation of North Korean society had "decisively changed the relationship of forces between revolution and counter-revolution in favor of revolution." Summarizing the southern situation he said: "The main trend of developments in South Korea today is that while the forces of revolution in favor of peaceful unification and democracy are growing stronger day by day, the forces of counter-revolution are desperately trying to find an escape in a militaristic-terroristic adventure."[23]

Kim described the April demonstrations as a "great victory" and "a great turning point in the struggle of the South Korean people against American imperialism and for national salvation." The demonstrations were said to have contributed to an "unprecedented rise in the political consciousness of the people," to the "beginning of sharp struggle against the American imperialists," and to a movement led by youth and students for unification and North-South negotiations. The 1961 military coup is described as an act of desperation by "American imperialism and South Korean reaction." Its effect upon the revolutionary process is portrayed as beneficial: "The military fascist regime will only further strengthen the people's struggle and accelerate the final destruction of American imperialist overlordship in Korea."[24]

For propaganda purposes, at least, two main conclusions were drawn by the Korean Communists from these important instances of political violence: they failed to result in immediate Communist advantage both because of lack of a "Marxist revolutionary party" and because of the stabilizing influence of the American presence. The primary task for the present stage of the revolution is thus specified to be the accomplishment of the withdrawal of some 60,000 American military personnel from South Korea. This is to be effected by means of "struggle" by "an anti-American united front for the salvation of the Fatherland" participated in by "workers, peasants, urban petty bourgeoisie, youth, students, intellectuals, and also the national bourgeoisie."

By the summer of 1962, two trends in North Korean propaganda became apparent: one was an intensification in the stridency of the anti-American theme and the other was a return to a conciliatory tone in appeals in the military junta in Seoul. Respectfully addressing as "the South Korean authorities" those who had been called

[23] Kim Ilsŏng, "Otchetnyy doklad Tsentral'nogo Komiteta Trudovoy partii Korei IV s"ezdu partii" [Report of the Central Committee of the KWP to the IV Party Congress], *Kommunist*, No. 14 (September 1961), 127.

[24] *Ibid.*, 128.

"murderous beasts" for months, a June resolution of the Supreme People's Assembly called upon the junta to take "all necessary measures" to secure the withdrawal of American forces.[25] If such a step were taken the military leaders and all others were promised that "all past crimes against the people" would be forgiven. Under conditions of political instability in South Korea, where there is every expectation of future coups and counter-coups, now that the precedent has been set by the group lead by General Pak Chŏnghŭi and intelligence chief Colonel Kim Chŏngp'il, the Communists apparently consider it probable that even the present leadership might switch to a favorable compromising position to secure its own power and to rid itself of American influence. For their part the Korean Communists stand ready with a wide range of conciliatory proposals on record extending from discussions between the leaders of North and South, to economic and cultural exchange, reduction of armed forces to 100,000 men, a federal structure of government in which southern authority would be retained, and national elections under non-United Nations supervision. As an example of the tactics of enticement being employed in the summer of 1962, a year before the elections in South Korea, the Central Committee of the KWP was letting it be known abroad that "General Pak can have any position he wants in the government of a united Korea."

Conclusions

This review of Communist experience with political violence in Korea since 1945 suggests that those situations in which they took the initiative in provoking and leading violence led to general Communist failure while those situations in which they were peripherally involved seemed to bring consequences in long-run terms favorable to the attainment of Communist objectives. A common factor in all Communist failures was the involvement of American power on the Korean peninsula, a fact which helps to explain apparent Korean sympathy for the Chinese position in the Sino-Soviet dialogue about the tactics of "peaceful coexistence." The Communists were defeated in the early post-1945 struggle for power under the aegis of the United States Army Military Government. They were beaten in the pre-1950 guerrilla war by an American equipped, trained, and advised

[25] *Message of the Supreme People's Assembly of the Democratic People's Republic of Korea to the Supreme Council for National Reconstruction of the Republic of Korea, the Public and Political Figures and the Entire People of South Korea,* P'yŏngyang, June 21, 1962, 6.

army. Communist interpretations of these events, of course, exaggerate American influence and fail to account adequately for Korean determination to avoid Communist subjugation and for the great sacrifices which the Korean people have made toward that end. In 1950 the Communists were deprived of what was almost a quick and easy victory by unexpected American military intervention. The student uprising of 1960, on the other hand, brought an end to a staunch but uninspiring anti-Communist government which American policy had sought both to support and to moderate. The 1961 military coup brought to power a group basically impatient with the practices of a free society, and whose discrediting of less than a year of remarkable attempts to make such a society operative in Korea undoubtedly struck a major blow against the psychological defenses of South Korean society against Communist absorption.

From *ex post facto* Communist analyses of these instances of political violence, at least five categories of interpretation can be derived: analysis of the effects of violence (1) upon the Communist party organization; (2) upon the general populace or segments of it and assessment of its significance for party-people relationship; (3) upon "the revolutionary process" as a whole; (4) upon the enemy; and (5) upon international relations. Whether such a paradigm of Communist internal war analysis actually serves as an *a priori* model for an estimate of the situation in pre-violence decision making is a matter of conjecture, but it might serve as a reasonable, if simple, framework of anticipatory analysis.

If such a framework were applied to the difficult undertaking of anticipating future Communist violence in Korea on the basis of past experience, the following predictions might be ventured. It is *unlikely* that the Communists will initiate and lead violence in South Korea under conditions where the party organization is weak and subject to exposure and decimation through violent action; where popular attitudes against violence remain strong and closely identified with Communist behavior; where political, economic, and social conditions seem to be building pressures favorable to the attainment of Communist objectives either by relatively non-violent processes or by violence initiated by others; where the enemy is heavily armed, highly organized, and well-disciplined; and where violence would increase unfavorable international involvement. On the other hand, Communist violence in South Korea would seem *likely* under conditions where the party is strong and influential; where Communist violence, as the lesser of existing social evils, can be expected to raise Communist prestige; where violence can be expected to stiffen popular rebelliousness; where the enemy is weak or seriously divided; and where international intervention is deterred or otherwise made improbable.

From this point of view the present situation in the Republic of Korea seems closer to the former rather than to the latter model. Although a large number of former members of the South Korean Workers' Party, outlawed in 1948, still live in the area south of the Thirty-eighth Parallel, there is little evidence that the Korean Communists have yet been able to rebuild a strong party organization in the South. It is to be recalled that the principal leader of the South Korean Communists, Pak Hŏnyŏng, was executed in North Korea in 1955 by the Kim Ilsŏng leadership. This suggests that the former South Korean Communists might be less than responsive to directives and organizational efforts from P'yŏngyang. If the present KWP leadership were overthrown by a Communist faction which could disavow Kim's responsibility for the elimination of Pak Hŏnyŏng, then Communist organizational capabilities in the South might appear in a new light. Of course, as the years pass, the attitudes of members of the former South Korean Communist organization will become less important.

Communist brutality during the Korean war probably has done more than any other single factor to weaken the appeal of Communism in South Korea. The surprise Communist invasion following talk of "peaceful unification" bewildered and disillusioned many Koreans who were sympathetic toward or at least tolerant of Communist activity. The pre-1950 reservoir of good will which the Communists may have had, whatever its extent, was largely drained off through wartime killing. In this connection it is important to note that Koreans estimate propensity to respond favorably to Communist appeals as highest in the areas in southeastern Korea which did not fall under People's Army control between June and September of 1950. By the same token it is unlikely that the behavior of the Republic of Korea Army left a legacy of sympathy in North Korea after the advance toward and retreat from the Yalu between October and January of 1950.

Again the passage of time seems to promise the diminution of hostility to the symbols of Communism based upon memories of bloodshed. Those Koreans who were five years old at the time of the

Communist invasion are now seventeen; in another decade they will be well on the way toward leadership of a burgeoning population. As illustrated by the student outburst of 1960, traditional social controls, associated with respect for the norms of the older generations, are being weakened under the impact of education and widening world horizons as the new youth of Korea emerges as a major political force. Already there are signs that the "generational gap" so keenly felt by both younger and older Koreans may tend to work in favor of an accommodation with North Korea. Since youth tends to blame "the older generation" for many of Korea's problems—such as permitting the country to be dismembered, failing to provide for a high rate of economic growth, failing to eliminate corruption in government, and many other aspects of Korean life—it is also likely that Korean youth will come to distrust the views of their elders on the evils of North Korean Communism and on the necessity of an alliance with the United States.

Whether true or not, the idea that South Korea cannot solve its economic problems without the reintegration of the northern and southern economies is gaining momentum among the youth of South Korea. Although this is an idea intensively cultivated by Communist radio propaganda, those who hold it are not necessarily motivated by pro-Communist sentiments. The young men of Korea are animated by a keen sense of nationalism; many find their pride deeply hurt by the idea that for the indefinite future the economic viability of their part of the country will depend upon American assistance, which has averaged about 200 million dollars a year. The notion that the South Korean economy should discover strength through dependence on Japan is also not especially attractive. The idea that some economic rapprochement ought to be brought about with the North is thus gaining in appeal. Some think that this might be accomplished without submission to Communist control; a few are willing to risk it as "the lesser of two evils."

Thus psychological attitudes toward economic development would seem to be one of the key variables in anticipating the appeals of communism in South Korea. At present the North Korean leadership seems to believe that time is on their side: with control over a rich natural resource and power base and with a limited population of eleven million people they contemplate the eventual economic subversion of the twenty-seven million people in the South. They undoubtedly expect that sooner or later economic discontent will erupt in violence from which they can benefit. This might come about first through a *coup d'état* by a group willing to negotiate merely an economic agreement; and eventually through seizure of power by a group which would negotiate a coalition government on behalf of a partially intimidated and partially demoralized populace.

The slogan "economics first" put forth by the Democratic administration of Chang Myŏn and the insistence of the military junta that freedom was secondary to economic development have both tended to pin the fate of Korea upon economic competition between North and South. Whatever the comparative economic realities of the two parts of the country may be, popular beliefs about them eventually will be a deciding factor. The trend of present beliefs is not favorable to South Korea.

For the immediate future, any Korean government will undoubtedly possess an overwhelming capability to crush Communist efforts to instigate violence in the South. The postwar anti-Communist hostility of the armed forces, police (both public and secret), and administration, leave no question as to the fate of any overt revolutionary activity clearly identified as Communist. The strength of the "enemy," coupled with the anticipation that the Republic of Korea Government would call for increased assistance from the United States and the United Nations, probably now serve as the major deterrent to Communist agitation and revolutionary initiative in South Korea.

The extent of the international involvement of North Korea in the "socialist camp" is also of importance for anticipating the future of Communist attempts to dominate South Korea. The more widespread the belief that North Korea is not a "puppet" of the Soviet Union or of Communist China, the greater the attractiveness of the North. Recognition of this by the Kim Ilsŏng leadership is evidenced by the fact that both the military defense treaties signed by North Korea with the Soviet Union and Communist China contain provisions for their automatic cancellation in the event of Korean unification. Since 1960, there have in fact been signs of the growing "independence" of North Korea from both Soviet and Chinese controls. Apparently the more marked the Sino-Soviet contention, the more the P'yŏngyang leadership has been able to maneuver to its advantage. North Korea has not yet achieved, however, the degree of autonomy which would be highly attractive to the South. If the international Communist system continues to develop through conflict in the direction of increased autonomy for its component states, the appeals of North Korea will be greatly enhanced.

Although it appears that Communist-led violence is not likely under present conditions in South Korea, this implies neither that there will be no violence there in the immediate future nor that the Korean Communists have abandoned it as a means for achieving power. Under conditions of neither peace nor war, political violence is to be anticipated until the governance of non-Communist Korea rests firmly upon a broad consensus of its people. The leaders of the Korean Workers' Party can be expected to attempt to promote and to channel such violence insofar as it promises to bring them closer to the conditions under which their adherents can act decisively to bring the Republic of Korea under Communist control.

PART III

Evolving Communist Strategies for Revolution

9

Communist Attitudes Toward Asia, Africa and Latin America

THOMAS P. THORNTON

The Post-Stalin Revision of Soviet Attitudes

The Communist view of the world in the era of Stalin, and particularly after the Second World War, was based upon the doctrine of "two camps"—Communist and non-Communist—and there was no real third choice. In the European context, the Soviet Union had brought virtually such a situation about through its aggressive behavior after the war. The choice was clearly between hostility and subservience, and most of the Western countries were directly engaged and vitally interested in the outcome of the confrontation.

This outlook was unsuited, however, to the pattern of international relations which began to emerge around mid-century. Following the stabilization of the international system in the years after the Second World War, whole continents and regions emerged from colonial status and established independent governments. Between 1947 and 1960 colonialism died and was buried, even though the Portuguese declined to attend the funeral. Also, states which had long been independent in name but in fact were clients of United States, Great Britain, or other powerful nations, began to seek new and fuller forms of independence. The Communists had long predicted the collapse of the imperialist colonial system, but when it came they were slow to appreciate the significance of the change. Nothing in Marxist theory had prepared them for such a sudden and radical transformation, one in which they played no leading role outside of China and Vietnam.

It took several years for the Communists to accept the fact that the new nations were indeed independent, not mere stalking horses of their former colonial masters. These new countries introduced a radically different element into the international equation, and as long as the Communist leaders failed to recognize this they found themselves fighting not only their "natural" enemies, but a large section of the world which cared little about Communism and desired only to be left in peace. The recognition of this changed state of affairs was probably not lost upon Stalin in the later years of his life; as early as the Korean War, the Chinese found that the presence of an Indian medical team with the UN forces in Korea did not mean that India was a bulwark of anti-communism.[1] Even the large number of Communists in Indian jails was not indicative of any Indian anti-communism on the international level. India and the other new nations might well become hostile to the Soviet Union and China, but only if they were forced to do so. By the time of Stalin's physical death in 1953 and certainly by the time of his moral assassination in 1956, new patterns of Soviet behavior were being designed to exploit the potential of the new international situation.

The great shift in Communist policy can be seen best in the period 1955-1956. Chou En-lai's beguiling performance at Bandung was the most publicized portent of change, but at the Twentieth Congress of the Soviet Party a completely new approach towards the new nations was decreed. Gandhi, Nehru, Sukarno, and other nationalist leaders were quickly refurbished to become not lackeys of imperialism, but true representatives of their peoples' aspirations. The Soviet Union undertook to cement international relations with nations from Brazil to Egypt to Indonesia, and Khrushchev entered with gusto into a campaign of personal diplomacy, backed up with substantial offers of economic and military aid designed to bring Soviet international influence at least up to the level to which its power position entitled it. Consternation in the West was widespread as the Soviets and Chinese occupied the positions in the Middle East and Asia which could be denied them only by their own unwillingness to assume them.

The repercussions of peaceful coexistence and its meaning for the advanced countries of Western Europe and North America will be discussed in another chapter. In the areas of Asia, Africa, and Latin America, its course is well known and will be referred to from time to time in the next four chapters which discuss these areas. The purpose of the following pages is to discuss the theoretical positions which the Communists have assumed in the course of their policy reassessment since 1956. We are fortunate in the Russian case, in that the Twentieth Party Congress explicitly decreed a new orientation and increased interest in the problems of the emerging nations.[2] This has

[1] Allen S. Whiting, *China Crosses the Yalu: The Decision to Enter the Korean War,* (New York 1960), 167

[2] There are a few good sources on Soviet orientology in western languages. Some of the most useful are Walter Laqueur, *The Soviet Union and The Middle East* (New York 1959), 159-175; Hugh Seton-Watson "The Communist Powers

led to a spate of writing concerning not only individual countries, but also the entire "third world." This literature provides us with a valuable means of seeing behind the action level of Soviet behavior, even though we can have little knowledge of the innermost planning and policy formation.

Before entering into a more detailed discussion of the Communist approach to Asia, Africa, and Latin America, it should be noted that Soviet policy has two objectives in regard to the new states; variations of the Chinese approach will be brought out subsequently in the chapter. The first Soviet objective is to protect the security of the Communist international system; the Soviet leaders hope to achieve this by restricting the influence of the advanced countries and their allies and by promoting neutralism in the uncommitted countries. Their second concern is with the "transition to socialism" of the new countries—that is to say, with the establishment of Communist power. To some extent, these two concerns overlap, for the success of communism in a given country would of course mark the end of Western influence there. It is significant, however, that the concern with security takes clear precedence over the seizure of power. It is more important to the Soviet leaders that the new countries be drawn away from Western influence, than that they be brought under Communist rule. It is in this sense that the Soviet theoreticians categorize the non-Communist nations of the world primarily in terms of the foreign-policy orientation of these countries, determined by the relative degree of Soviet or Western influence.

In discussing the Communist attitude toward these countries it is therefore necessary first to describe the various types of countries as the Communist leaders see them. In the light of this typology, the differences in the economic objectives and domestic policies of the Communists will be easier to understand.

Types of Non-Communist Governments

Although the Russians no longer lump all of Asia, Africa, and Latin America together under the general heading of "the east" and treat them as an undifferentiated unit, by the nature of their doctrine the Communists generalize to a considerable extent the characteristics of all the states in these regions. There are a number of factors which the Soviets consider basic to their approach to any nation, and the

and Afro-Asian Nationalism" in *Unity and Conflict* ed. by Kurt London, (New York 1962); Paul Urban, "Orientalistik und Asienpolitik der Sowjets," *Osteuropa*, No. 12 (1958), 797-805; and Curt Gasteyger "The Soviet Union and the Tiers Monde," *Survey*, No. 43 (August 1962), 10-22.

countries of Asia, Africa, and Latin America, with their low level of economic development, weakly developed working class, agrarian problems, and colonial or semi-colonial past, tend to be analyzed in terms of fairly constant categories.

The Soviets classify the overall position which the various states hold in the international community in terms of six groups. Two of these, "imperialist" and "socialist," do not pertain to any of the countries under consideration here. With the possible exception of Japan, none of the Asian, African, or Latin American states is actually "imperialist," and those which are "socialist" (China, North Korea, North Vietnam, and Mongolia) fall outside the scope of this chapter. Cuba might perhaps be considered as a special case. The remaining categories are those states which have gained political independence but, unlike the "socialist" nations, are still tied to the international economy; nations which have gained political independence but have jeopardized it by entering into military alliances and similar arrangements with the United States or another NATO power; and those few areas which are still in fact colonies.[3] The final category, about which we will have much to say later, is that of the "national democracy."

This classification is Russian in origin; it is not utilized by the Chinese.[4] It arises from the bipolar international situation, and implicitly ascribes varying degrees of merit to each category of states. The dividing line between acceptability and unacceptability for the Soviets is in general the criterion of political neutralism. "Socialist" states and those which have no military ties with the West are good; others are bad, albeit in varying degrees. The Chinese, however, tend to draw the line of acceptability to include only the "socialist" states. Although they are willing enough to derive benefit from dealings with neutral states, they deny that there is any likelihood that these states can develop peacefully into the "higher stage of socialism." Thus, for the Chinese all states are basically "bad," except for those which adhere to the Communist system.[5] The most obvious manifestation

[3] *Fundamentals of Marxism-Leninism* (Moscow 1961), 501-502.

[4] The only exception seems to have appeared in May 1960, when a Chinese writer discussed various nations in these same categories, but claimed to derive the categories ". . . by using Chairman Mao's theory of the new democratic revolution as a yardstick!" Chiang Hsiang-shih in *Zhongguo Jingnian*, No. 9 (1960) (JPRS 3904), 3.

[5] This line of thought is set forth in my article "Peking, Moscow and the Underdeveloped Areas," *World Politics*, XIII (July 1961), 491-504. See also Donald S. Zagoria, *The Sino-Soviet Conflict, 1956-1961* (Princeton 1962), esp. Chapter 10.

of this divergence in attitudes has been towards India which the Soviets continue to court assiduously, and which the Chinese have treated with outspoken hostility.

Re-evaluation of the National Bourgeoisie

Central to the understanding of the Sino-Soviet dispute over the underdeveloped areas is the question of the "national bourgeoisie."[6] This group has been the subject of overwhelming Communist attentions and study ever since the time of Lenin. The attribute "national" is easily enough explained, in that it applies to persons who are in fact nationalists, subscribing neither to the internationalism of Communism nor to the "capitalist internationalism" which the Communists allege exists. The national bourgeoisie is found preeminently in areas which have been subjected to colonial (e.g., India and Nigeria) or semi-colonial (e.g., Honduras and China) rule. Insofar as nationalism is the prime characteristic of the national bourgeoisie—during the struggle for independence and in its supposed fight against "American neocolonialism"—the national bourgeoisie is regarded as a highly progressive force by the Communists and ardently supported, within the limits imposed by Soviet policy considerations.

The national bourgeoisie is still bourgeois, however—or at least it is supposed to be. Actually the national bourgeoisie is an undefinable class. Proletarians, peasants, capitalists, and even such categories as "comprador bourgeoisie" can be defined for better or worse in terms of economic roles which they play. "Bourgeoisie" as such can even be given a plausible, if flexible, definition, but "national bourgeoisie" cannot be considered a class in Marxian terms since it is described primarily by political, not economic criteria, and it can most certainly not be given a meaningful definition in objective terms. Communist writers have wrestled mightily to infuse meaning into the term, but with little success. Besides bourgeois (by definition capitalists), it can also be stretched to include all manner of intellectuals, small businessmen, landowners, and even crowned heads. Very generally, the national bourgeoisie consists mostly of medium and small bourgeois—what we would call the middle and lower-middle classes

[6] On the national bourgeoisie see Seton-Watson, and Lacqueur, "The 'National Bourgeoisie': A Soviet Dilemma in the Middle East," *International Affairs* (London) xxxv, (July 1959), 324-331. The origins of the reconsideration were described in a report "Diskussiya ob ekonomicheskikh i politicheskikh pozitsiyakh natsional'noy burzhuazii v stranakh vostoka" [Discussion on the Economic and Political Positions of the National Bourgeoisie in the Lands of the East], *SV*, No. 1 (1957), 174-184.

—in the developing areas.[7] It is probably an oversimplification to call the national bourgeoisie ". . . those Asian or African businessmen who can be manipulated for the aims of Soviet foreign policy,"[8] but in practice this is frequently what they are.

Virtually all of the underdeveloped areas are controlled by the national bourgeoisie. The only exceptions are the Communist states, Cuba (Castro had been a national bourgeois but was successfully metamorphosized by announcing his Leninism), some newly-independent African states, the remaining colonies, and a few unspecified "feudal" states. Everywhere else, the national bourgeoisie was the instrument of achieving national independence, and therefore enjoys the fruits of its victory. Having performed this historical service, however, it is destined to pass from existence in favor of a Communist social order in which neither nationalists nor bourgeois would have a role.[9] This prospect is not what the national bourgeois leaders envision, so the seeds of conflict between them and the Communists have begun to sprout. For the time being the Soviets are doing all they can to minimize dissension with the national bourgeoisie. As long as such leaders as Nkrumah, Nasser, Nehru, and Mrs. Bandaranaike are useful to Soviet foreign policy objectives their coolness towards domestic communism is overlooked.

Some distinction is made between big bourgeois on the one hand, and middle and small bourgeois on the other. The big bourgeoisie—large manufacturers, bankers, etc.—is said to have closer ties to the "feudal" landowners and the international capitalist system than do its smaller brethren.[10] Thus, once a country has become independent the big bourgeois tend to lose their nationalist ardor and are less useful as allies for the Communists. The middle and small bourgeoisie have more modest rural ties and do not profit directly from international commercial trade relationships. They are therefore more likely to join with the Communists on a variety of post-independence foreign and domestic issues. In practice, this distinction is rather meaningless, and few Communists look askance at prospective allies with large bank accounts.

[7] See, for instance, N. Savel'ev "O natsional'noy burzhuazii v stranakh yugo-vostochnoy Azii" [On the National Bourgeoisie in the Countries of Southeast Asia], *MEIMO* No. 4 (1961), 40-42; and Li Wei-han "Study Chairman Mao's Writings and Gradually Improve your World Outlook," *Renmin Ribao* (Sept. 25, 1960), translated in *JPRS* 5953, p. 16.

[8] Seton-Watson, 193.

[9] W. Markov, "Mouvement National et Classes Sociales dans le Tiers-Monde," *Cahiers Internationaux,* No. 117 (1961), 59.

[10] N. Savel'ev, *passim.*

The Chinese attitude toward the national bourgeoisie lays much greater stress on the negative characteristics of the group. Chiang Kai-shek was a national bourgeois in his time, and the Chinese Communists are painfully aware of the treatment which he dealt out to them.[11] They contest the Russian belief[12] that the national bourgeoisie at present tends towards socialism and will ultimately give way peacefully to Communist domination. In the Chinese estimation, the group is bourgeois first and national only afterwards—its ties to the international bourgeoisie are actually increasing and the longer it is left in power the more difficult the Communists will find it to oust it.[13] As a result, Chinese policy towards the countries ruled by the national bourgeoisie is scarcely more accommodating than their policy towards outright "capitalist" states. For the Soviets, collaboration with governments controlled by the national bourgeoisie has become a basic strategy—for the Chinese it is only a tactic of convenience.

Prospects for Communist Success

In their varying ways, the Soviets and Chinese both feel that the present situation in the developing countries is favorable to the expansion of communism. The establishment of many new countries with little political experience, the loosening of international economic ties, the economic and social dislocations attendant upon modernization, and the increase of Communist power as an international force —all of these appear as attractive opportunities for Communist expansion. The exploitation of these targets, however, is not a matter of unanimity between Moscow and Peking. It is unfortunate that the Chinese have written so much on the developing areas and yet said so little. Their voluminous output on this subject can be fairly reduced to the proposition that local Communists must take all steps possible

[11] Most interestingly and most recently in a series of articles by Li Wei-han, "The Struggle for Proletarian Leadership in the New-Democratic Revolution in China," *Hongqi*, Nos. 3 and 4 (1962); reprinted in, *PR* Nos. 8 through 12 (1962), and published as a pamphlet (Peking 1962).

[12] Expressed typically in Markov, 59. It is clear that the Soviet view is becoming increasingly cautious, however, and since about 1960 Soviet scholars—and to a lesser extent political figures—have been increasingly critical of national bourgeois governments. This "quantitative" change has not, however, brought the Soviet position "qualitatively" nearer that of the Chinese. Specifics of this shift are discussed in the chapters below. See also Georg v. Stackelberg, "Renewed Attacks on the National Bourgeoisie," *Bulletin of the Institute for the Study of the U.S.S.R.*, VIII (Aug. 1961), 3-9.

[13] Shih Tsu-chih "The Fundamental Path for the Liberation Movement in the Colonies and Semi-Colonies", *GWY*, No. 5 (1960), translated in JPRS 6024, and Wang Chia-shang "The International Significance of the Chinese Peoples Victory," in *Ten Glorious Years* (Peking 1960), 272-276.

to promote the seizure of power in their countries by armed force and, although this force should initially come from within the country in question, the Chinese themselves are prepared, and—even more—expect the Soviets to be prepared to lend concrete and substantial assistance to these "national liberation movements." Chinese writings show virtually no interest in the development of pre-Communist transitional forms, taking the fundamentalist view that the evil of "imperialism" must be crushed firmly and with all possible speed. It is an essentially simple view of the world.

The Soviet Union, on the other hand, more experienced and much more conservative, has devoted great effort to the elaboration of Marxist theories to explain the present situation of the developing countries and predict their future course of development. The objective of Soviet policy, of course, is to move the various states along the progression towards membership in the Communist system. In the cases of the few remaining colonies this involves immediately the completion of the "national liberation struggle" and the attainment of political independence. The politically independent countries which maintain military arrangements with Western powers (e.g., Thailand, Pakistan, Iran) should be detached from their military alliances, and no Western bases should remain upon their territory. Once this step has been completed, the state in question is a qualified member of the "zone of peace" and receives Soviet approbation.[14] The development of this vital qualitative change is at least inappropriate to Marxist analysis since it stems from an act of foreign policy rather than local economic or political factors; but a minimum level of neutrality accruing from the "zone of peace" obviously serves Soviet strategic interests.

There are examples enough of nations which do make the transition from allies of the West to neutralist—Iraq, Ceylon, Egypt—and the Communists are reasonably sanguine that some of the other militarily and politically committed states will also make the change. Once this hurdle is crossed, the more specifically Marxian problems arise concerning the movement of the state from its position of political neutralism and economic dependence upon the world market to a position of membership in the Communist international political and economic system. This, ultimately, is the question of seizure of power.

[14] The Soviets are even willing to accept states such as Morocco in which there are bases, when there are signs that they will soon be evicted.

The State of National Democracy

The "state of national democracy" is postulated in Soviet literature as the desirable form of this transition, although the Chinese have never recognized the term beyond their signing of the 1960 Moscow Declaration in which it was first set forth.[15] Only five countries have ever been mentioned as potential national democracies by the Soviets —Cuba, Guinea, Ghana, Mali, and Indonesia—and at least two of these appear no longer to be in consideration. The relatively unfriendly position which Guinea assumed vis-à-vis the Soviet Union in 1962 seems to have brought about a "demotion," while Cuba has passed to the stage of "building socialism." Ghana, too, has been given credit by Anastas Mikoyan for being in a "socialist" stage, but this claim does not seem to have received much subsequent support and was probably meant as a sop to Nkrumah's vanity.[16] Even though no Soviet source ever stated that Cuba was a national democracy (only the East Germans ever made this claim), it is probable that the category was set up to accommodate the Cuban case during the brief period in which Castro was clearly moving towards the Communist system, but had not yet declared himself to be a Communist. The efforts to extend the category to other countries is beset with theoretical problems, most of which have been sidestepped by Soviet writers. In practice, the countries identified with the naional democracy concept are characterized by little more than a friendly disposition towards the USSR and the important role played by the Soviets in their economies.

The *ad hoc* origin of the concept and the essentially un-Marxian basis upon which it has been applied has resulted in considerably less than lucidity in the Soviet writing on national democracy.[17] Many ques-

[15] On the initial reaction to the national democracy concept in China, see Zagoria, 362. A good analysis of the Soviet and Chinese stands on national democracy is contained in William T. Shinn, Jr., "The 'National Democratic State'—A Communist Program for Less-developed Areas," *World Politics*, xv (April 1963), 377-389.

[16] Among other evidence, Potekhin carefully omits any reference to Guinea in his article "On African 'Socialism'," *IntAff*, No. 1 (1963), 71-79. Mikoyan's statement on Cuba was released by TASS (in English and Russian) on January 12, 1962.

[17] See M. Dzhunusov, "Nekotorye voprosy teorii sotsial'noy revolyutsii v svete krusheniya kolonial'noy sistemy" [Some Questions of the Theory of Social Revolution in the Light of the Destruction of the Colonial System], available to me only in German translation, the source given as "Materialen der kirgizischen Staatlichen Universität, Lehrstuhl Philosophie, Frunze, 1961"—reprinted in *Sowjetwissenschaft, Gesellschaftswissenschaftliche Beiträge*, No. 10 (1961) 1095. Also, B. Ponomarev "O gosudarstve natsional'noy demokratii" [On the National Democratic State], *Kom-*

tions of its specific features and even of its basic nature are left unclear or are hedged about with meaningless jargon. Behind the mass of phraseology, however, emerges the fact that national democracy is intended to provide the Communists with a transitional form to "people's democracy," in which they would wield decisive power. This has been the path of the Eastern European Communists in seizing power, and although the Russians have never identified the Eastern European governments of the post-Second World War period as national democracies, one Czech writer has made the correspondence clear by comparing the Czech and Cuban revolutions.[18] Despite the difficulty of achieving theoretical clarity on the question of national democracy, there are certain general qualifications which describe the state, and these attributes are the main criteria by which Soviet writers judge the economic and political level of countries in Asia, Africa, and Latin America. By considering these points, we will have gone far towards recreating the framework within which Soviet analysis proceeds. According to the Moscow statement, a national democracy is ". . . a state which consistently upholds its political and economic independence, fights against imperialism and its military blocs, against military bases on its territory; a state which fights against the new forms of colonialism and the penetration of imperialist capital; a state which rejects dictatorial and despotic methods of government; a state in which the people are ensured of broad democratic rights and freedoms (freedom of speech, press, assembly, demonstrations, establishment of political parties and social organizations), the opportunity to work for the enactment of an agrarian reform and other domestic and social changes, and for participation in shaping government policy."[19]

Neo-Colonialism

The political independence of a country naturally refers in the first instance to its attainment of freedom from colonial control. Beyond this, however, it is intimately connected with the question

munist, No. 8 (1961) (translated in *JPRS* 4791 of Sept. 1961, 20-39, and *CDSP,* XII No. 22, pp. 3-7); and G. Starushenko "Cherez obshchedemokraticheskiye preobrazovaniya k sotsialisticheskim" [Through General Democratic Reforms to Socialism], *Kommunist,* No. 13 (1962), 105-109.

[18] Jan Kozak, "Znacheniye natsional'noy i demokraticheskoy revolyutsii v Chekhoslovakii dlya bor'by rabochego klassa za sotsializm (1945-1948 gg.)" [The Significance of the National and Democratic Revolution in Czechoslovakia in the Struggle of the Working Class for Socialism (1945-1948)], *Voprosy Istorii KPSS* No. 4 (1962), 92.

[19] *Statement of the Representatives of the Communist and Workers Parties* (Moscow 1960). *CDSP,* XII, part 49, p. 4.

of the "fight aganst imperialism and its military blocs," for this is the criterion by which the state achieves political acceptability in Soviet eyes. These are indispensable prerequisites of "national democracy."

Political and economic freedom is not considered to be only a formal matter. In current Communist doctrine, colonialism has been supplanted by "neo-colonialism," which is manifested in the continuing influence of advanced western economies upon the developing countries; the distribution of foreign aid from non-Communist sources; close economic and political relationships of the "national bourgeoisie" to foreign capitalist interests; and its most extreme form, military alliance between an advanced and a developing country.[20] The United States is said to be the principal neo-colonialist power, thereby providing the Communists with a means of enlisting anti-colonialist sentiment in the new countries in the cause of anti-Americanism, and providing an explanation of why the new countries do not automatically follow the millenial road to communism via national democracy. Without the *diabolus ex machina* of "neo-colonialism", the Communists would have to impute all blame to the national bourgeoisie for the failure of communism in the developing areas.

State Capitalism and Industrialization

The principal effects of neo-colonialism are economic in nature. It is the bounden duty of each developing country to press the pace of industrialization and break traditional dependence upon the Western nations for manufactured goods. To be a "raw-material appendage" of the world market is considered shameful and inappropriate for any of the developing countries.[21] The Communists point out, not entirely inaccurately, that the Western nations show relatively little interest in the development of basic industrial capabilities in these nations, and that local private resources are in most cases too small to finance extensive development. Also, capital in the developing countries is frequently over-invested in areas which do not stimulate rapid economic growth.

[20] I. M. Lemin "Ekonomicheskaya sushchnost' sovremennogo kolonializma" [Economic Essence of Contemporary Colonialism], *PV,* No. 4 (1959), 8-25 (also available in translation in *Sowjetwissenschaft,* No. 2 (1961). Lemin's article is representative of the better Soviet writings on "neo-colonialism." K. Ivanov writes regularly on the subject in *IntAff,* but his work is of little intellectual interest.

[21] Not surprisingly, the Albanians have had a similar reaction to the Russian attempt to make them a "raw-material appendage" of the Communist international economic system.

In most of the new countries, the leadership needs no encouragement to undertake ambitious and over-ambitious industrialization programs. The prestige value of steel mills, aircraft manufacturing plants, and the like, is great. Nationalists, too, want to liberate their countries from what they consider to be economic bondage. To accomplish at least some degree of industrial progress, it is inevitable that the governments take an active role in financing and directing economic development. There are few countries which do not have their "five-year plans," and whether they call themselves socialist or not, the scope of state economic participation is always large. The Communists call this phenomenon "state capitalism," and are in general quite pleased with its existence,[22] although state capitalism is not a form of genuine "scientific" socialism and Communist writers often reiterate that it cannot solve the economic problems of the modernizing countries. Since state capitalism is controlled by the national bourgeoisie, it is said to share in the dual nature of the national bourgeoisie. It is progressive insofar as it stimulates economic growth, lays the physical groundwork for progression to the higher production relationships of socialism, lays the psychological groundwork for this progression by making the masses familiar with socialist slogans, provides the industrial base for the development of a "revolutionary proletariat" of workers, and limits the role of local capital and (particularly) foreign investment in the developing countries. Nevertheless, state capitalism in, say, India is specifically designed to provide the base for development of the private sectors of the local economy. The Communists fear that, if this is effective, the public sector will become overshadowed and ultimately crowded out by the burgeoning private sector,[23] so that India and similar countries would develop along the lines of the Western capitalist powers, instead of toward "socialism."

Along with the construction of a nationalized industry, the Communists urge the nationalization of other branches of the economy,

[22] For a general introduction to the concept of state capitalism see R. Avakov and R. Andreasyan "Progressivnaya rol' gosudarstvennogo sektora" [The Progressive Role of the State Sector] *Kommunist*, No. 13 (1962), 92-96. A more detailed discussion, as well as application of the theory to India can be found in A. I. Levkovskiy, "Osnovnye problemy razvitiye gosudarstvennogo kapitalizma v sovremennoy Indii" [Basic Problems of the Development of State Capitalism in Contemporary India] in *Gosudarstvennyy kapitalizm v stranakh vostoka* (Moscow 1960).

[23] They would thus become "monopoly capitalist" states in which the government was run by and for the benefit of the monopolies. On this distinction see *Fundamentals*, Chapter 10, Part 2.

especially foreign trade, and the expropriation of foreign investment.[24] Although ideological considerations alone would prompt such a course, the Communists have more pressing reasons to urge it. Government state trading companies are much more likely to enter into trade agreements with their counterparts in Communist countries than are private trading firms, especially when owned by nationals of the former colonial powers who want to keep old trade patterns intact. By detaching the developing nations more and more from the international economic system and re-orienting their commerce, the Communists apparently expect that they will gain an exceptionally favorable position from which to influence the policy of these new nations.

The failure of this line of development, notably in Egypt and Guinea, has not deterred the Soviets from continuing to place great emphasis upon trade and aid as a means of increasing their political influence in the developing countries. They are willing to accept setbacks at the hands of "national bourgeois" leaders, trusting apparently that as time goes on the setbacks will become fewer and the successes greater until the "national democratic" state has almost totally oriented its economy away from free enterprise and dependence upon non-communist foreign trade.[25] The Chinese, however, have few illusions about state capitalism.[26] In their meager writings on the subject they accept its existence and note certain positive features, but in general emphasize the negative factors and gloomily predict that the private sector will crowd out the public sector as long as the national bourgeoisie maintains control of the economy and the political apparatus of the country; only "revisionists" would expect that state capitalism would serve as a transitional form to true socialism.[27]

Agrarian Relations

The omnipresent fact of life in the underdeveloped areas is the agricultural situation. In almost all of these countries the population is tied to the land, and even city dwellers have close connections to

[24] Colonial profits are, according to Lenin, a major underpinning of the capitalist economies. When they are withdrawn, it will only be a matter of time until these economies collapse and can be gathered in by the Communists. See, for instance, *Imperialism, The Highest Stage of Capitalism,* Part x.

[25] S. I. Tyul'panov, "K voprosu o gosudarstvennom kapitalizme v slaborazvitykh stranakh" [The Problem of State Capitalism in the Underdeveloped Countries], *Vestnik Leningradskogo Universiteta,* No. 5, *Seriya Ekonomika, Filosofiya, i Prava,* No. 1 (1961), 21. (Translation in *JPRS* 8370.)

[26] Ya Nan, "Certain Special Characteristics of the Indian Bourgeoisie," *GWY,* No. 1 (1960), translated in *JPRS* 8532, 152-162.

[27] "The Fundamental Path . . .", 48. "Revisionists" is the term used by the Chinese to attack the Soviet leadership by indirection.

the countryside. With very few exceptions in Asia, there is severe rural overpopulation and underemployment; in Latin America the situation is often similar; and in Africa other grave problems beset the agricultural sector. Technology varies only in degrees of primitiveness and with a few exceptions life is carried on at a minimum subsistence level. Land tenure forms are generally unsatisfactory and although agriculture generally bears the burden of supplying capital for national development, its output is not great enough to provide for a satisfactory growth rate. Such important countries as India and Egypt have food deficits, and in most others there is barely enough production for subsistence. Only in a few countries of Southeast Asia and Latin America is there a substantial exportable surplus of food grains.

Several of the African economies, a number of those in South and Central America and a few in Asia, do produce exportable crops (e.g. coffee, jute, cocoa, rubber, tin, tea, bananas) which are raised on plantations, often owned by foreign interests. Very few countries in the developing areas have a substantial class of small land-holders who are able to provide themselves with a satisfactory existence and reinvest a reasonable amount of capital into their holdings. Much more characteristic is the landless laborer or the owner of a minuscule plot who cannot raise enough to support himself and his family. An exception to this pattern is found in some African areas (e.g., Guinea) where land is communally held, but this too, often produces unsatisfactory returns.

Virtually all of the countries in which land reform is a pressing problem have taken steps to ameliorate the situation, but generally with only modest success. Typical is the Indian situation where land reform has been carried out spottily, met with stiff and successful opposition from large landowners, and cannot hope to create a significant improvement in the agricultural situation in the near future. The Communists claim that land reforms initiated by the national bourgeoisie have some positive value, but cannot strike to the root of agrarian abuses. These reforms, they say, are reforms "from above", designed to act as a palliative to mass unrest and prevent the rural underprivileged from taking matters into their hands and forcing through a reform "from below".[28] The Communists associate themselves strongly with the slogan of land reform "from below", along the

[28] R. A. Ul'yanovskiy, "Agrarnye 'reformy' v stranakh Blizhnego i Srednogo Vostoka, Indii i Yugo-vostochnoy Azii" [Agrarian 'Reforms' in the Countries of the Near and Middle East, India, and Southeast Asia], *NAIA*, No. 1 (1961), 14 and passim.

lines of the reforms in the Asian Communist countries—expropriation without compensation and redistribution on the principle of "land to the tiller." (They forbear to point out the next steps in this process, leading to complete peasant dispossession and state ownership.) They direct particular fire against foreign-owned landholdings, especially since these are typically plantations which employ landless laborers—the "agricultural proletariat." By attacking foreign land holdings, the Communists hope to bring the battle of anti-colonialism to the countryside.

The Communists also claim that the national bourgeoisie cannot implement satisfactory land reforms because of its ties to the land-owning class in most of the developing areas. In fact, leadership groups in many countries of Asia, Africa, and particularly in Latin America, are drawn from landowner elements. National bourgeois land reforms are allegedly undertaken to introduce "capitalist production relationships" into the agricultural sector rather than to solve the problem of the poor peasant.[29] This is not an unfair analysis in many respects, but the performance of the Chinese and North Vietnamese agricultural sectors does not indicate that Communist land reforms would be more effective, or even as effective in solving the agricultural problems of the developing areas.

In attacking "national bourgeois" land reforms, the Communists must proceed slowly for fear of alienating the nationalists upon whom they place such great value. Nevertheless, they must come to grips with the dictum constantly urged by the Chinese, that "the democratic revolution is essentially a peasants' revolution. Only by mobilizing the peasants to wage a resolute struggle against feudalism can a mighty anti-imperialist force be organized."[30] If the nationalist leaders can be deprived of their rural support, they will be virtually powerless to resist Communist pressure. In China and Eastern Europe, as well as in Russia in 1917, agitation for land reform was a key element of Communist success. Despite the mockery made of land reform in these areas, the slogan remains powerful, and will play a determining role in the future of many underdeveloped countries.

Domestic Politics

In addition to foreign political and economic qualifications, there are domestic political criteria for the national democratic state. These entail the granting of "democratic freedoms" and—apparently—the

[29] See *Fundamentals*, 276.
[30] Wang, 274.

participation of Communists in the government. The democratic freedoms need not of course apply to non-Communist groups; it is only necessary that Communists be granted extensive freedom to agitate. In some ways this is reminiscent of the hoary tactical precept that Communists may never lose their freedom of action when they enter into a coalition, but it more immediately arises from the fact that in many of the developing countries the Communist party is not even a legal organization. Freedom for Communists to act politically is not now a criterion of Soviet acceptance of a neutral state—Communists in Egypt, for example, are a major element in the population of Nasser's jails—any more than it was in the days of Lenin's flirtation with Atatürk.[31] For a national democratic state, however, a legal Communist party is a prerequisite for entrance of the Communists into the government.[32]

The Communists are aware of the pitfalls of joining governments which they do not control. The dangers involved in submitting to the leadership of such powerful and mercurial figures as Sukarno, Nkrumah, or Sékou Touré, are considerable. Even the Communist partnership with Fidel Castro has not been an unqualified success, and a party which enters into such an alliance will have to be well organized, determined, and have brilliant leadership. If it does not, if it falls short of Lenin's ideal, the Communists are in danger of being used, rather than using, their coalition allies. The Soviets are apparently willing to take this chance with the local parties. The Indonesian party, for one, has announced itself anxious to join in a Sukarno-led government as a step towards national democracy in Indonesia.[33] With the exceptions of Laos and Cuba, no Communist party has shared leadership in the underdeveloped areas, and it still remains to be seen how they will perform once installed within the locus of power.

[31] A. A. Guber, "Distinctive Features of the National-Liberation Movement in the Eastern Colonial and Dependent Countries," *IntAff*, No. 3 (1959), 74. "There are frequent cases when representatives of the national bourgeoisie who are in power and who pursue a policy designed to strengthen the political and economic independence of their country at the same time make sharp attacks on the Communist parties. In such cases, however, the Communists define their attitude to the Government above all in the light of the basic criterion—what is the role of this Government in the struggle against imperialism?"

[32] Obvious problems are presented by "progressive" countries (e.g., Mali) which lack a Communist party. In this case the Communists accord the ruling party a sort of "honorary Communist" status. See "Soviet Party Sets Tie to Mali Group" *New York Times* (Sept. 11, 1962).

[33] Guy J. Pauker, "The Soviet Challenge in Indonesia," *Foreign Affairs,* XL (July 1962), 623-624.

The Chinese, disdainful of the idea of "national democracy," would probably press for as rapid a take-over of an infiltrated government as possible. It lies in the nature of their doctrine to distrust non-Communist elements and to assume that the "bourgeoisie" will use any means available to frustrate a Communist accession to power. The Russians have been silent on what should or will happen once a national democracy is established, or what their objectives will be in a governmental coalition. In the long run they will, of course, intend to subvert it and fully incorporate the country into the Communist system, but in the nearer future it may be expected that they will act cautiously. Cuba, where influence was thrust upon the Communists, is probably not a good test case; it will be more interesting to see how they perform as coalition members in Laos where they share governmental responsibility. Under Soviet influence, it is probable that they will move slowly, so that a premature seizure of power will not frighten off other countries.

The seizure of power in Czechoslovakia was instrumental in the formation of NATO and a generally heightened level of awareness on the part of non-Communists. The short-term gain of communising, say, Maliv—even if this were possible—would not warrant creating apprehensions in the other new nations. We can hardly blame the Communists for being silent concerning the ultimate fate of the state of national democracy. Any nationalist leader who fails to realize the Communists' intentions, even without being told, must certainly be blamed. The examples of Kerensky and Beneš are not easily forgotten. The great danger for the nationalists lies in the assumption that they can ally with Communists and then discard them when they have served their purpose. This assumption, often deprecated, is by no means fallacious. Nationalists have probably been more often successful in using Communists than vice versa. The Chinese situation in the 1920's is the classic example, but in more recent times, the Communists have come off second best in relationship with non-Communist groups in such diverse areas as Syria, Japan, and Ceylon, and perhaps even Cuba may fall into this category. Who will use whom should be a question of who is better organized and better led; in most of the developing countries, it is a question of who is less poorly organized and led. Devotion to Leninism notwithstanding, the Communists rarely can hope for a favorable solution of the power equation in these terms. When the answer does come out in their favor, however, it is extremely difficult to reopen the calculations.

The United Front

We have yet to discuss the mechanisms by which the Communists hope to achieve the state of national democracy and, ultimately, complete control (or as the Chinese would prefer, control without the interim stage). These methods can be violent, non-violent, or both. In either event, the Communists start from the principle that they must have allies in their struggle, for unaided they nowhere possess the capability to make a bid for power unaided. The mechanism for collecting allies is the "united national front," sometimes called the "national front," "united front," or a "national-liberation front."[34] Whatever the name, the objective remains the same—the acquisition of non-Communist allies either by joining an already existing organization and gaining influence within it, or by gaining adherents for an organization established by the Communists themselves. The objective of the front is never said to be establishment of Communist control. Usually it is "anti-imperialism" in one guise or another, and a great variety of nationalistic issues is used to stimulate cohesion, such as the gaining of West Irian in Indonesia, linguistic nationalism in India, anti-Americanism in Latin America or Japan, and independence in the remaining colonies.

The Soviets accept the fact that for a long time the Communists may not be able to exercise hegemony over these fronts; in almost all cases, national bourgeois forces will be by far the stronger element and hold control.[35] Doctrinally, this is acceptable as a temporary measure. By participating in fronts, the Communists gain prestige and acceptance among other nationalist forces. This was the experience of their participation in the Popular Fronts of the 1930's, and their alliance with the Kuomintang from 1924 to 1927 gave the Chinese Communists great opportunities. The Soviets expect that the united

[34] In the Comintern era a "united front" consisted solely of working class individuals or groups—a "popular front" was a union of various classes. This distinction has apparently been discarded—the term "popular front" is now out of fashion.

[35] An intriguing exception are the African countries, where there is no significant middle class. Indonesia is also discussed in this connection, since its commerce was mainly in non-indigenous hands. See R. Avakov and G. Mirskiy, "O klassovoy strukture v slaborazvitykh stranakh" [On Class Structure in the Underdeveloped Countries], *MEIMO* No. 4 (1962), 77. It is scarcely a coincidence that Indonesia plus certain African countries are considered the most likely candidates for national democracy.

front out of power will become a united front in power—the national democracy—and then either peacefully or with some (probably small) degree of violence progress to the stage of full Communist control.

At this point, however, the Chinese raise their objections. Mindful of their own humiliation at the hands of Chiang Kai-shek, they reject the idea of national bourgeois leadership. According to their model, the united front should be led by the Communists from the earliest possible stages. Thus, there is no opportunity for the Communists to be robbed of the fruits of their labors as they were in 1927. In this method, there is no need for the intermediate stage of a national democracy. The revolution, once successful, proceeds directly to the task of establishing a peoples democracy under Communist domination. It is undoubtedly more difficult for Communists to form a front along the Chinese model than according to the Russian precepts—Communists are always more welcome as followers than as leaders—but once formed, such a front is a much more effective weapon for the seizure of power.

It may be legitimately questioned, however, whether the Soviets consider the seizure of power to be the principal task of the united national fronts. More often than not, the Communist members of these fronts are willing to forego power gains and are disinclined to use the front to agitate for domestic reform. With few exceptions, the role of the fronts appears to be as an adjunct to Soviet foreign policy, and all other objectives are subordinated to the anti-imperialist, anti-American slogan. Since the fronts are usually open to all classes and interest groups who are willing to join them, they cannot infringe seriously upon the positions of any of their members. "National bourgeois" members are unlikely to take kindly to policies which would damage their own prestige and position in the economy, and when faced with the choice of alienating a significant group within the front or abandoning an ideologically important position, the Communists' option is usually for the latter.[36] In the long run this can be rationalized, for the strengthening of the Soviet Union and weakening of the United States is probably the most effective means of promoting Communism on a world-wide scale. Local Communists with any length of service are familiar with this approach, and have learned to live with it. They continue to manifest their "proletarian

[36] On the care and handling of a skittish national bourgeoisie see Markov, 60; and G. Skorov, "Krusheniye kolonial'noy sistemy" [The Collapse of the Colonial System], *MEIMO* No. 3 (1961), 16, translated in JPRS 8407.

internationalism" by sacrificing local interests to the overall interests of the Soviet Union. In the past, those unwilling to do this have soon found their way out of the party, perhaps into Trotskyism. Now, however, the Chinese are beginning to offer an alternate "orthodoxy" which puts greater emphasis upon local agitation and action, particularly in distant areas where China has no political stake.

The united fronts are not usually permanent and organizationally discrete entities. While the "Fatherland Front" in South Vietnam is actually a fighting organization under military discipline, completely controlled by the Communists, the various fronts in Japan, India, Syria, or Angola range from temporary *ad hoc* alignments to figments of the Communist imagination. In Ghana, the Convention Peoples Party is Nkrumah's personal political organization and has no visible Communist participation. In Indonesia, the front is essentially in the imagination of President Sukarno, and if realized it would contain virtually all elements of the Indonesian population, many of them bitterly anti-Communist. The united front is more of a slogan than a fact, but it remains the Soviet-imposed goal for the Communist parties of the developing areas. It is the task of these parties to make the front a real and permanent thing, an organization which is strongly anti-American and could ultimately be utilized in a bid for power, if and when the Soviets consider the time to be ripe. Given a good issue, public opinion can crystallize almost overnight, and a group which provides the slogan and can maintain leadership can frequently rise to power rapidly from the most unauspicious of beginnings. The united front is not necessarily a body of forces currently and consciously rallied around a program—it is, however, the potential of forces which can be rallied around a suitable interest either with the participation or under the leadership of the Communists. Short of being conjured into existence, its main value is probably as a recruitment technique for the Communist parties.

Sources of Support

In many cases, the united front is the entire population—this is particularly true in colonial areas, where only the "comprador bourgeoisie" and some feudal landowners are considered hostile to national independence and therefore not available to the united front. In present-day Japan, only a portion of the leadership of the Liberal Democratic Party and the biggest of big business—estimated to be less than two percent of the population—is said to be outside the united front.[37] In Cuba, the united front was similarly all-encompassing. Put this way, the problem becomes meaningless, and the Communists do attempt to differentiate among the segments of the population, realizing that one group or the other is a more likely ally or a more valuable one. When time comes for action, even the Japanese Communists know that ninety-eight percent of the population cannot be turned out into the streets to demonstrate; Castro and the Cuban Communists realize that their government enjoys considerably less than unanimous support. The crucial problem is to define exactly what classes and groups are most likely to give effective support to the cause of Communism.

LABOR

The basic group available should by definition be the working class—the proletariat. Inconveniently, there is only a very small proletariat in most of the Asian countries (Japan is the main exception); little or none in some of the Central African countries; and rather more in North and South Africa; and a larger number in most of Latin America.[38] The Communists have often done effective work among the industrial proletariat of the underdeveloped countries, especially in Asia, but have in no case been able to turn their assets into a strong basis from which a move for power would be possible. In their writings they applaud labor unrest all through the developing areas; in truth, however, this unrest is mostly either spontaneous or stimulated by groups other than the Communists. Even should the Communists be able to gain control of the workers' movement in the developing countries, they would still be far from power. There are just not enough workers; those that do exist are without any noticeable class consciousness, are often unprotected by labor or civil rights legislation, and lack organization.[39] As the industrial workers grow in number, however, it must be expected that the Communists will have success among them. Communist labor leadership is radical and dedicated, and has often shown itself effective. One of the stated

[37] Cited by Paul F. Langer, *The Japanese Communists and their Struggle for Power* (Santa Monica, Calif., 1962), 32.

[38] A survey is given in "Pod'yem rabochego dvizheniya v stranakh Azii i Afriki" [The Upsurge of the Workers Movement in the Countries of Asia and Africa], *Kommunist*, No. 6 (1962), 103-111, translated in *JPRS* 13774.

[39] Markov, 48-49; also V. V. Balabushevich, "O nekotorykh osobennostyakh rabochego dvizheniya v stranakh vostoka na sovremennom etape" [On Some Peculiarities of the Workers Movement of the East at the Present Stage], *PV*, No. 2 (1959), 51-52.

reasons for the Communists' eagerness to promote rapid industrialization in the underdeveloped areas is the hope that the industrial proletariat created will become available to Communist organization.[40] But this is a long-term undertaking.

Until there is a more substantial proletariat and its conditions improve to the extent that extensive organization becomes possible, the Communists must seek their major support elsewhere in the population. The two main groups which present opportunities have already been discussed—the peasantry and the national bourgeoisie. Within the bourgeoisie, or closely related to it, are certain important subgroups, especially the intelligentsia and the military. The intelligentsia of the modernizing areas holds a crucial position.[41] In areas where education is rare, the semi-educated are one-eyed men among the blind; those with a substantial education find leadership thrust upon them. To the extent that the intelligentsia finds a meaningful role in the development of its country, it is a powerful force for stability and rational development. To the extent it fails to find a role—either because of lack of employment opportunity or because of alienation from the government—its leadership qualities become a definite challenge to the existing order.

ELITE GROUPS

Substantial portions of the intelligentsia in the modernizing areas have been unable to identify with the course of development of their societies. The Communists have been quick to seize upon the frustrations and disillusionment of these people and present them with a pseudo-scientific blueprint for the future—one in which the intelligentsia is promised a leading rôle. Communist writers believe that there is a general "leftward drift" among the educated of the modernizing areas,[42] and this assessment is probably correct. Radical solutions are being sought for the grave problems facing the modernizing societies, and communism is one of the most radical being offered. Communist theoretical writing on the intelligentsia is sparse—it is after all not a legitimate class in the Marxist sense, and is particularly far removed from the proletariat. This lack of theoretical discussion

[40] Balabushevich, 50.

[41] Seton-Watson, 204ff.

[42] Markov, 54. For two Western views on the role of the intellectuals, see Edward Shils, "The Intellectuals in the Political Development of New States" *World Politics* XII (April 1960), 329-368; and Hugh Seton-Watson, "The Role of the Intelligentsia," *Survey*, No. 43 (August 1962), 22-30.

has not, however, kept the Communists from directing major organizational efforts towards the intelligentsia, particularly the students, all through Asia, Africa, and Latin America. The current Communist leadership in most of the countries in the area is drawn from the educated middle class, the students of the 1930's, and unless the new generations can find a more satisfying place in their societies, the Communists will have continuing successes in recruiting among them.

In particular, the Communists are making special efforts to recruit potential members of the elite through offers of training and education, at institutions ranging from Lumumba University in Moscow, to schools specializing in trade union organization or sabotage and guerrilla warfare. The number of these students and trainees was probably well over 10,000—perhaps twice that number—in 1961-1962. It is doubtful that a large number of these students become committed to communism as a result of their education; most of them no doubt remain convinced nationalists, with at most a diffuse sense of appreciation toward their alma mater. Indeed, it is probable that the great majority are disillusioned by the regimentation, living conditions, and racial prejudice which they have experienced. A number of serious and well-publicized incidents have occurred in the USSR and the Eastern European countries which have alienated many foreign (especially African) students and have caused severe diplomatic repercussions. The Communists appear willing to accept these losses, however, in the hope that a small number of Communist-indoctrinated students will ultimately assume positions of influence in their homelands and prove amenable to manipulation.

The role of the military in the developing areas has in almost all instances been opposed to the development of communism. The Communists have had little success in infiltrating those armed forces which either stemmed from the colonial period (e.g., Burma, India, Sudan) or those which have a long tradition of independence (Latin American countries, Japan, Thailand). They have had more success with armies formed in the heat of the "national liberation struggle," such as Cuba, Indochina, or China.[43] In Algeria, however, where the conditions might have been favorable for infiltrating an anti-colonial army, they were apparently ineffective. In Indonesia, also, they have had very limited success in getting important positions within the military despite Soviet attempts to influence the military by supplying Indonesia with large quantities of armaments.

[43] Markov, 56.

Although the army generally stands as an obstacle to their aspirations, the Communists are not inclined to conduct a frontal assault against it. In the tradition of Communist history, the struggle is "not against the army, but for it."[44] The armies of the developing areas are becoming increasingly more attuned to the aspirations of the general population. Although by no means democratically selected, the officers corps are no longer the preserve of the anti-Communist landowners and nobility. The educated middle class is gaining increasing influence among the officers corps and they can be approached in much the same manner as can the educated middle class civilian. The Communists are attempting to infiltrate the middle and lower echelons of the military in the developing countries. Their success may be limited, but will be in inverse proportion to the success these countries have in solving the problems of modernization by means short of Communist totalitarianism.

MINORITIES

A final population segment which presents opportunities for the formation of a united front are the minority groups which are found in many of the new nations. "Minority," when applied to the Chinese of Singapore, the Indians of Bolivia, the West Indians of British Guiana, or the Negroes of South Africa, is obviously an inaccurate term, but to the extent that these have been traditionally denied the rights and privileges of regular citizenship they react as minorities and can be exploited as such. The Communists have enjoyed some of their greatest successes among minority groups.[45] The egalitarian promises of communism have a strong appeal to those who suffer from discrimination, one which appeals to the Chinese in Malaya no less than the Jews of Eastern Europe. The trouble with minorities, though, is that any group which identifies itself with them tends to incur the same animosity which the majority population feels towards the minority. The Communists would like to have their cake and eat it too, and have consistently tried to integrate their minority support into a general national united front. This is a herculean task, and unless some overriding issue (such as national independence) can be found on which the majority and minority are willing to unite, the prospects for success are dim. Especially in newly independent

[44] *Ibid.*, 57. "Les classes et les partis ne se battent donc pas *contre* l'armée de leurs pays, mais *autour* d'elle." (Italics in original)

[45] R. V. Burks, *The Dynamics of Communism in Eastern Europe* (Princeton 1961), 187ff.

countries where the feelings of nationalism run high, over-identification with a minority can become the kiss of death to any attempt at creating a united front. Ceylonese and Iraqi Communists, for instance, have been disinclined to support Tamil and Kurdish violence against the majority population.

These, then, are the factors out of which the Communists hope to establish their control in the countries of the underdeveloped world. Their view of history makes them optimistic for ultimate success, and their propaganda tradition inclines them to make grandiose claims about present conditions as well. The preceding chapter has indicated the basis of the Communist analysis and a very general outline of the objective phenomena with which the analysis purports to concern itself. Whether this analysis is accurate, whether it provides reliable guideposts for future action—these are questions which must be answered on the basis of study of the individual areas concerned.

10

Asia

THOMAS P. THORNTON

Divided Countries

The lowest level of international existence recognized in the Communist taxonomy is that of the non-Communist areas of Korea and Viet Nam—the Republic of Korea (ROK) and the Republic of Viet Nam (RVN), both of which are in direct competition with their northern Communist neighbors for control of their national areas. Together with the Taiwan problem, these comprise the unresolved Asian remnants of the Second World War and its aftermath. All Communist countries of course recognize their colleagues, the Democratic Peoples Republic of Korea (DPRK) and the Democratic Republic of Viet Nam (DRV), as the legitimate governments of all of Korea and Viet Nam, while the ROK and RVN are described as puppets of the "American occupation," depriving the Communist regimes of their rightful hegemony over the entire countries. Since the "national liberation" movements of Korea and Viet Nam are considered to have been led by the Communists, the ROK and RVN governments are denied the aura of successful national liberation and therefore need not be taken into consideration in the balancing act which Communist policy must otherwise execute between the interests of the local parties and the existing government.

Communist propaganda directed at the ROK and RVN is much more vituperative and unconditional than that launched even against such American allies as the Philippines or Pakistan. By their recognition of the DPRK and the DRV, the Soviets and Chinese have forfeited any possibility of influencing governmental policy in the ROK and RVN and whatever attempts are made to contact these governments are left solely in the hands of their Communist counterparts. Thus in most respects it is not the Soviet Union or China, but the DPRK and the DRV which are responsible for the execution of Communist policy in the southern parts of the two divided countries. What we know of Communist activity in the ROK and RVN (less in the former than in the latter) confirms that this activity is directed from the DPRK and DRV. There is ample evidence to show that the activities of the Communist guerrillas in South Viet Nam are based in and directed from North Viet Nam,[1] and during periods of reduced tensions (e.g., before the resumption of guerrilla activity in Viet Nam and during the liberal Chang Myŏn government in the ROK) the governments of the DPRK and DRV carry the full burden of united front appeals designed to garner support in the non-Communist areas. The heart of the Communist strategy towards the RVN lies in the guerrilla warfare which is proceeding actively as this book is being written. This strategy is discussed in Chapter 8 by Modelski and will not be further elaborated here. Similarly, the development of the North Korean approach to South Korea is treated by Paige in Chapter 9.

The question of the Republic of China on Taiwan may be touched upon briefly here. Even more than South Viet Nam and South Korea, Taiwan is treated in Communist writings as a completely integral part of Communist China, under temporary military occupation by the United States. The objective of ultimately taking control of Taiwan is set forth on the one hand as an international matter requiring the withdrawal of the United States guarantee; on the other it is considered as a domestic affair, a liquidation of the last remnant of the Chinese civil war.

Communist Chinese behavior indicates that they hope to force the United States to abandon the Republic of China through political pressure and thus be allowed a free hand in dealing with the problem. As a subsidiary tactic, Communist propaganda assiduously appeals to the patriotism of the islanders—particularly the mainlander element of the population—to rejoin the Chinese motherland and throw out the American "occupiers." It is difficult to estimate whether the Communists expect the latter tactic to bear fruit. At least as long as Chiang Kai-shek lives, a rapprochement with Peking is highly unlikely and the Nationalist government has been ruthless and apparently effective in eradicating Communist activity and even Communist sympathy on Taiwan. Peking undoubtedly feels that any attempt to stimulate mass discontent except against the American "occupiers" would be counterproductive. The mass is Taiwanese, and any rebellion by it would be for the purpose of establishing an independent Taiwan, not joining the island to China proper. An

[1] The official U.S. government statement is in the State Department blue-book *A Threat to Peace: North Viet-Nam's Effort to Conquer South Viet-Nam,* (Washington 1961).

independent Taiwan would be even more difficult to gather to the motherland than would be the present government which does not dispute the "Chineseness" of Taiwan—only the matter of which government should be in control. At some later time, should Chiang's successors become disenchanted with the United States, a direct approach to the Nationalist leadership might be a feasible course of action. In the foreseeable future, however, the Communists almost certainly will rely primarily upon attempts to force an American withdrawal from the arena.

Allies of the West

Although the Philippines, Pakistan, Thailand, and Malaya are involved in alliances with the United States or Great Britain and are therefore outside of the "zone of peace," they stand a significant step above South Korea and South Viet Nam in the Soviet categorization. They comprise the Asian group of states which has achieved political independence even though this independence is allegedly jeopardized by involvement in military alliances. The critical factor here is the universally recognized political independence of the four countries. Both the Soviets and the Chinese may deal directly with them and hope to influence the course of action taken by the four governments, in addition to any designs they may entertain of fomenting unrest at the sub-governmental level. Even in the sphere of economic relationships, the Chinese and the Soviets can find justification for attempting to influence developments since political freedom carries with it the potentiality for achieving economic "freedom"—i.e. economic orientation toward the Communist states rather than toward the international market.

Naturally the more or less hostile attitude which the four countries take toward the Soviet Union and China is a determinant of current relationships. The Communist desire to break SEATO and CENTO transcends other considerations, but especially the Soviets realize that their best prospects of achieving this lie in the estrangement of the Asian member governments from the alliance system rather than forcibly incorporating their governments into the Communist orbit. Coupled with threats and intermittent vituperation, the Soviets have extended offers of aid to Pakistan and Thailand and would probably also be willing to improve relations with Malaya and the Philippines should these two governments show themselves receptive.

Aside from their committed status, Malaya, Thailand, and the

Philippines do form a fairly logical unit. All three are heavily dependent upon the fluctuations of international trade and they are the three most prosperous nations in Southeast Asia.[2] On the other hand, their governmental systems are quite different. The Philippines is a moderately well-functioning democracy, although political participation at lower social levels is weak; Thailand is ruled by a military dictatorship; and Malaya's government is formed by a heterogenous single party. The inclusion of Pakistan in this same category is artificial. While the three southeast Asian states are relatively small counters in the game of international politics, Pakistan is a nation of some 85 million people, and the problems it faces are of a completely different order. Aside from the economic and geographic anomaly of a nation divided into two distant and incompatible parts, Pakistan is faced with over-population, a food deficit, limited natural resources, extreme poverty, and the need to find some stable basis for its economy.

The Communists consider the very existence of a separate Muslim state in the Indian subcontinent to be the result of British machinations, and this initial prejudice was reinforced when Pakistan joined SEATO and the Baghdad Pact (CENTO). Nevertheless, when the general Soviet reappraisal of Asia was made in 1955, overtures of friendship were made to Pakistan (although always subordinated to the primary Soviet interest in India) and at least until 1957 Soviet writers portrayed certain aspects of Pakistani political and economic development in bleak, but by no means black, colors.[3] There are still modest trade and aid connections between Moscow and Karachi, and the Soviets probably appreciate that Pakistan's interest in SEATO and CENTO results more from anti-Indian, than from anti-Communist sentiment. Nevertheless, in the past few years the Soviets have become increasingly critical of Pakistani policies. This hardening of attitude may to some extent spring from the replacement of the corrupt and inefficient civilian government in Pakistan in 1958 by a more purposeful military regime;[4] even more it may be based on

[2] Expressed in terms of per capita income. Cited from Lucian Pye's chapter on Southeast Asia in *The Politics of the Developing Areas,* ed. by Almond and Coleman (Princeton 1960), 101.

[3] See the review article in *Central Asian Review,* v (1957), 164ff.; for an interesting Soviet example, R. Gordon-Polonskaya, "Ekonomicheskoye polozheniye Pakistana" [The Economic Situation in Pakistan], *SV,* No. 2 (1957), 49-64.

[4] Soviet writing had shown a moderately favorable attitude towards the "bourgeois" Awami League; e.g. S. F. Levin, "Partiya Narodnaya Liga" [The Peoples' League Party], in *Pakistan: Istoriya i Ekonomika,* (Moscow 1959).

a Soviet estimate that there is relatively little to be gained by being friendly towards Pakistan, when compared with the prospects of currying support among the Indians. Whatever the causes, Pakistan is now portrayed by the Soviets as a particularly reactionary country, a prime example of the evils which can result from close military ties with the United States.[5]

The Communist party in Pakistan has very little influence, and in the politically neutral situation imposed by the military government there has been little opportunity for the Communists to act even indirectly on the overt political scene. Despite some signs of strength in the railroad unions, little hope is apparently held for the development of a useful working class movement.[6] It is not possible to assess the Communist attitude towards their own subversive potential in Pakistan, nor is much known about such forces. There is of course an underground party in existence, and given the economic and political problems faced by the country it is not without potential. Much the same influences which have developed a mass party in India can be found in Pakistan as well, and should the stringent measures of the military government be relaxed it may be expected that a Communist movement would develop at a considerable rate. Failure of the government to come to terms with the precarious state of the Pakistan economy would over time provide such a movement with a strong political issue; in the foreseeable future however, the Communists have no particularly good prospects for progress in Pakistan and probably are well aware of the fact.

In passing, it is noteworthy that as the Soviet line has hardened, the Chinese have now "discovered" Pakistan. The modest blooming of Sino-Pakistani relations results from the Chinese desire to embarrass India on the question of the Sino-Indian border dispute. It does not reflect any divergent Chinese estimate of the revolutionary potential of Pakistan nor a Chinese belief that the government of Pakistan is any less hostile. Both Karachi and Peking find it profitable to embarrass India by pretending a show of friendship for each other.

[5] See, for instance, Khrushchev's speech to the Twenty-second Congress of the CPSU, in *CDSP*, XIII (Nov. 1, 1961), 9.

[6] L. R. Gordon-Polonskaya, "Polozheniye rabochego klassa Pakistana (1947-1957)" [Condition of the Working Class of Pakistan] in *Pakistan*, 46-85 gives a picture of great weakness, especially towards the end of the article. The article by T. Ruziyev, "Polozheniye rabochego klassa i rabocheye dvizheniye v Zapadnom Pakistane (1947-1957)," [Condition of the Working Class and Workers Movement in West Pakistan], *Kratkiye Soobshcheniya Instituta Narodov Azii*, XLII (Moscow 1961), 84-98, is also pessimistic despite some bright spots in the railroad unions, 94-97.

The political situation of Thailand is somewhat similar to that of Pakistan, since political control in Bangkok is wielded by a military dictatorship with very little popular participation. Thailand did enjoy a period of relative democracy beginning with the 1932 revolution, but the fragile democratic structure never fully recovered from the blows of the Second World War and especially in the 1950's palace coups were the normal manner of effecting a change in leadership, with a minimum of stress to the system. The brief attempt by Pibun Songgram to stimulate a degree of political diversity was crushed by the assumption of power by Marshal Sarit Thanarat in 1958. Sarit has devoted considerable effort to Thai economic development and made substantial progress in laying the foundations of economic modernization for Thailand. At the same time, however, he has established a firmly authoritarian rule, stifling all opposition and abandoning even the modest progress towards political modernization which had taken place in Thailand in the years after 1932.[7] Thailand enjoys a tremendous advantage over Pakistan in that it is a fairly prosperous, food-exporting country with a sound agrarian base. Although the customary claims are made by Communist writers that the condition of the Thai peasantry is deplorable, it is noteworthy that the maximum figure for the holdings of a "poor peasant," according to Soviet reckoning, is 15 *rai,* approximately 6 acres.[8]

The Communists have very little to say about revolutionary potentialities in Thailand, although they look back with restrained approval to the pre-Sarit period, especially the government of Pibun Songgram, when incipient left-wing movements enjoyed some degree of freedom. There is no open Communist strength in Thailand and under present restrictive conditions no apparent basis for united front activities.[9] Despite occasional threats by Thai politicians to reappraise their relationships with the Communist countries unless the United

[7] Despite a rather emotional critique of American policy, Frank Darling's article "American Policy in Thailand," *Western Political Quarterly,* xv (1962), 93-110, presents an excellent summary of the development of political forces in Thailand, as does David A. Wilson's *Politics in Thailand* (Ithaca 1962.)

[8] V. V. Pavlovskiy, "Agrarnyy vopros v Tailande" [Agrarian Question in Thailand], *NAIA,* No. 2 (1961), 44. According to Pavlovskiy, 42.5% of the Thai peasantry falls under this limit. The acreage limit for "poor peasants" in other Asian countries ranges down to less than an acre, but the percentate figure remains suspiciously constant at about 40%. A general survey, "Soviet Writings on Thailand" appeared in the *Yuva Newsletter,* I (4) (1962), 14-23.

[9] The Communist potential in Thailand is conveniently summarized by J. H. Brimmel, *Communism in South East Asia: A Political Analysis* (Oxford 1959), 350ff.

States is more amenable to Thai desires, this is a rather unlikely course of action, and in any case it would hardly effect the internal situation in Thailand.

During the late 1950's, the Chinese sponsored a "Free Thai" movement nominally under the liberal leader Pridi Phanomyang who had taken refuge in China. This movement was probably ephemeral, but trained cadres drawn from the substantial Thai minority in China could easily be infiltrated into Thailand proper as a nucleus for guerrilla activities. Little has been heard of Pridi's group or any other Thai opposition since Sarit's accession to power, but it could probably be resurrected on fairly short notice. Probably the most significant, albeit latent, threat which the Communists pose is their potential among the population of Northeast Thailand. (See Chapter 7, above) This is by far the most backward area of the country, one in which the government is only beginning to project its image. In addition, the population there is closely related to the Lao on the other side of the Mekong and there are large numbers of Vietnamese refugees who are only gradually being repatriated to North Viet Nam. Economic conditions there are far from desperate, but they suffer in comparison to the remainder of Thailand, and in the absence of governmental control there is ample opportunity for Communist political agitation and perhaps even for the formation of an anti-government guerrilla base.

There is no evidence that the Communists are engaged in creating a guerrilla capability in Thailand at present, but the proximity of Communist forces in Laos would be a valuable asset should they do so. The role which Thailand took in supporting Boun Oum and Phoumi Nosavan in the Laotian civil war, and the stationing of American troops in Thailand, came in for extremely heavy propaganda attacks, especially from the Chinese. The official newspaper *Renmin Ribao*[10] alleged that Thailand is rapidly becoming a base for American aggression against Laos and Cambodia, and shows signs of becoming a "colony under U.S. military occupation"—i.e. declining to the status of South Viet Nam. It would probably be incorrect to read into this statement an implication that Thailand will become the target of Communist political violence, but in a situation where Communist forces may soon be on the thinly guarded Thai borders, the possibilities of military action cannot be ignored. If launched, such activity would probably find significant support among educated Thais dissatisfied with the autocratic and restrictive Sarit regime, rather than among the

[10] Quoted in *PR,* No. 21 (1962), 10.

peasantry, outside of the Northeast, which shows little signs of restiveness.

Malaya presents a considerably different problem for the Communists due to the fresh memories of the Communist terrorist insurgency which has only in the past few years reached a state of quiescence. The opportunities for Communist activity at the overt level are understandably slight, and the discredit which the insurgency reflected upon the Communists is not likely to wear off in the foreseeable future. In addition, Malaya is prosperous and the government is taking an active role in developing the economy and providing an international image.

On the basis of economic and historical factors Malaya should be little concerned with the possibility of Communist activity, but the country is beset by a grave ethnic problem. The large Indian minority is docile, but the government faces the problem of coming to terms with the Overseas Chinese, who constitute 37 percent of the population and provided almost the entire support for the Communists during the insurgency. The Chinese are particularly heavily represented among the workers on the plantations (the "agricultural proletariat") and have been the object of continuing Communist attentions. Soviet writers note that the Chinese work under more disadvantageous conditions than do the Indian or Malayan workers[11] and that the level of class consciousness among the Indians and Malayans is low compared to that of the Chinese;[12] stated more directly, this means that the Communists have failed to make communism appear to be a national, rather than a Chinese, movement.[13] The plea for a united national front (the Socialist Peoples Front) in Malaya between workers and peasants is expressed specifically in the terms that the workers are Chinese and Indian and the peasants are Malays,[14] thus leading this program a double urgency.

The government is plagued by the racial divisions of the country no less than are the Communists. Although the ruling party of Tengku Abdul Rahman is multi-racial, it is by no means certain that it will be able to continue to aggregate the disparate interests of the

[11] *Agrarnye otnosheniya v stranakh vostoka* (Moscow 1958), 366, article by V. S. Rudnev.

[12] N. A. Simoniya, *Overseas Chinese in Southeast Asia—A Russian Study* (Ithaca, 1961), 93.

[13] This problem confronted the Malayan Communists already in 1948. See Lucian Pye, *Guerrilla Communism in Malaya,* (Princeton 1956), and Chapter 6, above.

[14] Musa Ahmed (Chairman, Central Committee, Malayan Communist Party), "For the Complete National Independence of Malaya," *WMR,* No. 7 (1961), 62.

three racial groups or of the various social and political elements within Malaya. The Communists are aware of the potential divisive forces within the alliance and expect that a split will occur between its right and left wings.[15] The main Communists problems are to ensure that when such a split does occur it is not simultaneously along racial lines, and that the left wing will look to the Communists as allies.

The most difficult problem facing Malaya is the question of union with Singapore. The overwhelmingly Chinese population of Singapore, added to the minority in Malaya, would provide a Chinese majority in a unified state. This situation is unacceptable to the Malays, especially since extreme left-wing elements are on the ascendant in Singapore.[16] The Communists urge the union of Malaya and Singapore, and ultimately such a union is inevitable. Rahman's solution to the problem is to unify not only Malaya and Singapore, but also the British possessions in Northern Borneo (Brunei, Sarawak, and North Borneo, the populations of which are predominantly non-Chinese) into a Malaysian Confederation, with the Chinese in a comfortable minority.

Initial opposition to the plan came from the Communists and their supporters; it was alleged that the Federation would be a "neo-colonial" arrangement made to shore up Rahman's position and preserve the extensive British economic interests (rubber, tin, oil).[17] The Communists proved unable to deter the formation of the Federation, and a rather spurious Philippine claim to North Borneo also had little effect. A separatist movement based in Brunei, however, was able to cause considerable commotion through an attempted coup which was only quelled after units of the British Army arrived. In the early Spring of 1963, there was still some guerrilla activity in North Borneo, and Indonesia had begun to give at least political support to the rebels. Thus there was considerable danger that the Federation would not be realized, despite the determination of Rah-

[15] D. Volskiy, "Malaya," *New Times,* No. 26 (1959), 27.

[16] For a Soviet appraisal see Ya. Paley, "Singapur na puti nezavisimosti" [Singapore on the Path of Independence], *MEIMO,* No. 9 (1959), 132. A recent and authoritative American appraisal is provided by former consul-general Wm. P. Maddux in "Singapore: Problem Child," *Foreign Affairs,* XL (1962), 479-488.

[17] A Chinese attack in *PR,* No. 23 (1962), 21, places the entire argument in these terms and never even mentions the basic problem of dealing with the Malayan and Singapore Chinese populations; similarly, S. Zhuzha, "Novyy manevr kolonizatorov" [New Maneuver of the Colonizers], *MEIMO,* No. 7 (1962), 122-124. This is one of the very few articles to discuss the Borneo dependencies specifically. "Soviet Writings on Malaya, Singapore and North Borneo" are reviewed in the *YUVA Newsletter,* I (4), (1962), 1-13.

man and the British to push ahead. The immediate threat to the Federation was Indonesian rather than Communist, but the delicate structure which Rahman had built was tottering and if it were to collapse the Communists would have won their point by default. The problem of incorporating Singapore would be unresolved; the stability of North Borneo would be in question; and Indonesian influence in the area would provide the Indonesian Communists with opportunities for political agitation in these virgin areas and perhaps even limited participation in an Indonesian-sponsored guerrilla campaign against the North Borneo government. If the Federation is realized it will still face difficult political problems, but it seems to be the only possible means of bringing some degree of stability to the area.

The Philippines present an interesting problem for Communist analysis. Soviet writers rank the Philippines along with India as the two Asian colonies in which capitalist relationships were most highly developed prior to independence. The Manila government is considered to be only a tool of the United States which enables American monopolies to continue their colonial exploitation of the Philippines, but the Communists believe that significant sections of the Philippine national bourgeoisie are coming into conflict with American economic interests.[18] Soviet writers go to considerable pains to establish just who comprises the national bourgeois elements who can be expected to counter U.S. interests, and consider the high point of state capitalist activity in the Philippines to have been in the period 1953-1957.[19] By sheer coincidence, apparently, this was the time of Ramon Magsaysay's presidency and there is no doubt that Magsaysay did more than any other Filipino to stimulate national consciousness at all levels of the population. Magsaysay can receive no credit in Communist writings, however, for he was responsible for the crushing of the Hukbalahap insurrectionary movement by successfully challenging it in the countryside.

The main strength of the Communist insurrection derived from peasant support, but Soviet writing on Philippine agrarian matters shows little sophistication. Similarly, studies of the labor movement admit implicitly that the Philippine unions are not likely targets for

[18] N. Savel'ev, "Bor'ba natsional'nogo kapitala protiv Amerikanskikh monopoliy na Filipinakh" [Struggle of National Capital against the American Monopolies in the Philippines], *MEIMO,* No. 5 (1958), 122. For a general review of Soviet materials concerning the Philippines see *YUVA Newsletter,* II (1), (1963), 1-5.

[19] E. S. Troitskiy, "Gos.-kap. sektor v ekonomike Filippinii" [The State Capital Sector in the Philippine Economy], in *Gosudarstvennyy kapitalizm v stranakh vostoka* (Moscow 1960), 279ff.

Communist manipulation.[20] What little optimism Communist writers do manifest with regard to the Philippines is expressed in terms of a growing feeling of nationalism and anti-Americanism.[21] The Philippines have, by Asian standards, a democratic system. Although this system is not one of effective universal participation, the number of persons achieving political awareness in the Philippines is steadily increasing, and the traditional ruling group are losing their predominance. In such a situation, the Communists' best chance appears to be a policy of waiting and hoping that the developing national awareness will have a radical and anti-American focus which could lay the groundwork for a closer identification of Philippine interests with those of the Communist powers.

The Neutrals

The next group of states comprises those which have assumed a position of neutrality in the conflict between Soviet and American interests and includes Cambodia, Ceylon, Nepal, and Burma. The new (1962) government of Laos also probably belongs to this category, and India is the most prominent representative of neutralism not only in Asia, but among all of the underdeveloped countries.

The agrarian problem in India has received considerable attention, especially in view of the successes which the Communist Party of India (CPI) has had in organizing agrarian support. Land reform in India has proceeded unevenly and even in the best of cases leaves much to be desired. The Indian government is genuinely trying to find means of alleviating peasant misery against the opposition of landowning interests, but the plight of the landless and almost landless peasants (the Communists claim that 47 percent of the agrarian population owns less than one acre[22]) can be exploited by adroit Communist propaganda. The programs of the government, based upon the cooperative movement, take long to implement and cannot show the dramatic progress which the Communists promise.[23]

[20] G. E. Komarovskiy, "K voprosu o kharakteristike sovremennogo profsoyuznogo dvizheniya na Filippinakh" [Concerning the Characteristics of the Contemporary Trade Union movement in the Philippines], *PV,* No. 1 (1959), 62-69.

[21] Savel'ev, *IntAff,* No. 11 (1961), 84.

[22] J. A. Lyallpuri, "Polozheniye krest'yantstva i sel'skokhozyaystvennykh rabochikh v Indii" [Situation of the Peasantry and Agricultural Workers in India], *PV,* No. 2 (1959), 105.

[23] On the Soviet attitude to Indian land reform see *Agrar. Otnosh.,* 125-128; R. A. Ul'yanovskiy, "Agrarnye reformy v stranakh blizhnego i srednego vostoka, Indii i Yu-Vost. Azii" [Agrarian Reforms in the Countries of the Near and Middle East, India, and Southeast Asia], *NAIA,* No. 2 (1961), 24, 28, 36; and M. Maksimov and A. Maslennikov, "Puti resheniya agrarnogo voprosa v. Indii" [Paths for Solution of the Agrarian Question in India], *MEIMO,* No. 12 (1961), 52-65.

Soviet writers have paid even greater attention to the problem of industrialization and state capitalism in India.[24] Probably no other specific problem area in orientology has been so often and intensively dealt with by Soviet writers, and even the Chinese have attempted to bring their modest scholarly forces to bear on the problem. Despite the favorable conditions for "independent" economic development which obtained in 1947, all Communist writers claim that India has failed to realize this promise. The role of foreign investment has not been curtailed sufficiently and the private sector of the economy has been favored. Private investment, with few exceptions, has allegedly shied away from basic industrial development, thus dissipating the limited resources available. The large industrial groups in India are rapidly passing to the stage of monopolies, if indeed they were not already that prior to independence, and the tendency to joint ventures between the Indian government and foreign capital only contributes to the development of the "comprador" class in India.[25]

The political system in India[26] is treated more ambivalently due to the friendly governmental relations between India and the Soviet Union. Soviet and, to a lesser extent, CPI writers are guarded in their attacks on the government. They are particularly anxious to avoid incurring the hostility of Prime Minister Nehru and elements within the Congress party who are regarded as potential allies. They are aided in this by the nature of the Congress itself. Congress is a mass movement, not a political party in the Western sense, and it includes elements which are scarcely distinguishable from the Communists, as well as some of the biggest business and landowning interests in India. The personality of Pandit Nehru and the tradition of Gandhi have served to hold Congress together, and will no doubt keep it an overwhelming political machine until Nehru passes from the scene. The CPI knows that if it is to gain political support, it must be at the expense of Congress, and the ultimate inevitable split of the Congress will be the great opportunity to create a united front with a truly mass base. With this in mind, the CPI states its program in terms which

[24] An important Soviet work on Indian state capitalism is A. I. Levkovskiy's chapter "Osnovnye problemy razvitiya gosudarstvennogo kapitalizma v sovremennoy Indii" [Basic Problems of the Development of State Capitalism in Contemporary India], *Gos. Kap.*, 9-95.

[25] Ya Nan, "Certain Special Characteristics of the Indian Bourgeoisie," *GWY*, No. 1 (1961), translated in JPRS 8532, esp. 154, 160.

[26] A sound Soviet article discussing Indian state structure is L. P. Ul'yanova, "O kharaktere i osobennostyakh gosudarstvennogo ustroystva Indiyskogo Soyuza" [On the Nature and Characteristic Features of the State System of the Indian Union], *SGIP*, No. 6 (1960), 74-85.

appeal to large segments of the Congress rank and file, and even the leadership. The program of the Communist government in Kerala, for instance, was said not to be the building of socialism (impossible, given the Indian constitutional framework) but simply to fulfill the program which Congress has always advocated.[27]

The party which is the instrument of Communist ambitions in India should be the monolithic well-organized type of party advocated by Lenin if it is to capitalize on the weaknesses of Congress. It would be hard to imagine anything more remote from Lenin's ideal than the Indian party.[28] The CPI has a long tradition of factionalism and failures. The leadership has been hard put to control the hotheads who press for a more militant line and have come increasingly to look towards Peking for guidance and support. The Sino-Soviet dispute has ripped the party wide open, and strong elements within the party remain loyal to the Chinese, despite the difficult position in which the entire CPI has been placed by the aggressive actions of the Chinese along the Indian border. The radicals are not strong enough to control the party, but they exercise an apparently increasing influence through their demands for a strategy which would probably stop short of large-scale violence, but would certainly abandon the milder approach which has characterized the CPI over the past years.

The dismissal of the Kerala government in 1959 was not the only event which helped discredit those Communists who expect that the Indian government will be lulled into complacency by a rightist strategy. Indian government policy has moved away from the virtual hostility with which the United States was regarded in the mid-1950's. On a number of issues, most notably the question of UN action in the Congo, the USSR and India have been on opposite sides; equally significant has been the shift in the Indian position on the International Control Commission in Viet Nam, whereby the Indian representative has begun to side with the Canadian member rather than the Pole, and support investigations of Communist activities in South Viet Nam.

These developments, coupled with the rise of a strongly anti-Com-

[27] Ajoy Ghosh, "Kerala," *WMR*, II (1959), 35-42.

[28] There are a number of works on Indian Communism, the best of these is *Communism in India*, by Gene D. Overstreet and Marshall Windmiller, (Berkeley 1959). More recent developments are surveyed by Harry Gelman, "The Indian CP between Moscow and Peking," *Problems of Communism*, XI (November-December 1962), 18-27.

munist, free enterprise opposition party in India, the Swatantra, have caused the Soviets to reappraise their estimate of India. Friendship at the governmental level still remains strong and has been especially increased by the benevolent attitude assumed by the USSR in the Sino-Indian border conflict, but lower level estimates of the strength of the "progressive" factors on the Indian political scene (especially the disposition of the national bourgeoisie and the development of state capitalism) are quite somber. In itself, a reserved attitude towards the national bourgeoisie is obligatory and has always been part of Communist theoretical writing. Soviet theoreticians have never hesitated to take issue with Indian claims that the economic system of India is "socialist," nor with Indian criticisms of communism, even at the highest level,[29] but the Soviet estimates of India at the peak of their relationships (1958) paid hardly any attention to potential or actual Indian shortcomings.[30]

The Communist slogan for India still remains "national front," but the elements which are considered prospective recruits for the front are probably much narrower than was thought to be the case in the mid-1950's. Also, some of the best issues for the national front (e.g. Goa) are no longer in existence. Increasingly, the Indian Communists will have to rely upon issues which will not bind them to other groups within India, but will serve to differentiate them from some of the most important elements in the country. An effective party, free to attack the government on a broad front, might well be able to recruit a decisive mass of peasants, workers, and dissatisfied middle class to its banner, but the CPI enjoys neither of these qualities. Should Nehru be followed by a government based on the Communists, some socialists, and the left-wing of Congress, the possibility of introducing "national democracy" into India might appear on the Communist order of the day, but it would require a much stronger party than the present CPI to be able to exploit even the opportunities offered by such a coalition. The emergence of a right-wing successor govern-

[29] Pavel Yudin, a leading Soviet theoretician, responded strongly to Nehru's criticism of the Soviet system, in *WMR*, No. 12 (1958). At a rather lower level, a writer of the Lithuanian Communist Party found it necessary to answer the question "Is Socialism Being Built in India?" B. Taurutis, "Stroitsya li v Indii Sotsializm?" *Kommunist* (Vilna), No. 1 (1959), 52-55, with a firm, albeit sympathetic, negative, in response to a question from three low-level propagandists.

[30] To cite only two examples: S. Mikoyan, "Desyat' let vneshney politiki Indii [Ten Years of Indian Foreign Policy], *MEIMO*, No. 2 (1957), esp. p. 31; and G. Skorov, "Nekotorye ekonomicheskiye voprosy raspada kolonial'noy sistemy" [Some Economic Questions on the Collapse of the Colonial System], *MEIMO* No. 4 (1958), 58.

ment would permit the Indian Communists to direct their full fire against the government and perhaps make significant progress. In such a situation, however, it probably would be only a very short time before the party was banned, and the Indian army and bureaucracy would be able to make the ban quite effective.

Communist attitudes toward two other Asian neutral states, Cambodia and Nepal, can be summarized briefly. The latter kingdom has been the object of very little attention on the part of Soviet writers,[31] although the Soviets have established relations with it and the Chinese have found Nepal, like Pakistan, to be a useful pawn in their dealings with India. The country is extremely backward, constitutional government has been suspended since 1959, and the local Communist party is minuscule. The Chinese have recently attained a considerable position of importance in Nepal through their economic aid program and by skillfully exploiting Nepalese distrust of India. Particularly on the latter count, there was some danger that the King might accept a degree of Chinese protection against the democratic revolutionists who received succor in India. Communist support for an autocratic ruler against his democratically-minded subjects would have been somewhat bizarre, but stranger things have been accomplished under the name of Marxism. The eruption of hostilities between India and China in 1962 has reduced the danger considerably as the Indian government has directed its attentions elsewhere, and the King of Nepal has doubtless had second thoughts on the efficacy of Chinese friendship. The Chinese continue their courtship of Nepal, however, and could ultimately assume a countervailing position to the traditional Indian domination.

Cambodia and its mercurial leader Prince Norodom Sihanouk have been the object of much attention from both the Soviets and the Chinese at the governmental level. Both countries have mounted aid programs in Cambodia, but without any real success in influencing the Cambodian government. Sihanouk considers himself to be a one-man mass movement, and is probably correct in assuming that he embodies the aspirations of the Cambodian people.

The Communists have assiduously supported Sihanouk in his disputes with Thailand and South Viet Nam, which he occasionally is willing to blame on the United States. On the other hand, he has been firm in suppressing communism within Cambodia and has been visibly disturbed by the increase of Communist power in North

[31] I was unable to locate I. Red'ko's book *Nepal* (Tashkent 1958); a summary of it is available in *Central Asian Review,* VIII (1960), 107.

Viet Nam and Laos.[32] If Communism is to come to Cambodia, it will be in the form of a capitulation to the increase of the Communist military strength on the Southeast Asian land mass which would result from Communist victories in Laos, South VietNam, and elsewhere. In the interim, Sihanouk will probably be left undisturbed to follow his own eclectic brand of neutralism.

The tripartite government of Laos established in 1962 should probably also be considered among the Asian neutral states. Its neutrality is extremely precarious and in late 1963 it was still far from clear whether Souvanna Phouma would be able to keep the artificial coalition from splitting, which would result in a probable renewal of the civil war. Should Laos be able to remain independent and neutral, it will be as a result of Soviet desires to preserve Laos as a showplace of the *troika* system, for the Communist threat in Laos is external, and only in the much longer run—assuming that Souvanna Phouma is successful—could internal factors become decisive.

Burma occupies a favored position among the Asian neutrals.[33] The Chinese especially have recently been at great pains to affirm the friendship of the two countries, and general approbation of Burmese policy has been forthcoming from both Peking and Moscow, generally irrespective of whether U Nu or General Ne Win is in charge of Burmese affairs. This is somewhat surprising since Ne Win (1958-60; 1962-) has taken particularly stringent measures against domestic Communism. In general, however, both Nu and Ne Win have followed very similar policies, and notably in the foreign field they have made Burma the most punctillious of neutralists. The Chinese friendship with Burma has been cloyingly close; the reason for this from the Burmese side is clear—fear of Chinese power, poised overwhelmingly on the northern Burmese border, is a basic fact of Burmese political life. The Burmese see no alternative but to coexist peacefully with China on the best terms possible. For their part, the Chinese have found Burma to be a useful showcase of the benevolence with which China is prepared to handle its more tractable neighbors. The extremely favorable terms which Burma received in the settlement of disputed border claims was patently a Chinese

[32] An excellent summary of Cambodia's foreign policy is provided in *Cambodia and Neutrality*, by Michael Leifer (Canberra 1962).

[33] Although Lucian Pye's *Politics, Personality and Nation Building: Burma's Search for Identity* (New Haven 1962) is not a conventional survey of Burma, parts of it are most valuable for a good appreciation of the country. See especially part 2.

move to embarrass India for its intransigence in failing to reach a border agreement with China.

The prospects for domestic Communism in Burma are mixed. On the one hand, the Burmese party—or more accurately, parties—have never recovered from their defeat during the period of insurgency and are badly fragmented.[34] There are still guerrillas unreconciled to the government, but these are a negligible force. The overt activities of the Burmese Communists were concentrated in the National Unity Front, a left-wing group which gained considerable electoral support in the late 1950's. More recently, however, the Front has declined sharply in importance and the military government is not likely to permit it to regain strength. The potential for Communist strength in Burma cannot be disregarded, especially among the intelligentsia. Communist influence in Rangoon University is reportedly strong and the Burmese educated class is confronted with the same problems which have furthered the cause of communism in other developing countries. As long as Ne Win continues his firm rule, the possibilities of domestic communism gaining a strong position vis-à-vis the government are small. Failure of the Burmese government to find a means to mobilize the physical and moral resources of the country, coupled with application of Chinese pressure and a weakening of Western support, could alter this situation greatly. For the interim, the Soviets appear to be playing for the support of the military government with little expectation that any other political force has any prospects.[35]

The last of the Asian neutrals to be considered is Ceylon, where the prospects of the Communists are considerably enhanced by the chaotic conditions of Ceylonese politics.[36] Since the rout of the conservative United National Party in 1956, the predominant political force has been the Sri Lanka Freedom Party (SLFP), a "national bourgeois" group headed by S.W.R.D. Bandaranaike and, since his assassination in 1959, by his widow. The SLFP has had to cast about widely for political allies to maintain its parliamentary position, and has found support in the left wing, principally among the Trotskyite

[34] On Burmese Communism see John H. Badgley "Burma's Radical Left: A Study in Failure," *Problems of Communism,* x (March-April 1961), 47-55. Also *IntAff.,* No. 2 (1962), 117-118.

[35] The present Soviet attitude is reflected in M. Aleksandrov, "Sotsialisticheskaya Partiya Birmy" [The Socialist Party of Burma], *MEIMO,* No. 9 (1962), 121-124. A general survey "Soviet Writings on Burma" is provided in *YUVA Newsletter,* I (2), (1962), 1-21.

[36] W. Howard Wriggins, *Ceylon: Dilemmas of a New Nation* (Princeton 1960), provides the best general coverage of Ceylon.

parties. The Communists have not participated in the government of Ceylon, but generally support SLFP policies, which tend to be socialistic domestically and neutralist in foreign policy. On some occasions it has participated in electoral alliances with the SLFP and the Trotskyites, but despite a high degree of receptivity to Marxist slogans in Ceylon, the Communists have never been able to exert a significant influence in the country due to the superior position of the Trotskyites and the socialist posture of the SLFP.

Despite its Marxist aspects, the strength of the SLFP lies more in its effective exploitation of racial and linguistic issues than in ideological considerations. The SLFP's approach to government has been sufficiently socialistic that one Soviet writer ranks Ceylon among the three nations who are doing the most efficient job of nationalizing foreign capital,[37] and discussions of state capitalism in Ceylon are generally quite laudatory.[38] The principal area of foreign investment in Ceylon is in the agricultural sector, mostly in the form of plantations (tea and rubber). This situation is potentially promising from the Communist point of view, for not only is there a rural proletariat available for organization, but it is located to a considerable extent on foreign-owned property so that the organizational attack can appear to be nationalistic in nature. Although Communist writers have applauded the steps of the government to take over the foreign-owned plantations[39] they are less enthusiastic about other land-reform methods of the government.[40] The Communists have had little success in the agrarian sector of Ceylon, however, and from their statements it is clear that they have yet to develop an agrarian policy.[41]

On the issue of Tamil separatism, a major factor in Ceylonese politics, the Communists have wisely followed the majority Sinhalese. This is thus not an issue exploitable by the Communists, although it has been the most notable cause of violence in Ceylon in the past years. There continues to be good prospect for more violence in

[37] N. Shmelev, "Burzhuaznye ekonomisty o role gosudarstvennogo sektora v slaborazvitykh stranakh" [Bourgeois Economists on the Role of the State Sector in Underdeveloped Countries], *MEIMO*, No. 4 (1962), 88. The other two are Cuba and Indonesia. This is the closest Ceylon has ever come to inclusion in the "national democracy" category.

[38] L. G. Ivanov, "Stanovleniye gosudarstvennogo kapitala na Tseylone" [The Rise of State Capitalism in Ceylon], *Gos. Kap.*, 154-171; and I. Popova, "Tseylon; Mery po ogranicheniyu inostrannogo kapitala" [Ceylon: Measures to Limit Foreign Capital], *MEIMO*, No. 8 (1961), 104.

[39] Ul'yanovskiy, *NAIA*, No. 2 (1961), 19.

[40] Ul'yanovskiy, *NAIA*, No. 1 (1961), 26.

[41] N. Sanmugathasan, in *WMR*, No. 2 (1960), 71-73.

Ceylon, however, stemming not only from the Tamil-Sinhalese friction, but also from other social and economic problems which the SLFP government is unwilling or unable to solve.

Communist policy in Ceylon is logically based on the national front principle, since the instability of Ceylonese politics provides considerable latitude for rapid political realignments. Thus far a number of parties have been willing to enter into *ad hoc* election alliances with the Communists, but these have had no lasting effect. In order to become a desirable long term ally, the Communists will have to develop a much more potent political machine than they now possess.[42]

The entire left wing and the SLFP government are under continuing pressure from conservative elements and the Communists are anxious to prove themselves trusted and valuable allies in the face of this pressure.[43] In the highly personalized atmosphere of Ceylonese politics, with its plots and counter-plots, the Communists have fairly good medium-range prospects if they can bring their own house in order and establish themselves on a mass basis.

Indonesia—An Incipient National Democracy

Of all Asian countries, Indonesia is the most hopefully regarded by the Communists, but there are substantial grounds to doubt that the position of the Indonesian Communist Party (PKI) is as sound as might be desired. It is heavily dependent upon the good will of President Sukarno for protection against the persecution of the military; its great strength lies in a political machine designed to contest parliamentary elections, but the institution of parliament in Indonesia is in eclipse; it is primarily a regional party in Java; its strength is much broader than it is deep; and the party is now faced with a political situation in Indonesia radically different from that in which it gained its strength.[44]

Nevertheless the PKI has, in less than a decade, risen from insignificance to become the strongest party in the country and the largest Communist party outside of the Communist system. Together with

[42] Pieter Keunemann, "Success of the Policy for Unity," *WMR*, No. 10 (1960), 73.

[43] On the declining fortunes of the Trotskyites, see Calvin A. Woodward, "The Trotskyite Movement in Ceylon," *World Politics*, XIV (1962), 307-321.

[44] This section draws heavily on Ruth McVey's "Indonesian Communism and the Transition to Guided Democracy" in *Communist Strategies in Asia*, edited by A. Doak Barnett (New York 1963). The Soviet view of Indonesia is summarized in *YUVA Newsletter*, I (3), (1962), 1-23.

the army and President Sukarno it is one of the three determining factors in Indonesian politics. It has broad support in a series of front and labor organizations, and it is working hard to build up its strength outside of Java and among the peasantry—two of its weakest areas. No other political force in the country has a grassroots organization which comes anywhere near matching the PKI's in effectiveness.

Within these considerations, the PKI must choose its course of action. It has chosen violence once in recent years, and the results were catastrophic for the party—to resume violence would have little prospect of success and the loss would now be much greater in terms of gains already made. The PKI has achieved a considerable "stake in society" and has a vested interest in not taking any rash action which might endanger it. In recent years the PKI has based its appeal on nationalism, but the universal symbol of nationalism in Indonesia is President Sukarno. Any action taken against him would probably isolate the party from its mass support, and provide the army with an excuse to decimate the party.

Sukarno pictures himself as the leader of all the nation, including the Communists, and advocates an all-national government in which the PKI would have a significant role. On the face of it, the realization of such a government would fulfill the political requirement for national democracy, and Indonesia is in fact the only Asian country which is mentioned in Soviet sources as a likely candidate for that distinction. The Indonesian national bourgeoisie is said to be weak by Asian standards and the role of the "state capitalist" sector is of considerable importance. Dutch holdings in Indonesia were largely nationalized in 1957, so that this large segment of the economy is in the government's hands. The Communists are critical, however, of the government's reluctance to nationalize other foreign holdings (especially American) centered in the oil industry, and appear to have some doubts as to the government's handling of the confiscated Dutch assets.[45]

The agrarian problem in Indonesia is acute, particularly in such

[45] M. A. Andreyev, "O razvitii gosudarstvennogo kapitala v ekonomike Indonezii" [On the Development of State Capitalism in Indonesia], *PV*, No. 6 (1959), 29ff. More critical is A. Lavrent'ev, "Changes in the Country of Bandung," in *CDSP*, Vol. XIII No. 19, 7-9 (translated from *Aziya i Afrika Segodnya*, No. 3 (1961), 3-5), and especially a Chinese article, Yu Tseng, "Imperialist Economic Strength in Indonesia," *GWY*, No. 2 (1960), *JPRS* 8532, 170-178. The latter appeared, however, during the bitter Sino-Indonesian controversy concerning Overseas Chinese, and is not characteristic of current Chinese propaganda concerning Indonesia.

overpopulated areas as Java. Both the government and the PKI make clear their desire to see land reform effected, but until very recently their words have spoken considerably louder than their actions. A far-reaching land reform law has now been put on the books, but still remains substantially unimplemented. The PKI, for its part, has in the past been loath to agitate in the countryside for fear of disrupting the incipient national front on which the party places its hopes.[46] Most recently, however, the PKI has begun to take a more active line on agrarian problems.[47] In the absence of any other group which gives the impression of caring for the plight of the peasant, the Communists stand a good chance of improving their rural support, which has heretofore been mainly limited to estate workers.

The Soviet view of Indonesian land reform had tended to be rather critical, speaking mainly in terms of plans rather than accomplishments.[48] In line with increased Soviet enthusiasm for Indonesia, the picture is now being painted in somewhat brighter colors, but the lack of concrete progress cannot be glossed over. Even the most enthusiastic appraisals refer to the new reforms only as a beginning, and assert that only distribution of land to the tiller will solve the problem. The determining factor in the Soviet appraisal of Indonesia is of course not a matter of agrarian reform or nationalization, but of Sukarno's foreign policy orientation. Indonesia has frequently been willing to side with the Soviet Union on international political matters, and is a member of the left wing of the Afro-Asian movement. In 1959, the secretary general of the PKI could note with

[46] For instance, the unwillingness to press for nationalization of the holdings of the middle and small bourgeoisie. See Andreyev, "V bor'be za ekonomicheskuyu nezavisimost'" ["In the Struggle for Economic Independence"], *NAIA*, No. 3 (1961), 39, and for a general view, the excellent article of Donald Hindley, "The PKI and the Peasants," *Problems of Communism*, XI (November-December 1962), 28-36.

[47] Described in Ruth McVey's paper cited above. See also D. N. Aidit's report reprinted in *Indonesien, Burma und Malaya im Kampf um Unabhängigkeit und Demokratie* (Berlin 1961), 109-111 and P. Anan'ev, "Agrarno-krest'yanskiy vopros v Indonezii" [The Agrarian-peasant Question in Indonesia], *MEIMO*, No. 7 (1962), 117-121.

[48] Ul'yanovskiy's survey is far from enthusiastic on Indonesian accomplishments—*NAIA*, No. 1 (1961), 32. Similarly, Kessel'brenner, "Indonesia's Economic Prospects," *NT*, No. 34 (1961), 19, and Yu. A. Sotnikov, "O kolonial'nom nasledstve v agrarnom stroye Indonezii" [Colonial Heritage in the Indonesian Agrarian Structure], *SV*, No. 4 (1958), 82, show considerable restraint. Even the most favorable treatment of Indonesian land reform—Sotnikov's chapter on agrarian matters in the collection of essays *Respublika Indoneziya* (Moscow 1961), 301, refers only to "concrete preparations" made towards agrarian reform.

satisfaction that in the previous years, the political orientation of Indonesia had been clearly leftwards.[49]

This trend can readily be interpreted as a move toward national democracy, in which it would only remain for the PKI to assume a predestined role.[50] The two principal questions which are still undecided are whether the party is capable of exploiting the opportunity presented by Sukarno's recognition of the Communists as a major element in his political balancing act, and—more important—whether the estimate is correct at all; whether perhaps Indonesia is moving towards a nationalistic authoritarian dictatorship under Sukarno and, ultimately, the army. The PKI itself is viewing Sukarno's arrogation of power with skepticism, and has hedged its acceptance of the new state of things with reservations about its right to criticize specific manifestations. The possibility of persecution at the hands of the army is openly taken into account,[51] and the PKI must look toward the acquisition of West Irian with mixed emotions, since it will deprive it of the most important nationalist slogan for united front action. Nevertheless, unless the PKI is willing to shift its policy radically there is little choice open to it except holding firmly to Sukarno's coat tails and attempting to see that his "guided democracy" is guided in the proper direction.

Japan—A Special Case

The last of the Asian countries to be considered lies almost completely outside the Asian framework. Japan is not underdeveloped, it is not newly independent, and it played a distinctly imperialist role from the late nineteenth century to 1945. Yet it is Asian and in the view of the Communists it shares many of the characteristics of the other Asian countries. The Japanese Communist Party (JCP) itself has only recently adopted a line on the nature of the struggle which it has to wage, and this line in itself represents a rather tenuous compromise.

On the one hand Japan is described as a country with its own "monopolies" and a highly advanced economic system. It supposedly has expansionist ambitions which the Second World War did not permanently dispel. Finally it is strategically located, and although its

[49] Aidit, 42.

[50] A typically enthusiastic summary is M. S. Likhunov, "Bor'ba indonez. naroda za postroyeniye nezavisimogo gosudarstva" [Struggle of the Indonesian people to Build an Independent Government], *SGIP*, No. 12 (1960), 53-64.

[51] Aidit, 59.

present military strength is slight, it has considerable potential and there are strong forces within the country which wish to see Japan remilitarized.

In contrast, there is said to be the other Japan, characterized by workers on the brink of starvation,[52] medium and small businessmen being ruined by competition with American business, disgruntled intellectuals, virtual military occupation by the United States, an exploited peasantry, and a seething population which has no fonder desire than to clasp China and the Soviet Union to its bosom, while throwing the Americans, along with the pro-American Japanese government back across the Pacific. This estimate is grossly exaggerated, but in each instance there is a germ of truth. Industrial wages are low, small businessmen are subjected to considerable pressures, and there is a considerable amount of highly vocal anti-American and anti-government sentiment in Japan.

Faced with the problem of which estimate to choose, the Communists have chosen parts of both but have based their operational policy on the latter. The main objective of international communism in Japan (and the Japanese are among the least nationalistically-minded Communists) is to reduce the American position by a "national liberation" movement and only then go on to the problem of establishing Communist power in Japan. This policy was spelled out in the Moscow Declaration of 1960, and was adopted in the JCP program of 1961.[53] In order to achieve this national liberation, the JCP must of course rally the other elements of Japanese society around it and form a united national front.[54] The most important potential ally is the Japanese Socialist Party, the principal spokesman for radical discontent in Japan. The Socialists are in sympathy with the objective of removing the Americans from Japan and establishing more friendly relations with China and the Soviet Union, but they are more inter-

[52] V. N. Khlynov, "Polozheniye rabochego klassa Yaponii posle vtoroy mirovoy voyny" [Situation of the Japanese Working Class after the Second World War], in *Problemy Sovremennoy Yaponii—Ekon. i. Polit.* [Problems of Contemporary Japan—Economics and Politics], *Ucheniye Zapiski,* xxi (Moscow, 1958). A significant Chinese commentary is by Chang Hsiang-shan, "The Struggle of the Japanese People and the Japanese Communist Party," *Hongqi,* No. 20 (1962), translated in JPRS 16,602, 54-85.

[53] "Declaration of the Leaders of Communist and Workers Parties," *CDSP,* xii, No. 49, p. 4. See also Paul F. Langer, *The Japanese Communists and their Struggle for Power* (Santa Monica 1962), and for a discussion of earlier Japanese communism, Rodger Swearingen and Paul Langer, *Red Flag in Japan* (Cambridge, Mass. 1952).

[54] Toki Tsuyoshi (editor of the Japanese Communist journal *Akahata*) in *Renmin Ribao* (Dec. 12, 1961), translated in JPRS 12431, 24.

ested in reforming Japanese society. In addition, the Socialists have resisted perennial JCP attempts to form any sort of a permanent front, and reasonably so since the Socialists' mass support is much greater than that of the Communists.

The political spectrum of contemporary Japan is not unlike that of many European counrties between the two World Wars. The government is conservative; the Socialists aggregate the interests of radical discontent; and the Communists represent a sectarian fringe with very little voter appeal. As one writer has pointed out, the Japanese Socialists, lacking governmental responsibility or much prospect of attaining it, present such a radical program that it is almost impossible for the JCP to differentiate itself from them and find an independent platform to secure voter support.[55] Also, the JCP must be restrained in its attacks on the Socialists, since left-wing elements among the Socialists enjoy extremely good relations with the Soviets and the Chinese, who consider them to be the ideologically most advanced Socialists in Asia.[56] In view of the primacy which the Soviets and Chinese assign to the neutralization of Japan, they must look to the relatively strong Socialist party as the instrument of neutralization, rather than to the JCP which, with only 100,000 members, carries little weight on the political scene. The JCP is urgently concerned with building up its strength and an important plank in the party platform is the creation of a mass party. It is hardly likely however that the JCP can make a significant dent in the urban strength of the Socialists beyond the small group of workers and intellectuals who already pay allegiance to it. Indeed, even the Socialists may prove a slender reed, for it has been persuasively argued that Japan is actually in a post-Marxist stage, one in which the position of the entire left wing is increasingly anomalous.[57] It is hardly surprising that both the Soviets and the Chinese have been giving increasing attention to cultivating contacts in conservative and business circles.

The particular weakness of the JCP lies in its failure to crack the stronghold of Japanese conservativism, the agrarian sector. Although they claim that there is increasing differentiation between rich and poor in the countryside, the Communists grudgingly admit the effects

[55] Langer, 17.

[56] G. I. Podpalova, "Novye tendentsii v deyatel'nosti sotsialisticheskoy partii Yaponii" [New Tendencies in the Activities of the Japanese Socialist Party], *Probl. Sovr. Yaponii,* 154-187.

[57] R. A. Scalapino, "The Left Wing in Japan," *Survey,* No. 43 (August 1962), 111.

of the agrarian reforms instituted by the US military occupation.[58] Their program for Japanese agriculture consists of slogans rendered empty by the course of development since the war.

The Communist view of Japan is mainly conditioned by the existence of a highly developed economy, unique among the countries of the "third world." The economy is described as "monopoly capitalist" in nature and heavily infiltrated by American investment. Following the "law" of monopoly capitalism, Japanese industry is overexpanded in terms of the local market and must therefore seek semi-colonial markets abroad.[59] Were the JCP able to follow this line to its logical conclusion, it could direct its main fire at the domestic issues which the Socialists effectively exploit. For domestic consumption, however, the main enemy must be "US imperialism," and allies for the national front must be sought at virtually any level.

The picture of Japan as an exploiting, rather than an exploited nation is easier to draw for foreign audiences, and Soviet and Chinese propagandists assiduously point to Japan's imperialist past as a warning not only to the nations of Asia who have bitter memories of the Second World War, but also to the Western nations who frequently find themselves at a disadvantage in competing with Japanese traders.[60] Their objective is clearly to isolate Japan from its political and economic partners and force it into a situation in which it must turn to the Communist states.

Even should Japan be effectively isolated from the international community, the JCP would benefit only indirectly. On its own, its prospects are at best mediocre. If conditions in Japan improve, the conservatives will benefit. If difficulties arise, it is the Socialists who will receive the lion's share of the support from the disaffected. Propaganda about US domination of Japan notwithstanding, Japan presents the Communists with problems much the same as do the smaller European countries. The Soviets and the Chinese are responding with much the same tactics. On the one hand the major Communist effort is the propaganda barrage which threatens Japan with

[58] Sotomi Hakamada, "The Foundation of the United National Front," *WMR*, No. 2 (1961), 4-9.

[59] A good recent example is G. Prigov, "Chto proiskhodit v Yaponskom ekonomike?" [What is Happening in the Japanese Economy?], *MEIMO*, No. 3 (1962), 65-77.

[60] V. Arkhipov, "Yaponskiy kapital v stranakh blizhnego i srednego vostoka" [Japanese Capital in the Lands of the Near and Middle East], *MEIMO*, No. 9 (1959), 134; and D. L. Angora, "Nekotorye voprosy Yap.-Amer. otnosh. posle vtoroy mirovoy voyny" [Some Questions of Japanese-American Relations after the Second World War], *Kratkiye Soobshcheniya*, XLV (Moscow 1961).

the direst of consequences as a result of its alliance with the United States.[61] At the same time, allegedly lucrative trade prospects are held out to those Japanese who look to China as their traditional market, and to Siberia as a field for new endeavor.[62] By playing on the fears and hopes of the Japanese people, the Chinese and Soviets obviously hope to neutralize the obstacle which a Japanese-U.S. alliance poses to Communist policy in the Western Pacific. What happens otherwise within Japan is of secondary consequence in the short run; detached from the American alliance and effective support, Japan could be handled in the same way envisioned for the European countries.

Conclusion

The problems faced by communism in Asia are hauntingly similar to those which have marked the progress—and regress—of the movement since its inception. In Japan—how to compete with a dominant Socialist Party; in Korea, Taiwan, and some of the Western allies—how to create an effective organization in the face of efficient police controls; in Viet Nam—how to wage guerrilla warfare in an agrarian society against superior military forces; in India and Indonesia—whether to endanger the gains already made in the interest of a more aggressive Communist program; in Laos—how to subvert a government in which there is Communist representation; all through the area—how to exploit nationalism, how to make attractive to the peasantry a philosophy which is counter to its interests, and above all, how far to press for the expansion of communism in the face of an effective commitment by the United States and its allies to limit the spread of communism in Asia.

On the basis of their past experience, the Communists should do fairly well in solving some of these problems. Certainly they should know much about the subversion of governments, but their successes in this field came in a period when the non-Communist world did not fully appreciate the danger posed to it. Similarly, they have had wide experience in guerrilla warfare, but they have never come up

[61] Such approaches are legion. One of the most virulent appeared in *Pravda,* April 30, 1960, p. 3, and was elaborated on by G. P. Zhukov, "Aggressivnyy kharakter novogo Amerikano-Yaponskogo voyennogo dogovora" [The Aggressive Character of the New American-Japanese Military Treaty], *SGIP,* No. 9 (1960), 40ff.

[62] For Anastas Mikoyan's activities in Japan along these lines see 'Observer,' "Japanese Neighbor," *New Times,* No. 35 (1961), 3-4. The Chinese approach has been more brusque but contains basically the same mixture. Ryozo Kurai, "Present Status of Japan-Communist China Relations," in *Japan Annual of International Affairs* (Tokyo 1961), 91-157.

against a well and suitably organized opponent and defeated him. There are good prospects for the Communist approach to the peasantry, as long as Maoist slogans are used, and it does seem certain that the mistakes of the 1920's have been abandoned. Still, how can the Communists consistently appeal to any mass group in the new nations without casting their appeal so much in the terms of nationalism that it loses its Communist content? True, for the trained cadre the Communist content is always there, but when the time comes for action, how will the mass party respond if confronted by the choice between nationalism and communism?

In some of the other problem areas the prospects are much less bright. Large Communist parties (and Socialist parties before them) have become progressively less revolutionary as their size and power increase. Peaceful and even legal acquisition of power look so temptingly close to a large party that a resort to violence or even extremist slogans seems foolhardy. Yet except for the case of Kerala, no Communist party has ever achieved power in a significant area without the use or threat of violence. In most of the Asian countries the Soviet and Chinese power centers are sufficiently distant that this component of violence must come from within the local party, but any attempt to build a capability for violence is an open invitation for anti-Communist elements, particularly among the military, to crush the party. The failures of the 1948 insurgencies weigh heavily upon the Communist Parties of Asia, stark warnings against the application of the Chinese revolutionary model in areas where conditions are different. Organizationally, the policy of the peaceful coexistence period has undeniably brought results, but have these successes brought the victory of communism closer? The question can be answered in the affirmative only conditionally.

Generally the Communists must welcome any accretion to their strength, but the gains of the past few years have been almost solely in terms of non-violent potential—increased membership, greater acceptance of Communist legitimacy, improved state relations with the Soviet Union and China. Communism is becoming a normal part of life for some Asian societies and sub-societies—a means of articulating discontent or even a form of accommodation to a modernizing world. Not only the greater degree of acceptance of local Communists, but the increasing role of the Soviet Union as a trade partner, a source of economic and political aid, and a development model, have caused great concern in Western countries. In such a case as Indonesia, there is no doubt that the Soviet Union is at least as important an element of the political equation as is the United States, and the Soviet or Chinese role in India, Cambodia, Ceylon, and of course Laos is often considerable. It is argued that some of these Asian nations are slipping into communism and are inextricably bound up with the Communist bloc. Yet both the apparent development of "national democratic" tendencies, and the increasing influence of the USSR leave the essential question of the transfer of power unanswered.

India, one of the most democratic and free of Asian nations, has demonstrated that the Communists cannot expect to translate simple electoral strength into power in the face of entrenched opposition; there is little reason to expect that they could be successful in Ceylon or even Indonesia, should the electoral system be reactivated. Efforts to build "mass parties" dissipate Communist efforts over such a broad area that it is difficult to believe that they are simultaneously forming hard-core, conspiratorial parties of the Leninist type, and what we know of the inner workings of most Asian Communist parties does not indicate that this type of development is taking place. Without a Leninist "new type" party, a seizure of power is unlikely by any minority, no matter how large, and even a majority would find it most difficult to achieve power in the face of military opposition.[63] There is even less evidence that Asian Communists are undergoing military training which would enable them to survive a military confrontation. In areas adjacent to China and North Viet Nam this is less important, since "volunteers" could be provided, but the simple fact of American naval supremacy in the Far East renders virtually impossible the movement of "volunteers" to nonadjacent areas.

It is also unclear exactly how the Soviet Union is going to translate its political influence into political power. In Afghanistan, or perhaps Laos, the Communist presence is so overwhelming that either country could probably be fairly easily taken over. In Indonesia, however, should Sukarno be threatened by the extent of Soviet and local Communist influence, he is well aware that the United States would help him pull his chestnuts out of the fire. A man who flies a Russian airplane, holds a Russian gun, or works in a sugar mill donated by East Germany does not thereby become a Communist. Technical training, even if given in Moscow, is a far cry from political indoctrination. From our own experience we should by now realize that foreign aid programs are an ineffective means of influencing public or even leadership opinion in foreign countries.

[63] For this problem in Indonesia see Hindley, 36.

Again and again, the matter resolves itself to the question of whether the Communists are willing and able to use violence to achieve the seizure of power. Without qualification it may be said that Soviet writings on Asian countries are concerned solely with the prospect of a peaceful development of the Communist movement in the foreseeable future. The preponderance of local Communist writing is couched in the same terms, as well as that of the Yugoslavs, even though Kardelj thinks that a violent transition to power is more likely in the underdeveloped areas where "individual contradictions are more powerfully brought out."[64] Obviously, the Communists are not likely to broadcast any specific plans for internal war, but when compared with writing of any other period except the Popular Front of the 1930's, the absence of all but the minimum mandatory reference to the possibility of violence is striking. Enthusiastic endorsement of the traditional Marxist symbols of violence is simply lacking except from the Chinese and their sympathizers—but the Chinese and their supporters are not in control of most Asian Communist movements.

It would be a grievous mistake to dismiss the role of violence in Communist attempts to expand their influence in Asia. First of all, the present Soviet policy is far from permanent. It is closely associated with Khrushchev and his departure from power could occasion a radical change. It is also not inconceivable that in many Asian countries Chinese theories may gain predominance and the local parties would act counter to Soviet wishes. Furthermore, the Communists will willy-nilly find themselves injected into internal war situations in Asia over the next years, for they, no more than we, could prevent completely the outbreak of civil strife in the modernizing areas, even should they desire to do so.

Last of all, it is obvious that the Communists—Soviet, Chinese, or local—would not pass up a target of opportunity if one presented itself. To say this is to say both much and nothing; Russia was a target of opportunity in 1917, as were China in 1945 and Laos in 1960. There are several very general factors which play a role in what constitutes an "opportunity" for the Communists. Foremost among these is the requirement that the international environment be propitious—that the target country not be able to receive effective foreign support, and hostilities not be likely to escalate. In a hypothetical extreme case, this would be all that is necessary for the imposition of Communist rule from without. In practice, however, there are certain

[64] Edvard Kardelj, *Socialism and War* (London 1961), 86.

internal preconditions which are required to provide the opportunity for forceful Communist action. Basic is the stipulation that the Communists enjoy a favorable balance of forces for the type of action envisioned (small local preponderance is adequate for a coup d'état—a much larger base is required for guerrilla warfare). Also of great importance is that the incumbent regime be isolated psychologically from popular support, so that it will not be able to summon popular opposition to the Communists.

In all of this calculation, the Communists themselves play a small role, albeit the crucial one. It is the essence of a target of opportunity that it be presented to the Communists, not created by them, and it is on this basis that the Communists have historically had their greatest successes. The Communists are generally too weak to make their own opportunities and are often overly cautious even when they seem to have adequate potential strength. The future of Asia is to an overwhelming extent dependent upon the actions taken by the non-Communist countries. In the first line, these actions must be taken by those most directly concerned—the Asians themselves. The role of the West, in the light of the conditions of "opportunity" which have been set forth above, would consist of ensuring that it possesses a credible military presence in Asia, and endeavoring to see that the governments which it supports have the maximum rapport with their peoples. In such conditions, the Communists will be forced to their own resources to create targets of opportunity for exploitation.

One cannot predict precisely when and where internal war will break out, the outcome of the Sino-Soviet dispute and the Khrushchev succession, or fortuitous circumstances which will present targets of opportunity. Therefore one cannot make specific predictions about the likelihood of the Communists utilizing internal war. To some extent we can, and have, noted countries whose current or probable situations will make them inviting targets for such activity—these are the danger spots. Also, we can hardly avoid the conclusion that the Soviets and most local Communists are becoming less and less adapted to the utilization of violence as a means of political change. Certainly Khrushchev, and probably most other Soviet leaders, would be disinclined to substantially risk the Soviet power base for the sake of acquiring even such an important country as India or Japan. Their estimate is, almost certainly, that the power of the Soviet Union's military force and its example of successful modernization will ultimately weigh so heavily that the nations of Asia will fall to communism automatically. In theory, the Soviets may feel that some degree of force may be necessary to effect the change, but the time for that is still comfortably distant. The Soviet Union feels that time is on its side—whether Asia becomes Communist a few decades sooner or later is immaterial. The prime consideration is that the USSR be able to continue its national development as the heart of the international Communist movement.

The Chinese would find it difficult to argue with this viewpoint on theoretical grounds. In very practical terms, however, they can make two telling criticisms. First, there is the danger that the Soviet Union will go the way of the Second International—it will become so involved in non-revolutionary problems of the status quo, and the image of the revolution will undergo such a change, that Leninism will become as irrelevant as Marxism. Second, the Chinese can point to the failure of Soviet policy in Asia over the past decade. Since the settlement of the Indochinese fighting in 1954, the Soviets have devoted large amounts of effort, prestige, and money, to the forwarding of the Communist cause in Asia, principally to court the friendship of the "national bourgeoisie." None of this effort has brought Communists to power or—in the Chinese view—even near to power. The only success has been in Laos, and this came about through the use of violence along lines typified in the Chinese experience and only after relatively non-violent methods of subversion had failed.[65]

The prospects for Communist revolutionary strategy can be focussed upon these questions. Are a number of nations so impressed by the example of the Soviet Union that they are even now on the threshold of moving to the stage of national democracy and, ultimately, communism? Or have the forces opposed to communism become so aware of the danger which is posed that they are taking measures which are becoming increasingly effective in delimiting the Communist threat and, ultimately, annihilating it? As long as the Communists believe the answer to the first question is more strongly affirmative than that to the second, the likelihood of violence, except in rare targets of opportunity, is low. If the balance of opinion shifts, the prospect of revolutionary violence all through Asia, and immediate moves for power in such exposed areas as Burma and Thailand will become real and pressing. The Communists have had successes and failures with both strategies—their opponents have had successes and failures in combating both.

[65] There are two particularly good works dealing with China's policy toward Asia —R. G. Boyd, *Communist China's Foreign Policy* (New York 1962), and A. Doak Barnett, *Communist China and Asia* (New York 1959).

11

The Middle East and North Africa

MANFRED HALPERN

Introduction

Since the First World War, the region from Morocco to Pakistan has seldom been free from political violence. During the past four decades, the area now occupied by nineteen independent states has witnessed at least ten wars of "national liberation," at least thirty *coups d'état* committed to the achievement or reversal of radical changes in political and social structure, and at least twice as many as that if one were to count all unconstitutional changes of government engineered by men interested solely in the fruits of power. This area has seen at least seven attempts by force to establish separatist states, at least ten assassinations of kings, presidents, premiers, or foreign ministers, and at least thrice this number of narrow escapes. In Algeria, organized guerrilla forces engaged in daily acts of violence for eight years and in Lebanon for half a year. Such forces fought somewhat more intermittently in Morocco for three years, in Tunisia for five years, and in Israel for about twelve years. Riots—many powerful enough to topple governments, undo treaties, prevent alliances, alter governmental programs, kill men by the hundreds, and destroy property by the millions of dollars—have been too numerous to count.

This revolutionary activity in the Middle East and North Africa has, moreover, a new meaning. Traditional Islam endured for about 1,300 years (from 622 A.D. to the arrival of the modern age in this region a few decades ago) *because* of continual internal warfare, which served to sustain and renew the balance of tensions which constituted the Islamic system. Thus religio-political rebellions in the past again and again restored stronger and more acceptable authority without altering the structure of institutions or the forces which would lead to renewed decay of authority and rebellions against it. Early in the twentieth century, such homeostatic rebellions became useless as the traditional Islamic system shattered under the pressures of modernization. In the wake of this social distintegration there followed a period of violence without conclusive political results as the Middle

Eastern equivalents of *caudillo,* warlord, political opportunist, or status quo-minded oligarchies rose to power. Most internal warfare in the Arab world since the 1950's has been initiated with the purpose of altering the structure and values of society; in Turkey, Iran, and what was to become Pakistan, this movement began several decades earlier. Yet the Communists remained bystanders in most of the internal warfare which has accompanied this pervasive revolution of rapid political and social modernization. In every case so far in which the Communists have tried to seize control of this revolution through political violence they have failed.

We shall analyze this remarkable record of failure in the face of excellent opportunities in this region by focusing first on the three most dramatic situations of Communist incapacity under inviting circumstances, namely in Iraq (1958-1960), Syria (1954-1958), and Iran (1953). Then we shall make a general survey of Communist involvement, or rather non-involvement, in internal warfare in the Middle East and North Africa, to see how characteristic such Communist incapacity is, and what its causes may be.[1] Finally, we shall conclude with some observations that may help to explain why the Communists have so far failed in the art and science of revolutionary violence when others in this region seem to have succeeded, and why Communist difficulties may be prolonged.

Iraq: 1958-1960

There was a tendency between 1958 and 1960, especially in the United States, to exaggerate the potentialities for a Communist takeover in Iraq. The US began landing troops in Lebanon in 1958, the day after the July 14 overthrow of the Western-allied regime of Nuri al-Sa'id in Iraq, in part because it was thought it might be necessary

[1] Walter Z. Laqueur provides a detailed survey of the history of Communist parties in the Arab world, Israel, and Turkey in *Communism and Nationalism in the Middle East* (New York 1956), and an analysis of shifting Soviet interpretations and activities in this general area in *The Soviet Union and the Middle East* (London 1959). An analysis complementing the present chapter by concentrating on Communist theory and practice that do not involve political violence may be found in Chapter 9 of Manfred Halpern, *The Politics of Social Change in the Middle East and North Africa* (Princeton 1963). A helpful discussion of neutralism and the developing relationship of the great powers with the Arab Middle East is provided by Charles D. Cremeans, *The Arabs and the World: Nasser's Arab Nationalist Policy* (New York 1963). Morroe Berger, *The Arab World Today* (New York 1962) discusses the underlying social problems of this region. There is no Soviet work dealing concretely and analytically with the role of the Communist movement in the Middle East and North Africa from any of the viewpoints covered by the titles of the first three Western books mentioned.

to be prepared for intervention in Baghdad against a Soviet-controlled, communist-neutralist coalition. Only Communists, and not the usual Arab, said one of the highest State Department officials privately, could have organized a coup so efficiently and kept it secret so well in the capital of the Baghdad Pact defense treaty organization.

Myths aside, however, the Iraqi Communists held advantages that no other Communist party possessed in 1958 in the entire region. It is one of the oldest Communist parties in the Middle East and the oldest party in Iraq (founded in 1927), and during the 1940's it had become one of the largest Communist parties of the region (7,000-10,000 members). It had cemented sympathetic relations with other opposition elements during prolonged common repression under Nuri's regime. The Iraqi Communists' opportunity in 1958 came at a time when the Soviet Union's prestige as an alternate source of arms, economic aid, and political support for Middle Eastern nationalists was as high as was resentment of the West, raised by the Anglo-French intervention at Suez, and more recently by American landings in Lebanon and the return of British troops to Jordan. Above all, for the first time in the area, a ruler chose deliberately to sustain his regime by utilizing the Communist party as a counterbalance against his other political opponents. Threatened by splintering among his own former supporters who now variously conspired to unite Iraq with Egypt, or else with a reformed United Arab Republic under socialist Syrian leadership, or to keep Iraq independent but under a multi-party coalition, General Abd al-Karim Kassim sought help from the Communists shortly after achieving power. He armed a Popular Resistance Force, encouraged trade unions and peasant associations, and established a military tribunal to judge political crimes—all under predominantly Communist control.

Yet by February 1960, the Communists could not get General Kassim's permission to legalize their party (a nationalist Communist splinter group received formal license instead), even though they had agreed to eliminate the word "revolutionary" from their party's Charter.[2] By the summer of that year, the party complained that the trade and peasant unions it controlled had been disbanded, that its control of the Lawyers' Association (dating from the 1940's) was lost, and its daily newspaper banned in half the provinces of the country.

[2] In a letter to the government dated February 8, 1960 republished in the *Iraqi Review* (a Communist weekly) for February 24, 1960. The original Charter was published in the Communist daily, *Ittihad al-Sha'ab,* January 10, 1960.

Communists who had used violence to defend General Kassim against uprisings by various nationalist opponents were now being left unprotected to be beaten or killed by irate neighbors, and were even being court-martialed. In discouragement, the party declared that it was "in favor of a constitutional political development that will ensure stability."[3]

What had happened to bring the party so quickly to such low fortune? The Communists had begun with considerable insight to assess the reasons for their declining influence as early as August 1959. The Report of the Enlarged Session of the Central Committee of the Iraqi Communist Party makes clear some of the principal reasons for the Communist failure.[4] The Communist party did not always know what it was doing: "The Party did not resort during this period to the procedure of deep scientific analysis of the swift and intricate developments in the situation. It adopted some of its tactics in the light of daily development of events . . . in isolation from their class roots and their general connections. The swiftness with which some negative trends in the political situation attained prominence took our Party somewhat by surprise." In an earlier statement, the party had already confessed that "the rapid changes in the situation and their development are far more complicated than can be fully absorbed at the right time, even by the most experienced of parties."[5]

The vanguard also acknowledged that it was led, and so also misled, by its followers. "It was impossible," declared the Enlarged Central Committee, "for any force to control the zeal of the masses, especially the politically backward sections who suddenly joined in gigantic numbers in the political struggle," looting, torturing, and dragging dead bodies through the streets.

This self-criticism, however, was strongly reminiscent of the party's difficulties seven years earlier, during the most serious riots in Baghdad in the decade preceding the 1959 rebellions. Analyzing its own role during the November 22-26, 1952 violence, when nationalist reformist parties had initiated mob outbreaks in order to compel a temporarily divided conservative oligarchy to grant them additional parliamentary seats in a forthcoming rigged election, the Communist party had made a similar point. A "true national front" was formed "practically"

[3] *Iraqi Review* (August 19, 1960); see also the issue for August 31. The *Iraqi Review,* and the daily *Ittihad al-Sha'ab,* the latter with a circulation of 15,000, were banned altogether by October 1960.

[4] Dated August 24, 1959, published in the *Iraqi Review* (September 6, 1959).

[5] "Statement on the Central Committee Session," *Iraqi Review* (August 6, 1959).

only in the "fire of battle," they said then, and the party leadership was urged "to prepare to accommodate these rushing masses which are determined to realize their objectives."[6]

Why had the Communists failed, in the interval, to maneuver themselves into the forefront of a popular movement which had been getting ahead of them? The Enlarged Central Committee in 1959 offered a number of explanations, all of which may be summed up by saying that it tried too hard too soon—an odd thing to say for a revolutionary party one year after others had succeeded in making a revolution. Yet for the Iraqi Communists, it was indeed an appropriate conclusion. If hindsight allowed the Enlarged Central Committee to say that "there is no doubt that the army was able to bring down with such amazing speed the pillars of the old regime . . . because the conditions for the revolution were fully mature among the people," its own state of preparedness was probably closer to Premier Khrushchev's when he confessed his surprise a week after the Iraq coup: "No one expected that the Baghdad Pact would so soon cease to exist."[7]

After attaining considerable strength in the 1940's, especially among teachers, lawyers, civil servants, and students, Communist party capabilities were severely harmed by governmental roundups and trials that began in 1947. The hanging of the party's leader "Fahad" (Yusuf Salman Yusuf), ". . . that thinking brain, left a vacancy in our party which all our party's efforts during the last seven years failed to fill."[8] By 1954, and seven reorganized Central Committees later, factionalism, which had always plagued the Iraqi party, had grown far worse.

In 1954, the Iraqis did join the rest of the world's Communists in placing the achievement of unity with the national bourgeoisie against American "imperialism" ahead of the goal of domestic revolution, but that adhesion remained only a formal statement of orthodoxy. In 1959, the Enlarged Central Committee admitted that "we are facing under the present circumstances chiefly the task of combating the 'leftist' ideas from which our Party suffered during the past period and which are still in the minds of the majority of party comrades."

[6] *Evolution of the Political Situation after the Liberation November Uprising and the Duties of our Communist Party to Develop the Popular Struggle and Realize its Objectives,* published by *Al-Qu'idah* in December 1952 and signed by Basim, pseudonym of the party's chief Sharif al-Shaykh.

[7] In a speech on July 22, 1958, reported in *Pravda* on the following day.

[8] *The National Struggle Front Against War and Imperialism,* issued by the People's Education Bureau of the Iraqi Communist Party, July 28, 1954.

Apparently the "leftists" had again seized control of the party. After the first eight months of the revolution, said the Enlarged Committee, the Political Bureau had neither held regular meetings nor consulted the Central Committee. At the same time, the continued secrecy in organization, the lack of sufficient communication among small cells, and "the basic and serious obstacle . . . the shortage in the number of organized cadres" had allowed "leftist" ideas to predominate, "undermining the importance of the National Front, resorting to sectarian tactics not accepted by the masses, and running behind extremist spontaneous actions which might occur among the masses." The demand for a coalition government to include Communist ministers, though based on the experience of other countries, was erroneous. The use of mass pressure to attain this goal "exaggerated the strength of our Party and distorted its intentions in the view of the government, of considerable sectors of the Iraqi and Arab bourgeoisie, and of many moderate forces. As a result, they became panicky . . ."

The Communists had resorted to arms, perhaps most dramatically in Kirkuk in July 1959, not in order to gain immediate power, but in order to force their way into acknowledged partnership in an ongoing revolution. The sharp reaction of the government should have been predictable (said the Enlarged Central Committee in retrospect) now that the "national bourgeoisie" was no longer in opposition but had itself become the ruling class.[9] At this point, however, the Communists were not permitted to draw any lessons that might improve their ability to resort to political violence against the "national bourgeoisie" in the next round. On the contrary, said the Iraqi Communists in a statement approvingly republished by *Pravda* on August 17, 1959, we erred by "underrating the role of authority and the other nationalist forces and their ability to safeguard the Republic." We should have avoided unnecessary excitement; the government could be relied on to remain neutralist. The chief enemy was not at home but abroad. For the sake of defeating "American

[9] The possibility that Moscow was also incapable of offering clear-cut guidance in the midst of this revolution, or else was itself divided in opinion, is suggested by the contrast between the approving, if hurt tone of S. Danilov's "Provocation in Kirkuk," *IntAff,* No. 9 (1959), and the praise for the Iraqi Communist Party appearing at the same time in *Sovremennyy Vostok,* No. 9 (1959) for casting aside "secondary differences of opinion and renewing cooperation with other different national forces," and recognizing the necessity for "prolonged coexistence between parties and national forces of different political trends," trans. from *Mizan Newsletter,* 1 (November 1959), 3-5.

imperialism," it remained essential to "maintain solidarity with the government and other patriotic forces."

By the spring of 1961, General Kassim had disbanded even the legal nationalist Communist party, believing that he no longer required it as a foil to those Communists who tried, however erringly, to follow the Kremlin line. He paid no attention to the USSR when it ended its long abstention from independent public comment on Iraq by publishing a series of protests by Soviet organizations against the persecution of Iraqi Communists, beginning with the telegram of the Soviet Afro-Asian Solidarity Committee, published in *Pravda* on February 10, 1961 under the title, "We Cannot Keep Silent." Instead, it was the Soviet Union which felt compelled by its anti-American policy to continue giving economic and military aid to Iraq, and to insist that the Iraqi Communists continue to affirm their solidarity with General Kassim even if in an increasingly masochistic vein. It must have been painful for Salam Adil, the First Secretary of the Iraqi Communist Party, to report to Moscow in the fall of 1961 that "at present there languish in prison more than 50 fighters condemned to death by a military tribunal for displaying heroism in the struggle against reactionary forces during the imperialist intrigues; and 286 courageous fighters were killed in broad daylight—Communists and democrats. The country's economic position is deteriorating, the standard of living is falling, unemployment is increasing, and the dominance of feudal overlords is springing up again in the country. The government is avoiding fulfilling the law on land reform, and has worked out no program of industrialization, while state revenue is being spent on secondary projects."[10] If the cold war has imposed a number of difficult allies and some unrewarding expenditures in foreign aid on the United States, what more burdensome collaborators and costs has it brought upon the USSR!

Meanwhile, internal warfare broke out again in Iraq, but not under Communist leadership. Kurds, led by Mullah Mustapha Barzani, began in the summer of 1961 to renew on a much larger scale their recurrent battle for greater autonomy. Barzani, upon his earlier defeat by Iraqi and Iranian forces in the 1940's, had spent over a decade in the USSR before Kassim permitted him, together with several thousand followers, to return in 1958. His cause, however, overlaps quite imperfectly with that of the USSR. While the Iraqi Communists

[10] *Pravda* (October 25, 1961), trans. in *Mizan Newsletter,* III (November 1961), 15.

and the USSR have persisted in expressing their sympathy for Kurdish discontent, there are obvious limits to the advantages they can hope to reap from any endorsement of Kurdish violence. They need only recall that conflict between Kurdish and Arab Communists over the issue of Kurdish rights and Arab nationalism has several times in the past succeeded in splitting the Iraqi Communist Party. Moreover, since the five to seven million Kurds are distributed not only over Iraq (over one million), but also the USSR (about 100,000) as well as Turkey (between two and four million), Iran (over one million), and Syria (nearly half a million), the Communists cannot bluntly endorse Kurdish rights without linking the USSR directly to a challenge of the national integrity and nationalist sensitivity of neighboring states about ten times more numerous in population than the Kurds. The threat of outside support for Kurdish warfare (under the Kassim regime, Barzani managed on his own to seize control of almost one-third of Iraq) might intimidate a weak Iraqi regime, although in fact, Soviet hints in that direction during 1963 failed to accomplish such a result. Indeed, if Arab, Turkish, or Iranian nationalists came to believe that the Kurdish minority were acting with Soviet backing, they would turn against, and certainly not toward, the USSR in foreign affairs.

Before the Kurdish uprising had yet been settled, violence broke out anew in Baghdad, overthrowing Kassim and destroying the Communist party. A coup engineered by socialist and pan-Arab nationalists on February 8, 1963 ousted and killed Kassim who, having failed at the only kind of politics he knew—playing his opponents against each other—had found himself morally and politically isolated. For some time already, his opponents no longer balanced each other out. Communist excesses during 1958 and 1959 had caused Kassim to cut their strength drastically, while Communist violence and Kassim's unscrupulous tactics and lack of positive accomplishments helped to unite the nationalist left. From about 1961 forward, his overthrow became only a matter of time and opportunity.

When that time came, the Communists once again found themselves surprised spectators of revolution. They decided to fight—this time to overthrow the new revolutionary regime. If violence now contradicted all previous self-criticism and indeed proceeded against the heaviest odds the Communists had ever encountered in Iraq, the reasons were visceral. The Communists knew that the victory of men whose supporters and kin they had attacked, massacred, or sent to jail by trial in "people's courts" would now spell their own deaths. When the Communists attacked the new February regime in some towns, or were being attacked by forces of the new regime in other towns, they were fighting for their very lives. Apparently almost no one in the Central Committee survived.

Their fight was encouraged by a clandestine Communist radio station broadcasting in Arabic from East Germany calling upon all, "whether Arabs or Kurds," to "overthrow the usurpers . . . before all the opportunities are lost." The Soviet Union, however, immediately recognized the new regime but, in adhering so remarkably to such stoic official courtesy, it could not altogether hide its deep bitterness and pain at so extraordinarily costly and dramatic a defeat. After the Soviet bloc had offered nearly half a billion dollars in credits and aid and invested the labor of over 2,000 technicians in Kassim's Iraq, the local Communist party had not only lost a fine opportunity but almost its very life, while the officials and newspapers of the new regime almost daily attacked the USSR for its meddling in Iraqi affairs. On February 16, the Soviet Communist Party's Central Committee spoke out to condemn the "mass reprisals and bloody terror," and on March 14, Moscow for the first time encouraged a mass demonstration against the embassy of an Arab nation when some 1,500 demonstrators broke windows and threw ink on the Iraqi Embassy building. Protest meetings also took place in other Soviet cities. It was, all things considered (including the likely American reaction to a similar loss), a restrained and carefully harnessed public reflection of the profound and unresolved political and intellectual frustration of Communist leadership in coping with revolution.

Syria: 1954-1958

During the four years preceding the Iraqi revolution, the Syrian Communist Party had never wavered from the orthodox and nonviolent line of organizing a national front. It also failed. This case is worth examining, for the lesson which the Communists drew from the failure of violence in Iraq—to persist in seeking collaboration with a "national bourgeoisie" that is unreliable at home and neutralist abroad—had to be assimilated in the knowledge that it had also paid no domestic dividends whatever in neighboring Syria.

In the case of Syria, Western diplomats and journalists had not merely one year, as in Iraq, but four, in which to alarm themselves and the world about the dangers of Syria becoming a Soviet satellite.

It remains uncertain, however, whether Western observers have yet fully appreciated how much Communist opportunities in Syria were the result of Western policies and also of Syrian forces not sufficiently analyzable in orthodox Leninist or Western terms; and how much the Communist failure to achieve an enduring communist-neutralist coalition was the result of local nationalist strength and Soviet restraint.

The most effective pressure making for collaboration between Communists and neutralist nationalists came from the West. Concerned with the military defense of the Middle East, but neglecting the social revolution transforming Middle Eastern society, the United States between 1954 and 1955 succeeded in fashioning the Baghdad Pact. Iraq, the only Arab nation to join this alliance, interpreted this new international backing in local terms: together with its Turkish ally, it marshalled troops on Syria's frontiers and utilized other subversive means from 1955 until early 1957, in attempts to convert a Syria moving toward reform and neutralism, into a conservative, pro-Iraqi state or, if possible, into an Iraqi province. In April 1955, also, the Syrian Nationalist Social Party, fascist and self-styledly pro-American, assassinated Colonel Adnan Mulki of the General Staff, a mainstay in the socialist-neutralist forces. In November 1956, shortly after the Anglo-French-Israeli intervention at Suez, a plot to smuggle Iraqi arms into Syria was discovered and led to widespread arrests.

In the face of such pressures from Western or pro-Western quarters, it was not surprising that most Syrians welcomed the first major Soviet pronouncement since the Second World War injecting the USSR actively in Middle Eastern politics. The Soviet government declared on April 16, 1955, that it "would not remain indifferent, since the setting up of military bases in this region directly affects the security of the USSR." Syrians were also cheered when the Western monopoly and control on arms supplies to the Middle East was broken and they received Soviet weapons in February 1956. They also listened apprehensively when the Soviet Foreign Minister declared at the time of the Iraqi arms plot that he had "incontestable information" that the UK, France, and Israel intended to attack Syria and other Middle Eastern countries.

The Syrian Communists should have been able to prosper in this climate. Their leader, Khalid Bakdash, is the most experienced and best trained Communist leader in the Middle East. No Middle Eastern Communist has spent more years in the USSR (his first sojourn lasted from 1931 to 1933), nor visited it more frequently and for more prolonged periods since, nor remained Secretary General for as long (nearly three decades). His second in command, Yusuf Faysal, has spent much time in Prague. In 1954, the Syrian Communist Party was the largest Communist party in the entire Middle East and North Africa and, with 10,000 members in a country of 4,000,000, was far larger in proportion to population than any other in non-Communist Asia except Indonesia.

Thanks to Soviet discipline, the party had been in difficulties in the past. During the Second World War, it could not support Syrian nationalists because it was backing France's fight against fascism, and in 1947 it endorsed Soviet support for the creation of Israel. It has, in fact, been outlawed ever since 1947, but it has retained a steady following, especially Moslem Kurds who admire their fellow-Kurd Bakdash; Armenian and Orthodox Christians still looking to Russia for protection; and a high quota of intellectuals. Its illegal status was also eased by the epidemic of opportunistic political alliances which symptomized Syria's travail during this period. During the 1950's these involved the Communists in links with Moslem extremists like Maruf Dawalibi (the Grand Mufti's political secretary in Germany during the Second World War), wealthy landowners like Khalid al-Azm, and socialists like Akram Hourani. By September 1954, Bakdash, polling 50,000 votes, had in fact been elected to Parliament under the guise of a "National Union" ticket and was seated on the foreign affairs and oil committees of the Chamber of Deputies.

Bakdash had worked hard to achieve such respectability despite the formalities of the law. In February 1954, during the last days of Colonel Adib al-Shishakli's dictatorship, the Communist party had declared itself in favor of a "republican parliamentary system," saying the party would support it "without making their part in it a condition for such support, or any other condition, except that this government should proceed to achieve the democratic and national objectives which are the goal of the people"—namely the removal of those domestic ills whose prime cause is American imperialism. After Shishakli's overthrow, Bakdash observed, accurately, that this revolution had been radically different from those which had preceded it in Syria. "All preceding 'state revolutions' took place as the result of an agreement between a limited number of persons isolated from the people. But the dictatorship crumbled as a result of a broad popular movement, in the process of which a brotherly unity was established between the people, the soldiers' masses and honorable officers."[11] The Communists sought to ease their entrance into this coalition by suspending their fight with the socialists over control of the trade union movement. The Communist party's position was also being enhanced by the proclivity of Western and "pro-Western" nations in thought and practice to lump together as "anti-Western" pro-Communists, pro-Socialists, and pro-Egyptians—distinctions which proved to be crucial for Syria's fate.

But the Communists never achieved the status of dominant partner in a "national front" government. Akram Hourani's Socialists were willing to use the Communists, but were unwilling to be used by them. In 1954, Hourani and Bakdash fashioned an electoral alliance, but while Communists kept their promise to vote for Socialists, Socialists voted only for Bakdash and neglected most of the other 21 Communist candidates. Four more Communists might have been elected but for government intervention. The Communists were to fall for this trick again in the 1956 elections, and in the increasingly successful Socialist coups for control of the army (March and August 1957) the Communists were left to be spectators.

In the final round, the Communists therefore turned away from the Socialists. The latter, with a more radical domestic line and a (then) increasingly pro-Egyptian policy, made it difficult for the Communists to align them with others to form a united national front. With an explicit leftist and nationalist ideology of their own, the Socialists also could and would compete on favorable ground with the Communists.

The Communists during 1957, strengthened by the backing of General Afif Bizri (currently in exile in Prague), and by their considerable influence in the Popular Defense Corps and the Youth Militia which had been organized during the previous summer, offered their support to Khalid al-Azm instead of to the Socialists. Al-Azm was a wealthy landowner with no ideology and limited organization of his own—but with an overwhelming ambition to become President of Syria. He had useful contacts in conservative circles and he would be largely dependent on Communist and Soviet support. It was the kind of gambit that old-fashioned British imperialists

[11] Quoted by A. F. Sultanov and others, *Sovremennaya Siriya* [Contemporary Syria] (Moscow 1958), 162, trans. in *Mizan Newsletter*, 1 (August 1959), Appendix, 4.

had been fond of (but in which they had already begun to be disillusioned).

This strategem served the Communists well for a time. Syria is a country more fundamentally divided than France; indeed, more so than most Arab countries, and since no veto group has been able to steal a march on others for long, virtually each one has its representatives in the army. In Syria, the army has therefore reflected the uneasy deadlock of social forces rather than, as in other Arab countries, acted as a vanguard of social change. Because of this unstable deadlock, and also because the very recent shattering of traditional values has left many without any sense of norms, political opportunism has been especially rife in Syria, and correspondingly, political bandwagons swell and collapse with startling rapidity. By the beginning of 1958 many Syrian nationalists feared that with the prestige earned by al-Azm in expanding Soviet military and economic aid and the added appeal this had given the Communists, the latter might well, with al-Azm's connivance, win the forthcoming municipal elections.

Against the double danger that such a victory would cause the Communists to insist on sharing in the national government and bring about outright Western intervention, the Syrian nationalists threw themselves into Egyptian arms instead. Upon the establishment of the United Arab Republic in 1958, Khalid Bakdash fled the country while hundreds of Communists were arrested. Though Syria has since experienced many changes of government (including one in which al-Azm formed a "pro-Western" government, only to be forced to flee for refuge in the Turkish Embassy), Bakdash has never been allowed to return to Syria.

It might be asserted that with a little greater luck, this Communist attempt to collaborate with the "national bourgeoisie" might have paid off. Such an interpretation would not answer one crucial question. Why did the Communists fail to resort to violence in collaboration with al-Azm and General Bizri, the two principal pillars of the government then existing, at a moment when all their hopes and accomplishments were being threatened? The answer most probably derives from the national interests of the USSR. The Soviets did not believe it useful at that time to press for the establishment of a satellite government in Syria, or even a government solely dependent on the USSR. Certainly such a move would have then driven most surrounding states closer to the West, raised the likelihood of Western counter-intervention, and undermined Soviet diplomacy in Europe and Asia without easing the road to other gains in the immediate area. On the contrary, it would have confronted the USSR with much larger risks in having to participate directly in regional hostilities between Syria and Israel, Iraq, Turkey, Lebanon, Jordan, Saudi Arabia, and Egypt. The Syrian Communists could not move to secure their gains through violence because they could not afford to win too much too soon.

Iran: 1953

This view is reinforced by an examination of the Communist reluctance to engage in sufficient violence in Iran during the final days of Premier Mohammed Mosadeq—allowing the victory in the internal war then in progress to go to forces supported by the West. Earlier Iranian history, by contrast, provides ample evidence that the Communist party is willing to engage in revolutionary violence. In a number of Iranian provinces—in Gilan (1919 and for a few days in 1953), in the Kurdish area of Mehabad (1946), and twice in Azerbaijan (1920 and 1945)—Communists established separatist regimes through political violence.[12] There is, however, another way of reading this score of uprisings, namely that each failed after a few months when the USSR, more concerned with its relationship to the governments of Iran or the West than with the fates of local Communists, refused to sustain the revolutionary regimes. In 1953, the Communists may well have known in advance that they could not call on the USSR for aid against forebidding odds and hence desisted in the face of their opponents' American support.

Yet they might not have had to retreat quite so ignominiously had they, and the USSR, not also been suffering from an inability to make up their minds. To be sure, the overthrow of the Communist regimes in Azerbaijan and Mehabad in 1946, and the concommitant ouster of four Communist cabinet ministers from the national government, had demoralized the party. Its difficulties were compounded in early 1949, when it was blamed on dubious grounds for an attempted assassination of the Shah, declared illegal, and had many of its leaders arrested or forced to flee. But by the end of the Mosadeq period, it

[12] For an analysis of these instances of internal warfare, see George Lenczowski, *Russia and the West in Iran, 1918-48* (Ithaca 1950); also Archie Roosevelt, Jr., "The Kurdish Republic of Mehabad," *Middle East Journal,* I (July 1947), 247-69; William Eagleton, Jr., *The Kurdish Republic of 1946* (London 1963); and Robert Rossow, Jr., "The Battle of Azerbaijan, 1946," *Middle East Journal,* x (Winter 1956), 17-32.

had become the country's largest single party—smaller than Mosadeq's own National Front, but more united than that coalition of groups which ranged from Mullah Abolkasim Kashani's opportunistic religio-political extremism to Dr. Mozaffar Baghai's undoctrinaire socialism. The Communists could not decide, however, whether they really ought to collaborate with Mosadeq's National Front or not, and as a result they never overcame Mosadeq's suspicions of their intentions and they falsely assessed the balance of forces in almost every crisis.

The Tudeh Party (as the Communist party is known in Iran) attacked the National Front until mid-1952, including the first year of Mosadeq's rule, or at least pursued a clearly independent line more extreme than Mosadeq's. Thus a Communist-sponsored demonstration by the "National Association for Struggle against the Imperialist Oil Companies in Iran" on July 15, 1951 was suppressed by Mosadeq at the cost of about 100 dead and 500 injured. Then, catching up with the new Soviet appreciation of the role of the "national bourgeoisie" in Asia and Africa, the Tudeh Party enthusiastically joined the riots on July 21, 1952 which successfully restored Mosadeq's rule after a five-day interval during which the Shah had attempted to replace him with a pro-British Premier. Since the National Front emerged victorious from this struggle for power, it gave a cool reception to Tudeh's call for a "coalition." On the contrary, it reacted to Tudeh's efforts to capitalize on riots which the National Front had initiated by refusing Tudeh's plea to be legalized, and instead soon reimposed martial law on Teheran and other areas.[13]

A year later, with a membership of 40,000-80,000, and a hard core of about 7,000, the Tudeh Party stated its demands with greater hopes. In an open letter to Mosadeq published on July 27, 1953, it called for a united front, abolition of martial law, dissolution of the royal court and parliament, calling of new elections, an end to contracts with Americans in Iran, and cooperation with the USSR. By this time, the Shah, the army, the landowners and traditional bourgeoisie, the Kashani wing of the National Front, and the Western powers were all clearly aligned against Mosadeq. Mosadeq, however, rejected this appeal.

On August 16, the army struck against Mosadeq but failed to

[13] The clandestine "Azerbaijan Democratic Radio" (broadcasting from Soviet soil since 1947) continued to attack Mosadeq until the spring of 1952 and then gradually centered its attacks on the Shah instead. Oddly enough, it left the air on August 3, 1953, just prior to the most crucial event in recent Iranian and Tudeh history.

muster enough strength to overthrow him. Instead, the Shah was forced to flee to Rome. This time, Tudeh asked Mosadeq for arms "to defend the Republic," but Mosadeq refused to become dependent on them in what seemed to be his hour of victory.[14] Tudeh on August 17 therefore tried to seize the initiative in order to coerce Mosadeq into a united front. Its mobs in Teheran clashed with troops loyal to Mosadeq and raised red flags. The following day, Mosadeq retaliated by turning the army sharply against all Tudeh demonstrators, and routing them. On August 19, elements of the Iranian army and rightist organizations who shared the conviction of the American government that Mosadeq might yet join with Tudeh, or at least yield to the Communists, overthrew Mosadeq and restored the Shah. On that day, the Tudeh Party stayed home.

Tudeh's first reaction was to blame the defeat of August 19 on Mosadeq's "vacillating policy" and on his having turned the security forces against the Communists.[15] Later it changed its mind, arguing that Mosadeq was still the "legal" Prime Minister, and asserting that it would "give full support to a united front government without demanding a position within that government."[16]

Almost a decade later, when Tudeh strength had shrunk to about 10 percent of its former size, Soviet writers referred to that "critical moment" when the party "was in fact fighting on two fronts—against imperialism and against Mosadeq."[17] In the Soviet view, it was the fault of the National Front, representing "the middle classes of the national bourgeoisie," that it sought, "to take advantage of the oil nationalization movement in order to distract the people's attention from democratic demands and to direct all its anger against the colonizers . . ."[18]

Actually, four difficulties had beset the Tudeh Party at that turning point. It fought Mosadeq too hard for its own safety; it would almost certainly have been unable to win the dramatically shrewd (rather than waywardly theatrical) Mosadeq to its cause either by force or persuasion; it could not hope to triumph over "imperialism"

[14] The Soviet radio twice rebroadcast Tudeh's August 16 appeal for a united front.

[15] *Mardom* (Tudeh's clandestine newspaper), August 28, 1953.

[16] *Mardom,* September 23, 1953.

[17] R. Avakov and G. Mirskiy, "O klassovoy strukture v slaborazvitykh stranakh" [On the Class Structure of the Underdeveloped Countries], *MEIMO,* No. 4 (1962), 81.

[18] A. K. Lavrent'yev, *Imperialisticheskaya politika SShA i Anglii v Irane* [The Imperialist Policy of the USA and England in Iran] (Moscow 1960), trans. in *Mizan Newsletter,* III (September 1961), 7-11.

by its own strength; and it could not look for Soviet intervention to counterbalance American intervention. Under Mosadeq, Iran was in the midst of a social, political, and economic revolution, but nothing in Communist theory or practice sufficed to allow the Communists to participate under such conditions.

The Middle East and North Africa since the Second World War

The three situations which we have examined in Iraq, Syria, and Iran are uncharacteristic of Communist experience in the Middle East and North Africa since the Second World War in only one respect. The Communists here tried harder for higher stakes—though nowhere for as much as sole power—and failed. Elsewhere in this region, despite almost continual internal warfare in the midst of a social and anti-colonial revolution, the Communists either could not or did not try, or were foiled in the first round. It may be instructive to survey briefly this area of 230,000,000 people in which, in 1963, there was not a single government in power except through victory in internal warfare, and discover what the Communists had failed to do while all this was going on.

When the Algerian guerrilla war for national independence and social reform began in 1954, the territory was legally part of France, the home of Western Europe's second largest Communist party. Algeria's own Communist party had 15,000 members; until 1955 it was legal (the nationalist groups were not) and controlled the local CGT-affiliated trade union movement.[19] Algerian peasants, who constitute the backbone of the nationalist army, might be assumed to make easier recruits for the Communists than, say, the Vietnamese. Many of the peasants had left their eroded lands for temporary periods as unskilled (and racially discriminated against) labor in France, or fought with the French army in Indochina. Many of the urban slum dwellers have had a similarly broadening experience. Yet the Communists have been unable to infiltrate the nationalist movement.

The Communists clearly had no advance warning of the outbreak of guerrilla warfare in October 1954. Earlier that year, on July 1, the Soviet bloc had begun to beam a clandestine "Voice of National Liberation and Peace" from Budapest to North Africa, but its main concern in that summer was to welcome the French pledge to negotiate for Tunisian and Moroccan independence, regretting only

[19] The *Confederation Général du Travail* is the Communist labor union in metropolitan France.

that the Communists were not being included in these negotiations. After the fighting began in earnest, the Communists continued to suffer from the same handicap which has always beset American policy toward the Algerian nationalists. Both great powers saw justice in the Algerian cause, but considered their influence in France to be the greater good. Since the end of the Second World War, the Communists in Algeria and France had hedged their support of independence for any North African state whenever their hope of tactical gains in France made such advocacy seem imprudent. As late as 1956, the Communists, in the hope of finding grounds for collaboration with the French Socialists, voted confidence and special powers to the Guy Mollet government which was to harden French policy in Algeria and attack Suez. Little wonder that such a party, which also constantly reaffirmed in Algeria its own links to a movement in France and the USSR, and which attracted a largely European electorate, was denied all organizational links with the guerrilla movement. Its own "Liberation Fighters" were short-lived: the nationalists made it plain to the Communists that they would brook no competition. In fact, with American trade union assistance, the nationalists established their own trade unions in February 1956, thus ending their last entanglement with a Communist-controlled organization.

The Chinese Communists confined themselves to sending medical aid and relief to the Algerian guerrillas until the fall of 1958; the USSR also limited its aid until the fall of 1960. After these dates, both sent arms—but arms also came from West Germany, Egypt, and Tunisia, among others. The new Algerian government is composed of radicals—but they are self-made in every respect.

In neighboring Tunisia and Morocco, the Communist parties suffered from exactly the same difficulties, living passively through the years of guerrilla warfare, and reaching the first year of independence and social reforms (1956) in both countries with only five percent of the membership they had possessed a decade earlier, and control over the dominant trade union movement lost. The Communists could only engage in perceptive commentaries. At the end of 1951, for example, the leader of the Moroccan Communist Party, Ali Yata, had reported from Algerian exile to his Central Committee that "the political conjuncture has never been as favorable for the development of the party as it is today. But our party is not advancing. It is, as it were, paralyzed." (The United States was then constructing several large military bases in Morocco, and the nationalist movement was steadily gaining momentum.) Ali Yata noted, however, that the party had become so panicky that excessive secrecy prevented the organization from getting anything done. From November 1950 to the end of 1951, the Central Committee had held only one meeting lasting one day. For two years, no sectional or regional meetings had been held except in Rabat. Sections having primarily Arab membership neglected Morocco's European minority, ridding themselves in an "arbitrary and authoritarian" manner of comrades who had retained some colonial prejudices "instead of helping such men to change their minds." In sections of predominantly French membership, Ali Yata often found a "paternalistic, colonialist" attitude shown toward Moslem members. He touched on one aspect of his most fundamental difficulty, namely that by endorsing nationalism the Communist party had come to sound merely like a small nationalist splinter group, but he failed to add clearly just how much its "nationalism" remained suspect.

Violence on the eastern Mediterranean island of Cyprus persisted almost as long as in Algeria, from 1954 to 1960, when a settlement provided for independence rather than the union with Greece which the majority of Cypriots had fought for. The Communists are stronger in Cyprus than in Greece. They received nearly 40 percent of the Greek Cypriots' vote (who constitute four-fifths of the inhabitants) during the 1960 legislative elections. They control the municipal council in three of the five major cities, and the island's trade union confederation. Yet on Cyprus, which continues to grant the British use of a large military base, the Communists left nationalist violence exclusively to the Greek Orthodox Church and the right-wing National Organization of Cypriot Fighters (EOKA). They even refrained from calling the trade union confederation out on strike against any strategic plant, construction activity, or defense works. In Limassol, where the Communists are strongest, violence was less frequent than in any other major town.

Just as France is more important to the USSR than Algeria, so is Greece more important than Cyprus. The first task of the Greek-speaking Communists in Cyprus, like that of their comrades in Greece, is to reassure the Greek Government and people (after their bitter experience with Communist guerrillas in the 1940's) that the Communist party and the Soviet bloc no longer stand for violence. Their aim is a united front against pro-American politicians in Greece—a purpose fulfilled with particular amplitude in the February 1956 elections, when such a coalition won a popular but not a parliamentary majority in Greece. The Communists' chief goal is not in uniting Cyprus with Greece but in separating Greece from the West, and for the sake of that achievement violence must by all means be avoided.

Palestine suffered at least 12 years of sporadic but often extreme violence before Israel emerged independent in 1948. During that period, however, the Communists isolated themselves from events by remaining anti-Zionist without supporting, except occasionally by words, the anti-Zionist warfare of the Arabs. Now they live in a state in which, by virtue of their small following and the society's organization, Communist-initiated internal warfare has not the remotest chance.

In neighboring Jordan, *coups d'état,* assassination, and riots have been endemic since 1951. Jordan is an artificially created country that cannot be self-supporting, and contains a large and powerful force of educated, urbanized Arabs dispossessed of their property in Palestine and without loyalty to the ruling pro-British dynasty.

Yet only once, and then almost by accident, have Communists held the leading role in a major act of internal warfare. When British efforts to win Jordanian adherence to the Baghdad Pact stimulated a deep and intense sense of immediate danger among all nationalist Jordanians, the National Socialists, a reformist group, seized the initiative in December 1955 to unite and direct all opposition groups in violent demonstrations against the Pact. When the demonstrators won their case, the National Convention (as the joint opposition leadership, including Communists, called themselves) tried through renewed riots on January 7, 1956, to oust the government altogether. In the ensuing disorders, mobs disregarded Arab Legion fire for the first time and moved in on small detachments of armed troops. At this point, the more moderate nationalists withdrew, fearing a bloodbath, and for the rest of that day, Communists were largely left in charge of the remaining mobs.

The Communists have participated in other riots, before and since. But they are not invited to join those conspiracies that have aimed directly for control of government. The Jordanian nationalists do not mind being augmented by Communists when they want to make a big demonstration against the government, but they have no illusions about the special international character of the Communist movement.

It was in Egypt in 1952 that the movement for full independence and socialism first attained power in the Arab world. Half a year before Colonel Gamal abd al-Nasser took control, the Cairo riots of January 26, 1952, burst out as a bloody symptom of deep discontent—the most costly disorders in terms of life and property in Egypt since it became independent. Although the government remained doubtful of its course, and seemed unable to deploy sufficient forces in time to control the outburst, the Communists failed to take effective advantage of their opportunity. They showed themselves to be almost completely unprepared and powerless. A number of Communists probably joined in the riots, but the most successful of the various extremists in assuming leadership of the Cairo throngs was Ahmad Hussain's Socialist Party, a fascist and opportunistic group.

Egypt's Communist party was at that time divided into seven factions. Since then, it has never been able to reduce its factions for long to less than three, and under the Nasser regime, most of its members have lingered in jail. One Communist newspaper printed on May 21, 1952, two months before Nasser's coup, makes it evident how distant the Communists' largest faction was from being able to cope with the problems of Egypt. About to be faced by a regime whose first major domestic contribution would be land reform, the Communists acknowledged that their contact with the peasantry "is slight if not nonexistent." The injunction "to shift the center of gravity in our revolutionary struggle to rural areas," was, however, a tactic dictated by desperation. "In these periods of terror, tyranny is felt mostly in the big towns where the main governmental machinery is found. This is why opportunities for the revolutionary struggle are diminished." The better known elements should therefore be sent to the countryside. However, "so far, we have no plans for propaganda for peasants except a report on the future revolution."

In the spring of 1954, the Communists joined with the faction-ridden nationalist Wafd Party and the religio-political totalitarian Moslem Brotherhood in a campaign of propaganda and riots designed to substitute General Mohammed Nagib and parliamentary rule for Colonel Nasser's authoritarian rule. In the fall of that year, the Communists joined with the Moslem Brotherhood (who were about to fail in an attempt to assassinate Nasser) in rejecting the Anglo-Egyptian agreement for British evacuation of the Suez Canal Zone and an independent Sudan as "a deal with the imperialists." Both campaigns failed, and the latter has since been adjudged as a "left-wing sectarian error."[20]

History has since passed the Egyptian Communists by. "The most progressive forces," complained a Soviet writer in 1962," are deprived of any real possibility of participating in active social and political life," adding without any sense of irony, that "the social and economic measures introduced in the UAR are effected 'from above,' by decree."[21]

Communists, though in control of the trade union movement in the Sudan, did not react violently against a military coup in 1958 which overthrew a parliament in which they were represented. They saw no role for themselves in the Lebanese civil war in 1958 between pro-Western and pro-Egyptian forces. They lacked the strength to take any position whatever during the Turkish coup of 1960 which attempted to instill new vigor and momentum in Turkey's ongoing revolution.

This survey of Communist lack of involvement in internal warfare in the Middle East and North Africa has left out Libya, Saudi Arabia, Yemen, Kuwait, and Afghanistan. These, however, are countries without Communist parties although, as Yemen demonstrated in 1962 and Saudi Arabia may demonstrate soon, not necessarily countries without revolutionary potentials.

Conclusions and Projections

Our conclusions so far have been derived from local experience. That is a form of analysis obviously being slighted by Communists, and with telling consequences. After experiencing local failure the Communists invariably fall back to a line that may or may not produce domestic gains for the Communist party but which is intended to establish a more favorable climate for the foreign policy of the USSR. Such a procedure cannot lead to improved revolutionary theory or practice. The USSR, through the requirements of its foreign policy, has become a major brake on Communist revolutions in the Middle East and North Africa.

[20] For a Soviet view of Communist relations with the Moslem Brotherhood, see A. M. Goldobin, "The Dissolution of the Moslem Brotherhood in Egypt in 1954," *Istoriya Stran Vostoka* [History of the Countries of the East], (Leningrad 1962), trans. in *Mizan Newsletter*, IV (September 1962), 17.

[21] V. Tyagunenko, "Tendentsii obshchestvennogo razvitiya osvobodivshikhsya stran v sovremennuyu epokhu" [Tendencies of Social Development in the Newly Liberated Countries in the Contemporary Epoch], *MEIMO*, No. 3 (1962), trans. in *Mizan Newsletter*, IV (April 1962), 4.

Except for two countries immediately bordering on the USSR (Turkey and Iran), this contradiction between Soviet policy and Communist revolution did not become evident in the Middle East and North Africa until the 1950's. Eager to acquire plants rather than peasants, the USSR had earlier slighted this part of the world in which three-quarters of the people are peasants, yet live in great poverty because they are able to cultivate only four percent of the total land area between Morocco and Pakistan. The USSR does not need the area's oil, and lacks tankers for carrying it away. In 1950, an editorial in the Cominform journal on the "Mighty Advance of the National Liberation Movement in the Colonial and Dependent Countries" did not mention the Middle East and North Africa at all.[22] In 1952, a similar editorial devoted only a single paragraph to this region, and failed to mention Egypt, Morocco, Algeria, or Pakistan among the countries it cited.[23]

All this has changed. By now, Egypt is second only to India among all non-Communist recipients of Soviet economic aid, second only to Indonesia in Soviet military aid. Afghanistan, Syria, and Iraq follow not far behind. Since the USSR first became an alternative supplier of credits, arms, and political support to the Middle East in 1955, however, this new relationship has also imposed new limitations on both Soviet and Communist potentials. The USSR, by winning a place for itself in the area, has made neutralism a still more viable and popular attitude. But while the neutralists of the area have demonstrated that they are prepared to rely on Soviet countervailing force to protect their independence against threats that stem from the West or its allies, they value their own independence highly enough to prefer to collaborate with both the West and the USSR in order to enlarge their freedom of action. They clearly do not intend to allow the special positions vacated by the UK and France to be filled by any other great power that would use its weight to acquire political or military prerogatives. They take their nationalism seriously enough to confront the USSR with the obvious danger that should Kremlin-controlled Communists take control of one country in the region, the rest would almost certainly move more closely to the West for support.

In one important respect, the limitations upon Soviet actions in the Middle East and North Africa have thus actually increased since 1955. For if the internal political instability and intensity of nationalist

[22] *For a Lasting Peace, For a People's Democracy!*, January 27, 1950.
[23] *Ibid.*, February 29, 1952.

feeling in most states of this region increase the risks of miscalculation in their dealings with the great powers, the USSR now also has new reasons of its own to refrain from taking full advantage of such possibilities. It can cement government-to-government relations in this highly nationalist region only at the cost of minimizing its support and encouragement for the Communist party.

The Communist parties in turn are now even more limited than before (even, for example, from the perspective of Egyptian jails) in becoming sharply critical of any regime—whatever its domestic policy—which has entered into closer relations with the USSR, and still more limited in advocating violence. The corresponding Communist emphasis on forming broad national fronts against American imperialism also makes it more difficult for the party to increase its own membership by competing with other opposition groups on the basis of its own distinct platform. And because it remains smaller than any nationalist movement, its efforts to create united fronts often merely expose to competitors its hopes of capturing popular issues, instead of demonstrating its capacity to marshal public sentiment on its own.

In some countries, the new Soviet policy has lent greater respectability to local Communists and given them greater opportunity to gain entrance into the circle of highly opportunistic or politically insecure politicians. This may well be the moment of greatest promise for Middle Eastern and North African Communists, for in the next and higher stage of political development, when (as in Egypt or Tunisia) a strong, socialist regime is coming to grips with the roots of instability, it may be too late. But the Communists labor under considerable handicaps even during that earlier period when no one has yet achieved control over the revolutionary forces and loyalties remain uncrystalized.

The Communists are prevented by current Soviet requirements, based on a sound appreciation of the international risks entailed in a more adventurous policy (and perhaps also by Soviet fears, incited by China, Yugoslavia, and Albania, of the course of Communist revolutions not imposed by the USSR) from trying to seize full control over Middle Eastern countries by their own strength. Instead, they must find "national bourgeois" allies. That tactic involves the Communists in three difficulties. The first is that the "national bourgeoisie"—in the sense of a property-owning middle class whose stake and therefore ideological commitment lies in the domestic rather than the "imperialist" economy—ceased more than two decades ago to be the revolutionary vanguard of Middle Eastern and North African nationalism. Since the 1940's, the motor force of politics in this area has been a new *salaried* middle class of army officers, teachers, bureaucrats, journalists, augmented by professional men and a would-be salaried middle class of diploma-holders without jobs. The core of the Communist party itself has been composed of such men, but the Communists find it hard to accept this reality without acknowledging that a class not directly defined by production and property relations, and certainly not proletarian, can play a decisive historical role—in short, without shattering that ideological myth which justifies the very structure of Soviet society and the Communist movement.

The second difficulty for the Communists is that the most effective form of internal warfare employed by the new salaried middle class after the achievement of national independence is the *coup d'état*. Since the purpose of such attempts is almost invariably to assure rapid modernization through centralized planning based on the mobilization of the masses through a single-party regime, it hardly ever occurs to the exceedingly small group of leaders who stage such coups to invite an obviously competitive and internationally-linked movement to join with them.

The third handicap under which Communists suffer as they seek to make headway under current conditions is that the army has been the favored instrument in the Middle East for coups made in the interests of the salaried middle class. While many of the best educated, ambitious, and patriotic young men sought a career in this most rapidly expanding, least corrupt, and most powerful bureaucracy in the Middle East, relatively few Communist intellectuals entered it. Nationalism did not motivate them, and as a result, the confining discipline, discomforts, and repressive political duties of army life deterred Communists in larger numbers than it did others. There have been individually important Communist officers in all Middle Eastern armies (especially in Iran, where 400 were arrested in 1954), but Communists have so far remained, at best, among the least influential political factions in Middle Eastern armies.

The real issue, however, is not size. If all Communist parties in the region are small, it is also true that every act of political violence during the past decade which succeeded in becoming the first step in transforming the structure of an independent Middle Eastern country was carried out by far smaller bands. These nationalist, neutralist, reformist juntas, however, found no difficulties in establishing a moral and ideological connection with the rest of their society. The Communists, by contrast, are known by now as a particularist sect bound to another nation. The Communists may therefore be right in concentrating first on the search for allies if they are ultimately to arrive in power.

These burdens, onerous enough for the Communists in the present, are likely to become heavier in the future. While the Communists remain compelled to reject violence except in collaboration with the "national bourgeoisie," others, aware that the Middle East and North Africa are already ripe for revolutionary action, are likely to move on in several more countries to capture power and modernize their society. In contrast to Europe and much of East Asia or Latin America, however, the Communist parties cannot challenge such regimes with a more radical program or a more attractive mystique of revolutionary violence. These socialist and nationalist authoritarian rulers usually score far higher on both these grounds than do the Communists themselves. In contrast to parts of Southeast Asia, Communist assistance was not required in the national-independence struggle of the Middle East. In contrast to some of their Latin American counterparts, the modernizing leaders of the Middle East and North Africa have shown themselves more aware of the implications of ideological choices. In the quest for rapid modernization, the Communists, publicly fighting among themselves, can no longer offer a uniquely relevant way. Yugoslavia—not the USSR or China—has become one of the most attractive exemplars for the Middle East and North Africa, mixed with the experience of other Afro-Asian states and a clear-headed recognition that there is no ready-made theory or model anywhere for the tasks at hand.

Doubtless it has never been Communist doctrine to prefer violence, but rather to use it only when it seemed more promising than any other means. But how long can a revolutionary movement eschew revolutionary violence and avoid serious schisms, loss of membership, or a change of character, particularly in an area of the world in which internal warfare and revolutionary change are the order of the day? For it is explicit in Soviet Communist thinking that it is imprudent to alter the present strategy until an altered international balance of power makes it impossible for the United States to intervene against Communist internal warfare in areas like the Middle East and North Africa. A decisive shift of that kind, however, is unlikely to occur soon and may not occur at all.

In the meantime, the most radical and revolutionary segments of Middle Eastern and North African opinion are unlikely to be attracted to a party that is preparing to wait, while splintering among orthodox and activist Communists (already evident for some years in Iraq, Syria, and Egypt) may get worse. In these circumstances, Communists may nonetheless initiate internal warfare in this region, but under terms that could scarcely please the USSR—namely with Chinese support or after reformist regimes have been defeated by economic scarcities which, even now, exceed those of China. Aside from Communism as the politics of despair, Communist violence could also break out during a crisis in the process of modernization, or succeed without violence, if individual Communists should succeed in dominating a small junta. But that is merely to say that accidents can happen, which is not much to say about a movement which claims to know the direction of history and what to do about it.

12

Latin America

JAMES M. DANIEL

The argument still frequently heard among Latin Americans is that communism cannot have broad appeal nor succeed in the area because of its irreconcilability with Christianity; that the deeply ingrained Roman Catholicism of the people would prevent them from accepting the atheistic creed. It is further argued that communism is bred by poverty and that, therefore, the best means of fighting communism is to raise the standard of living of the people. These arguments are not wholly valid, however, because in a number of countries the people as a whole are not deeply religious nor committed to the Roman Catholic Church—this was true in Cuba and is true in Brazil, for example. Furthermore, the revolution in Cuba occurred in a country with one of the most prosperous economies and one of the highest standards of living in Latin America.

The fact is that communism has considerable, if so far largely unrealized, appeal. R. J. Alexander notes that "the surprising thing is . . . that, in spite of the very profound feeling of revolt and change which has swept Latin America since the First World War, the Communists have made comparatively little progress."[1] He concludes that one of the most important deterrents to the advance of communism in the region has been the appearance of indigenous movements of broad appeal which have developed mass bases, such as Haya de la Torre's APRA in Peru and Betancourt's *Acción Democratica* party in Venezuela. These left-of-center parties have arisen in

[1] Robert J. Alexander, *Communism in Latin America* (New Brunswick, N. J. 1957), 11. This work has been heavily relied upon for the historical background of Communist activities in Latin America. See also Corporation for Economic and Industrial Research, *United States–Latin American Relations; Soviet Bloc Latin American Activities and Their Implications for United States Foreign Policy; A Study Prepared at the Request of the Subcommittee on American Republics Affairs of the Committee on Foreign Relations, United States Senate,* 86th Congress, 2d Session, Committee Print No. 7, (Washington, D. C. 1960), hereinafter referred to as CEIR, *Soviet Bloc Latin American Activities.* Ludwig Lauerhass, Jr., *Communism in Latin America, A Bibliography: The Postwar Years 1945-1960* (Los Angeles 1962), is an excellent listing of recent literature on the subject. For the popular front period, see Victor Alba, *Historia del frente popular; Analisia de una tactica politica* (Mexico 1959).

conjunction with the social revolution through which Latin America has been moving during the past several decades, a revolution comprised of four basic components: nationalism, economic development, political democracy, and changes in class structures (particularly as affected by agrarian reform and the organization of urban labor). The Communists have attempted to use each of these factors to their own ends, and their successes have been particularly in those countries which have not developed strong indigenous left-of-center parties such as Chile (1946), Guatemala (1944-1954), and Cuba (1959).

The Communist movement in Latin America dates from soon after the October Revolution and the establishment of the Communist International. The International attracted a number of Latin American groups, including the Brazilian Anarchists, the Uruguayan and Chilean Socialists, and the revolutionary generals of Mexico (which was in the throes of the unique indigenous revolution that began in 1910). Some of these groups, at the insistence of the International, converted themselves into Communist parties, while others, disillusioned by the rigid discipline demanded by the Comintern, broke away. Those parties which remained in the Comintern have since that time faithfully hewn to the required line and "are an integral part of the international Communist movement."[2] Thus the Communist parties of Latin America have gone through much the same phases which characterize the history of the world Communist movement. Their greatest successes have come during those periods when international communism permitted greatest flexibility, including alliances with non-Communist groups—the period of the popular front of the 1930's, the latter part of the Second World War, and the past few years when united fronts with other leftist parties have been encouraged. The Latin American parties have been rocked by internal frictions corresponding to those which have occurred in the Communist party of the Soviet Union, but these frictions have often been traceable to struggles for personal power in the jargon of the contenders in whatever struggle happened to be in progress in the CPSU. Personalism is a powerful factor in the internal politics of the Communist parties as it is in Latin American politics generally.

Popular Front: Cuba and Chile

During the popular front period the Communists scored a notable success. In Cuba they had attempted to establish an alliance with the

[2] Alexander, 30.

Auténtico Party of Dr. Grau San Martin, but were rebuffed. They then turned to Fulgencio Batista, who, though lacking broad popular support, desired at that time (1938) to be elected president by means of relatively honest elections. This was neither the first nor the last time that a Latin American Communist party cooperated with a dictator to achieve its ends. In this case the move was successful, for the alliance with Batista outlasted the popular front period and led to the appointment, in March 1943, of Juan Marinello as Minister without Portfolio, the first time a Latin American Communist had attained a cabinet post. This accomplishment was short-lived, for in 1944 Batista retired from the presidency in favor of Grau. During Batista's second tenure (1952-1959) he permitted the Communists a relatively free hand in the labor union field, but otherwise tended to restrict their activities. The Communists continued to support Batista until the summer of 1958, when they concluded an agreement with Fidel Castro in the Sierra Maestra.[3]

After the German attack on the USSR in 1941, and in the period immediately following the war, the Communists were afforded opportunities to make advances in Latin America. These arose from international communism's general policy of cooperating with governments or parties which supported the "Great Fatherland War," and from the genuine admiration for and goodwill toward the USSR which was generated by the Soviet struggle against the German forces. In 1946, Gabriel González Videla won the Chilean presidential election with Communist support,[4] and as a result, he awarded three of the nine cabinet posts to the Communists. The Chilean Communists made significant advances during this period, particularly in labor. González Videla had promised to permit the organization of unions of agricultural workers, and the Communists seized on this promise to expand their work in rural areas. They demanded more and more concessions from González Videla and in fact began to act as if they controlled the government. They set out to terrorize their opponents, especially in labor unions, and instigated street fights against the Anarchists and Socialists. In short, the Communists attempted to consolidate control too quickly and openly, resulting in the unification of all elements outside of the government and, at length, in the defection of the two other government parties, the Radi-

[3] Theodore Draper, *Castro's Revolution: Myths and Realities* (New York 1962), 53-56.

[4] Alexander, 200-202.

cals and Liberals. These had become concerned over the trend of events, and in April 1947 resigned from the government, forcing the President to dismiss the Communists from the cabinet.

Guatemala

It was also during the period of cooperation late in the Second World War that bases were laid for the rise of Communist power in Guatemala.[5] On July 1, 1944, the thirteen-year rule of General José Ubico came to an end when he was forced to resign from the presidency. He was succeeded by a military triumvirate, one of whom, General Federico Ponce Vaides, forced Congress to name him Provisional President, whereupon he set out to become another Ubico. He in turn was overthrown on October 20 by a swift coup, one of the leaders of which was Captain Jacobo Arbenz Guzmán, who had resigned from the Army in protest against Ponce's dictatorial inclinations. These three then formed a provisional junta until elections could be held. The coup, supported by students and young army officers, reflected a widespread desire for economic and political reforms.

After the overthrow of Ubico, and particularly after the liberal-minded junta came to power, intellectuals who had fled from the sterile rule of Ubico began returning from abroad, where many of them had become strongly nationalist and influenced by Marxism. Their nationalism made it easy to blame the backwardness of their country on "imperialist exploitation," while communism provided a pat "scientific" explanation of imperialism and a concrete cause dedicated to its overthrow. Even before the October coup, labor unions, forbidden under Ubico, began to be organized. As there were no Guatemalans experienced in labor organization, assistance was obtained from other Central Americans, mainly Salvadoran exiles who had associations with communism. At the same time two leftist parties

[5] The account of the Guatemalan experience, unless otherwise noted, is based on Ronald M. Schneider, *Communism in Guatemala:* 1944-1954 (New York 1959); and U. S. Department of State, *A Case History of Communist Penetration—Guatemala,* Department of State Publication 6465, Inter-American Series 52 (Washington, D. C. 1957). Both are well-documented, using materials which became available after the fall of the Arbenz regime. Quite readable, but published soon after the event, before many documents came to light, and written in a journalistic and sometimes exaggerated style, is Daniel James, *Red Design for the Americas: Guatemalan Prelude* (New York 1954). For a short analytical treatment, see Victor Alba, "Friends of the Communists: Some Curious Examples," *Problems of Comunism,* x (Jan.-Feb. 1961), 19-27. Many other treatments of the Guatemalan experience are available, but the above, particularly the Schneider book, are the most reliable.

were formed, and as there was no Communist party, Communists were to be found in both of them.

Juan José Arévalo, an educator with radical ideas who had lived in exile in Argentina for the past fifteen years, returned to Guatemala in late 1944 and was elected president, taking office in March 1945. During his years in exile he had developed the philosophy of "spiritual socialism," a vague doctrine based on equality of opportunity and education, freedom of self-expression, and the dignity of the individual. Publicly, Arévalo's attitude was anti-US. Once in office he enjoyed great popularity, but he was unable to present a well-planned and realistic program and his administration was inexperienced and ineffectual. The new constitution which became effective in March 1945 provided for extensive social and agrarian reforms. With an able president, devoted public servants, and funds for development, it would have been a good constitution. Instead, the government drifted, and the enthusiasm of the young revolutionaries did not counterbalance their inexperience. They knew what they were against, but had no positive, dynamic program to offer.

Arévalo rejected the materialism of communism, but found bases for cooperation with the Communists in social reform and opposition to imperialism. He encouraged the participation of Communists as individuals in the administration of political and labor groups, but discouraged the open formation of a Communist party. In general, the Communists were able to work freely, becoming the champions of labor and dominating or infiltrating most of the labor organizations. These were merged in 1951, on the advice of the Communist-oriented Latin American Confederation of Labor (CTAL), into the *Confederación General de Trabajadores de Guatemala* (CGTG) in which key positions were held by Communists, and which represented practically all industrial, commercial, and transport labor as well as numbers of agricultural workers, including those on United Fruit Company plantations. The Communists also began in 1947 to form front groups of leftist youths and women, both of which organizations became affiliated with international Communist groups.

In the meantime, Arévalo's leftist orientation alienated the traditional elite, while the inertia of the administration disillusioned many of the revolutionaries. The anti-Communists foolishly attacked all social legislation, including social security, land reform, and other legislation which had broad appeal, as Communist measures. Thus Arévalo was forced to rely increasingly on the Communist-infiltrated bureaucracy and labor, and to seek the support of young army officers. The administration's *Partido Acción Revolucionario* (Revolutionary Action Party—PAR), formed by the fusion of the two leftist parties established earlier, lacked mass support, so that the Communist labor leaders became useful allies of the administration, by producing votes and "popular" demonstrations.

The Communists now decided to come together in a formal organization. On September 28, 1947 the *Vanguardia Democrática* was organized as a conspiratorial group. The Guatemalan Communists had ample contact with world communism through the visits of Communist leaders from other Latin American states, but direct contact with foreign Communist leaders did not occur until the spring of 1949 when José Manuel Fortuny and Victor Gutiérrez attended the first World Congress of Partisans of Peace in Paris. Gutiérrez also went to Milan for the WFTU congress, and Fortuny went on to tour Eastern Europe. In September 1949, some months after their return from Europe, the *Vanguardia Democrática,* at its first party congress, changed its name to *Partido Comunista de Guatemala* (PCG) and Fortuny and others resigned from the PAR. In June 1950 Gutiérrez founded the *Partido Revolucionario Obrero de Guatemala* (Revolutionary Workers Party of Guatemala—PROG) with the aim of further indoctrinating political and labor leaders. Fortuny apparently wished to proceed rapidly with the establishment of an open Communist party, whereas Gutiérrez felt that additional groundwork was required.

The PCG and PROG now worked loyally together as well as wtih the PAR in the presidential campaign of Colonel Jacobo Arbenz, who, however, was careful to retain the Communists as junior partners, not only because they were in fact a minority in the coalition, but also because he wanted to avoid alienating the moderates. Arbenz was inaugurated president on March 15, 1951 and the Communists began to capitalize on the foundations they had laid during Arévalo's regime.

It was during the administration of Arbenz that the Communists flourished in Guatemala. The motives of Arbenz in encouraging and supporting the Communists during his administration are difficult to establish. Their control and manipulation of labor at the polls and in the streets was undoubtedly an important factor. Furthermore, the Communists had a program—they knew where they were going and had some ideas on how to get there—whereas the moderates and non-

Communist left had no concrete and realistic program. As was shown during the administration of Arévalo, they were ineffective in their attempts to implement the program which they developed. Finally, there may well have been a personal motivation. Arbenz had in 1939 married the daughter of a wealthy Salvadoran family which disowned her for marrying out of her class. Guatemalan society snubbed the couple; so that it may have been simple desire for revenge rather than concern for the masses which drove Arbenz to the left. Furthermore, his wife is reported to have been a student of Marxism and is said to have influenced him in favor of communism.[6]

Whatever the reasons, the Communists now felt free to step up their activities, and during the course of the Arbenz administration broadened their influence by maintaining a close relationship with the administration. They infiltrated key government agencies, particularly at the middle and lower levels, and established interlocking directorates between the Central Committee of the Communist party and the labor, youth, women, and student organizations. Toward the end of the Arbenz administration, they attained the leading place in the National Democratic Front, the coalition of administration parties which grew out of the Democratic Electoral Front formed for the 1953 elections. The PCG came into the open in April 1951 when Fortuny signed a press statement as Secretary General of the PCG, and in July Gutiérrez flatly stated that he was a Communist. In November 1951, Gutiérrez attended the WFTU congress in Berlin and went on to visit Moscow. On his return in January 1952, he announced the dissolution of the PROG and advised its members to join the PCG. In December of that year the Second Party Congress of the PCG decided to change the name of the party to *Partido Guatemalteco del Trabajo* (Guatemalan Labor Party, PGT) in order to avoid the Communist label. At the same time it was decided to expand the membership, with the result that a party which had consisted of a few dozen labor leaders and intellectuals became by early 1954 a well-organized party of 4,000. The congress also adopted statutes modeled on the standard organization of Stalinist Communist parties.

The Communists then undertook the suppression and intimidation of the opposition. When the party had emerged openly as the Communist party in 1951, the anti-Communists tended toward unity

[6] James, *Red Design for the Americas,* 56-57, considers the personal factors the key ones.

and began to grow in influence. In March 1952 there was a mass demonstration of anti-Communists in Guatemala City which dramatized their strength. During the course of 1952, anti-Communist leaders began to be arrested and held without charges by a police force already controlled by the Communists. After an abortive uprising in Salama in March 1953, the police took the opportunity to arrest not only those involved but also many opposition leaders, charging them with complicity. Arrest, torture, attacks on non-Communist labor leaders, attacks on anti-Communist radio stations and other individuals or centers of opposition became increasingly characteristic of the regime, so that by early 1954 there was a veritable reign of terror in the country.

The Communists realized at the outset of Arbenz' administration that they had not thus far succeeded in reaching the peasantry, aside from those estate workers organized in the CGTC, a relatively small part of the rural labor force. It was the land reform program which gave them the means to do so. Land reform had been dealt with in the Constitution of 1945, but no implementing legislation had been passed. A month after the return of Gutiérrez from Moscow in 1952, the Central Committee of the PCG devoted its first plenary session of the year to agrarian reform, which Fortuny called the party's first task. When the National Congress convened on March 1, the Communists used their influence to get Gutiérrez elected Chairman of the Special Committee on Agrarian Reform, and on March 10 Arbenz introduced the Agrarian Reform bill. Arbenz allowed the Communists complete freedom in applying pressure for the passage of the bill, and they organized meetings and instructed local labor leaders to send petitions to the President in support of the bill. The law was quickly passed, and provided that peasants were to receive the use of land, not ownership, thus making the *campesinos* servants of the politicians and their tenure of the land subject to the whims of the authorities.

Agrarian reform soon became an instrument of political action in the hands of the Communists and those who shared their views. The Department of Escuintla, on the Pacific slope, became the main area of action. The Department contained large coffee plantations, national farms, and the most important United Fruit Company division in Guatemala. Though the agrarian reform law was aimed at land which was not in production, it was applied extensively to productive land. The Arbenz regime expropriated some 234,000 acres, many of the expropriations being accompanied by threats or actual violence against the landowners. By the end of the Arbenz administration the Communists virtually controlled the Department of Escuintla and were building considerable strength in several others. By means of the agrarian reform program the Communist party was able to reach the "agricultural proletariat" who worked for wages on the plantations, but it was never able to reach the bulk of the rural population—the Indians who lived in self-contained communities and followed traditional ways of life.

By early 1954 the Communists controlled much of the government and had direct access to the President, but they were still in the early stages of converting the country into a Communist state. The Communists were, of course, counting on the remaining three years of the Arbenz administration in order to build a mass base throughout the country. Their main problem would be the succession in the presidential election of 1956. In early 1954 Carlos Manuel Pellecer, a Communist leader in the CGTG, wrote that this period was characterized by "the organization and education of the proletarian armies under conditions of development more or less peaceful, parliamentarism, alliance with other parties, united front, flexibility without major clashes. The conquest of proletarian dictatorship is not part of the order of the day."[7]

The Communists did not control the Army, which remained relatively free of Communist influence, but as an alterative to outright control they seemed to realize the necessity for creating a counterforce. Arbenz, perhaps at the suggestion of the Communists, decided in late 1953 or early 1954 to establish a people's militia. The suggestion may well have originated in Moscow, as Fortuny spent two months there in late 1953. In January 1954 a personal emissary of Arbenz was in Czechoslovakia, apparently concluding a deal for arms destined for a militia, and in June 1954 plans for the militia were being completed. The Communist secretary general of the union of rural workers was to be the Commanding General of the People's Militia, and other leading Communists and Arbenz supporters were to comprise the upper echelons of the officer corps, while the sergeants of the army were to become junior officers. It was no doubt considered that the strategem would weaken the army initially and that in time the militia would displace the army altogether.

On May 15, 1954 a Swedish ship arrived in Guatemala from

[7] Department of State, *A Case History . . . Guatemala,* 36-37.

Poland carrying some 2,000 tons of rifles, machineguns, artillery, and other arms. The arrival of the arms led to the downfall of the Arbenz regime, for Colonel Carlos Castillo Armas, in exile since 1951, decided to invade with the small organization he had built up with US assistance before the arms could be distributed. Arbenz learned of Castillo's plans and countered with an intensified reign of terror. Constitutional guarantees were suspended and hundreds were arrested, tortured, and executed on suspicion of anti-communism. Castillo with 200 men invaded Guatemala from Honduras in late June to be greeted by crowds as the local Communists fled. The Army was apathetic, and, when Arbenz announced that he was sending a militia of 5,000 armed workers to the front, the Army officers viewed this as a usurpation of their functions by Communist labor leaders and demanded the President's resignation. In the meantime, the people did not rise against the regime, as Castillo hoped, but neither did they defend the government, as the Communists and Arbenz had thought they would. Arbenz therefore resigned on June 22, 1954 and sought asylum in the Mexican Embassy along with 800 of his followers.

Though the Guatemalan episode ended in the failure of the Communists, it was of unquestionable value for the lessons they could (and apparently did) learn from it. Since the Soviets themselves seem to base their conceptions of events in Latin America on analyses of local Communists, it is reasonable to suppose that the Guatemalan Communists' analysis of their failure is largely accepted by the Russians. This analysis appeared in a pamphlet published by the Central Committee of the PGT in June 1955.[8] The Central Committee concluded that "the working class and not the bourgeoisie must be the class leading the struggle for national liberation." Stated otherwise, the Communists had converted mainly intellectuals, students, professional people, and persons of the middle and lower-middle class, and only a relatively small number from these groups. For all of its work in labor and other mass groups, the party did not have mass support and did not represent the thinking of the Guatemalan people as a whole. The PGT also concluded that commercial ties with the Soviet Bloc should have been increased, ostensibly to weaken Guatemala's economic dependence on the United States, but mainly as a means of making the country dependent on the Soviet Bloc. A third conclusion was that the state should allow the exercise of democratic rights only to its friends and should be empowered to employ dictatorial methods

[8] *Ibid.*, 66-69.

against its enemies. Finally, the Communists admitted that they had "committed a serious error in undertaking democratic revolutionary changes while leaving the old army intact."

The PGT, which had gone underground upon the fall of Arbenz, by mid-1956 formulated a new program which reiterated some of the lessons learned.[9] The emphasis must be on forging the unity of labor and *campesinos*. Coups, adventurism, and provocation were rejected as being "harmful to the advancement of the democratic forces." Ultimate triumph must come by means of revolution, but it must be a mass revolution. For the time being the PGT must concentrate on organization and work through legal channels until conditions would guarantee the success of a people's insurrection. This, concluded the PGT sadly, would be a long task.

We may add a postscript taken from an article written by Jacobo Arbenz for *Pravda* in 1960: "In Guatemala the revolutionary movement did not take on the same scope in mobilizing the masses as in Cuba today."[10]

Cuba

Prior to the death of Stalin, and for some time thereafter, the Soviets paid little attention to Latin America. There is some evidence, as we have seen, that the Soviets assisted the Guatemalan Communists with advice,[11] but there was no attempt to increase economic ties with that country or to provide financial, material and technical assistance, as has been done in the case of Cuba. It seems likely, however, that the events in Guatemala had some part in awakening the interest of the Soviets in Latin America and in showing them the possibilities for Communist expansion in the area. Premier Bulganin's interview in the New York magazine *Visión* in January 1956 in which he expressed the Soviet Union's interest in the area,[12] and the greatly increased trade efforts in 1954 and the years following,[13] may have resulted from the interest in Latin America generated by the Communist experience

[9] Scheider, 320.

[10] Jacobo Arbenz, "Cuba's Example Inspires," *Pravda* (October 26, 1960), in *CDSP*, XII, No. 43 (November 23, 1960), 12-13.

[11] See also Schneider, 276.

[12] *Visión*, New York (January 16, 1956), summarized in Department of State, *A Case History . . . Guatemala*, 4.

[13] Robert Loring Allen, *Soviet Influence in Latin America: The Role of Economic Relations*, (Washington, D. C. 1959), *passim*, but especially the table of Soviet-Latin American trade, 9. See also CEIR, *Soviet Bloc Latin American Activities*, 57-84.

in Guatemala. The lessons learned in Guatemala by the Communists are linked directly with the later events in Cuba through the person of the Argentine Ernesto "Che" Guevara, who arrived in Guatemala as a young doctor in the Spring of 1954, and during the waning months of the Arbenz regime served in the National Agrarian Department.[14]

By the time Guevara met him in Mexico City in 1955, Fidel Castro was already a seasoned revolutionary. He had participated in the *bogotázo* in 1948, the terrible rioting in the Colombian capital touched off by the assassination of the popular Liberal Party leader Jorge Eliecer Gaitán;[15] he had been among those who met at Cayo Confites that same year in a plot to invade the Dominican Republic; and on July 26, 1953 he was involved with about 165 young men in a futile assault on the Moncada Barracks in Santiago de Cuba. Most of them were killed outright or executed soon after their capture, but 31, including Fidel and his brother Raúl, were imprisoned. In May 1955 they were amnestied by President Batista and some weeks later Fidel went into exile in Mexico.[16] There he organized a guerrilla warfare school under Alberto Bayo, the Communist veteran of the Spanish Civil War, and prepared to return to Cuba. This he did in November 1956 with 82 companions aboard the *Gramna.*[17] Within a week after the landing in eastern Cuba, 70 of the conspirators had been killed or captured and only twelve reached the Sierra Maestra to start the guerrilla warfare which brought Castro to power.[18]

[14] Daniel James, *Cuba: The First Soviet Satellite in the Americas* (New York 1961), 59; Edwin Lieuwen, *Arms and Politics in Latin America* (New York 1961), 264.

[15] James, *Cuba,* 45. James, as well as many others, ascribes the riots to the Communists. In fact, however, the Communists were taken completely by surprise and did little to capitalize on the disorders. See Alexander, 250.

[16] James, *Cuba,* 45-51.

[17] *Ibid.,* 63.

[18] Much has been written on the Castro regime, a great part of it being so biased for or against the regime as to make it worthless. While the definitive study will not be written for some time to come, there are available a few works worth attention. A brief factual summary of events to early 1961 is available in Lieuwen, 264-283. James, *Cuba,* is written in journalistic style and tends to exaggerate, but is detailed and useful if taken with some caution. The little pamphlet issued by the U.S. Department of State, *Cuba,* Department of State Publication 7171, Inter-American Series 66, (Washington, D. C. 1961), is factual. By far the best analysis of the events in Cuba is Theodore Draper, *Castro's Revolution, Myths and Realities* (New York 1962), a collection of essays dealing particularly with Castro's relationship with the Communists and the transformation towards socialism which Cuba has undergone. Draper effectively puts to rest the myth that Castro was forced into the arms of the Communist countries by US refusal of assistance. A similar interpretation is offered in R. Hart Phillips, *The Cuban Dilemma* (New York 1962). All of these

From the nucleus of survivors from the *Gramna,* Castro's group in the Sierra Maestra grew to no more than 500 in early 1958, but expanded more rapidly in the closing months of the year. The bulk of the guerrillas was recruited from among the peasants, or *guajiros,* but included numbers of urban middle class refugees from Batista's increasing oppression. Cuban and Soviet propaganda is quite correct in characterizing Castro's rebel army as one drawn from the masses (though, of course, so was Batista's—for what modern army is not?) but its leadership was altogether of bourgeois origins. In fact, most of the opposition to Batista came from the middle class, the professional class, landowners (particularly in eastern Cuba), and even the upper class.

Economic conditions were good during 1957 and 1958, and the masses, both urban and rural, were not interested in revolution. It should also be recalled that Castro's was not the only anti-Batista group, but all of the opposition tended to unite around him, partly because he was a striking figure of powerful personality, partly because the opposition realized that to topple Batista it would be necessary to achieve some sort of unity, and partly because Castro's announced program was moderate, including the restoration of the Constitution of 1940, the guarantee of political freedom, and the promise of early elections. The program appealed precisely to those middle and upper class groups who were most strongly in opposition to Batista. In effect, Castro's was a middle class revolution. Batista's armed forces fought either apathetically or not at all (or even rebelled, as in the case of the Cienfuegos naval revolt of September 1957) because the aims which appealed to the middle class also appealed to sizable sectors of the officer corps. Quite as important to Castro's victory as the apathy of the armed forces was the urban resistance movement, against which the terror of the Batista police was brought to bear and which suffered far more casualties than did the *barbudos* in the mountains. Draper points out that "it was the desertion of the middle class—on which Batista's power was based—that caused his regime to disintegrate from within and his army to evaporate."[19]

The middle class revolution was victorious on January 1, 1959,

---

and various other sources have been used in the following section but none will be cited specifically except in the case of quotations or opinions expressed by various authors. Draper's essay "Castro and Communism," *The Reporter,* XXVIII (January 7, 1963), 35-48, is an excellent analysis of the missile crisis of late 1962 and its effects on Castro's relations with the USSR.

[19] Draper, *Castro's Revolution,* 23.

but it appears that the first steps in the betrayal of the revolution had already been taken. Whether or not Fidel Castro was a card-carrying Communist or even a Marxist in 1953 or 1959 or 1961 is an academic matter now, though the argument has raged in the press and in other quarters in this country and elsewhere (possibly even Moscow, as well). There is no question that those closest to him—Che and Raúl, but others in his entourage as well—were either Communists or so greatly influenced by Marxism-Leninism that they may as well have been. Whatever ties the Fidelistas had with Communists, the *Partido Socialista Popular* (Popular Socialist Party—PSP—as the Communist party has been known in Cuba) did not support the revolution until late in 1958. The PSP refused to support Castro's call for a general strike in April 1958, but it is likely that even at that time agreement was being reached in the PSP concerning the possibility of achieving power through Fidel. In July, Carlos Rafael Rodriguez visited the Sierra Maestra and returned there, probably in September, to remain until the victory of the revolution. His second trip was made as official representative of the PSP, suggesting that an agreement had been reached between the Communists and the Fidelistas. The contribution of the Communists to the victory of the revolution was slight.

One of the first tasks undertaken by the Castro regime in the six months after it came to power on January 1, 1959, was to destroy the old Army and Air Force, replacing them with the rebel Army and rebel Air Force composed of the *barbudos* who had fought with Fidel. Those personnel who were favorable or neutral toward the revolution were merely retired or dismissed, while the leaders of those services and of the Navy as well were tried by the Revolutionary Tribunals and either executed or imprisoned. During the course of 1959 the leftist turn of the government began to cause disaffection within the rebel armed forces, leading to the defection or arrest of several prominent officers and shaking Castro's faith in his army.

At the same time, Castro had embarked on various foreign adventures, particularly landings of Cubans and exiles in Panama and the Dominican Republic in April and June, earning the hostility of a number of Central American and Caribbean governments. Simultaneously the American press and government, both generally sympathetic to Castro at first, showed signs of disillusionment. Thus faced with foreign and domestic hostility, Castro decided on a massive build-up of armed strength. He appointed his brother Raúl as Minister of the Revolutionary Armed Forces in October 1959 and at about the same time began the organization of the civilian militia. At first Castro had no difficulty in obtaining arms from Western Europe, but by the spring of 1960 Cuba, in financial difficulties, could no longer pay for her purchases. In July 1960, Raúl journeyed to the Soviet Union and other Communist countries with a request for arms and soon armaments were flowing in an increasing stream. By midsummer of 1960 there were 45,000 men in the armed forces and some 200,000 in the militia and, because of Fidel's uncertainty as to the loyalty of the armed forces, the militia had taken over many of the functions of the army.

During the first six months of the new regime, there were only occasional indications of the radically leftward turn the government would soon take. There were few known Communists in the government, and Castro's 26th of July Movement controlled the labor organizations. The PSP during this period quickly reorganized and awaited its opportunity. In March 1959 the new regime began the seizures of properties of Batista collaborators, a term broadly interpreted to mean any who had profited during the dictatorship, however indirectly the profits could be attributed to collaboration. Within a month there followed decrees greatly reducing rents and interest rates, and in May 1959 the Agrarian Reform law was decreed. The law, administered by the National Institute for Agrarian Reform (INRA), began to turn the revolution into a class struggle, pitting peasants against landowners. The director of INRA, Captain Antonio Nuñez Jiménez, a Communist long associated with Castro, began to bring Cuban and foreign Communists into all levels of the organization.

Abruptly, in mid-1959, the government moved sharply leftward. Already the upper and middle classes and the political moderates were having grave misgivings concerning policies of the government, particularly the Agrarian Reform law and its implementation. In June and July moderates were forced out of the government, including President Manuel Urrútia and five cabinet members. These were replaced by leftists, and Osvaldo Dorticós was appointed president. Dorticós had been a Communist party member in his youth and may well have been at the time he was appointed. He has, in any case, wholeheartedly supported the leftward trend. In November, Guevara was appointed President of the National Bank and thus became the economic commissar of the country. By this time various PSP leaders (Juan Marinello, Carlos Rafael Rodríguez, Blas Roca, and Lázaro Pena) had worked their way into the inner councils of the government, though they themselves did not hold government positions.

At the same time, the Communists were challenging the 26th of July Movement's control of the Cuban Confederation of Labor. At the convention of the Confederation in November 1959, a completely non-Communist executive committee was elected, whereupon Fidel Castro himself came before the convention to demand "unity," in effect forcing the Secretary General to appoint Communist sympathizers to the executive. Next the Communist delegates brought a motion to purge all officials associated with the Batista regime. They then brought charges against 26th of July leaders who had engaged in labor activity, however innocent, during the Batista period. Finally in the spring of 1960 the non-Communist Secretary General was forced to resign and the Communist victory in the labor movement was completed.

Economically, Cuba was breaking away from the United States and drifting toward the Communist countries. The Soviet Union apparently edged into the Cuban economy hesitantly at first, no doubt being uncertain as to the advantages which might accrue. But by the end of 1959 it had agreed to buy 500,000 tons of sugar. In February 1960 , First Deputy Premier Anastas Mikoyan on his visit to Cuba concluded a trade agreement for 5 million tons of sugar over a five year period in return for petroleum, iron and steel, machinery, technicians, and $100 million in credits. A series of aggravations (such as refusal to negotiate differences, and the expropriation of US owned properties without adequate compensation), led President Eisenhower in mid-1960 to cut the Cuban sugar quota, a subsidy which Guevara in March had called "a form of economic enslavement." Castro replied by seizing the US-owned oil refineries which had refused to process Soviet crude oil, whereupon the United States suspended all imports of Cuban sugar. In October, the United States embargoed all trade with Cuba, except for food and medicine; and in January 1961 broke diplomatic relations. Relations between the two countries were further exacerbated by the support given by the United States to the ill-fated attempt of Cuban exiles to establish a beachhead in Cuba in April 1961.

While Cuba became ever more dependent on the Soviet Union as her trading partner, the internal economy was being increasingly socialized. The agrarian reform, as it was implemented, did not provide the peasants with land except in a few instances, but rather joined them together in cooperatives and they became in effect tenants of the government. "Peoples stores" were opened on the cooperatives, selling articles at cut rates, thus forcing small merchants out of business. In the fall of 1960, after the seizure of the oil companies (sugar mills, the telephone and electric companies, hotels, and considerable tracts of land had already been taken over in the spring), other properties, both Cuban and foreign, were expropriated rapidly, and these included lands, factories, and mines. Only small shops remained in private hands by the end of the year.

One of the extraordinary features of Castro's regime is that the dictator has ruled without a party organization of his own. The 26th of July Movement was an amorphous grouping with no detailed formal organization. From time to time during the early period of the Castro regime, there were suggestions or discussions concerning the desirability of converting the movement into a political party, but all such suggestions were turned down by Castro. As 1959 wore on and brought the persecution of political opposition, as political activity was banned in 1960, and as anti-communism became synonymous with counterrevolution, the field was left open to the Communist party, the only remaining functioning party. By mid-1960 Castro was heading toward a fusion of the remains of the 26th of July Movement, the student *Directorio Revolucionario* (also an amorphous group which had dwindled to a shadow) and the Communist PSP.

Since the 26th of July Movement was reduced, in effect, to the top leadership, it was more a question of merging Castro and those around him into the Communist party. Because of the PSP's past relationship with Batista, for whom Castro harbors an implacable antipathy, it would be inappropriate for Castro simply to join the PSP. Instead, in August 1960, Secretary General Blas Roca of the PSP suggested the creation of a united party, merging all remaining revolutionary groups. The device was also obviously necessary because the mass support of the regime was directed at Castro, so that any government party would have to be Castro's party rather than one whose leadership he had taken over from Blas Roca. The support of the regime is centered primarily in the mass organizations (women, students, children, and others), which long since have passed to the control of the Communists.

For the past two years steps have been taken toward the merger. In a preparatory phase, the *Organizaciones Revolucionarias Integradas*

(ORI—Integrated Revolutionary Organizations) was to be formed, followed by its conversion into the *Partido Unido de la Revolución Socialista* (PURS—United Party of the Socialist Revolution). By roughly mid-1961 the ORI was functioning, though it is difficult to determine precisely when it came into being as news concerning it was released piecemeal and after the fact. A similar policy is followed regarding the PURS, which is to be "built on Marxist-Leninist principles" and will depend on "democratic centralism" in its organizational structure.[20] In March 1962 the establishment of the directorate of the ORI was announced,[21] with Castro as First Secretary and Raúl as Second Secretary.[22] In 1963 organizational work for the PURS went forward rapidly, and complete conversion of the ORI into the United Party appeared to be only a matter of time.

Important extensions of Communist power came in 1962 with the appointment in January of Juan Marinello as rector of the University of Havana;[23] in February of Carlos Rafael Rodriguez as president of INRA;[24] and with the creation in February of a three-man committee to direct the economy, composed of President Osvaldo Dorticós, Minister of Industry Che Guevara, and Carlos Rodriguez.[25]

We have not covered here all of the areas into which the Communists penetrated and which they came to control, but some of the main ones have been indicated. As to the question of how they have come to wield such power, the answer mainly revolves around the person of Fidel Castro, who in January 1959 held all of the reins of power in his own hands. It was Castro who handed the revolution to the Communists, betraying the very groups which had brought him to power. There is at present no satisfactory answer as to why he did so. His announcement of December 1, 1961, that he was a Marxist-Leninist and had held these views since his university days[26] is not to be taken too seriously. Castro is of the mold of the egocentric, demagogic Latin American *caudillo* type (he is, after all, the *Líder Maximo*) with something new added—Marxism-Leninism. Once he had made his decision in early 1959 to alter the nature of the revolution he found that he had increasingly to rely upon Communists to operate the bureaucracy and the economy, because in late 1959 and

[20] *Ibid.*, 123-124.
[21] *New York Times* (March 10, 1962).
[22] Washington *Evening Star* (March 23, 1962).
[23] Washington *Post and Times Herald* (January 11, 1962).
[24] *New York Times* (February 15, 1962).
[25] *New York Times* (February 25, 1962).
[26] Washington *Evening Star* (December 2, 1961).

especially during 1960 the middle class technical and managerial personnel fled the country in rising numbers.

In Cuba, as in the earlier cases we have examined, the power of the Communists and their success has depended on the permissiveness or active support of the executive. It is difficult to say whether enough control has been transferred from Castro to the Communists to make the process irreversible. His abrupt dismissal in March 1962 of Anibal Escalante, who had just been appointed to the directorate of the ORI, and the accompanying blast at "old Communist militants" who, he said, held "the belief that those revolutionaries who don't belong to them are not able to occupy important posts,"[27] indicates that Fidel still controlled Cuba's destiny. In fact it is now clear that the "old Communists" reached the zenith of their influence in early 1962 and that the dismissal of Escalante served to notify them that they were not to be permitted to take the country over completely. Thereafter, more "new Communists" and non-Communist members of the 26th of July movement appeared in prominent positions formerly held by "old Communists." The withdrawal by Khrushchev of missiles during the crisis in the fall of 1962 was viewed by Castro as a sign of weakness and tended to alienate him further from the Moscow-oriented Communists. Most Communist leaders, such as Blas Roca and Rodriguez, have, however, made their peace with Castro by vigorously supporting his call for revolution in Latin America, a stand much closer to that of Peking than that of Moscow. Despite the reduction of the influence wielded by "old Communists" Communists are to be found in every sphere of national life. They are, moreover, significantly augmented by large numbers of advisers and technicians from the Soviet Union, Czechoslovakia, China, and other Communist countries. Important as the Communists continue to be, it appears that after five years of revolution the Communists probably still need Castro more than he needs them, though the mutual dependence is great on both sides.

Now we may examine the lessons the Communists learned in Guatemala, to see whether they have been applied to Cuba:

1. The working class and not the bourgeoisie must lead the revolution. The Cuban revolution was led by the middle class, but Fidel Castro delivered it, if not to the working class, to the Communists. He had or developed the mass support that the Communists could never have obtained alone.

[27] Washington *Evening Star* (March 27, 1962).

2. Commercial ties with the Communist countries should be increased. Cuba's pattern of trade has been completely overturned and trade with the USSR probably amounted to $750 million in 1962.[28]

3. The state should allow the exercise of democratic rights only to its friends and should employ dictatorial methods against its enemies. The second part of the conclusion certainly has been applied in Cuba, but the regime does not allow democratic rights even to its friends.

4. The traditional (or "old") army should not be allowed to remain intact. The Cuban Army was demobilized early in 1959 and the rebel Army, after being superseded temporarily by the militia, was retrained and re-equipped.

We have seen what happened in Cuba, but it is of interest to note the views of the Soviets and other Communists as to what occurred. The Soviet view has changed considerably, and understandably so, over the past few years. Until quite recently the view was that Cuba had passed beyond the stage of national democracy to one in which a non-Communist government was cooperating with the Communists in building socialism. In the May Day slogans for 1962, Cuba was said to be "embarked on the path of building socialism," and was listed directly after Czechoslovakia (the last of the people's democracies in Russian alphabetical order) and before Yugoslavia. By 1963, Cuba was described in the May Day slogans as having already begun to build socialism, and was listed alphabetically among the people's democracies. According to the Soviets, the PSP "gave the lives of many of its best sons for victory" and the party militants "fought for the establishment of a revolutionary underground in the towns and villages."[29] Castro and the *Gramna* survivors organized a "broad insurrectionary movement against the Batista regime."[30] By that time the people had become familiar with Castro's plan for economic development, agrarian reform, industrialization, and nationalization, as well as his criticism of free enterprise. Thus, the strong implication that Castro's pre-1959 pronouncements were already permeated with socialism.[31] "The entire Cuban people have acquired broad democratic rights and freedoms, the road has been opened for them to

[28] Gavin Young, "Fidelistas Are Proud to be 'Odd Men Out.'" Washington *Post and Times Herald* (July 15, 1962), E4.

[29] "Splocheniye sil kubinskoy revolyutii" [The Rallying of the Forces of the Cuban Revolution], *Pravda* (April 11, 1962).

[30] L. Surogin, "Landmarks of the Cuban Revolution," *Int. Aff.*, No. 5 (1960), 101.

[31] *Ibid.*, 101-102.

better living conditions, happiness and prosperity," Khrushchev has said.[32] The existence of the "world Socialist system" ensured the success of the struggle against imperialism.[33] "Cuba has now completed its agrarian reform and nationalization of the property of the foreign monopolies . . . and is carrying out the first Socialist revolution in Latin America."[34] The present process of organizing the PURS is described in these terms: "The striving for unity of all revolutionary forces has found vivid expression in the movement for the establishment of a single Marxist-Leninist party."[35] The key to the Soviet interpretation (which is the one accepted in Communist quarters generally) is, of course, the pre-dating of Castro's trend toward socialism, and the ascribing of his mass support to such ideas. Given this modification of history, all that follows from January 1959 to the present is perfectly reasonable.[36]

The Chinese Communist view seems to coincide with that of the Soviets. Castro and the Cubans, after his overly frank statement in December 1961 that though he had been a Marxist for some years he had not revealed his views because he needed the support of moderates to win power, have been content to emphasize the revolutionary role of the peasants, under the leadership of the workers and revolutionary intellectuals, and the importance of guerrilla warfare.[37] Luis Carlos Prestes, the Brazilian Communist, is realistic without being too frank: "In Cuba, specific conditions permitted a democratic

[32] N. S. Khrushchev, Report to the Twenty Second Congress of the CPSU, October 18, 1961, *CDSP*, XIII, No. 40 (November 1, 1961), 9-10.

[33] G. N. Shevyakov, "Soviet Co-operation with Cuba," *Int. Aff.* No. 3 (1962), 74.

[34] *Ibid.*, 75.

[35] "The Rallying of the Forces of the Cuban Revolution," *Pravda* (April 11, 1962).

[36] There are also Western interpretations which maintain either that Castro's movement was Communist from the start: especially Nathaniel Weyl, *Red Star Over Cuba* (New York 1960), and Earl E. T. Smith, *The Fourth Floor: An Account of the Castro Communist Revolution* (New York 1962); or that Castro was driven into the arms of the Communists by American opposition to his reforms: C. Wright Mills, *Listen, Yankee: The Revolution in Cuba* (New York 1960), Herbert L. Matthews, *The Cuban Story* (New York 1961), William Appleman Williams, *The United States, Cuba, and Castro* (New York 1962), and Maurice Zeitlin and Robert Scheer, *Cuba: Tragedy in Our Hemisphere* (New York 1963).

[37] Fidel Castro, "Second Declaration of Havana," February 4, 1962 (*Prensa Latina*, February 4). The emphasis on the role of the peasants may echo Mao's dependence upon them for his revolution. See Joseph R. Fiszman, "The Appeal of Maoism in Pre-Industrial Semicolonial Political Cultures," *Political Science Quarterly*, LXXIV (1959), 79. In this connection it may be noted that Che Guevara drew on the works of Mao Tse Tung in writing his book, *Guerrilla Warfare* (New York 1961). There is considerable affinity on the part of the Cubans for the Chinese, as they feel that their guerrilla experience may be compared with that of the Chinese Communists. See also P. S. H. Tang and J. Maloney, *The Chinese Comunist Impact on Cuba* (Chestnut Hill, Mass. 1962).

bourgeois revolution to be replaced later by the construction of socialism," but he is careful not to go into detail as to the nature of the specific conditions.[38]

British Guiana

If Communism comes to British Guiana,[39] it will be imposed from above, as was the case in Guatemala and in Cuba. The question of communism revolves about the person of Dr. Cheddi Jagan, premier of the little country and leader of the People's Progressive Party (PPP), who openly states that he is a Marxist but denies allegations of membership in the Communist party. Jagan has been deeply influenced by his wife, the former Janet Rosenberg, whom he met and married while studying at Northwestern University. Whether or not she was a member of the Young Communist League at the time (which she denies), she held radical views and was active in left-wing organizations. The couple returned to Georgetown in 1943 and Jagan soon became active in a militant labor movement. In 1946 he founded the Political Affairs Committee, with the purpose of providing political indoctrination to workers. Out of this organization developed the PPP, established in 1950. Since then the PPP has been the dominant force in local politics. In the PPP, Jagan has been able to bring together elements of all races in British Guiana (the population of which is about half East Indian and one-third negro) and, despite the party's ultimate goal of a socialist state, most social classes.

In 1953 a new constitution was promulgated aimed at leading the colony toward self government. For the first time a majority of the members of the legislature were to be popularly elected, and ministers, directly responsible to the governor, were to be appointed from the assembly. The PPP swept the elections held in April 1953 and the Jagans, among others, were given ministerial positions. The PPP, not satisfied with the degree of autonomy granted by the 1953

[38] Prestes, in a lecture delivered in Rio de Janeiro, June 28, 1962, quoted in *Prensa Latina.*

[39] The best book generally available is Raymond T. Smith, *British Guiana* (London 1962), which includes a section on politics. The White Paper, *British Guiana: Suspension of the Constitution,* Cmd. 8980 (London 1953), should be consulted for the events of 1953. It is, of course, a justification of the steps taken by the government. For recent events, see "The Atlantic Report: British Guiana," *The Atlantic,* CCX (July 1962), 22-25; and J. Robert Moskin, "Memo on a Marxist," *Look* XXVI (August 14, 1962), 66, 68-69. Curiously enough, the article by Moskin was reprinted in the Havana weekly *Bohemia* (September 28, 1962), 76-77, 85.

constitution, now set out to create a constitutional crisis to force a further liberalization. There followed several months of turbulence until October when the governor declared an emergency. The British government suspended the constitution, British troops were brought in, and PPP leaders were arrested. The British government considered these drastic steps necessary to preserve law and order, to safeguard private property, and to prevent the establishment of a one-party Communist regime. The government issued a White Paper concerning the crisis which listed various actions of the ministers that led to the crisis. These included fomenting strikes for political purposes, attempting to oust trade unions by legislative action, threats of violence against opponents, the removal of a ban on the entry of West Indian Communists, and the attempt to remove a ban on the entry of subversive literature.

A split occurred in the PPP in 1955, when Lyndon Forbes Burnham, a negro lawyer, broke with the Jagans' extremist faction in the PPP, and ultimately formed the People's National Congress. The break raised for the first time the element of race in politics, for Burnham draws most of his support from the urban negro element, while Jagan's support comes mainly from the rural East Indians. Thus in the 1957 elections under an interim constitution, the Jagan faction won nine seats (all from rural constitutencies), while the Burnham faction won three, all in Georgetown.

Under the interim constitution Jagan and the PPP acted circumspectly, biding their time. In 1961 a new constitution was promulgated, granting considerably more autonomy than that of 1953 and looking toward complete independence in May 1962. Elections held in August gave the PPP a clear majority, and Jagan was chosen Premier. He soon turned to the United Kingdom and the United States, seeking loans to finance land projects and to develop state-owned industry. When assistance was not forthcoming as quickly or in the volume he desired (and because his avowed Marxism discouraged foreign private investors), he determined that taxes would have to be raised to finance his projects. The taxes and other features of his proposed budget presented in February 1962 created resentment in urban areas, which would be hardest hit by the measures and where most of Burnham's support lay. Burnham and other opposition leaders cooperated to organize a successful general strike which led to destructive rioting in Georgetown. Jagan, who had strongly criticized the government for the use of troops in 1953, now ironically was forced to request that British troops be brought in to restore order and that the date of independence be postponed.

The responsibility of the office he holds, as well as the demonstration of the strength of the opposition, may lead Jagan to move slowly in his program of socialization. Nonetheless, he has visited Castro and has agreed to sell rice to Cuba as well as to send sugar workers to assist with the Cuban harvest, he has accepted Moscow's offer to provide scholarships, and has negotiated with Polish and Czechoslovakian trade unions. Jagan has stated that he will accept aid from any country and, for the time, appears to wish to follow a neutralist policy. Thus far Marxism has appealed only to a relatively small group of intellectuals and activists in the PPP, so that if Jagan should decide to move leftward he will have to contend not only with the opposition parties, but also with factions within his own party, which includes moderate and conservative members of the East Indian community.

The Communist View of Latin America

Having dwelled in some detail on the more notable Communist experiences in Latin America, and before examining the possibilities the Communists may see in the use of political revolution there, we need to pause and try to see the area and its economic, political and social processes through red glasses—to see the area as the Communists do. The fact is that the Soviet Communists see very little of the picture. A recent article in *Voprosy Istorii* [Problems of History] deplores the general lack of Soviet scholars with an interest in Latin America and the unsatisfactory number of books and other studies produced on Latin America. "Our scientists," states the writer, "have not yet undertaken any serious attempts at a complex study of [Latin America's] problems . . . We are still publishing far too little scholarly material presenting a deep analysis of the economic and political processes now going on in Latin America."[40] The writer recognizes an "extremely significant shortcoming" in Soviet studies of Latin America, "the absence of a differentiated approach to specific Latin American countries."[41]

A review of Soviet studies on Latin America shows that the best articles on Latin America were usually written by native Communists and that the Soviet periodicals tend to rely to a consilderable extent on articles or transcripts of speeches of such luminaries as Blas Roca

[40] S. S. Mikhaylov, "Izucheniye Latinskoy Ameriki v Sovetskom Soyuze" [The Study of Latin America in the Soviet Union], *Voprosy Istorii*, No. 4 (1962), 98-106, in JPRS No. 13980, 24-36.

[41] *Ibid.*, 33.

and Fidel Castro of Cuba, and the persuasive First Secretary of the Uruguayan Communist Party, Rodney Arismendi. Naturally, the Soviet government itself relies also on other sources of information to which we do not have access, such as the embassy staffs. In the articles by local Communists, a number of weaknesses are evident: they have a natural desire to present themselves, the activities of their parties, and the receptivity of the masses to their doctrines in the best light, and therefore tend to overstate their achievements and popularity (such as the inclination to imply that the Communist party militants were in the forefront leading every strike, no matter what the facts may be); they have been presented by Marxism with a rigid explanation for the source of the ills of their countries so that their analyses must be made within that framework, with the result that they, like the Soviets, frequently make little differentiation between the great variations in the state of development among the Latin countries.

Latin America is far from being a homogeneous area. Politically, the countries range from relatively stable democracies, such as Costa Rica and Uruguay, to dictatorships such as Haiti. Economically, they range from primitive Haiti to the relatively industrialized and complex economies of Argentina, Brazil, and Mexico. Socially, they range from the almost entirely European and substantially middle class population of Uruguay, to Bolivia with its large proportion of Indians barely touched by the process of modernization.

The Communist view of Latin American politics is rather uniform for the entire area.[42] The proletariat and the peasantry are repressed and deprived of political rights. Usually the small landholders and small businessmen are included in the repressed groups, as are sometimes the lower middle class as a whole, as well as intellectuals and "progressive" elements. The upper middle class is seldom included in the repressed groups. The nationalistic elements of this class may be recognized, but it is generally considered that their interests, as busi-

[42] The following is a composite of views stated frequently by local Communists as well as the Soviets. See for example, the "Second Declaration of Havana;" the "Draft Program of the Chilean Communist Party," *El Siglo*, Santiago (December 17, 1961), 9-13, in *Translations on International Communist Developments*, No. 120, JPRS 12718, 1-56; *Hoy*, Havana (August 24, 1961), 3, in *Translations on International Communist Developments*, No. 75, JPRS 12228, 1-7; S. Mikhailov, "The Giant Wakes Up," *IntAff*, No. 5 (1962), 92-94; and Trinidad Martillo, "The Latin American Situation," *IntAff*, No. 5 (1959), 56-63. See also A. Shulgovskiy, "Imperializm i ideologiya natsional-reformizma v Latinskoy Amerike" [Imperialism and the Ideology of National-Reformism in Latin America], MEIMO, No. 8 (1961), 45-59; and V. Ya. Avarin and M. V. Danilevich (eds.), *Natsional'no-osvoboditel'noe dvizheniye v Latinskoy Amerike na sovremennom etape* [The National-Liberation Movement in Contemporary Latin America] (Moscow 1961).

nessmen and property owners, coincide with those of the ruling circles and that they will normally act in concert with the rulers. The ruling circles are composed of the big landowners (latifundists), big industrialists and financiers, and the military, who act either in co-operation with or at the direct orders of U. S. monopoly capital or the US government.

Basically, of course, governments (or political parties) are viewed as democratic and progressive or as dictatorial and against the interests of the people, depending on the policies of the government toward the Communist party, the Communist international system, and Cuba. Thus the moderate leftist, anti-Communist President of Venezuela, Romulo Betancourt, was "supported by the people and democratic forces" in a coup attempt against his government in April 1960,[43] but he is now a "reactionary dictator who kills and seizes patriots."[44] The radical change in Betancourt's status has come as a result of his stiffening attitude toward Cuba and local extremists since early 1960. The liberal and reformist army-backed Directorate which ruled El Salvador in 1961 until elections were held was considered a "tool of the imperialists and the local oligarchy, ruling with bayonet and rifle."[45] Parties which are reformist but anti-Communist (such as Haya de la Torre's APRA in Peru, Betancourt's *Acción Democratica* in Venezuela, and the ruling *Movimiento Nacionalista Revolucionario* in Bolivia) represent "the most rotten kind of reformism" and have "betrayed the peoples' movements."[46] These examples are typical.

The Communist view of the economic dynamics of Latin America is almost as stylized as their view of political developments.[47] Each of

[43] V. Adrianov, "Venezuela: The Lesson of Recent Events," *IntAff*, No. 6 (1960), 83-84.

[44] Article on Venezuelan events, *Krasnaya Zvezda,* quoted by Tass, June 22, 1962; Luiz Carlos Prestes in a lecture in Rio de Janeiro quoted by *Prensa Latina* (June 28, 1962).

[45] José Sánchez Verde, Address at the 22nd Party Congress of the CPSU on 28 October 1961, *Pravda* (October 30, 1961).

[46] "Draft Program of the Chilean Communist Party," *El Siglo,* Santiago (December 17, 1961), para. 14, JPRS 12718, 19.

[47] See note 42. The article by the Uruguayan Communist Trinidad Martillo is the best analysis of the subject which I have seen either in the Soviet or Latin American Communist press. See also the interview with the articulate Uruguayan Communist leader Rodney Arismendi in *El Popular,* Montevideo (December 24, 1961), 3, in *Translations on International Communist Developments,* No. 98, JPRS 12498, 31-42. See also speech of Anastas Mikoyan to 22nd Party Congress of the CPSU on 20 October 1961, in *CDSP,* XIII, No. 51 (January 17, 1962), 13-14; and "Old Promises in New Wrappings," *Izvestia* (April 12, 1961), in *CDSP,* XIII, No. 15 (May 10, 1961), 30.

the Latin American countries depends on one or two raw material exports for its foreign exchange. Prices paid for these goods by American imperialism are kept at a low level, while imperialism raises the prices of finished products it sells in return. In addition, wealth is drained from the country by means of remittance of profits on investments as well as interest and repayments on foreign loans. The aim of American imperialism is to prevent the industrialization of Latin America and thus assure continued dependence on the United States as a market for raw materials and as a source of finished products. The big landowners, industrialists, and financiers are allied with imperialism, and in cooperation with it make excessive profits. Their aims are to hold wage levels down in order to maintain their sources of cheap labor, while at the same time real wages are lowered as a result of inflation. Such industry as exists is either owned outright by foreign monopolies or is developed by them in conjunction with local capitalists. The large enterprises squeeze out the medium and small producers or enterprises, thus concentrating ever more economic power in their hands. Similarly, the big landowners squeeze out smallholders, buying up their land and forcing them either to move to the slums of the cities or to become tenant farmers. Therefore, the economic situation and standard of living of urban and rural workers continues to deteriorate while the capitalists prosper, and since the Second World War the gap between the wealth of the exploiters and the poverty of the exploited has widened.

There is some basis in reality for these views, distorted though they often are. The dependence of most Latin American countries on one or two main exports is well known; and world prices for these products have generally been low or declining in recent years. Also, profits on capital invested in Latin America are substantially higher than on investments in the United States, but the risks are also considered to be greater. Latin American industry is heavily capitalized by foreign investors and firms, but most countries require that over half the capital be from native investors and have required that an ever increasing proportion of employees at all levels be their own nationals. Thus the foreign contribution usually consists primarily of production machinery and technical knowledge. It is also true that landholdings have tended to increase in size, particularly in certain countries such as Chile. This is a result of the natural movement to the city which has been in progress for some decades, but may also stem partly from a deliberate policy of individual landowners to squeeze out their neighbors and acquire their lands. The standard of living in Latin America has risen in recent years, substantially in some countries such as Mexico, but on the other hand salaried and wage workers have suffered a great deal in those countries which have been experiencing severe inflation, such as Chile, Brazil, Bolivia, and Argentina.

The Communist views of Latin American society are linked, of course, with their views on political and economic developments.[48] The increasing foreign and domestic economic pressures on the exploited masses have led to rising class antagonisms and anti-imperialist feeling. Most urban dwellers live in slums under hopeless conditions. Unemployment is chronic and underemployment is permanent. On the other hand, bankers, speculators, those at the top levels of large enterprises, importers, and venal government and military officials form a new and morally corrupt plutocracy. "Regression or stagnation has permeated the entire social and cultural fabric of the various republics,"[49] while the plutocracy lives a "life of princes in the midst of the desperate situation of the people."[50]

This view, too, is overdrawn, though poverty is the lot of a major portion of the Latin American population. The movement to cities, along with high rates of population growth, has aggravated underemployment and added to the numbers of slum dwellers. The economic disparity between the poor and the rich has always been marked, and in recent years the disparity has perhaps become more obvious because of the conspicuous consumption of the newly rich—the entrepreneurs who have made fortunes during and since the Second World War. The fact is, however that now there is greater social mobility than ever before and it seems to be increasing. Horatio Alger still lives in many a Latin American who has risen from humble origins to become an industrialist or financier, or who on a more modest scale has become a professional man, an intellectual, or a middle class functionary.

Communist Uses of Internal Conflict

The appeal of communism, based on its avowed intentions to alleviate the conditions outlined above, is potentially relatively broad. To this must be added the appearance of sweet reasonableness and the line of peaceful coexistence of the post-Stalin Soviet Union; the offers to

[48] Again, see note 42, and particularly the article by Martillo.
[49] Martillo, "The Latin American Situation," *IntAff*, No. 5 (1959), 61.
[50] "Draft Program of the Chilean Communist Party," *El Siglo* (December 17, 1961), JPRS 12718, 12.

trade those export commodities on which the Latin American countries depend for the finished goods or petroleum which they require; and the attractive sight of Fidel slapping the "Colossus of the North," while "building socialism" with considerable material aid from the Communist countries and aligning his country with them. Effective Soviet propaganda, particularly concerning space successes, has given the impression that in less than half a century the USSR has evolved from backwardness to an industrial, technological and military position superior to that of the United States—and that other backward countries can do the same, if they will only ride the wave of the future and follow the path of Marx. The Communists have attempted to capitalize on the rising nationalism coupled with xenophobia, which cut across class lines and reach from the lowest very often to the highest levels of the political, economic, and social structures. Added to all of these factors is the reluctance of the political and economic leadership of most countries to effect long overdue reforms (witness the difficulty under the Alliance for Progress program of persuading governments to institute land and tax reforms) and their tendency to label all such reforms as Communist.

The means by which the Communists hope to develop these appeals and gain power range from the peaceful revolution (such as advocated by the parties in Chile and Uruguay)[51] to the violent (the Cuban Communists).[52] Even those advocating the peaceful road often add, more or less as a postscript, some sentiment such as "the peaceful way does not imply passiveness,"[53] or the "stubborn opposition of the ruling class may one day make it necessary to adopt the way of violent revolution."[54] In other countries, parties are split by factions supporting one or the other of the "roads." Thus in Ecuador an extremist faction of the party has supported guerrillas, and in Brazil the supporters of violent revolution have left Prestes' party to form a rival Communist group. The difference in viewpoint is to a large

[51] Speech of Secretary-General Luis Corvalan to the 12th National Congress of the Communist Party of Chile, *El Siglo,* Santiago (March 14, 1962), in *Translations of International Communist Developments,* No. 160, JPRS 13649, 19-20; Arismendi, *El Popular,* Montevideo (December 24, 1961), 3, in JPRS 12498.

[52] "El camino válido para América: la revolución," *Revolución* (December 1, 1961). This is an account of a lecture given by Carlos Rafael Rodriguez on November 30, 1961. Statements of Fidel Castro, Che Guevara, Blas Roca and others agree that all of Latin America should follow the Cuban example.

[53] "The Peaceful Way Does Not Imply Passiveness," *El Siglo,* Santiago (March 18, 1962), 10, in *Translations on International Communist Developments,* No. 160, JPRS 13649, 155-157.

[54] Arismendi, *El Popular,* Montevideo (December 24, 1961), 3, JPRS 12498.

extent a practical matter. In countries where the party is too small or weak to accomplish much either at the polls or through violence, the peaceful road is chosen. This is also true in those countries in which the party hopes to gain at the polls, as in Uruguay, and particularly in Chile, where the Communists have joined with other parties in a coalition which has prospects of winning the elections in 1964. The Chileans understandably adopt a "don't rock the boat" attitude, since violence would only damage their position and prospects. In Venezuela, on the other hand, the Communist party (or a large faction of it) sees chances of gains through violence and has supported extremist violence.[55] The main difference in the thinking of the advocates of the two "roads" lies in the utilization of guerrilla warfare to gain their ends. The advocates of a peaceful road are quite willing to use strikes, mass demonstrations, agitation, and the other forms of violence short of measures which would lead to significant repressive reaction from the government.

The Communists have several means at their disposal to make use of internal conflict to gain their objectives. Labor, the peasants, and students are used in mass actions, while the ultimate method, guerrilla warfare or civil war, may make use of all of these groups and others as well.

Urban labor is, of course, the favorite group of the Communists and most stress is laid on acquiring its support and encouraging its militancy. Though Communist influence in the labor movement in Latin America is considerable, it is only in a few countries that they have outright control of important unions or significant segments of the labor movements. Thus it is often the case that if they cannot call or control a strike, they may influence a strike in progress and give it political overtones. To legitimate wage or working condition demands may be added calls for the diplomatic recognition of and trade with all nations, friendship with Cuba, release of imprisoned Communists, legalization of the Communist parties in those countries where it is outlawed, land reform, and anti-U. S. slogans such as denunciations of imperialism, neo-colonialism, and the Alliance for Progress. The Communist purpose in strikes is not necessarily violence, but simply to disrupt the economy as much as possible, to demonstrate

[55] See, for example, statement of Communist Deputy Eduardo Machado quoted in "Puerto Cabello Revolt Stimulated by Extremist Congressman," *La Esfera,* Caracas (June 5, 1962); "Contents of Secret PCV Manifesto Revealed," *La Esfera,* Caracas (June 13, 1962).

the party's concern with the welfare of labor, and if possible to identify the labor movement with its aims.

Urban labor also plays an important role in mass demonstrations, which may be joined by other groups as well, notably students. Such demonstrations may be spontaneous or leftist but non-Communist inspired, in which case the Communists may seek to influence them to their ends, or they may be incited by Communist agitators. There are any number of causes which in the United States might lead merely to a flurry of letters to the editor, but which in Latin America may result in demonstrations—an unpopular bill before the congress, a rise in bus fares, the execution of a convicted spy in the United States, the passage of some law in the U. S. Congress (such as one regulating sugar quotas), or an attempt to raise scholastic standards in the high schools or colleges.

The first purpose of the Communists is to divert the demonstration or influence it by linking the grievance with anti-American and pro-Communist sentiments. As in the case of strikes, the purpose is to imply that the masses of the people support the Communist program and to identify the Communist program in the eyes of the people with popular causes. The Communists may go even further, attempting to incite the demonstrators to violence, attacking police or security troops which may try to control the mob, or smashing and looting shops or other enterprises, particularly those which are linked in any way with American capital. At some point in the demonstration, the mob will almost certainly be led or urged by the agitators to attack the American Embassy, of which many of recent construction thoughtfully provide large and inviting expanses of plate glass. The goading of police or military security personnel frequently leads to violent retaliation resulting in deaths. The funerals of these martyrs then provide additional occasions for demonstrations. Violence is used in demonstrations in order to pressure the government or to frighten police and moderates with the power of the people. Strikes, demonstrations, and violence were typically used successfully by Communists and other extremists in Ecuador in November 1961 when President Velasco resigned and part of the military sought to prevent Vice President Arosemena from taking office, fearing that he would favor the Communists.

The students play a significant part in Communist plans. For almost two centuries the universities in Latin America have been centers of what might be called leftist (and more recently Communist) thought, and university students have a long tradition of participation in political activities.[56] Communists may be found in greater or smaller numbers on the faculties of most state or federal universities. University autonomy, much prized by the institutions of higher education, gives the university the right of regulating its affairs free of outside interference—including the provision that police or other government security forces may not come on the campus. (It may be noted that the University of Havana lost its autonomous status after Castro brought the Communists to power.) Normally there are no limitations concerning the time taken to complete courses of study, resulting in the many "young student leaders" (as they are usually described) in their forties or fifties, including many experienced Communist agitators. A considerable number of the universities in Latin America are not educational institutions as we understand the term in this country. A Mexican writer described the University of Havana in 1957: "in recent years the principal activity there has been politics. . . . More than lawyers, physicians, architects, engineers, chemists, the venerable house of learning has specialized in preparing political bosses. . . ."[57] The same could be said for a number of universities, including several in Mexico, where concern with politics, rather than studies, is the order of the day. The Communists have had moderate success in their work among university students, and more recently have been drawing on high school or even primary school youngsters in demonstrations and riots. In 1962, Caracas was rocked by several severe anti-government riots in which university and high school students participated.

It has been only in very recent years that the Communists have begun to develop a more than perfunctory interest in the peasants. Castro's reliance on the peasants during his successful revolution has no doubt been a contributory factor. The recent statements of most of the parties and party leaders stress the necessity for more work among the *campesinos,* both in indoctrination and in organizing unions of rural workers.[58] In working among the peasants the Com-

[56] M. D. Rosenberg, "Collegian Real Power in Politics of Latins," *Washington Post and Times Herald* (July 2, 1961) is a good, brief summary of the role of the student and the university in Latin American politics.

[57] R. S. Sosa Ferreyro in *Excelsior,* Mexico City (June 30, 1957), as quoted in James, *Cuba,* 33.

[58] See, for example, speech by Oscar Astudillo, Secretary of the Communist Party of Chile, to the 12th National Congress of the Party, *El Siglo,* Santiago (March 14, 1962), 1-6, in *Translations on International Communist Developments,* No. 160, JPRS 13649, 95-101, especially 99; address of Rodney Arismendi to the 22nd

munists play on their legitimate desires for land reform, pointing to the USSR, China, and Cuba as the examples which should be followed in this field (without, however, being too specific concerning the communes in China and avoiding the fact that Cuba's cooperatives are more similar to the Soviet state farms than to the usual concept of a cooperative). Although the Communists have not been altogether responsible for recent invasions of private land by squatters, they have encouraged the movement and in some cases have been among the leaders. Poor peasants are gathered and at times transported some distance to a property chosen in advance, and preferably held by foreign interests, though lands of native large landholders are also fair game. The peasants are then placed on the land, living off of it or neighboring farms while their leaders demand that the government parcel the land out to the squatters. Such movements have occurred in the recent past in Mexico, Peru, Brazil, Costa Rica, Honduras, Colombia, and other countries, and have at times led to violence.

Guerrilla warfare is the road to revolution strongly recommended to the Latin Americans by Cuba and Communist China and, in somewhat muted tones, by the Soviet Union. Castro's success has persuaded many Communists as well as non-Communist extremists of its virtues. The Soviet view is that guerrilla warfare may be resorted to if sufficient progress cannot be made toward Communist goals by peaceful means, and the Soviets point out that "guerrilla warfare is the most typical form of armed struggle in national-liberation wars."[59] According to Khrushchev it is the local party (as the vanguard of the proletariat) which must decide "what forms and methods of struggle will be selected . . . under concrete historical circumstances."[60] As we have seen, most parties (certainly most party leaders, who are overwhelmingly attached firmly to Moscow) follow this line—that the revolution can be peaceful, but open warfare may be a last resort.

During 1962, there were guerrilla outbreaks, most of them very modest in scope, in Venezuela, Ecuador, and Guatemala. The extent

---

Congress of the CPSU on October 24, 1961, *Pravda* (October 26, 1961); address of Rodney Arismendi at opening of 18th Party Congress of Uruguayan Communist Party, Montevideo, *Prensa Latina* (June 30, 1962); and address of Pedro Saad of Ecuador at the 22nd Congress of the CPSU on October 25, 1961, *Pravda* (October 28, 1961).

[59] Y. Dolgopolov, "National-Liberation Wars in the Present Epoch," *IntAff*, No. 2 (1962), 21.

[60] N. S. Khrushchev's report on new victories of the world Communist movements, *Kommunist*, No. 1 (January 1961), in *CDSP*, XIII, No. 3 (February 15, 1961), 16-19; No. 4 (February 22, 1961), 8-15, 24.

of complicity of the Communists in Guatemala seems to be quite small, though there is a possibility that Cuba was involved to some extent. In Ecuador, the Communist party leadership has opposed violence, and the small guerrilla outbreak in April 1962 was mainly the work of the pro-Castro Ecuadorian Revolutionary Youth Union, though individual Communists seem to have participated. In Venezuela the Communists were involved in the small-scale guerrilla outbreaks in various part of the country during the first half of 1962.[61] These guerrilla groups were heavily influenced by Cuba and may have received assistance from Castro's government.[62] Recruiting for the guerrilla bands was done on university campuses, particularly at the Central University of Venezuela in Caracas. University autonomy gave the leftist groups a free hand in operating on the campus, safe from interference by security forces.[63] Communists, along with other leftist extremists, were also influential in inciting the rebellions of military personnel, mainly Marine Corps, at Carupano in May 1962 and Puerto Cabello in early June.[64] The latter, a particularly bloody affair, was joined by large numbers of civilian leftist elements.

In Colombia, guerrilla warfare—amounting almost to civil war at times—has been in progress for over a decade. The *violencia,* as it is called, began originally as warfare between partisans in the country side of the two major political parties, the Conservative and the Liberal. In recent years the political character has tended to disappear and the violence has become banditry on a large scale, including complete control of sizable areas by various leaders. The Communist Party has pondered for some time the advisability of supporting certain of the leaders and it appears, from the evidence, that it is now providing some assistance to a few of them.

Cuba has supported all of these armed activities in its propaganda, and probably has provided some assistance, both arms and training, to various groups involved. China has also shown approval in its propaganda.[65] The attitude of the Soviet Union seems to be to support the uprisings once started, but not to encourage the use of armed conflict.

An intensification of the Communist use of internal war techniques

[61] See *Daily Journal,* Caracas (April 4, 1962); *El Nacional,* Caracas (April 15, 1962); *El Universal,* Caracas (April 21, 1962); *El Nacional* (April 25, 1962).

[62] *El Universal,* Caracas (April 22, 1962).

[63] *El Nacional,* Caracas (April 21, 1962); *Daily Journal,* Caracas (April 12, 1962).

[64] "Contents of Secret PCV Manifesto Revealed," *La Esfera,* Caracas (June 13, 1962).

[65] See, for example, the editorial "Salute to Heroic Cuban People," *Da Gong Bao* (April 19, 1962).

in Latin America may be expected in the future. Favorable political, economic, and social conditions for the use of such tactics will undoubtedly exist to a greater or lesser degree throughout the area as those nations undergo the stresses of modernization. Unless the communization of Cuba soon ends in a complete fiasco (and the USSR has shown a willingness to subsidize the country heavily), Castro's example will continue to be an attractive alternative for leftist extremists. Of equal importance is the greater attention being given Latin America by the Soviet Union, as indicated by the significant increase in the study of the area by Soviet scholars, the increase in the publication of Soviet books concerning the area, and the creation in early 1962 of a Latin American Institute of the Academy of Sciences.[66] That interest in the area is higher not only among scholars but in the Communist party of the Soviet Union as well has been demonstrated by the dispatch of the Soviet delegations to the 12th Congress of the Chilean Communist Party in March 1962 (the first to a Latin American party congress), and to the 18th Congress of the Uruguayan Communist Party in June and July 1962. The more detailed studies by scholars will equip the Soviet Union to better understand the political, economic, and social processes in the region and to correct the rather superficial analyses upon which they now depend. The Soviet Union will then be in more favorable position to seize on advantageous situations.

[66] Mikhaylov, 100-102.

13

Sub-Saharan Africa

WILLIAM H. LEWIS

The African Dilemma

Africa and Africans are now caught up in the universality of history. No longer will the continent's chronicles reflect simply the struggle of clan groups, tribes, and ethnic confederations for political supremacy within a narrowly defined geographic area; or the strivings of royal dynasties to survive the onslaughts of marauding pastoralists. Sub-Saharan Africa has now entered the mainstream of world history—culturally, technically, and politically. The resulting implications for Africa, however, are probably no more serious and far-reaching than are the possible consequences for the West. For better or for worse, Africa has become one of the central theaters of competitive coexistence, and is part of the continuing struggle which this political euphemism connotes.

The existing world order has not only introduced the Sub-Saharan regions to the universalism of contemporary history, but it has also established the broad perimeters within which the primary actors—the Africans—must shape their future political and social roles. These perimeters are the new collectivities of political reality, the modern nation-states which defy tribal landmarks, ethnic configurations, and traditional patterns of living and of interrelationship. Within these compartments, Africans are faced with the need to establish a wholly revised hierarchy of loyalties, as well as reciprocal rights and obligations. Indeed, an entirely new identity must be shaped for diverse groupings of peoples who, traditionally, have maintained relationships predicated upon rivalry rather than cooperation.

The search for identity comes at a time when the entire basis of life in Africa has been severely shaken. All human relationships have been placed in flux by the impact of the West's technological revolution. Particularly affected in much of the continent are the sub-strata of existing social and political systems—the traditional beliefs and customs that form the basis of family and tribal structure. The personal and societal disorganization which have accompanied this change have often been profound. In addition to the depersonalization of society—

particularly in such highly Westernized sectors as modern mines and plantations, commercial emporia, and coastal urban agglomerations—the African is faced with a high ambiguity of norms, a sense of cultural discontinuity, and a loss of personal orientations.

For Africa's emergent leadership and the fragile collectivities which they must govern, the primary concern for the future is the fashioning of new social norms, political identities, and developmental goals. The vehicle most frequently chosen is the mass party; the doctrine enunciated is African socialism; and the label of identity, the "African personality." The inherent obligation of the political party to direct social change is accepted. It is considered imperative to avoid "polycentrism" in nations enfeebled by crosscutting rivalries and division, and to enforce the authority of the central government as an instrumentality of the mass party. On the other hand, Africans are far from agreement as to the models to be followed in the restructuring of their societies, the priorities to be established in pursuing their goals, and the pace at which they must progress.[1]

At the core of the problem is the tremendous dependence of the present generation of African leaders upon external sources for the economic and financial resources needed to carry their nations more fully onto the threshold of the modern world. Dependence at a time of independence—particularly upon former colonial masters—is a melancholy paradox, one which not all African leaders are willing to accept with grace. Nevertheless, the Western presence in the continent remains ubiquitous. All of the new African leaders and their governments use one or another of the Western languages in both official and informal communication. In West Africa alone—Guinea aside—over 80 percent of all foreign trade is accounted for by Western Europe and the United States. The bulk of non-indigenous teachers, technicians, advisers, military training officers, and other specialized personnel originate from the former metropoles. Grants-in-aid totalling more than $50 million have been extended to Ghana, Nigeria, and Sierra Leone by the United Kingdom since they slipped their colonial moorings. In the French-speaking areas of West and Equatorial Africa, the De Gaulle government is providing approximately $300 million annually in direct assistance. Indeed, French aid might be reckoned at substantially higher levels if marketing prefer-

[1] The main features of the contemporary African scene are ably presented in George W. Shepherd, *The Politics of African Nationalism* (New York 1962); W. E. Abraham, *The Mind of Africa* (Chicago 1963); and Vernon McKay, *Africa in World Politics* (New York 1963).

ences, advantageous exchange arrangements, and other special subventions are taken into consideration. To these general figures must be added United States aid which has grown prodigiously, and the contribution of the common market fund (Fedom) which has risen to approximately $100 million annually.[2]

Acute embarrassment and varying types of political self-compensation are bound to be the by-products of this dependent relationship. The bulk of Africa's leaders seek to compensate for their dependence by compulsive efforts to forge closer bonds among themselves, presently expressed in the Pan-African unity movement. This frustration is also reflected in the polemics of the so-called African radicals, and in the attacks upon white settler policies in such southern African areas as the Federation of the Rhodesias and Nyasaland, the Portugese territories, and the Republic of South Africa. It is also likely to seek other outlets as well.

The Communist World: Alternatives and Problems

The Communist world offers an attractive alternative for some Africans, for the Communist countries have demonstrated the feasibility of policies of modernization other than those developed in the West. Unfamiliar as they are with the historical circumstances under which the Communists came to power in Russia, China, and elsewhere, or with the vast differences between the Communist countries and the new nations of Africa, African radicals are not infrequently attracted by Communist propaganda. Moreover, in proffering seemingly unlimited financial credits, skilled technicians, and dramatic aid projects, the Communist countries offer African leaders a means of escaping the stigma of "neo-colonialist" dependence upon the West. At the same time, in international councils the balance of forces between the Communist countries and the West gives the new states of Africa greater importance and freedom when they act as an uncommitted third force.

For the Communist world, Africa constitutes a new frontier, a new area of opportunity for political revolution. On the other hand, this great promise contains innumerable pitfalls and perils. In this continent are diverse areas inhabited by more than 200 million people, speaking more than 1,000 languages and dialects, divided into almost 2,000 distinct clan, tribal, and ethnic groups which have been undergoing social change at varying rates of speed and differing degrees of

[2] *The Economist* (January 20, 1962), 28-31.

intensity. Here too are peoples that retain customs, traditions, and world views which, at least until recently, have seemed chaotic and incomprehensible to Marxists. Finally Africa has been a region virtually closed to Communist scholars, and unknown to Soviet theoreticians, and almost outside the boundaries of Marxist interest as defined during the Stalinist period. Thus, as the continent emerged as a testing ground between the Communist world and the West, the former suffered from certain disadvantages in knowledge and insight which weakened it in the face of the contrasts, contradictions, and paradoxes which are contemporary Africa.[3]

Prior to 1946, the Communist leaders of the Soviet Union had established virtually no priorities for themselves in Africa, their primary preoccupation being one of consolidation of their own internal power. If there was to be any confrontation with the capitalist world it was to be in Europe or Asia. Africa was generally regarded as fitting neatly within the broad framework of the Negro question, with emphasis placed upon the formation of a *rassemblement* of Negro workers from the Americas and Sub-Saharan Africa.[4] Indeed, between the First and Second World Wars, several Comintern Congresses established Negro commissions from which representatives from the African area were notably absent. It has in fact been noted that the "Communist concept of the Negro world was based neither on scholarly analysis nor on deep emotions such as later gave rise to the idea of 'negritude,' stressing the cultural links between Negroes on both sides of the Atlantic Ocean."[5] The unfounded hope of the Communist theoreticians was that the national Communist apparatus of the United States and South Africa would develop the racial cadres needed to form the nuclei of Marxist movements in the untouched regions of middle Africa.

Race, however, has proved an unhappy touchstone for the Com-

[3] The best historical introduction to Russia's interest in Africa is Sergius Yakobson, "Russia and Africa," *Russian Foreign Policy: Essays in Historical Perspective,* ed. by Ivo J. Lederer (New Haven 1962), 453-487. The emergence of a new school of African studies in the USSR is described in "Soviet Views on Africa," *Soviet Survey,* No. 28 (April-June 1959), 37-45; and Mary Holdsworth, *Soviet African Studies, 1918-59: An Annotated Bibliography* (London 1961). Current Soviet publications may be followed in the monthly *Mizan Newsletter,* especially IV (May 1962) devoted to *Africa Today: The Soviet View.*

[4] David L. Morison, "Communism in Africa," *Problems of Communism,* X. (November-December 1961), 20-26. See also Fritz Schatten, *Afrika-Schwarz oder Rot?* (Munich 1961); Pieter Lessing, *Africa's Red Harvest* (London 1962); and Aderogba Ajao, *On the Tiger's Back* (Cleveland 1962).

[5] Walter Kolarz, "The West African Scene," *Problems of Communism,* X (November-December 1961), 27-35.

munists, placing them at a dual disadvantage in Africa. White Europeans, for example, who had been in the vanguard of the Communist movement in South Africa, found themselves ousted from the then powerful Industrial and Commercial Workers' Union in the late 1920's as a result of the deep suspicions with which black Africans tended to regard them. In other areas as well, white direction of the embryonic Communist apparatus tended to foster internal strains for black Africans who felt needless risks were incurred in identifying themselves with what were then two clearly "subversive" forces—communism and nationalism; the perils of nationalism were sufficient.

For the Communist world on the other hand, to emphasize racial issues was to run the risk of losing the potential support of the growing numbers of Europeans settling in Kenya, the Rhodesias, and South Africa. As a result, for the most part the "colonial question" passed Africa by during the 1930's, with primary attention being focused by the Comintern upon India, the Levant, and one or two areas in Southeast Asia.

The Second World War and its aftermath, however, fostered a partial restructuring of priorities, and Africa became a much more clearly defined target area. Part of this change may be attributed to the consolidation of the Communist position in Russia and the occupation of large portions of Eastern Europe by Soviet armies, thus creating a suitable buffer zone of satellites against Western "machinations." More significant was the sudden power vacuum created in large portions of Africa by the demise of Italy as a colonizing force. The imperium of Rome was to be replaced by new authorities designated by the Big Four Foreign Ministers. Suddenly, and largely through fortuitous circumstance, the Soviet Union became directly involved in the disposition of such pivotal areas as Tripolitania, Cyrenaica, Fezzan, Eritrea, and former Italian Somaliland. In addition, membership in the United Nations afforded the Soviet Union opportunities to help shape the destinies of trust territories such as Tanganyika, Ruanda-Urundi, the Camerouns, and the Togolands.

Despite these new advantages, direct contact with Africa was spasmodic and indecisive. Opportunities to diffuse Communist doctrines and strategy over a wide region of Africa, especially the non-trust areas, remained restricted. Since the dissolution of the Comintern in 1943, the only vehicles available for penetration were the Communist parties and labor organs in the metropoles. These, however, scored few major successes between 1946 and 1960. The Belgian

Communist Party, for example, had virtually no direct access in the Congo until early in 1959—only 18 months before independence. The efforts of the British Communists proved equally ineffectual, as was demonstrated by the complete absence of Africans at the February 1947 Conference of the Commmunist Parties of the British Empire held at Beaver Hall in London—a conference devoted to the resolution of tactical dilemmas in India, Malaya, and Palestine.[6]

Only in French-speaking Africa were any notable successes registered, and these ultimately proved not only ephemeral but exceedingly disillusioning. The efforts of the French Communist Party began to bear fruit in 1943 with the organization of *Groupes d'Études Communistes* at Dakar, Conakry, Abidjan, Bamako, and Bobo-Diolasso. Formed to provide French-speaking Africa's emerging intellectuals with the opportunity to engage in "guided" discussions of Marxist ideas as interpreted by local French Communist monitors, the GEC's also offered Africans a new political idiom and operational concepts for planning "directed" social change.[7] After the Second World War, the graduates of the GEC's became the founders and leaders of Africa's leading indigenous political formation, the *Rassemblement Démocratique Africain* (RDA). Created in 1946 by Felix Houphouët-Boigny and Gabriel d'Arboussier, among others, the RDA immediately entered into a parliamentary alliance in Paris with the French Communist Party, a Fourth Republic arrangement which persisted until 1950, when it was unilaterally dissolved by the RDA.

The alliance was forged to enhance the parliamentary position and bargaining power of the RDA as well as to gain access to those ideas, techniques, and resources which were necessary to strengthen African nationalism. It foundered precisely because the metropole partner could provide none of the desired assets. The parliamentary power of the French Communists evaporated rapidly after 1948: concomitantly, official French attitudes towards the RDA were growing more stringent. Once, again, African nationalists were confronted with the prospect of double jeopardy, and precisely at a time when it was becoming apparent that the metropole Communist leadership was as assimilationist in orientation as previous colonial administrations. "The French Communists themselves were hoping not only to retain, but to extend power in the center and thus, as it were, to

[6] Theodore Draper, *American Communism and Soviet Russia* (New York 1960).

[7] Thomas Hodgkin and Ruth Schachter, "French-Speaking West Africa in Transition," *International Conciliation*, No. 528 (May 1960), 375-436.

capture the colonies via Paris. They therefore discouraged separatist and revolutionary tendencies in Africa, advocated a liberal program of evolution, and told the colonial peoples that 'the French Union is the most favorable framework for the realization of their aspirations.' "[8]

Indeed, the alliance with the French Communists even adversely affected the position of black African labor organizations. The Communist *Confederation Général du Travail,* for example, argued vehemently during this period in favor of the basic identity of interests of the French workers and the African masses—an identity which involved the sacrifice of African interests in order to avoid economic privation among the French working classes. African trade unionists such as Guinea's Sékou Touré could only react with ill-grace to these demands for inordinate sacrifice. Thus the political defection of the RDA from the alliance was emulated by African trade unionists who, in 1954, created the independent *Union Général des Travailleurs d'Afrique Noire.*

Commensurate with the failure of the metropole Communist organs to consolidate their influence among Africa's emergent political and economic elites was the inability of Soviet theoreticians to accept the possibility of African political evolution and eventual emancipation outside the framework of the Marxist dialectic. The dictum that imperialism is the last phase of capitalism, one that must be succeeded by the socialist revolution, engendered a sense of determinism and political faith which bordered on the pathological. At the center of Communist dogma was the presumption that only the working class has the capabilities for fostering the true national and socialist revolution in Africa and Asia. The national bourgeois leadership was inherently unreliable, corruptible, and devoted to the interests and privileges of its own class. Since the leadership of Africa's emergent political organisms were distinctly "bourgeois," they were consistently belittled as imperialist lackeys and petty stooges of the colonial powers.

Revision of Communist Doctrine

Historical reality, however, has overtaken Communist doctrine and forced a re-examination of the norms to be applied in Africa. The real revolution in Africa over the past decade has been reflected in the large number of states that have emerged from colonial status without the type of massive confrontation envisaged by Marxist de-

[8] Kolarz, 29.

terminists. The startling ease of transition in most instances, the maintenance of close ties with the former metropoles, and the unforeseen stability of the indigenous regimes have upset previous calculations. Even more significantly, at the head of Africa's national liberation movements have remained the very elitist-bourgeois elements excoriated by the Soviet ideologists. Indeed, these leaders have entered into successful alliances with the African urban workers and peasants, alliances which have resulted—in most instances—in the implantation of "mass" one-party regimes whose popular base appears to be unshakeably broad. Africa's new leaders have thus assumed supreme political power in twenty-five states, with little or no Communist advice, involvement, or direction, and are consolidating their positions with relative ease.

Even more troublesome have been the African "borrowings" from the political rhetoric and economic dicta of the Communist world. This eclecticism is particularly prevalent in nationalist discussion of Western imperialism—viz., the "whole policy of the colonizer is to keep the native in his primitive state and to make him economically dependent." Similar African adaptations of Marxist doctrine are reflected in the conception of nationalist parties as the socialist *avant-garde* and in the priority given to the adoption of "democratic socialism"—or "Democratic Centralism," as preferred in Ghana—throughout Africa. President Kwame Nkrumah has clearly underlined, on the one hand, that the African intelligentsia, not the urban proletariat, must serve as the guiding force of nationalist organs. President Sékou Touré, in contrast, has adopted a more catholic view seeking to bridge the gulf between Guinea's intellectual elite and the "masses" via the country's ruling *Parti Démocratique de Guinée* (PDG)—an emphasis upon popular egalitarianism which apparently leaves little room for tactical maneuver by small "picked bands of professional revolutionaries."[9]

Nevertheless, by mid-1960, even the most doctrinaire Communist theoreticians had to acknowledge that many of the "bourgeois" nationalists were appropriating for themselves primary roles as Africa's radical activists, roles which lent them international notoriety and influence far out of proportion to their actual power and resources. For Communist leaders, these new radicals—Nkrumah, Touré, Keita, etc. —posed serious dilemmas. Their radicalism clearly was not founded

[9] Thomas Hodgkin, "A Note on the Language of African Nationalism," *African Affairs* (St. Anthony's Papers), x (1961), 22-40.

upon ideologies which were compatible with Marxism; if anything, African radicalism was a state of mind rather than a fixed doctrine. Fragmentary ideas, bits and pieces of shibboleth—some of them inspired by eighteenth century Western thinkers—and a blend of contemporary British and French liberalism, local pragmatism, and Marxist idiom formed the crazy-quilt pattern of what might be loosely termed an ideology.

The Nature of the Radical Left in Africa

Several tactical advantages promise to accrue to the Soviet Union, however, if short-term accommodations are informally struck with Africa's radicals who clearly represent an indigenous vehicle for protest against past colonial injustices and future Western "neo-colonialist machinations." Their fulminations promise to strike a responsive chord among the continent's emergent second and third generation working classes and intellectual elites. Indeed, virtually all African leaders already subscribe, in varying degrees, to the assortment of attitudes represented by African radicalism, to the extent that these attitudes stem from feelings of cultural inferiority, grievance against former colonial regimes, and a sense of injustice derived from poverty and backwardness.

Even more attractive has been the growing congruence of interest between Africa's radicals and the Communists. Unlike such moderates as Leopold Senghor, Houphouët-Boigny, and the late Sylvanus Olympio, with a strong sense of their African heritage—including the colonial period—the radicals appear to the Communists bent upon an almost suicidal dismissal of the past. The leadership of the "Radical Left" is characterized by a self-proclaimed determination to expunge any vestigial colonial attachments involving remaining military ties, heavy reliance upon former metropoles for economic and technical assistance, and other forms of dependency which accord the West near monopolistic controls. In addition, their expressions of "rebellion" are reflected in denunciations of Western colonial policies in white settler territories before the United Nations, support of Communist positions on issues of major interest to the West, and in the contribution which they make to the general "demoralization" of the West in Africa.

Domestically, Africa's radicals appear determined to circumvent the troublesome present by an alliance with the future. They tend to approach domestic concerns with a policy of iconoclastic activism—

militantly nationalistic, revisionist, and revolutionary. The goal of these leaders is the creation of a monolithic party-state apparatus and the elimination of all independent centers of power. They demand mass loyalty to the political directorate of the national party which seeks to "tinker" with some traditional institutions and to suppress others. The African radicals also insist upon the elimination of ethnic divisions, tribal rivalries, and special privileges predicated upon class, education, or religious affiliation. They are doctrinaire in their commitment to planned social change and modernization, largely predicating their hopes upon centralized direction, rigid controls, and full government participation in the economic sphere. Feeling that there are shortcuts which can be taken in bridging rapidly the historical and material gap between African backwardness and the modern world, Africa's radicals are willing to utilize Communist models and prescriptions for social advancement.

The promising opportunities afforded by the emergence of the "Radical Left" in Africa, as well as the reduction in barriers to normal relations once posed by colonial fiat, have engendered an important shift in Communist approach and emphasis. Fixed tactical doctrine has been discarded for a tractable pragmatism, calculated to provide the flexibility needed to keep pace with the frequent shifts and lurches which form part of an almost normal rhythm of political life in Africa. Thus, the Soviet leadership is devoting greater priority to broad strategy, de-emphasizing the tactical rigidities of the Stalinist period. Recognizing that the preconditions for the classical revolutionary situation have not materialized, they have placed greater stress on imaginativeness in policy and approach. With this shift, a basic reallocation of responsibilities has emerged. The top echelons of the Communist oligarchy have assumed the burden of coping operationally with the intricacies of Africa's evolving politics, while the Soviet Union's new generation of Africanists has been assigned the responsibility of fathoming its complexities.

"National Democracy"

Conceptually, the gap between strategy and tactics is being bridged by extensive recourse to such doctrinal hyphens as the theory of "national democracy" and the "national liberation movement." In addition to the virtue of providing symbolic linkages between Marxist-Leninist determinism and African realities, these concepts legitimize tactics and provide a broad overview of a vague strategy. Moreover, while containing both prognoses and prescriptions, they avoid the pitfalls of stereotyped dialectics and offer, instead, prospects of progress for Africans.[10]

Although certain ambiguities are encountered in official Communist definitions of the concept of "national democracy," in broad application it applies to states which are still in transition to "people's democracy." Significantly, as used in 1955 by the leading Soviet Africanist Potekhin, the concept accepts the realities of the African political revolution of the 1950's: "The historical situation is at present such that national democracy is coming to be the political form of liberation of peoples under the yoke of imperialism. This guarantees the leading role of the proletariat and opens the path to socialism. This means that with the liquidation of the colonial regime a socialist and not a bourgeois nation will emerge in such countries. The rate of formation of the Socialist nation will be determined by the rate of transition of the democratic revolution into a socialist one."[11] This general approach, not adopted in official Soviet circles until 1960, accepts the fact that representatives of "progressive forces" which have led their African states to independence are "at the helm" for the present. Their leadership is acceptable to the Communists so long as they "ensure their nation's advance along the road of social progress."[12]

The prerequisites of "progress" are: the consolidation of political independence; "elimination of the survivals of feudalism;" "the carrying out of agrarian reforms in the interest of the peasantry;" creation and development of a national industry; democratization of social life; "pursuance of an independent and peaceful foreign policy;" and the development of economic and cultural cooperation with the socialist countries of eastern Europe.[13] The preconditions and prescriptive paths are clearly, if not rigorously, established. Nationalist revolution rather than Communist power is the precondition, and this makes it possible to enlarge the prospects of transition to a "higher form of social order." The "national democracy" is led by progressive bourgeois elements

[10] Stefan T. Possony, *Analysis of Khrushchev Speech of January 6, 1961* (Washington, 1961), 15-16.

[11] I. I. Potekhin, *Formirovaniye natsional'noy obshchnosti Yuzhno-Afrikanskikh Bantu* [The Formation of the National Community of the South African Bantu] (Moscow 1955), 47.

[12] See especially I. Plyshevsky, "Some Problems of the Independence Struggle in Africa," WMR, No. 7 (1961), 35-36.

[13] The national democratic concept is discussed in Chapter 9, above, where there is also the original definition of national democracy provided in the Moscow Declaration of 1960.

which must transform a once colonial, but presently capitalist, state into a socialist collectivity. This must be accomplished through the eradication of tribalism, feudalism, and other reactionary interests. Thus, for the present, revolutionary reforms are accepted as an adequate substitute for socialist revolution.

As the "progressive bourgeoisie" struggles with the reforms which are to radically transform their society, the Communist apparatus must seek to organize urban workers and the rural peasantry, to create among them a sense of solidarity, and to instill a will to struggle for "true" socialist regimes.[14] For this purpose, recourse is made to various international conferences and operational agencies sponsored by the Soviet Union. The leading instrumentality in Africa is the World Federation of Trade Unions; it combines in its appeals "special group interest with general political objectives, such as anti-imperialism, peace, freedom of association, social welfare measures, anti-capitalism, nuclear disarmament," and related matters.[15]

Obviously, the new approach to African realities would entail a suicidal effort by progressive leaders to "revolutionize" the prevailing societal order. At the same time, workers and peasants are to be permitted certain freedoms, including the opportunity to form separate —but allied—political organizations. The Communist perspective implies ultimate failure on the part of Africa's progressives to fashion programs of action which will succeed. In the ensuing atmosphere of frustration and uncertainty, the resources of the state will be placed in the hands of the workers and peasants who, hopefully, will accept direct guidance from their "socialist" *confrères*.[16]

During this crucial transitional period the basic sin is conceptual rigidity. National democracy, by definition, is essentially "a list of tactical objectives" and operational criteria rather than a rigorously conceived design. According to Potekhin, "it is not a question of classifying all the liberated states in some definite categories . . . Such an approach would be stereotyped and harmful . . . In real life there are already liberated countries which . . . have created the prerequisites for establishing a national democracy."[17]

A cautionary footnote is taken even by Potekhin, however, concern-

[14] I. Yernachov, "Ideas of the Age," *New Times*, No. 24 (1962), 8-11.

[15] George E. Lichtblau, "The Communist Labor Offensive in Former Colonial Countries," *Industrial and Labor Relations Review*, xv (April 1962), 376-401.

[16] "Resolution of the 22nd Congress on the Report of the CC CPSU (Khrushchev's Report)," quoted in *Mizan Newsletter*, III, 10 (November 1961), 10.

[17] Potekhin, 49-50.

ing the various approaches to socialism being adopted by Africans. Accepting the tremendous appeal which socialism has as a slogan among even the most moderate African leaders—such as Leopold Senghor, Mamadou Dia, Julius Nyerere—Potekhin cannot resist the temptation to remonstrate with them concerning misguided interpretations and applications: ". . . 'feudal socialism,' used by the aristocracy as a false slogan in its struggle against the bourgeoisie; petty bourgeois socialism, which idealized the existing commodity production system and sought to perpetuate it; conservative or bourgeois socialism, which sought to remedy social ills only so as to strengthen the structure of bourgeois society—a type of socialism with which the capitalists of the whole world are today in agreement; and utopian socialism, which, though honest in intention, is not based on the revolutionary struggle of the proletariat but on the philanthropy of the bourgeoisie. . ."[18] His admonition is to proceed with the fashioning of a scientifically socialist state by completing such specifically assigned tasks as the formation of a broadly based working class and an attendant sense of class consciousness. Even Potekhin acknowledges that, commensurately, there must occur a parallel emergence of a more fully formed African national bourgeoisie, since "such a class now has new opportunities of development in African countries which have acquired independence."[19]

Counterbalancing any normative prescriptions which may occasionally creep into Soviet ruminations about Africa's current stage of evolution, is the tendency to avoid categorizing states as national democracies and non-democracies. Instead, primary emphasis is devoted to analyzing the foreign and domestic policies of the newly emergent countries in order to "popularize their progressive initiatives," as well as to condemn any retrograde or reactionary undertakings. Thus, Mali is increasingly applauded for its advanced social planning while Senegal is criticized for its retention of "colonialist connections." Similarly, official acts of repression against "progressive warriors" by moderate governments in Chad, Senegal, and the Ivory Coast are condemned as blocking the access of working class elements to positions of power and influence. The Ivory Coast leadership in particular is castigated for having become puppets of France, being

[18] I. I. Potekhin, *Afrika smotrit v budushcheye* [Africa Looks Ahead] (Moscow 1960), quoted in supplement to *Mizan Newsletter*, III, 4 (April 1961), 2; see also Potekhin's article "On 'African Socialism,'" *IntAff*, No. 1 (1963), 71-79.
[19] *Ibid.*

corrupt, opening the country to speculators, and helping to form the "imperialist Brazzaville group."[20]

Main Trends in Communist Policy

For its part, the Soviet government has tended to adopt a more relaxed attitude in the face of the manifold contradictions and incompatibilities encountered in Africa, leaving to its academics the role of "defenders of the faith." The fulminations that emanate from official sources are directed against vestigial Western influence and the threat of neo-colonialism. The problems tentatively posed by "muddled African thinking" about socialism, the "African personality," Pan-Africanism, and "negritude," have been put aside in favor of the promising opportunities afforded the Soviet Union to establish a presence in the continent. In contrast to other areas, the Communists are not confronted with the necessity of "fighting their way into Africa." The preconditions for competitive coexistence with the West obtain by virtue of the revolutionary liquidation of the European colonial presence in West and Central Africa, as well as the mounting predisposition of the new African states to accept the fruits of coexistence.

The impressive expansion of the Communist presence in Africa is reflected in the growth of diplomatic accreditations of Communist countries from 42 at the end of 1960 to 77 by March 1962; almost half of Africa's independent states (14) had agreed to establish diplomatic ties with one or more Communist states during this period. In addition, Communist economic assistance agreements doubled during 1961, rising from $279 million at the end of 1960 to $602 million by January 1962. The number of Communist technicians serving in the area rose by more than 275 percent and was more than 2,000 in January 1963. Concomitantly, during the academic year 1961-1962, approximately 3,000 African students matriculated in Communist universities and other Communist educational institutions. This represented an increase of 1,800 over the previous academic year.

In the field of propaganda and communication, the Communist countries have more than doubled their weekly radio broadcasts to non-Arabic speaking Africa. Broadcasts which totalled 96 hours in December 1960 rose to 200 hours one year later. Simultaneously, news services have been expanded; the number of cultural agreements with African states has risen from 11 to 30; Bloc exhibits increased

[20] See *Mizan Newsletter*, III, 9 (October 1961), and IV, 5 (May 1962).

by 25 percent; and the flow of films, newspapers, and journals reflected similar growth ratios.

Significantly, however, the number of Communist parties functioning in Sub-Saharan Africa has remained quite limited. At present, only Nigeria, South Africa, Basutoland, and the Malagasy Republic have formally organized Communist parties. Their combined membership probably does not exceed 5,000 in an area where active membership in nationalist political organs runs to substantially more than 20 million Africans. The South African Communist Party, outlawed since 1950, was controlled largely by white Europeans. For its part, the Nigerian Communist organ is an ephemeral entity which stands little prospect of being able to compete effectively with the inherently more powerful and well-established Hausa-Fulani and Ibo political consortiums. The parties in Basutoland and the Malagasy Republic have even more shadowy existences.

Even within the more "progressive" states of Ghana, Guinea, and Mali, the present leadership has expressed itself as unalterably opposed to the formation of indigenous Communist parties. The latter are regarded as supra-national organs which, if implanted, threaten to inculcate Africans with doctrines and ideologies which will compete with the prevailing one-party system. Thus, Sékou Touré, Kwame Nkrumah, and Modibo Keita have all expressed formal opposition to the possibility of legally constituted Communist organizations. Each has persistently declared that Africa's new nations are too brittle to afford themselves the luxury of more than one powerful, formally organized party. Power, they contend, must be consolidated at the center by only one force, one party, one leadership.

The Soviet Union has acceded with relatively good grace to these African "realities." During his West African sojourn in January 1962, Soviet First Deputy Premier Mikoyan applauded Ghanaian attempts to build socialism as a model for other newly independent African states. Going further, he acknowledged Ghana's right—for the moment—to develop its own African type of socialist system: "Dr. Nkrumah knows how to build the new life in Ghana. He called this 'socialism in conditions of Africa'—African socialism. The programmatic part of the rules of the Convention People's Party of Ghana says that this type of socialism is impossible without a broad development of industry and the development on agriculture on this basis. This correct thesis is so broad, so general, that it concerns all. . ."[21] That Guinea and Mali are accorded similar recognition is reflected

[21] *Tass*, January 17, 1962.

in the attendance of party representatives from these states, as well as Ghana, at the 22nd Congress of the CPSU in 1961 as "fraternal delegates"—a not inconsiderable indicator of Communist recognition and honor.

A disinclination to become embroiled in dialectical controversy, prudence in the face of crises which appear promising but which are essentially episodic, circumspection in interpreting events which could be considered seminal—these have become primary characteristics of the Soviet approach to Africa. They are manifested in the lionization of Emperor Haile Selassie during his July 1959 sojourn in the Soviet Union, and in the proffering of a $100 million line of credit to him. They are further shown in the subsequent scrupulous Soviet avoidance of involvement in the abortive December 1960 coup attempt by a temporary alliance of Ethiopia's reformist intellectuals, civil servants, and military. Similarly, the Communist world has been loath to condemn Mali for its continued franc zone membership and recent acceptance of French credits for the construction of an expanded Sotuba dam complex. Even Togo's Sylvanus Olympio and Senegal's Mamadou Dia were the recipients of Soviet blandishments, despite their position as adversaries of Nkrumah and Modibo Keita.

Far from constituting contradictions within the official Soviet hierarchy of strategy and tactics, these *démarches* conform perfectly to contemporary Soviet perceptions of desirable means and goals. It is the West which confronts the Communist countries globally and serves as its main competitor for power. In Africa, it is thus the West which is primarily under attack; Africa is a means rather than an end. If the West can be dislodged and demoralized in Africa, its *élan,* indeed its very unity, will be undercut. Within this frame of reference direct seizure of power by Communist groups, even if possible, would not serve the immediate purposes of the Soviet Bloc.

It would appear, on the contrary, that primary emphasis is to be devoted to providing newly independent African regimes with alternative sources of technical assistance, development financing, and military material. This by no means implies the acquisition of monopolistic controls by the Communist countries which quite clearly do not have the capacity to feed Africa's insatiable appetite. The thrust of Soviet policy is thus largely psychological—i.e. to create an image among Africans of the Communist world as a ubiquitous and economically powerful competitor capable of supplanting the West as a munificent friend whenever Africans feel disposed to accept Communist generosity.[22]

Secondly, the Communist countries clearly wish to reinforce those indigenous African forces which are seeking to establish state systems, normative standards, and patterns of international behavior which fall outside the matrix erected by the West during the nineteenth and early twentieth centuries. The Communists anticipate that African standards, when rigorously applied in such bodies as the United Nations, will immobilize the West on critical issues and erode its confidence. If in the process the United Nations should suffer irreparable damage, a signal victory will have been won, for additional impetus would thereby be given those forces in Africa and Asia which prefer to radically reorder their societies. Indeed, Africans seeking strictly African solutions to local problems would be fashioning a new edifice of international values which could threaten the foundations of international order as conceived by the West.

Because of these broader goals and anticipations, Communist involvement in Africa's recent upheavals has been minimal. Indeed, even at moments when Communist interest appeared at least tangentially at stake, or when the possibility of substantial gains in one or two territories have been in the offing, the Communist countries have tended to adopt a restrained posture, retaining their political equilibrium and eschewing short-term advantages for longer-run anticipations.

The rebellious wing of the *Union des Populations du Cameroun* (UPC), operating as a clandestine terrorist organization in the Bamileke and Sanaga-Maritime regions, has failed to receive the level of Communist assistance which it anticipated when it raised the standard of dissidence in 1957. While supplied with some small quantities of Communist arms—several leaders have also received guerrilla warfare training in mainland China—the UPC has been successfully contained by local French and Camerounian security forces. Indeed, its leadership has been seriously divided since 1960 and, with the rising power and influence of President Ahmadou Ahidjo, the terrorist wing of the UPC is likely to become moribund. Having committed none of its prestige and few of its major assets to

[22] A. M. Sivolobov, *Natsional'noye-osvoboditel'noye dvizheniye v Afrike* [The National Liberation Movement in Africa] (Moscow 1960), translated in JPRS 10683, 1-69.

the UPC, the Communist countries have devoted little of their time to any political eulogies.

Guinea and the Congo

Where the Soviet Union has expended considerable energy, personnel, and funds, notably in Guinea, its political dividend has been marginal at best. Communist penetration in Guinea began in earnest after President Sékou Touré led his country out of the French Community during the 1958 referendum on the Fifth Republic's new constitution. Guinea's negative vote led President de Gaulle to accept Touré's cry: "We prefer poverty in liberty to riches in slavery." French technicians and advisers were immediately withdrawn, various subventions quickly terminated, and Guinea set adrift, bereft of those basic governing institutions necessary for nation building.

The Soviet Union quickly sprang into the void, proffering large quantities of technical assistance and advice. Over 1,000 Russian and East European specialists were lodged in Conakry, Kan Kan, and other towns. Relatively large development projects were initiated with blatant fanfare, and Guinea appeared to have become the first African state to be subjected to decisive Communist influence. Concomitantly, the ruling *Parti Démocratique de Guinée* attempted to orchestrate the new rhythm of political life which was emerging. Indeed, the PDG became the primary instrument for mobilizing and uniting this small West African nation, which embraces 2.6 million people speaking 20 distinct languages and dialects. Operating on the assumption that almost any routine human activity can be organized and manipulated for the greater cohesion of the nation, the theoreticians of the PDG Politburo felt that their primary responsibility was to give meaning and perspective to the programs of change and modernization which they wished to introduce to the illiterate African masses.

The slogans and campaigns of the PDG have, however, come up against a number of imposing realities. The Guinean peasantry has met PDG efforts at rural reorganization with obstinate resentment. Even in those sectors where local farmers have accepted government fiat, food production has declined appreciably. By 1961, popular discontent was rising over worsening economic conditions. Food and other commodities were in scarce supply, wages were frozen despite mounting prices, and unemployment had become serious in certain commercial sectors as a result of the withdrawal of French investment. Those massive Communist credits which had been extended were producing few economic gains. The primary priorities of the Soviets, Czechs, and Poles had been allocated to such showy projects as sports stadia, a radio station, and improvement of municipal services in Conakry.

A serious blow to the ruling PDG materialized in the form of teacher-student strikes at the end of 1961—characterized by the PDG Politburo as a counter-revolutionary "uprising"—with apparently clear evidence of Russian embassy involvement. The Russian ambassador, Daniel Solod, subsequently was requested by the Guinean government to depart Conakry in view of his "support" for extremist groups wishing to push Guinea even more deeply into the Russian "orbit." Since this denouement Soviet-Guinean relations have been correct, but ample evidence is crystallizing that President Sékou Touré intends to adopt a more completely "neutral" position. In addition to seeking a rapprochement with President de Gaulle, Touré has also turned to the United States for a larger share in its aid program, and has launched serious efforts to produce a reconciliation between Africa's Casablanca and Monrovia "blocs."

Since their presence in Africa, while expanding, continues to rest upon slender foundations, the Communist countries have been extremely wary in supporting general opposition movements. Even where "working class" interests may have been violated—as during the mid-1961 Ghanaian labor strikes—the Communists have borne their grievances in silence. The Ghanaian episode is instructive in this respect. Labor dissidence erupted in Ghana during September 1961 as a result of an austerity program introduced several weeks earlier to limit excessive expenditures on luxuries and to move the country onto a sounder agricultural and industrial footing. Far-reaching sacrifices were called for on the part of salaried workers at a time when living standards were already suffering a general decline.

The Ghanaian government's program was greeted with widespread and serious outbursts of violence from one of the most vaunted wings of the Convention People's Party (CPP) apparatus—the labor unions. Railway workers, as well as port workers and oil distribution personnel, struck and effectively paralyzed the national communications and transport system for a period of ten days. The CPP-dominated regime felt constrained to declare a limited state of emergency, dispatched heavily armed police to the striking areas, and threatened severe reprisals. Subsequently 50 strikers were summarily arrested and imprisoned, local union officials were expelled, and their organizations placed "under trusteeship." Ironically, several weeks later, a CPP delegation at the 22nd Congress of the CPSU received a warmly cordial reception.

The Congo, frequently held to be the area where the Communist countries suffered their first major debacle in Africa, has probably been responsible for existing Communist caution. Deeply torn by cross-cutting tribal, ethnic, and economic forces, the Congo has proved an unexpectedly refractory area for the Communists. Whatever defeats the latter may have suffered in their initial adventures in support of Patrice Lumumba and Antoine Gizenga, however, have not automatically resulted in any clear-cut Western victories. By 1963 the efforts to unite the Congo seemed within sight of success.

The Communist policy on the Congo—gropingly and instinctively set during the first six months of the crisis—may even yet be proven the wisest in terms of tactics and strategy. While in no way over-extending themselves materially, the Communist countries have expressed themselves clearly in support of: (1) full and unencumbered Congo unification; (2) liquidation of all vestigial colonial influences in the form of mercenaries, mining monopolies, etc.; and (3) the creation of a powerful Congolese army capable of securing the nation's sovereignty against all threats, internal or external. Thus, they have allied themselves with symbolic African unity as against the forces of balkanization, Congolese legitimacy rather than provincial particularism, and unfettered independence as opposed to neo-colonialism. The Communist countries have also successfully fashioned an image of themselves as champions of the Congo's "great leader" and martyr, Patrice Lumumba.[23]

Unfortunately, a number of the tactical advantages the West possessed at the outset of the Congo crisis may have slipped away through policy differences—differences which the Communists have sought to portray as disagreements over interment of the corpse rather than revival of the victim. This dissension together with the prevailing confusion of authority in the Congo, also provided the first real opportunity for the Cold War to divide Africa. Out of the chaos of the region, Africans were compelled to make difficult policy choices which led them into clusterings of states or blocs. The Casablanca grouping, a loose cluster of protest-oriented leaders, was formed in January 1961, to be followed but a few months later by the more conservative Monrovia grouping. While by no means firmly grounded blocs, these group-

[23] Harvey Glickman, "The Roots of the Congo Crisis," *New Forces in Africa*, William H. Lewis, ed. (Washington, D.C. 1962), 67-87.

ings underscore the tendency of Africans to divide deeply during moments of crisis or when confronted with "post-colonial" issues.

In addition, it has been pointed out that the Congo crisis may have been the popular watershed for the United Nations in Africa. "That the Congo's troubles permitted the Soviet government to threaten to paralyze the UN through transformations in its apparatus is well-known, as is the basis for the attack in the charge that the UN operation in the Congo has become an agency of American policy. Repulsing the Russians on this score, however, has not resolved the difficulties concerned. In supporting the Kasavubu delegation at the UN before a conciliation commission could go to the Congo and in underwriting the finances of the UN's operation in the Congo, America has been burdened by the image of 'master-minding' the initial stages of restoring order. Added to other setbacks of the UN in attempting to administer a country in the process of finding a government, all this has combined to damage the prestige and perhaps the future capabilities of the UN in Africa."[24]

For its own part, the Communist countries have learned four valuable lessons from the Congo. The first is the realization that, in some African areas, local political forces are too ill-formed and volatile to warrant full-scale support. The marriage of broad principle with symbolic leaders in areas such as the Congo offers greater hope of political dividends than collaboration and identification with one or two cliques. Indeed, the complete failure of abstract categories in the Congo was reflected in the mid-1962 threat posed to Premier Cyrille Adoula's regime by the incongrous and illogical alliance of supporters of Antoine Gizenga and Katanga's President Moise Tshombe.

Secondly, they have learned that they are too distant geographically to be able to intervene effectively in southern or central Africa. The lending of diplomatic support to Gizenga at Stanleyville during 1961 produced extreme embarrassment when a new embassy was required at Leopoldville with the Adoula-Gizenga detente of late 1961. Materially, the Communists were frustrated in attempts to fly arms and equipment to Stanleyville by the tremendous distances to be traversed. The Russian government has since initiated far-reaching efforts to correct this deficiency by negotiating special overflight and landing rights for its civil aircraft in Cairo, Khartoum, and several areas in North and West Africa, but these too could be easily interdicted.

Thirdly, the Communists have come to realize that they have not

[24] *Ibid.*, 69-70.

yet developed the capabilities for launching the types of offensives which the Congo situation requires. Consequently, greater priority is being given to working through more effective instrumentalities—i.e., the radical states of Ghana, Guinea, Mali, and the United Arab Republic. The Communists have initiated a vigorous program to become the principal armorer and supplier of material for these states in order to bolster their ability to serve as the indirect vehicle of Soviet policy. The targets of the Communists are the continent's liberation movements, especially those which are forming in central and southern Africa in anticipation of a monumental struggle for independence. Thus, the fourth lesson learned from the Congo is that African movements cannot be seized, organized, or directed from abroad. They must be nurtured by Africans, from within, and with the assistance—direct or indirect—of other Africans.

The Congo problem does not persist in isolation. For the West and the United Nations, the Congo could well represent a critical turning point in southern Africa. The Congo is closely tied to neighboring areas, particularly Portuguese Angola where a nationalist rebellion erupted early in 1961, and the Rhodesias, one of the frontiers of white settler Africa. Geographically and otherwise it is the gateway to the south, and it is consequently the key to white settler fears and hopes for the future. Independence, which has come with relative ease in West and much of Central Africa, can only threaten to topple the privileges and status of the white man in the south. Consequently, there is a hope of continued chaos and confusion in the Congo among neighboring white dominated regimes. Instability and fragmentation in this turbulent area would stem the tide of black notionalism for the present generation of whites—so it is hoped.

For the Communists, on the other hand, the Congo represents a springboard to the entire region to the south and the east. Indeed, it is these latter regions which are crucial for the future Communist policy in Africa. Representing the core areas of European domination, they are all regions where a bloody confrontation between "colonialism" and African nationalism may be anticipated. The broad advantages which could accrue to the Communists in such a confrontation must appear promising, especially since white settlers cannot be expected to sacrifice their privileged status with alacrity. The Communists, consequently, can be expected to press for a denouement as early as possible.

The tactical and strategic opportunities for the Communist countries in the south cannot be too greatly exaggerated. In addition to placing the West on the defensive politically, they almost certainly will seek to undermine further the unity of the West and to demoralize it on issues which threaten its vital interests throughout the continent. Among Africans, they would hope to bolster communism as the defender of legitimate African aspirations, a struggler against the forces of colonialism, and a supporter of racial equality. Thus, southern Africa may well become the main testing ground in the period directly ahead, one where the Communists will enjoy immense tactical advantages.

Conclusion

The total Communist experience in Africa to date suggests, however, that African nationalism has not always embraced Communist advances without reserve. The present generation of African leadership, while quick to appropriate Marxist slogans and susceptible to Soviet offers of economic assistance, has tended to resist working alliances with the Soviet Union or with the local Communist apparatus. The Soviet experience in Guinea, where the pendulum of policy is swinging into a more clearly neutral position, has been far from reassuring. Similarly, President Kwame Nkrumah's attacks upon pro-Communist associates have produced some disillusionment. Even where Communist efforts have been directed toward the penetration of the highest echelons of African nationalist leadership for the seizure of power from "above," serious setbacks have been registered in the Congo, in the Ivory Coast, and, most recently in Mozambique.

Even in the Republic of South Africa, where *apartheid* is producing a widening psychological gulf between whites and blacks, African nationalist leadership has not yet fully grasped the nettle of Communist collaboration. The bulk of Africans seek privileges comparable to those enjoyed by whites, rather than a direct confrontation in terms of political hegemony or independence. While *Afrikaner* obduracy is forcing radical blacks to initiate a campaign of terrorism, their sabotage acts do not have the support of the overwhelming majority of the non-Europeans.

Even among the Communists themselves, consensus and coordinated action have been far from complete. Throughout Africa, Chinese Communist and Soviet rivalry has been blatant—particularly in Mali, the Horn area, and East Africa. The Chinese have tended in most instances to support extremist political groups in the Somali Republic, Zanzibar, Kenya, and the Cameroon, to the consternation and diplomatic embarrassment of the Soviet Union. Even among the East European states, an increasing predisposition to take independent courses, however modest, has been manifest in Africa. Indeed, the extension of Czech aid and credits in Guinea, Mali, and elsewhere in West Africa has engendered some Soviet discomfiture. In some respects, Africa has served as a window on the world for several eastern European nations—notably Czechoslovakia, Poland, and Hungary.[25]

Finally, Africa threatens to serve as a basic test of Communist tactical flexibility, political resiliency, and economic resourcefulness. Thus far, Communist setbacks have led to increasing caution and circumspection. As new targets of opportunity unfold, Soviet prudence at least is likely to slow governmental reflexes somewhat. However, in the area of economic assistance Soviet reflexes are not likely to be defective. The basic consideration will be the Communists' ability to meet the requirements of more than twenty-five African states with needs which are boundless, and with expectations which are insatiable. Even in this area, however, the Communist world suffers from a glaring lack of experience in the realities of African economics, and its own limitations in human and physical resources. Thus, Africa, shaped like a gigantic question mark, presents opportunities and risk which are incalculable for both the Communist world and the West.

[25] This problem is discussed in Ho Wei-yang, "Die Politik der Chinesen in Afrika," *Aussenpolitik,* XII (March 1961), 162-168; Kurt L. London, "Communism in Africa: The Role of China," *Problems of Communism,* XI (July-August 1962), 22-27; Leon M. S. Slawecki, "The Two Chinas in Africa," *Foreign Affairs,* XLI (January 1963), 398-409; and Curt F. Beck, "Czechoslovakia's Penetration of Africa, 1955-1962," *World Politics,* XV (April 1963), 403-416.

14

The Advanced Countries

RAYMOND L. GARTHOFF

The Political Role of Communism

A proletarian revolution in the advanced countries was at the very center of Marx's own expectation, and of subsequent Marxist thinking until after the consolidation of Bolshevik rule in Russia. The decade beginning in 1914, however, marked a major watershed in socialist analysis of the world revolution, as orthodox Marxism underwent three severe shocks. First was the discovery that most socialists persisted in retaining national consciousness and patriotism in a war among "bourgeois" states. Earlier disagreements within the socialist movement between revisionists and the old school were, for a time, overlaid by a new split into socialist nationalists and radical internationalists. The second shock was caused by the initial success of the socialist revolution in relatively underdeveloped and autocratic Russia, contrary to all Marxist expectations, including Lenin's. Moreover, it was revolution by *coup d'état* rather than a real proletarian uprising and was consolidated only by reliance on the peasantry. The third startling development was the failure of the socialist revolution in the advanced countries, above all in Germany. Not only was the revolution not supposed to begin in Russia, it was not supposed to be suspended even temporarily upon success in any single country, and least of all in Russia.

Adjustments in Marxist thought were swayed largely by the interrelated facts that success in practice facilitates rationalization in the reinterpretation of theory; that the group which has succeeded has great advantage over other groups in achieving a dominant role if it chooses—and the Russian Bolsheviks did so choose; and finally that a "going concern" develops needs and aims of its own, which can deeply affect the actions and viewpoints of the practitioners of any ideology. Ideologies—not excepting Marxism-Leninism—do tend to be part of the "superstructure" of deeper underlying political and economic realities.

Subsequent decades have seen the USSR develop into the second most powerful country in the world. This accomplishment has been achieved by placing the interests of the Soviet Union above assistance to the world Communist revolution in the many and significant times, places, and ways in which these two objectives have conflicted. Naturally, in instances where they converge, each reinforces the other. But, to coin for them a slogan: "What is good for the Soviet Union is good for the Communist world revolution" is not an inaccurate expression of the practical policy of successive Soviet leaders.

If the First World War left both an unexpected victory and other unexpected defeats for the Marxists, so did the Second World War. The postwar "victory" of socialism imposed on Eastern Europe under the shadow of Soviet military occupation was trumpeted as a sign of the wave of the future, but it was in fact a mere consolation prize for the failure of the Communists to hold and extend their foothold in the advanced countries. During the wartime heyday of the Soviet-Western alliance, the Communists were able to achieve a much greater degree of popular support in the advanced countries than ever before, or since. In France, Belgium, and Italy, they were able to seize control of much of the popular resistance movements; in Britain, Canada, and the United States they succeeded in infiltrating some sectors of society and government, and influenced public opinion in many ways favorable to the Soviet Union; and in Denmark and Norway they gained significantly in influence. In Japan, which may also be considered as an advanced country in this context, they attempted with only limited success to take advantage of postwar unrest.

Only in France, Belgium, and Italy were the Communists able to make major gains, however, for the collapse of the incumbent governments during the war gave them an unprecedented opportunity to put to use their skill at organization and propaganda. In France, the Communists emerged soon after the Nazi invasion as the most influential force in the resistance movement. Their National Front, and its military arm the *Francs-Tireurs et Partisans,* were in the forefront of the resistance effort. As advocates of active resistance, in contrast to a policy limited to sabotage, they attracted many who were disillusioned by the fall of France and enraged by German occupation policies. At the end of the war, the Communists were influential in the National Council of Resistance, and after the Allied invasion they defied Eisenhower and DeGaulle by seizing power in many localities and undertaking a campaign of terror against rival political groups. They had hopes of seizing Paris as well, but there they were anticipated by DeGaulle. Two Communists were nevertheless admitted to DeGaulle's government, and the party soon gained a virtual monopoly of the trade union movement.

In Beligum a much weaker party than the French likewise gained a dominant position in the resistance movement, and at the end of the war there was no statesman of the calibre of DeGaulle capable of establishing governmental authority in Brussels. In September 1944 two Communists participated in the formation of a weak coalition government, but in November they resigned in preparation for a general strike supported by armed formations which apparently aimed at the overthrow of the government. The situation was saved by the deployment of British troops, and the Communists later reentered the government, but they never regained their influence.

It is by no means certain that the Communists aimed to seize power immediately in France and Belgium at the hour of liberation, but they doubtless expected to use the leverage which control of Paris and Brussels would have given them to gain a dominant position in the postwar governments. Probably from the outset Stalin realized that the strength of the Western powers as a whole, and the relative weaknesses of the Communist movements within the advanced countries and of the Soviet Union vis-à-vis the United States, made it unrealistic to expect Communist seizures of power. There was nevertheless a powerful pressure group at Stalin's elbow, headed by Zhdanov, which advocated a vigorous policy of exploiting all opportunities to gain power. It would have been characteristic of Stalin to encourage probing actions so long as they did not expose the Soviet position to serious risks, and to extract whatever benefits could be gained from them if they were successful. In these as in so many other cases before and since, however, the critical factor was not the aims of the Communists but the determination of their rivals. Moreover Stalin's crude and obsessive pursuit of narrowly defined Soviet security interests, and his suspicious lowering of the Iron Curtain in 1946, soon squandered Russian popularity and influence in the West.

In Italy, after the fall of Mussolini in 1943, the Communists proved to be effective resistance leaders. The return of Togliatti from Moscow in 1944 enhanced their prestige, and their participation in the wartime governments of Badoglio and Bonomi gave them an early entry into official circles. Upon the defeat of the Axis, effective power in Italy was held by the Allied armies, and after the establishment of a stable government by DeGasperi in

1946 the opportunities for Communist infiltration and subversion were progressively reduced. In Denmark and Norway, Communist leaders likewise gained access to the postwar governments, but their party organizations were much weaker than the Italian and they were never in a position to contemplate the seizure of power. In the Netherlands their political role was even more restricted. In Western Germany, under very different circumstances, the prestige of the Communists was at a very low ebb in the hour of defeat. They made no significant gains in postwar elections, and the party was later banned in the course of the political struggle between East and West Germany. In Great Britain the Communists made substantial gains in membership during the war, and were successful in winning positions of influence in several of the leading trade unions. The overwhelming victory of the Labor Party in 1945 nevertheless proved to be a crushing blow to Communist political aspirations, and their influence declined rapidly thereafter. In the European countries that were only indirectly affected by the war, the political role of the Communists proved to be even less important. The Communists made significant new gains only in newly independent Iceland, due to their strength in the trade union movement and to the weakness of the Social Democrats. They participated in coalition governments in 1944-1947 and 1956-1958, and exerted a considerable influence on domestic and foreign policy.

Throughout Western Europe the governments established at the end of the war, with the backing of the Allied armies, undertook effective programs of reform and reconstruction which won the support of the bulk of the politically active citizens. In the cases where Communists participated as minority members of coalition governments in the immediate postwar period—in France, Belgium, Italy, Denmark, and Norway—the majority parties were sufficiently realistic to prevent them from using their governmental positions as a basis for a decisive infiltration of the key sources of power in the bureaucracy. The popular vote of the Communists was as high as 32 percent for the Communist-sponsored People's Democratic Front in Italy in 1948, and 28 percent for the Communist party alone in France in 1946, but this did not constitute effective political strength. By the time Stalin's challenge to the West in 1946 compelled European political leaders to take sides, all but the Communists and certain sections of the Socialist parties were prepared to close ranks. This decision was greatly facilitated by the unprecedented vigor and foresight of American policy as reflected in the Truman Doctrine and the Marshall Plan. By the middle of 1947 the Communists were excluded from the five coalition governments in which they had participated, and they turned to strikes, sabotage, and propaganda in their efforts to undermine the new plans for European recovery.[1]

In the advanced countries outside of Europe, communism never gained a significant position of political influence. Even in Japan, where the complete collapse of the wartime government ushered in a period of political disorganization, the Communists failed to make significant gains. This failure was largely due to the foresight of the American occupation forces under General MacArthur. The Soviet Union was excluded from an active role in the occupation. Communist-led strikes were forbidden and support was deliberately given to the socialist and moderate parties. Most important of all, General MacArthur initiated a sweeping program of political, economic, and social reforms which went a long way toward meeting the accumulated frustrations of the Japanese people. Although many of these reforms were received with considerable scepticism on the part of Japanese political leaders, if only because they were imposed by an army of occupation, they were destined to have a profound effect on Japanese political life and were in large measure accepted with significant adaptations. A final blow to Communist hopes was the emergence of the Socialist party as the principal and successful representative of the populist, radical, and neutralist sentiments which were so influential in Japanese public opinion.[2]

The story of the failure of the Communist Party of the USA, if not typical of all the advanced countries, is of particular importance in view of the leading role of the United States in the "capitalist" world. After more than two decades of stormy beginnings and a gradual rise during the Great Depression, sometimes tactically facili-

[1] See Mario Einaudi, Jean-Marie Domenach, and Aldo Garosci, *Communism in Western Europe* (Ithaca 1951); Franz Borkenau, *European Communism* (New York 1953), 441-483; and Hugh Seton-Watson, *From Lenin to Khrushchev* (2nd ed., New York 1960), 218-225, 291-300, and 185-392, for general accounts. There are also a number of specialized accounts of national parties: A. Rossi, *A Communist Party in Action* (New Haven 1949), Hadley Cantril and David Rodnick, *On Understanding the French Left* (Princeton 1956), Charles A. Micaud, *Communism and the French Left* (New York 1963), and Henry Pelling, *The British Communist Party* (London 1958). The situation in Iceland is discussed in Donald E. Nuechterlein, *Iceland: Reluctant Ally* (Ithaca 1961), and M. S. Olmsted, "Communism in Iceland," *Foreign Affairs*, XXXVI (January 1958), 340-347.

[2] See especially Rodger Swearingen and Paul Langer, *Red Flag in Japan: International Communism in Action, 1919-1951* (Cambridge, Mass. 1952).

tated but strategically blunted and foreclosed by the New Deal, the CPUSA reached its peak in mid-1945. It then had about 80,000 members, two Communist city councilmen in New York, and two American Labor Party fellow-travellers from that city in the national House of Representatives. In July of that year, the "soft" line was dropped, and with it Browder, the party's wartime leader, and a more assertive stance was adopted under pressure from Moscow. By 1948, a policy of stimulating the creation of a third party and then bending it to Communist control succeeded. But, as in the more bloody case of the Communist seizure by internal purges of a dominant role in the Loyalist government during the Spanish Civil War, "the operation was successful, but the patient died." The embrace of the Progressive Party by the Communists was its kiss of death, and in the process the Communists lost badly such influence as they had in politics, and especially in the CIO and other trade unions. The Party declined constantly to 54,000 in 1950, 25,000 in 1953, and since 1958 it has been well under 10,000 members.[3] Even of these, according to one recent published report by a former FBI man, some one in six may be an FBI informant![4]

The CPUSA has failed with hard as well as soft tactics, with penetration and with agitation, in depression and in prosperity. The cold war confrontation with the USSR has also contributed to this isolation and decline. But the basic reason for its total failure has been its irrelevance to American political life. Similarly in Canada, Australia, and New Zealand, despite the occasional prominence of individual leaders and activities, the Communists have failed to gain significant political influence.

Over four decades, the lesson of 1917-1923 has been confirmed: if the whole world is going to become socialist, the advanced countries would be the last to fall. Thus the current generation of Communist leaders has come to believe that the advanced countries will in the first instance be economically, politically, and militarily isolated by a gradual sweep of socialism over the rest of the globe. The "rear" of these countries—the former colonial and economically under-

[3] For discussions of the CPUSA we have an excellent trilogy: Theodore Draper, *The Roots of American Communism* (New York 1957); Draper, *American Communism and Soviet Russia* (New York 1960); and David Shannon, *The Decline of American Communism* (New York 1959). For a general bibliographical guide, see Robert Delaney, *The Literature of Communism in America* (Washington 1962).

[4] Peter Kihss, "1,500 from F. B. I. Said to Inform on U. S. Reds," *The New York Times* (October 18, 1962).

developed areas of Asia, Africa, and Latin America—is seen as the next stage for the advance of communism.

Another legacy of the Second World War was the victory of communism in mainland China. Here, too, the fruits of victory are by the early 1960's bittersweet; Peking is now less of an ally of Moscow than it is a competitor. Indeed, the bonds of common ideological aspiration and interest have been badly frayed by controverting ambition and conflicting national interest. Significantly, one of the symptoms and contributing causes of conflict is precisely a divergence of policy with respect to the advanced countries. The Soviet policy of waging conflict through "peaceful coexistence" has clashed with Chinese desires to prod the "paper tiger" of imperialism more vigorously than the Soviets consider prudent.

Chinese and Soviet differences over policy toward the advanced countries also find their counterpart in disagreements over the strategy to be pursued in the rest of the world. While the Soviets affirm their interest in the "national liberation movements" in colonial and neocolonial areas, and sometimes provide significant support, this assistance is selective and is geared to congruence of local objectives with broad Soviet foreign policy aims. The Chinese argue for greater priority, energy, and militance to be devoted to such campaigns.

Parenthetically, we might note that while Communist hopes for the rapid disintegration of colonial rule and a decline in Western influence in the independent underdeveloped countries have been realized, their expectations of unrest and Communist advance in the wake of colonial departure have been signally disappointed. Chaos in the Congo, temporary alienation of Guinea, uneasy repression in Angola, and controversy over West New Guinea have been but limited exceptions to the extraordinary shift of dozens of nations with hundreds of millions of people from colonial status to independence without leaving the "free world." Only Cuba is in the Communist fold. But while this trend must be sorely disappointing to the Communists, they evidently still see prospects for eventual extension of their authority throughout this area—by power of example, diplomatic influence, and revolution waged by guerrilla campaigns or subversion.

Communist Prospects in the Advanced Countries

The advanced countries of Western Europe (Great Britain, West Germany, France, Italy, Belgium, the Netherlands, Luxembourg,

Switzerland, and the Scandinavian countries), North America (the United States and Canada), and the Pacific (Japan, Australia, and New Zealand) represent diverse cultural, political, and economic backgrounds and current roles. Nonetheless, in the context of the world as a whole, the generally shared cultural traditions and political development (except for Japan), and economic, political, and military alliance ties (except for a few small European neutrals) stand out as enormously more significant. The advanced industrial countries are, strategically, the hard core of the "capitalist" world. Tactically, of course, differences among them are not insignificant.

It has long been a premise of Communist thinking that the "capitalist" countries are inevitably at one another's throats in competition for economic raw materials and markets. The development of the Common Market does not fit the Communist stereotype. As recently as ten years ago, Stalin was weighing the likelihood of war among "capitalistic" powers; now the Communists must weigh the prospects for possible eventual unity of many of the principal "capitalist" nations, and more of moment is the form and degree of conflict between the *Communist* powers.

We have noted the growing strength of the advanced countries, individually, and as a group. There are, of course, variations. Internal political instability may recur in France or Japan, and there is a large Communist party and voting minority in Italy. But in none of these cases can the Communists see any real prospect for gaining power in the foreseeable future. Even in France and Italy the voting strength of the Communist parties—which, above all in those countries, is no index of revolutionary potential—is respectively about twenty and twenty-five percent. Moreover, the trend of party membership, party unity, and voting strength is running against the Communists almost everywhere. In all the advanced countries taken together, except for Italy, there are fewer than one-half million Communists, and in Italy less than one and a half million. This represents only about forty percent of comparable Communist strength in 1946.[5]

Communist political influence can be brought to bear only in-

[5] The estimated current Communist strength here cited is compiled from the Department of State publication *World Strength of the Communist Party Organizations*, Intelligence Report No. 4489 R-14 (Washington 1962), *passim*. For earlier figures, including those for 1946, see *Communism's Postwar Decade*, Supplement to the *New Leader* (December 19, 1955), S6-S7.

directly, and usually even then ineffectually, in the advanced countries. In Italy, the "opening to the left" may yet isolate the Communists. Moreover, the Communist movement in Italy has grown "satisfied," and supports the *status quo* in those local areas where its strength is generally settled. In France, their only hope is to provoke a polarization of political forces into Left vs. Right in the uncertainty that is bound to follow DeGaulle, and then to press their influence within the Left coalition. In Great Britain, they spur on pacificist movements. But beyond these limited forms of indirect maneuver, the Communists have practically no political leverage. Their general tactic, therefore, is to support the most "left" elements and hope either to infiltrate or otherwise influence others. In general, though, in the rare cases when the Communists do acquire some real influence, the outcome is usually to kill the infiltrated movement by their support —as was the case with the Progressive Party in the United States in 1948. Finally, as so often occurs when a small group has no external prospects, there is a tendency to splinter in internal debate and conflict. Until fairly recently such tendencies were usually limited to personal maneuver in the leaderships, but now the Sino-Soviet split has had among its repercussions the first chance since the fall of Trotsky for struggle in the Communist movement with alternate outside sources of support and allegiance. And, as a result, some Communist parties (including a few in advanced countries such as Belgium) have divided into rival pro-Moscow and pro-Peking factions. There have also been recurrent "revisionist" deviations, especially in the small American and British parties.

In the fall of 1962 a world conference of Marxist-Leninist specialists on the subject of the decline of capitalism was held in Moscow, sponsored jointly by the Institute for World Economics and International Relations, the USSR Academy of Sciences, and the journal *Problems of Peace and Socialism (World Marxist Review)*. It fell to the lot of this conference to analyze the broad trends in the advanced countries, and to square the facts with the Marxist-Leninist line. The conferees could not, of course, totally ignore the relative prosperity, economic advance, and trend to economic cooperation highlighted by such developments as the success of the European Economic Community. Nonetheless, while citing Lenin on the continuing advance of capitalism for a limited time, they sought to argue that basic flaws in the system and contradictions among the capitalist states would eventually lead to the decline and downfall of the capitalist system. The standard themes of growing monopoly capitalism, spreading unemployment, and increased class stratification and conflict were all asserted.[6] A similar account appears in a collective volume on the class struggle published following the conference of Communist parties held in Moscow in November 1961. These same hackneyed themes were repeated, and strikes were defined as the chief form of class conflict in the capitalist countries at this stage. The book also offered unusual statistics on the class structure of the advanced countries: the "bourgeoisie" was said to comprise 1-4 percent of the population, the "middle class" 45-50 percent, and the "proletariat" 45-50 percent.[7] Other discussions in the same volume stressed that while the class struggle was allegedly sharpening, peaceful transition had now become "the fundamental form" of achieving socialism in the capitalist countries.[8]

In general, Communist ideologists and economists find excuses for the continuing successes of capitalism, and present elaborately selected data to exaggerate its failings. But Communist policy-makers cannot always accept a grossly distorted image in place of real live phenomena. They may remain confident in their future expectations, but they must sometimes recognize the realities of prosperity, economic advance, and political cooperation in the West. As they look ahead into the longer range of practical policy planning—over the next decade or more—they see only marginal possibilities for direct Communist political action in the advanced countries.

One possible exception is France, where the persistent instability of several successive Republics, and a strong Left current in which the Communists have a certain base for maneuver, offers some hopes. There may even be concrete residual assets from the 1930's and 1940's in the form of experienced cadres and even materiel for violent action,

[6] "Theses on Imperialist 'Integration' in Western Europe (The Common Market)," TASS, *Radio Moscow* (August 27, 1962), and other press and radio accounts of the Conference.

[7] V. S. Semenov, "Narastaniye klassovoy bor'by v stranakh kapitala" [Growth of the Class Struggle in the Capitalist Countries], in *Velikaya khartiya kommunisticheskikh i rabochikh partii* [Magna Carta of the Communist and Workers' Parties] (Moscow 1961), 209-272, esp. 212-215. See also S. Vygodsky, "Faktor uglubleniya obshchego krizisa kapitalizma" [A Factor Deepening the General Crisis of Capitalism], *Mezhdunarodnaya zhizn'*, No. 4 (April 1962), 38-45; and A. A. Arzumanyan, ed., *Rabochoye dvizheniye v kapitalisticheskikh stranakh, 1951-1961* [The Workers' Movement in the Capitalist Countries, 1951-1961] (Moscow 1961).

[8] Ts. A. Stepanyan, "xx vek—vek torzhestva Kommunizma" [The Twentieth Century—Century of the Victory of Communism], in *Velikaya khartiya*, 24-79, esp. 47-49.

though this latter is but speculative. Another possible exception lies in the semi-developed southern fringes of Europe: Spain, Portugal, Southern Italy, and Greece. If these countries are counted as part of the advanced capitalist camp, they are its least economically developed and politically secure areas. But, we must repeat, these are but marginal possible exceptions to the general situation in the major advanced nations.

Equally significant in recent years has been the marked decline in the appeal of communism to intellectuals. In the 1930's and the 1940's a number of intellectuals in France, Great Britain, and the United States were drawn to the Communist party—some as members, but the majority as sympathizers. The initial motives were in most cases a search for an alternative to the social order that had collapsed as a result of the Great Depression, and a means of countering the facism of Italy, Germany, and Spain whose danger to the West they were early to recognize. The attraction of communism lay less in the reality of the Soviet Union, which few had visited or seriously studied, than in Communist propaganda which impressed uninitiated Westerners as a sincere program for the creation of a liberal and just social order.

The extent to which this mirage was the fundamental attraction is reflected in the promptness with which these intellectuals abandoned communism when the reality of Soviet policies was revealed. Stalin's purges of Communists in Russia, and in Spain during the civil war, and especially the conclusion of the Nazi-Soviet Pact, were for most intellectuals a decisive revelation of the tactics of Marxism-Leninism. For some, however, especially in France and Great Britain, the wartime coalition restored a measure of faith which was not decisively undermined until 1956 when Khrushchev admitted the realities of Stalinism at the Twentieth Party Congress, and revealed the nature of his own policies a few months later in Hungary.[9]

A by-product of the attraction of communism for some intellectuals was their active role in the many Communist-inspired front organizations designed to mobilize public opinion in the advanced countries against nuclear testing, NATO, American economic aid to Europe, the creation of the Common Market, and other policies opposed by the Soviet Union. The existence of a climate of opinion

[9] Gabriel A. Almond, *The Appeals of Communism* (Princeton 1954); Raymond Aron, *The Opium of the Intellectuals* (London 1957); Neal Wood, *Communism and British Intellectuals* (New York 1959); and Daniel Aaron, *Writers on the Left: Episodes in American Literary Communism* (New York 1961).

receptive to such propaganda is illustrated by the fact that when the veteran Communist leader Aksel Larsen was expelled from the Danish party in 1958, he continued his political activity as head of a movement working for pacifism and neutralism. The appeal of neutralism was particularly strong in Japan, where the traditional value system had been shattered by military defeat and the use of atomic bombs against Hiroshima and Nagasaki had produced a profound shock. Despite the limited political role of communism in Japan, the pervasive influence among intellectuals and students of the ideological frame of reference of Marxism-Leninism was reminiscent of the Western experience of a generation earlier.[10]

A more serious challenge to the Western governments was the infiltration of bureaucracies by party members and sympathizers who were prepared to cooperate with the Soviet intelligence services as spies. Although the number of prominent Western scientists and civil servants working for the Soviet Union was very small, and the extent of their revelations is, because of the nature of the situation, not a matter of public knowledge, it seems likely that the Soviet Union gained significant information from this activity. In the scientific field this form of espionage was limited primarily to the immediate postwar years, but in the political field it continued on into the 1960's.[11] No doubt much of this spying may be explained in terms of the age-old motives of personal gain or blackmail, but a few cases reflected a residue of ideological loyalty which survived the many revelations of Communist reality. By the 1950's, in any event, the appeal of communism was limited to a very small range of educated Westerners. The achievements of Communist policies were generally recognized, but the human costs were by now so well known that Communist propaganda had little influence.

The vitality of the advanced countries has not only affected the status of the Communist parties in those countries; it has also challenged the Communist ideology itself. Efforts to express or codify development of Western economic ideology have not been very effec-

[10] Evron M. Kirkpatrick, *Target: The World* (New York 1956) and *Year of Crisis* (New York 1957); and Frederick C. Barghoorn, *The Soviet Cultural Offensive* (Princeton 1960).

[11] David J. Dallin, *Soviet Espionage* (New Haven 1955) provides a general introduction to this subject. Two well-documented cases are *The Report of the Royal Commission . . . to Investigate the Facts Relating to and the Circumstances Surrounding the Communications by Public Officials and Other Persons in Positions of Trust of Secret and Confidential Information to Agents of a Foreign Power* (Ottawa 1946); and *Report of the Royal Commission on Espionage* (Sydney 1955).

tive, but nonetheless the Communists—even in the USSR itself—have been greatly agitated by such ideas as "people's capitalism," and by the effects of social democracy in power in a number of Western countries. And, of course, the very problem of explaining away Western prosperity and economic advance is persistently difficult.

Soviet Strategy and the Advanced Countries

The advanced countries have, as we have noted, moved in Communist expectations from being first in line for revolution to last place. Consequently, they are seen not as the target for current attempts to extend Communist sway, but rather as obstacles to Communist efforts to extend influence and control in other parts of the world. Thus, for the present, the Communists seek to neutralize, rather than to overthrow, the advanced states. By a wide variety of means they attempt to deter or distract the advanced countries from bringing their great power to bear effectively against erosion of their own traditional influence and against Communist extension of influence by various means into the underdeveloped, often politically uncommitted, and sometimes unstable areas of the world.

In view of the strength of the major advanced countries, the Communists realize that, even though they believe this strength to be on the wane, they are forced to combat internal authority within the advanced countries by cautious and indirect means. Direct action is focused on two other spheres: building internally the economic and military power of the USSR, and of the other Communist countries under the leadership of Moscow; and extending Marxist-Leninist influence, and the influence of the USSR, in the most vulnerable parts of the non-Communist world. During the decades ahead, while building their own power, the Soviets seek gradual political and economic isolation of the advanced countries; gradual undermining internally of their political, economic, and moral strength; and infiltration of political and social institutions by Communist and "progressive" forces.[12] These courses of action involve military and political threats and pressures as deemed appropriate, but neither war nor direct political violence. Along with military pressure, complementing but far outweighing it in importance, are campaigns for disarmament, disen-

[12] Among the many volumes analyzing the methods and techniques of the Communist conspiracy in the advanced countries, see Philip Selznick, *The Organizational Weapon* (New York 1952 and 1960); Robert Strausz-Hupé and others, *Protracted Conflict* (New York 1959); and William R. Kintner and Joseph Z. Kornfeder, *The New Frontiers of War* (Chicago 1962).

gagement, accommodation, and relaxation of tensions on terms favorable to the Communist countries. By manipulating pressures within the advanced countries, while controlling reciprocal pressures in their own countries, the Communists seek to use indigenous peace movements and other appropriate vehicles to relax Western efforts and to bring about concessions.

War between the Communist states and the advanced countries is now ruled out as a course which Soviet leaders would choose.[13] General nuclear war in the foreseeable future would utterly devastate the Communist countries, no matter what it did also to other parts of the world. Limited war would carry unnecessarily great risks of escalating into general nuclear war. Of course, local hostilities might occur due to miscalculation as to the Western reaction, but the Communists would seek to prevent or to dampen down such occurrences. They also believe that they face the possible contingency of a Western surprise attack, and hence recognize the need to be cautious of premature pressure on vital interests of the advanced countries, as well as the need to build strong Soviet strategic nuclear offensive and defensive capabilities to deter such possible Western resort to arms, or in the extremity to lessen its terrible blow. Especially in the long run, the Communists would have to consider a possible desperate attempt of the cornered and dying "imperialist beast" to lash out with its formidable strength, which could bring great peril and enormous destruction even if (in their view) foredoomed to failure.

Bolshevism had always been based on the concept of Communist victory through internal revolution, rather than war between nations. After the success of the revolution in Russia in the wake of the First World War, and in China and Eastern Europe after the Second World War, postwar Stalinist discourse strongly implied that a third world war was a logical, if indeed not *the* logical, path to the complete extension of socialism throughout the world. However, in the post-Stalin period, spurred on by increasing recognition of the consequences which would ensue from a global nuclear war, this implication of expanding Communism by war or by revolution spurred by war has been rejected. Similarly, Leninist doctrine has been solemnly

[13] For a fuller discussion, see R. L. Garthoff, "War and Peace in Soviet Policy," *Russian Review*, xx (April 1961), 121ff.; and for an authoritative Soviet statement see N. S. Khrushchev, "Za novye pobedy mirovogo Kommunisticheskogo dvizheniya" [For New Victories of the World Communist Movement], *Kommunist*, No. 1 (1961), 3-37.

revised by rejection of the inevitability of war.[14] The following passage from an authoritative article in *Kommunist* expresses well the new view: "It happened that after the First World War our country fell away from the imperialist system, and so did China and other people's democracies after the Second World War. But do these facts indicate some internal law in the maturing of socialist revolutions? No. Marxist-Leninist theory has never held that war constitutes a source or prerequisite, necessary for the emergence of revolutions . . . But the question of the relation of war and revolution has assumed a different character in our times . . . The creation of modern weapons of mass destruction, of atomic and hydrogen weapons and the means of their delivery to any point on the globe, has fundamentally altered the nature of war, making it many times more destructive. . . . [A world war] would cause the complete destruction of the main centers of civilization and the annihilation of whole peoples. It would bring untold suffering to all mankind. Only madmen could want such a catastrophe to happen. . . . The working-class does not think of creating a Communist civilization on the ruins of the centers of world culture, on desolated territories contaminated by thermonuclear fall-out, which would be the inevitable consequences of such a war. . . . It is, therefore, obvious that a contemporary nuclear war, however one looks at it, can in no way be a factor that would accelerate the revolution and bring nearer the victory of socialism. Quite the contrary, such a war would throw mankind, the revolutionary workers' movement throughout the world, and the construction of socialism and Communism back for many decades."[15]

The Communists believe that, in some particular cases, they may be able to apply specific measures of neutralization to Western power. Apart from general efforts to capitalize on divisions and differences within the alliances of advanced countries, the Soviets no doubt anticipate that the special case of divided Germany will permit the alienation of West Germany from the alliance either by a deal with the other advanced countries to weaken their ties to Germany, or by a deal with Germany weakening its ties to the other allies. The Rapacki Plan for denuclearization of Central Europe—removing effective

[14] For a longer historical analysis, see the discussion by R. L. Garthoff in Ivo Lederer (ed.), *Russian Foreign Policy: Essays in Historical Perspective* (New Haven 1962), 243-277, esp. 252-253 and 270-272, and A. Butenko, "Voyna i revolyutsiya" [War and Revolution], *Kommunist,* No. 2 (1961), 49-60.

[15] A. Belyakov and F. Burlatskiy, "Leninskaya teoriya sotsialisticheskoy revolyutsii i sovremennost' " [Lenin's Theory of the Socialist Revolution and the Present Time], *Kommunist,* No. 13 (1960), 15-16.

Western military presence from Germany—is an excellent example of a ploy directed to that end. Efforts in connection with the persistent Berlin friction to force increasing Western reconciliation to the indefinite division of Germany, by recognizing the German Democratic Republic, is another prominent case in point. The disastrous attempt in 1962 to create a missile base in Cuba on the doorstep of the United States was yet another.

While weakening and neutralizing the efforts of the advanced countries, the Communist powers believe that their expected gains in other areas, described in other chapters of this volume, would not only add to their relative weight but would also subtract from the strength and confidence of the capitalist states. Not only do they regard the advanced countries as dependent economically on other areas, but they think their own expected increasing economic advances will persuade many to see in them a greater vitality. Thus they believe that the socialist world system will extend its influence at the expense of the advanced countries, and that the decline of the old system will contribute directly to the growth of the socialist system. At the same time, despite some temporary continuing economic progress by the capitalist states in the next few decades, a superior Communist system is expected gradually to outstrip them and to attract others—including many within the advanced countries themselves—by the power of successful example.

The Communist Image of Final Victory

The final victory of communism in the whole world is only very dimly seen—not even seen, really, but assumed. How do the Communist leaders visualize the final push, the final fall of the powerful advanced countries? They do not. They believe in it, but they do not have a clear image of how or when the advanced countries would fall. Guiding ideological works—including the most authoritative recent work of all, the new *Program of the CPSU* adopted in 1961—do not have an answer. All the old Marxist-Leninist doctrine is there, tailored when appropriate or necessary to meet the current Soviet outlook, but with nothing more than articles of faith on the ultimate victory. The most poignant, if not very concrete, expression of this credo appeared in Khrushchev's 1962 Supreme Soviet election speech when, in an aside from his prepared text, he declared: "This victory will come. It will, it will. No prayers, alms, or bribes will help the capitalists—and they do offer bribes. It is a question of time.

We have patience. One must be patient and wait—and not only be patient and wait. Our work, the construction of communism, is like yeast used to raise leaven. . . . You and I, our Communist Party, the fraternal Communist parties, and our practical construction of communism are the yeast of the world for, so to speak, insuring the victory of communism."[16]

The question of the ultimate victory of communism intrudes into current Soviet thinking most directly in ideological discussions of the achievement of "communism" within the USSR itself. Now that the Soviet Union is officially "building communism" it must, at least in their theoretical "building," deal with awkward questions such as the withering away of the state. Since the existence of the state is required so long as there exist a number of capitalist states, "communism" either cannot come about until there is no longer a capitalist system, or else "communism" must occur before the state withers away.

It is clear that the Communist leaders have not thought about the ultimate stage of the revolution in operative policy terms. This is certainly not surprising; it is realistic. But it is not often realized, and it is extremely significant. It contrasts with their attention (and disagreements) over the forms and extent of aid to "national liberation movements" in the less advanced countries.

Khrushchev personally has predicted that the time will come in the days of his grandchildren—which would mean roughly within little more than half a century. It is most doubtful that any responsible Communist leader would expect the fall of the advanced countries within the next few decades. The Communists have a strong expectation of the final achievement of a Communist world, but they do not have a timetable, a deadline, or prophecies on timing to reinterpret when they go wrong. It is not unlikely that as time moves ahead the hazy distant image of ultimate victory will continue to recede time and again, perhaps until it is finally recognized to be a mirage.

The manner and form of the fall of "capitalism," in contrast to its alleged decline, is also not predetermined in Communist eyes. Soviet writings indicate that in the "capitalist" citadels peaceful assumption of power is the principal means envisaged. The *Fundamentals of Marxism-Leninism,* published in 1959, stresses the possibility and the preference for peaceful transition to socialism. "Thus," it states, "peaceful revolution has become feasible not because the nature of the ruling classes has changed or that they now display an

[16] N. S. Khrushchev, *Radio Moscow* (March 16, 1962).

inclination to cede power voluntarily, but because in a number of countries it has now become possible to achieve a preponderance over the reactionary classes that will make them conscious of the futility of resisting, leaving them with no choice but that of capitulating to the revolutionary people. And so, in this case too, the outcome of the revolution is decided by the actual relation of forces."[17] The distinction between this view, and that of despised "reformists" or "revisionists," is explained by the *Fundamentals* to reside in reformist denial of the class struggle and of the very possibility of non-peaceful roads to socialism. But the protestation is a weak one, as the Chinese and Albanian Communists charge. Even when arguing for "striking at the heart of capitalism," the Soviets lamely fall back on convincing peoples by the power of example. Thus, for instance, the *World Marxist Review,* which provides guidance to Communist parties under Moscow's direction, has stated: "A realistic view of things—and the Communists have always been noted for their realism—impels the conclusion that the outcome of the struggle between the two social systems in the world today cannot be decided by blows, however painful, at the periphery; by 'nibbling,' as Alsop puts it, at the edges of the capitalist world. No, the complete and final victory of socialism throughout the world will come only when it strikes a mortal blow at the very heart of capitalism, that is, by demonstrating its superiority as a social system all along the line, and by convincing the people in the capitalist countries of that superiority. This is how the people will be won for socialism. With capitalism gripped by deepening contradictions, this conviction of the superiority of socialism will generate such a mighty upsurge of revolutionary struggle that imperialism will have to give way, and socialism will win the final victory in the struggle between the two systems."[18]

This is the general line, although particularly before the Sino-Soviet controversy erupted there were reminders of the need for active, rather than passive, exploitation of the superiority claimed for Soviet socialism. Thus an editorial in *World Marxist Review* in early 1960 declared: "It would be a mistake to think that in the capitalist countries profound social changes will take place automatically, merely as a result of the strength and prestige of the socialist countries. . . . Only resolute action by the masses will compel the bourgeoisie to make

[17] *Fundamentals of Marxism-Leninism,* 528-529.

[18] J. Armstrong, "Global Poker versus Grand Strategy," *WMR,* No. 6 (June 1962), 61.

social and political concessions."[19] But even such indications of vague "resolute action" refer to actions within the advanced countries. Nor is this mere double-talk or deception. The Soviets will surely continue to instigate and to support subversion and other forms of revolutionary activity, where they consider it expedient. But there is every good reason in logic and in history to believe in Soviet sincerity when they protest their desire "to ensure a situation in which internal processes in particular countries do not lead to *military* clashes of the two opposing systems."[20]

The Soviet attitude toward outside assistance for revolutions is doubtless based in predominant measure on their policy calculations of feasibility. Their frequently repeated statements that one cannot export revolution (or counterrevolution) is probably valid as a general policy statement, even though such statements are based most on considerations of prudence and of propaganda, and least on Marxism-Leninism. But we are, after all, interested in operative Communist thinking rather than scholastic ideology. In a recent article in *Kommunist,* we find the very interesting statement: "The socialist revolution is not a ballistic missile, and cannot be sent overseas."[21]

Perhaps the most revealing indication of attitudes in the Soviet leadership on transition to communism in the advanced countries is to be found in a statement by Khrushchev commenting on the meaning of his earlier declaration "We shall bury you." Khrushchev expressed what were probably his real views when he explained: "We are convinced that communism will win, as it provides better conditions for the development of the productive forces of society, provides the conditions for the fullest and most harmonious development of the society in general and for every individual in particular. Capitalism fights against communism, but it is impossible to arrest the process of the development of mankind. Sooner or later communism will win everywhere in the world, and, consequently, communism will bury capitalism. This is how my statement should be understood. It is not a question of someone burying someone physically, but of a change in the social system in the course of the historical development of society. When we say that communism will bury capitalism, this does not mean, of course, that the Soviet people, the Communists of the

[19] Editorial, "On the Threshold of 1960," *WMR,* No. 1 (January 1960), 6.

[20] A. Sovetov, "Leninist Foreign Policy and International Relations," *IntAff,* No. 4 (1960), 9.

[21] G. Starushenko, "Mirnoye sosushchestvovaniye i revolyutsiya," [Peaceful Coexistence and Revolution], *Kommunist,* No. 2 (1962), 86.

Soviet Union, will inter capitalists of this or that country. No, communism is winning in the Soviet Union, and many other countries are now following the road of Communist development. Communism is growing out of the dedicated labor and struggle of the peoples of the socialist countries for a new, better, the most just, creative life on earth. Such is the teaching of life, of history: a more progressive social system inevitably comes to replace a system which is outliving itself, a progressive system buries a moribund one. This is how we regard the historic process of the development of society. I have spoken of this more than once. I spoke of this in the United States, too, when I visited your country. We do not impose our communist convictions by force on anybody. We believe that in America, too, mighty forces will grow—they already exist there and are growing and developing all the time. These progressive forces which are growing within the American people itself will ultimately win. In place of capitalism, which reigns in America today, the American people will themselves establish a new social system, and this system will be communism. Thus, it can be said that one system, asserting itself, buries another system, which is outliving itself. It is not that one people buries a part of another. This would be monstrous; this would mean war between states. The question of the victory of one social system over another is one of class struggle. It is a new class which is developing and gaining in strength now—the working class, the people themselves—that will, so to speak, reign in the world, including the United States."[22]

In a recent Soviet broadcast to Communist China, it was remarked that: "Many Communist parties—including those in Italy, France, the United States, Japan, Britain, Norway, and other countries—consider peaceful transition to socialism their goal."[23] The CPSU Program adopted at the Twenty-Second Party Congress, a formal document of great official weight, reiterated the view frequently presented in recent years that the Communist preference is to achieve power by peaceful means, and it even went so far as to speculate that in some cases the capitalists would sell the means of production to the proletariat.[24]

[22] N. S. Khrushchev, Interview with Gardner Cowles, broadcast TASS account, *Radio Moscow* (April 25, 1962).

[23] "The Marxist-Leninist Viewpoint on the Paths of Transition from Capitalism to Socialism in Various Countries," *Radio Moscow* (March 27, 1962), in Mandarin to China. Also, Vladimirova, "Marxism-Leninism," *Radio Moscow* (August 30, 1962), in Albanian.

[24] "Program of the CPSU," *Pravda* (November 2, 1961).

Revolution by insurrection, *coups d'état,* guerrilla warfare, and civil war is of course the broad alternative path. Soviet, and much more emphatically Chinese and Albanian, ideological sources endorse this alternative if it proves necessary. Soviet accounts usually now refer to this alternative delicately as "the non-peaceful transition to socialism," and stress its occurrence only when the imperialists most unreasonably compel it by waging civil war against the working classes. Also, some Soviet accounts have interpreted the peaceful path and "parliamentary means of struggle" broadly enough to include the Czech *coup.*[25]

Although other ideological and policy differences and the clash of ambitions have been the leading causes of splits within the Communist world, diverging views on the current and future prospects and means of Communist action against the advanced countries have played an important role in these controversies. As a reflection of a generally more militant attitude, the Chinese and Albanians have assumed a greater, and earlier, role for political violence in the advanced countries than have the Soviets or, of course, the Yugoslavs. In assessing the current situation in the advanced countries, the Albanians have on a number of occasions alleged that a revolutionary situation was ripe. Shehu declared in a speech in mid-1962: "In recent years, crippling strikes have been staged in the United States, West Germany, Britain, France, Italy, Spain, Greece, Japan, Argentina, and elsewhere. Today we observe with satisfaction a democratic, anti-imperialist, and revolutionary movement in the capitalist world headed by the working class."[26] Another Albanian Politburo member, in speaking of the alleged strike movement, mentioned nearly the same list of advanced countries (Belgium was included, and Japan and Greece omitted).[27] Hoxha, in a speech which emphasized revolutionary transition, implied inclusion of North America in his prediction when he said: "The American peoples and the Communist and worker's parties of that continent will undoubtedly follow heroic Cuba's example in its efforts to put power into the hands of their peoples."[28] In this same speech, Hoxha downgraded the possibility of peaceful assumption of power in the capitalist states.

[25] "The Twenty-Second Congress of the CPSU and the Nature of the Present Era and Paths for Advancement of Society," *Radio Moscow* (May 10, 1962); and Vladimirova, "Marxism-Leninism," *Radio Moscow* (August 30, 1962).

[26] Mehmet Shehu, Speech to the People's Assembly, *Zeri i Popullit,* broadcast by *Radio Tirana* (July 16, 1962).

[27] Gogo Nushi, Election Speech, *Radio Tirana* (May 25, 1962).

[28] Enver Hoxha, Election Speech, *Radio Tirana* (May 30, 1962).

The Chinese Communists have likewise implied that revolutionary war will be necessary in the advanced countries. They cite Lenin's remarks that as a general rule the seizure of power by the proletariat "can happen only by means of a violent revolution" and they have extended that idea into the concept of "uninterrupted revolution" in the course of the transformation of a bourgeois democratic revolution into a socialist revolution.[29] The actual course of history in the advanced countries is not easily reconcilable with this thesis. Moreover, the Chinese eye is focused above all on the development of a revolutionary movement in the less advanced countries. The celebrated article in *Red Flag* on the anniversary of Lenin's birthday in 1960, which touched off the open polemics between the Chinese and Russians, said that: "The shortening of the period between capitalist economic crises is a new phenomenon. It further signifies that the world capitalist system is drawing nearer and nearer to its inevitable doom." And the article went on to state, "No matter which way one looks at it, none of the new technology such as atomic energy, rocketry, and the like, has changed the basic character either of the epoch of imperialism or of the proletarian revolution as pointed out by Lenin, contrary to the allegations of modern revisionists. The capitalist-imperialist system absolutely will not crumble of itself. It will be pushed over by the proletarian revolution within the imperialist country concerned, and the national revolution in the colonial and semi-colonial countries."[30] It is, however, probably safe to say that the Chinese Communists have not really posed seriously the question of the means for effecting socialist revolution in the advanced countries. They do not dissent from the theoretical principle held by the Soviet Marxist-Leninists that the question of "peaceful" or "non-peaceful" transition from capitalism to socialism will vary from case to case, depending on particular circumstances.

The Yugoslav view on the question of transition to Communist rule in the advanced countries has been most definitively given in Kardelj's *Socialism and War*. "It is," he said, "quite certain that in highly developed countries there is greater feasibility of a more peaceable path than in less developed countries, where internal contradictions are more powerfully brought out. For this reason it is no accident that in many European countries the working class has adopted a

[29] Lu Ting-i, "Get United Under the Banner of Lenin," *Radio Peiping* (April 22, 1960).

[30] *Red Flag* article on the ninetieth anniversary of the birth of Lenin, broadcast on *Radio Peiping* (April 20, 1960).

mainly social-democratic outlook. . . ."[31] Kardelj cites both Marx and Engels in support of his thesis of peaceful transition to communism in the advanced capitalist countries (quoting Marx as mentioning the United States, Great Britain, and Holland, and Engels as mentioning the United States, France, and England).

A statement by Luigi Longo of the Italian Communist Party (PCI) is quite interesting as an example of forthright insistence on the "peaceful" path to the very acquisition of power. At the Conference of Communist Parties held in Moscow in November 1961, in the course of the Sino-Soviet controversy over the general line of the international Communist movement, Longo (usually identified as a "militant") said: "It is possible, in a number of countries, to realise the transition from capitalism to socialism by peaceful means, advancing continuously on the road of development of democracy, without a prior revolutionary rupture and civil war. . . . The Chinese comrades ask us to indicate what country is advancing along this road. We reply in all tranquility and firmness that the PCI itself has been moving for some time in this direction. . . ."[32]

The Soviet position on the roles of war, and on violent and nonviolent revolution, has been set forth in clear detail in the Open Letter of July 14, 1963, prompted by the debate with the Chinese Communists. The Central Committee of the CPSU stated:

"We would like to ask the Chinese comrades, who suggest building a bright future on the ruins of the old world destroyed by a thermonuclear war, if they have consulted the working class of the countries where imperialism dominates? The working class of the capitalist countries would be sure to ask them: 'Do we ask you to trigger a war and destroy our countries while annihilating imperialists?'

"Is it not a fact that the monopolists, the imperialists are only a comparatively small group, while the bulk of the population of the capitalist countries consists of the working class, working peasantry, working intelligentsia. The atomic bomb does not distinguish between the imperialists and working people; it hits big areas and therefore millions of workers would be destroyed for each monopolist.

"The working class, the working people, will ask such revolutionaries: What right do you have to settle for us the questions of our existence and our class struggle? We are also in favor of Socialism,

[31] Edvard Kardelj, *Socialism and War* (London 1961), 86.

[32] Luigi Longo, *Interventi della delegazione del PCI alla conferenza di Mosca degli 81 partiti communisti ed operai* (Rome 1962), 40; cited in *Survey,* No. 42 (June 1962), 109.

but we want to gain it through the class struggle and not by unleashing a world war. . .

"And what is the position of the Chinese comrades on this issue? It is the keynote of all their statements and the letter of the C. C. P. Central Committee of 14 June.

"The Chinese comrades regard as the main criterion of revolutionary spirit the recognition of an armed uprising always, in everything, and everywhere. Thereby the Chinese comrades actually deny the possibility of using peaceful forms of struggle for the victory of the Socialist revolution, whereas Marxism-Leninism teaches that the Communists must master all forms of revolutionary class struggle—both violent and non-violent. . . .

"The question arises: What is the explanation for the incorrect propositions of the C. C. P. leadership on the basic problems of our time? Is it the complete divorce of the Chinese comrades from actual reality, a dogmatic, bookish approach to the problems of war, peace, and the revolution, their lack of understanding of the concrete conditions of the modern epoch; or it is the fact that behind the rumpus about the world revolution raised by the Chinese comrades, are other goals which have nothing in common with revolution?

"All this shows the erroneousness, the disastrous nature, of the course that the C. C. P. leadership tries to impose on the world Communist movement. What the Chinese leaders propose under the guise of a 'general line' is nothing but an enumeration of the most general tasks of the working class, made without due consideration for time and the concrete correlation of class forces, without due consideration for the peculiarities of the modern stage of history.

"The Chinese comrades do not notice, or do not wish to notice, how the tasks of our movement change in conditions of the present-day epoch. Reducing the general line to general tasks which are valid for all stages of transition from capitalism to Socialism, they deprive it of its concreteness, purposefulness, and genuine effectiveness. . .

"The Socialist revolution takes place as a result of the internal development of class struggle in every country, and its forms and ways are determined by the concrete conditions of each given nation. The general regularity lies in the revolutionary overthrow of the power of capital and the establishment of a proletarian dictatorship in this or that form. It is the task of the working class and the Communist parties to make maximum use of the now available opportunities for the peaceful road to a Socialist revolution, not connected with a civil war, and to be at the same time ready for the non-peaceful method, for the armed suppression of the resistance of the bourgeoisie. . . ."[33]

It is evident that the disparate Soviet, Chinese, Albanian, Yugoslav and other Communist views differ chiefly in spirit rather than in detailed positions. They are corollaries to views on more active policy questions such as selection of the strategy for extending communism in the underdeveloped areas, and definition of the role of war in the general transition of the non-Communist world to Communist rule. The Soviet contention that war must be avoided is carried to the point of assigning preservation of peace as the priority task of the international Communist movement. The Chinese, in contrast, urge that priority be given to the revolutionary struggle. The capitalists, argue the Chinese, will not really intervene and make war; but if they do, it will be their own doom. The Russians are not satisfied with reasonable assurance of the doom of the capitalists when it means also—as they know—reasonable assurance of their own demise.

The Prospects of War and Revolution

Revolutions carry much lower risks than international wars. Consequently, the Soviets are more ready to support them in those peripheral situations where they hold promise. But revolutionary war waged within the advanced countries would be quite another matter. The Communists do not, at present, see circumstances in prospect which would make such actions feasible.

It is not unlikely that serious Communist consideration of comprehensive disarmament has included attention to the possibilities of "unleashing" revolutionary war in many circumstances in which it would be quite out of the question in a nuclear-armed world. Soviet disarmament proposals and positions have been intended chiefly for political warfare rather than serious negotiation. Nonetheless, the Soviet leaders have insisted on standing their ground on general disarmament as a desirable objective, even at the expense of further debilitating discord over this very issue with the Chinese Communists, and moreover on an issue on which their doctrinal position is not unassailable. While the Soviets see serious obstacles and disadvantages to general disarmament, they also would expect along with other advantages to see the national liberation movements sweep ahead

[33] *New York Times* (July 15, 1963), 12-13, 14.

much more rapidly than if the imperialists retain their powerful military strength. Ultimately, revolutions would thus be facilitated in engulfing the economically weakened and militarily neutralized advanced countries themselves. However, they do not see general disarmament as a practical possibility at any time now foreseeable.

The Soviet leaders also consider another unlikely but possible course of events. What if a general nuclear war should actually occur? Apart from frail hopes for Soviet survival and net military advantage in the Eurasian periphery, the Soviet leaders would hope that the "capitalist system" would itself be atomized, and that "revolution" in the radioactive debris would create a new socialist society—but for the distant English-speaking countries at least, the burden would probably still rest on local popular reaction rather than projectable Soviet military power. The role of revolutionary war in Communist strategy in such circumstances, however, would be but one of many crucial uncertainties in the post-nuclear world, even in the eyes of the Communists. Overt external war, and internal revolutionary war, are neither accepted nor rejected as possible future courses, though both are distinctly subordinate in current Soviet thinking to the continued pursuit of victory through "peaceful coexistence." Revolution, though, would be preferred to overt war, and is probably rated as more likely.

The Communists thus do not clearly foresee the role of revolutions in the final push against what they regard as the weakened bulwarks of the disintegrating capitalist order. The trend of their current discourse clearly does not highlight this issue, but beyond this we can do little more than note that the general absence of focus on it leaves rather vague and undefined the Communist views on the final stages of achievement in the advanced countries of the worldwide victory of communism.

15

The Anticipation of Communist Revolutions

CYRIL E. BLACK

The Communist Experience with Revolutions

In the course of the past half century Communist leaders have gained control of fourteen countries with one third of the world's population, and in other countries there are some seventy-seven active Communist parties with a membership of over six million. At the same time, the Communists have met with failure in formal attempts to seize power in fifteen or twenty countries; and no more than two of some fifty-five former colonial countries that have gained their independence since the Second World War—North Korea and North Viet Nam—have come under Communist control. The Communist system of states has been rent by profound disagreements over ideology and policy, moreover, and in most other states the Communist movement is not particularly influential. Both the successes and the failures are thus impressive.

What can be learned from this record? To what extent can it serve as a basis for anticipating—in the sense both of foreseeing and forestalling—future Communist efforts? In seeking answers to these questions, let us review the Communist experience with revolutions and examine the conditions under which they have been successful.

The revolutionary methods which the Communists have over the years found most useful in achieving their ends may be described in terms of four patterns according to the extent of political violence and of outside assistance involved: (1) In a violent domestic revolution, the local Communist party seizes power as a result of an extended civil war and generally with assistance short of armed occupation by a foreign Communist state. (2) In a "revolution from without," extensive political violence is likewise involved but the decisive influence is exerted by a foreign Communist army which installs the local Communists in power. (3) In a "revolution from above," a manipulative revolution, foreign Communist influence is exerted by essentially non-violent means to assist a local Communist party in establishing a position of decisive political influence. (4) In an electoral revolution, finally, a Communist party is voted into office without any more than incidental political violence.

The two outstanding examples of violent domestic revolutions undertaken by Communists are the Russian and the Chinese, and the differences between these two cases reflect the variety of tactics that are possible.[1] In Russia a relatively non-violent revolution was carried out by a *coup d'état,* but it developed into a civil war involving a combination of domestic and foreign enemies that lasted more than three years. In China the revolution started as an urban movement in the 1920's, but later moved to the countryside where it continued in the form of an intermittent civil war with the incumbent government until victory was achieved in 1949. Only after the vitality of the Chinese government had been undermined by the protracted war with Japan and by its own inadequate policies were the Communists able to seize power in a final vigorous campaign.

Under somewhat different circumstances, and with a greater degree of outside assistance, Communists came to power as a result of revolutionary wars in Yugoslavia and Albania in 1944, and in North Viet Nam in 1954. It is interesting to note that in the case of Yugoslavia most of the outside aid came from Great Britain and the United States, while in the case of Albania it came principally from Yugoslavia. In North Viet Nam, the Communists received some assistance from China. What these five cases have in common, despite some significant differences, is that the Communists came to power essentially by their own efforts and without the assistance of a foreign Communist army of occupation. In all five instances an international war played a vital role in the defeat of the incumbent governments, but within each country the Communists depended primarily on their own resources.

There have been numerous unsuccessful efforts at violent domestic revolutions, and these are also instructive. In the aftermath of the First World War there were armed uprisings in Germany (Berlin, Bavaria) and in Hungary in 1919, in Germany in 1921, in Bulgaria and Germany (Hamburg) in 1923, in Estonia in 1924, in Java in

[1] These two revolutions are compared in Robert Vincent Daniels, "The Chinese Revolution in Russian Perspective," *World Politics,* XIII (January 1961), 210-230; Karl A. Wittfogel, "The Russian and Chinese Revolutions: A Socio-Historical Comparison," *Yearbook of World Affairs,* XV (1961), 41-66; and Cyril E. Black, "Political Modernization in Russia and China," Kurt London, ed., *Unity and Contradiction: Major Aspects of Sino-Soviet Relations* (New York 1962), 3-18.

1926, and in Sumatra in 1927. Since the Second World War there have been similar attempts in Greece, the Philippines, South Korea, Malaya, and in several of the Indian states.

In these various cases of success and failure, the central basis of comparison is the ability of the Communist leaders to assess correctly the domestic and international balance of forces. This is never easy. In the two most important revolutions, neither Lenin nor Mao had the full support of fellow Communists in their decision to make the attempt. The other successful revolutions in Yugoslavia, Albania, and North Viet Nam depended to a greater extent on the outcome of the international struggle, although the final victory was achieved in terms of domestic factors. The failures, on the other hand, have in every instance been due to miscalculations of the balance of forces within the countries concerned.

"Revolution from without," is a term that was prominently employed in connection with the Soviet effort to establish a Communist government in Poland in 1920, but it did not become a part of the official terminology of Marxism-Leninism.[2] This is not difficult to understand, since a formal recognition of the role of external force in Communist revolutions would fatally undermine the argument that communism is a spontaneous result of domestic social forces. Revolution from without is nevertheless a term that accurately describes the establishment of Communist governments in countries in which the incumbent government has been defeated by a foreign Communist army which remains in occupation of the country until a local Communist government is firmly entrenched.

Soviet attempts to export revolution by force after the First World War met with mixed results. This was tried in Poland and in the province of Gilan in Iran in 1920, but both attempts met with failure due to military defeat. It succeeded in Georgia and Azerbaijan in the early 1920's, but these were countries that had been an integral part of the Russian empire and during their brief independence had not been recognized as members of the international community. The establishment of Communist governments in Tannu Tuva in 1921 and Outer Mongolia in 1924 also represented revolutions from without, but these regions were still under Chinese suzerainty although they had been Russian protectorates since 1880 and 1911 respectively. The Communists thus had considerable experience before 1939 with

[2] On this question see Warren Lerner, "The Russian Plan to Sovietize Poland in 1920" (M. A. essay, Faculty of Political Science, Columbia University, 1954).

the problems of exporting revolution, but they had as yet no clearcut success with this method. The necessary precondition was the preponderance of Communist military power, and in the interwar period this was achieved only in regions that had been part of the Russian empire or under its protection.

The Second World War gave the Soviet Union unprecedented opportunities for engineering revolutions from without. As a consequence of the Nazi-Soviet pact, Soviet armed forces occupied Estonia, Latvia, and Lithuania under the provisions of the mutual assistance agreements concluded in September and October, 1939, and in the following July all three "asked to be admitted" to membership in the USSR. The Baltic states were soon to become a battlefield in the German-Russian war and they were not brought under effective Communist control until after 1945. This same method was attempted in Finland in 1939, but it failed due to the military resistance of that country. In these cases Soviet military preponderance was due to the explicit division of Eastern Europe into spheres of influence under the terms of the Nazi-Soviet pact, and to the weakness of the Western allies.

Further opportunities came at the end of the war, when the Soviet armies in their pursuit of the defeated Germans overran Poland, Rumania, Bulgaria, Hungary, the greater part of Czechoslovakia, and East Germany. In Asia, Tannu Tuva was annexed in 1944, and North Korea was occupied in 1945. In the case of the East European states and Korea, Soviet spheres of influence were established by agreement with the Western allies. In each instance popular front governments were established in which the Communists had decisive control through their monopoly of the instruments of force. They then proceeded to undermine first the opposing political groups and then their partners in the popular fronts coalition by the methods that Rákosi has described so well with the term "salami tactics." It is thus significant that in eight of the countries under Communist rule —Bulgaria, Czechoslovakia, East Germany, Hungary, Mongolia, North Korea, Poland, and Rumania—the establishment of Communist governments is directly attributable to the presence of a foreign Communist army. In addition, three formerly independent states—Estonia, Latvia, and Lithuania—were absorbed by the Soviet Union after successful revolutions from without.

Two attempts were made to produce revolutions from without in western Iran in 1945, and the attack on South Korea in 1950 may also be considered in this category if one regards North and South Korea as separate countries. The Korean War had a sobering effect on the Soviet leaders, however, and there appears to have been a reappraisal of the possibilities of revolutions from without before Stalin's death. By 1956 a major change had occurred in Soviet strategic thinking and in that year, at the Twentieth Party Congress, Khrushchev formally advanced the view that international war was no longer "inevitable." It was now recognized that nuclear weapons had become far too destructive to be regarded as an acceptable means for achieving revolutionary gains abroad, and in current Soviet doctrine great emphasis is placed on revolutionary methods short of international war. From a doctrinal point of view, this conclusion is formulated as follows: *"Whereas world wars are unthinkable without revolutions, revolutions are quite possible without wars."*[3]

This is the Soviet view, but it is not fully accepted by the Chinese Communists. The latter are still inclined to regard international war, and hence "revolution from without," as an active possibility. The Chinese Communists have not, however, had experience with this method. The invasion of Tibet in 1950 and the suppression of the uprising in 1959 are sometimes cited as a case of revolution from without. Nevertheless Tibet was already a constituent part of China and, as an intermittent dependency of China since 1720, it had never been recognized as a member of the international community.

"Revolution from above" is a term chosen to describe a method of achieving political power in which influence exerted by a foreign Communist state on the leadership of an incumbent non-Communist government is the decisive factor. Domestic Communist organizations may or may not play a significant role in this method, and the effort is made to avoid any more than incidental political violence. Revolution from above, like revolution from without, is not discussed as such in Communist literature and has even less basis in Marxist-Leninist theory. The plausibility of such a revolutionary method may nevertheless be inferred from recent innovations in Soviet and other Communist policies toward the uncommitted countries.

This method is particularly applicable in countries which, for one reason or another, have been abandoned or neglected by the West and have found it necessary to turn to the Communist countries for political support and technical assistance. In such cases the Communist countries may be called on to supply and train the police and

[3] *Fundamentals of Marxism-Leninism,* 606, italics in original.

the armed forces, to become the principal partners in commerce, to provide various forms of technical assistance, and to train its civil servants. If this were carried far enough, a point might well be reached at which the Communists could train a group of native leaders in the Marxist-Leninist ideology and outlook, and install them in the government to form a "national democracy." A local Communist party, with appropriate mass organizations, could then be organized "from above" preparatory to taking full control. In contrast to the undermining and subversion which one usually associates with Communist tactics, this new method is sometimes referred to as "overmining" and "superversion."

There has as yet been no example of a fully successful revolution from above as described here; but perhaps Cuba, when events in that country have run their course, will fulfill the requirements of this model. The origins of the Cuban revolution are still a matter of bitter dispute among informed persons, but it seems clear that Castro's original revolutionary movement was not Communist-organized. A few of Castro's close associates in the mountains were Communists, but the Cuban Communist Party supported Batista and did not make formal contact with Castro until a few months before his final victory. The Cuban Communists thus gained their position of influence not by seizing power but by receiving it as a gift from Castro after he came to power. This step appears to have been an effort by Castro to bolster the revolutionary movement in anticipation of pressure not only from the United States but also from the bulk of the moderates who were Castro's original allies. The Communists may thus be said to have gained their initial foothold "from above," in the sense that they joined a revolutionary government as allies rather than having to seize power. As Cuba came increasingly under Soviet influence, first through political and economic cooperation and later as a result of a program of massive military aid, the Communists within the government became correspondingly stronger despite a sharp struggle between them and Castro's "new Communists." The events in Cuba are in many respects unprecedented, and they leave much to be desired as a clearcut example of Communist methods. The precise nature of these events is in fact still a matter of dispute among experts. It is nevertheless clear that they represent a departure from the pattern of Communist takeover familiar in Europe and Asia, and serve to illustrate in rough outline one form that a revolution from above might take.

The fourth pattern, the electoral revolution, also draws more on theory than on practice since there has as yet been no successful example of a revolution of this type on the national level. Indeed, Communist success with non-violent electoral methods is limited largely to the rather marginal cases of San Marino and Kerala.

In San Marino, an independent republic with a population of some 15,000 located near Rimini, Italy, a coalition of Communists and leftwing Socialists gained a majority in the 60-member Grand Council in the elections of 1947. For a decade the coalition government administered one of the smallest states in the world in an orderly fashion, implementing a reform program that was only to a moderate degree more radical than that of the Christian Democrats in Italy. In 1957 the coalition lost its majority as a result of the defection of six Socialist councillors, and in the subsequent election it was defeated. The Communists, due no doubt in part to strong Italian pressure, surrendered political power after electoral defeat as non-violently as they had acquired it ten years earlier.

In the state of Kerala in southern India, in a period of great political instability and discontent—and after failing in an earlier attempt to seize power by violent methods—the Communists won the support of some 35 percent of the voters in 1947 and a sufficient number of seats in the legislature to give them a majority with the assistance of five independents. The popularity of the Communists evaporated during their twenty-eight months in office as a result of corruption and misrule, however, and in July 1959 their government was dissolved by the president of India in exercise of his constitutional powers. This was thus not a happy episode for the Communists, and it is not surprising that it should not be cited as an example to be followed by others.

The case of Czechoslovakia is sometimes mentioned as an instance of an electoral revolution on the grounds that the Czech party came to power in 1948 without civil war as a result of the skillful and essentially non-violent manipulation of political forces. What this argument ignores, however, is that the Communists gained their decisive positions not in 1948, but in 1945. The original postwar government of Beneš was the result not of elections but of negotiations in Moscow at a time when Soviet armed forces were completing the occupation of the greater part of Czechoslovakia. The positions of strength in key ministries gained by the Communists at this stage were an essential factor in their relative success in the first elections held in 1946 and in their ability to withstand the efforts of the other parties to oust them from the government in 1948.[4] Similarly other Communist electoral victories in Eastern Europe, including that in Yugoslavia in 1945, were won by Communist parties which were already in control of the machinery of government.

In addition to the cases of San Marino and Kerala, there are a number of instances of Communists winning municipal elections in France, Italy, and elsewhere. These are all nevertheless only regional and local successes—if one may disregard for these purposes the technical status of San Marino as a "state"—and they do not add up to a significant body of Communist experience with the techniques of electoral revolution.

Reference should also be made to the numerous cases in which Communist parties have been members of governing coalitions but have failed to gain a dominant position. Communists have participated in a number of coalition governments—notably in Spain (1936-1939), Finland (1945-1948), France (1945-1947), Italy (1945-1947), Iceland (1944-1947, 1956-1958), Chile (1946-1947), and Guatemala (1950-1954)—under circumstances in which they were either dislodged by their colleagues or went down to defeat with the whole coalition. In citing these cases several important distinctions should nevertheless be made. In none of these instances did the Communists gain extensive influence in the government or in non-governmental organizations. Moreover in most of these cases, and especially in France, Italy, Iceland, and Chile, the Communists did not envisage the seizure of power as an immediate goal. In Finland and Guatemala, on the other hand, it seems clear that the Communists were defeated only by the firm resistance of the Social Democrats and the Agrarians in the former case, and by Castillo with the support of the United States in the latter.

There are today fourteen countries under Communist government, diverse though they may be in other respects, and it is interesting to note that except for Cuba they all came to power as a result either of violent domestic revolutions or of revolutions imposed from without.

[4] It is significant that both Czech and Soviet theorists acknowledge the crucial role of the Soviet army in 1945; on this question see especially Yan Kozak, "Znacheniye natsional'noy i demokraticheskoy revolyutsii v Chekhoslovakii dlya bor'by rabochego klassa za sotsializm" [The Significance of the National and Democratic Revolution in Czechoslovakia in the Struggle of the Working Class for Socialism], *Voprosy Istorii KPSS*, No. 4 (July 1962), 72-91.

In five countries—Albania, China, North Viet Nam, Russia, and Yugoslavia—Communists seized power primarily as a result of their own efforts. In eight others—Bulgaria, Czechoslovakia, East Germany, Hungary, Mongolia, North Korea, Poland, and Rumania—Communism was imposed in the aftermath of occupation by Soviet armies. In Cuba, Castro co-opted the Communist party to power early in the revolution, and it proceeded to strengthen its position by means which we are here calling revolution from above. There has as yet been no successful Communist revolution at the national level (apart from San Marino) by means of elections. The experience of Communist leaders with revolution has thus been almost exclusively with violent methods, whether from within or from without. If they now wish to turn to non-violent methods, whether from below or from above, they have no successful experience to draw on except for the rather ambiguous case of Cuba, and they will have to rely largely on theory and on experiments in countries in which they have had little operational experience. Before turning to a discussion of the prospects for revolution in the years ahead, it is consequently important to analyze the conditions which have been conducive to Communist success in the past.

The Conditions of Communist Success

The Communist experience with revolutions suggests that success has been achieved only when three conditions have been present: a critical weakening of the authority of the incumbent government, the ineffectiveness of alternative political reform movements, and an international balance of power favorable to the Communists.

The defeat or significant weakening of the incumbent government in an international war played a decisive role in all instances of successfully completed Communist revolutions except that of Cuba. In Russia, the Bolsheviks overthrew not the Tsarist government but the Provisional government, the authority of which, like that of its predecessor, had been undermined by military defeat. In China, the Communists renewed in 1945 a civil war against a Nationalist government which was exhausted physically and morally as a result of its long struggle against Japan. In the other three cases in which Communists relied primarily by their own efforts—Yugoslavia, Albania, and North Viet Nam—the role of international war was even more decisive. In the countries where Communists came to power after the Second World War as a result of revolutions from without—

Bulgaria, Czechoslovakia, East Germany, Hungary, North Korea, Poland, and Rumania—the political support of Soviet armies of occupation was by all odds the most important factor in the success of the revolution. Twenty years earlier, Soviet troops had also brought communism to Mongolia.

One of the significant differences between orthodox Marxism and Marxism-Leninism is that the latter defines a "revolutionary situation" in terms not only of the objective changes in the economic and social structure of a society but also in terms of a "national crisis" which weakens or destroys the authority of the incumbent government. It is usually an international war that provokes such a crisis, and Marxist-Leninist doctrine in contemplating the future suggests that "military adventures," "the renewal of fascism," and "an atomic catastrophe" may result in the creation of revolutionary situations. The Soviet theorists have thus concluded from their own experience that wars and military crises have provided the most fertile soil for revolution.[5]

Wars are becoming dangerous, however, and if Communists were to rely on such crises alone for making gains they might find it very slow going. It is therefore important to note that incumbent governments can be weakened not only by war but also by their own ineptitude. They may corrode their own authority by prolonged mismanagement of their affairs, and in effect create revolutionary situations by default. Indeed, most of the modernizing revolutions in recent years have resulted from the excessive mismanagement and corruption of incumbent governments. Thus the governments of Nuri in Iraq, of Farouk in Egypt, of Bao Dai in South Viet Nam, and of Trujillo in the Dominican Republic—and this is by no means a complete list—fell essentially of their own weight. Particularly striking is the case of Batista in Cuba, where a political leader who originally gained prominence as a reformer gradually alienated most of his supporters at home and abroad by virtue of his corrupt and tyrannical methods. Castro won less from his own strength than from his enemy's weakness. It would not be difficult to draw up a list of other countries where such revolutions are imminent. Contemporary Soviet doctrine recognizes the possibility that "unbridled political reaction may also bring about a revolutionary situation,"[6] but it devotes only passing attention to domestic crises of this type. In all

[5] *Fundamentals of Marxism-Leninism,* 607-610.
[6] *Ibid.,* 609.

probability the principal reason for this neglect is that situations of this sort have not lent themselves as readily as international wars to the type of national fervor which permits the Communists to gain positions of influence through "united front" coalitions.

A second condition necessary for Communist success in organizing political revolutions is the ineffectiveness of alternative movements of political reform. In a great majority of the cases in which traditional, conservative, or colonial governments have been overthrown, it is not the Communists who have benefited but other political movements which have been more successful in formulating and implementing a modernizing program. These other leaders are often referred to as "nationalists," but such a term describes only one aspect of their program and does not do justice to their concern for economic and social reforms. The fundamental aim of a Nehru, a Nasser, or a Betancourt is to create effective administration, to promote economic growth, and to encourage social betterment. Nationalism is only a means of consolidating national sovereingty, and in this sense the Communists are no less nationalistic than the "nationalists." In many respects Kemal Atatürk was the prototype of the present generation of modernizing leaders, and the type of program which they favor has never been summarized more effectively than in one pithy sentence in Article 2 of his constitution: "The Turkish State is republican, nationalist, populist, 'etatist,' secular, and revolutionary"—although not all have found republicanism or secularism necessary.

The significance of the poor showing of the Communists in so many of these countries is less the lack of able leadership, although this has no doubt been a factor, than the fact that the alternative political movements have an effective revolutionary ideology which has had a greater relevance and appeal than Marxism-Leninism. This ideology, judging from the many examples in the Middle East and Asia, is inspired principally by the European radical republican tradition. Such programs may well contain elements of Soviet influence—such as widespread resort to centralized planning—but in their origin and value system these programs are Western rather than Communist. Similarly in Africa, the leaders of the new states are predominantly West European in outlook, and have been much more attracted by the models of Arab, Israeli, and Indian socialism than by the Russian or Chinese systems. Among the various Communist countries only Yugoslavia has had a significant influence among the new states and

Yugoslav domestic institutions are in particular disfavor among other governing Communist parties.[7]

One should nevertheless not conclude from this record that communism has no chance of success in these countries, for their leaders are confronted by many difficult problems which may cause the downfall of a whole series of alternative policies before they are mastered. The Communists take a long-range view of these matters, and are concentrating their attention in particular on the students who form the reservoir from which political leadership will be drawn in the next generation. The competition between Communists and rival political movements is not one that can be resolved in the course of a specific revolutionary situation or even during the first generation after a new state is created, but one that will continue as long as Marxism-Leninism survives as a militant political doctrine. In attempting to anticipate Communist revolutions, the vitality of modernizing ideologies and political movements other than Marxism-Leninism is one of the most critical factors to be considered.

It is significant in this connection that such alternative movements are, on the whole, weakest in Latin America. One often thinks of the Latin American countries as having had their revolutions in the nineteenth century, but these were independence movements which did not have, or at least did not sustain, significant modernizing programs. No doubt in a few Latin American countries, such as Mexico, Argentina, Uruguay, Costa Rica, Chile, and Venezuela, the critical turning point between "traditional" and "modern" political systems has been passed. In most of the other countries, however, despite the glitter of the cities, the incumbent political leaders are not prepared to adopt policies making for rapid modernization. These matters are no doubt relative, but it would seem that with the exception of a few countries Latin America as a region will be more vulnerable to Communist revolutionary efforts than the Middle East and North Africa, Sub-Saharan Africa, or most parts of Asia.

In anticipating Communist revolutions one must consider not only the stability of the incumbent governments and the vitality of rival political reform movements, but also the international balance of

[7] Useful discussions of this general problem may be found in Edward Shils, "Political Development in the New States," *Comparative Studies in Society and History*, II (1959-60), 265-292, 379-411; Robert C. Tucker, "Towards a Comparative Politics of Movement-Regimes," *American Political Science Review*, LV (June 1961), 281-289; and Martin L. Kilson, "Authoritarian and Single-Party Tendencies in African Politics," *World Politics*, XV (January 1963), 262-294.

power. In all but two of the revolutions which Communists have won by violent means, Cuba again excepted, the assistance of foreign Communists in the form of armies of military occupation or military support from adjacent countries has been a vital factor in success. In the remaining two, Russia and China, the international situation was a factor in that the opponents of Communism failed to receive effective assistance. Much has been made in Russia since the 1930's of the successes of the Red Army against the intervention of the Western Allies, yet Lenin himself maintained that his revolution succeeded less because of Soviet strength than because of the indecisiveness of Western intervention, which he attributed to "the internal decay of capitalism."[8] In China after 1945, the main trend of Western policy was not to support the Nationalists against the Communists, but to urge the two contending groups to reconcile their differences.

Experience since the Second World War has confirmed the importance in a revolutionary situation of the role of the two rival coalitions. There are no doubt certain limits beyond which neither the Communists nor the Western countries are willing to go. In countries which are associated with one of the two coalitions—as are, for example, the East European countries with the Soviet Union, and most South American and several Middle Eastern and Asian countries with the United States—political and economic assistance may be offered by the rival system to insurgent movements if they gain influence on their own initiative, but they cannot expect to receive decisive military support. Thus, the Communist countries can provide assistance to Communist or pro-Communist movements in Greece or Iran, but cannot risk a military show-down over missiles in Cuba; similarly the West can give economic aid to an independent-minded Yugoslavia or Poland, but cannot risk war over Hungary. In this respect the West has had a bolder policy, offering military commitments to a number of countries bordering on the Communist system, while the Communist countries have made similar commitments only to other Communist states to which they have direct access, and they have been careful not to make formal military commitments in treaties with countries like Cuba and Indonesia. In the less sensitive uncommitted countries geography and political opportunity have been the determining factors. Both the Communist and the Western

[8] John M. Thompson, "Lenin's Analysis of Intervention," *American Slavic and East European Review*, XVII (1958), 141-160.

countries have taken the initiative in recent years in countries of easy access of them—the Communists in South Korea, South Viet Nam, and Laos, and the Western countries in Greece and Lebanon—but always under circumstances in which they expected to avoid an international war. The miscalculations of the Communists in regard to Korea in 1950 and Cuba in 1962 point to the danger of these ventures, and also reflect their continuing willingness to take bold initiatives—until challenged effectively.

The influence of the balance of power on a revolutionary situation may be exerted negatively, however, as well as positively. If one state or one of the two rival coalitions withdraws its support from an incumbent government—as was the case with the Soviet Union in Yugoslavia in 1948 and in Albania in 1961, the Western states in Egypt in 1956, France in Guinea in 1958, and in a sense also the United States in Cuba in 1959—such a government faces the choice of attempting to survive on the basis of its own resources or of turning elsewhere for assistance. In such cases the previously existing balance of power is upset not by assault but by default, and this may have a determining effect on the domestic relationship of forces in a country threatened with a revolutionary situation. The abrupt withdrawal of support may be due primarily to unbridled indignation, but it generally has the calculated objective of bringing the incumbent government to terms or of overthrowing it. This was certainly the purpose of Stalin's action against Tito in 1948, and it may explain some of the other instances just cited.

So far as the Western states are concerned, such action is particularly likely to follow efforts of nationalistic and reformist leaders to nationalize foreign properties and in other respects to threaten the long-standing position of foreign interests. In cases of this sort, unless it has made careful preparations for such an eventuality, a Western government may suddenly be confronted with the choice of accepting a humiliating abrogation of the interests of its nationals or of initiating recriminatory sanctions to the point of severing diplomatic relations. If the latter policy is followed, it may result in a long-term loss of influence with far greater implications than the immediate loss of property. In Latin America, for example, where the United States has investments amounting to over eight billion dollars—about one quarter of its total foreign investments and by far the largest holdings outside of the advanced countries—the first impulse of many modernizing leaders is to expropriate American property. The steps from such an action to a worsening or severance of relations with the United States and to a rapprochement with the Communist countries are likely to be short and rapid.

Revolution and World Politics

The importance of revolutions as a subject for political analysis derives from two key considerations: revolutions arising from crises of modernization will be a frequent occurrence in the years ahead; and revolutions have become the decisive arena of conflict between the Western and Communist systems of states. The revolutions of the eighteenth and nineteenth centuries—and the wars of national liberation and unification which were also in effect revolutionary wars—no doubt affected the relations of the great powers to a significant degree. Nevertheless the arbiter of the balance of power was international war. Due to the unacceptable destruction that international war would in all likelihood bring today, however, the major contestants have turned to the manipulation of domestic revolutions as a means of maneuvering for power. A new pattern of world politics is thus emerging, in which revolution is replacing war. In the light of the Communist experience with revolutions and the conditions which in the past have brought them success, what are the prospects for Communist revolutionary activity in the years ahead?

For the first time in history, two rival groupings or coalitions of states have commitments that are literally worldwide. Under these circumstances every instance of revolution, whether on the territory of a member of one of the coalitions or on that of one of the uncommitted countries, is viewed with great concern on both sides. It has already been noted that members of both coalitions have evidenced an unwillingness to intervene in the countries which the opposing coalition is committed to defend, but this does not mean that the balance of power may not be affected by revolutions. Revolutions may result either in the defection from a coalition of a country committed to it, or in the adherence of a country formerly uncommitted. Thus Iraq in 1957, Cuba in 1959, and Laos in 1962 severed close relations with the West as a result of revolutions; and Greece, Iran, the Philippines, and Thailand joined the Western coalition under the threat of revolutionary situations.

It may still be possible for remote countries to enjoy the luxury of domestic revolutions without becoming fatefully involved in world politics, and there are numerous examples of such internal conflicts in recent years that have passed almost unnoticed. Nevertheless, the recent cases of the Congo and Laos illustrate the sense in which the prestige of both coalitions tends to become involved in these struggles. It is moreover always possible that victory in one revolution will lead to a succession of further victories as a result of the prestige of the victor and without recourse to violence. Thus it seems possible that an eventual consolidation of Communist power in Laos may lead to a series of relatively easy victories in Southeast Asia. No doubt neither coalition has any desire for an international war, and each is prepared to permit its opponent to gain influence in a number of countries without provoking a conflict. As the rivalry develops, as it is likely to despite deep fissures in both coalitions, the situation arising from each successive civil conflict will tend to become more tense.

The pattern of world politics that has thus emerged since the Second World War is one in which two loosely organized coalitions are vying for influence within the countries of the "third world." The nucleus of the Western coalition is formed by the fifteen members of the North Atlantic Treaty Organization and the advanced countries in the Pacific region with which the United States has defense agreements: Australia, New Zealand, and Japan. Four other countries—Austria, Spain, Sweden, and Switzerland—share most of the political attitudes of the Western group. The Communist coalition consists of the eight members of the Warsaw Pact, and the Asian countries with which the Soviet Union has defense agreements: China, Mongolia, and North Korea. Four other countries—North Viet Nam, Cuba, Finland, and Yugoslavia—adhere to a greater or lesser degree to the policies of this coalition. Despite serious internal conflicts, these two coalitions offer reasonably clearcut and contrasting models of organization and policy to the "third world." This "third world" consists of over ninety independent countries, and some fifty colonial territories which are likely to gain independence in some form in the decades ahead. These countries are generally referred to as "underdeveloped," or "developing," or "modernizing," but these terms conceal a wide range of levels of development and degrees of political stability. Some are governed by able and well-trained political leaders, controlling an orderly system of administration, and implementing relatively realistic and effective programs. Others are headed by traditional oligarchies whose outlook has changed little over the centuries, or by nationalist leaders without programs or organized support. The difference between an India and a Tunisia on the one hand, and a Congo and a Saudi Arabia on the other, is very great indeed.

At the same time, even the most orderly of these governments are beset by many problems that may easily lead to domestic crises. The United States, Germany, and France were unable to solve their domestic problems in the nineteenth century without resort to extensive civil strife. There is no reason to assume that these countries will do any better. The authority of the governments in the new states is heavily dependent on their success in creating effective bureaucracies, raising capital through taxation, promoting economic development, and improving social conditions. In most of these countries the demands on the governments outstrip their resources by a considerable margin, and the expectations of the inhabitants are rising much more rapidly than their productivity. The types of social turbulence that may result from crises of modernization are not yet well studied, but there can be no doubt that—although it may be poor in other respects—the "third world" is rich in situations that are likely to lead to revolutions.

The Communists are fully cognizant of these opportunities for revolutionary activity, and Soviet expositions of "peaceful coexistence" go out of their way to assert that this policy does not involve any relaxation of revolutionary ardor on the part of the Communist movement. In a semi-official reference work edited by Foreign Minister Gromyko, this policy is interpreted as follows: "Peaceful coexistence is a specific form of class struggle between socialism and capitalism. The socialist system is victorious in worldwide competition with capitalism, because the socialist mode of production has a decisive advantage over the capitalist mode of production. There is no contradiction whatsoever between the Marxist-Leninist position concerning the inevitability of the victory of communism and peaceful coexistence. It does not affect the internal relations of states, and it does not affect the revolutionary struggle for the reconstruction of societies.

"Peaceful coexistence of the states of the two systems does not presuppose a compromise on ideological questions. It is impossible to reconcile the bourgeois and the Communist world outlooks, and indeed this is not required of the peaceful coexistence of states."[9]

[9] "Mirnoye sosushchestvovaniye" [Peaceful coexistence], *Diplomaticheskiy Slovar* [Diplomatic dictionary], A. A. Gromyko and others, eds., (3 vols.; Moscow 1960-), II, 299.

The policy of peaceful coexistence is designed to avoid the dangers of international war, according to current Soviet doctrine, but military power plays a vital role in this policy. Its principal purpose is to counterbalance Western military power, so that the extension of communism to other countries can be confined to violent or non-violent domestic political methods. In addition, the Soviet leaders employ their military power as a means of threatening members of the Western alliance system and uncommitted states. The use of nuclear deterrence by the Soviet alliance system resembles the corresponding policy of NATO insofar as both policies seek to avoid nuclear war, and to restrict to political violence of a local or domestic character those international conflicts that cannot be resolved by negotiation. The two policies differ, however, to the extent that the USSR and its allies assume the ultimate victory of communism through domestic political revolutions, and are more inclined than the members of NATO to assume that aggression on their part is "just" on the ground that the objective forces of history are on the side of Marxism-Leninism.

"Peaceful coexistence" has had considerable success as a general slogan designed to reflect Communist goodwill toward the outside world, but as a practical policy it has led to great controversy among the various Communist parties. It should be noted that none of the Communist parties has set forth its objectives in such positive and forceful terms as has the Soviet, although all except the Yugoslav signed the Statement of the conference of Communist and Workers parties which was drafted in Moscow in November 1960.[10] The Yugoslav Communists also see "socialism" in some form as ultimately inevitable, but envisage a much more varied development that includes Western as well as the Communist institutional forms. They have not, however, committed themselves to any specific pattern or program of change. The Communist leaders of China, for their part, have

[10] This Statement of the conference of Communist and Workers' Parties held in Moscow in November 1960, *Pravda* (December 6, 1960), 1-4, trans. in *CDSP*, XII (December 28, 1960), 3-9, and (January 4, 1961), 3-8, represented a compromise of Soviet and Chinese views and is regarded by the Russians as a document of fundamental importance for the international Communist movement. More authoritative, but representing only the views of the Soviet party, is the 1961 Program of the Communist Party of the Soviet Union, *Pravda* (November 2, 1961), 1-9, trans. in *CDSP*, XIII (December 9, 1961), 3-16, and (December 13, 1961), 3-21. The open letter of the Communist Party of the Soviet Union of July 1963, *Pravda* (July 14, 1963), 1-4, trans. in *New York Times* (July 15, 1963), 11-14, likewise reflects only the Soviet viewpoint. The controversy as it concerns the relationship of war and revolution is ably summarized in Frederic S. Burin, "The Communist Doctrine of the Inevitability of War," *American Political Science Review*, LVII (June 1963), 334-354.

been engaged in a long controversy with the European Communists over the question of appropriate Communist strategy and tactics in foreign policy. This is one of the central issues between China and the Soviet Union, and it is significant that the Chinese have expressed in unambiguous terms the view that peaceful coexistence and a general nuclear war are not the only alternatives available. There is a third alternative, and this is a policy that adds local wars to the methods that the Soviet leaders are prepared to use. Unlike the Soviets, the Chinese believe that local wars can be prevented from growing into general wars, and that they should be employed boldly in the interest of the expansion of communism.[11]

The Soviet policy of "peaceful coexistence," and the more cautious and bolder variants of this policy advocated respectively by Yugoslavia and China, are set forth in their speeches, party programs, and other official documents. It must nevertheless be recognized that evidence of this type has its limitations, and it would be a mistake to estimate Communist intentions on the basis of official statements alone. The view is in fact sometimes advanced that the doctrinal statements of Communist leaders should be interpreted more as ritual than as policy, and that the confrontation of "the West" and "Communism" belongs to the same category as that between Christianity and Islam, or Catholicism and Protestantism—confrontations in which differences in doctrine can be overcome in most practical matters. In this case, however, it must be recognized that the actions of Communist leaders have in general matched their words, and that in the years since the Second World War there has been no significant relaxation of militancy. The events between 1950 and 1962 in Korea, Laos, the Congo, and Cuba reflect the determination of the Communist leaders to take bold action when they believe—mistakenly more often than not—that they will meet with no greater resistance than can be overcome by means short of war. So long as this militant attitude is maintained by the Soviet leaders and their allies, and the preponderant

[11] Edvard Kardelj, *Socialism and War: A Survey of the Chinese Criticism of the Policy of Coexistence,* trans. by Alec Brown (London 1960), provides an authoritative statement of the Yugoslav view in the course of a debate with the Chinese theorists; original theoretical work in such countries as Poland and Czechoslovakia is concerned with domestic rather than foreign policy. Donald Z. Zagoria, *The Sino-Soviet Conflict, 1956-1961* (Princeton 1962), especially 350-355, summarizes the Chinese argument; this argument is reviewed in some detail in the letter of June 14, 1963 from the Central Committee of the Communist Party of China to the Central Committee of the Communist Party of the Soviet Union, published in *PR,* VI (June 21, 1963), 6-22.

evidence supports the view that this attitude is not likely to be relaxed in the forseeable future, one must anticipate a continuing Communist pressure in all countries where political revolution appears to be feasible.

In order to maneuver their way successfully through the myriad of political obstacles that block the road to power, Communist leaders must pursue a correct policy. The highest importance is therefore given to what Soviet theorists call *"the struggle for the purity of the Marxist-Leninist world outlook . . ."*[12] This purity was guarded until recently by the Communist party of the USSR. In 1957, however, changes in the doctrine were negotiated by the leaders of Communist parties who assembled in Moscow to celebrate the fortieth anniversary of the Russian revolution. Since that date there have been a number of conferences of national party leaders, in the course of which the Sino-Soviet dispute has emerged as a central problem. Communist leaders are in agreement that there are two dangers to guard against. One is what they call "revisionism" or "right-wing opportunism"—too great a willingness to cooperate with "bourgeois democracy" and the danger of failure through lack of revolutionary zeal. At the other extreme are "dogmatism" and "sectarianism"—an inflexibility of revolutionary tactics that leads to isolation from the masses and to the danger of failure through excess of revolutionary zeal. The meaning of these terms is always relative, however, and their definition depends on the outlook of the user. The Communist party of the USSR was referring to its Yugoslav colleagues as "revisionists" in the late 1950's. By 1963, the USSR and Yugoslavia had reached a substantial accommodation, and the Chinese regarded the leaders of both countries as "revisionists" while the latter referred to the Chinese and Albanian Communists as "dogmatists."

Communists thus face a formidable task in understanding this complex world and in negotiating successfully its many dangers, and it has not been easy to find the necessary personnel. Of the approximately 42.5 million Communist party members in 1962 in 91 countries, according to Soviet statistics, some 36.5 million were in the Communist countries. Of these about half were in China. The remaining 6 million were distributed among seventy-seven parties, of which thirty-seven were illegal.[13] Among the legal parties in Europe,

[12] *Fundamentals of Marxism-Leninism,* 431, italics in original.

[13] Official Soviet figures are summarized in *World Strength of the Communist Party Organizations,* U. S. Department of State, Intelligence Report No. 4489, R-15 (January 1963), 2.

those in France, Italy, Finland, and Iceland still have a substantial membership and exercise considerable influence with the voters, although they have not participated in the governments since the late 1940's in the first three countries or since 1958 in Iceland. In the Middle East and North Africa the only influential legal Communist party is in Cyprus. In Asia legal parties play an active role in Laos, India, and Indonesia, and are vocal but relatively ineffectual in Ceylon and Japan. In Latin America, legal parties play a predominant role in Cuba and British Guiana and have significant influence in a half a dozen other countries. In Sub-Saharan Africa the influence of organized Communist parties, whether legal or illegal, is relatively small.

If it is difficult to estimate the influence of legal Communist parties, it is even more difficult to evaluate the role of the illegal parties. In South Viet Nam the Communist party is engaged in an active internal war against the incumbent government. In South Korea, Taiwan, and Thailand, the Communists face the opposition of security-conscious—though frequently inept—governments. In Greece, Malaya, Burma, and the Philippines, the Communist parties have been defeated in major internal wars but still retain some influence. An important factor in the role of the Communist parties in these countries is the influence of neighboring Communist states, and the international prestige of communism is often more important than domestic considerations in determining Communist political power.

In considering the opportunities for revolutions under Communist leadership in the years ahead, it is also important to recognize that Soviet leaders tend to subordinate support for Communist revolutions to their overall security needs. When faced with the choice of detaching a country from Western influence by supporting a nationalist revolution, or of encouraging communism under circumstances where the probability of success is not high, Soviet leaders have normally pursued the former course. Thus in the Middle East, from Atatürk in the 1920's to Nasser in the 1960's, Soviet policy has regularly sacrificed local Communist parties in order to support nationalist governments that seemed likely to pursue anti-Western policies. A similar approach prevailed in China until the very eve of the Communist victory, and appears also to be the principal consideration in Indonesia today.

The precedence given by Soviet policy to considerations of balance of power over revolution—or, to put it differently, to nationalist at the expense of Communist revolutions—need not be regarded as the abandonment of Marxism-Leninism. It represents rather a belief that in underdeveloped countries nationalism must precede communism, and that the reduction of Western influence through the support of nationalist revolutions is only the first step in the process of evolution —or rather of successive revolutions—that will lead ultimately to the desired goal. At the same time this distinction between nationalism and communism—and the timing and degree of support that should be afforded to one or the other—is always a matter of judgment. It is indeed on this very issue that the Chinese Communists have objected most strongly to Soviet policy. The Chinese assert that the gradualist approach represents nothing less than a betrayal of communism, and they favor a worldwide revolutionary drive uniting the national liberation movements with the forces of communism to effect the final overthrow of "imperialism." Just what such a policy might mean in practice is not clear, but the sharp confrontation of Soviet and Chinese attitudes on this subject provides a good example of the dilemmas facing those desiring to employ Marxism-Leninism as a guide to policy.

Since the Chinese approach does not differentiate significantly among the countries of the "third world," and the smaller Communist parties have not developed distinctive programs of revolutionary activity, Communist-led revolutions can best be discussed in terms of Soviet doctrine as modified by the Communist experience with revolution in recent years. In discussing the prospects for revolution in the years ahead Soviet doctrine places almost exclusive emphasis on "peaceful transition to socialism," which it defines as *"the transition of individual countries to socialism without an armed rising and civil war."*[14] In support of this method, Soviet theorists argue that "it was not the fault of the Bolsheviks that a peaceful transition to the socialist stage of the revolution did not take place in Russia."[15] They also note that the revolution of October 25/November 7 was "perhaps the most bloodless revolution in history"[16]—referring to the assault on the Winter Palace—and they blame the subsequent civil war on the refusal of "the capitalists" to accept Lenin's victory.

Although the Bolshevik revolution is not a case of "peaceful transition," the opening engagement of the revolution is cited to convey an idea as to the meaning of this term. "Peaceful transition"

[14] *Fundamentals of Marxism-Leninism,* 616, italics in original.
[15] *Ibid.,* 615.
[16] *Ibid.,* 613.

is not necessarily peaceful in the sense in which the transfer of power from one political party to another in a democratic society is peaceful, but may involve the threat of violence and readiness to use violent methods in the event of unforeseen opposition. "Peaceful transition" assumes the use of political violence, but it is violence on a limited scale and of short duration, and differs from "non-peaceful transition" in that no prolonged civil war is anticipated. A number of arguments are advanced by Soviet theorists in support of the validity of this doctrine. They claim that the Communist states are now strong enough to offset their rivals, and that a quick Communist *coup d'état* could be isolated from the type of foreign intervention which contributed to the prolonged civil strife in Russia after 1917 and which led to many Communist failures in later years. Moreover, the Soviet leaders believe that communism now has a large following because of the industrial and technological successes of the Soviet Union, and will continue to attract adherents abroad. Communist leaders also claim that in many countries the "bourgeoisie" is becoming more isolated and that it is becoming correspondingly easier for Communists to influence public opinion.

This Soviet conception of "peaceful transition" embraces the two patterns already described as revolution from above and electoral revolution. Indeed, Soviet theory supports this distinction indirectly in its doctrine of the "national democratic state," which places particular emphasis on the bargaining power of Communist parties in coalition governments in an international environment of sharp rivalry between "socialist" and "imperialist" coalitions.[17] The possibility of Communists coming to power as a result of ordinary electoral politics, on the other hand, is a minor theme in Soviet theoretical writing.

The Anticipation of Revolutionary Situations

The situations conducive to Communist revolutions from above in the years ahead, are those in which established Communist governments may be able to influence domestic developments in a country in such a way as to permit a Communist party to gain effective power without resort to prolonged civil war. It has already been noted that Cuba has most of the elements of such a pattern, in so far as Castro

[17] William T. Shinn, Jr., "The 'National Democratic State': A Communist Program for the Less-Developed Areas," *World Politics*, xv (April 1963), 377-389, summarizes Marxist-Leninist theory on this subject; and Alexander Sobolev, "National Democracy—The Way to Social Progress," *WMR*, xi (February 1963), 39-48, provides an authoritative statement of the Soviet view.

invited the Communists to share his power in anticipation of domestic and foreign opposition. They have subsequently made significant gains in domestic political power in the course of Cuba's increasingly close association with the Soviet Union. At the same time, to the extent that the "old Communists" of the Cuban Communist Party have failed to displace the "new Communists" led by Castro, the events in Cuba do not represent a successfully completed case of a Communist revolution from above.

Indonesia likewise occupies an important position in Soviet writing as a country where the Communist party has grown rapidly and has come to play a prominent role in the tense maneuverings within the governing coalition formed by Sukarno and the army. The prevailing Soviet view asserts that the Indonesian Communist Party has already succeeded in mobilizing the political energies of the working class, and has established itself as a member of the governing coalition. This view also maintains that the Communists deserve credit for having gained acceptance for an economic program involving the exclusion of Western interests and the expansion of state-supported and cooperative enterprises. It remains for them to gain greater influence with the peasantry, and to strengthen their role in the government with a view to leading the country definitively on the road to "socialism."

Western observers are not in full agreement as to the trend of events in Indonesia, but the prevailing opinion is that the political gains of the Communists in recent years have not been of critical significance. The party has grown greatly in size, but the formal and informal channels to effective political power have been successfully blocked by Sukarno and the army. The two cabinet posts assigned to the Communists in 1962 are of an advisory character without an administrative apparatus, and press and propaganda outlets are closely supervised by the government. Opportunities for infiltration into the army and the state bureaucracy are also limited. The massive Soviet military aid, designed to bolster Indonesia in its conflict with Dutch and British influence, has tended to strengthen the army at the expense of the Communists. Moreover Sukarno's foreign policy has been moving away from extreme nationalism toward a gradual accommodation with the West and with the Philippines and Malaysia. At the same time, the Indonesian Communists have been increasingly impressed by the Chinese approach to revolution, and such political leverage as they can acquire may in the end be used against Soviet interests. The situation in Indonesia is indeed one of the most relevant to the Soviet concept of "national democracy," but its principal lesson thus far has been that an effective nationalist government can be a frustrating obstacle to Communist efforts.

Of a somewhat analogous character is the situation in Guinea, Ghana, and Mali, where there is no domestic Communist organization of significance but where extensive economic and military aid has made the Communists a major foreign influence. In Guinea the Communists overreached themselves, and their influence was drastically reduced by government action. It is nevertheless not difficult to imagine situations in which a Communist aid program could be carried to the point of decisive political influence on a government, without significant assistance from a domestic Communist organization. Similarly in British Guiana and in a number of countries in Latin America and Southeast Asia, Communist leaders may achieve sufficient influence to be able to use the leverage of Soviet or other Communist aid as a means of attaining effective power.

Under very different circumstances, outside Communist influence exerted directly on the government has also come to play an increasing role in Finland. Here there is a strong Communist party, but its influence has been more than counterbalanced by a long tradition of vigorous anti-communism on the part of the large Social Democratic and Agrarian parties. Recently, however, as the result in part of a delicately balanced electoral situation, and in part of a conviction that there is no alternative to making an accommodation with the USSR, the Agrarian president Kekkonen has gone out of his way to cultivate Soviet friendship at the price of agreeing to restrict the political activities of certain prominent Social Democrats. If the Soviet leaders succeed in undermining by these methods the prestige of the Social Democrats, the most effective domestic alternative to communism, it would not be difficult for them later to turn the pressure on the Agrarians and eventually to open a path for the participation of the Communist party in the government and the formation of what would in effect be a "national democracy."

Simple electoral revolutions are much less likely to occur than revolutions from above, if only because effective electoral and parliamentary systems are limited almost entirely to countries where the Soviet, Chinese, and other Communist programs have little appeal. In Italy and France where the Communist parties have a much larger following than in many other countries where Communists have a reasonable chance of gaining power, the Communist vote represents a protest against the existing economic and social order rather than an expectation of an electoral victory. So long as the incumbent governments in these two countries remain vigorous and self-confident, the likelihood of a Communist electoral victory is very slight. There are nevertheless a few countries, such as for example Chile and Cyprus, where a Communist party might win a parliamentary majority in free elections either alone or more likely as a member of a coalition. It should also be recognized that the boundary between an electoral revolution and a revolution from above need not be very sharp, and there will doubtless be situations in which Communists can combine electoral strength with the cruder forms of maneuver associated with revolution from above.

These two non-violent patterns of revolution will be the most common in the foreseeable future, but despite the menace of nuclear war there are circumstances in which violent domestic revolutions involving prolonged civil wars may well occur. Revolutions of this type have been in progress in Laos and South Viet Nam for several years, in circumstances in which domestic Communist forces bear the main burden of the struggle despite the great importance of foreign assistance. In these two instances, which may in a sense be considered to represent unfinished business left over from the Second World War, the authority of the incumbent governments was never fully established after the collapse of the French colonial system. In the absence of effective alternative modernizing movements, the Communists were able to gain considerable political influence. The remoteness of Southeast Asia from the centers of Western power further facilitated the Communist task. The United States, which represents the Western coalition in this region, has been able to match the material aid provided by the Soviet Union, China, and North Viet Nam in this struggle. It has nevertheless failed as yet to elaborate effective domestic policies for these countries.

A similar situation exists in the Caribbean where Cuba, in a position somewhat analogous to that of North Viet Nam, provides a base from which aid can be given to Communist movements in nearby countries. Here the military power of the United States is potentially overwhelming, but its employment is constrained by the traditional opposition of Latin American countries to North American intervention and by the presence of Soviet military forces in Cuba. Cuban agents have been very active, and there are in fact few countries in

Central America that do not offer fertile opportunities for subversion.

Revolution from without, on the other hand—the establishment of a Communist government as a result of the occupation of a country by a foreign Communist army—is possible only under conditions of international war. This is unlikely in the foreseeable future. There are a number of small countries on the periphery of the Communist orbit which could be invaded without the provocation of a nuclear conflict, but the risks of such a procedure are sufficiently great and the opportunities offered by less costly methods are sufficiently attractive to make outright invasion unlikely.

In discussing the prospects of Communist revolutions in an era of rapid change, one must consider the consequences of a decisive break in Sino-Soviet relations and a settlement of outstanding differences between the Soviet Union and the West. The chances are that such an eventuality would not have a profound effect on Communist revolutionary activity. At this stage in the development of the Communist revolutionary movement, the experienced cadres are sufficiently widely diffused that they can manage their own affairs. Soviet support has not been a decisive factor in Laos and South Viet Nam, and in Cuba the Communists joined the government before Russia became active in the Caribbean. Even the severance of diplomatic relations between the Soviet Union and China would not necessarily result in a significant relaxation of Soviet pressure on Finland or a withdrawal of Soviet troops from Cuba, nor would the Soviet Union be likely to join with the West in actively opposing Chinese support of revolutions in Asia, Africa, or Latin America. The main effect in the next few years of continued Chinese intransigence is likely to be not an abatement of Communist revolutionary activity but rather a greater diversity in the nature and support of such efforts.

It must also be recognized that in so far as it concerns war and revolution the Sino-Soviet ideological dispute has a certain unreality to it. China, the advocate of violence, is pursuing a cautious policy and has not challenged the West for a number of years. The Soviet Union, the advocate of caution, has been actively supporting revolutions in Laos and Cuba. It would be prudent not to take this ideological controversy at face value but to assume that it conceals a more profound difference in policy which cannot be argued in public because it would reveal China's fundamental weakness. This more profound issue is the need of China for economic assistance in far greater amounts than the Soviet Union and its Communist associates have provided in the past or would be able to provide without very substantial and probably unacceptable reductions in their own plans for domestic development.

Communist China is thus in a sense caught in a trap of its own making. The Chinese economy has been brought to a virtual standstill for several years due to agricultural experiments which disrupted the traditional pattern of production without putting into effect a viable alternative. China cannot hope for assistance in the necessary amount from the Communist countries. It cannot turn to the West for assistance without making concessions of a practical and ideological character that would undermine the authority of the Communist leaders. Under these circumstances, the Chinese critique of Soviet foreign policy should be interpreted more as a cry of rage and frustration than as a rational contribution to the strategy and tactics of revolution. The effect of the Chinese stance in creating diversity and divisions within international communism should nevertheless not be underestimated, particularly in the countries of Asia where Chinese influence can be directly brought to bear.

The Soviet theory of "peaceful coexistence," on the other hand, provides a rational basis for anticipating Soviet policy. It states in effect that "socialist" revolutions will inevitably occur in those countries which are not yet under Communist rule, that they will occur in the less-developed countries first, that they should be given all assistance commensurate with the larger security interests of the Communist countries, and that international war would inflict unacceptable damage to all concerned and should be avoided. The practical question which this doctrine raises, and it is one that is no doubt of constant concern to officials in Western governments responsible for evaluating Soviet policies, is how Soviet and other Communist leaders are likely to estimate the risks of supporting revolutions in any given situation. Western specialists can point to a pattern of acceptable risks established by past Communist actions and can calculate the balance of forces as seen from the West, but how can one know whether the Communist leaders see things this way? Both great wars of the twentieth century, after all, had their origins in differences in estimates on the part of European political leaders on the basis of information available to all informed persons.

The prudent approach for Western observers is to familiarize themselves as fully as possible with the thinking of Communist leaders as expressed in their writings, speeches, and private conversations, and to interpret this thinking in the light of the continuing experience with the implementation of Soviet policy. If the major revolutionary crises in recent years may be taken as a guide—especially those in Korea, Southeast Asia, and Cuba—it is clear that the gap between Communist and Western estimates of revolutionary situations has not yet been bridged. In these major crises Western observers have been consistently surprised by the high expectations that revolutionary situations have aroused on the part of Communist leaders, and by their relatively low estimate of the Western willingness to respond to challenges. Western specialists continue to find it difficult to accept the fact that the Communist leaders really believe what they say about the inevitability of revolutions and of the decline of the West. So long as this intelligence gap remains, further surprises are likely to occur. Western estimates of Soviet policy must in any event rest heavily on the currently fluctuating balance of forces and personalities, for rules and patterns claiming to offer a guide to Communist policy over a long period are bound to be too general to be of practical value in specific cases.

More important even than the estimate of Communist intentions in anticipating revolutionary situations is the evaluation of the stability of incumbent governments. In all fourteen cases of successful Communist revolutions, the incumbent governments fell or were very seriously undermined before the full force of Communist power was brought into play. In thirteen of these cases the collapse came primarily as a result of international wars. In the case of Cuba, it came as a result of the transfer of support on the part of moderate political leaders from Batista to Castro.

The advanced countries of the West face these Communist challenges from positions of great strength, and at first glance one is inclined to wonder why they should be particularly concerned. Of the independent countries of the "third world," twenty-three in Latin America and Asia are associated with the Western alliance system through the Organization of American States, the Central Treaty Organization, and the Southeast Asia Treaty Organization. At the same time, all of the colonial countries are ruled by members of the Western system or countries associated with them. The Western countries also have vast resources at their command, and when they wish to take vigorous action they are more than a match for the Communists. To this extent it may be said that the Western countries, when they are in full agreement as to policy and are prepared to commit the necessary resources, have it in their power to confine to very narrow limits the choices available to the Communists. This degree of consensus does not always prevail, however, and not infrequently the Western countries are divided as to courses of action and degree of commitment.

This position of apparent strength nevertheless conceals two profound weaknesses. One is the fact, already noted in some detail, that the countries of the "third world" are still at an early stage of modernization. They will in all likelihood be confronted in the years ahead with the same burdensome problems of domestic and foreign policy with which the more advanced countries have been wrestling since the eighteenth century. In addition, the very fact that the Western powers have normally enjoyed a privileged position and own much property in the countries of the "third world" tends to make them the first target of the strong emotions that normally characterize the striving for national power and identity.

The second weakness, the tendency of the more advanced countries to regard revolutionary movements as conflagrations or infections, is even graver. The Western countries seem to have forgotten that they too were at one time undeveloped and unstable, and expect the new states to conduct their affairs with a dignity and lawfulness which they themselves were never able to achieve in their formative years. Modernization cannot take place without strife, and the concern of the West should be not with the existence of strife but with the policies of the leaders striving for power. The British and to a lesser extent the French have had considerable success in guiding their former colonies to independence. The United States has sympathized with the new countries in principle, and in regions where its own interests have not been directly involved, but elsewhere it has often appeared to seek stability at the expense of modernization.

Now that the balance of power has come to depend to such a great extent on the outcome of domestic revolutions, a form of strife that is likely to characterize world politics for several generations, the advanced countries of the West should recognize that the unrest caused by rapid modernization deserves much more careful consideration in terms of national policy than it has thus far received. In the past these problems have been met more often than not on an emergency basis. The crises represented by the Soviet sponsorship of revolution in Iran in 1945 and the construction of medium range missile sites in Cuba in 1962 were met by implicit threats of international war by the United States. On at least two occasions, in Guatemala in 1954 and in Cuba in 1961, direct assistance was given to groups desiring to overthrow incumbent Communist-supported governments. In Greece in 1947-1949, in South Korea in 1950-1953, and more recently in Laos and South Viet Nam, military assistance was afforded to governments threatened by major Communist armed assaults. Similarly the United Kingdom and France have not infrequently resorted to the emergency use of force since the Second World War in response to Communist and other threats.

Some of these efforts have been successful and others have not, but each was a crisis measure in a situation which had been allowed by default to get out of control. There may be cases where such methods are unavoidable in the best of circumstances, but the resort to force in most of these cases reflects a lack of foresight and a failure to understand the revolutionary character of our age. Technical assistance, both direct and through the United Nations, has of course become a general practice in recent years. Even this form of assistance has been granted on a haphazard basis, however, and in amounts too small to meet the needs of the situation.

Modernization in the "third world" is too large and too important a problem to be tackled by these piecemeal methods, and no long-term success can be expected from emergency measures taken at the last moment in reaction to Communist policies. What is called for is a much more systematic and comprehensive cooperative effort on the part of all of the advanced countries of the West. This effort should be inspired by a conception of the nature of the modern world which the West wishes to attain. It should seek to employ so far as possible the institutions and methods which, combined with favorable natural conditions, have made the Western countries such a congenial environment for the development of human welfare. All this is more easily said than done, but it is not difficult to perceive the principal tasks called for by the promotion of long-term modernization with a minimum of violence. A first task is to identify the political, economic, and social changes confronting a given country and to elaborate methods by which these changes might be made. This involves reviewing the methods of land reform, education, and taxation and investment, that have been successful elsewhere in similar circumstances, and then suggesting which of these, or which variant of them, is most suited to the value system and social structure of the country in question. Another task is to convince the incumbent government that it should undertake these reforms. This is perhaps the most difficult task, for most political leaders are aware of the risks involved in such experimentation and are loth to undertake it. If all efforts to persuade the incumbent government should fail, the question will arise of recognizing other political leaders who may seek to take charge of the government and of urging upon them restraint in the use of violence. Such leaders capable of implementing successful policies of modernization will normally have gained their experience in the civil or military bureaucracy or in urban or agrarian mass organizations.

Accompanying these primarily political tasks is the problem of making available long-term technical assistance in large amounts in a broad range of fields. The most important of these is in the education of trained personnel. Even a relatively small country needs thousands of mechanics, accountants, technicians, teachers, and medical workers, and hundreds of more highly trained engineers, legal and financial specialists, and political and military leaders. They also need machines, schools, books, and equipment of all sorts. This personnel and equipment is not of much use without a general program, but neither can a general program be implemented without trained personnel. All of this requires financial aid, which serves both as a vital stimulus to development and also as a means of bargaining with the political leaders. A final task is that of assisting the country to find a framework of international political, economic, and social relations so that it can carry on trade and other foreign relations in an orderly and fruitful manner.

Efforts of this sort are still in their infancy, and the West has great advantages in personnel and experience if it wishes to use them. Indeed, a partial beginning has already been made by various agencies of the United Nations, and by such organizations as the Colombo Plan, the French Community, and the Alliance for Progress. The Communists have also made a start in this direction with their aid program in support of the doctrine of "the peaceful transition to socialism," although their principal experience has been with "non-peaceful" methods. The best chance for a stable world today lies in these efforts to encourage modernization with a minumum of violence, and only those that can meet this challenge successfully can hope to see their institutions and values prevail in the emerging modern world.

Bibliographical Essay

The principal monographs and articles dealing with individual topics and regions are cited in the footnotes. The following bibliographical references are provided for those wishing to study in greater detail the problems discussed in this volume.

Bibliographies. The best starting point for research on world communism is Thomas T. Hammond, ed., *A Bibliography on Soviet Foreign Relations and World Communism* (Princeton 1964), which lists some 7,000 books in 25 languages with comments by a variety of specialists. This volume also lists the most important specialized bibliographies on the Communist movement in the various countries of the world. R. N. Carew Hunt, *Books on Communism* (London 1959) provides a briefer and more general selection of books in English.

Bibliographical introductions to the Chinese Communist movement are provided by E. Stuart Kirby, ed., *Contemporary China: Economic and Social Studies, Documents, Bibliography, Chronology* (4 vols., Hong Kong 1955-60), a continuing publication; *The Thought of Mao Tse-tung: A Selected List of References to the Published Works and Statements Attributed to Mao Tse-Tung and to the Literature on the Chinese Communist Leader,* Department of State, External Research Paper 138 (April 1962); *Communist China: Ruthless Enemy or Paper Tiger? A Bibliographic Survey,* Department of the Army, Pamphlet No. 20-61 (January 1962); Allan B. Cole, *Forty Years of Chinese Communism,* "Service Center for Teachers of History, Publication Number 47" (Washington, D.C. 1962), which includes a brief bibliography; Tung-Li Yuan, *Russian Works on China, 1918-1960, in American Libraries* (New Haven 1961); and Chun-tu Hsueh, *The Chinese Communist Movement 1937-1949: An Annotated Bibliography* (Stanford 1962).

Bibliographical guides to political developments around the world are provided by the *Foreign Affairs Bibliography,* of which three volumes have appeared: *1919-1932* (New York 1933), *1932-1942* (New York 1945), and *1942-1952* (New York 1955); and American Universities Field Staff, *A Select Bibliography: Asia, Africa, Eastern Europe, Latin America* (New York 1960). There are also bibliographical references in Robert M. Slusser and Jan F. Triska, *A Calendar of Soviet Treaties, 1917-1957* (Stanford 1959).

The Academy of Sciences of the U.S.S.R. issues bibliographies of Soviet writings on the countries of Asia, of which five have appeared thus far: Turkey (1959), India, (1959), Japan (1960), Southeast Asia (1960), and China (1960). Current Soviet and Western writings on Asia are listed in the Soviet periodical *Novaya sovetskaya i inostrannaya literatura po stranam zarubezhnogo Vostoka* [New Soviet and Foreign Literature on the Countries of the Non-Soviet East] (Monthly 1960-). Soviet materials for the period 1950-1959 are covered in *Literatur über Entwicklungsländer* (Hanover 1961), published by the Verlag für Literatur und Zeitgeschehen.

The *Monthly Index of Russian Accessions,* published by the Library of Congress (1948-) includes an invaluable subject index of monographs and of articles in leading Soviet periodicals. Of similar value are the *East European Accessions Index* (monthly 1951-), and the *Southern Asia Accessions List* (monthly 1956-). The Library of Congress has also published *Latin America in Soviet Writings, 1945-1958,* compiled by Leo A. Okinshevich and Cecilia J. Gorokhov (Washington, D. C. 1959). Current Soviet publications since 1960 are listed in *Soviet Periodical Abstracts: Asia, Africa and Latin America,* published quarterly by the Slavic Languages Research Institute (New York 1961-).

Somewhat more specialized are the surveys of Soviet writings on Asia and Africa issued by the Central Asian Research Centre in association with the St. Antony's College (Oxford) Soviet Affairs Study Group: *Mizan Newsletter* (monthly 1959-), dealing with the Middle East and Africa, and *Yuva Newsletter* (quarterly 1962-), dealing with Southeast Asia. The Royal Institute of International Affairs has sponsored two valuable bibliographies: A. R. C. Bolton, *Soviet Middle East Studies: An Analysis and Bibliography* (London 1959), and Mary Holdsworth, *Soviet African Studies, 1918-59: An Annotated Bibliography* (London 1961). The extensive bibliographical work of the Istituto Giangiacomo Feltrinelli of Milan, which is particularly concerned with labor movements and socialism, may be followed in its *Annali* (1958-).

Communist Press and Translations. One of the most important sources for the detailed study of the Communist movement is the daily press and other periodical publications which it supports. Most of the Communist newspapers and journals in the countries where the movement is active are listed in Walter H. Mallory, ed., *Political Handbook and Atlas of the World: Parliaments, Parties and Press* (New York 1927-), published annually by the Council on Foreign Relations.

The most influential Communist publications are those of the Soviet and Chinese parties. The Soviet party daily *Pravda* [Truth] and the journal *Kommunist* present in an authoritative manner the views of the Central Committee. *Mirovaya Ekonomika i Mezhdunarodnye Otnosheniya* [World Economics and International Relations] is particularly valuable for foreign policy. *International Affairs* (not to be confused with the

British journal of the same name) and *New Times*, both published in Moscow in English, are in a more polemical vein. The *World Marxist Review*, published monthly in Toronto since 1958, is the English-language edition of *Problemy mira i sotsializma: teoreticheskiy i informatsionnyy zhurnal kommunisticheskikh i rabochikh partiy* [Problems of Peace and Socialism: A Theoretical and Informational Journal of the Communist and Workers' Parties]. This is the principal Communist international journal, and is the successor to *For a Lasting Peace, For a People's Democracy* (1947-1956) and *The Communist International* (1919-1943). Also useful for the earlier period, but in a more journalistic vein, is the weekly *World News and Views* (1922-1953), the English-language edition of *Inprekorr, internationale Presse-Korrespondenz*. The scholarly journal *Narody Azii i Afriki* [Peoples of Asia and Africa], successor to *Sovetskoye Vostokovedeniye* [Soviet Oriental Studies] and *Problemy Vostokovedeniye* [Problems of Oriental Studies], deals more particularly with the underdeveloped countries.

A valuable aid in English is the *Current Digest of the Soviet Press* (1949-), published weekly in New York under the joint auspices of the American Council of Learned Societies and the Social Science Research Council. It provides translations of selected articles from the Soviet press, as well as a weekly index to *Pravda* and *Izvestiya* and a quarterly index which lists translated articles published not only in the *Current Digest* but also in the major Soviet publications printed in English and in the British journal *Soviet Studies*.

For China the party daily *Renmin Ribao* [People's Daily] and the journal *Hongqi* [Red Flag] may be supplemented by *Guoji Wenti Yanjiu* [Study of International Affairs]. The *Peking Review*, published in English in Peking, provides translations of policy statements. A much wider selection of translations is available in *Current Background, Extracts from China Mainland Magazines*, and *Survey of the China Mainland Press*, published in mimeographed form by U. S. Consulate-General in Hong Kong. There is also a *Union Research Service* published by the Union Research Institute in Hong Kong.

A very extensive program of providing mimeographed translations of monographs and periodical materials published in the Soviet Union, China, and other countries has been undertaken by the U. S. Joint Publications Research Service, administered by the Office of Technical Services of the Department of Commerce. The materials on China translated from the inception of the project in late 1957 to July 1960 are listed in Richard Sorich, ed., *Contemporary China: A Bibliography of Reports on China Published by the United States Joint Publications Research Service* (New York 1961). The entire range of these translations has been listed since October 1958 in the *Monthly Catalog of United States Government Publications.*

Documentation. There are a number of collections of documents on international communism which provide materials which are otherwise not readily available. The most important of these collections for the Soviet Union are Jane Degras, ed., *Soviet Documents on Foreign Policy* (3 vols.; New York 1951-53); Olga H. Gankin and H. H. Fisher, eds., *The Bolsheviks and the World War: The Origins of the Third International* (Stanford 1940); Xenia J. Eudin and Robert C. North, eds., *Soviet Russia and the East, 1920-1927: A Documentary Survey* (Stanford 1957); Xenia J. Eudin and H. H. Fisher, eds., *Soviet Russia and the West, 1920-1927: A Documentary Survey* (Stanford 1947); and Robert V. Daniels, ed., *A Documentary History of Communism* (New York 1960). *Sowjetwissenschaft: Gesellschaftswissentschaftliche Beiträge* (monthly 1949-), published in East Germany, provides translations of Soviet materials often not available elsewhere in Western languages.

There are also some important documentary collections relating to the Communist movement in China: Conrad Brandt, Benjamin Schwartz, and John K. Fairbank, eds., *A Documentary History of Chinese Communism* (Cambridge, Mass. 1952); Boyd Compton, ed., *Mao's China: Party Reform Documents, 1942-44* (Seattle 1952); *Communist China, 1955-1959: Policy Documents with Analysis* (Cambridge, Mass. 1962), with an introduction by Robert R. Bowie and John K. Fairbank; and Dan N. Jacobs and Hans H. Baerwald, eds., *Chinese Communism: Selected Documents* (New York 1963).

Among documentary collections that deal with the international Communist movement, one should note: *Kommunisticheskiy internatsional v dokumentakh, 1919-1932* [The Communist International in Documents, 1919-1932] (Moscow 1933); *The Communist Conspiracy: Strategy and Tactics of World Communism;* Part I *Communism Outside the United States* (5 vols., Washington D.C. 1956), an extensive collection prepared by the Committee on Un-American Activities of the U. S. House of Representatives (House Reports 2240-2244 of the 84th Congress, 2d Session) which includes a number of documents and pamphlets not available elsewhere; Jane Degras, ed., *The Communist International, 1919-1943: Documents* (2 vols.; New York 1956-60); Royal Institute of International Affairs, *Soviet-Yugoslav Dispute: Text of the Published Correspondence* (London 1948); Vaclav L. Benes, Robert F. Byrnes, and Nicolas Spulber, eds., *The Second Soviet-Yugoslav Dispute* (Bloomington, Ind. 1959); The Russian Institute, Columbia University, *The Anti-Stalin Campaign and International Communism* (New York 1956); Paul Zinner, ed., *National Communism and Popular Revolt in Eastern Europe* (New York 1956); G. F. Hudson, Richard Lowenthal, and Roderick MacFarquhar, eds., *The Sino-Soviet Dispute* (New York 1961); Alexander

Dallin, and others, eds., *Diversity in International Communism: A Documentary Record, 1961-1963* (New York,1963); and Thomas P. Thornton, ed., *The Third World in Soviet Perspective* (Princeton 1964).

Periodicals. Much of the writing on contemporary affairs is in scholarly periodicals, and there are several hundred of these in which one may find relevant interpretations and information. Only a few of these can be mentioned here. Among those that frequently publish articles on the world Communist movement, one should note in particular: *Foreign Affairs* (quarterly 1922-), Council on Foreign Relations, New York; *Est et Ouest* (semimonthly 1949-), Association d'études et d'informations politiques internationales, Paris; *International Affairs* (quarterly 1922-), Royal Institute of International Affairs, London; *New Leader* (biweekly 1924-), American Labor Conference on International Affairs, New York; *Problems of Communism* (monthly 1952-), United States Information Agency, Washington, D. C.; *St. Antony's Papers* (triennial 1956-), St. Antony's College, Oxford; *Kyosan Ken Mondai* [Communist Bloc Problems] (monthly 1957-), Oa Kyokai, the Japanese Association on Communist States in Europe and Asia, Tokyo; and *World Politics* (quarterly 1948-), Center of International Studies, Princeton University, Princeton, N. J.

The journals principally concerned with the Soviet Union and Eastern Europe also frequently publish articles on Communist policy in other parts of the world: *Bulletin* (monthly 1954-), Institute for the Study of the USSR, Munich; *Cahiers du Monde Russe et Soviétique* (quarterly 1959-), École pratique des hautes études, Paris; *East Europe* (monthly 1952-), Free Europe Committee, New York; *Europe de l'Est et Union Soviétique* (quarterly 1958-), Centre d'études des relations internationales, Paris; *Journal of Central European Affairs* (quarterly 1941-), University of Colorado, Boulder, Colo.; *Osteuropa* (monthly 1951-), Deutsche Gesellschaft für Osteuropakunde, Stuttgart; *Slavic Review* (quarterly 1940-), American Association for the Advancement of Slavic Studies, Seattle; *Slavonic and East European Review* (quarterly 1922-), School of Slavonic and East European Studies, University of London; *Soviet Studies* (quarterly 1949-), Department for the Study of the Social and Economic Institutions of the USSR, University of Glasgow; *Studies on the Soviet Union* (quarterly 1961-), Institute for the Study of the USSR, Munich; and *Survey: A Journal of Soviet and East European Studies* (monthly 1956-), Congress for Cultural Freedom, London.

There are also a few other journals, concerned primarily with Asia and Africa, which are likewise concerned with communism:*L'Afrique et l'Asie* (quarterly 1948-), Centre des hautes études administratives sur l'Afrique et l'Asie modernes, Paris; *Central Asian Review* (quarterly 1953-), Central Asian Research Centre, London; *China Quarterly* (1960-), Congress for Cultural Freedom, London; *Journal of Asian Studies* (quarterly 1941-),

Association for Asian Studies, Menasha, Wisc.; *Middle East Journal* (quarterly 1947-), Middle East Institute, Washington, D. C.; *Pacific Affairs* (quarterly 1928-), Institute of Pacific Relations, Honolulu; and *Tiers Monde* (quarterly 1960-), Institut d'étude du développement économique et social, Paris.

Marxism-Leninism. Although the theory of Marxism-Leninism offers no detailed blueprint of Communist plans for the future, it provides an indispensable insight into the Communist view of the dynamics of the modern world.

The theoretical outlook of the Soviet leaders is set forth in three fundamental texts. The first is the *History of the Communist Party of the Soviet Union* (Moscow 1960), translated from Soviet edition of 1959 edited by B. N. Ponomarev. The differences between this history and the earlier Stalinist version of 1938 are discussed by S. I. Ploss in *World Politics,* XIII (October 1960), 77-98. The second text, and probably the most generally useful in providing an understanding of the Communist world view, is *Fundamentals of Marxism-Leninism* (Moscow 1961), a translation of the basic manual published in 1960 under the editorship of O. V. Kuusinen. A revised edition of this work, which has been printed in over a million copies for use in Soviet higher educational institutions, was published in 1962. The third text is the *Program of the Communist Party of the Soviet Union* of 1961, translated from *Pravda* (November 2, 1961) in the *Current Digest of the Soviet Press,* XIII (December 9, 1961), 3-16, and (December 13, 1961), 3-21. The text of the new *Program,* with commentaries, is available in Herbert Ritvo, *The New Soviet Society* (New York 1962), Leonard Schapiro, ed., *The USSR and the Future* (Munich 1962), Jan F. Triska, ed., *Soviet Communism: Programs and Rules* (San Francisco 1962), and Thomas P. Whitney, ed., *The Communist Blueprint for the Future* (New York 1962).

The Chinese Communists have not published any basic theoretical works. The Chinese Communist view of their own history is reflected, however, in the *Brief History of the Chinese Communist Party* (Peking 1958) by Wang Shih and others. An English translation has been published as No. 8756 (August 1961) of the U. S. Joint Publications Research Service series. An understanding of Chinese Communist ideology may also be gained from the extensive historical work that has been produced since the revolution. This important body of material is reviewed in Albert Feuerwerker and S. Cheng, *Chinese Communist Studies of Modern Chinese History* (Cambridge, Mass. 1961).

The writings of the principal Communist leaders provide a further insight into Marxism-Leninism. Of these, by all odds the most important are the works of V. I. Lenin, which are available in several editions in Russian and in English translation. Extensive selections of the works of

J. V. Stalin, N. S. Khrushchev, and Mao Tse-tung have also been published in English. Likewise available, although generally not in English translations, are the works of Dimitrov, Gheorghiu-Dej, Ho Chi Minh, Kardelj, Kim Il-sŏng, Nagy, Ranković, Tito, and others.

Of the smaller Communist countries, only Yugoslavia has developed a distinctive ideology. This is set forth in the party program of 1958, available in English in *Yugoslavia's Way: The Program of the League of the Communists of Yugoslavia,* translated by Stoyan Pribichevich (New York 1958). The Yugoslav attitude toward foreign policy is discussed in some detail in Edvard Kardelj, *Socialism and War: A Survey of the Chinese Criticism of the Policy of Coexistence,* translated by Alec Brown (New York 1960). Current trends in Yugoslav official thinking may be followed in the quarterly English-language journal *Socialist Thought and Practice* (Belgrade 1961-), which provides a translation of the new constitution in No. 10 (June 1963), 5-125. There is also a semimonthly *Review of International Affairs* (Belgrade 1950-), published in English by the Federation of Yugoslav Journalists. Ideological developments in certain other countries may be followed in *Philosophes Roumains Contemporains* (Bucharest 1958), Nikolaus Lobkowicz, *Marxismus-Leninismus in der ČSR: Die tschekoslowakische Philosophie seit 1945* (Dordrecht 1961), Z. A. Jordan, *Philosophy and Ideology: The Development of Philosophy and Marxism-Leninism in Poland Since the Second World War* (Dordrecht 1963), and W. E. Griffith, *Albania and the Sino-Soviet Rift* (Cambridge, Mass. 1963).

A branch of Marxist-Leninist theory of particular relevance to revolution is that concerned with guerrilla warfare. Some of the principal Communist writings on this subject of contemporary interest are: Mao Tse-tung, *On Guerrilla Warfare* (New York 1961), *Che Guevara on Guerrilla Warfare* (New York 1961), and Vo Nguyen Giap, *People's War, People's Army: The Viet Cong Insurrection Manual for Underdeveloped Countries* (New York 1962). Alexander Orlov's *Handbook of Intelligence and Guerrilla Warfare* (Ann Arbor, Mich. 1963) is an interesting reconstruction by a former MVD intelligence officer of the training material that he used in the Soviet Union. Frank S. Meyer, *The Moulding of Communists: The Training of the Communist Cadre* (New York 1961) and Allen W. Dulles, *The Craft of Intelligence* (New York 1963) provide valuable information on the training and deployment of Communist personnel. The considerable Western interest in Communist guerrilla methods is reflected in George K. Tanham, *Communist Revolutionary Warfare: The Vietminh in Indochina* (New York 1961), Franklin M. Osanka, ed, *Modern Guerrilla Warfare: Fighting Communist Guerrilla Movements, 1941-1961* (New York 1962), Otto Heilbrunn, *Partisan Warfare* (New York 1962), and Peter Paret and John W. Shy,

Guerrillas in the 1960's, 2d ed. (New York 1962), which has a good bibliography.

A number of critiques by Western students have been written which provide general introductions to Marxism-Leninism. The most comprehensive of these are two books by Henri Chambre: *Le Marxisme en Union Soviétique: Idéologie et institutions* (Paris 1955), and *From Karl Marx to Mao Tse-tung* (New York 1963); Herbert Marcuse, *Soviet Marxism: A Critical Analysis* (New York 1958); Gustav A. Wetter, *Dialectical Materialism: A Historical and Systematic Survey of Philosophy in the Soviet Union* (New York 1958), translated from the German edition of 1952; and J. M. Bochenski, *Soviet Russian Dialectical Materialism* (Dordrecht and Stuttgart 1963), translated from the 3rd German edition of 1960. Other commentaries are R. N. Carew Hunt, *The Theory and Practice of Communism*, rev. ed. (London 1957); Alfred G. Meyer, *Leninism* (Cambridge, Mass. 1957) and *Communism* (New York 1960); George Lichtheim, *Marxism: An Historical and Critical Study* (New York 1961); Clinton L. Rossiter, *Marxism: The View From America* (New York 1960); Gerhard Möbus, *Behauptung ohne Beweis: Zur Analyse und Kritik des Marxismus-Leninismus* (Osnabrück 1961); and Robert V. Daniels, *The Nature of Communism* (New York 1962).

Histories of World Communism. In view of the extensive footnote references that have been provided in the individual chapters, no attempt will be made here to cite the many works that deal with the history of the Communist movement in individual countries. Mention should be made, however, of a few comprehensive works that provide general introductions to this subject. The two pioneering works of the late Franz Borkenau, *The Communist International* (London 1938), recently reprinted under the title *World Communism* (Ann Arbor, Mich, 1962), and *European Communism* (London 1953), by a former member of the German Communist party, were based on an extensive personal knowledge of the movement. Hugh Seton-Watson, *From Lenin to Khrushchev* (New York 1960), published originally in England as *The Pattern of Communist Revolution*, provides a general survey of the movement. Stefan T. Possony, *A Century of Conflict: Communist Techniques of World Revolution* (Chicago 1953) is a well-documented survey both from the political and the military point of view. Robert Strausz-Hupé, and others, *Protracted Conflict* (New York 1959) places particular emphasis on contemporary Communist strategy. Theodor Arnold, *Der revolutionäre Krieg* (Pfaffenhofen/Ilm 1961) is concerned primarily with Communist uses of political violence. Günther Nollau, *International Communism and World Revolution: History and Methods* (New York 1961) offers a comprehensive interpretation. Joseph M. Bochenski and Gerhart Niemeyer, eds., *Handbook on Communism* (New York 1962) deals principally with Europe.

List of Contributors

JAMES H. BILLINGTON is Professor of History and Research Associate of the Center of International Studies, Princeton University. He is author of *Mikhailovsky and Russian Populism* (1958) and *A History of Modern Russian Culture* (forthcoming). He has made a number of visits to the U.S.S.R. and also to Finland, where he was a Fulbright Research Professor in 1960-61.

CYRIL E. BLACK is Professor of History and Faculty Associate of the Center of International Studies, Princeton University. He is the author of *The Establishment of Constitutional Government in Bulgaria* (1943) and *Modernization: Essays in Comparative History* (forthcoming), and has edited *The Transformation of Russian Society* (1960) and *Rewriting Russian History* (rev. ed. 1962).

R. V. BURKS is Professor of History at Wayne State University, Detroit. He was a Fulbright Fellow in Greece in 1951-1952, and was Policy Director of Radio Free Europe from 1961 to 1965. He is the author of *The Dynamics of Communism in Eastern Europe,* (1961).

JAMES M. DANIEL is a Field Staff Member of The Rockefeller Foundation, and Visiting Professor of History at the Universidad del Valle, Cali, Colombia. In 1963-64 he was a Visiting Research Associate at the Center of International Studies, Princeton University.

RAYMOND L. GARTHOFF is Special Assistant for Soviet Bloc Politico-Military Affairs, Department of State; and Lecturer on Soviet Affairs, the Johns Hopkins School of Advanced International Studies. He is the author of *Soviet Military Doctrine* (1953), *Soviet Strategy in the Nuclear Age* (rev. ed. 1962), and *Soviet Communism and World Power* (forthcoming); and has written extensively on problems of Soviet foreign policy.

MANFRED HALPERN is Associate Professor of Politics and Research Associate at the Center of International Studies, Princeton University. He is the author of *The Politics of Social Change in the Middle East and North Africa* (1963), and has written numerous articles on Middle Eastern affairs.

ANDREW C. JANOS is Assistant Professor of Political Science at the University of California at Berkeley. From 1960 to 1963 he was a Research Associate at the Center of International Studies, Princeton

University, and he is the author of a forthcoming study of *Power and Violence in Internal Conflict*.

WILLIAM H. LEWIS is Chief, Division of Research and Analysis for North and East Africa, Department of State; and Associate Professor of History at Georgetown University. He has travelled extensively in Africa, and has edited *New Forces in Africa* (1962) and *Emerging Africa* (1963).

RUTH T. MCVEY is a Research Associate at the Center for International Studies, Cornell University. She is author of *The Soviet View of the Indonesian Revolution* (1957), *The Calcutta Conference and the Southeast Asia Uprisings* (1958), and *The Rise of Indonesian Communism* (1965); and the editor of *Indonesia* (1963).

GEORGE MODELSKI is Professorial Fellow in the Department of International Relations at the Australian National University, Canberra. He was a Visiting Research Associate at the Center of International Studies, Princeton University, in 1960-1961 and 1964-1965, and is the author of *Atomic Energy in the Communist Bloc* (1959) and *A Theory of Foreign Policy* (1962), and editor of *SEATO: Six Studies* (1962).

GLENN D. PAIGE is Associate Professor of Politics at Princeton University. He served in 1959-1961 as Research Adviser to the Graduate School of Public Administration at Seoul National University, Korea, and has contributed to *Communist Strategies in Asia,* edited by A. Doak Barnett (1963).

THOMAS P. THORNTON is a senior research specialist in the Department of State, and Associate Professorial Lecturer in the Institute of Sino-Soviet Studies, George Washington University. In 1961-62 he was a Visiting Research Associate at the Center of International Studies, Princeton University, and he is editor of *The Third World in Soviet Perspective* (1964).

Index of Names